CW00735513

Rolls Series

Rerum Britannicarum Medii Aevi Scriptores, or The Chronicles and Memorials of Great Britain and Ireland during the Middle Ages, usually referred to as the 'Rolls Series', was an ambitious project first proposed to the British Treasury in 1857 by Sir John Romilly, the Master of the Rolls, and quickly approved for public funding. Its purpose was to publish historical source material covering the period from the arrival of the Romans to the reign of Henry VIII, 'without mutilation or abridgement', starting with the 'most scarce and valuable' texts. A 'correct text' of each work would be established by collating 'the best manuscripts', and information was to be included in every case about the manuscripts used, the life and times of the author, and the work's 'historical credibility', but there would be no additional annotation. The first books were published in 1858, and by the time it was completed in 1896 the series contained 99 titles and 255 volumes. Although many of the works have since been re-edited by modern scholars, the enterprise as a whole stands as a testament to the Victorian revival of interest in the middle ages.

Year Books of the Reign of King Edward the Third

The records of the medieval English courts were compiled into manuscript 'year books', organised by regnal year of the monarch, and further subdivided into the four law terms. The year books of the reign of Edward III (1312–77), beginning at the eleventh year (1337) and continuing to the twentieth (1346), were to have been edited for the Rolls Series by Alfred Horwood (1821–81), who had previously edited the year books of Edward I, but he died while the first volume was in proof. The work was taken over by L.O. Pike (1835–1915), the set of fifteen books being published between 1883 and 1911. (Horwood chose his start date because the year books of Edward II and the first part of the reign of Edward III already existed in modern editions.) This volume contains reports from Easter Term, 19 Edward III, to Michaelmas Term, 19 Edward III.

Year Books of the Reign of King Edward the Third

Year XIX

EDITED AND TRANSLATED BY
LUKE OWEN PIKE

CAMBRIDGE
UNIVERSITY PRESS

CAMBRIDGE UNIVERSITY PRESS

Cambridge, New York, Melbourne, Madrid, Cape Town,
Singapore, São Paolo, Delhi, Mexico City

Published in the United States of America by Cambridge University Press, New York

www.cambridge.org
Information on this title: www.cambridge.org/9781108048019

© in this compilation Cambridge University Press 2012

This edition first published 1906
This digitally printed version 2012

ISBN 978-1-108-04801-9 Paperback

RERUM BRITANNICARUM MEDII ÆVI SCRIPTORES,

OR

CHRONICLES AND MEMORIALS OF GREAT BRITAIN AND IRELAND

DURING

THE MIDDLE AGES.

A 673. Wt, 8381,

THE CHRONICLES AND MEMORIALS

OF

GREAT BRITAIN AND IRELAND

DURING THE MIDDLE AGES.

PUBLISHED BY THE AUTHORITY OF HER MAJESTY'S TREASURY, UNDER
THE DIRECTION OF THE MASTER OF THE ROLLS.

On the 26th of January 1857, the Master of the Rolls submitted to the Treasury a proposal for the publication of materials for the History of this Country from the Invasion of the Romans to the reign of Henry VIII.

The Master of the Rolls suggested that these materials should be selected for publication under competent editors without reference to periodical or chronological arrangement, without mutilation or abridgment, preference being given, in the first instance, to such materials as were most scarce and valuable.

He proposed that each chronicle or historical document to be edited should be treated in the same way as if the editor were engaged on an Editio Princeps; and for this purpose the most correct text should be formed from an accurate collation of the best MSS.

To render the work more generally useful, the Master of the Rolls suggested that the editor should give an account of the MSS. employed by him, of their age and their peculiarities; that he should add to the work a brief account of the life and times of the author, and any remarks necessary to explain the chronology; but no other note or comment was to be allowed, except what might be necessary to establish the correctness of the text.

The works to be published in octavo, separately, as they were finished ; the whole responsibility of the task resting upon the editors, who were to be chosen by the Master of the Rolls with the sanction of the Treasury.

The Lords of Her Majesty's Treasury, after a careful consideration of the subject, expressed their opinion in a Treasury Minute, dated February 9, 1857, that the plan recommended by the Master of the Rolls "was well calculated for the accomplishment of this important national object, in an effectual and satisfactory manner, within a reasonable time, and provided proper attention be paid to economy, in making the detailed arrangements, without unnecessary expense."

They expressed their approbation of the proposal that each Chronicle and historical document should be edited in such a manner as to represent with all possible correctness the text of each writer, derived from a collation of the best MSS., and that no notes should be added, except such as were illustrative of the various readings. They suggested, however, that the preface to each work should contain, in addition to the particulars proposed by the Master of the Rolls, a biographical account of the author, so far as authentic materials existed for that purpose, and an estimate of his historical credibility and value.

Rolls House,
    December 1857.

𝔜ear 𝔅ooks

OF THE REIGN OF

KING EDWARD THE THIRD.

Year XIX.

Year Books

OF THE REIGN OF

KING EDWARD THE THIRD.

Year **XIX.**

EDITED AND TRANSLATED

BY

LUKE OWEN PIKE,

OF BRASENOSE COLLEGE, OXFORD, M.A., AND OF LINCOLN'S INN, BARRISTER-AT-LAW ;
AUTHOR OF "A HISTORY OF CRIME IN ENGLAND,"
"A CONSTITUTIONAL HISTORY OF THE HOUSE OF LORDS," ETC.

PUBLISHED BY THE AUTHORITY OF THE LORDS COMMISSIONERS OF HIS MAJESTY'S
TREASURY, UNDER THE DIRECTION OF THE MASTER OF THE ROLLS.

LONDON:
PRINTED FOR HIS MAJESTY'S STATIONERY OFFICE,
By MACKIE & CO. LD., 59, Fleet Street, E.C.

And to be purchased, either directly or through any Bookseller, from
WYMAN AND SONS, Ld., Fetter Lane, E.C. ; or
OLIVER AND BOYD, Edinburgh ; or
EDWARD PONSONBY, 116, Grafton Street, Dublin.

1906.

CONTENTS.

INTRODUCTION.

INTRODUCTION.

THIS volume contains reports of Easter, Trinity, and Reports of
Michaelmas Terms in the nineteenth year of the reign the year
fo Edward III., which have never before been printed. III. not
The manuscripts which have been used to establish previously printed.
the text are the Lincoln's Inn MS., the Harleian MS. The
No. 741 in the British Museum, and the two MSS. in manu-
the University Library at Cambridge numbered Hh. 2. used to
3 and Hh. 2. 4. The three first have already been establish
described in the Introductions to previous volumes of the text.
Year Books. The Cambridge MS. Hh. 2. 4 (or 1632),
has also been already mentioned,[1] but may require some
further notice in relation to the reports now published.
Of Easter Term it contains only the last seven cases
(Nos. 40–46 as printed below). It has a complete set
of reports of Trinity Term. The heading of Michaelmas Term has originally been "*De Termino Michaelis*
"*anno Regni Regis Edwardi tertii a Conquestu vicesimo*
"*nono*," but the word "*decimo*" has been afterwards
substituted for "*vicesimo*." The reports really are of
Michaelmas Term in the nineteenth year of the reign,
but they are incomplete, as they extend only to the
case No. 60 which is on fo. 252, b. of the MS. At
some time, however, other reports must have followed,
as there is a catch-word at the foot of the folio relating to the case No. 61 as found in other manuscripts.
Folio 253 begins with reports of Michaelmas Term
23 Edward III. The writing is in a hand of the
fourteenth century, and the manuscript is consequently
of value as being approximately contemporary with the
reports themselves.

---

[1] *See* Y.B., Mich. 13-Hil. 14 Edw. III., Introd. pp. xxi-xxiv, and Y.B.
Hil.-Trin., 17 Edw. III,, Introd. pp. xxxi xxxii.

The corresponding records compared.
The reports found in the manuscripts have, as usual, been compared with the corresponding records. The system on which the comparison has been made, the manner in which the records have been used when found, and the difficulties attending the search have been explained in the volume of Year Books (Rolls edition) containing the reports of Easter and Trinity Terms 18 Edward III.[1]

References to Fitzherbert's Abridgment, and the *Liber Assisarum*.
As in all previous volumes edited by me, every case which occurs in Fitzherbert's *Abridgment* has been traced, and noted, as well as those which are to be found in the *Liber Assisarum*.

Matters illustrating the social history of the period.
The reports of the three terms now published, with the associated records, are, perhaps, more than usually rich in matters illustrating the every-day life of the people. We obtain glimpses of the Knights Hospitallers in their Commanderies, where they had been settled after the Knights Templars had been suppressed, and of the customs of the manor of Temple Combe.[2] We find a parson letting his church to farm, with all its appurtenances, rights, and obventions, for a term of three years, at a rent of ten pounds *per annum*.[3] We are told of a man who was indicted in the King's Bench for threatening and striking jurors, and who there had sentence that his right hand should be struck off, and that his lands and chattels should be forfeited.[4]

A Latin text of the Statute of Gloucester, c. 11.
We are also introduced to a Latin version of the eleventh chapter of the Statute of Gloucester,[5] for the protection of tenants for years, which (notwithstanding the clerical error of *admittere* for *amittere*) appears to be, on the whole, somewhat better than that which is given by Fleta.[6]

---

[1] Introd. pp. xviii-xxxiv.
[2] Below, pp. 352-357.
[3] Below, pp. 402-406; 405, note 2.
[4] Below, p. 452.
[5] Below, p. 441, note 1.

[6] Fleta (1685), p. 120. The statute appears in French both in the Statutes at Large and in the Statutes of the Realm.

The subject of villenage again comes into some Villenage:
use of the
prominence. It again clearly appears that any cattle words
which a villein might possess were regarded as being *nativus*
the lord's, from a strictly legal point of view, and that *villanus.*
to take them was to levy a good distress on the lord.[1]
There is an example of a writ of Naifty[2] by which a
lord attempted to recover possession of two villeins.
This could be done only when the villein had run
away from his lord's land, and it was a part of the form
of the writ that he had to be described as "*nativum*
" *et fugitivum*,"—always, be it observed, as "*fugitivum*,"
and always not as "*villanum*" but as "*nativum*." It
is, perhaps, possible by closely marking the use of the
word "*nativus*" in the writ of Naifty and elsewhere,
and of the word "*villanus*," where it occurs, to ascertain
in what respects they differed.

In the report the French word used to express the The
lord's villein who had fled is "*neif*" (in the masculine), *nativus* (or
and the land from which he had fled as being the *neif*) in
lord's "*neif terre*." The word "*villeyn*" is used only Naifty.
once in relation to the "villein issues" of which the
lord was alleged to have been seised. It is clear, however, that villein issues are those which are extracted
from a "*nativus*" or "neif," and it would seem that
for a moment the reporter lapsed from that extreme
accuracy with which he began when he made the
"*nativus*" uniformly "neif." Colloquially a male "neif"
was commonly called "villein" in French.

The form of the writ which one lord brought against The
another in relation to villeins and suit to a mill was *villanus*
in the writ
" *quod permittat villanos suos facere sectam ad molen-* of *Quod*
" *dinum suum*." The word used here is always "*villanos*" *facere*
and never "*nativos*." It seems, therefore, certain that *sectam.*
when the words were used in a strictly legal and not
merely colloquial manner, there was some well recognised distinction between them. What was it?

---

[1] Mich., 19 Edw. III., No. 79 | [2] Easter, 19 Edw. III., No. 40
(below, pp. 472-478). | (below, pp. 110-112).

8381 b

Suit to a mill was a service which did not necessarily indicate that the person performing it was of villein condition. In addition to the form of writ which was brought against a lord " *quod permittat villanos suos* "*facere sectam*," there was the writ of *Secta ad molendinum*, which required a particular person of free condition to do suit to the mill of another. When, therefore, the action was brought against a lord requiring him to permit his "*villanos*" to do the suit to another person's mill, the "*villani*" were probably persons who held in villenage, whether of free condition or not. The suit in this case might be due by custom from the villein lands, the *neif terre*, the *bondagium*, just as in the other case it was due from lands held by free tenure.

The *nativus* always of unfree condition, the *villanus* possibly not.

It is possible, therefore, that in the reign of Edward III. a *villanus* was a person who might or might not be free, but held his lands in villenage, while a *nativus* was one of unfree condition. The case of writ of Naifty now under consideration contains in the record a passage which seems to show that a distinction was recognised between a *nativus* and a *villanus*. The lord claimed his *nativi* on the ground that his father had been seised of their father, as of his *nativus*, as of fee and right, alleging that his father had also brought a writ of Naifty against their grandfather who confessed himself in Court to be "*nativum* "*et villanum ejusdem Adæ*" (the lord's father). It is true that tautology (though rare) is not unknown in the records, especially in ecclesiastical matters, but it is reasonable to suppose that in this case strict legal terminology was observed and that the *villanus* was regarded as being something different from the *nativus*.

The *nativus* in the action of Waste.

For a writ of Waste there was the form "*vastum* *venditionem, et destructionem, et exilium*." In the declaration the *exilium* appeared in the form "*exulando* "*quosdam A. B. et C., nativos suos, quorum quilibet* "*tenuit in villenagio.*" [1] Thus we have *nativos* both in the action of Waste and in the writ of Naifty, and apparently for the same reason, that is to say, that the *nativus* was not a free man, though the *villanus* possibly might be. It was not waste to expel a free man who was holding *in villenagio* because he did not belong to the lord, but it was waste to expel a *nativus* holding *in villenagio* because he did belong to the lord.

It is unfortunate that there is not in the English language any word to express the meaning of *nativus* as distinguished from *villanus*, since the word "neif" has been restricted to the female; and imperfection of language is apt to lead to confusion of thought. It is curious that the writ for the recovery of the bond-man is called in English a writ of Naifty, and not a writ of villenage, or villainy, just as it was called in Latin a writ *de nativo habendo*, or a writ *de naivitate*, [2] upon which the defendant pleaded denying "*omnem* "*nayvitatem,*" [3] and not *omne villenagium*. Enough, however, it may be hoped, has now been said to show that the Latin words of the records ought to be care-fully weighed by any one who wishes to secure accuracy in dealing with the conditions in which our forefathers lived, as free men or otherwise.

(marginal note: No English word strictly equivalent to the Latin nativus.)

The case of *Monstraverunt* [4] with which this volume commences has also some relation to the subject of villenage. It contains in the declaration a curious illustration of the manner in which statements might be deliberately invented, and even find a place on the Plea Roll. The action was brought by Walter Blake, Robert Revesone, John Cryps, Richard "The Loder," Robert Hankyn, Alan Gybone, William "The Herte,"

(marginal note: A case of Monstra-verunt: plaintiffs attribute their own surnames to ances-tors who lived in the time of the Conqueror.)

---

[1] There is an illustration in Y.B., Mich., 15 Edw. III., No. 62 (p. 427, note 5), and the expression "*exu-* "*lando nativos*" frequently occurs in the records.

[2] Below, p. 111, note 4.
[3] Below, p. 113, note 1.
[4] Below, p. 2.

Richard Walters, John Streen, Robert Leovon (or Leofwine), and Adam le Blake, tenants of Ancient Demesne, against the Abbot of Eynsham, on the ground that he was demanding of them customs and services other than those which they ought to perform. All the plaintiffs, except Adam le Blake, asserted not only that they had had ancestors or "consanguinei" who had held the lands which they held, by certain specified services, in the time of William the Conqueror (nearly three centuries before), but also that those ancestors or "consanguinei" had borne the same surnames as themselves. Walter Blake's "cousin" of the Conqueror's time was William le Blake, Robert Revesone's was John Revesone, John Cryps's was Walter Cryps, Richard "The Loder's" was William "The Loder," Robert Hankyn's was another Robert Hankyn, Alan Giboun's was Gilbert Giboun, William "The Herte's" was Philip "The Herte," Richard Walters's was John Walters, John Streen's was Richard Streen, and Robert Leovon's was Adam Leovon.

The surnames of the ancestors were invented, family names not being usually hereditary at the time.
This was a very clumsy fabrication. It is easily demonstrable that surnames had not, in ordinary cases, been fixed and hereditary for many generations after the Conquest, even in the highest classes, much less among tenants in Ancient Demesne. A lord of the manor of Dale might be described as Johannes de Dale, and his son as Radulphus de Dale, simply because they both were "de" or of Dale, but, if there was a different mode of identification, the son's name differed from the father's, as in the cases of Henry Fitz-Hugh and Hugh Fitz-Henry. In the lower walks of life the son was not uncommonly known by a name entirely different from that of his father, and a brother by a different name from that of his brother.[1]

The name of "Blake" or "Le Blake" was simply

---

[1] With regard to the late development of hereditary family names or surnames, in ordinary cases, *see* Y.B., 13-14 Edw. III., Introd. pp. lxxviii-lxxxiv.

a nick-name, a description of a person by a personal characteristic. He was Black or The Black, and if by any chance Walter Black's *consanguineus* William was called by the same nick-name as himself in the time of the Conqueror, it was impossible that he could have known it. Robert Revesone in the time of Edward III. was simply Robert son of the Reeve, or *præpositus*, his father actually being or having actually been a reeve. His assumed *consanguineus* John Revesone suggests the idea of a family of Revesone, each called by that name in a line of descent, and not one of them being the reeve from whom the first Reveson of the line must have originally had the name. Not even nine generations took them back to the original Reeve. So also all the other names are obviously invented for the purposes of the case. The only trustworthy inference to be drawn is that surnames were in the year 1345 really becoming hereditary, even among the lower classes, and that the framer of the declaration was not aware how recently this had happened.

It was alleged on behalf of these tenants in Ancient Demesne that their ancestors or *consanguinei* had each held one messuage and two virgates of land in the manor of Eynsham, in the time of the Conqueror, by certain definite services. These were fealty, the payment of ten shillings *per annum* in the case of some of the tenants, and five shillings in the case of others, and after the death of each tenant double one year's rent, in lieu of all services and customs. They complained that the Abbot of Eynsham exacted from them other services and other customs, which were, in fact, those which would be exacted from villeins. He demanded of every tenant holding one messuage and one virgate of land that they should plough his land with one plough and eight oxen or other beasts of the plough three times a week, that they should sow and harrow his land, that they should manure the whole land of the manor with their carts, and mow all the Abbot's meadows, and turn and bind his hay and

The complaint of the tenants against the lord.

carry it to his house, and should hoe, reap, and
bind his corn, and carry it to his manor-house, and
thresh it, at Christmas, Easter, and other Feast-days.
On a vacancy of each of the tenements he took a fine
from the tenant at his will. He took ransoms of flesh
and blood from the tenants and their issue, and
tallaged them high and low at his will, and made
them his reeves or bailiffs (*præpositos*) at his will. He
also set at nought the King's Prohibition against doing
all these things, which had been duly delivered to him.

Allegation of the lord that certain of the tenants were villeins.   All this appears in the record, in which there are
no pleadings beyond the declaration. According to
the report, however, the Abbot alleged that three of
the plaintiffs were his villeins and that he was "seised"
of them, and that he had the right to tallage them
high and low. Some technical objections were also
raised against the declaration. One of those was that
the record to certify the Court as to the manor being
Ancient Demesne had not been produced; and the
Court held that it could not do anything until it was
apprised by the record (Domesday Book) that the
manor was of that nature.

The action abandoned by the plaintiffs.   Before the proof was brought in the plaintiffs
abandoned the action (*non sunt prosecuti*), thus admit-
ting, for the time, at any rate, that they could not
establish their claim. They appear to have been ill-
advised. It had long been an established rule that a
manor could be proved to be Ancient Demesne only
by Domesday Book. It may have been necessary to
assert that the tenure by which the plaintiffs alleged
that they held their tenements was that which had
existed in the time of the Conqueror and under his
successors; but it was idle to attempt to show this by
giving the names of *consanguinei* or ancestors identical
with those of the existing tenants. It is, of course,
possible that the names of the ancestors were understood to be fictitious, like those of the later John Doe
and Richard Roe, but this is not probable. It is not
only in the record that the names are mentioned. In

the report also it is said that "one A. cousin of the "aforesaid Walter" held in the time of the Conqueror, which indicates that the names of the ancestors were stated as those of real persons in the declaration. In other reported cases, however, in books of entries, and in the *Natura Brevium* the form used in the declaration appears as "their ancestors" without any names. The reasonable inference, therefore, is, as already suggested, that in this case they were invented for the occasion, and not introduced in accordance with precedent.

It has been pointed out in previous volumes that "the law's delays" are not by any means of recent origin, as some have supposed, but can be traced back almost as far as the law itself. Various attempts were made to stop them by statute. One of the devices to gain time was that which was technically known as "fourcher," which, however, could only be practised when there were more defendants or tenants than one. In certain cases one had not to answer until the other or the others appeared. One of those against whom the action was brought (A.) would then agree with another (B.) that they should fourch against C. who brought the action. The way in which the fourcher was arranged was as follows:—A. made default and B. either appeared or was essoined. As A.'s default was no fault of B.'s, B. had a day over or his essoin was adjudged, and a day given, and the same day (an *Idem dies*) was given for A.'s appearance. On that day A. made his appearance or was essoined, but B. made default, and then A. had a day given over, or his essoin was adjudged, and a day given thereon, and the same day was given to B. The next time A. again made default, and B. appeared, or was essoined, and so on in turn. The law's delays: fourcher.

Three chapters of the Statute of Westminster the First are directed against the abuse of the essoin. In the forty-second it is provided, in order to prevent The abuse of essoins checked by statute.

inconvenience to jurors, that, on writ of Assise, Attaint, and *Jurata utrum*, after a tenant (where the action was brought against one tenant alone) had once appeared in Court, he could not be essoined, though he might, if he pleased, appoint an attorney to act for him. If he then failed to do that, or to appear in person, the assise or the jury would be taken against him by default. But this, though it checked the improper use of essoins, did not affect the practice of fourching.

By the forty-third chapter of the Act it was provided in the interest of demandants, who had in former times been delayed in obtaining their right, that when several parceners were tenants, one of whom could not answer without the others, and when there were several tenants who were joint feoffees, and no one of them knew what was his several, such tenants should have an essoin on one day only, in the same manner as a sole tenant, so that they should never be able to fourch. By the Statute of Gloucester (6 Edward I.), c. 10, this provision was extended to real actions brought against husband and wife. The forty-fourth chapter of Westminster the First was directed against the use of essoins falsely representing that tenants were *ultra mare* when they were in fact within the four seas of England.

None of these provisions, however, affected personal actions brought against more defendants than one, and a curious illustration of the fact occurs in the present volume.[1] John Gisors brought a writ of Debt against several defendants. One of them made default, and the process known as the Grand Distress issued in order to make him appear on a certain future day. The same day (*Idem dies*) was given to the others who had appeared, that is to say, they were to appear again on the day on which the defaulter was to appear in virtue of the Grand Distress. When the day came

Marginal notes:
Fourcher in real actions also checked by statute.

But not in personal actions: an illustration: fourching for seven years.

---

[1] Easter Term, No. 4 (p. 12).

he appeared, and so saved any further ill consequences as affecting himself. But, when he appeared, one of the other defendants made default, and then the Grand Distress issued against the second defaulter, and all the rest had *Idem dies*. The second defaulter then appeared in answer to the Grand Distress, but one of the others made default. It appears in the report that this game was carried on for no less than seven years.

The plaintiff naturally became somewhat impatient, and his counsel prayed that the issues belonging to the last defaulter might be forfeited, although he had previously had *Idem dies* when one of the others had made default. The meaning of this prayer is to be sought in the process of Grand Distress itself. When a defendant had failed to appear in response to a summons or attachment, the Grand Distress was directed to the Sheriff in the following form:—We command you that you do distrain [A.] by all his lands and chattels in your bailiwick, so that neither he nor anyone on his behalf do put hand upon them until you have some other command from us, and that you do answer unto us for the issues of the same, and that you do have his body before our Justices [on a day named] to answer [B.] in respect of a plea of [stating the nature of the action], and to hear his judgment in respect of several defaults. And have you there this writ, &c.

If the defendant appeared on the appointed day in obedience to this writ, he, so to say, purged his previous default on the summons or attachment, and began anew. That which had been seised by the Sheriff was, if not replevied, held on behalf of the King as a sort of pledge for the defendant's appearance, but, as soon as he had appeared, he was entitled to have it all restored to him. What counsel prayed in the case of Gisors was practically that the last default might be regarded as a default after default, and that the issues might be regarded as no longer belonging to the defaulter, but forfeited to the King.

A remedy prayed in vain by counsel explained.

The defendants left still fourching.

This, however, Hilary, J., said could not be done. There was no statute which touched the point. And so we see the defendants, after seven years of successful fourching, left fourching still *in infinitum*.

A Commission of Sewers touching the river Lea.

There is in the present volume a case [1] showing the proceedings on a Commission which would in later times have been called a Commission of Sewers. In one of the MSS. [2] of the report, indeed, there is a marginal note " Commission de Sewers " but in a very much later hand. It is of interest as showing how the old manuscript reports were used, generation after generation, before there was any printed edition of the Year Books.

The Commission of Sewers as understood in later times appears in Registers of Writs and in Fitzherbert's *Nouvelle Natura Brevium* [3] (1581) under the head of Oyer and Terminer, though the form of it was not "*ad audiendum et terminandum.*" Whatever may have been the date at which this form first came into existence it was set forth as the form to be followed in the Statute 6 Henry VI., c. 5, which provided that in the ten years next following " severalx commissions de sewers soient faites as " diverses persones par le Chaunceller Dengleterre " pur le temps esteant." This appears to be the first occasion on which the expression " Commission of " Sewers " was used in a statute. According to the form the enquiry to be made extended, among other things, " *ad wallias, fossata, gutteras, seweras, pontes,* " *calceta, et gurgites, ac trencheas supervidendum.*"

---

[1] Trin., 19 Edw. III., No. 22 (pp. 178-184 and Appendix).

[2] Cambridge Univ. MS. Hh. 2. 3.

[3] Fo. 113. By the Act 8 Hen. VI., c. 3, and subsequent Acts, power was given to Commissioners of Sewers to execute their own ordinances, and thence possibly their commission came to be regarded as one of Oyer and Terminer.

The later annotator of the margin of one manu- The form script report of the reign of Edward III. was thus of the correct in his definition.[1] The Commission was as Commis-follows:—Because we have been given to understand sion. that several persons of the counties of Essex and Middlesex, in divers places in the river called "The "Lea," which runs from the town of Ware to Waltham Cross, and thence to our City of London (in which river ships and boats have during all bygone times been used to pass with victuals from divers parts unto the said city for the sustentation of the community of that city and of other persons frequenting the same) have fixed and placed piles, hurdles, locks, and other divers contrivances for the taking of fish, and also do in certain other places cause that river to run through divers trenches made in their lands, and have diverted the true course of that river, by reason whereof the transit of such ships and boats along the river aforesaid is impeded, to the grave damage and manifest loss of the said community of that city and of others so frequenting the same city Now we, willing to provide for the security of our people from damage in this respect, have appointed you and two of you to enquire more fully, by the oath of good and lawful men of the counties aforesaid by whom the truth may be best known, as to the truth touching all and singular the premises and other circumstances affecting them. And therefore we command you that on certain days and at certain places which you or two of you shall appoint for this purpose you do make inquisitions touching the premises, and that you do without delay send them, distinctly and openly made, to us under your seals, or the seals of two of you, and under the seals of those by whom they have been made.[2]

It will be seen that the Commissioners in this The in-case were not only not appointed *ad audiendum et* quisition taken

returned into the Chancery.

---

[1] As to this *see* Callis's *Reading upon the Statute* 23 H. VIII., c. 5, *of Sewers*, pp. 8-9.

[2] Appendix, pp. 485-6.

terminandum, but had no power except to take inquisitions and return them into the Chancery.

The inquisition returned by the Commissioners is nevertheless described as having been taken "*Coram* "*Johanne de Cherletone et sociis suis Justiciariis domini* "*Regis.*" It was taken at West Smithfield without the Bar on the Sunday next after the Feast of St. Luke the Evangelist in the eighteenth year of the reign.

Annoy-
ances to
persons
passing
with ships
and boats.

It was to the following effect:—"There is a certain "ditch called 'Louediche' near Old Ford in the vill "of Stepney in the County of Middlesex between the "meadows of Maud late wife of Geoffrey Aleyn on "both sides. This used to be, at the head of the said "ditch next the Lea, of the width of six feet only, and "of the depth of two feet only, and used to be closed "with five piles previously placed there by Stephen "Asswy the tenant of two mills called 'Landmilnes' "for the purpose of keeping the river Lea in its right "course so that the water in the Lea should not be "diminished. This ditch extends from the said river "Lea to the water called 'Rothulvespond.' It was "widened[1] two feet by handiwork during the time "when John Hauteyn was tenant of the said meadows, "to wit, in the time of King Edward the Second, and "it was widened four feet by handiwork in the time "of the present King Edward the Third, during the "time when Gilbert de la Bruere was tenant of the "meadows aforesaid. The said ditch was also widened "two feet, in the time of the present King Edward "the Third, by Geoffrey Aleyn and Maud his wife, "during the life of the same Geoffrey. And the said "ditch was in like manner widened four feet by the "same Maud who is now tenant of the meadows afore-"said, during her widowhood after the death of the "said Geoffrey. And the said ditch was made two

---

[1] The Latin is "*oblargatum*," which might mean narrowed, but the word appears to have been written by mistake for *elargatum*, which is found in the corresponding place in the verdict of the petty jury.

" feet deeper than it used to be by the same Maud, to
" the annoyance of all persons passing with ships and
" boats in the said river Lea." The jurors found
further that "Letitia de Markam, late Prioress of Strat-
" ford, and Isabel Blounde, the present Prioress, placed
" eighteen piles in the river Lea aforesaid, near Strat-
" ford Bridge in the vill of Bromley in the time of the
" present King Edward the Third, to the annoyance
" and obstruction of those passing by the said river with
" their ships and boats. Moreover the same Isabel now
" Prioress placed elsewhere in the said river at Bromley
" twelve piles in the time of the present King Edward
" the Third to the annoyance as above. Furthermore
" the same Isabel now Prioress placed in the river
" aforesaid at Bromley twenty piles, and in another
" place in the same vill twenty other piles, in the time
" of the present King, to the danger and annoyance of
" all persons passing with their ships and boats."

They found that " Richard de Wight, formerly Abbot Damage to
the city of
London.
" of Stratford, made a certain hedge or obstruction in
" the river Lea at the entrance to the river Thames
" in the vill of West Ham, by reason of the strength
" of which obstruction the river Lea is diverted from
" its right course over the county of Middlesex, and the
" right course of the river is altogether closed for the
" space of twelve perches, each perch containing sixteen
" feet and a half, and the land there is so raised and
" heightened that hardly any ship can pass in the
" river Lea aforesaid, and the Thames fish are unable
" to enter the river Lea aforesaid, by reason of the
" masterfulness and wrong of the Abbot, to the damage
" of the King and of the community of the City of
" London, and to the annoyance of the people as
" above, and this annoyance is continued by William
" de Coggeshale, the present Abbot."

They found that " John de Triple, in the time of
" the present King, placed in the course of the river
" Lea at Stepney Marsh thirteen piles, to the annoy-
" ance as above,"

They found that " Richard de Bynteworth, late
" Bishop of London, placed nine piles in the aforesaid
" course of the river over against Trendlehope in
" Stepney, in the fourteenth year of the reign of the
" present King, and Ralph, the present Bishop of
" London, still continues the same nuisance, to the
" annoyance as above."

They found that " Isabel the present Prioress of
" Stratford placed seven piles in the river aforesaid
" near Redhope in Bromley to the annoyance as above."

They found that " Ralph formerly Prior of Christ
" Church, London, placed eleven piles at Warewal in
" Bromley in the time of King Edward the Second,
" to the annoyance as above, and Nicholas the present
" Prior continues the same nuisance. The aforesaid
" Ralph formerly Prior of Christ Church also placed
" six piles in the course of the river aforesaid, at his
" mill in Bromley in the time of King Edward the
" Second, to the annoyance as above, and Nicholas
" the present Prior continues the said nuisance. The
" aforesaid Ralph formerly Prior of Christ Church also
" placed seventeen piles in the course of the river
" aforesaid near his manor of Bremlehalle (or Bromley
" Hall) in Bromley, and thirteen other piles in another
" place in the same vill near to the seventeen piles
" aforesaid, in the time of King Edward the Second,
" to the annoyance as above, and the said nuisance is
" continued by Nicholas the present Prior."

Injury to
mills, and
floods
caused by
a lock.

They found that "There is at Stratford in the parish
" of Bromley a certain lock of the river Lea called
" 'Fourmulleloke,' which was first placed there by
" Henry de Bedike in the time of King Edward the
" First, of which lock Thomas Bedike, the Prioress of
" Haliwell, and Isabel the present Prioress of Stratford
" are tenants. This lock shuts off and holds back the
" river aforesaid to a height of four feet more than
" the rest of the locks placed higher up in the river
" Lea aforesaid hold it back. It causes the river
" aforesaid to flow back, and to be diverted, so that

" the mills which are placed higher up the said river
" cannot grind while the water there is so held back,
" to the annoyance of the city of London aforesaid.
" By the same lock the river is diverted so that it
" flows back upon the adjacent meadows, by reason
" whereof the growing hay is to a great extent de-
" stroyed, to the annoyance of the tenants and of the
" city of London. Furthermore the King's high-way
" at Stratford is flooded by reason of the same lock,
" to the annoyance of all persons passing by it, and
" in like manner to the annoyance and obstruction of
" all persons passing by the said river Lea with ships
" and boats. And that nuisance and obstruction have
" been continued from that time to the present."

The inquisition having been returned into the
Chancery was sent by *Mittimus*[1] into the King's Bench
with a command to the Justices of that Court to cause
to be done further that which of right and in accordance with the law and custom of the realm they should
see ought to be done.

The inquisition sent from the Chancery to the King's Bench by Mittimus.

The Court of King's Bench thereupon directed to
the Sheriff of Middlesex a *Venire facias* to cause
Matilda late wife of Geoffrey Aleyn, the Prioress of
Stratford, the Abbot of Stratford, John de Triple, the
Bishop of London, the Prior of Christ Church,
Thomas Bedike, and the Prioress of Haliwell, to
appear[2] and answer to the King wherefore the
annoyances or nuisances mentioned should not
be removed. On the appointed day none of them
appeared, and new process of Distress and *Habeas
corpora* issued to bring them into Court on the Saturday next before the Feast of the Nativity of St. John
the Baptist, that is to say on the 18th of June.

Process against the offenders to bring them into the King's Bench.

On the 18th all the persons concerned appeared,
except the Bishop of London and Thomas Bedike. On

Objection that the alleged nuisances were private, and not public, over-ruled,

---

[1] Appendix, p. 485.

[2] According to the report (p. 178)
on the Saturday next after the
Quinzaine of the Trinity (the 11th

of June), but according to the record (Appendix p. 489) on the Monday next after three weeks from
the Trinity (the 13th of June).

behalf of Maud, widow of Geoffrey Aleyn, several technical objections were taken, according to the report, one of them that the supposed nuisance was not a public but a private nuisance, and that the King ought therefore not to have been made a party. The argument was that as the City of London was a community (in French "*comune*," in Latin "*communitas*") it could have an action by that description as a single individual would have one. The Court held that there was nothing in the point, because the words of the presentment were "to London and the people" ("*ad* "*damnum et jacturam Communitatis Civitatis Londoni-*" *arum et aliorum ad eandem confluentium*").

Various pleas as to the facts, on which issue was joined.

With regard to the facts it was, according to the record, pleaded on behalf of Maud, after a recital of the words of the presentment, that she did nothing and continued nothing by way of widening the ditch to the annoyance of the King's City of London in the river Lea, or to the obstruction of persons passing by land, or passing by the river with ships and boats. For the Prioress of Stratford there was a like plea with the omission of any reference to passengers by land. For John de Triple it was pleaded that he did not place anything in the course of the river to the annoyance or obstruction of ships and boats passing by the river, as had been presented. For the Prior of Christ Church it was pleaded that all the piles placed in the river Lea by his predecessors were placed there to protect the Prior's lands and those of other persons of those parts lying by the river, and not to the annoyance or obstruction of persons passing by the river with ships and boats. Issue was joined on behalf of the King on all these pleas, and a *Venire* issued for a jury to come on the Wednesday next after the Feast of the Nativity of St. John the Baptist, or on the 29th of June.

Various technical points raised and

On that day Maud the widow of Geoffrey Aleyn, the Prioress of Stratford, John de Triple, and the Prior of Christ Church duly appeared, as well as the jurors;

and counsel immediately proceeded to raise various over-ruled
technical points, some of which show that the practice before the jurors
relating to a Commission of Sewers was not very well were charged.
established. One was that the jurors ought to have
view, and that, as it was not expressed in the *Venire*
that they were to have it, the process was bad.
Thorpe, J., said that the suit for the King was in lieu
of a *Quod permittat* for the purpose of abating a
nuisance, and pointed out that view was not given on
a *Quod permittat* though it was on an Assise of
Nuisance. Pole for one of the parties maintained that
the suit was of the nature of an Assise, but Thorpe
showed conclusively that it could not be so. The presenting jurors had made a definite statement as to
the facts, and if they stood in the place of the jurors
of an Assise they had already given their verdict, and
the parties would consequently be put without answer.

After the jurors had been charged, according to the Verdict in the main
report they could not agree, but, after dinner (*apres* in accord-
maunger), the verdict was taken "at St. Clement's ance with
"Church," meaning probably the church of St. Clement the pre-
Danes in the Strand, not far from the Temple. sentment.

The particular spot at which the verdict was given
is not mentioned in the record. In it however the
findings are stated to have been as follows. There
was a certain ditch called "Louedich" near Old Ford
in the vill of Stepney which lay between the meadows
of the aforesaid Maud on both sides, the widening
and deepening of it had been effected in the manner
alleged in the presentment, and, "the course of the
"river aforesaid by reason of the nuisance aforesaid
"is so much dried up that the nuisance cannot in
"any way be suffered without the flow of the river
"being continually diminished."

With regard to the Prioress of Stratford the finding
was "that seven piles have been placed in the river at
"Redhope by Isabel the present Prioress, and that forty
"piles were placed there by Letitia formerly Prioress and
"have been continued there by the present Prioress."

As to the Prior of Christ Church the finding was "that he has continued the nuisance of eleven piles "placed in the river in Warewal in Bromley by Ralph "formerly Prior, as well as that of seven piles at his "mill of Bromley placed there by his predecessor "aforesaid, and that of seventeen piles placed "by his predecessor aforesaid in the river "aforesaid near Bromley Hall, and of thirteen "other piles placed in the river aforesaid by his "predecessor aforesaid." In each of these cases it was found that what had been done was "to "the annoyance of all persons passing by the river "aforesaid."

With regard to John de Triple it was found "that "he did not place any piles in the river aforesaid "to the annoyance or obstruction as had been "presented."

Plea, in arrest of judgment, that the verdict had been taken out of Court, but the Chief Justice claimed the power to take jurors about in carts.
Pole now pleaded in arrest of judgment that the verdict had been taken out of Court, and not at a proper time. The reply of Scot, C.J., was characteristic of the age. "We can take a verdict by candle-light "if the jury will not sooner agree; and, if the Court "were to move we could take the jurors about "with us in carts, and so Justices of Assise have to "do."

Judgment for the nuisances to be removed at the cost partly of the parties and partly of the Crown.
Judgment was then given "that the ditch aforesaid "so widened in width and deepened in depth by the "aforesaid Maud in her own time be stopped up and "put right at the cost of Maud herself, and that the "same Maud be in mercy for the widening and "deepening of that ditch, and that the other nuisances "aforesaid effected in the ditch aforesaid during the "times at which the aforesaid Geoffrey, Gilbert, and "John Hauteyn were tenants of the same ditch be in "like manner stopped up and put right at the cost "of the Lord the King, and that the aforesaid nine-

" teen piles placed by the aforesaid Isabel now Prioress
" be removed and destroyed at the cost of the Prioress
" herself, and that the aforesaid Prioress be in mercy,
" &c., and that the aforesaid forty piles placed by the
" aforesaid Letitia formerly Prioress be removed and
" torn up at the cost of the Lord the King, and that
" all the nuisances continued by the aforesaid present
" Prior of Christ Church be in like manner removed
" at the cost of the Lord the King."

A writ was to be sent to the Sheriff directing him that he should cause it to be publicly proclaimed throughout the whole of his bailiwick that all persons of his county to whose annoyance, hindrance, and obstruction the matters aforesaid had been done in the river aforesaid should be on the spot on some certain day appointed to them by the Sheriff himself in aid of the Sheriff to remove, stop up, and utterly tear away the nuisances, hindrances, and obstructions effected in the same river by the aforesaid Maud, and the aforesaid Prioress and Prior, and that he should make known in the King's Bench on the Quinzaine of Michaelmas in what manner this had been done. *A great flood delays the execution of part of the work.*

R. Thorpe (counsel for the King) prayed a *Capias* against those who had actually effected the handiwork of the nuisances, on the ground that it must have been done technically "with force and arms." This was, like the prayer of the parties to have view, founded on the analogy of an Assise, but as the proceedings had not taken the form of an Assise the *Capias* was not granted.

The report ends at this point, but the record gives some further information. After several delays, the Sheriff at length returned that he had done as required in relation to the ditch called "Louediche" near Old Ford "so that it is now, in width and depth, as it " used to be in times gone by. The expenses and " costs incurred on the King's behalf in relation to " the removal of the nuisances caused by John, Gilbert, " and Geoffrey amounted to forty pence.

"But," added the Sheriff, "I have not been able in "any way to cause the other nuisances and obstructions "included in this writ, which were effected and con- "tinued in the aforesaid river Lea by Isabel late "Prioress of Stratford, and Letitia late Prioress of "Stratford, and also by Nicholas now Prior of Christ "Church, to be removed and torn away in accordance "with the tenour of this writ, by reason of the great "flood and rising of the river, which were continuous "in those parts from the day of the receipt of this "writ until now at the return of it."

Another writ was therefore sent to the Sheriff directing him, as before, to cause those nuisances to be removed, but with that the record ends.

Import-
ance of
the navi-
gation of
the Lea to
the city of
London. It is evident from the record of this case that the navigation of the river Lea was, at the time, regarded as a matter of considerable importance to the city of London. Provisions of all kinds could be brought in readily and cheaply by water-carriage, and any obstruc- tion of the water-course would naturally be greatly resented. It is, perhaps, difficult to realise in the twentieth century the every-day life of the fourteenth. When, however, that which was grown in England sufficed for English mouths, and the Englishman was content with the fruit and vegetables of each season as it came in turn, the interruption of even one source of supply was a serious mischief. The Lea was the water-way for the produce of a considerable portion of the counties of Hertford, Essex, and Middlesex, and though not perhaps of the same value as the Thames, must have been of greater value than any road for conveyance by land.

The word
"arraign"
as applied
to a
prisoner. In the volume of Year Books Easter and Trinity 18 Edward III. (Rolls edition) some remarks were offered on the word "arraign" as applied to an Assise. There are cases in the present volume which appear to call for some remarks on the word "arraign" as

applied to a prisoner. Though the derivation of the word used in the one sense is different from the derivation of the word used in the other sense, the word is quite correctly used in both senses, as was the French word "arreyner" in the fourteenth century.

The Latin forms of the word "arraign" as applied to a prisoner were noted many generations ago by Sir Matthew Hale in scholarlike fashion. He pointed out their meaning in relation to the case of Roger Mortimer of Chirk, and of his nephew the better known Roger Mortimer who found favour in the eyes of Queen Eleanor the consort of Edward II.[1] That King on the 14th of July, in the sixteenth year of his reign, appointed by special commission certain "Justices" to pronounce judgment on the uncle and nephew in the form prescribed by himself. The proceedings and others connected with them form a useful introduction to the study of arraignment.

Sir Matthew Hale, the case of the Mortimers, and the word "arraign."

The Commissioners were Walter de Norwyz (or Norwich), William de Herle, Walter de Friskeney, John de Stonore, and Hamo de Chigwell. Of these Walter de Norwyz had been appointed a Baron of the Exchequer in the fifth year of the reign.[2] In the tenth year he was Chief Baron, and was a member of the King's Secret Council.[3] In the thirteenth year he was Treasurer,[4] which office he seems to have held alternately with the Bishop of Exeter until the sixteenth year.[5] He had served all his life in the Treasury of the Exchequer, or in offices connected with it,[6] and does not appear to have had any experience in either the King's Bench or the Common Bench. It is evident, however, that he enjoyed the confidence of the Sovereign.

The Commissioners to pass sentence on the Mortimers without arraignment.

---

[1] *Rot. Lit. Pat.* 1 Edw. III., p. 2, m. 3.

[2] *Rot. Lit. Pat.* 5 Edw. II., p. 2, m. 19.

[3] *Rot. Lit. Pat.* 10 Edw. II., p. 2, m. 11.

[4] *Rot. Lit. Claus.* 13 Edw. II., m. 15.

[5] *Rot. Lit. Pat.* 13 Edw. II., m. 19; *Rot. Lit. Pat.* 15 Edw. II., p. 1, m. 19; *Rot. Lit. Claus.* 16 Edw. II., m. 20.

[6] *Rot. Lit. Pat.* 10 Edw. II., p. 2, m. 11.

William de Herle was a man who lived to make a high reputation, and left behind him a name which was always mentioned with respect after his death. At this period, however, he had only recently been appointed a Justice of the Common Bench,[1] after having previously been one of the King's Serjeants.[2]

Walter de Friskeney had only recently been appointed a puisne Baron of the Exchequer.[3] He afterwards became a Justice of the Common Bench,[4] and subsequently a Justice of the King's Bench.

John de Stonore was now a puisne Judge of the Common Bench, having been recently appointed,[5] and having previously been one of the King's Serjeants.[2] He rose, however, afterwards to be Chief Justice of the Common Bench, in which capacity his name continually appears in the Year Books.

Of Hamo de Chigwell little is known. It was, however, without doubt supposed that he was a man upon whom the King could depend to do as he was bidden.

Such was the constitution of the Court commissioned to pass sentence on (not to try) the Mortimers. No member of it had, as a judge of the King's Bench, had at the time any experience in criminal proceedings. This fact may, perhaps, be regarded as some excuse for that which they did, though some of them must, as lawyers, have known what was the law.

The sentences for crimes which were recorded by the King. The King sent to them the judgments which were to be pronounced. One was against Mortimer the uncle. It recited, with many details, that he had, with others, levied war against the King, that the crimes which he had committed were notorious, and that the King recorded them against him. Therefore the Court was commanded to give judgment that for the treasons of which he was guilty he should be drawn, and for

---

[1] *Rot. Lit. Pat.* 14 Edward II., p. 1, m. 15, and m. 17.

[2] *Liberate Roll*, 9 Edw. II., m. 1.

[3] *Rot. Lit. Pat.* 14 Edw. II., p. 1, m. 17.

[4] *Rot. Lit. Pat.* 17 Edw. II., p. 1, m. 22.

[5] *Rot. Lit. Pat.* 14 Edw. II., p. 1, m. 15.

the arsons, robberies and homicides he should be hanged. The judgment to be passed on the nephew was in similar form. The Court thereupon required the then Constable of the Tower, Roger de Swynnerton, to bring in the prisoners, and to execute the judgment.

This was on Monday the morrow of the Feast of St. Peter *ad Vincula* (the 2nd of August), the letters patent giving the authority being dated the previous 14th of July. On the following day, however, Tuesday next after the Feast of St. Peter *ad Vincula* (the 3rd of August), and, in virtue of the King's letters patent dated the 22nd of July, the Commissioners announced the commutation of the sentence, and gave judgment against the Mortimers of perpetual imprisonment in the Tower.

The prisoners were thus condemned without arraign-ment, and unheard, and this was a ground for the annulment of the judgment in the first year of the reign of Edward III., five years afterwards. In the mean time, however, another event happened which affords a curious illustration of the doctrine of arraign-ment. " Stephen de Segrave was attached by his body " by the King's Marshal for that, whereas the Lord the " King had committed to him the custody of the " Tower of London and of the prisoners for the time " being therein, as in an indenture between the said " Lord the King and the said Stephen (here recited in " French) appears, in which indenture it is contained " that the aforesaid Stephen received the aforesaid " prisoners into his custody, and among them Roger " de Mortimer, the nephew, who has been convicted " of sedition, and sentenced to imprisonment in the " Tower, yet the aforesaid Roger has feloniously and " seditiously escaped. And the aforesaid Stephen being " *arraigned* (*arrenatus*) on the premises as to whether " he could say anything for himself wherefore he ought " not to be subjected to such sentence as the aforesaid " Roger would have if he were present, the aforesaid " Stephen denies all sedition, consent, and agreement,

Escape of Mortimer the nephew, and arraign-ment of the Con-stable of the Tower thereon.

" and [confesses] the escape of the said Roger, but
" says that it was not by his consent, agreement,
" or will. But he says that he was misled by
" a certain yeoman of his in whom he had con-
" fidence, and whom he trusted as himself, but who
" was in connivance with Roger for the purpose of
" effecting this escape, Stephen himself being wholly
" unaware of the fact. This Roger and the yeoman
" between them mixed a drink specially designed for
" the purpose, which they gave to the warders under
" the said Stephen within the Tower aforesaid to
" drink. By reason of this drink the same warders
" fell into such a sleep that they were unable to
" keep their watch and ward over the said Roger
" as they ought, while the aforesaid Roger and like-
" wise the yeoman aforesaid with him feloniously
" and seditiously escaped out of the Tower aforesaid
" from the custody of the said Stephen. And Stephen
" puts himself thereof upon the King's mercy."[1]

Asked "si quid pro se dicere sciat," the Constable explains. We see here that Segrave was arraigned "*si quid pro se dicere sciat.*" The words are identical with those used in a writ of *Scire facias* in which the person is to be warned, or have notice to come and show wherefore a certain judgment should not be rendered. The prisoner being in court has not to be warned by writ, but he is in precisely the same position as the garnishee in a *Scire facias* after appearance. This arraignment is the equivalent of the questions asked of the garnishee, and he can deny the charge or explain it away, as Segrave did.

Prayer for annulment of the judgment on the Mortimers. Roger de Mortimer, the uncle, probably died in the Tower, but Roger de Mortimer, the nephew, after his escape, remained at large. Some three years later he returned in triumph with Queen Eleanor, and after Edward II. had been put to death, he bestirred

---

[1] *Placita coram Rege*, 17 Edw. II., *Rex*, R° 37. Printed in the *Abbreviatio Placitorum*, fo. 343, b.

himself to have the judgment passed on his uncle and himself annulled. He made petition to the King and Council in full Parliament that the record, process, and judgment passed upon Roger de Mortimer, his uncle, whose heir he was, might be brought before the King and his Council, and the errors therein amended, and they were accordingly brought in by the Chancellor, and Mortimer was asked to assign the errors on which he relied.

He said :—"When any one belonging to the King's "Realm has in time of peace committed any offence "injuriously affecting the Lord the King or any other "person, by reason of which he is liable to lose life "or member, and has thereupon been brought to judg- "ment before judges, he ought first of all to be "arraigned,[1] and his own answers with regard to the "offence charged against him ought to be first heard "before proceeding be had to judgment concerning him. "But in the records and processes[2] aforesaid it is con- "tained that the aforesaid Roger, the uncle, and "Roger, the nephew, being brought before the Justices, "were sentenced to be drawn and hanged, and were "afterwards sentenced and delivered over to perpetual "imprisonment, *absque hoc* that they had been "arraigned as to the accusation, or that they were "permitted to answer to any of the matters charged "against them, which is contrary to the law and "custom of the realm, &c., and therefore the pro- "ceeding to judgment against them was erroneous."[3] *[margin: The right to be arraigned, and to give an answer.]*

It was in relation to this passage, which he quoted in the original Latin in full, that Sir Matthew Hale pointed out that the meanings of *arrenare*, *ad*

---

[1] In this passage the expression "put to reason" has been used instead of "arraigned" in a publication in which "arrame" is uniformly substituted for "arraign," as applied to an assise.

[2] "Trials" is substituted for "processes" in the same publica- tion. The whole essence of the complaint, however, was that there had not been any trial.

[3] *Rot. Lit. Pat.*, 1 Edw. III., part 2, m. 3.

rationem ponere, and *rationi ponere* are identical.[1]
Roger Mortimer, the nephew, also alleged that
whereas the King had "recorded" that he and his
uncle had committed the offences for which sentence
was passed upon them, the King had no power so
to record except with regard to his enemies in time
of war in the realm, when he was riding with
banners displayed. At the time of these sentences,
however, he was not so riding, and the Courts of
Chancery, King's Bench, and Common Bench were
sitting for the administration of justice. If the King
could record the guilt of the person brought up for
judgment, arraignment was out of the question, as
the matters had passed beyond that stage. It was
therefore necessary to show that the King had not
this power in the particular circumstances in order
to establish the fact that want of arraignment was
an error. Another point was that the sentences on
the Mortimers were not by lawful judgment of their
peers, and so contrary to *Magna Charta* and the law
of the land.

Judgment on the Mortimers annulled because pronounced without arraignment. For these reasons (including the sentence
without arraignment) the judgments on both
the Mortimers were annulled and revoked, and
the younger had restitution of his lands, &c.
That, however, was quite as much because his
party was in power as because the law was on
his side.

A second sentence on Mortimer, the nephew, pronounced without arraignment, and reversed for the same cause. Roger Mortimer, the nephew, having incurred the
King's displeasure, was a second time condemned
unheard, and attainted, only three years after the
reversal of the previous judgment against him.[2]
Again there was a reversal in Parliament, twenty-four
years after his execution, and again the reason
assigned was the condemnation without arraignment.

---

[1] *The History of the Pleas of the Crown* by Sir Matthew Hale, part II., c. 28, pp. 216, *et seq.*

[2] *Rotuli Parliamentorum,* 4 Edw. III., No. 1 (Vol. II., pp. 52-53).

It was declared in Parliament that the judgment was erroneous, because he was put to death, and suffered disherison, without having been put to answer (*mesne en respons*).[1]

The Rolls of Parliament also throw some light upon the usual formality in cases in which the accused actually was arraigned. He was "*allocutus, et ad rationem positus*,"[2] or addressed and required to give an account of himself, or, as we have already seen, asked whether he could show cause why sentence should not be pronounced on him. *Latin words used to express arraignment.*

Cases in the present volume carry us a little further, and enable us to see, according to the French forms, exactly how far the meaning of arraignment extended in the time of Edward III., and why the right of the prisoner to his answer is so strongly put forward in the Roll of Parliament and in the Patent Roll. *Cases of arraignment in the present volume: the French forms.*

"John de Neuton was arraigned[3] (*arreyne* in one MS., *arrene* in others) in the King's Bench by Thorpe, J., for that he had been outlawed for a certain felony." Outlawry for felony was at this period equivalent to conviction of felony, for which the penalty was death. It appears, however, from this case, that even when captured the felon was not executed without a hearing. He was "arraigned," and the meaning of this was that having been brought into Court he was asked by the Judge whether he could show any good cause (again in the form of the writ of *Scire facias*) why he should not be led away to the gallows. Neuton answered that, at the time at which the writ of Exigent (or *Exigi facias*) for his outlawry issued, he was in Britanny with the English forces engaged in the *Proceedings in the arraignment of one who had been outlawed for felony.*

---

[1] *Rotuli Parliamentorum*, 28 Edw. III., No. 8 (Vol. II., p. 256).

[2] *Rotuli Parliamentorum*, 23 Edw. I., m. 2 (Vol. I., p. 135). In one passage in the Rolls of Parlia-ment there occurs the phrase "*arrenatus et ad rationem positus*," 21 Edw I. (Vol. I, p. 95, b), but this may be a clerical error.

[3] Below, p. 174.

war there. The Judge asked him whether he was a clerk, in which case he would have been delivered over to the Ordinary, and whether he had a charter of pardon of outlawry, in which case he might have been released. He could not answer either question in the affirmative, and the Court adjourned, apparently for the purpose of considering the outlaw's excuse of absence beyond the seas.

On the following day he was brought into Court again, and again arraigned. In this part of the report the French word used in the manuscripts is "*aresone*," "*arresone*," or "*aresoune*," and it might almost seem, at first sight, that there is some difference of signification intended between "*aresone*," and "*arrene*," between the word meaning arraign when written without an *s* and when written with one. That, however, is seen to be impossible when it is found that the prisoner was "*aresone*" *as above*, and that he was questioned whether he could say anything (or show cause, as in the writ of *Scire facias*) why the Court should not proceed to execution against him. Neuton seems to have had but a poor opinion of the value of consistency, for he now answered that at the time of the issue of the Exigent, and before, and afterwards, he was in prison in York. The Judge's remark upon this was:—"Yesterday you "said you were in Britanny, and therefore you cannot "be permitted to say that you were in prison at "York." He was then ordered out to execution. His fate thus depended on his answer to the arraignment—to the question whether he could show cause why he should not be executed.

Of one who had been found in the realm after abjuring it. In the case[1] which immediately follows this in the reports it is stated that one Gilbert Gower was arraigned (*arrene* in one MS., *arreyne* in the others) for having been found in the King's realm after he had abjured it. He was arraigned—that is to say, he

---

[1] Below, pp. 174-176.

was asked whether he could show cause why the Court should not proceed to execution—or (omitting certain parenthetical words) "*arreyne sil savoit rienz dire* (a French translation of the form in the writ of *Scire facias*) *pur quei homme nirreit a execucion.*" In answer he produced a general charter of pardon of all kinds of robberies, felonies, and homicides, but there was no mention in it of abjuration. The offence for which he had taken sanctuary, and which he had confessed, was that of aiding and abetting in a homicide. Again the Court adjourned, and on the following day Thorpe, J., arraigned (*arrena*) him "as above." He said in answer that he was not guilty, and further that he was not the person who had made abjuration, but that it was another, and that his name had been entered through malice. This averment was not admitted in opposition to that which appeared on the Coroner's roll. The Court, however, took care to ascertain that, as Gower was an accessory only, his principal had been attainted. Then the Judge said "Take him away," and the reason given was that abjuration was not mentioned in the charter of pardon, though homicide was. The prisoner, however, had the benefit of every chance which the law allowed him. He was arraigned, he was asked what cause he could show to save his life, and, as those which he stated were insufficient in law, he had to die.

A third case,[1] immediately following this in the reports, again shows clearly the sense in which the word arraign was used. A thief had been convicted, and as he was going to the gallows he was rescued by force. He was, however, afterwards recaptured and relodged in prison. He was not hanged in virtue of the previous conviction and sentence, but was brought into Court and "*arrene*" (or "*arreyne*") *sil savoit rienz dire*, wherefore he should not be executed. He

Of one rescued on his way to the gallows, and afterwards recaptured.

---

[1] Below, pp. 176-178.

then claimed benefit of clergy, was delivered to the Ordinary, and so escaped death.

The answer of the accused upon arraignment not at first restricted as in later times.

In these three cases it is abundantly evident that the meaning of the French words which were eventually represented by the English "arraign," was to ask a prisoner what cause he could show why the law should not take its course. They were, however, all of a somewhat exceptional character. No one of them was a simple case of arraignment upon indictment, but each of them was an arraignment after the prisoners had already been convicted or had confessed. There consequently arises a question how far the inferences which may be drawn from these cases are applicable to arraignment in general. And this leads us back to the time when the petty or trying jury was young, and the trial by ordeal or compurgation had not long been abolished.

With regard to the answer of the accused Fleta tells us that what he said with respect to appeals may be said with respect to indictments.[1] In an appeal he had "*defendere omnem feloniam, et verba* "*per ordinem dedicere secundum quod in appello* "*fuerint versus eum proposita.*"[2] This is more fully and clearly expressed by Bracton: "The appellee (in "a case of homicide) denies (*defendit*) all felony, and "that the peace of the Lord the King was broken, "and whatsoever is against the peace of the Lord the "King, and the death, and everything which is "alleged against him, and the whole appeal, word "by word, as brought against him."[3] And in the case of an indictment the accused, says Bracton, "comes and denies the death and the whole "matter."[4]

The words of Bracton and Fleta, however, relate obviously only to cases in which the accused absolutely denied the charge against him, and do not

---

[1] *Fleta*, 52, § 39.
[2] *Fleta*, 52, § 34.
[3] *Bract.*, 138, b.
[4] *Bract.*, 143, b.

cover all the possibilities. The words of Britton show that the prisoner was asked, in general terms, what he had to say in his defence. "On a presentment "of this felony (conterfeiting the King's seal and "coin) we will that the sheriff do cause to be taken "without delay all those who shall be indicted "thereof, and their bodies to be safely kept in prison, "and that they be brought into our Court of King's "Bench or before our Justices in Eyre. And, in order "that no one may be without warning to prepare "an answer, we will, with regard to those who are "so taken, that they have time to provide their "answer to the extent of fifteen days at least, if they "so pray. . . . . And when they come for judg-"ment into our Court of King's Bench or before our "Justices in Eyre, let them be there arraigned "(*aresounez*) . . . . in accordance with the form of "the presentment. And if they will not speak in "exculpation of themselves ('*si il ne se veulent aquiter*')[1] "let them be put to" the *prison forte et dure*.

Thus it seems the accused knew the charge against him, and was supposed to be prepared with his defence when brought into Court. He was then immediately "*aresoune*," or formally asked what he had to say in answer. He might stand mute, in which case he was put to the *prison forte et dure,* he might claim benefit of clergy, he might confess, he might absolutely deny the presentment word by word, or he might say something in explanation. In later times the general issue "Not Guilty" pleaded to the indictment took the place of the cumbersome repetition and denial of each word of the presentment or indictment, and explanation might be given, on the plea of "Not Guilty," by evidence at the trial.

It may, however, be hoped that it is now suffi- He was ciently plain what is the meaning of the Latin asked to give an expressions "*ad rationem ponere*," "*rationi ponere*," and account of himself, and gave it.

---

[1] *Brit.,* Lib. I., c. 5, § 2.

"*arrenare*," and of the French word which takes the various forms *arraisonner, aresouner, aresoner, aresner, arener, areyner*, &c. The idea to be conveyed had nothing to do with any ratiocinative process restricted to the mind of the accused. *Ratio* had more significations than one even in classical Latin, and account was one of them. *Ad rationem ponere* in the sense of to put one to render his account is not very far from the original meaning of arraign. The presentment or indictment was put to the accused in the affirmative, and if he wished to obtain an acquittal he had to go through the same form in the negative, and possibly to add an explanation. That was his account,[1] and if he then put himself on the country as to the truth of it, the jury settled the question. As Blackstone said, at a later time, "to arraign is nothing but to call the prisoner "to the bar to *answer* the matter charged upon him." That is precisely what it was from the very first. The only difference was in the form of the answer required, and in the fact that while Blackstone limited the answer to the "matter charged upon him in the "indictment," an answer could be required in different circumstances, as in the three cases in the present volume.

Like the word "arraign" applied to an *assisa*, the word "arraign" applied to a prisoner underwent a change of meaning before the reign of Elizabeth.

It is, perhaps, worthy of remark that as the word "arraign," applied to an *assisa* or a *jurata*, underwent a change of meaning between the time of Edward III. and that of Sir Edward Coke, so also it underwent a change, when applied to a

---

[1] With regard to the etymology of the word arraign as applied to a prisoner there appears to be no doubt, though the derivation of a French form from the Latin, and the subsequent derivation of a Latin form from the French are curious. "*Ad rationem ponere*" is the equivalent of the French "*arraisonner*." Ducange, indeed, gives a Latin form "*arrationare*," adding "*Gallis olim arraisonner.*" I have never met with the form *arrationare* in English records, but when a substitute for *ad rationem ponere* or *rationi ponere* is used, it is *arrenare*. This is quite common, and seems to have been formed from the French *arrener*. There are other Latin law-terms apparently formed from the French, *e.g. naivitas* from *naifte*, or *neifte*.

prisoner, before the reign of Elizabeth. In earlier times, as appears in the present volume, it was the judge who questioned or arraigned the prisoner.[1] In later times it was the clerk who asked him to plead "Guilty" or "Not Guilty." In Elizabeth's time "the clarke speaketh first to one of the "prisoners: 'A.B., come to the barre, hold up thy "hand.'[2] The clarke goeth on: 'A.B., thou by the "name of A.B., of such a towne, in such a countie, "art endicted that, such a day, in such a place, "thou hast stolen with force and armes an horse, "which was such ones, of such a colour, to such a "valor, and carried him away feloniously, and con- "trarie to the peace of our soveraigne Ladie the "Queene. What sayest thou to it, art though guiltie "or not guiltie? If he will not aunswere, *or not* "*aunswere directly guiltie or not guiltie*, after he hath "beene once or twise so interrogated, he is judged "mute. . . . .'"

"If he pleade not guiltie, as commonly all theeves, "robbers, and murtherers doe . . . . the Clarke "asketh him how he will be tryed, and telleth him "he must saie by God and the Countrie, for these "be the words formall of this triall after Inditement, "and where the Prince is partie: if the prisoner doe "say so, I will be tryed by God and the Countrie, "then the Clarke replyeth, 'Thou hast beene "endicted of such a crime, &c. Thou hast pleaded "not guiltie: being asked how thou wilt be tryed, "thou hast aunswered by God and by the Countrie. "Loe these honest men that be come here be in the "place and stead of the Countrie: and if thou hast "any thing to say to any of them, looke upon them

---

[1] In Britton's time it appears to have been the Sheriff, or the King's Serjeant. Lib I., c. 5, § 2.

[2] It is, however, stated in Hawkins's *Pleas of the Crown* (5th edition), p. 308, that "there is no "necessity that a prisoner at the "time of his arraignment hold up "his hand at the bar, or be com- "manded to do so; for this is only "a ceremony for making known "the person of the offender to the "Court; and if he answer that he "is the same person it is all one."

"well, and nowe speak, for thou standest upon thy "life or death.'"[1]

Here we have, beyond all doubt, arraignment in the more modern sense, though there is a curious omission of the pleas which had previously been and were afterwards possible, as well as the general issue or plea of "Not Guilty." The prisoner could, of course, plead to the jurisdiction, demur to the indictment on a point of law, plead in abatement of it, as on the ground of misnomer, or plead one of the special pleas in bar—*autrefoitz acquit, autrefoitz convict, autrefoitz attaint*, or a pardon. He could not, however, enter upon a general explanation such as that of Segrave cited above. In Segrave's position he could have demurred on the ground that what he was charged with having done or omitted to do was neither sedition nor felony, or he could have pleaded "Not Guilty," and afterwards adduced his statement of the facts in support of the plea.

Probably in or about the reign of Henry VI.

The precise time at which the change was effected can hardly be shown with certainty, but may probably have been when benefit of clergy ceased to be claimed before trial, and was claimed only after conviction, and in arrest of judgment. This appears to have been in or about the reign of Henry VI. Chief Justice Fortescue, who lived in that reign, throws but little light on the matter, as he merely mentions the jury-process in a case in which the accused (*rettatus*, or *rectatus*) "crimen suum coram judicibus dedicat." It is true that one of the translators has rendered "*rettatus*" "on his arraignment,"[2] but this appears to be only an illustration of the use of a technical term of which the meaning was not understood. The disappearance, however, of the claim of benefit of clergy as a declinatory plea before trial may well have coincided with more strict rules affecting the proceedings on arraignment in general.

---

[1] Sir Thomas Smith *De Republica Anglorum* (1583), pp. 78-79.

[2] Fortescue *De Laudibus Legum Angliæ* (1616), fo. 61 b.

There are other words which, like *arraign*, under-went a change of meaning either during the time when French was spoken in the Courts in England, or after they had been borrowed from the French and become part of the English language. They will be mentioned in due course in the Glossary, which is steadily progressing. It was necessary to comment, in the mean time, on the use of the word *arraign* in the Year Books and elsewhere, both because there appeared to be considerable misapprehension with regard to its meaning and derivations, and because the use of it in the reports appeared to need explanation.

Other words which have changed their meaning to be noted in the Glossary.

In Michaelmas Term [1] there again appears a case which has recurred at intervals from the thirteenth year of the reign to the nineteenth. Gilbert Talbot brought a writ of Cosinage against Ralph de Wilynton and Eleanor his wife demanding, as the reports and records express the names, the castle of Keyr Kenny and the commote of Iskenny. Though evidently in Wales there is nothing in report or record to show in what part of Wales the subject of the demand was.

A case of Cosinage relating to the Marches of Wales.

It is not for an editor of Year Books to introduce any small matters of genealogy or topography, but there are some features in this case which are of legal and historical importance, and which can hardly be brought out clearly without an attempt to identify persons and places. The reports are, even with the assistance of the record, hardly intelligible without explanation.

The castle of " Keyr Kenny " and the commote of "Iskenny" identified with Carreg Cennen Castle and Iskennen in the modern Carmarthenshire.

There is in the modern Carmarthenshire a river Cennen (which is in Welsh pronounced Kennen), a hundred of Iskennen, and a Carreg Cennen Castle, and, even were there nothing else to show it, there

------

[1] No. 60. Below, p. 420.

could be but little doubt that the name of the
commote is preserved in the hundred, and that "le
"chastel de Keyr Kenney" the "castrum de Keyr-
"kenny" is Carreg Cennen Castle. The "Keyr" of
the Latin and French may have been written by
mistake, or may possibly represent the Welsh "Caer"
(a fortress), but the difference does not seem to be
of importance. As will be seen below, the identity
of the "castrum de Keyrkenny" with Carreg Cennen
Castle can be clearly established. Talbot's claim was
that his "consanguineus," described as "Lewelinus
"ap Rees Vaghan," had been seised in his demesne
as of fee of the commote and castle, in time of
peace, in the time of Edward I., and had died
without heir of his body. The fee, as alleged,
resorted from him to his aunt and heir "Wenthana"
(an Englishman's representation in Latin of the
Welsh name Gwenllian), who was the sister of
"Rees Vaghan" his father. The descent was traced
from her to Richard [Talbot] as son and heir, and
from him to the demandant Gilbert.

Mistakes
in Peer-
ages: a
supposed
daughter
of a Prince
of Wales,
or of South
Wales.

It is stated in some Baronages and Peerages
that Gilbert's grandfather, Gilbert Talbot, married
Gwenllian or Gwendoline, daughter of Rhys ap
Griffith "Prince of Wales,"[1] and in them the descent
is traced from her to Richard, and from Richard to
Gilbert, who is thus made great-grandson of a Prince
of Wales.

Gilbert Talbot, the demandant in the action of
Cosinage, however, did not himself claim descent from
Rhys ap Griffith, Prince of Wales, or any other Rhys
ap Griffith, but, as already shown, from an aunt of
Llewelyn ap Rhys Vychan. Moreover, when the
statement that his grandmother, Gwenllian, was a
daughter of Rhys ap Griffith, Prince of Wales, is
traced back to its source, there appears to be no

---

[1] e.g. Dugdale's *Baronage of
England* (1675), Vol. I., pp. 325-6;
Burke's *General and Heraldic*
*Dictionary of Peerages, Extinct,
Dormant, and in Abeyance* (1831),
p. 511.

evidence whatever for it. It has been copied from Peerage into Peerage, though sometimes more or less abridged and sometimes amplified. It seems to have had its beginning in a passage in Dugdale's Baronage. Gilbert Talbot, it is there stated, "having married "Guenthlian, or Guendoline, daughter of Rhese ap "Griffith, Prince of Wales, ... departed this "life in 2 Edward I. [1274] . . . . leaving "Richard his son and heir, twenty-four years of "age."[1]

The most curious feature of this statement is, perhaps, that the only reference given in support of it is to the very plea roll which is a part of the case now under consideration,[2] and in which there is no mention whatever of Gwenllian's father, or of Rhys ap Griffith, or of any Welsh Prince of Wales. In some of the later Peerages—in that, for instance, of Collins, who, however, copies Dugdale's references— Rhys ap Griffith becomes Prince, not of Wales, but of South Wales.[3] In Banks's *Dormant and Extinct Baronage* (1807), Gwenllian becomes "Julian, daughter "and at length heir of Rhese ap Griffith, Prince of "South Wales."[4] In Burke's *Extinct Peerage* (1831) she becomes "Guentian, daughter and at length heir "of Rhese ap Griffiths, Prince of Wales,"[5] but in his *Peerage* (1832) she is "Gwendaline, daughter of Rhese "ap Griffith, Prince of South Wales,"[6] without any mention of heirship. In "G. E. C.'s" *Peerage* (1896) she again becomes "Gwendoline, daughter and finally "heir of Rhys ap Griffith, Prince of South Wales."[7]

---

[1] Dugdale, *Baronage of England* (1675), Vol. I., pp. 325-326.

[2] It is to the "*Plac. de Banco*, T. Hill, 19 Edw. III., *Rot.* 132."

[3] Collins, *Historical Peerage of England*. By Sir Egerton Brydges (1812), Vol. III., p. 3.

[4] Banks, *The Dormant and Extinct Baronage of England*, Vol.I., pedigree facing p. 176. The words

"at length heir" seem to have been taken from "tandem hæres" in Dugdale's pedigree of the Talbots. (*Baronage,* Vol. I., facing p. 325.)

[5] Burke, *Peerages Extinct, &c.,* p. 511.

[6] Burke, *Peerage and Baronetage,* Vol. II., p. 433.

[7] "G. E. C.," *Complete Peerage,* Vol. VII , p. 359, note a.

It may be said with truth that there was no Rhys ap Griffith "Prince of Wales" at any time near that of Gilbert Talbot, the grandfather. It has even been said that, in the strict sense of the term, there was no Prince of South Wales during that period. About the year 1114 the whole of Wales, except the extreme North West, and, perhaps, a strip of land extending along the West coast southwards as far as the westernmost part of Carmarthenshire "was divided between Norman and Welsh lords who "came to be called Lords Marchers. The subsequent "history of South and Central Wales resolves itself "into the records of quarrels between these lords and "the rise and fall of baronial families."[1]

The history of these Lords Marchers is very obscure, but they seem to have assumed quasi-regal rights within their lordships however small,[2] which were not regarded as constituting any part of any principality of Wales. In the year 1354 it was "agreed and established that all the lords of the "Marches of Wales shall be perpetually attendant "and annexed to the Crown of England, as they and "their ancestors have been in all previous times, and "not to the Principality of Wales in whosesoever "hands the same Principality may be."[3]

Position of Rhys ap Griffith commonly called Prince of South Wales.

Among these turbulent barons there had been a Rhys ap Griffith, who was of the blood of the earlier princes of South Wales, and who at one time exercised authority over a considerable portion of that territory. He made his peace with King Henry II., who appointed him Justiciary of South Wales; and his own fellow-country-men afterwards called him "Arglwydd" or Lord, which may have

---

[1] *The Welsh People*, by Prof. Rhys and Mr. Brynmor-Jones, p. 300.

[2] This was, at any rate, alleged in a plea to an information of *Quo Warranto* against Thomas Corne-

wall, in the reign of Elizabeth. Coke's *Booke of Entries*, fo. 550. The Statute 27 Hen. VIII., c. 26, is to the like effect.

[3] Stat. 28 Edw. III., c. 2.

indicated a recognition of a kind of feudal superiority. He was, indeed, again and again described as Prince of South Wales by his kinsman and contemporary Giraldus Cambrensis,[1] and may well have been recognised by his compatriots as Prince of South Wales *de jure*, if not *de facto*. He neither was nor claimed to be Prince of Wales, but when "Rhys ap "Griffith" is mentioned, without further description, as Prince of South Wales, it is always he who is meant.

This Rhys ap Griffith led a very active life, fighting battles and taking castles, from the year 1137, in which his father died, to the year 1197, in which he died himself at an advanced age.[2] There appears to be no doubt that he really had at least one daughter named Gwenllian, but he could not have had a daughter Gwenllian who married Gilbert Talbot, the grandfather of the demandant in our case of Cosinage. In one of the Welsh Chronicles it is stated that Gwenllian, daughter of Rhys, died in the year 1190,[3] and, as Rhys ap Griffith is mentioned in the sentence next preceding, the daughter was presumably his. In another chronicle, however, it appears that Gwenllian, daughter of Rhys the Great (as Rhys ap Griffith was sometimes called), and wife of Ednyfed Vychan, died in the year 1236.[4]

His daughter Gwenllian or Gwendoline, could not have been married to Gilbert Talbot, the demandant's grand father.

---

[1] *Giraldus Cambrensis* (Rolls edition), Vol. I., pp. 43, 57, 203, 208; Vol. IV., p. 100 ; Vol. VI., p. 85, &c. In the last passage the words are " ad Rhesum Griphini "filium . . . dextralis Kambriæ "dominium est devolutum."

[2] *Brut y Tywysogion* (Rolls edition), p. 244, and *Annales Cambriæ* (Rolls edition), p. 60. *See also The Welsh People*, by Rhys and Brynmor-Jones, pp. 309-315.

[3] *Brut y Tywysogion* (Rolls edition), p. 236.

[4] *Annales Cambriæ* (Rolls edition), p. 81. " Guenllian filia "Resi Magni, uxor Edneveth

" Vethan, obiit." The husband's name is obviously mis-spelt, *Vechan* having been misread *Vethan.* Ednyfed Vychan was not an unknown person. He is mentioned in the Myvyrian Archæology of Wales, and he has a prominent position in the pedigree of Lloyd of Plymog (Burke's *Heraldic Illustrations*, XL.). Professor Tout in his article *Rhys ap Gruffydd*, in the Dictionary of National Biography appears to recognise the Gwenllian who married Ednyfed Vychan, and died in 1236, as Rhys's only daughter of that name (p. 90)

It is possible that there was only one Gwenllian, daughter of Rhys ap Griffith, and that the date is wrongly given in one of the chronicles, but in any case she could not have been the wife of Gilbert Talbot, the grandfather of the demandant Gilbert, as she must have died at least fourteen years before the latter Gilbert's father, Richard Talbot, was born.

There remains the possibility that Rhys ap Griffith had yet another and younger daughter named Gwenllian. But even if he had a posthumous daughter born in 1198, she would have been fifty-two years of age when Richard Talbot was born, and the improbabilities practically amount to impossibility.

It ought, perhaps, to be mentioned that there was another Rhys son of Griffith, who appears to have been the grandson of Rhys ap Griffith, or Lord Rhys, the Justiciary. He, however, never enjoyed even the position held by his grandfather. He died, while still a young man, in the year 1222.[1] He seems to have been always known and described as Young Rhys, "Rys ieuanc," rather than as Rhys ap Griffith. There is nothing whatever to show or even to suggest that the Rhys the Little or Rhys Vychan or "Rees Vaghan" of the record was his son, or Gwenllian his daughter, and there is sufficient to show the contrary.

The Gwendoline so married was a daughter of Rhys Mechyll.

The field of Welsh pedigrees of this period is extremely slippery, because the same names occur again and again, and one generation may easily be confused with another, and even one family with another. Hereditary surnames were unknown, and territorial descriptions, such as we find in England, were but very rarely used in Wales. A man was commonly described as the son of his father, though often with a nickname for further identification, such as "the hoarse," "the red," "the little" or

---

[1] *Brut y Tywysoyion* (Rolls edition), p..310, &c.

"the younger." It may, however, be not impossible to discover who was the father of that Gwenllian whom Gilbert Talbot married. She was, according to the record, the sister of Rhys Vychan, or Rhys the Little, whose name was not unknown to the Welsh chroniclers, and if we can ascertain who was his father we shall know who was hers. That can be done, and Carreg Cennen Castle can be identified with the castle of Keyr Kenny at the same time. In the year 1248 Rhys Vychan, or the Little, son of Rhys Mechyll, regained possession of the Castle of Carreg Cennen, which his mother had treacherously given up.[1] Gilbert Talbot's father-in-law was therefore Rhys Mechyll, and not Rhys ap Griffith.

There is some reason to believe that Rhys Vychan died in the year 1271. At any rate a son of Rhys Mechyll, also named Rhys, but described in the text of the chronicle as Young Rhys, died then at Dynevor Castle.[2] The point is of some importance because in the year 1282 we find Griffith and Llewelyn, described as the sons of Rhys Vechan, engaged in another capture of Carreg Cennen Castle, together with a "Resum Vechan filium Resi filii Mailgonis" and several other persons.[3] From the collocation of the words it would appear that Rhys Vechan, the father of Griffith and Llewelyn, was one person, and Rhys Vechan, the son of Rhys the son of Mailgon, was another, who was described by the name of his father and grandfather to distinguish him from the older and better known Rhys Vychan.

Rhys Vychan's two sons became lords of Iskennen in accordance apparently with Welsh law.

Griffith and Llewelyn are here described as lords of Iskennen,[4] from which fact it seems to be clear

---

[1] *Brut y Tywysogion* (Rolls edition), p 334; edition of Messrs. Rhŷs and Evans, p. 371.

[2] *Brut y Tywysogion*, A.D., 1271 (p. 358, Rolls edition).

[3] *Annales Cambriæ* (Rolls edition). p. 106.

[4] The words as printed are " dominos Deyskennen," but they should obviously be read " dominos " de Yskennen."

that their father was dead. In the following year (1283) they were, with others, taken and thrown into prison in London.[1] It is worthy of notice that it is not the one brother Llewelyn who is said to be lord of Iskennen, but the two brothers jointly. This seems to show that the Welsh law had prevailed, and that the seignory had not descended from the father to the eldest son.

Demand-
ant's claim
founded
on the
seisin of
one only
(Llewelyn)
In the record there is no mention of Llewelyn's brother Griffith, but the whole claim is founded on the seisin of Llewelyn alone, and treated as if the law of England had prevailed. Llewelyn ap Rhys Vychan is made to appear as what would in England have been called a baron, possessing a fee of considerable extent, but not as a Prince of Wales or of any portion of Wales, except in so far as a great landowner may be called a prince.

His grand-
father's
wife not a
daughter
but a great
grand-
daughter
of Rhys ap
Griffith.
It appears, nevertheless, to be the fact that Gilbert Talbot, the demandant, might have traced a descent from Rhys ap Griffith "Prince of South Wales" in another way, though not through his daughter Gwenllian. Gilbert's grandmother, Gwenllian, and her brother, Rhys Vychan, were children of Rhys Mechyll. He, according to one of the chronicles, was a son of Rhys Gryg or Rhys the hoarse, and Rhys the hoarse was a son of Lord Rhys or Rhys ap Griffith.[2] Thus Gilbert's grandfather married not a daughter, but a great-grand-daughter of Rhys ap Griffith "Prince of South Wales," and this was, in all probability, the origin of the story.

The
reports of
the case :
a plea to
the juris-
diction.
Knowing, as we now do, who the demandant was, what were his connexions with the princely or other families of Wales, what was the subject of dispute, and where the lands claimed were situated, we are in a better position to follow the arguments and statements in the reports and the record. The defence

---

[1] *Annales Cambriæ*, p. 107   [2] *Brut y Tywysogion*, A.D., 1244, p. 330 (Rolls edition).

to the action began as follows[1]: "We tell you,"
said Derworthy, "that, whereas Gilbert Talbot
" demands on the seisin of his cousin, as having
" been seised in the time of King Edward I., the
" fact is that King Edward I. conquered the whole
" of Wales, and we tell you that the castle of Carreg
" Cennen is in Wales, outside the *corpus* of every
" county of England, and we do not understand that
" in this Court of Common Pleas you will take
" cognisance of the plea. And, as to the commote,
" that is not a term of law in England by which
" anything can be demanded." Paruynge, the future
Chancellor, who was for the demandant, said that the
castle and the commote constituted one great seignory
holden *in capite* of the King and his crown, and
that pleas concerning it ought not to be held any-
where but in his own Court.

The question of jurisdiction having been apparently Other
settled or waived for the time, a charter was pleaded pleas:
on behalf of the tenants, Ralph de Wilyntone and seisin
his wife, whereby the King (Edward III.) enfeoffed and issue
them; and aid was prayed of the King and granted. joined
Afterwards the King sent his writ *de procedendo* to thereon.
the Justices, and the tenants vouched to warrant
the heir of John Giffard. The ground of the
voucher was that the lands were seized into the
King's hand by reason of the forfeiture of John
Giffard, whose heir[2] sued them out of the King's
hand when the proceedings against Thomas, Earl of
Lancaster, and his adherents were reversed, but,
nevertheless, confirmed the King's estate in them
with warranty to the King and his heirs and assigns.
Ralph de Wilynton and his wife therefore claimed to
be warranted as the King's assigns. No documents,

---

[1] Y.B., Mich., 13 Edw. III., No.
79, p. 176.

[2] In the three reports of this part
of the case, one in Michaelmas
Term, 13 Edw. III., No. 79, and

two in Michaelmas Term, 14 Edw.
III.(No.95). there are three different
statements as to who was the heir,
but the names and relationships
were imm aterial to the reporter.

however, were produced in support of this statement, and on the other hand it was alleged that in the admitted charter to Wilyntone and his wife it was expressed that the King had previously been seised by reason of the forfeiture of John Maltravers. The voucher was not allowed, and issue was joined on a traverse of Llewelyn's seisin.

Aid prayed of the King on the ground of his charter to the tenants.

Jury process to try that issue was continued until the morrow of St. Martin in the seventeenth year of the reign, when Ralph de Wilyntone and Eleanor his wife made default, and, after some essoins, Eleanor prayed, before judgment, on a second default of her husband, to be admitted to defend, alleging that the castle and commote were her right. She was admitted, and produced the King's charter to which reference has already been made. It was to the effect that he gave and granted to John de Wilyntone, since deceased, and Ralph, his son, and Ralph's wife, Eleanor, the castle of Carreg Cennen (which had belonged to John Maltravers, the King's enemy and rebel, and had come into the King's hand by forfeiture as an escheat) to hold to the three grantees and the heirs of Ralph's body, together with the lands and tenements and commote of Iskennen, as well as knights' fees, advowsons of churches, liberties, and customs belonging to the castle, lands, tenements, and commote. The whole was to be held of the King and his heirs and other chief lords of the fee. There were remainders to Henry, son of Henry de Wilyntone, in tail, and to the right heirs of Ralph. On the ground of this charter Eleanor again prayed aid of the King.[1]

A new plea to the jurisdiction, the King having granted the Principality of Wales,

When the King's writ *de procedendo*, which followed, was received by the Justices of the Common Bench, there was again a plea to the jurisdiction. Grene, who was counsel for the tenants said :—" The tene- " ments are in the Welshry, and, before the conquest

[1] Y.B., Hil., 19 Edw. III , No. 12 (pp. 420-424 ; 425, note 3).

" of Wales, were pleadable in the court of the Prince since the
" of Wales; and we tell you that, while the writ action com-
" was pending, the King has granted the Principality menced, to
" of Wales to his son, to hold with all the his eldest son.
" franchises as fully as Llewelyn [ap Griffith, Prince
" of Wales] held them, and the Prince now has his
" Justices, Chancery, &c., there, and we do not under-
" stand that you will take cognisance in this Court."[1]

The King also sent a writ to the Justices, reciting his grant by charter to his eldest son, Edward (the Black Prince), of the Principality of Wales, and commanding them in no wise to attempt unduly anything contrary to the form and effect of that charter, to the prejudice of the Prince, or of his right and franchises, but to allow to the Prince in their Court the franchises and other matters included in the charter. This writ was used in support of the plea to the jurisdiction.[2]

For the demandant it was then pleaded that the Met by the
Court had been seised (*seisita*) of the plea long before reply that there was
the King had divested himself of the Principality of nothing to show that
Wales, and that Eleanor had been admitted to defend the tene-
her right after he had so divested himself, had then ments were part
prayed aid of the King, and had so confirmed the of the
jurisdiction of the Court. There was nothing to show Princi-pality.
to the Court by any mandate from the King or from the Prince that the tenements were part of the Principality, or that the Justices ought to stay proceedings. Therefore it was not to be understood that it lay in the mouth of Eleanor, who had already confirmed the jurisdiction of the Court to deny or question it. If, however, it should appear to the Court that she ought to be admitted to question the jurisdiction, the demandant was prepared to say sufficient to maintain it, and, since she said nothing else in defence of her right, he prayed judgment.[3]

---

[1] Below, pp. 420-422.

[2] Y.B., Hil., 19 Edw. III., p. 425, note 3.

[3] Below, p. 422, and Y.B., Hil., 19 Edw. III., p. 425, note 3,

But supported by the statement that they were within it.

It was then pleaded on behalf of Eleanor that the tenements in demand were within the Principality, which the King had granted to the Prince with everything appertaining to the Principality, such as his own Chancery, cognisance of pleas, and all other things belonging to the regality of the Principality, as appeared in the writ already mentioned. It was, therefore, not to be understood that the Court would take cognisance of this plea, contrary to the King's grant to the Prince of the Principality with all things belonging to it, as testified in the writ.

There followed an adjournment for the Court to consider whether it should proceed further in the plea or not.[1]

The charter by which the Principality was granted to the Black Prince.

Thus it was contended, on the one hand that the castle and commote were within the Principality of Wales, and within the jurisdiction of the Prince, and on the other hand that no claim of the cognisance of the plea had been made on behalf of the Prince, and therefore that the Court was not apprised that the tenements were within the Principality. As a matter of fact they were not within the Principality of which Llewelyn was Prince, and the Principality was not in express words granted to Edward the Black Prince to hold with all the franchises as fully as Llewelyn held them. There was a little rhetorical artifice in Grene's statement to that effect.

It included other lands and lordships, and in particular the county of Carmarthen.

Edward III. created[2] his eldest son Prince of Wales, and granted to him the Principality of Wales and certain other lordships and lands as fully as he himself held or ought to hold them, and by such services as Edward II., when Prince of Wales, held

---

[1] Y.B., Hil., 19 Edw. III., p. 425, note 3.

[2] The charter has already been printed in Selden's *Titles of Honour*, pp. 595-598, from *Rot. Chart.* 17 Edw. III., No. 27, and it has, therefore, not been reprinted here, or in the notes to the reports of the case. Portions of it have also been printed in Coke's *Fourth Institute*, p. 243, and in the Third Report on the Dignity of a Peer, p. 187.

them of Edward I. Llewelyn is not mentioned at all. In addition to the Principality the Prince was to have all the King's lordships or seignories and lands of North Wales, West Wales, and South Wales, and various lordships or seignories, castles, and towns mentioned by name, and in particular "dominio, "castro, villa, et comitatu de Kermerden," and he was to enjoy all the franchises (enumerated) "tam "ad dictum Principatum quam ad nos in dictis "partibus spectantibus quoquo modo." This would appear to have given him every jurisdiction which the King had in any part of Wales, but not to have affected any jurisdiction which the Lords Marchers may have possessed.

It might, perhaps, be thought that, as the county of Carmarthen was expressly mentioned, and as Carreg Cennen Castle and the hundred of Iskennen are in the modern Carmarthenshire, the Prince's jurisdiction could be clearly established. When we find also in the so-called *Statutum Walliæ* made shortly after the conquest of Wales by Edward I. (in the twelfth year of the reign) a mention of the Sheriff of Carmarthenshire with a statement that his jurisdiction was to extend over the county " cum "cantredis, et commotis, ac metis et bundis suis " antiquis," it might seem that no doubt could arise about the commote of Iskennen. There is, however, some reason to believe that the county of Carmarthen was not, at this time, generally understood to extend eastwards beyond the river Towy. *The boundaries of the county at that time not exactly defined.*

There are, indeed, in the Rolls of Parliament[1] of the time of Edward I. expressions which seem to treat certain liberties, and apparently that of Iskennen, as being within the boundaries of the county though not part of the geldable, but it is not clear that there was any geldable of the county east of the *The commote of Iskennen not added to it before the reign of Henry VIII.*

---

[1] *Rot. Parl.* 21 Edw. III. (*Placita in Parliamento*, No. 18, m. 6), Vol. I., p. 105.

Towy. These expressions cannot, at any rate, out-weigh the positive words of the Act of Henry VIII. It is there definitely stated that "there be many " and dyvers Lordshippes Marchers within the said " Countrey or Dominion of Wales lieng betwene the " Shires of Englande and the Shires of the said " Countrey or Dominion of Wales, and beyng noo " parcell of any other Shires where the Lawes and " due correccion is used and had." It was therefore enacted *inter alia*, that certain lordships, towns, parishes, commotes, hundreds, and cantreds, and all honours, lordships, castles, manors, lands, tenements, and hereditaments lying or being within the precinct or compass of the said lordships, &c., should stand and be geldable for ever, and should be united and joined with the county of Carmarthen as a member, part, or parcel of the same. Among several lordships and commotes east of the Towy so added to Carmarthenshire we find "Eskennyn,"[1] which is, without doubt, the Iskenny of the reports and record, the Iskennen which gives its name to the modern hundred, the Isgenen of some old maps.

The action abandoned.
As both the reports and the records conclude with an adjournment, the probability is that the demandant abandoned the claim. It assumed that the English law as to realty and its descent was in force, in that part of Wales or its marches in which the commote and castle were situated, at the time of the death of Llewelyn ap Rhys Vychan.[2] He does, in fact, appear to have survived the conquest of Wales, but he had been engaged with David, the brother of Llewelyn, Prince of Wales, or of North Wales, in the last struggle made against the English,[3] and was,

---

[1] Stat. 27 Henry VIII., c. 26, s.13.

[2] In the opinion of Messrs. Rhys and Brynmor-Jones the whole of Wales, except the extreme north-west corner, may have been feudalised by this time (*The Welsh People*, p. 304). The mention, however, of Griffith and Llewelyn together as lords of Iskennen after the death of their father Rhys Vychan seems, in this particular case, to point the other way.

[3] *Annales Cambriæ* (Rolls edition), p. 106,

without doubt, regarded, like David himself, as a traitor. If he was not executed like David, he probably died in prison in London, and his lands would almost certainly have been forfeited to the crown of England, and any subsequent title to them would have depended upon a grant from the King. It appears, indeed, on the Rolls of Parliament, that Edward I. did, in the eleventh year of his reign (A.D. 1283), within a year of the conquest of Wales, grant the commote to John Giffard,[1] whose descendant the tenants in the action would, if they had been permitted, have vouched to warrant. It is true that the commote is described as "Hyskynny" in the roll, and that the grantee is described as John Giffard of "Ilkenny" in the printed text, but the commote which is meant is clearly that of Iskennen, and Talbot could not have had any good claim to it by descent.

I have again the pleasure of offering my best thanks to the Benchers of the Honourable Society of Lincoln's Inn for the loan of their most valuable MS.

L. OWEN PIKE.

Lincoln's Inn,
    11th August, 1906.

---

[1] *Rot. Parl.* 21 Edw. I. as above.

TABLE OF CASES IN THE PRESENT VOLUME. [1]

[1] This table includes only cases in which the name of one party at least is given in the report, or in which the names of the parties have been ascertained from the record, and not those in which all the parties are represented merely by letters in the report. An index of matters is printed at p. 497, and an index of persons and places at p. 527.

TABLE OF REFERENCES TO THE LIBER ASSISARUM.

Year of Reign and Number of Case in the Liber Assisarum.								Page in the present Volume.
19.	Li. Ass.	No.	1	-	-	-	-	13
,,	,,	,,	2	-		-	-	15
,,	,,	,,	3	-	-	-	-	35
,,	,,	.,	4	-	-	-	-	105
,,	,,	,,	5	-	-	-	-	139
,,	.,	,,	6	-	-		-	179
,,	,,	,,	7		-		-	237
,,	,,	,,	8	-	-	-	-	267
,,	,,	,,	9	-	-	-	-	353

TABLE OF REFERENCES TO FITZHERBERT'S ABRIDGMENT.

Title and Number in Fitzherbert's Abridgment.					Page in the present Volume.
Abbe, 13	-	-	-	-	- 423
Administratours, 20	-	-	-		13
Aide, 27	-	-	-	-	- 305
,, 144	-	-	-	-	- 51
Ayde de Roy, 5	-	-	-	-	- 361
,, 65	-	-	-	-	- 51
Amendement, 65	-	-	-	-	- 331
Annuite, 26	-	-	-	-	- 107
Assise, 83	-	-	-	-	- 15
,, 84	-	-	-	-	- 105
Attourne, 77	-	-	-	-	- 329
Avowre, 122	-	-	-	-	- 199
Barre, 279	-	-	-	-	- 179
,, 280	-	-	-	-	- 403
,, 281	-	-	-	-	- 473

THE CHANCELLOR, JUSTICES OF THE TWO BENCHES, TREASURER, AND BARONS OF THE EXCHEQUER DURING THE PERIOD OF THE REPORTS.

Chancellor.

Sir Robert de Sadington.

John de Offord (from and after the 26th of October, 1345).[1]

Justices of the Court of King's Bench.

Sir William Scot, Chief Justice.

Sir Roger de Baukwell.

Sir William Basset.

Sir William de Thorpe.[2]

Justices of the Court of Common Pleas.[3]

Sir John de Stonore, Chief Justice.

Sir Roger Hillary.

Sir Richard de Kelleshulle, or Kelshulle.

Sir Richard de Wylughby, or Willoughby.

Sir John de Stouford.

Treasurer.

William de Edyngton.

Barons of the Exchequer.

Sir William de Shareshulle, or Sharshulle, Chief Baron until the 10th of November, 1345.[4]

Sir John de Stouford, Chief Baron from the 10th of November [5] to the 8th of December, 1345.

Sir Robert de Sadington (late Chancellor), appointed Chief Baron on the 8th of December, 1345.[6]

Sir William de Broclesby.

Sir Gervase de Wilford.

Sir Alan de Asshe.

---

[1] *Rot. Lit. Claus.* 19 Edw. III., p. 2, m. 10, d, and *Rot. Lit. Pat.* 19 Edw. III. p. 2, m. 7.

[2] *Rot. Lit. Pat.* 19 Edw. III., p. 1, m. 14 (grant to as Justice, 20 May, 1345).

[3] As ascertained from the Feet of Fines of the three Terms.

[4] Sharshulle was re-appointed to the Common Bench, as Second Justice, on the 10th of November, 1345 (*Rot. Lit. Pat.* 19 Edw. III., p. 2, m. 2). His name, however, does not re-appear in the Feet of Fines until Hilary Term, 20 Edw. III.

[5] *Rot. Lit. Pat.* 19 Edw. III., p. 2, m. 2. On the appointment of Sadington to be Chief Baron on the 8th of December, 1345, Stouford seems to have been re-appointed Justice of the Common Bench, and his name re-appears in the Feet of Fines of Hilary Term, 20 Edw. III.

[6] *Rot. Lit. Pat.* 19 Edw. III., p. 3, m. 11.

NAMES OF THE "NARRATORES," COUNTORS, OR COUNSEL.

Richard de Birton.
Roger de Blaykeston.
Adam Bret.
Hamo Derworthy.
John de Gaynesford.
Henry Grene.
John de Haveryngton.
James Huse, or Husee.
John de Moubray.
Henry de Mutlow, or Motelowe.
William de Notton.
Richard de la Pole.
Peter de Richemunde.
John de la Rokel, or Rokele, or Rokelle.
Hugh de Sadelyngstanes.
Thomas de Seton.
William de Skipwith.
Robert de Thorpe.
William de Thorpe.[2]

CORRECTIONS.

Page 58, note 1, column 2, line 1, *for* "per" *read* "par."
  ,, 131, margin, *after* "*Quare impedit*" *add* "[Fitz., Collusion, 33.]"
  ,, 178, line 18, *for* "Shipwith" *read* "Skipwith."
  ,, 267, note 1, column 1, line 3, *for* "Trin." *read* "Easter."
  ,, 301, note 3, column 2, last line, *for* "egui" *read* "equi."
  ,, 413, note 1, column 2, line 23, *after* "concessimus" *dele* the comma.
  ,, 426, line 17, *for* "W.¹" *read* "W.³."
  ,, 433, notes, column 2, line 12, *for* "libræ" *read* "libras."
  ,, 489, line 4, *for* "septimanus" *read* 'septimanas."

[1] Mentioned in the Plea Rolls of the Common Bench as receiving chirographs of Fines. The fact that the counsel mentioned in the reports could be identified with the "narratores" mentioned in the rolls was discovered through the minute inspection of the rolls which was necessary for my proposed calendar of them. *See* the Vol. of Y.B., 16 Edw. III., Part 2 (published in 1900), p. xi.

[2] A Justice of the King's Bench in May, 1345.

EASTER TERM

IN THE

NINETEENTH YEAR OF THE REIGN OF
KING EDWARD THE THIRD
AFTER THE CONQUEST.

EASTER TERM IN THE NINETEENTH YEAR OF THE REIGN OF KING EDWARD THE THIRD AFTER THE CONQUEST.

=====

No. 1.

A.D. 1345.
*Monstra-
verunt.* (1.) § Walter Blake and several others,[1] as tenants of Ancient Demesne of the manor of Eynsham, brought a *Monstraverunt* against the Abbot of Eynsham, containing a statement that the Abbot demanded of them customs and services other than those which they ought to perform or were wont to perform in the time during which the said manor was in the hands of the progenitors of our lord the King, and tortiously so, because, whereas when the said manor was in the hand of King William the Conqueror, one A.,[1] cousin of the aforesaid Walter, in the time of the said William the Conqueror, held so many acres of land by the service of so much rent *per annum*, and of doubling his rent after the death of each tenant, in lieu of all services, and so in the case of each particular tenant,[1] the present Abbot came and demanded of them other customs and services, that is to say, sowing, hoeing,

---

[1] For the names, *see* p. 3, note 2.

DE TERMINO PASCHÆ ANNO REGNI REGIS EDWARDI TERTII A CONQUESTU DECIMO NONO.[1]

No. 1.

(1.) [2] § Wauter Blake et plusours autres, comme A.D. 1345. tenantz del aunciene demene del maner de E.[3] *Monstra-verunt.* porterent *Monstraverunt* vers Labbe[4] de Eynesham, [Fitz., contenant coment Labbe les demande autres custumes *Monstra-verunt,* 5.] et services qe faire[5] ne deivent ou faire[6] soleint en temps qe le dit[7] maner estoit en meyns des progenitours nostre seignur le Roi, et pur ceo atort qe, par la quant le dit maner fuit en la meyn le Roi William le Conquerour, un A. cosyn lavantdit[8] Wauter, en temps le dit William le Conquerour, tient taunt des acres de terre[9] par taunt de rente par an, et pur doubler sa rente apres la mort de chesqun[10] tenant, pur touz[11] services, *et sic de singulis,* la vint[12] Labbe qore est et les demande autres custumes et services, saver, semer, sarcher,[13] sier des

---

[1] The reports of this Term are from the Lincoln's Inn MS. (called L.), the Harleian MS., No. 741 (called H.), the Cambridge MS. Hh. 2, 3 (called C.), and the Cambridge MS. Hh. 2, 4 (called D.).

[2] From H., L., and C., but corrected by the record, *Placita de Banco,* 19 Edw. III., R° 91. It there appears that the action was brought by Walter Blake, Robert Revesone, John Cryps, Richard "The Loder," Robert Hankyn, Alan Gybone, William "The Herte," Richard Walters, John Streen, Robert Leovon, and Adam le Blake, "homines et tenentes

" Abbatis de Eynesham, de manerio " suo de Eynesham," against the Abbot of Eynsham.

[3] MSS. of Y.B., B.

[4] Labbe is omitted from C.

[5] C., fere.

[6] faire is from L. alone.

[7] dit is omitted from C.

[8] H., le dit.

[9] L., and C., des terres, instead of de terre.

[10] H., chescun mort de, instead of la mort de chesqun.

[11] L., and C., toux.

[12] The words la vint are omitted from H.

[13] So in all the MSS.

No. 1.

A.D. 1345. cutting corn, threshing, ploughing, and harrowing, and the right to tallage them high and low, and ransom of flesh and blood, whereupon they delivered to him the King's Prohibition, forbidding him, &c., and he, on that account, did not desist, tortiously, and to their

No. 1.

blees,[1] bater, arrer,[2] et hercer, et les tailler haut et
bas,[3] rechat de char et saunk, sur quei, &c., ils live-
rerunt[4] la Prohibicion le Roi, &c., defendant,[5] &c., et il
par taunt ne lessa point,[6] atort,[7] et a lour damage.[8]—

---

[1] H., bleds.

[2] C., arrere.

[3] H., baas.

[4] H., livererent.

[5] H., defendaunt.

[6] H., and C., &c.

[7] L., attort.

[8] The declaration was, according to the record, " quod quidam " Willelmus le Blake, consan- " guineus prædicti Walteri Blake. " tenuit unam mesuagium et " duas virgatas- tèrræ, cum perti- " nentiis, in . . . . manerio " de Eynesham, quod est de " antiquo dominico coronæ Regis, " &c., tempore Willelmi Regis " Conquæstoris, &c., progenitoris " domini Regis nunc, per fidelita- " tem, et servitium decem solido- " rum per annum, et post mortem " cujuslibet tenentis duplicandi " redditum prædictum, pro omni " servitio et consuetudine, et qui- " dam Willelmus Bodde tenuit " unum mesuagium et duas virgatas " terræ, cum pertinentiis, in eodem " manerio de Eynesham, tempore " ejusdem Regis, per consimilia " servitia, et quidam Johannes " Revesone, consanguineus prædicti " Roberti Revesone, tenuit unum " mesuagium et duas virgatas " terræ, cum pertinentiis, in præ- " dicto manerio, per consimilia " servitia, et quidam Walterus " Cryps, consanguineus prædicti " Johannis Cryps, tenuit unum " mesuagium et duas virgatas " terræ, in eodem manerio, per " consimilia servitia, &c., et " quidam Willelmus The Loder, " consanguineus prædicti Ricardi " The Loder, tenuit unum mesua- " gium et duas virgatas terræ, cum " pertinentiis, in eodem manerio, " per consimilia servitia, &c., et " quidam Robertus Hankyn, con- " sanguineus prædicti Roberti " Hankyn, tenuit unum mesuagium " et unam virgatam terræ, cum " pertinentiis, per fidelitatem, et " servitium quinque solidorum per " annum, et post mortem cujuslibet " tenentis duplicandi redditum " nomine relevii, &c. Et quidam " Gilbertus Giboun, consanguineus " prædicti Alani Gyboun, tenuit " unum mesuagium et unam " virgatam terræ, cum pertinentiis, " in eodem manerio, per consimilia " servitia, &c., et quidam Philippus " The Herte, consanguineus præ- " dicti Willelmi The Herte, tenuit " unum mesuagium et unam " virgatam terræ, cum pertinentiis, " in eodem manerio, per consimilia " servitia, &c., et quidam Johannes " Walters, consanguineus prædicti " Ricardi Walters, tenuit unum " mesuagium et unam virgatam " terræ, cum pertinentiis, in eodem " manerio per consimilia servi- " tia, &c., et quidam Ricardus " Streen, consanguineus prædicti " Johannis Streen, tenuit unum " mesuagium et unam virgatam " terræ, cum pertinentiis, in eodem " manerio, per consimilia servitia, " &c., et quidam Adam Leovon, " consanguineus prædicti Roberti " Leovon, tenuit unum mesuagium " et unam virgatam terræ, cum " pertinentiis, in eodem manerio,

No. 1.

A.D. 1345. damage.—*Huse* denied tort and force, and, as to three, he said that they were the Abbot's villeins, to be tallaged high and low, &c., and that the Abbot was seised of them, &c.; judgment whether they ought to be answered. And, as to three others, he denied the damages, and demanded judgment of the count, because they had counted for those three in common,

No. 1.

Husc[1] defendi[2] tort et force, et, quant a iij, il[3] dit A.D. 1345. qils sount les villeins Labbe, a[4] tailler en haut et bas, &c., et il seisi de eux,[5] &c.; jugement sil deivent estre respondu. Et, quant as autres iij, il defendi[2] les damages, et demanda jugement de count, de ceo qils avoint counte pur eux[6] en comune, la

---

" per consimilia servitia, &c.,
" idem Abbas exigit ab eis alia
" servitia et alias consuetudines,
" videlicet, de quolibet tenentium
" prædictorum tenente unum
" mesuagium et unam virgatam
" terræ, de arando terram ipsius
" Abbatis cum una caruca et octo
" bobus, vel octo affris, ter in
" septimana, et de seminando et
" herciando eandem terram, et
" facit eos compostare totam
" terram dicti manerii cum
" carectis ipsorum tenentium, et
" falcare omnia prata ipsius
" Abbatis, et fena levare, et unire,
" et ad domum dicti Abbatis
" cariare, et blada sua sarculare,
" metere, et unire, et ad manerium
" ipsius Abbatis de Eynesham
" cariare, et facit eos eadem
" blada triturare, tam in diebus
" Natalis domini, Paschæ, et
" omnibus aliis dupplicibus festis,
" quam in aliis diebus ferialibus,
" ubicumque eos assignare voluerit
" cariare et affragium facere, ita
" quod redire possint eodem die,
" et post vacationem cujuslibet
" tenementorum prædictorum capit
" finem de tenente eorundem
" tenementorum ad voluntatem
" ejusdem Abbatis, et capit
" redemptiones carnis et sanguinis
" de eisdem tenentibus et eorum
" exitibus, et plures alias extor-
" siones, fines, tallagia, et diversa
" servitia innumerabilia per graves
" districtiones et intolerabiles ab

" eisdem hominibus extorquendo
" talliat alto et basso ad volunta-
" tem suam, et præpositos suos de
" eis facit, per quod iidem homines,
" taliter indebite prægravati, Pro-
" hibitionem domini Regis, die
" dominica proxima ante festum
" Sancti Augustini, anno regni
" Regis nunc decimo octavo in
" præsentia Johannis le Peyntour,
" Hugonis de Loughtebourghe, et
" Willelmi Jonesman the Peyntour,
" et aliorum, apud Eynesham,
" liberarunt eidem Abbati, inhi-
" bendo ne idem Abbas alias
" consuetudines vel alia servitia
" ab eis exigeret quam facere
" deberent, et ipsi et antecessores
" sui facere consueverunt, &c.,
" idem Abbas, spreta prohibitione
" domini Regis prædicta, ipsos
" homines ad faciendum con-
" suetudines et servitia supradicta
" graviter, et intolerabiliter, ac per
" extorsiones innumerabiles, dis-
" trinxit, contra prohibitionem,
" &c., unde dicunt quod deteriorati
" sunt et damnum habent ad
" valentiam mille librarum. Et
" inde producunt sectam, &c."

[1] H., *Husee.*
[2] H., defend.
[3] H., vous, instead of quant a iij, il.
[4] C., au.
[5] L., and H., deux, instead of de eux.
[6] H., eaux.

No. 1.

A.D. 1345. whereas one of them, to wit A., was dead at the time at which the count was counted.—*Grene.* You shall not be admitted to that, because you have denied the damages of him, as well as of the others, and have so accepted him as being one entitled to an answer.— HILLARY. Do you think that he shall not be admitted to allege the death of any one after having denied damage? As meaning to say that he would. But even though the exception be to the abatement of the count, that affects only the one who is dead, so that it is necessary to answer the others.—*Blaykeston.* The defect in this bad count is not that of the one who is dead, but that of the other two who are parties; and if the count is to abate by reason of their mistake it should rightly abate in its entirety.—*Seton, ad idem.* If several persons bring a writ, and one be dead on the day on which the writ is purchased, the writ will abate with regard to them all; for the same reason the count will abate when it is counted for one who is dead on the day on which the count is counted.—STONORE. It is a special case on this writ of *Monstraverunt,* that one person can sue on behalf of himself and of all the other persons of the vill, even though they be not named; and, even though they be not named in the writ, yet all the others shall have advantage through the suit of one; and the one who appears may be admitted, and shall answer by attorney for all the others, although that attorney was never admitted as theirs, so that this suit and this writ are not like any others.—*Seton.* That, Sir, is true; but one who appears is not, on that account, entitled to count on behalf of a person who is dead, and, if he do so, it is right that the count do abate. —*Thorpe.* And if

No. 1.

ou un[1] de eux,[2] saver A.,[3] al temps del count counte A.D. 1345.
fuit mort.—*Grene.* A ceo ne serretz resceu, qar
vous avetz[4] defendu les damages de luy[5] si bien
come de les[6] autres, et issint accepte luy estre responable.—HILLARY. Quidetz vous qe apres defens
il[7] ne serra pas resceu dallegger[8] sa mort? *quasi
diceret sic.* Mes, tut soit il[9] al abatement de count,
ceo nest forqe a luy qest mort, issint qil covient
respondre a les autres.—*Blayk.* En celuy qest mort
nest pas la defaut de ceo malveis count, mes en[10]
les autres deux[11] qe sount parties; et si[12] le count
abate par[13] lour mesprissioun[14] il est resoun qil
abate en tut.—*Setone,*[15] *ad idem.* Si plousours portent
un brief, et un soit mort jour du brief purchace,
le brief abatra vers touz[16]; par mesme la resoun
le count quant il est counte pur un qest mort jour
de count counte.—STON. Cest un cas a per luy en
cest brief de *Monstraverunt,* qun purra suir pur luy
et touz[16] les autres de la ville, tut ne soient[17] il
pas nomes[18]; et coment qils ne soient pas nomes
el brief et par la suite dun touz[16] les autres averount avantage; et cestuy qe vient purra estre resceu,
et respoundra par attourne pur touz[16] les autres,
coment qe unqes ne fuit resceu lour attourne, issint
qe ceste[19] suite ne[20] brief est semblable a nulle
autre.—*Setone.* Sire, il est verite; mes celuy qe vint
par taunt ne deit pas counter pur mort persone,
et sil face, il est resoun qe le count abat.—*Thorpe.*

---

[1] un is omitted from H.
[2] L., and H., deux, instead of de eux.
[3] H., A., et B.
[4] L., and C., avietz.
[5] L., and C., lun.
[6] H., des, instead of de les.
[7] H., qils.
[8] C., de allegger.
[9] il is omitted from C.
[10] en is omitted from H.
[11] deux is omitted from C.
[12] H., issi.
[13] H., pur.
[14] C., mespressioun.
[15] L., and C., STON.
[16] L., toux.
[17] H., suent.
[18] nomes is omitted from H.
[19] H., en cesty.
[20] H., le.

No. 1.

the count abates, according to your contention, with regard to one who is dead, it therefore abates with regard to all the plaintiffs, and consequently with regard to those in whose persons you allege villenage, and, therefore, if you hold to your exception, you waive the villenage.—*Blaykeston.* As to the villeins we do not say anything but that they ought not to be answered; but as to the persons of free condition we say that they have counted badly. And suppose three persons bring a writ of Trespass against me, and I say, as to one, that he is my villein, and therefore shall not be answered, and, as to the others, I plead to their count, I shall be admitted to do so; so in the matter before us.—*Pole.* In the case which you give an exception of villenage alleged against one abates writ and action against all.—*Quære.*—And, in this case, if you abate the count as to the other three, it cannot stand good with regard to the villeins.—HILLARY. In that case issue can be taken on the villenage without affirming the count with regard to those in whom villenage is alleged; and if, while the inquest is pending, the count abates, on such cause, with regard to all those who are of free condition, it will abate with regard to the villeins also, but not otherwise.—Afterwards *Huse* took exception only as to the death, having regard to the person who was dead; and, as to the two others, he prayed that they should produce the record to certify the Court that the manor whereof, &c., is Ancient Demesne.—And the COURT was of opinion that nothing could be done until they were apprised by record that the manor was Ancient Demesne.—Afterwards the plaintiffs *non pros.*

No. 1.

Et si le count abate,[1] a vostre entent, vers celuy A.D. 1345. qest mort, *ergo* vers touz[2] les pleintifs, et *per consequens* vers ceux en queux vous alleggez le villenage, par qai si vous tenetz[3] a vostre excepcion vous weyvetz le villenage.—*Blayk.* Nous ne[4] dioms, quant as villeins,[5] rienz mes qils ne deivent estre respondu; mes, quant a les fraunkes nous dioms qils ount malement counte. Et mettetz qe iij[6] portent un brief de Trans vers moy, et jeo die, quant a un, qil est mon villein, par quei il ne serra pas respondu, et[7] quant a les autres jeo plede a lour count, jeo serroy[8] resceu; *sic in proposito.*—*Pole.* En le cas qe vous donetz excepcion de villenage allegge vers un abat brief[9] et accion vers touz.—*Quære.*—Et, en ceo cas, si vous abatez le count quant as autres iij, ceo ne poet esteer[10] vers les villeins.—Hill. Homme poet en le cas prendre issue sur le villenage saunz affermer le count vers eux en queux le villenage est allegge; et si pendaunt lenqueste le count abat sur tiel cause vers touz les fraunkes, il abatra vers les villeins auxi, et autrement nient.—Puis[11] *Huse*[12] prist lexcepcion soulement de la mort, eaunt[13] regarde a celuy qest mort; et quant a les deux autres il pria[14] qils meissent avant le[15] recorde pur ascerter[16] la Court qe le maner dount, &c., est aunciene demene.— Et Court est del avys qe homme ferreit rienz sanz estre appris par recorde qe le maner est aunciene demene.—*Postea non prosecuti sunt.*[17]

---

[1] H., abatra.

[2] L., toux.

[3] H., teignes.

[4] H., vous.

[5] H., a la villenage, instead of as villeins.

[6] H., les iij.

[7] L., mes.

[8] L., serra; H., serrai.

[9] L., le brief.

[10] H., estre; C., estere.

[11] Puis is omitted from H.

[12] H., *Husee.*

[13] H., eiaunt.

[14] The words autres il pria are omitted from H.

[15] le is from H. alone.

[16] H., asserter.

[17] On the roll the words " Postea " prædicti Walterus Blake et alii " querentes non sunt prosecuti " immediately follow the declaration.

Nos. 2–5.

A.D. 1345.
Note.

(2.) § Note that in the case in which persons who had taken, through the Ordinary, administration of the goods of one deceased, not being the executors appointed by the testator, and who had brought a writ against the Prior of the Hospital of St. John of Jerusalem, HILLARY gave judgment that they should take nothing, because they were not executors, and an action is not given them by Statute.[1]

Account.

(3.) § Note that, on a writ of Account brought against William de Langeforde, *Birton* said :—You have here William de Langeforde, knight, by attorney, and he prays that you do count against him.—And, because the plaintiff would not count, HILLARY gave judgment that the plaintiff should take nothing, notwithstanding the variance in the addition of "knight."

Debt.

(4.) § Note that John Gisors sued by writ of Debt, for seven years, against several defendants, who, after the Grand Distress, fourched by *Idem dies*, that is to say, when the Distress was returned upon one, he appeared and took a day by *Idem dies*, and one who had a day by *Idem dies* now makes default.—*Birton* prayed that the issues of those who now make default, which were previously returned upon them, might be forfeited, although they had a day by *Idem dies*.— HILLARY. We cannot do that in the absence of any Statute.[2]

Novel
Disseisin.

(5.) § Novel Disseisin, before BAUKWELL and THORPE, in respect of a moiety of a mill. It was found that

---

[1] 13 Edw. I. (Westm. 2), c. 23 ; 4 Edw. III., c. 7.

[2] The remedy prayed was not given by the Statute against fourcher by essoin (3 Edw. I., Westm. 1, c. 43).

Nos. 2–5.

(2.)[1] § *Nota* qe autrefoith ces qavoint pris adminis- A.D. 1345.
tracion des biens le mort par Lordener,[3] et ne furent *Nota.*[2]
pas assignes par le testatour, qe porterent autrefoith [Fitz., *Adminis-*
brief vers le Prior del Hospital de Seint Johan, &c., *tratours,*
HILL. agarda qils preissent rienz, *quia non executores,* 20.]
et actio pro eis non datur per statutum.

(3.)[4] § *Nota* qen[6] brief Daccompte porte vers Acompte.[5]
William de Langeforde, *Birtone* :—Vous avetz[7] cy
William de Langeforde, chivaler, par attourne, et
prie qe vous countez vers luy.—Et pur ceo qe le
pleintif ne voleit pas, HILL. agarda qil prist rienz,
non obstante la variaunce del adjeccion de chivaler.

(4.)[4] § *Nota* qe Johan Gisors suyt par[8] brief de Dette.[5]
Dette, par vij aunz, vers plusours qapres la graunt[9] [Fitz., *Forcher,*
destresse, fourcherunt par *Idem dies*, saver, quant a 10.]
la destresse retourne sur un, il apparust et prist
jour par *Idem dies*, et celuy qad jour par *Idem dies*
fet ore defaut.—*Birtone* pria qe les issues de ces
qore fount defaut autrefoith retourne sur eux, tut[10]
eient ore jour par *Idem dies*, soient forfetes.[11]—HILL.
Ceo ne poms faire saunz estatut,[12] &c.

(5.)[4] § Novele disseisine, devant BAUK. et THORPE, Novele
de la moite dun molyn. Trove fuit qe deux freres disseisine.
[19 Li.
Ass., 1 ;
[Fitz.,
Particion,
8.]

---

[1] From L., H., and C. This is
the conclusion of the report No. 44
in Hilary Term next preceding.
From the roll there cited (*Placita
de Banco,* Hil., 19 Edward III.,
R° 345, d) it appears that the
action (of Covenant) was brought
by Andrew de Welles, parson of the
church of Shipham (Somerset), and
John Danyel, administrators of
Nicholas de Wedergrave, against
Philip de Thame, Prior of the
Hospital of St. John of Jerusalem
in England.

[2] In H. are added the words
residuum dil Covenant.

[3] C., lordeigner.

[4] From L., H., and C.

[5] In H. the marginal note is
Nota.

[6] H., qe ; the word is omitted
from C.

[7] L., and C., avietz.

[8] par is omitted from H.

[9] H., graund.

[10] tut is omitted from C.

[11] H., forfaitz.

[12] C., and H., statut.

No. 6.

A.D. 1345. two brothers purchased the entirety of the mill to hold to them and their heirs, and that afterwards there was a dispute between them as to the repairing of the mill, whereupon an agreement took place between them, through the mediation of their third brother, on whose decision they put themselves. And he came to the mill-post, and marked the post, in the middle, with an adze, and said that one of them should repair the mill on one side, and the other on the other side, for ever. And the Assise said that their intention was that severance should be made in this manner for them and their heirs, for ever, and that the same mill was afterwards leased at a certain rent, and that one took a moiety of the rent, and the other took the other moiety severally. Afterwards one of them died, and, his issue, being under age, levied parcel of the rent by his mother. The other, who survived, came and forbade the tenant of the mill to pay the rent, and so the

Judgment. heir of the one who died first was ousted.—And, notwithstanding that this severance was not made by specialty, judgment was given that the severance was good, and that the plaintiff should recover the moiety, &c.

Novel
Disseisin.
     (6.) § Novel Disseisin, between a woman who was plaintiff and a man who was defendant, before SHARS-HULLE and STOUFORD. It was found by verdict that the father of the woman who was the plaintiff gave the tenements to the man who was the defendant, with his daughter who was the plaintiff, in frank-marriage, while they were both under marriageable age, and that afterwards, when they arrived at their full age, the man sued a divorce, and this with the full consent of the woman, and that, at his suit, the divorce was effected, and

No. 6.

purchacerent tut[1] le molyn a eux et lour heirs, et A.D. 1345
qe puis sur le reparailler du molyn y avoit debat
entre eux, par quei acorde se prist entre eux par
la mediacion de lour terce frere,[2] en qi ordinaunce
ils soi mistrent, qe vint a la post del molyn et
dola dun dolet en la post en mylieu,[3] et dit qe lun[4]
deux[5] reparaillast le molyn dune part, et lautre
dautre part a touz jours. Et Lassise dit qe lour
purpos fuit qe la severaunce par la manere pur eux
et lour heirs fuit fet a touz jours, et qapres mesme
le molyn fuit lesse a certein ferme, lun prist la
moite de la rente et lautre prist[6] lautre moite
severalment. Apres lun moruyst, et lissue de luy
deinz age par sa mere leva parcelle de la rente.
Lautre qe survesquit vint et defendist le tenant du
molyn de paier la rente, et issint fuit il ouste, saver
leir celuy[7] qe primes devia.—Et, *non obstante* qe *Judicium*.[8]
ceste severaunce ne se fist pas par especialte, fuit
agarde qe la severaunce fuit bone, et qe le pleintif
recoverast la moite, &c.

(6.)[9] § Novele Disseisine entre une femme pleintif Novele
et un homme defendant devant SCHAR. et STOUFF Disseisine.
[19 Li.
Trove fuit[10] par verdit[11] qe le pere la femme plein- Ass., 2;
tif[12] dona al homme defendaunt ove se fille qest[13] [Fitz.,
Assise,
pleintif les tenementz en fraunk mariage, quant ils 83.]
furent *infra annos nubiles* lun et lautre, et[14] qe puis
a lour plein age le homme[15] suyt[16] divors,[17] et ceo
par le bon[18] gree la femme, et qe a sa suite divors[19]

---

[1] L., tote; H., tout.

[2] H., un A. (interlined) instead of lour terce frere.

[3] L., mislieu; H., my luy.

[4] H., qun, instead of qe lun.

[5] C., de eux.

[6] prist is from H. alone.

[7] celuy is omitted from H.

[8] This marginal note is from C. alone.

[9] From L., H., and C.

[10] H., fust.

[11] H., verdist.

[12] pleintif is from L. alone.

[13] L., qe estoit.

[14] et is from H. alone.

[15] C., lomme, instead of le homme.

[16] H., suiwist.

[17] H., le devors.

[18] C., boun.

[19] H., devors; C., divorce.

No. 7.

A.D. 1345. that after the divorce he kept himself in possession of the entirety, ousting the woman, whereupon she brought the Assise. And because it was on her account that the gift was made, and the form of the gift was brought to an end by the divorce at the suit of the husband, judgment was given that she should recover the entirety.

Covenant.   (7.) § Covenant in respect of a certain manor[1] was brought against the Prioress of Haliwell (or Holywell), and the count was that her predecessor, with the consent of the Convent, leased to the plaintiff for a certain term, and that she ousted him within the term, &c.— *Grene.* In the deed containing the covenant, of which *profert* is made. it is supposed that the plaintiff was to hold the manor on certain conditions, that is to say, so long as he should pay a certain rent, and that he should not commit waste, and that he should do certain other things. And we tell you that he has broken all the covenants and conditions, and therefore we entered

---

[1] As to the tenements alleged to have been leased *see* p. 17, note 5.

No. 7.

se[1] fit, et apres la[2] divorce[3] il se tient einz en A.D. 1345.
lentier, oustant la femme, de quei ele porte Lassise.
Et pur ceo qele fuit cause del doun, et la fourme
fuit termine par la[4] divorce[3] a la suite le baroun,
fuit agarde qele recoverast lentier.

(7.)[5] § Covenant dun certein maner fuit porte vers Covenant.
la Prioresse de Haliwell, countaunt qe sa predeces- [Fitz., Double
soresse, del assent le[6] Covent, lessa al pleintif pur Plee, 20.]
certein terme, et qele luy ousta deinz le terme, &c.[7]
—Grenc. En le fait del covenant, qest mys avant,
est suppose qe le pleintif tiendreit le maner sur
certeins condicions, saver tanqil paiast certein rente,
et qil[8] ne feist wast, et feist autre chose. Et vous
dioms qil ad enfreint touz les covenauntes et condicions, par quei nous entrames par force de la

---

[1] se is omitted from H.

[2] H., le.

[3] H., devors.

[4] la is from L. alone.

[5] From L., H., and C., but corrected by the record, *Placita de Banco*, Easter, 19 Edw. III., R⁰ 53. It there appears that the action was brought by Richard de Ware against Elizabeth, Prioress of Haliwell, in respect of one messuage, 100 acres of land, 5 acres of meadow, and 100 acres of pasture in Camerwelle (Camberwell, Surrey) demised to him by Theophania, Elizabeth's prede-cessor.

[6] H., sa.

[7] The declaration was, according to the record, " quod cum prædicta " Theophania prædecessor, &c., " die Mercurii in festo Sanctæ " Agathæ Virginis, anno regni " domini Regis nunc Angliæ " decimo, per scriptum suum " indentatum dimisisset prædicto " Ricardo prædicta tenementa,

" cum pertinentiis, tenenda sibi,
" heredibus, et assignatis suis,
" usque ad finem decem annorum
" tunc proxime sequentium et
" plenarie completorum, reddendo
" inde annuatim eidem Priorissæ
" et Conventui suo, durante
" termino prædicto, octo marcas
" ad festum Sancti Jacobi Apostoli,
" per quam dimissionem idem
" Ricardus fuit seisitus de tene-
" mentis prædictis usque diem
" Lunæ proximum ante festum
" Sancti Michaelis Archangeli
" anno regni domini Regis nunc
" quartodecimo quod prædicta
" Elizabeth nunc Priorissa ipsum
" Ricardum de tenementis illis
" amovit, unde eadem Priorissa,
" licet sæpius requisita, &c.,
" conventionem prædictam præ-
" dicto Ricardo tenere recusavit,
" et adhuc contradicit, unde dicit
" quod deterioratus est, et damnum
" habet ad valentiam ducentarum
" librarum."

[8] H., sil.

No. 7.

by force of the condition; judgment whether an action, &c.—*Birton.* State in particular in what respect he has failed [to perform the covenants].—*Grene.* In the whole, for our plea is the consequence of your statement, and of the specialty of which you make *profert.* — *Gaynesford.* Still, you must plead the particulars.—HILLARY. He need not do so.—And this HILLARY said as by judgment.—Therefore *Birton* said that the plaintiff had kept and performed all the covenants; ready, &c.—And the other side said the contrary.

No. 7.

condicion ; jugement si accion, &c.[1]—*Birtone*. Mettetz ^{A.D. 1345.} en certein en quei il ad failli.—*Grene*. En tut, qar nostre plee vynt de vostre livere, et de lespecialte qe vous mettetz avaunt.—*Gayn*. Unqore vous plederetz en certein.—HILL. Noun fra pas.—*Et hoc dixit quasi par agarde*.—Par quei *Birtone* dist qil ad tenu touz les covenauntes et parfourny ; prest, &c.—*Et alii e contra*.[2]

---

[1] The Prioress's plea was, according to the record. "non "dedicit quin prædictus Ricardus "recepit tenementa prædicta ex "dimissione prædictæ Theophaniæ, "quondam Priorissæ, &c., ad "terminum prædictum, reddendo "inde per annum prædictas octo "marcas,et etiam ad quasdam alias "conditiones in prædicto scripto "indentato ex dimissione prædicta "fideliter observandas, videlicet "redditum prædictum ad terminum "suum prædictum constitutum "solvere, nec non idem Ricardus et "heredes sui sufficienter et compe- "tenter sustentarent et defender- "ent sumptibus suis propriis "omnes domos prædicto mesuagio "pertinentes contra ventum et "pluviam, et facerent et custodi- "rent clausturam prædictis mesu- "agio et terris spectantem, et "fossata ibidem mundarent, ita "quod prædicta Priorissa et "Conventus, in nullo, occasione "prædicta, graverentur nec dam- "num incurrerent, sed indemnes "versus quoscunque conservaren- "tur, et etiam prædicti Ricardus. "heredes, seu assignati sui nihil "caperent de boscis, sepibus, seu "arboribus prædictis tenementis "spectantibus nisi per visum et "liberationem prædictorum Prior- "issæ et Conventus aut eorum

"attornatorum, et hoc rationabili- "ter pro housbote, heybote, et "ferbote tantum pro familia in "dicto mesuagio necessariis "existentibus ita quod, si idem "Ricardus conditiones et conven- "tiones prædictas vel aliquam "earundem non observaret, quod "bene liceret prædictæ Priorissæ "et successoribus suis tenementa "prædicta ingredi, et omnia bona "et catalla ibidem inventa in "manu sua detinere, non obstante "prædicto scripto nec aliquo juris "remedio, quousque prædictæ "Priorissæ fuerit de omnibus in "prædicto scripto non observatis "fuerit [*sic*] satisfactum. Et dicit "quod, pro eo quod idem Ricardus "nullam conventionum prædicta- "rum observavit, prædicta Priorissa "tenementa prædicta intravit "virtute scripti prædicti, sicut ei "bene licuit, et petit judicium si "prædictus Ricardus responderi "debeat, &c."

[2] According to the record, after the plea, "Ricardus dicit quod ipse "bene et fideliter observavit omnes "conventiones in prædicto scripto "contentas, quas ad ipsum per- "tinuit observare, et quod ipse, "prædicto die quando ipse soluisse "debuit, obtulit eidem Priorissæ "duas marcas de firma prædicta, "quas idem Ricardus eidem

No. 8.

A.D. 1345.   (8.) § Detinue of charter against the Prior of
Detinue of Wymondley,[1] in which charter it was contained that
charter.

[1] The name is given as Wymondesleye in Dugdale's *Monasticon*, but it does not appear that there is any good authority for the letter *s*.

No. 8.

(8.)[1] § Detenue de chartre vers le Priour de Wymondeleye[3] contenant qen la seisine les aunces-

"Priorissæ ad terminum in præ-
"dicto scripto indentato contentum
"soluisse debuit, et eas ei adhuc
"offert in Curia, &c. Et hoc
"paratus est verificare, et petit
"judicium, &c."

"Et prædicta Priorissa dicit
"quod prædictus Ricardus non
"obtulit ei prædictas duas marcas,
"nec aliquam conventionum præ-
"dictarum prout debuit observa-
"vit." It was upon this rejoinder
that issue was joined.

The verdict was "quod, prædicto
"die Sancti Jacobi Apostoli anno
"regni Regis nunc quartodecimo,
"præfatus Ricardus soluit præ-
"dictæ Priorissæ sex marcas de
"prædicto redditu octo marcarum,
"et non plus, quia adhuc residuum
"ejusdem redditus promptum non
"habuit, sed dicunt quod die
"Lunæ proximo post festum Sancti
"Michaelis tunc proxime sequens,
"ante horam nonam ejusdem
"diei, prædicta Priorissa intravit
"in tenementis prædictis occasione
"non solutionis prædictarum
"duarum marcarum residuarum
"de prædictis octo marcis, et post
"horam nonam ejusdem diei
"præfatus Ricardus obtulit eidem
"Priorissæ prædictas duas marcas,
"quas eadem Priorissa vel adtunc
"recipere recusavit. Quæsiti si
"ante præfatum diem Lunæ præ-
"dicta Priorissa exigebat prædictas
"duas marcas, vel ante illum diem
"præfatus Ricardus obtulit eidem
"Priorissæ easdem duas marcas,
"&c., dicunt quod ante diem illum
"nec prædictus Ricardus eas
"obtulit, nec prædicta Priorissa
"exigebat. Quæsiti si prædictus
"Ricardus omnes alias conventi-

"ones supradictas tenuit, dicunt
"quod sic."

Judgment was then given "Quia
"per juratam prædictam comper-
"tum est quod prædictus Ricardus
"in omnibus prædicto scripto
"contentis, solutione prædictarum
"duarum marcarum de prædicto
"redditu residuarum dumtaxat
"excepta, con[ventiones] præ-
"dictæ Priorissæ tenuit, quas
"quidem duas marcas prædicto
"die Lunæ quo prædicta Priorissa
"tenementa prædicta ante horam
"nonam ingressa fuit idem
"Ricardus post horam nonam
"ejusdem diei præfatæ Priorissæ
"ibidem obtulit, et quas eandem
"Priorissa adtunc admittere recu-
"savit [et] eadem Priorissa
"prædictum Ricardum contra
"formam conventionis prædictæ
"possessionem prædictorum tene-
"mentorum hucusque habere non
"permisit, ad damna centum
"solidorum, &c., ideo considera-
"tum [est quod] prædictus Ri-
"cardus recuperet damna præ-
"dicta, et prædicta Priorissa in
"misericordia, &c."

[1] From L., H., and C., but
corrected by the record, *Placita de
Banco*, Easter, 19 Edw. III., R⁰ 144.
It there appears that the action
was brought by Joan late wife of
John Boteler against the Prior
of Wilmondeleye (Wymondley).
There is on R⁰ 66 an incomplete
record ending with the declaration,
which, however, is not there in
quite the same form as in the
complete record on R⁰ 144.

[2] The words de chartre are from
C. alone.

[3] L., and C., Wymondwold; H., W.

No. 8.

A.D. 1345. one A.,[1] while the tenements were in the seisin of the plaintiff's ancestors, confirmed, by that same deed which the plaintiff demands, and bound himself and his heirs to warrant to the plaintiff's ancestors and the heirs of their bodies, those tenements which they already had by gift from another person in the same form, which deed was delivered by the plaintiff's ancestors to the Prior's predecessor, to wit, one William, in whose possession, &c., to be re-delivered to them and the heirs of their bodies, which deed, after the death of the predecessor, came into the hands of the present Prior, wherefore the husband and the wife[2] who now sue, and her coparcener, a woman, with her husband,[3] who have been summoned and severed, have many times prayed the re-delivery.—*Moubray*. Judgment of the count, because you see plainly how the

---

[1] For the name *see* p. 23, note 6.

[2] The wife alone was plaintiff, her husband being dead according to the record, p. 21, note 1.

[3] For the names *see* p. 23, note 6.

No. 8.

tres un A. conferma par mesme le fet quel il demande,
et obligea luy et ses heirs a garrantir a ses auncestres
et les heirs de lour corps, &c., queles tenementz ils
avoint devant[1] dautri doun par mesme la fourme,
quel fet fuit baille par les auncestres le pleintif al
predecessour le Priour, saver, un W.[2] vers qi, &c.,
a rebailler a[3] eux et les heirs de lour corps, quel
fet, apres la mort le predecessour, devynt[4] en la
mein le Priour qore est, par quei le baron et la
femme qore suent et lautre parcenere la femme ove
soun baron, qe sount somons et severetz, sovent[5] ount
prie, &c.[6]—*Moubray.* Jugement de count, qar vous

---

[1] In L., the word devant is omitted in this place, but inserted after the words dautri doun.

[2] MSS. of Y.B., E.

[3] The words a rebailler a are omitted from H.

[4] H., devient ; C., demurt.

[5] C., et sovent.

[6] The declaration was, according to the roll (R⁰ 144), " quod cum " Johannes filius Reginaldi Dar-" gentein, ... apud " Ixnynge in Comitatu Suffolciæ, " tradidisset cuidam Willelmo " quondam Priori de Wilmondeleye, " prædecessori prædicti Prioris " nunc, quandam chartam custodi-" endam, in qua continetur quod " quidam Reginaldus Dargentein, " avus prædictæ Johannæ, et " etiam cujusdam Elizabethæ " uxoris Gilberti de Ellesfelde " sororis ejusdem Johannæ, quæ " alias, simul cum prædicto Gil-" berto, viro suo, summoniti " fuerunt ad sequendum simul " cum prædicta Johanna placitum " prædictum versus prædictum " Priorem, et tunc secuti non " fuerunt, per quod consideratum " fuit quod prædicta Johanna

" sequeretur, sine, &c., concessisset, " et charta sua confirmasset mane-" rium suum de Novo Mercato, " exceptis advocatione veteris " capellæ ejusdem manerii, et feria " in festo Apostolorum Simonis et " Judæ annuatim tenenda, et etiam " redditu triginta ferrorum equo-" rum de fabrica sua in eodem " manerio, in seisina prædicti " Johannis et cujusdam Johannæ " tunc uxoris ejusdem Johannis, " et obligasset se et heredes suos ad " warantizandum manerium præ-" dictum, exceptis, &c., ipsis Jo-" hanni et Johannæ et heredibus " de corporibus ipsorum Johannis " et Johannæ procreatis, quod " quidem manerium, exceptis, &c., " prædictus Johannes et Johanna " prius habuerunt de dono prædicti " Reginaldi tenendum sibi et " heredibus de corporibus eorun-" dem Johannis et Johannæ " exeuntibus, et chartam prædictam " . . . . . . retradendam " ipsis Johanni, vel Johannæ uxori " ipsius Johannis, seu heredibus " de corporibus eorundem Johannis " et Johannæ procreatis, cum inde " ab ipsis requisitus fuisset, qui

No. 8.

words of the writ are *quandam chartam*, and they have counted of a confirmation, in which case the words of the writ by which such a count would be warranted should be *quoddam scriptum confirmationis*, and not *chartam*, which properly requires livery of seisin.—*Grene*. It is all one.—HILLARY. That does not seem to be so.—*Gaynesford*. Who can say that a confirmation is not a charter?—*Skipwith*. If you recover this confirmation by this writ, you will on another occasion, have another writ, and will demand the confirmation, and then it will not be an answer for us to say that you have recovered your charter.—STONORE. Yes, it will be.—*Moubray*. We tell you that we never had any predecessor named William. And afterwards *Moubray* said that William de Bereforde, in a different place and a different county, delivered the same writing to the Prior's predecessor, Elias, on a certain condition, to redeliver it to the plaintiff, or to others to whom the law should adjudge that it ought to be redelivered, and he said that the Prior was ready to deliver it to whomsoever, &c. And he said further that others had a writ of Detinue pending against him.—*Grene*. We

No. 8.

veietz bien coment le brief voet *quandam chartam*, et ils ount counte dun conferment, qar le brief de quei tiel counte[1] serreit garranti serreit *quoddam scriptum confirmationis*, et noun pas *chartam*, qe demande proprement livere de seisine.—*Grene.* Tut est un.—Hill. Ceo ne semble il pas.—*Gayn.* Qi purra dire qun conferment nest pas une chartre?— *Skip.* Si vous recoveretz par cest brief cest conferment, vous averetz autrefoith autre brief, et demanderetz le conferment, et donqes ne serra ceo pas respons a[2] nous a[3] dire qe vous avietz recoveri vostre chartre.— Ston. Si serra.[4]—*Moubray.* Nous vous dioms qe nous navioms unqes predecessour W.[5] par noun. Et puis dit qe W. de Bereforde, en autre lieu et autre counte, livera mesme lescript a E.[6] soun predecessour sur certein condicion a bailler a celuy qe se pleint, ou as autres a qi la ley lajuggeast, et dist qil est prest pur liverer a qi, &c. Et dit outre qe les autres ount brief vers luy de Detenue pendant.[7]—*Grene.* Nous voloms averer

---

" quidem Johannes filius Reginaldi, " et Johanna uxor ejus sæpius in " vita sua prædictam chartam " a prædicto Willelmo quondam " Priore, prædecessore, &c., exeger- " unt, idem Willelmus Prior " chartam illam ipsis Johanni seu " Johannæ, uxori ipsius Johannis, " in vita sua reddere recusavit, " per quod post mortem prædicti " Willelmi quondam Prioris, præ- " decessoris, &c., eadem charta " devenit in manus prædicti Prioris " nunc, et prædicti Johannes et " Johanna uxor ejus jam obierunt, " post quorum mortem prædicta " Johanna quæ modo queritur, " simul cum prædictis Gilberto et " Elizabeth qui modo non sequun- " tur, heredes prædicti Johannis " per formam, &c., sæpius prædic-

" tam chartam a prædicto Priore " qui nunc est exigebant, idem " Prior qui nunc est chartam illam, " licet sæpius requisitus, ipsi " Johannæ quæ nunc queritur, " seu etiam prædictis Gilberto et " Elizabeth qui modo non sequun- " tur, liberare recusavit, et adhuc " recusat, unde dicit quod deteri- " orata est et damnum habet ad " valentiam centum librarum. Et " inde producit sectam, &c."

[1] C., brief.

[2] H., pur.

[3] The words nous a are omitted from L.

[4] H., fra.

[5] MSS. of Y.B., E.

[6] MSS. of Y.B., W.

[7] The plea as it appears on R⁰ 144 is, after a recital of a portion

No. 8.

will aver the delivery in accordance with our count.—
Thorpe. Issue cannot be taken, in this case, on the
manner in which the delivery was made, because you
well know that when a writing is delivered on condition
to deliver to another, unless it be by indenture, it is
not the practice to count any other count than a
common count; and if the manner of the delivery
could make an issue, no one could ever be garnished
[by *Scire facias*] in Detinue of writings. The conclusion is false.—STONORE. There is nothing more upon
which a traverse can be made than the condition, for
you are speaking of another delivery made by another
person and in another place, in respect of which he can
never have an action.—*Grene, ad idem.* And, in the case
which *Thorpe* has put, if the plaintiff be willing he
can have a traverse on the condition, that is to say,
on the manner of the delivery.—*Thorpe* maintained
the delivery to have been as he had alleged, *absque
hoc* that the charter had been delivered as the plaintiff
counted; ready, &c.—And the other side said the contrary.—And because the original writ was brought in
the county in which the defendant alleged the delivery
to have been, the writ issued to the Sheriff of that
county, that is to say, of Hertford, to cause the jurors to
come, and not to the Sheriff of Suffolk in which county
the plaintiff counted that the delivery was made, and

No. 8.

le baille solonc nostre count.—*Thorpe.* Sur la manere
coment le baille se fist, en ceo cas, issue ne se
poet prendre, qar vous savetz bien quant escript est
baille par condicion a bailler a autre, sil ne soit
par endenture, homme ne use pas counter autre
counte forqe comune counte ; et si la manere du
baille purreit fere issue jammes ne serra homme
garny en Detenue descriptz. *Consequens falsum.*--
STON. Il ny [1] ad plus [2] qe fait travers qe la condicion, qar vous parletz dune baille fait par autre
persone et en autre lieu, de quei il navera jammes
accion.—*Grene, ad idem.* Et,[3] en le cas qe *Thorpe*
ad mys, si le pleintif voille, il avera travers a la
condicion, saver, sur la manere du baille. —*Thorpe*
meintent le baille come il avoit allegge sanz ceo
qil fuit baille come le pleintif counte ; prest, &c.—
Et alii e contra.[4]—Et pur ceo qe loriginal fuit porte
el counte ou le defendant alleggea le baille, brief
issit a cel Vicounte, saver de Herforde de faire
venir pays, et noun pas au Vicounte de Suffolk ou
le pleintif counta le baille estre fait, *et hoc* par

---

of the declaration, " quod quidam
" Willelmus de Bereforde habuit
" custodiam chartæ prædictæ, &c.,
" qui quidem Willelmus chartam
" illam tradidit cuidam Eliæ quon-
" dam Priori de Wylmondeleye,
" prædecessori Prioris nunc, apud
  Wylmondeleye in Comitatu Hert-
" fordiæ, sub tali conditione custo-
" diendam, &c., videlicet ad deliber-
" andum chartam illam præfatis
" Johanni Dargentein, vel Johannæ
" uxori suæ, sive heredibus prædicti
" Johannis, seu heredibus de cor-
" poribus eorundem Johannis et
" Johannæ exeuntibus, cui vel
" quibus per legem adjudicatum

" fuerit deliberandum, et non
" præfato Willelmo quondam Priori,
" prædecessori, &c., apud Ixnynge
" in Comitatu Suffolciæ, sicut
" prædicta Johanna superius in
" narratione sua supponit."

[1] ny is omitted from H.

[2] L., pais.

[3] Et is from C. alone.

[4] According to the roll, issue was
joined upon the plea as quoted
above p. 25, note 7, and then the
Prior " profert hic in Curia chartam
" prædictam et paratus est illam
" deliberare cui Curia consider-
" averit, &c."

No. 9.

this by judgment, by HILLARY.—And afterwards WILLOUGHBY directed that jurors should be caused to come from both counties.

Præcipe quod reddat.

(9.) § A *Præcipe quod reddat* demanding two parts of a mill was brought against the wife of J. Comyn. —*Moubray.* We cannot render her demand, because we hold only a moiety of the two parts of the mill, and one A., wife of H. Comyn, holds a third part of a moiety, and the Abbot of N. holds the rest of the mill; judgment of the writ.—*Thorpe.* And, inasmuch as he does not allege non-tenure with certainty, giving as a good writ against the others, and the non-tenure does not extend to our demand, judgment; and we pray seisin.—*Seton.* When non-tenure is alleged, it is not with the object of giving a good writ against another person, in whom the tenancy is affirmed by the exception, because he might abate it by a plea of joint tenancy or non-tenure, when he appeared; but the object of an exception of non-tenure is to give a good writ with certainty against the person himself who takes the exception, and that we have done; and if we were to allege greater or less non-tenure, the demandant would still have no other way of maintaining his writ than by averring tenancy to the full.—HILLARY. But every alleged non-tenure must be non-tenure of the demand, and not of anything else, and if an allegation were to be definitely made that another holds parcel of the demand, against which other the demandant could have a good writ, the Court holds him to be tenant; now your exception of non-tenure does not

No. 9.

agarde de HILL. Et puis WILBY comaunda pays de A.D. 1345.
lun counte et de lautre.[1]

(9.) [2] § *Præcipe quod reddat* porte vers la femme *Præcipe quod reddat.*[3]
J. Comyn demandant les deux parties dun molyn.—
Moubray. Nous ne poms sa demande rendre, qar [Fitz., Nontenure, 15.]
nous tenoms forqe la moite de deux parties del
molyn, et un A., la femme H. Comyn, tient la terce
partie de la moite, et le remenant del molyn tient
Labbe de N.; jugement du brief.—*Thorpe.* Et,
desicome il nallegge pas la nountenure en certein,
donant a nous boun brief vers les autres, ne la
nountenue ne sestent pas a nostre demande, jugement; et nous prioms seisine.—*Setone.* Quant nountenue est allegge ceo nest pas al entent de doner[4]
boun brief vers autre persone, en qi par lexcepcion
la tenance est afferme, qar il le purra abatre par
jointenance[5] ou nountenue quant il vendra; mes
excepcion de nountenue est pur doner boun brief
en certein vers mesme la persone qe doune lexcepcion, et ceo avoms nous fait; et si nous alleggeassoms de plus ou de meins la nountenue, unqore le
demandant navera autre meintenance de soun brief
qe[6] daverer pleinement tenauntz.—HILL. Mes chesqune nountenue[7] covient estre de la demande [et
noun pas dautre chose, et si nous alleggeassoms[8]
en certein qautre tient parcelle de la demande],[9] vers
qi il purreit aver boun brief, Court vous tient tenant; ore vostre nountenue[7] sestent pas a la demande

---

[1] According to the roll the *Venire* was originally to have been directed to the Sheriff of Hertford alone, but the reading is by interlineations made to be "tam "prædicto Vicecomiti Hertfordiæ "quam Vicecomiti Suffolciæ."
  Nothing further appears on the roll except adjournments.
  [2] From L., H., and C.

[3] The words *quod reddat* are from H. alone.
  [4] L., nous doner.
  [5] H., yoyntenance.
  [6] qe is omitted from C.
  [7] H., nountenure.
  [8] C., alleggeoms.
  [9] The words between brackets are omitted from H.

Nos. 10, 11.

extend to the demand, nor do you state with regard to what quantity he would have a writ against any other person than you.—*Moubray.* If a writ were brought against me to demand a manor, and I were to allege non-tenure of parcel, I should say definitely of how much, because in another writ brought against myself the parcel ought to be excepted, and in such a way that I should give a good writ against myself; but in the case of a different demand, where nothing has to be excepted, there is no necessity to do so.— STONORE. It is absolutely necessary that you give a good writ against the others if you wish to abate this writ.—And afterwards *Moubray* alleged non-tenure, as above, and also that a woman held a third part of a moiety which amounted to a fourth part of the demandant's demand, and that the Abbot held the rest; judgment of the writ.—And on the demandant's non-denial the writ abated.

Debt.

(10.) § Executors brought a writ of Debt.—*Derworthy.* Produce the will.—*Sadelyngstanes.* We have a day by *Prece partium inter talem*, plaintiff, and *tales executores, &c.*, and so you have accepted us as being entitled to be answered.—*Prece partium* does not make you executors, and the will is the ground of your action, and that is not affirmed by *Prece partium.*—STONORE. The will is not the ground of action, but the obligation is. —HILLARY. On a writ of Formedon in the remainder will not the demandant be put to show a specialty after *Prece partium* ?—*Sadelyngstanes.* Yes, that is the ground of the action.—And by judgment *Derworthy* was put to answer without the will having been shown.

Debt.

(11.) § Debt on obligation brought against the Abbot of Eynsham.—*Moubray* made *profert* of a collateral

Nos. 10, 11.

ne vous ne donetz pas de quel quantite il avereit A.D. 1345.
brief vers autre qe vers vous.—*Moubray.* Si brief
fuit porte vers moy a demander un maner, et jeo
alleggeasse nountenue de parcelle, jeo dirrei en certein de come bien, pur ceo qe la parcelle en autre
brief porte vers moy mesme coviendreit estre forpris,
et issint qe jeo durroy bone brief vers moi mesme;
mes en autre demande, ou forprise ne serra pas fait,
il ne bosoigne[1] pas.—STON. Il covient a force qe
vous donetz bone brief vers les autres si vous voilletz
abatre cest brief.—Et puis *Moubray, ut supra,* alleggea
nountenure,[2] et auxint qune femme tient la terce
partie de la moite qamount a la quarte partie de sa
demande, et Labbe le remenant; jugement du brief.
—Et sur nient dedire le brief abatist.

(10.)[3] § Executours[4] porterent brief de Dette.— Dette.
Derr. Moustrez testament.—*Sadl.* Nous avoms jour [Fitz., Monstrans
par *Prece partium inter talem* pleintif et *tales execu-* de faits, fins, et
tores, &c., issint nous avetz[5] accepte responable.— records,
Derr. *Prece partium* ne vous fait pas executours, et 173.]
testament est cause de vostre accion, quel par *Prece
partium* nest pas afferme.—STON. Testament nest pas
cause daccion mes est obligacion.—HILL. En brief
de remeindre apres *Prece partium* ne serra pas le
demandant mys de moustrer especialte?—*Sadl.* Oyl,
cest cause daccion.—Et par agarde *Derr.* saunz testament estre moustre fuit mys de[6] respoundre.

(11.)[7] § Dette de xl*li.* porte vers Labbe Deynes- Dette.
ham[8] par obligacion.—*Moubray* moustra par endenture

---

[1] C., busoigne.

[2] L., and C., qamount forqe a iij parties.

[3] From L., H., and C.

[4] L., Deux executours.

[5] avetz is omitted from C.

[6] C., a.

[7] From L., H., and C., but corrected by the record, *Placita de*

Banco, Easter, 19 Edw. III., R° 70.
It there appears that the action
was brought by Thomas Mundy,
of Woodstock, against the Abbot of
Eynsham, in respect of a debt, on
obligation, of £40.

[8] L., de Eynesham; C., Deygnes-ham.

No. 12.

indenture executed by the plaintiff to the effect that if the Abbot paid £20 [on a certain day] the obligation should lose its force, and tendered the averment that the Abbot paid the £20.—*Richemunde.* And, inasmuch as he does not produce any acquittance, judgment.—*Moubray.* And we pray judgment.—*Richemunde* tendered the averment that the Abbot did not pay.—*Moubray.* And we demand judgment whether he shall now be admitted to an averment which he previously refused.—Stonore to *Moubray.* Will you not accept the averment? That is extraordinary, because it makes in your favour, as it seems.—*Moubray.* We would rather abide judgment.

Naifty.

(12)[1] § Writ of Naifty. The parties on both sides appeared by attorney. The plaintiff counted that the defendant's grandfather acknowledged himself, in a Court of record, to be the villein of the plaintiff's ancestor, and made the descent from that ancestor to him the plaintiff, &c.—*Skipwith* denied tort and force, and all servile condition, &c., and said that the defendant's father was a bastard; judgment whether he shall be put to answer as one being of the blood of the grandfather.—*Grene.* Your father was legitimate; ready, &c. — And the other side said the contrary.

---

[1] There is a fuller report of the same or a like case below (No. 40).

No. 12.

le pleintif fet de coste qe sil paiast xx*li*. qe lobli- A.D. 1345.
gacion perdreit sa force, et tendist daverer qil paia[1]
les ˉxx*li*.[2]—*Rich.* Et desicome il ne moustre pas
acquitance, jugement.—*Moubray.* Et nous jugement.
—*Rich.* tendist daverer qil paia pas.—*Moubray.* Et
nous jugement sil serra resceu[3] ore al averement quel
devant il ad refuse.—STON. a *Moubray.* Ne voilletz
pas laverement? Il est[4] merveille, qar il fet[5] pur
vous a ceo qe semble.—*Moubray.* Nous voloms meuth
demurer en jugement.[6]

(12.)[7] § Brief de Neifte.[8] Les parties dune part Neifte.[8]
et dautre par attourne. Le pleintif counta qe soun
aiel, en Court de record, se reconissat[9] estre le villein launcestre celuy qest pleintif, et fit la descente
de par le pleintif, &c.—*Skip.* defendi tort et force
et tut servage, &c., et dit qe le pere le defendaunt fuit bastard; jugement sil come celuy qe fuit
del sank laiel serra mys a respondre.—*Grene.* Vostre
pere fuit mulure[10]; prest, &c.—*Et alii e contra.*

---

[1] L., paye; C., paiast.

[2] According to the record, the Abbot, confessing the obligation to be. that of himself and his Convent, " dicit quod idem Thomas postea " . . . . . concessit quod si " prædicti Abbas et Conventus " soluissent eidem Thomæ, vel " suo certo attornato, heredibus, " vel exeuntibus suis, ad prædictum " festum Paschæ, apud Wodestoke, " viginti libras quod tunc prædic- " tum scriptum quadraginta libra- " rum pro nullo haberetur, et dicit " quod ipse in prædicto festo " Paschæ apud Wodestoke soluit " eidem Thomæ prædictas viginti " libras."

Profert was made of the deed of defeasance.

[3] H., ressu.

[4] H., nest pas.

[5] H., est fet.

[6] According to the record, the plaintiff confessed the deed of defeasance, but said "quod prædic- " tus Abbas non soluit ei prædictas " viginti libras, sicut idem Abbas " superius in responsione sua " prætendit verificare." Issue was joined upon this.

The jury found " quod prædictus " Abbas non soluit præfato Thomæ " prædictas viginti libras nec " aliquid denariorum inde. Quæ- " siti ad quæ damna, &c., dicunt " quod ad damnum ejusdem " Thomæ viginti librarum. Judgment was given for the plaintiff to recover the damages, and he had execution by *Elegit.*

[7] From L., H., and C.

[8] H., naifte.

[9] H., conisast.

[10] H., mullure.

No. 13.

A.D. 1345.
Error:
Novel
Disseisin.
See the
beginning
in an
Assise of
Michael-
mas Term
in the
eighteenth
year.[1]

(13.) Novel Disseisin which the Prior of Sempringham heretofore brought, before BAUKWELL and THORPE, against two persons, one of whom pleaded that the plaintiff had released to him all manner of personal actions, and the other pleaded joint tenancy. And the plaintiff said that the one who pleaded joint tenancy had not anything in the freehold, but that the other was tenant. And this was found by the Assise. Therefore the other pleaded, as before, the release in bar, but he did not, in pleading, take upon himself the tenancy. And the plaintiff said that he had been seised and disseised since the execution of the release. And upon this the Assise was taken, without any title having been made. And the verdict passed for the plaintiff, and he recovered. And upon that judgment, that the Assise should be taken without any title having been made, error was assigned. And the record was maintained by plea on the ground that the one who pleaded the release did not at any time take upon himself the tenancy, and that, even had he done so, such a release still does not bar the right, because if any one be disseised, and release to the disseisor all personal actions, his right in the land is still not extinguished, so that if he subsequently entered upon his disseisor, and was ousted, he would have an Assise in respect of that ouster, and consequently there was no need in this case, to make a title for the plaintiff, but only to say that he was seised and disseised after the release.—And, on the other hand, there was touched the point that by such a release an action grounded on disseisin is extinguished, and that consequently judgment ought not to be given that the Assise should be taken, except on the ground of subsequent seisin or title.— And, notwithstanding, the record was by judgment confirmed.

[1] The reference appears to be to Y.B., Mich., 18 Edw. III., No. 14.

No. 13.

(13.) [1] § Novele disseisine qe le Priour de Semp- A.D. 1345.
ringham porta autrefoith devant BAUK. et THORPE Errour: [2]
vers deux, dount lun pleda qe le pleintif avoit re- Novele
disseisine.
lesse a luy totes maneres daccions personels, et lautre *Vide*
principium
pleda jointenance. Et le pleintif dit qe celuy qe en un
pleda la jointenance navoit rienz en le franctene- Assise,
Michaelis
ment einz lautre. Et ceo trove par assise. Par quei *xviij.* [3]
lautre, *ut prius*, pleda par le relees en barre, mes [19 Li.
Ass., 3;
il enprist pas tenance en pledaunt. Et le pleintif Fitz.,
dit qe seisi et disseisi puis la confeccion, &c. Et *Title,* 35.]
sur ceo lassise pris saunz title fere. qe passa pur
le pleintif, et il recoveri. Et de cel agard del assise
saunz title errour est assigne. Et le recorde par
ple fut meintenue par tant qe celuy qe pleda le
relees a nulle temps enprist tenance, et, tut ust il,
unqore tiel relees ne barre pas en dreit, qar si
homme soit disseisi, et relest chesqun accion personel
al disseisour, unqore soun dreit en la terre nest pas
esteint, issint qe sil entra apres sur son disseisour,
et fuit ouste, il avereit Assise [de cel ouster, et *per*
consequens en ceo [4] cas il bosoigne pas de fere title
pur celuy qest pleintif, mes] [5] a dire qe puis le relees seisi et disseisi.—*Et e contra* fuit touche qe
par tiel relees accion de disseisine est esteint, et
per consequens Assise nient agarde sanz seisine ou
par title puis. — Et, *non obstante*, le recorde est
afferme par jugement.

---

[1] From L., H., and C.

[2] The word Errour is from
H. alone, from which MS. the
following words Novele disseisine
are omitted.

[3] The words following disseisine
are from H. alone.

[4] C., tiel.

[5] The words between brackets
are omitted from H.

Nos. 14, 15.

A.D. 1345.
Forjudger.
(14.) § Two parceners were forjudged on a writ of
Mesne. One of them and the heir of the other
brought a writ of Error, supposing that the ancestor
of that other was dead at the time at which the
judgment was rendered. And it was said that such
suit [of a writ of Error] is not given for one who
sues after having been a party.

Right.
(15.) § John de Hardeshulle and Maud, his wife,
brought a writ of Right of Advowson in respect of
the church of Roade against the Abbot of St. James
of Northampton, counting that it was the right and
inheritance of John, and that they were seised thereof
as of the fee and right of John, in time of peace,
&c., and presented to the same church their clerk,
who was admitted, &c., and took the esplees as in
greater tithes and lesser tithes, oblations, obventions,
and other kinds of issue of tithes, &c., as of the right
of the church of Our Lady of Roade aforesaid, and to
show that such is John's right, John and Maud have
suit and good proof.—*Grene* denied the right of John,
and had license from the Court to come to terms on
payment of money to the King. And he stated the
words of the concord of the fine in the following
manner :—John and Maud acknowledge the advowson
of two parts of the church, and also the advowson of
the tithes of two virgates and twenty acres of land,
together with the advowson of a third part of the
same church, to be the right of the Abbot and the
right of his church, and release the same, for themselves and the heirs of John, to the Abbot and to his

Nos. 14, 15.

(14.) [1] § Deux parceners furent forjugges en brief A.D. 1345. de Mene. Lun et leire [3] lautre porterent brief derrour Forjuger. [2] supposant qe launcestre lun al temps del jugement rendue fuit mort. Et fuit dit qe pur luy qe suyt qe fuit partie al jugement tiel suite nest pas done.

(15.) [4] § Johan de Hardeshulle et Maude sa femme Dreit. [5] porterent brief de Dreit davoweson del eglise de [Fitz., *Fynes*, Rodes vers Labbe de Seint Jakes de Northamptone, 46.] countaunt qe cest le dreit et leritage Johan, et dount ils furent seisiz come de fee et dreit Johan, en temps de pees, &c., et presenterent a mesme leglise lour clerk, qe fuit resceu, &c., pernant les esples, come en grosses dismes et menues dismes, oblacions, obvencions, et autres maneres dissue des dismes, &c., come de dreit del eglise de nostre Dame de Rodes avandit, et qe tiel soit le dreit Johan, [6] Johan et Maude en ount suite et dereine bone.—*Grene* defendi le dreit Johan, et avoit conge de Court dacorder pur deners donant au Roi. Et dist la pees [7] en tiel manere qe Johan et Maude conissoint lavoeson de ij parties del eglise, et auxint lavoeson des dismes de deux verges et xx acres de terre, ov [8] lavoeson de la terce partie de mesme leglise, estre le dreit Labbe et le dreit de sa eglise, et relessount ceo, de eux et les heirs Johan, al Abbe et a ses successours

---

[1] From L., H., and C. The full report of the case is in Trinity Term next following (No. 59), where the record is cited. It is *Placita coram Rege*, Easter, 19 Edward III., R° 55. The writ of Mesne had been brought by John de Wenlyngburghe against John Gisors and his brother Henry, and judgment had been given that they should lose his service. The writ of Error was sued by the same John Gisors and by John and Henry, sons and heirs of the above-named Henry, on the ground that Henry the father was dead at the time at which the judgment was given.

[2] The marginal note in H. is Errour.

[3] leire is omitted from H.

[4] From L., H., and C.

[5] The marginal note is omitted from H.

[6] Johan is from C. alone.

[7] H., la pees est, instead of dist la pees.

[8] L., and H., en.

No. 16.

successors for ever; and for that acknowledgment the Abbot grants and renders the advowson of a third part of the church aforesaid, except the advowson of the tithes aforesaid, to John and Maud and to the heirs of John for ever.—And the lady was examined, and the fine was admitted, &c.

Quare impedit. (16.) § The King brought a *Quare impedit* against the Prior of Pentney, counting that the Prior held the advowson of the King, as of his Crown, and presented, and afterwards appropriated it without the King's license, wherefore the right of patronage, by the law of the land, accrued to the King.—*Grene.* We tell you that, in the time of King John, the Prior's predecessor was seised of the advowson, and held it of the Count de Perche, and presented, &c., and now the advowson is held of W. Philip, cousin and heir of the said Count[1]; and we tell you that our Lord the King, by his charter, which is here, gave license to the Prior to appropriate the advowson, and for him and his successors to hold it to their own use; judgment whether the King can be

---

[1] For the facts, as stated in the record, *see* p. 41, note 1.

No. 16.

a touz jours; et pur cele reconissance Labbe graunt A.D. 1345.
et rende lavoeson de la terce partie del eglise
avandit, forpris lavoeson des disͣmes avanditz, a
Johan et a Maude et as heirs Johan a touz jours.
—Et la dame examine et la fine resceu, &c.

(16.)[1] § Le Roi porta *Quare impedit* vers le Priour *Quare*
de Penteneye,[2] countaunt qe le Priour tient lavowe- *impedit.*
soun du Roi, come de sa Coroun, et presenta, et *Double*
puis[3] sanz conge du Roi lappropria, par quei dreit *Plee, 21;*
del avowere par la ley de la terre acrust au Roi.[4] *Graunte,*
58.]
—*Grene.* Nous vous dioms qen temps le Roi Johan
le predecessour le Priour fuit seisi del avoeson, et
le tient de Count de P.,[5] et presenta, &c., et ore
lavoeson est tenue de[6] W.[7] de P.,[8] cosyn et heir le
dit Counte; et vous dioms qe nostre seignur le Roi
par sa chartre, qe cy est, dona conge au Priour del
approprier, et pur luy et ses successours de la
tenir en propre oeps; jugement si le Roi a ceste

---

[1] From L., H., and C., but
corrected by the record, *Placita de
Banco*, Easter, 19 Edw. III.,
Rᵒ 392. It there appears that the
action was brought by the King
against the Prior of Pentney in
respect of a presentation to the
church of Bilney (Norfolk).

[2] MSS. of Y.B., Benteseye.

[3] The words et puis are omitted
from C.

[4] According to the record, the
declaration was " quod idem Prior
" fuit seisitus de advocatione
" ecclesiæ prædictæ ut de feodo et
" jure Prioratus sui prædicti tem-
" pore . . . . domini Regis
" nunc, et præsentavit ad eandem
" quendam Edmundum Bozoun,
" clericum suum, qui ad præsenta-
" tionem suam fuit admissus et
" institutus . . . . . qui

" quidem Prior dictam advoca-
" tionem de ipso rege tenuit in
" capite. Et postmodum prædicta
" ecclesia vacavit per resigna-
" tionem ejusdem Edmundi, [et]
" idem Prior dictam ecclesiam sibi
" et Prioratui suo, absque licentia
" domini Regis, contra legem
" Angliæ. &c., appropriavit in pro-
" prios usus tenendam . . . . . .
" per quod ipsi domino Regi
" accrevit jus præsentandi ad
" eandem, &c., et ea ratione
" ad ipsum dominum Regem ad
" ecclesiam prædictam pertinet
" præsentare."

[5] L., and C., B.; H., K.

[6] de is omitted from C.

[7] L., B.

[8] The words de P. are omitted
from H.

No. 16.

A.D. 1345. admitted to make this declaration.—*R. Thorpe.* Show how William is the Count's cousin.—STONORE. If he were to demand through the Count it would be necessary for him to show it, but not in the present case.—*R. Thorpe.* By the appropriation it is supposed that the advowson is not held of the King, and we tell you that the advowson is held of the King; and, inasmuch as the King was not apprised, at the time of the grant, that it was held of him, and so the suggestion was false, and the King was deceived, judgment for the King; and we pray a writ to the Bishop.—*Grene.* And, inasmuch as your title is that the advowson is amortised without the King's license, and we have shown the reverse by record, judgment. —*Thorpe.* Enter the plea.—*Grene* did not dare to

No. 16.

moustraunce, &c.[1]—*R. Thorpe.* Moustretz coment W.[2] A.D. 1345. est cosyn al Counte.—Ston. Sil demandast par my luy il fra, mes ore nient.—*R. Thorpe.* Par lappropriacion est suppose qe ceo nest pas tenu du Roi, et vous dioms qe lavoweson est tenu du Roi ; et desicome le Roi nestoit my appris, al temps del graunt, qe ceo fuit tenu de luy, et issint la suggestion faux, et le Roi desceu, jugement pur le Roi ; et prioms[3] brief al Evesqe.—*Grene.* Et, desicome vostre title est qe lavoeson est amorti saunz conge du Roi, et le revers avoms moustre par record, jugement.— *Thorpe.* Entretz le plee.—*Grene* nosa demurer, mes

---

[1] The plea was, according to the record, "quod quidam Petrus de "Pelevile quartus, filius Petri de "Pelevile secundi, fuit seisitus de "manerio de Bilneye, ad quod "advocatio ecclesiæ prædictæ fuit "pertinens, tempore Regis Jo-"hannis, &c., et illud tenuit de "quodam Comite de Perche, et "per chartam suam concessit, "dedit, et confirmavit Deo et "ecclesiæ beatæ Mariæ Magdalenæ "de Penteneye et Canonicis "ibidem Deo servientibus et servi-"turis, pro salute animæ suæ et "antecessorum et successorum "suorum, advocationem ecclesiæ "de Bilneye, cum pertinentiis, et "totam culturam in eadem villa quæ "vocatur Ellernewonge. habendas "et tenendas illis et successoribus "suis in liberam puram et per-"petuam eleemosynam. Et obli-"gavit se ad heredes suos ad "warantiam. Et profert hic præ-"dictam chartam præfati Petri, "quæ hoc testatur, &c. Et dicit "quod postmodum dominus Rex "nunc de gratia sua speciali "concessit et licentiam dedit, pro "se et heredibus suis, quantum in

"ipso fuit, cuidam Egidio Priori "de Penteneye, prædecessori præ-"dicti Prioris nunc, et ejusdem "loci Conventui, quod ipsi eccle-"siam de Westbilneye quæ est de "advocatione sua propria, ut "dicitur, quæ est eadem ecclesia "ad quam dominus Rex nunc "clamat præsentare, &c., appro-"priare et eam appropriatam in "proprios usus tenere possint "sibi et successoribus suis in per-"petuum, statuto de terris et "tenementis ad manum mortuam "non ponendis edito non obstante. "Et profert hic literas domini "Regis nunc patentes quæ hoc "testantur, &c., unde dicit quod "ipse sic tenet ecclesiam illam in "proprios usus ut de advocatione "sua propria, &c., de quodam "Willelmo Philip, consanguineo "et herede prædicti Petri, in "puram et perpetuam eleemosy-"nam in forma prædicta, et non "de domino Rege immediate "prout idem dominus Rex in "demonstratione sua supponit. "Et hoc paratus est verificare, &c."

[2] L., B.

[3] prioms is from L. alone.

No. 17.

abide judgment, but imparled, and then said that the advowson was held of William Philip, and not of the King, as of his Crown; ready, &c.—*R. Thorpe.* Held of the King; ready, &c.—*Grene.* Not held of the King, as of his Crown; ready, &c.—*R. Thorpe.* If you will confess that it is held of the King, but not as of his Crown, and will abide judgment whether the appropriation be not sufficiently good, we will answer to that, and will abide judgment without putting the facts to a jury; and if you will traverse in general terms to the effect that the advowson is not held *in capite* of the King, that is a different issue; and since you will do neither the one nor the other, we pray a writ to the Bishop.—STONORE to *Grene.* Do you imagine that by such a license from the King, in general terms, where he did not grant his own right, you will be able to debar the King from his presentation, on the ground that the advowson is not held of the King as of his Crown, but possibly by reason of some escheat? as meaning to say that he would not do so.—*Grene.* No, Sir, but it is sufficient for us to traverse his title as comprised in his count and his declaration.—And afterwards they were at issue as to whether the advowson was held immediately of the King, or not, &c.—So note.

Ad terminum qui præteriit.

(17.) § Entry *ad terminum qui præteriit.*—*Sadelyng-*

No. 17.

enparla, et dit qe lavoeson est tenu de W. de[1] P.,
et noun pas du Roi come de sa Coroun; prest, &c.
—[*R. Thorpe*. Tenu du Roi; prest, &c.—*Grene*.
Noun pas tenu du Roi come de sa Coroun; prest,
&c.][2]—*R. Thorpe*. Si vous volletz conustre qe cest
tenu du Roi, mes noun pas come[3] de sa Coroun, et
demurer en jugement si lappropriacion ne soit assetz
bone, nous respoundroms a cella, et demuroms en
jugement sanz enqueste; et si vous vollez traverser
generalment qe lavoweson nest pas tenue en chief
du Roi, cest autre issue; et de puis qe vous ne
voilletz ne[4] lun ne lautre nous prioms brief al
Evesqe.—STON. a *Grene*. Quidetz vous par tiel licence
du Roi general, ou il graunta pas son dreit demene,
de forclore le Roi de son presentement, par tant qe
ceo nest pas tenu du Roi come de sa Coroun, mes
par cas par cause dasqun[5] eschete? *quasi diceret non.*
—*Grene*. Nanil, Sire, mes il nous suffit de traverser
son title compris deinz son counte et sa moustrance.
—Et puis ils furent a issue le quel il fuit tenu du
Roi ou noun, simplement, &c.—*Sic nota.*[6]

(17.)[7] § *Ad terminum qui præteriit.*—*Sadl.* Quei *Ad terminum qui præteriit.* [Fitz., *Taile*, 1.]

---

[1] L., B., instead of W. de.

[2] The words between brackets are omitted from L.

[3] come is from C. alone.

[4] ne is from H. alone.

[5] dasqun is omitted from H.

[6] The words "simplement, &c. —*Sic nota*" are from H. alone. According to the record, the replication, upon which issue was joined, was "quod prædictus Prior "tenet advocationem prædictam "de domino Rege immediate, &c."

A verdict was found at *Nisi prius* "quod ecclesia de Westbil- "neye est eadem ecclesia de "Bilneye ad quam dominus Rex

"nunc clamat præsentare, et quod "prædictus Prior tenet prædictam "ecclesiam in proprios usus ut de "advocatione sua propria de præ- "dicto Willelmo Philip, consan- "guineo et herede prædicti Petri, in "puram et perpetuam eleemosy- "nam, et non de domino Rege "immediate, prout idem dominus "Rex in demonstratione sua "supponit."

Judgment was thereupon given: —"Ideo prædictus Priori eat inde "sine die, salvo jure Regis cum "alias, &c."

[7] From L., H., and C.

No. 17.

stanes. What have you to show the lease?—STONORE. Do you not say anything else?—*Sadelyngstanes.* Your ancestor, on whose seisin you bring the action, gave, by this deed, in frank marriage to this same person with his daughter, and we are their issue; judgment whether you can have an action against us.—And the deed, being read, was found to be in the form alleged, but to have and to hold for their lives.— *Seton.* You see plainly that, according to the deed, in the *Habendum et Tenendum* clause, in which the nature of the gift is definitely declared, it is only a term for life, which term is passed according to their own confession; judgment, and we pray seisin.—*Seton* (continuing). When the intention of the donor is not definitely determined in the first clause, and it is definitely determined in the *Habendum et Tenendum* clause, you will adjudge the effect of the deed to be in accordance with the definite words, and not by the first words which are indefinite.—HILLARY. If I give to you and to your heirs by the *Dedi* clause, and for your life only by the *Habendum et Tenendum* clause, do you not have a fee simple? So also if I give to you and your wife in tail, or for term of life, to have and to hold to you alone for your life, will not the gift be such as the first clause purports? as meaning to say that it will.—WILLOUGHBY. I saw Sir Ralph de Hengham give judgment, with regard to such deeds as have the clause of gift contrariant to the *Habendum et Tenendum* clause, in accordance with the purport of the first clause.—*Stouford.* It is all one deed and one livery; therefore the judgment must be in accordance with the whole deed.—*Huse.* When a gift is made conditional in the first clause without expressly determining what is the estate, and the intention of the donor is definitely declared in the subsequent *Habendum et Tenendum* clause, the deed will be judged in accordance with the definite determination, and not in accordance with that which is indefinite.—HILLARY. A gift in frank-

No. 17.

avetz vous[1] du lees?—STON.[2] Autre chose ne ditetz? A.D. 1345.
—*Sadl.* Vostre auncestre de qi seisine, &c., par ceo
fait dona en fraunk mariage a mesme celuy ove sa
fille, entre quex nous sumes issue; jugement si vers
nous accion poietz aver.—Et le fet lieu voleit qe le
doun fuit par la manere, a aver et tener pur lour
vies.—*Setone.* Vous veietz bien qe par le fet en la
clause de *habendum et tenendum*, ou le doun est
desclarre en certein, nest qe terme de vie, quele
terme est passe de lour conissance; jugement et
prioms seisine.—*Setone.* Quant en[3] la primere clause
nest pas determine[4] la volunte le donour en certein,
et en le *habendum et tenendum* il est determine en
certeine, vous ajuggeretz le fet solonc les paroles en
certein, et noun pas par les primers qe sount en
noun certein.—HILL. Si jeo doune a vous et a voz
heirs par la clause de *dedi*, et par le *habendum et
tenendum* forqe soulement a vostre vie, navetz fee
simple? Auxint [si] jeo doune a vous et vostre
femme en taille, ou terme de vie, a aver et tener
a vous soulement a vostre vie, ne serra le doun
tiel com la primere clause purport? *quasi diceret sic.*
—WILBY. Jeo vie[5] Sir Rauf de Ingham[6] ajuger
tieles fetes qe furent contrariauntz en la clause del
doun et del aver et tener solonc purport de la
primere clause.—*Stouff.*[7] Tut est un fet et un livere;
par quei il covient juger sur tut[8] le fet.—*Huse.*
Quant un doun est fait condicionel en la clause
saunz expressement determiner quel estat, et en la
clause subsequent de *habendum et tenendum* est desclarre en certein la volunte le donour, homme
ajugera le fet solonc la determinacion en certein, et
noun pas solonc ceo qest en noun certein.—HILL.

---

[1] vous is from L. alone.
[2] H., *Setone.*
[3] H., a.
[4] C., termine.

[5] H., vy.
[6] H., H.
[7] H., STON.
[8] L., tote.

No. 18.

marriage is as definite as a gift in fee tail; and the estate can be enlarged by the *Habendum et Tenendum* clause, but not restricted.—*Rokel*. If I give a man certain land without any other words, he will have a freehold; and if I say in the *Habendum et Tenendum* clause only for a term of years, he will have only a term of years; so in the matter before us.—HILLARY. The cases are not similar.

Continuation: Admeasurement of Pasture.

(18.) § Continuation of the Admeasurement of Pasture in Foxton.—*Moubray*. We have demanded judgment inasmuch as the land to which he claims that common is appendant, and all the rest of the land in Foxton in which he claims common, was always, since time of memory, in the hands of John de Siggestone and his ancestors, except the land which we hold, until the time of the present King, when the said John enfeoffed the plaintiff of the parcel to which he claims the common as appendant, and so common cannot be said to be appendant by reason of the unity of possession, nor consequently does Admeasurement lie by reason of that land which has remained in the lord's hand. Nor does Admeasurement lie against us by reason of common in our land, because that would be to suppose that we had common in or could surcharge our own soil, and could so be admeasured in our own soil, which is impossible.— *Seton*. We understand that in the wastes which are in the lord's hand (notwithstanding that the land which we hold, to which we claim common appendant, was entirely in the hand of the lord, at which time he could not common there, though he could feed his beasts) by the conveyance of the parcel of the demesne lands made to us by the lord, because this

No. 18.

Doun en fraunk mariage est auxi en certein come
doun en fee taille; et homme poet enlarger lestat
par le *habendum et tenendum*, mes restreindre nient.
—*Rokele.* Si jeo doune a un homme[1] certein terre
saunz plus il avera franctenement; et si jeo die en
le aver et tener forqe terme daunz il navera qe
terme daunz; *sic in proposito.*—HILL. *Non est simile.*

(18.)[2] § *Residuum* del Amesurement de pasture en[4] *Residuum:*
Foxtone.[5]—*Moubray.* Nous avoms demande jugement *Amesurement.[3]*
desicome la terre a quel il cleyme, &c.,[6] et tut le
remenant de la terre en Foxtone ou il cleime, &c.,
fuit tut temps puis temps de memore en meins de
Johan Siggestone et ses auncestres, sauf la terre qe
nous tenoms, tanqen temps cesti Roi, qe le dit J.
feffa le pleintif de la parcelle a quele il cleime, &c.,
et issi en la terre le seignur pur la une possession
ne poet comune[7] estre dit appendant, *nec per consequens* par cause de cele terre qest remys en la
meyn le seignur Amesurement ne git pas. Ne par
cause de la comune en nostre terre ne git pas
Amesurement vers nous, qar ceo serreit a supposer
qe nous ussoms comune ou qe nous purroms sour-
charger[8] nostre soille demene, et issint en nostre
propre soille destre amesure, qe ne poet estre.—
Setone. Nous entendoms qen les wastes qe sount en
la mein le seignur, *non obstante* qe la terre qe nous
tenoms a quel nous clamoms, &c., fut tut en la
mein du seignur, a quel temps il ne poet y comuner
mes pestre, qe par[9] la demise de la parcelle de la
demeyns fet a nous par le seignur, pur ceo qe ceo

---

[1] The words a un homme are omitted from H.

[2] From L., H., and C.

[3] Amesurement is from C. alone.

[4] H., de; the word is omitted from L.

[5] The report is in continuation of Y.B., Trin., 16 Edw. III., No. 52, and Trin., 18 Edw. III., No. 43 (Foxton *v.* Foxton).

[6] &c. is from L. alone.

[7] comune is from H. alone.

[8] L., and C., charger.

[9] par is omitted from C.

No. 18.

was a hide of Ancient Demesne, to which, &c. (of common right, as ought to be adjudged), common ought to be adjudged to us as appendant, &c., and the lord who was our feoffor had common appendant in the defendant's land; so, therefore, have we who are enfeoffed by him.—WILLOUGHBY. Would the lord have had Admeasurement against him?—as meaning to say that he would not, because in that case the lord would have been admeasured in his own soil, and so, after admeasurement, debarred from approvement with regard to the rest.—*Grene.* It seems that the lord would have had admeasurement against him by reason of his common surcharged, and he, *e converso,* against the lord: for when there are several commoners in one vill, and one brings Admeasurement against another, even though the whole common be cast to a certain amount, still judgment on the Admeasurement holds good only between the parties themselves, and each of the other commoners has to bring a new writ of Admeasurement after he has felt himself aggrieved, and the admeasurement will be made in such a way that one will be admeasured in the land of the other, and *e converso,* and so no one will be admeasured in his own soil. And although the lord himself cannot have admeasurement against his tenants, he has another remedy: for if the commoners surcharge his soil, he will have the beasts or will impound them.—But this was altogether denied, except after admeasurement has been made.—SHARSHULLE to *Grene.* If there are only two neighbours in one vill who intercommon, each in the land of the other, does Admeasurement lie?—*Grene.* Yes, Sir, when they are commoners; and Admeasurement lies for every commoner, and the law is the same if there are only two as if there were twenty, because admeasurement holds good only between parties.—*Huse.* The law is different when there are several commoners from that which it

No. 18.

fut auncien terre hide a quele, &c., de comune dreit A.D. 1345.
[come deit estre ajuge, qe comune nous][1] deit estre
ajuge appendant, &c., et en la terre le defendant
le seignur qe fut nostre feffour avoit comune appendant; *ergo* nous qe sumes feffe[2] par ly.—WILBY. Ust
le seignur eu amesurement vers luy? *quasi diceret
non*, qar donqes ust il este amesure en son soille
propre, et auxi apres amesurement forclos au remenant dapprowement.—*Grene.* Il semble qe le
seignur ust eu Lamesurement vers luy pur sa comune
charge,[3] et *e converso* il devers le seignur: qar quant[4]
plusours comuners sount en un ville, et un port
Amesurement vers un autre, coment qe tote la comune
soit jettu[5] a certein, unqore le jugement sur Lamesurement se tient forqe entre mesmes les parties,
et chesqun autre des comuners, apres qe se sent
greve covient porter novel Amesurement, et lamesurement se fra issint qe lun serra amesure en la terre
lautre, et *e converso*, et si serra nulle amesure en
son soille propre. Et coment qe seignur mesme ne
poet vers ses tenantz aver amesurement, il ad autre
remedye: qar si les comuners surchargent son soille
il avera les avers ou les enparkera.—*Quod fuit omnino
negatum*, sil ne soit apres amesurement fet.—SCHAR.
a *Grene.* Sils y soient forqe deux veisyns en une
ville qentrecomunent chesqun en autri terre git Lamesurement?—*Grene.* Oyl, Sire, quant[6] ils sount
comuners; et pur chesqun comuner git Amesurement
et mesme la ley sil y soient forqe deux comme sils
fuissent xx, qar lamesurement se tient forqe entre
parties.—*Huse.* La ley est autre quant ils sount

---

[1] The words between brackets are omitted from H.

[2] feffe is omittted from C.

[3] H., dreit charger

[4] quant is omitted from C.

[5] H., joynt.

[6] H., qar.

Nos. 19, 20.

A.D. 1345　is when there are only two, for, as between two, one cannot say that the other has surcharged his common, because his common is the other's freehold, and he cannot surcharge his own freehold; but, if there were several, the supposition would be good with regard to the common which all would have in the freehold of the other commoners. — SHARSHULLE to *Grene.* Certainly he has answered you well.

Note.　　　(19.) Note that an alien Prior was tenant by his warranty, in respect of his own lease, where land was demanded. And he alleged that the King had seised the possessions, fees, and rents of his Priory, and that by this lease, by reason of which he had warranted, certain rent was saved to him, which rent, among others, was seised into the King's hand, and therefore he did not understand that the Court would proceed without consulting the King. — *Notton, ad idem.* Through a recovery the rent would be lost to the King, and that is not right, when the King has not been consulted.—HILLARY. Do you expect to have aid by reason of the rent when it is the land which is demanded? You will not have it; therefore answer.

Formedon.　(20.) § A writ was brought against Joan late wife

Nos. 19, 20.

plusours qe quant il y ad qe deux, qar entre deux A.D. 1345.
lun ne poet pas dire qe lautre ad surcharge sa
comune, qar sa comune est le franctenement lautre,
et son franktenement demeyne[1] ne poet il sour-
charger[2]; mes si plusours y fuissent le supposaille
serreit bone pur la comune qe toutz[3] averount[4]
en le franctenement des autres comuners.—SCHAR. a
Grene. Certes il vous ad bien respoundu.

(19.)[5] § *Nota* qun Priour alien fut tenant par sa *Nota.*
[Fitz.,
garrantie, de son lees demene, ou terre fut en de- *Ayde de*
mande. Et il alleggea[6] qe le Roi avoit seisi pos- *Roy,* 65.]
sessions, fees, et rentes de sa Priorie, et par cel
lees par quel il ad garranti certeine rente ly fut
sauve, quele rente entre autres fut seisi en la mein
le Roi, par quei sanz counseiller au Roy nentent
pas qe Court irreit avant.—*Nottone, ad idem.* Par my
le recoverir la rente descrestreit au Roy, et ceo nest
pas resoun, le Roi nient counseille.—HILL. Quidetz
vous aver eide par cause de rente la ou la terre est
en demande? Vous laveretz pas; par quei responez.

(20.)[7] § Brief porte vers Johane qe fut la femme Forme de
doun.[8]

---

[1] demeyne is from H. alone.

[2] L., and C., charger.

[3] L., and C., tut deux.

[4] H., avereint.

[5] From L., H., and C.

[6] H., dit.

[7] From L., H., and C. The record may be that found among the *Placita de Banco,* Easter, 19 Edw. III., R° 137. It there appears that an action of Formedon in the reverter was brought by John Kyriel, knight, against Joan late wife of Henry Gysors, in respect of the manor of " Scoteneye ' juxta veterem Romenhale " (Scotney-by-Old-Romney, Kent). The count was, according to the record, to the effect that Nicholas

Kyriel, the demandant's grand- [Fitz.,
Aide,
144.]
father, gave the manor to Robert
de Fyneaux and Margery his wife
in special tail. " Et de ipsis
" Roberto et Margeria, quia
" obierunt sine herede de corpori-
" bus suis exeunte, revertebatur,
" jus, &c., præfato Nicholao avo,
" &c., ut donatori, &c. Et de
" ipso Nicholao descendit jus
" reversionis, &c., cuidam Nicho-
" lao ut filio et heredi, &c. Et
" de ipso Nicholao descendit jus
" reversionis isti Johanni ut filio et
" heredi, qui nunc petit, &c. Et
" inde producit sectam, &c."

[8] The marginal note is omitted from C.

No. 20.

A.D. 1345. of Henry Gisors.—*Notton* showed how the tenements demanded and other tenements were in the seisin of a common ancestor, from whom they descended to Joan, against whom the writ was brought, and to one K., as to daughters, and that between these daughters partition was made. And he showed that by the custom of Gavelkind in Kent, in which county the tenements are, a husband shall hold a moiety of his wife's inheritance, after the wife's death, so long as he shall keep himself unmarried. And we tell you (said he) that, in satisfaction for this land allotted to Joan, R., late husband of the other parcener, holds, by custom, a moiety of that which was allotted as his wife's purparty, and we pray aid of him.—*Skipwith*. He does not show any definite tenancy in the person of whom he prays aid, as being tenant by the curtesy of England, nor in any other definite manner; judgment.—This exception was not allowed.—*Skipwith*. Then we tell you that Henry died without heir of his body, and therefore the right descended to Joan against whom the writ is brought; judgment, since R.'s tenancy is only by custom, and that indefinite, that is to say, so long as he keeps himself unmarried, whether she, who has the fee and right of the same person that held in her right, ought to have aid.— *Grene*. Then it is so; and we demand judgment, inasmuch as he does not deny that R. holds with us in estate of parcenery as tenant by the curtesy of England, and this aid prayer is made with the object of recovering *pro rata portione*, as he, in respect of his tenancy, shall, according to law, make satisfaction *pro rata*, just as a parcener would; and we pray aid. —*Skipwith*. Suppose that a person other than she against whom the writ is brought were heir to R.'s wife, it is certain that she would not have aid of one holding in that manner, without having aid of the heir also, and then the aid would be granted entirely by reason of the estate of the heir, being a parcener

No. 20.

H. Gisors.—*Nottone* moustra coment ces tenementz A.D. 1345. et autres tenementz[1] furent en la seisine un comune auncestre, de qi descendirent a J. vers qi le brief, &c., et une K., come as filles, entre queles purpartie, &c. Et par usage de[2] Gavelkynde[3] en Kent, ou les tenementz sount, le baroun del heritage sa femme, apres la mort la femme, tendra la moite tant qil[4] se tendra desmarie. Et vous dioms qen allowaunce de ceste terre allote a J., R., qe fut baroun a lautre parcenere tient la moite, par usage, de ceo qe fuit allote a sa purpartie, et prioms eide de luy.[5]—*Skip.* Il ne moustre nulle certein tenance en luy de qi il prie eide, come tenant[6] par la ley Dengleterre nen autre manere en certein; jugement. —*Non allocatur.*—*Skip.* Donqes vous dioms qe H. murust[7] sanz heir[8] de son corps, par quei le dreit descendi a J. vers qi le brief est porte; jugement, del houre qe sa tenance est forqe par usage, et ceo en noun certein, saver tanqil se tient desmarie, si ele qad le fee et dreit mesme celuy qe tient en son dreit eide deive aver.—*Grene.* Donqes est il issint; et demandoms jugement, desicome il ne dedit pas qe R. tient[9] ovesqe nous en estat de parcenerie come tenant par ley Dengleterre, et ceste eide prier est pur cause de recoverir *pro rata portione*, le quel de sa tenance par ley fra *pro rata* si avant come parcenere; et prioms eide.—*Skip.* Jeo pose qautre fut heire a sa femme qe[10] celuy vers qi le brief est porte, *certum est* qil navera pas eide del tenant par la manere saunz aver eide del heire ovesqe, et donqes leide serreit tut par cause del estat leire

---

[1] tenementz is from L. alone.
[2] H., del.
[3] L., and H., Gavilkynde.
[4] C., tanquele, instead of tant qil.
[5] H., R.

[6] tenant is omitted from C.
[7] C., muruyst.
[8] H., and C., issue.
[9] H., tient pas.
[10] L., and H., et.

No. 20.

and holding in parcenary, and the tenant of the free-hold would be joined in the prayer solely because satisfaction to the value would be made in respect of his freehold; therefore, when the tenant is herself the heir, the reason for the aid is wanting. Besides, suppose a writ were brought against the person of whom aid is prayed, it is certain that he would have aid firstly, by reason of the reversion, of the heir in whose right he held, and afterwards they would both have aid over of the parcener, in order to save the estate of the heir, in whose right they held; but one who is immediate tenant by the curtesy of England would never have aid by reason of parcenary, nor consequently would another have aid of him.—*Setone.* Tenant by the curtesy of England will be vouched with the heir, and he will make good the value of his tenancy; why then will he not, on the other hand, have the advantage of recovering the value.—*Skipwith.* He will never recover the value so as to hold by the curtesy of England land other than that which belonged to his wife, unless because the heir, in whose right the recovery took place, would have the advant-age.—STONORE. Why should you have aid of one who holds in your own right? I never heard of such a case, but it is quite inconsequent. And suppose a woman held a moiety in dower, as she would do by custom in these parts, would the heir have aid of her? —*Grene.* Tenant in dower never holds in parcenary, but tenant by the curtesy of England does.—*Skipwith.* Aid of a tenant by the curtesy of England will never be grantable in such case; and he is now in a worse case, because the person of whom aid is prayed does not hold by the curtesy of England, but by custom.— *Birton.* Suppose that he of whom aid is prayed and his wife had had judgment to recover *pro rata* against their co-parcener, would not the husband have execu-tion of such a judgment after the death of the wife?

No. 20.

qest parcenere, et tient en parcenerie, et le tenant A D. 1345.
de franctenement joint soulement en la priere pur
ceo qe de dreit[1] de son franctenement value se freit;
donqes quant le tenant mesme est heire cause del[2]
eide y faut. Ovesqe ceo, jeo pose qe brief fuit porte
vers celuy de qi leide est prie, *certum est* qil ust
eide primes, par cause de[3] reversion, del heir en
qi dreit il tenist, et apres les deux outre pur sauver
lestat leir en qi dreit il tiendrent[4] averount eide de
la parcenere ; mes immediate tenant par ley Dengleterre navereit jammes eide par cause de parcenerie,
nec, per consequens, autre de luy.—*Setone.* Tenant
par ley Dengleterre ove[5] leir serrount vouches, et
il fra sa tenance en value ; pur quei navera il
areremein lavantage de recoverir en value. — *Skip.*
Jammes ne recovera en value a tenir autre terre
par ley Dengleterre forqe ceo qe fut a sa femme,
sil ne fut par tant qe leire, en qi dreit le recoverir
se fit, ust lavantage.—STON. Pur quei averetz vous
eide de celuy qe tient en vostre dreit demene ? Jeo
nay pas oy tiel cas, mes il ensuit[6] arere. Et jeo
pose qune femme tenist en dowere la moite, come
par usage en celes parties ele freit, avereit leire
eide de luy?—*Grene.* Tenant en dowere tient jammes
en parcenerie, mes tenant par ley Dengleterre fet.—
Skip. Del tenant par ley Dengleterre eide ne serra
pas[7] grantable el cas ; et si est il ore en pire cas,
qar il ne tient pas[8] par ley Dengleterre de qi leide
est prie, mes par usage.—*Birtone.* Jeo pose qe sa
femme et luy de qi eide est prie ussent eu jugement de recoverir *pro rata* vers lour parcenere, navera
le baron execucion apres la mort la femme de tiel[9]

---

[1] The words de dreit are from H. alone.
[2] H., de cel.
[3] C., del.
[4] C., tiendrient.

[5] L., od.
[6] H., ensuist ; C., suffit.
[7] L., jammes.
[8] pas is omitted from C.
[9] H., C., cel.

No. 21.

as meaning to say that he would. Therefore he is in an estate of parcenary, and you have adjudged that a writ *de participatione facienda* lies against him; why then not aid-prayer?—HILLARY. If the reversion were to any one but yourself, you would never have aid of tenant by the curtesy of England, without praying in aid, together with him, the person in whom the right rests, and consequently, if you ought to have aid, you ought to have prayed it of yourself.—*Grene.* Possibly we shall have aid of ourself in this case; but it is, at any rate, right that aid should be granted of one, whoever he may be, who holds in estate of parcenery; for it is not in accordance with justice that we should lose all our portion, and that he should hold his entirely in that manner without making satisfaction to the value. And suppose the reversion had been to another, and not to us, and he had granted the reversion to a stranger, I should have aid of both.— *Skipwith.* Never, where the right is out of the blood by alienation.—HILLARY. No, certainly, she shall not have *pro rata* in her case any more than if her coparcener had aliened her purparty.—And, according to the opinion of the COURT, she shall not have aid.— Therefore she traversed the gift.

Nuper obiit.

(21.) § Note that, in the case of *Nuper obiit* brought by three persons, in which one of the tenants declared himself to be the villein of the Archbishop of York, which confession was entered, and in which judgment was deferred because one of the demandants did not prosecute his suit, that one was now summoned to prosecute, and did not prosecute his suit; and therefore he was severed. And also another of the demandants who previously sued did not now appear. And he was

No. 21.

jugement? *quasi diceret sic.* Donqes est il en estat A.D. 1345.
de parcenerie, et vous avetz[1] ajuge qe brief *de par-*
ticipatione facienda gist devers luy; pur quei nient
donqes eide prier?—HILL. Si la reversion fuit a
autre qe vous mesmes, jammes naveretz eide del
tenant par ley Dengleterre, saunz prier en eide
ovesqe celuy en qi le dreit reposa, et, *per consequens,*
si vous duissetz aver eide, et vous la duissetz[2] aver
prie de vous mesmes.—*Grene.* Par cas nous averoms
eide de nous mesmes en le[3] cas; mes au meins
de qi qe tient en estat de parcenerie est il resoune
qe leide soit graunte; qar resoune ne voet pas qe
nous perdoms tut[4] nostre porcion, et qil teigne en-
terement par la manere saunz value faire. Et jeo
pose qe la reversion fuit a autre qe a nous, qe ust
grante la reversion a estraunge persone, javeray eide
de eux deux.— *Skip.* Jammes, la ou le dreit est
par alienacion hors du sank.—HILL. Noun certes,
nient plus navera il *pro rata* en son cas, qe si soun
parcenere ust aliene sa purpartie.—Et, *per opinionem*
CURIÆ, il navera pas leide.—Par quei il traversa le
doun.[5]

(21.)[6] § *Nota* qe le *Nuper obiit* porte par iij, ou *Nuper*
obiit.
un des tenantz se dist estre le villein Lercevesqe
Deverwyke, quel conisaunce fut entre, et jugement
respite pur ceo qun des demandantz ne suit pas,
et ore celuy somons a suyre ne suit pas; par quei
il est severe. Et auxint un autre des demandantz
qautrefoith suit ne vint pas a ore. Et il est severe,

---

[1] L., avietz.

[2] The words et vous la duissetz
are omitted from H.

[3] L., ceo.

[4] L., tote.

[5] As aid was not granted, the
prayer and the allegations in
support of it do not appear on the
roll. The count is there followed
immediately by the plea *Non dedit,*
upon which issue was joined. The
award of the *Venire* follows, but
nothing further.

[6] From L., H., and C. The
report is in continuation of Y.B.,
Mich., 18 Edw. III., No. 72.

Nos. 22, 23.

A.D. 1345. severed, so that no one now prosecuted but one. And the villein, being called, did not appear. And, not-withstanding his non-appearance, on the allegation of the other tenants who held in common with him who made the confession of villenage, the whole writ abated. —The beginning is above.

Conclusion of the Quare impedit between the Earl of Lancaster and the Sub-prior of Trent-ham, of which the commence-ment is above.

(22.) § RICHARD WILLOUGHBY. Because the Earl has affirmed possession of a presentation in his ancestor, Earl Edmund, which has been confessed, and also by the King, by reason of the non-age of Thomas, Edmund's son, which you allege to have been in right of the King, and that is impossible, inasmuch as his ancestor was in possession, and the possession was in Thomas himself by presentation, and that presentation you allege to have been made by reason of Thomas's masterful power, and inflexibility,[1] which cannot be understood in law, and then you say that the King seized, &c., and restored to the present Earl all the inheritance, and saved to himself the patronage of the Priory, which is legally impossible, and you do not show that you are or that any one whose estate you have has been in possession, therefore let the Earl have a writ to the Bishop, and let him have a writ of enquiry of damages directed to the Sheriff.—See the beginning above, &c.

Quare impedit.

(23.) § Robert de Hungerforde brought a *Quare impedit*

---

[1] The Latin words of the roll (*Placita de Banco*, Easter, 18 Edw. III, R°. 318), which represent the French words " per seignurie et mestrie" of the report, are "per vim et rigorem ipsius Thomæ."

Nos. 22, 23.

issint qe nulle suyt a ore sauf un. Et le villein[1] A.D. 1345.
demande ne vint pas. Et, *non obstante* sa noun
venue, par lalleggeaunce des autres tenantz qe tiendreint en comune ove luy qe fit la conissance de
villenage, tut le brief abatist par agarde.—*Principium*
supra.

(22.) [2] § RICHARD [4] WILBY.[5] Pur ceo qe le Count *Residuum*
ad afferme possession de presentement en son aun- *del Quare*
impedit
cestre, le Count Edmund, qest conu, et auxint par *supra*
entre le
noun age Thomas son fitz [6] par le Roi, quel vous Count de
ditetz estre en le dreit le Roi, qe ne poet estre, Lancastre
et le
desicome son auncestre fut en possession, et apres Supprior
en Thomas mesme par presentement, quel vous de Trent-
ham.[8]
ditetz estre par seignurie et mestrie, qe ne poet par [Fitz.,
ley estre entendu, et puis ditetz qe le Roi seisist, *Quare*
impedit,
&c., et rendist au Count qore est tut leritage, et 156.]
qil sauva a luy lavowere de la Priorie, qe ne poet
estre de ley, et vous moustretz pas qe vous estes
en possession ne nulle qi estat vous avietz,[7] par
quei le Count eit brief al Evesqe, et au Vicounte
bref [8] denquere de damages.[9]—*Vide principium supra,*
&c.

(23.) [10] § Robert Hungerforde [11] porta *Quare impedit* Quare
impedit.

---

[1] villein is omitted from C.

[2] From L., H., and C. The report is in continuation of Y.B., Easter, 18 Edw. III., No. 15. (Henry, Earl of Lancaster, *v.* the Sub-prior and Convent of Trent-ham.)

[3] The marginal note is, except the words *Quare impedit*, from C. alone. In H. it is *Judicium*, with a reference to a folio of the MS. for the "*principium.*"

[4] RICHARD is omitted from H.

[5] H., WILBY agarda.

[6] MSS. of Y.B., frere.

[7] H., avetz.

[8] bref is from H. alone.

[9] For the judgment, as it appears on the roll, *see* Y.B., Easter, 18 Edw. III. (Rolls edition), p 65, note 6.

[10] From L., H., and C., but corrected by the record, *Placita de Banco*, Easter, 19 Edw. III., R⁰ 188, d. It there appears that the action was brought by Robert de Hungerforde, knight, against the Prior of Farley, and Robert de Segbroke, his clerk, in respect of a presentation to the church of Bysshopestrowe (Bishopstrow, Wilts).

[11] C., Hungreforde.

No. 23.

A.D. 1345. against the Prior of Farley, and the parson of the church [of Bishopstrow], and counted that a certain Prior, predecessor of the present Prior, was seised, and presented, and leased to him for his life [the advowson, &c.], and that he presented, and that on a subsequent voidance of the church, a dispute having arisen, he brought a *Quare impedit* against that Prior's successor, and recovered, and that the Bishop made donation in accordance with the right which had devolved upon the Bishop by lapse of time, and that, on the resignation of the donee, the church is now void, and that so it belongs to him to present.—*Thorpe.*

No. 23.

vers le Priour de Farleye, et la persone del eglise, A.D. 1345. contaunt qe le Priour[1] predecessour, &c., fuit seisi, et presenta, et luy lessa pur sa vie, et il presenta, et puis a lautre voidaunce sur debat il porta *Quare impedit* vers les successours, et recoveri, et Levesqe dona en son dreit par temps passe, par qi resignement, &c., et issint appent a luy.[2]—*Thorpe.* Nous

---

[1] H., leglise le Priour.

[2] The declaration was, according to the record, " quod quidam " Willelmus de Balsham, quondam " Prior de Farleghe, prædecessor, " &c., fuit seisitus de advocatione " ecclesiæ. prædictæ, ut de jure " ecclesiæ suæ Sanctæ Mariæ " Magdalenæ, tempore pacis, tem- " pore domini Regis nunc, qui ad " eandem præsentavit quemdam " Johannem de Bradeforde, cleri- " cum suum, qui ad præsentati- " onem suam fuit admissus et " institutus, ... qui " quidem Willelmus de Balsham " postmodum depositus fuit et " amotus. &c., post cujus deposi- " tionem et amotionem prædictus " Prior nunc fuit electus in Priorem, " &c., qui quidem Prior nunc " et ejusdem loci Conventus per " scriptum dederunt et concesser- " unt ipsi Roberto advocationem " ecclesiæ prædictæ et sex solidatas " et octo denariatas redditus annu- " atim percipiendas per manus Jo- " hannis de Bradeforde et Elenæ " filiæ Gregorii Beaufitz pro terris " et tenementis quæ dicti Johannes " et Elena de præfato Priore tenent " ad terminum vitæ suæ in " Horspole in villa de Bisshope- " strowe. Concesserunt etiam pro " se et successoribus suis quod " prædicta terræ et tenementa quæ " prædicti Johannes et Elena " tenent ad terminum vitæ suæ, et

" quæ post mortem eorundem " Johannis et Elenæ præfatis " Priori et Conventui et eorum " successoribus reverti deberent, " ipsi Roberto remanerent, habenda " et tenenda, simul cum advoca- " tione prædicta, de prædictis Priore " et Conventu et eorum successori- " bus, ad totam vitam ipsius " Roberti, virtute cujus concessi- " onis prædicti Johannes et Elena " se attornaverunt, &c. Et profert " hic prædictum scriptum prædic- " torum Prioris et Conventus quod " prædictam concessionem testa- " tur, &c. Et postea, vacante " ecclesia prædicta per resignati- " onem præfati Johannis de " Bradeforde per prædictum Willel- " mum de Balsham quondam " Priorem, &c., præsentati, con- " tentio mota fuit inter prædictum " Priorem nunc et ipsum Robertum, " per quod idem Robertus tulit " breve suum de *Quare impedit* " versus eundem Priorem nunc de " ecclesia prædicta, quod fuit " returnabile hic a die Paschæ in " unum mensem anno regni " domini Regis undecimo, et " antequam idem Robertus præ- " sentationem suam, &c., recu- " perare potuisset dominus R., " Episcopus Sarum qui nunc est, " per lapsum temporis jure sibi " devoluto, contulit ecclesiam " illam cuidam Johanni de " Budestone, clerico suo, et eum

No. 23.

A.D. 1345. We tell you that the King seized the fees and advowsons of the Priory because the Prior is an alien, and afterwards brought a *Quare impedit*, and recovered against the Prior, and presented. And his presentee was admitted, and instituted, and so the church is full, and so was for six months before the present writ was purchased; judgment of the writ. And, as to the parson, *Thorpe* alleged the same matter, and said :—Judgment whether such a writ lies against him. —*Mutlow*. To that allegation of plenarty the law does not put us to answer, for the allegation of plenarty does not lie in the mouth of any one but of him who can show himself to be patron, because by giving such an answer he would be in a position to give a writ of Right against himself, and to abate every possessory writ. And, inasmuch as we have by deed, and also by recovery against himself, disproved his title, and affirmed right and possession in ourselves, we do not understand that the law puts us to answer to the recovery had against him [by the King], to which we are strangers. And, as to the parson who disclaims, we pray a writ to the Bishop.—*Thorpe*. Then it is so. And we demand judgment, because he has not denied the plenarty, which plenarty we show to be in our right, even though we did not present, because the King presented in right of the Priory, and so this allegation of plenarty lies in our mouth, just as an heir will allege plenarty through a presentation made by his guardian; judgment.—*Mutlow*. The church was not full before the six months preceding the purchase of the writ; ready to aver this wheresoever we ought.—And note that *Thorpe* said that one who alleges plenarty, even though he waive his exception, shall not afterwards be admitted to traverse the plaintiff's title.—*Quære.*—*Skipwith*. Then we tell you, not confessing the lease, &c., that, whereas they say that the church is void through the resignation of him

No. 23.

vous dioms qe le Roi seisist fees et avoesouns de A.D. 1345.
la Priorie pur ceo qe le Prior est alien, et puis
porta *Quare impedit*, et recoveri vers le Prior, et
presenta. Et son presente resceu et institut, et
issint leglise pleine, et fut par vj moys avant le
brief purchace; jugement du brief. Et quant a la
persone, alleggea mesme la chose; jugement si vers
luy tiel brief ygise.—*Mutl.* A cel plenerte ley ne
nous mette pas a respondre, qar plenerte gist en
nully bouche forqe de celuy qe se purra moustrer
patroun, pur ceo qe par tiel respons il serreit a
doner brief de dreit vers luy, et abatre chesqun
brief de possession. Et desicome par fait, et auxint
par recoverir vers luy mesme, nous avoms desprove
son title, et afferme dreit et[1] possession en nous, et
al recoverir taille vers luy nous sumes estrange, et
nentendoms pas qe ley a ceo nous mette a respondre.
Et quant a la persone qe descleyme, nous prioms
brief al Evesqe.—*Thorpe.* Donqes est il issint. Et
demandoms jugement, del houre qil nad pas dedit
la plenerte, quel plenerte moustroms estre en nostre
dreit, tut ne presentames nous pas, qar le Roi presenta en le dreit la Priorie, et issint gist ceo en
nostre bouche, come leire alleggera plenerte par[2]
presentement fait par son gardein; jugement.—*Mutl.*
Nient plein avant les vj moys avant le brief purchace; prest ou averer le devoms.—Et *nota* qe
Thorpe dist qe celuy qe allegge plenerte, tut weyva
il son chalenge, il ne serra pas apres resceu de
traverser le title del pleintif.—*Quære.*—*Skip.* Donqes
vous dioms, nient conissant le lees,[3] &c., qe la ou
ils dient qe leglise est voide par resignement de

"induxit in eadem, ...
"per cujus resignationem prædicta
"ecclesia modo vacat, super quo
"brevi ipse Robertus præsentati-
"onem suam per judicium Curiæ
"recuperavit, et ea ratione pertinet

"ad ipsum Robertum de Hunger-
"forde ad prædictam ecclesiam
"præsentare."

[1] C., de.
[2] H., et.
[3] C., lesse.

No. 23.

to whom the Bishop made donation in their right, the truth is that the plaintiff recovered by *Quare impedit*, with damages, &c., and the King, in respect of the same voidance, afterwards recovered the presentation against us, and his presentee was admitted, as above, *absque hoc* that the person whom you allege to have been inducted, by the Bishop's collation, in your right, was instituted and inducted, as you have said ; ready, &c. And we demand judgment inasmuch as, in respect of the same voidance, you had by your judgment against us the effect of a presentation, whether you ought to be answered a second time as to such a writ.—*Pole*. You shall not be admitted to that, because the first plea, that is to say the plenarty, was to our action, and particularly against us who are a purchaser, and that only for term of life.—WILLOUGHBY. He has now affirmed your writ.—*Pole*. Still this second plea is in the first place an allegation of plenarty, and is also to our action.—WILLOUGHBY. Answer.—*Mutlow*. We tell you that he was admitted and instituted as we have said ; ready, &c.—*Skipwith*. Not instituted on the collation of the Bishop, as they say ; ready, &c.—And in that manner the issue was taken by judgment, and not in general terms whether instituted or not.—And of this enquiry shall be made by the country.

No. 23.

celuy a qi Levesqe dona en lour dreit, nous dioms qe voirs est qil[1] recoveri par *Quare impedit,* &c., et lour damages, &c., et le Roi de mesme la voidaunce apres recoveri vers nous le presentement, et son presente resceu, *ut supra,* sanz ceo qe celuy qe vous ditetz estre inducte par collacion Devesqe en vostre dreit fuit institut et inducte, come vous avetz dit; prest, &c. Et demandoms jugement, desicome de[2] mesme la voidaunce vous avietz par vostre jugement vers nous leffecte del presentement, si autrefoith a tiel bref deivetz estre respondu.—*Pole.* Vous ne serretz a ceo resceu, qar le primere plee fut a nostre accion, saver la plenerte, et nomement vers nous qe sumes purchaceour, et auxint forqe pur terme de vie.—WILBY. Il ad ore afferme vostre brief.—*Pole.* Unqore cest second plee est dallegger la plenerte primer et auxint a nostre accion.—WILBY. Responez. —*Mutl.* Nous vous dioms qil fuit resceu et institut come nous avoms dit; prest, &c.—*Skip.* Nient in-stitut al collacion Levesqe, comme ils dient; prest, &c.—Et par cele manere fuit lissue par agarde pris, et nient generalment le quel institut ou noun.—Et serra enquis par pays.[3]

---

[1] C., qelc.

[2] L., par.

[3] On the roll the pleas come immediately after the declaration as follows:—"Robertus de Seg-"broke dicit quod ipse est persona "ecclesiæ prædictæ impersonata "in eadem ad præsentationem "domini Regis, nec aliquid clamat "in advocatione ejusdem, nec "ipsum impedivit præsentare ad "eandem. Et de hoc ponit se "super patriam et Robertus "similiter. Et Prior dicit quod "ubi prædictus Robertus de "Hungerforde in narratione sua "supponit quod per resignationem "præfati Johannis de Bradeforde "ecclesia prædicta vacavit, et, "contentione mota inter prædic-"tum Robertum de Hungerforde "et ipsum Priorem super præ-"sentatione ad eandem, præfatus "Episcopus contulit ecclesiam 'prædictam prædicto Johanni de 'Budestone per lapsum temporis, "&c., per cujus resignationem, "&c., idem Prior dicit quod "dominus Rex nunc ratione guerræ "inter homines de Anglia et illos "de Francia motæ seisivit in "manum suam Prioratum de Far-"leghe, una cum feodis militum, "et advocationibus ecclesiarum

Nos. 24, 25.

A.D. 1345.
Dower.

(24.) § Dower of a moiety, by custom, of a fifth part of the tronage in the town of Boston. Exception was taken to the demand because the demandant did not define by her demand that which she would take, and also because that which was demanded is an office, in which case she ought to demand a moiety of the office, &c.

Error.

(25.) § Error on a Mort d'Ancestor taken in the County of Chester. In this Assise it was pleaded by the tenant that the demandant ought not to be answered as to such a writ, because he previously brought a Formedon in the descender in respect of the same tenements against the same person, on a gift made to the same ancestor, and that Formedon is a writ of a higher nature, to which writ he appeared. Against this the demandant said, in order to have the Assise, that he prosecuted the writ of Formedon until

Nos. 24, 25.

(24.) [1] § Dowere de la moite, par usage, de la A.D. 1345. quinte partie del tronage [2] en la ville de Seint Botolf. Dowere. La demande chalenge de ceo qele ne mist pas en certein par sa demande ceo qele prendreit, et auxint cest un office, en quel cas ele demandereit la moite del office, &c.

(25.) [3] § Errour en Mortdauncestre pris el Counte Errour. de Cestre, en quel Assise fuit plede par le tenant [4] [Fitz., Estoppel, 227.] qe le demandant ne devoit pas a tiel brief estre respondu, pur ceo qautrefoith de mesmes les tenementz il porta un Fourme doun en descendre dun doun fait a mesme launcestre, qest brief de plus haut nature, a quel il apparust,[5] vers mesme la persone. Countre quei il dit, pur aver Assise, qil pursuyst avant en le brief de Fourme doun si qe

---

" eidem Prioratui spectantibus, eo
" quod idem Prior alienigena est,
" et, pro eo quod ecclesia illa
" adtunc vacans fuit per resigna-
" tionem prædicti Johannis de
" Bradeforde, idem dominus Rex
" tulit breve suum de *Quare*
" *impedit* versus ipsum Priorem, et
" præsentationem suam ad eandem
" per judicium Curiæ recuperavit,
" et ad eandem præsentavit præ-
" dictum Robertum de Segbroke,
" qui ad præsentationem suam
" adhuc est persona impersonata
" in eadem, absque hoc quod præ-
" dictus Episcopus prædictam
" ecclesiam contulit præfato Jo-
" hanni de Budestone per lapsum
" temporis, prout prædictus Ro-
" bertus de Hungerforde superius
" in narratione sua supponit."
Issue was joined upon this also, and the *Venire* was awarded, but nothing further appears upon the roll.
[1] From L., H., and C.
[2] C., trowage.

[3] From L., H., and C., but corrected by the record, *Placita coram Rege*, Easter, 19 Edw. III., R° 85. The action was brought by William son of Bernard de Tranemol against Richard de Wheloke and Margaret his wife.
" Rex mandavit Edwardo Prin-
" cipi Walliæ, Duci Cornubiæ, et
" Comiti Cestriæ, filio suo caris-
" simo, vel ejus Justiciario Cestriæ,
" aut ejusdem Justiciarii locum
" tenenti, breve suum clausum in
" hæc verba," *i.e.* the writ of Error.
Then follow the record and process of the Assise "in hæc verba "—
" Placita Comitatus Cestriæ tenta
" apud Cestriam coram Thoma de
" Ferariis, Justiciario Cestriæ, die
" Martis in Crastino Conceptionis
" beatæ Mariæ anno regni Regis
" Edwardi tertii a Conquestu
" decimo octavo."
[4] The words par le tenant are from L. alone.
[5] C., apparuyst.

No. 25.

the gift was traversed; and it was found that the alleged donor did not give, and judgment was therefore given that the demandant should take nothing by his writ. And therefore he was restored to this action of Mort d'Ancestor. And he prayed the Assise. Against this the tenant said again that the demandant ought not to have the Assise, because he previously brought a Mort d'Ancestor, as he now does, as to which the tenant alleged the user of a writ of a higher nature. Against this the demandant alleged nothing in order to have the Assise. Therefore judgment was given that the demandant should take nothing by the Assise. And (said Counsel for the tenant) we demand judgment whether there ought to be Assise contrary to this judgment, which still stands in force. And the demandant said that the tenant's first plea was in bar of the Assise, to which he had given a sufficient answer in order to have the Assise, and therefore the tenant ought not to be admitted to this second bar. Therefore the judgers awarded the Assise, and it passed

No. 25.

le doun fuit traverse; et trove qil ne dona pas, par

A.D. 1345.

quei agarde fuit qil ne prist rienz. Et par tant il restitut a cest accion de Mortdauncestre. Et pria Assise. Countre quei le tenant de rechief dit qe par tant ne devereit il Lassise aver, qar autrefoith il porta Mortdauncestre, come ore fait, a quei il allegea le user de brief de plus haut nature. Countre quei il dit rienz pur aver Assise. Par quei fuit agarde qil prist rienz par Lassise. Et demandoms jugement si countre cel agarde esteaunt en sa force Assise devereit estre. Et le demandant dist qe son primer plee fut barre dassise, a quei il ad [done] suffisaunt respons pur aver Assise, par quei a ceo secounde barre il ne serra resceu. Par quei les jugeours agarderent Lassise qe passa pur le demandant.[1]—

[1] According to the Chester record, as set out on the King's Bench roll, "Assisa venit " [at Chester] recognitura si " Bernardus de Tranemol fuit " seisitus in dominico suo ut " de feodo de uno mesuagio " et una bovata terræ, cum " pertinentiis, in Tranemol, die " quo obiit, et si obiit postquam " Ranulphus quondam Comes " Cestriæ fuit cruce signatus, et si " idem Willelmus propinquior " heres ejus sit, &c., quæ quidem " tenementa Ricardus de Wheloke " et Margareta uxor ejus tenent, " qui .veniunt et dicunt quod " prædictus Willelmus alias in " Comitatu hic, scilicet die Martis " proxima post clausum Paschæ " ultimo præteritum, tulit quoddam " breve de Forma donationis de " prædictis tenementis modo in " visu positis, ad quod breve idem " Willelmus comparuit, et petunt " judicium si ad istud breve Mortis " antecessoris, quod est de inferiori " natura responderi debeat, &c. " Et Willelmus dicit quod quo-" modo prædicti Ricardus et " Margareta allegant quod ad " istud breve responderi non " debeat, placitum illud non potest " intelligi de alio effectu quam ad " præcludendum ipsum ab Assisa " ista, &c. Et bene concedit quod " ipse tulit prædictum breve de " Forma donationis, prædictis die " et anno, de prædictis tenementis, " per quod breve supposuit quod " quidam Henricus de Staundone, " capellanus, dedit Bernardo de " Tranemol et Elenæ uxori ejus " et heredibus de corporibus " ipsorum Bernardi et Elenæ " exeuntibus, sed dicit quod ad " illud breve prædicti Ricardus et " Margareta venerunt et dixerunt " quod prædictus Henricus non " dedit prædictis Bernardo et " Elenæ prædicta tenementa, cum " pertinentiis, sicut prædictus " Willelmus per breve suum " supposuit, ita quod postea,

No. 25.

A.D. 1345 for the demandant.—*Mutlow* assigned error inasmuch as the judgers awarded the Assise notwithstanding the first plea, that is to say, the user of a writ of a higher nature, on the ground of a replication which the demandant made to the effect that the action was tried with a result adverse to him. Another error assigned was that the tenant was ousted from pleading the second plea in bar of the Assise since the first plea was only to the writ.—*Skipwith.* As to the first error

---

" continuato processu usque ad
" Comitatum hic, ...
" per quandam inquisitionem inde
" inter eos summonitam et
" captam compertum fuit quod
" prædictus Henricus non dedit
" prædictis Bernardo et Elenæ
" prædicta tenementa, cum perti-
" nentiis, in forma prædicta, per
" quod consideratum fuit in eodem
" Comitatu quod prædictus Willel-
" mus nihil caperet per breve suum,
" sed esset in misericordia pro
" falso clameo, &c., et quod præ-
" dicti Ricardus et Margareta irent
" inde sine die, et petit inde
" judicium, desicut compertum
" fuit per inquisitionem prædictam
" quod ipse non habuit actionem
" per prædictum breve de Forma
" donationis, et actio sua penitus
" adnullatur, si ad hoc breve
" Mortis antecessoris responderi
" non debeat, seu ab Assisa ista
" præcludi debeat in hac parte, &c.
" Et consideratum est per judica-
" tores quod eidem Willelmo ad
" istud breve respondeatur, non
" obstante allegatione prædicta, et
" quod per allegationem illam non
" præcludatur ab Assisa ista, &c.

" Et Ricardus et Margareta
" adhuc dicunt quod prædictus
" Willelmus alias in Comitatu hic,
" scilicet die Martis proxima ante

" Festum Sanctæ Margaretæ Vir-
" ginis anno regni domini Regis
" nunc sextodecimo, tulit quoddam
" breve Mortis antecessoris de præ-
" dictis tenementis modo in visu
" positis versus ipsos Ricardum et
" Margaretam, ad quod breve iidem
" Ricardus et Margareta venerunt
" et dixerunt quod ad illud breve
" Mortis antecessoris responderi
" non, deberet, quia dixerunt quod
" prædictus Willelmus alias in
" Comitatu hic tulit breve de
" Forma donationis ad quod præ-
" dictus Willelmus comparuit, et
" petierunt judicium si ad illud
" breve de Morte antecessoris quod
" fuit de inferiori natura responderi
" deberet, &c., ad quod breve præ-
" dictus Willelmus tunc venit et
" dixit quod per illud breve Mortis
" antecessoris petiit liberum tene-
" mentum suum et feodum sim-
" plex, et petiit judicium si per
" prædictum breve de . Forma
" donationis, quod tangit feodum
" talliatum, et quod est de inferiori
" natura, ab Assisa illa tangente
' feodum simplex repelli deberet,
'· &c., per quod consideratum fuit
" quod prædicti Ricardus et Mar-
" gareta irent inde sine die, et
" prædictus Willelmus nihil caperet
" per breve suum, sed esset in
" misericordia pro falso clameo,

No. 25.

Mutl. assigna errour en tant come il agarderent A.D. 1345.
Lassise *non obstante* le primere plee, saver, luser
dun brief de plus haut nature, par tiel replicacion
qil fist qe laccion fuit trie contre luy. Autre errour,
de ceo qil fuit ouste de pleder le secounde plee en
barre Dassise del houre qe le primer plee ne fuit
forqe au brief.[1]—*Skip.* Quant al primere errour qe

" &c. Et petunt judicium si ad
" istud breve de Morte antecessoris
" responderi debeat, &c. Et Wil-
" lelmus dicit quod prædicti
" Ricardus et Margareta ad istud
" placitum modo admitti non
" debent, ex quo alias allegarunt
" quod idem Willelmus tulit
" quoddam aliud breve de Forma
" donationis de prædictis tenemen-
" tis modo in visu positis, sicut
" superius allegatum est, et
" petierunt judicium si ad istud
" breve responderi deberet, quod
" quidem placitum fuit de effectu
" ad præcludendum ipsum Willel-
" mum ab Assisa ista, &c., ad
" quod placitum idem Willelmus
" respondit competenter pro Assisa
" illa, ut præmittitur, habenda,
" &c., et super hoc consideratum
" fuit per Judicatores quod idem
" Willelmus ad ·istud breve respon-
" deri deberet, non obstante
" allegatione prædicta, nec per
" allegationem illam præcluderetur
" ab Assisa ista, et istud placitum
" quod prædicti Ricardus et Mar-
" gareta modo allegant est novum
" placitum ad præcludendum ipsum
" ab Assisa ista, ad quod de jure
" admitti non debent, et petit inde
" judicium et Assisam, &c. Ideo
" consideratum est per Judicatores
" quod, non obstante allegatione
" prædicta, Assisa capiatur, &c.
" Juratores de consensu partium
" electi dicunt super sacramentum

" suum quod prædictus Bernardus,
" pater prædicti Willelmi, fuit
" seisitus in dominico suo ut de
" feodo de prædictis tenementis,
" cum pertinentiis, die quo obiit,
" et quod obiit postquam, &c., et
" quod idem Willelmus propinquior
" heres ejus est. Ideo considera-
" tum est quod idem Willelmus
" recuperet versus prædictos Ri-
" cardum et Margaretam seisinam
" suam de prædictis tenementis,
" cum pertinentiis, per visum
" recognitorum ejusdem Assisæ,
" et, quo ad damna, relaxantur per
" prædictum Willelmum."

[1] The assignments of error in
the King's Bench were, according
to the roll, " quod prædicti Judica-
" tores erraverunt in hoc quod, cum
" prædicti Ricardus et Margareta
" allegarunt quod idem Willelmus
" tulit breve suum de Forma
" donationis de tenementis præ-
" dictis de seisina prædicti Ber-
" nardi, de qua seisina idem
" Willelmus tulit breve suum
" Mortis antecessoris versus eosdem
" Ricardum et Margaretam, ad
" quod quidem breve de Forma
" donationis idem Willelmus ap-
" paruit, et petierunt judicium si
" ad illud breve de inferiori natura
" responderi debuisset, ubi idem
" Willelmus expresse cognovit
" quod ipse tulit prædictum breve
" de Forma donationis versus
" eosdem Ricardum et Margaretam

No. 25.

A.D. 1345. which you assign, you see plainly how the demandant
in the Assise said that the writ of Formedon was
determined and tried with a result adverse to him,
and in that case it is law and it is right that he
should be admitted to any other action which may be
consistent with that which was then tried with a result
adverse to him.   Moreover, even though there was no
gift, it may still be consistent with that fact that the
alleged donee died seised as of fee, so that the judgers
acted rightly in that judgment.   And as to the other
point, with respect to which he said that the first plea
was only to the writ, and that the judgers therefore
erred when they ousted him from pleading in bar

" de tenementis prædictis, ad quod
" quidem breve idem Willelmus
" supposuit quod Henricus de
" Standone, capellanus, dedit tene-
" menta prædicta prædicto Ber-
" nardo, patri ipsius Willelmi, et
" Elenæ uxori ejus, et heredibus
" ipsorum Bernardi et Elenæ
" exeuntibus, ad quod breve iidem
" Ricardus et Margareta dixerunt
" quod prædictus Henricus non
" dedit prædicta tenementa præ-
" dictis Bernardo et Elenæ, sicut
" idem Willelmus per breve suum
" supposuit, super qua inquisitione
" partes prædictæ posuerunt se
" hinc inde in Juratam patriæ, per
" quam quidem Juratam comper-
" tum fuit quod prædictus Henricus
" de Standone non dedit prædicta
" tenementa prædictis Bernardo et
" Elenæ, sicut idem Willelmus per
" breve suum supposuit, per quod
" consideratum fuit quod prædictus
" Willelmus nihil caperet per
" breve suum, sed esset in miseri-
" cordia pro falso clameo, &c.,
" et petiit judicium, ex quo actio
" sua per breve de Forma donati-
" onis per veredictum prædictum

" pro nulla reperta fuit et omnino
" adnullata, si ad istud breve
" Mortis antecessoris responderi
" non debuisset, ubi Judicatores
" prædicti consideraverunt quod ad
" breve suum Mortis antecessoris
" responderi debuit, ubi Judicatores
" prædicti prædictum breve cassasse
" debuissent, eo quod exceptio ad
" utendum brevi de altiori natura
" allegata contra petentem aufert
" ipsum ad utendum brevi de
" inferiori natura de seisina ejus-
" dem de qua seisina breve de
" altiori natura tulebatur, et ponit
" eundem petentem ad breve de
" eadem natura, licet actio in brevi
" quo utebatur de altiori natura
" ut nulla reperta fuit.
" Item   Judicatores   prædicti
" erraverunt in eo quod, cum
" prædicti Ricardus et Margareta
" placitaverunt in barram Assisæ
" prædictæ per hoc quod idem
" Willelmus alias tulit breve suum
" Mortis antecessoris versus eos
" de seisina prædicti Bernardi, de
" qua quidem seisina idem Willel-
" mus tulit Assisam prædictam de
" tenementis prædictis, ubi iidem

No. 25.

vous assignetz, vous veietz bien coment le demandant A.D. 1345.
en Lassise dist qe le brief de Fourme de doun fuit
termine et trie countre luy, en quel cas il est ley
et resoun qe a[1] chesqune autre accion qe poet
estere[2] ove ceo qadonqes fuit trie[3] countre luy qil
soit resceu. Mes tut ny avoit[4] il pas doun, uncore
puit estere ovesqe ceo[5] qil muruyst seisi come de
fee, issint qen cel agarde ils firent bien. Et quant
al autre point, qil dist qe le primer plee ne fuit
forqe au brief, par quei ils errerunt quant ils luy
ousterunt de pleder en barre apres, jeo die qe le

"Ricardus et Margareta allegarunt
"quod ipse ad idem breve Mortis
"antecessoris responderi non
"debuit, eo quod idem Willelmus
"alias tulit versus eos breve de
"Forma donationis de eisdem
"tenementis, ad quod breve idem
"Willelmus apparuit, et petierunt
"judicium si ad breve Mortis
"antecessoris quod est de natura
"inferiori responderi debuit, ad
"quod idem Willelmus adtunc
"venit et dixit quod id quod ipse
"petiit per breve Mortis ante-
"cessoris fuit feodum simplex, et
"per breve suum de Forma
"donationis, quo ipse utebatur,
"ipse petiit feodum talliatum, et
"sic breve suum de Forma dona-
"tionis fuit de natura inferiori,
"et non intendebat quod ipsi ad
"utendum breve suum Mortis
"antecessoris ipsum repellere
"potuerunt, per quod breve ipse
"petiit feodum simplex, et sic
"breve suum Mortis antecessoris
"fuit de altiori natura quam fuit
"praedictum breve de Forma
"donationis en le descendere, et
"petiit judicium si de Assisa sua
"praedicta repelli debuit, in qua
"Assisa consideratum fuit quod

"praedicti Ricardus et Margareta
"irent inde sine die et praedictus
"Willelmus nihil caperet per
"breve suum sed esset in miseri-
"cordia pro falso clameo, et
"petierunt judicium si idem
"Willelmus ad illud breve Mortis
"antecessoris responderi debuit,
"quod quidem judicium per ipsum
"Willelmum ad tunc non fuit
"dedictum, ubi Judicatores prae-
"dicti consideraverunt Assisam,
"&c., non habito respectu ad
"placitum illud nec ad judicium
"prius per eos redditum in brevi
"de eadem natura de eisdem tene-
"mentis, et de seisina ejusdem,
"quod quidem judicium adhuc
"stat in suis robore et virtute, et
"in tantum Judicatores praedicti
"erraverunt, quos quidem errores
"praedicti Ricardus et Margareta
"petunt corrigi, et judicium inde
"redditum adnullari et revocari,
"&c."

[1] a is from C. alone.

[2] C., eisteer.

[3] H., trove.

[4] H., and C., navoit, instead of
ny avoit.

[5] C., ovesqe ceo esta, instead of
unqore puit estere ovesqe ceo.

No. 25.

afterwards, I say that the first plea was in bar, because the demandant would never have the Assise, contrary to the first plea, unless he destroyed the force of it.— *Thorpe, ad idem.* Although the manner of pleading be to conclude to the writ on a plea which trenches on the action, such as the user of a writ of higher nature, nevertheless the plea is to the action. And suppose the plea was only to the writ, and that the tenant could afterwards have been admitted by law to have a plea in bar, still that which he pleaded was not in bar ; for, although the demandant was previously barred as to the Mort d'Ancestor, when possibly the writ of Formedon was pending, against which bar he could not then have said anything in maintenance of his writ, because suit was then pending on the Formedon, and consequently the judgment was good, nevertheless when the action on the Formedon was afterwards tried with a result adverse to the demandant, and judgment was rendered thereupon, as above, the demandant was then restored to the action by Assise, and consequently that was not a bar. Therefore, whether he could not be admitted, as by law he would not, or he could be admitted, the judgment was good.

No. 25.

primer plee fuit barre, qar countre le primer plee
il navereit jammes Lassise sil nust[1] destruit[2] la force
de cel.[3]—*Thorpe, ad idem.* Tut soit ceo manere de
concludre au brief sur plee qe trenche al accion,
come est user de brief de plus haut nature, nepurqant il est al accion. Et mettetz qe ceo fuit forqe
au brief, et qil pout apres aver avenu par ley daver
plee en barre, unqore ceo qil pleda ne fuit pas
barre; qar tut fuit le demandant autrefoith barre al
Mortdancestre, quant le brief de Fourme de doun
fuit par cas pendant, countre quei adonqes il ne
poet rienz aver dit en meintenance de son brief, pur
ceo qe la suite adonqes pendist sur le Fourme doun,
et *per consequens* le jugement bone, nepurquant quant
laccion apres sur le Fourme doun fuit trie countre
le demandant, et jugement sur ceo rendu, *ut supra,*
adonqes fuit il restitut al accion par Assise, et *per
consequens* ceo ne fuit pas barre. Par quei le quel
il [ne] pout aver avenu, come de ley il ne freit
pas, ou qil pout aver avenu, le jugement fuit bone.[4]

---

[1] C., myst.

[2] C., destreut.

[3] According to the roll the defendant in Error pleaded " quod " Judicatores prædicti in nullo " erraverunt in captionem Assisæ " prædictæ, immo Assisam bono et " legitimo modo consideraverunt, " et petit quod judicium illud " tanquam bonum et rite redditum " affirmetur."

[4] The judgment of the Court of King's Bench was, according to the roll, as follows:—" Quia, visis et " examinatis recordo et processu " prædictis, videtur Curiæ quod " Judicatores erraverunt in hoc " quod, cum prædicti Ricardus et " Margareta placitaverunt in bar- " ram Assisæ in hoc quod idem " Willelmus alias tulit breve Mortis

" antecessoris de seisina ipsius " Bernardi, de qua quidem seisina " idem Willelmus tulit Assisam " istam, &c., de tenementis præ- " dictis, ad quod quidem breve " consideratum fuit quod prædicti " Ricardus et Margareta irent inde " sine die, et quod prædictus " Willelmus nihil caperet per breve " suum, sed quod esset in miseri- " cordia pro falso clameo, quod " quidem judicium ad tunc non " fuit per ipsum dedictum, non " habito respectu ad placitum illud " nec ad judicium prius per eos " redditum in brevi de eadem " natura et seisina ejusdem, quod " quidem judicium videtur Curiæ " quod adhuc stat in suo robore et " virtute, et in tantum Judicatores " prædicti erraverunt in hoc quod

Nos. 26, 27.

A.D. 1345.

Ad terminum qui præteriit.

(26.) § Edward Trenchaunt and his co-parcener brought an *Ad terminum qui præteriit*, demanding the Bedelary of the Soke of Winchester, on the seisin of their ancestor, laying the esplees as for 6*d.* on every livery of seisin, &c. View was counterpleaded by *Grene*, because the profit is not one issuing from any definite freehold.—HILLARY. What of that?—*Grene.* What will be put in view?—HILLARY. Let him have view.—See more below.[1]

Quare impedit.

(27.) § The King brought a *Quare impedit* against the Bishop of Lincoln in respect of the prebend of Carlton-cum-Thurlby, counting that the prebend became vacant while the temporalities were in his hand, by reason that the Prebendary was created Bishop of Utrecht, which is beyond sea.—And exception was

---

[1] The conclusion of this case is in Y.B., Hil., 20 Edw. III., No. 21, the record being among the *Placita de Banco* of that Term, R° 331. The action was brought by Edward Trenchaunt, and Richard Chanyn, and Margaret, Richard's wife, against Walter de Theddene, in respect of "ballivam de soka "Wyntoniæ."

Nos. 26, 27.

(26.)[1] § Edward Trenchaunt et sa parcenere porte- A.D. 1345.
rent *Ad terminum qui præteriit*, demandant la Bedelrie *Ad*
del[2] Soke de Wyncestre, de la seisine lour auncestre, *qui*
liaunt les esplees a chesqune seisine livere vj*d*., &c. *præteriit.*
La viewe fuit countreplede par *Grene*, pur ceo qe [Fitz., *View*, 77.]
ceo est un profit issaunt de nul certein[3] franctenement.—HILL. De ceo quei?—*Grene*. Quei serra mys
en viewe?—HILL. Eit la viewe.—*Vide infra plus.*[4]

(27.)[5] § Le Roi porta *Quare impedit* vers Levesqe *Quare*
de Nichole de la provandre de Carletoun, countaunt *impedit.*
coment la provandre se voida esteauntz les tempor- *Triall*,
altes en sa mein, par tant qe le[6] provandrer[7] fuit 57.]
cree en Evesqe de Urtene, qest de dela [la mer].[8]

" ipsi non posuerunt prædictos,
". Ricardum et Margaretam [*sic*]
" ad respondendum ad illud
" novum placitum, et in hoc
" erraverunt, ideo consideratum
" est quod judicium illud per
" Judicatores illos erronice reddi-
" tum revocetur et adnulletur, &c.
" Et mandatum est præfato
" Principi, vel ejus Justiciario, ve*l*
" Justiciarii locum tenenti, quod
" præfatis Ricardo et Margaretæ
" de tenementis illis versus ipsos
" per ipsum Willelmum recuperatis
" seisinam de tenementis prædictis,
" simul cum exitibus medio tem-
" pore perceptis, rehabere, faciat,
" &c."

[1] From L., H., and C.

[2] H., de la.

[3] certein is from H. alone.

[4] The words *Vide infra plus* are
omitted from H., and the words
Sic nota de visu, &c., substituted.

[5] From L., H., and C., but
corrected by the record, *Placita de
Banco*, Easter, 19 Edw. III., R° 324.
It there appears that the action
was brought by the King against

Thomas, Bishop of Lincoln, in
respect of a presentation to the
prebend of Carleton and Thurleby
in the church of St. Mary, Lincoln.
There is also an imperfect record
of the case on R° 120 with a
different declaration and plea.

[6] H., and C., la.

[7] C., provendrere.

[8] The declaration was, according
to the record (R° 324), " quod
" quidam Johannes de Dalderby,
" quondam Episcopus Lincolni-
" ensis, fuit seisitus de advocatione
" præbendæ prædictæ ut de feodo
" et jure Episcopatus sui prædicti,
" tempore . . . . Edwardi
" Regis patris domini Regis nunc,
" et eandem præbendam contulit
" cuidam Johanni de Northburghe,
" clerico suo, et ipsum installavit
" in eadem, ... et post-
" modum, vacante præbenda præ-
" dicta per mortem prædicti
" Johannis de Northburghe, idem
" Episcopus præbendam illam
" contulit cuidam Nicholao de
" Cabuthe, clerico suo, et ipsum
" installavit in eodem. . . . . .

No. 28.

A.D. 1345. taken to this on the ground that such a cause of voidance cannot be tried in this Court.—The exception was not allowed, because voidance shall be tried generally, and not specially a voidance for a particular cause.—Therefore they were at issue on the question of voidance in general terms.

Formedon. (28.) § Formedon in respect of rent. After view *Thorpe* said that the manor of Harrington was put in view, and that one A.[1] held so much of it, and one B.[1] so much of it, and that they were not mentioned in the writ; judgment of the writ.—*Grene.* He does

---

[1] For the names *see* p. 79, note 5.

No. 28.

A.D. 1345.

—Et ceo fuit chalenge pur ceo qe tiel cause en ceste[1] Court ne poet estre trie.—*Non allocatur*, qar voidaunce serra generalment trie, et noun pas certein voidaunce especialment.—Par quei sur la voidaunce sount a issue generalment.[2]

(28.)[3] § Fourme de doun de rente. Apres la vewe *Thorpe* dit qe le maner de H.[4] est mys en vewe, et un A. tient tant et B. tant, nient nomes el brief; jugement du brief.[5]—*Grene.* Il ne plede ne[6] come

Fourme de doun. [Fitz., Briefe, 468.]

" . . . . Et postea temporalia " Episcopatus prædicti devenerunt " in manus domini Regis nunc " per mortem Henrici de Burg- " hershe nuper Episcopi Lin- " colniensis, successoris prædicti " Johannis de Dalderby præde- " cessoris, &c., quo tempore eadem " præbenda vacavit per cessionem " prædicti Nicholai, eo quod idem " Nicholaus creatus fuit in Episco- " pum de Utright, et ea ratione ad " ipsum dominum Regem ad " præbendam prædictam pertinet " præsentare."

[1] C., ceo.

[2] According to the record (R° 324) the plea was " quod . . . . eadem " præbenda non fuit vacans tem- " pore quo temporalia Episcopatus " prædicti fuerunt in manu domini " Regis post mortem prædicti " Henrici nuper Episcopi, sicut " per narrationem ipsius domini " Regis supponitur."
Issue was joined upon this and the *Venire* awarded, but nothing further appears upon the roll.

[3] From L., H., and C., but corrected by the record, *Placita de Banco*, Easter, 19 Edw. III., R° 324, d. It there appears that the action was brought by John son of Richard de Haryngtone

against Roger de Cobeldike and Matilda his wife, in respect of £20 of rent in Haryngtone and Aswardby (Harrington and Aswarby, Lincolnshire), which John de Haryngtone gave to Richard de Haryngtone and Amice his wife in special tail. The descent is traced in the count from Richard and Amice to the demandant as son and heir.

[4] MSS. of Y.B., B.

[5] The plea in abatement of the writ was, according to the record, " quod tenementa in visu posita, " unde prædictus Johannes sup- " ponit prædictum redditum pro- " venire, sunt manerium de " Haryngtone, cum pertinentiis, et " dicit quod Decanus et Capitulum " ecclesiæ beatæ Mariæ Lincolniæ, " et Thomas de Stowe, capellanus, " tenent inde tria tofta, unam " carucatam et unam bovatam " terræ et dimidiam, cum pertinen- " tiis, et quidam Johannes filius " Philippi de Haryngtone tenet " inde unam carucatam terræ, cum " pertinentiis, ... qui " quidem Decanus et Capitulum, " Thomas, et Johannes filius " Philippi non nominantur in " brevi."

[6] ne is from C. alone.

No. 28.

not plead either as tenant of the land out of which the rent is to be taken, or as taker of the rent, nor does he say what kind of rent it is, as for instance rent charge, so that non-tenure of parcel of the land could abate the writ; judgment whether the law puts us to answer.—HILLARY. When you have a good writ he will say that there is no rent, and, even though there be a rent, he will not tell you what kind of rent.—WILLOUGHBY. He does not deny that he holds the rest of the manor, so that he cannot be under-stood to be either taker or tenant of the rent, and therefore it is so (as the tenants say).—*Grene.* Our demand is rent service; judgment whether such a plea lies in your mouth. — *Thorpe.* The land is not holden of you; ready, &c.—*Grene.* That is not a traverse: for if my ancestor, being tenant in tail, alienes, I am out of the seignory until I have recovered; and, therefore, even though I be out of the seignory, still it does not therefore follow that you will have such a plea.—HILLARY and WILLOUGHBY agreed that for the time during which the alienation stands not revoked by action the land is not holden of the issue in tail.—HILLARY to *Grene.* Does not a plea of non-tenure of the land lie in respect of rent service as well as in respect of rent charge? Certainly it does.—*Grene.* No, for in respect of rent service, even though he had nothing in my demand nor in the land, but held of me, the writ would lie against him. —HILLARY. But, if he hold only part of the land out of which the rent is to be taken, and others hold the rest of the land, and you demand against him the whole of the rent, as well that which is issuing from the rest of the land as that which he holds himself, and you do not allege any other special fact by reason of which your writ would be good, will not your writ abate through his exception? as meaning to say that it would. Therefore it is so (as the tenants

No. 28.

tenant de la terre dount, &c., ne come pernour de A.D. 1345. la rente, ne il ne dit pas quel rente ceo est, come rente charge, issint qe nountenue de parcelle de la terre purreit abatre le brief; jugement si la ley nous mette a respondre. — HILL. Quant vous averetz bone brief il dirra qil y ad nulle rente, et tut y eit il rente il vous dirra pas quele rente.— WILBY. Il ne dedit pas qil ne tient le remenant du maner, issint qil ne poet estre entendu pernour ne tenant de la rente, par quei il est[1] issint.— *Grene.* Nostre demande est rente service; jugement si tiel plee en vostre bouche gise.—*Thorpe.* La terre nest pas tenu de vous[2]; prest, &c.—*Grene.* Cella nest pas travers : qar si moun auncestre tenant en taille aliene, jeo su hors de seignurie tanqe javeray recoveri ; et pur ceo, tut soy jeo hors de la[3] seignurie, unqore de ceo nensuit pas qe vous averetz tiel plee.—HILL. et WILBY sacorderunt qe pur le temps qe lalienacion esta nient repelle par accion qe la terre nest pas tenu[4] del issue en la taille.— HILL. a *Grene.* Ne git pas nountenue de la terre de rente service si bien come de rente charge? Certes si fait.—*Grene.* Noun, qar rente service, mes qil nust rienz en ma demande nen la terre, mes tenist de moy, le brief girreit vers luy.—HILL. Mes sil tiegne forqe parcelle de la terre dount, &c., et autres tiegnent[5] le remenant de la terre, et vous demandetz vers luy tote la rente, si bien ceo qe est issaunt del remenaunt de la terre come de ceo qil mesme tient, et nalleggetz autre fet especial pur quei vostre brief serreit bone, nabatera vostre brief par sa excepcion? *quasi diceret sic.* Par quei il est[1]

---

[1] H., est il, instead of il est.
[2] H., nous.
[3] la is from C. alone.

[4] C., tenuz.
[5] L., and H., tenent.

No. 29.

say).—*Grene.* Fully tenant of the land as the land was holden at the time at which the gift was made to our ancestor; ready, &c.—*Thorpe.* We have nothing to do with the time of the gift; but we will maintain the non-tenure of the lands put in view out of which you suppose the rent to be taken.—*Grene.* You will hold yourself to the land out of which the rent is taken, without having regard to the view, for view will not abate a good writ.—*Thorpe.* Certainly it will do so, for the demandant must on his part maintain his demand according to the manner in which he demands, and also according to the manner in which it is put in view.—And the COURT agreed to this.—Therefore *Grene* was put to answer as to the land put in view, for the tenant can elect his exception either with regard to the demand or with regard to the view.— *Grene.* Fully tenant of the tenements put in view, out of which we suppose the rent to issue.—*Thorpe.* You must take the issue: fully seised of the tenements put in view.—And that he was compelled to do.—And he did so.

Quare impedit.

(29.) § *Quare impedit* in respect of the Priory of Leighs, counting that one Ralph Gernon was seised of the manor of "la Geronere," to which the advowson was appendant, and presented such a canon, elected by the Convent, who, on his presentation, was admitted and installed, which Ralph gave the manor with the appurtenances to William Gernon, his son, and to Isabel, William's wife, and to the heirs issuing from

No. 29.

issint.—*Grene.* Pleinement tenant de la terre solonc A.D. 1345.
ceo qe la terre fuit tenu al temps del doun fet a
nostre auncestre; prest, &c.—*Thorpe.* De temps de
doun navoms qe faire; mes des tenementz mys en
vewe dount vous supposez, &c., nous voloms meintenir la nountenue.—*Grene.* Vous prendretz a la
terre dount la rente, &c., saunz aver regarde a la
vewe, qar la vewe nabatera pas un bone brief.—
Thorpe. Certes si fra, qar le demandant de sa part
covient meintener la demande solonc ceo qil demande,
et auxint solonc ceo qil est mys en vewe.—*Ad quod*
Curia *consensit.*—Par quei *Grene* fuit mys de respondre a la terre mys en vewe, qar le tenant
eslirra sa excepcion a la demande ou a la vewe.—
Grene. Pleinement tenant des tenementz mys en
vewe, dount nous supposoms la rente sourdre.—
Thorpe. Vous prendretz lissue qe pleinement tenant
des tenementz mys en vewe.—Et a ceo fuit il chace.
—*Et ita fecit, &c.*[1]

(29.)[2] § *Quare impedit* de la Priorie de L.,[3] countant *Quare*
impedit.
qun Rauf fuit seisi del maner de la Geronere, a
quei lavoeson fuit appendant, et presenta · un tiel
chanoun eslieu par le Covent, qe a soun presentement fuit resceu et installe, le quel Rauf dona a W.
Gernoun son fitz et Isabelle sa femme et les heirs
de corps W. issauntes le maner ove les appurtinances.

---

[1] The replication, upon which issue was joined, was, according to the record, " quod . . . . " iidem Rogerus et Matilldis, die " impetrationis brevis sui, . . . " . . . tenuerunt integre præ- " dictum manerium de Haryngtone " in visu positum."
After some adjournments the demandant confessed that the Dean and Chapter and the others held a portion of the tenements as alleged in the plea.

Judgment was therefore given for the tenants.

[2] From L., H., and C., but corrected by the record, *Placita de Banco*, Easter, 19 Edw. III., R° 157, d. It there appears that the action was brought by John Gernoun, knight, against Ada late wife of John de Sancto Philberto, in respect of a presentation to the Priory " de Lega " (Leighs, Essex).

[3] L., H.; H., and C., K.

No. 29.

A.D. 1345. William's body.[1] From William the manor with the advowson descended, in accordance with the limitation, to John as to son, and he aliened the manor, saving to himself fees and advowsons. And from John the descent was, in accordance with the limitation, to the Lady Saint Philbert as to daughter, who now brings this writ together with her husband.[2]—

---

[1] As to this statement *see* p. 85, note 3.

[2] According to the record she was the defendant, her husband being dead. The descent was from John son of William to John Gernoun, the plaintiff. *See* p. 85, note 3.

No. 29.

De W. descendi[1] par la taille le maner ove lavoe- A.D. 1345. son a J.[2] com a fitz, le quel aliena le maner, sauf a luy fees et avoesouns. Et de J.[2] descendi[1] a la Dame Seint Filbert par la taille com a fille, qore porte ceo brief ove son baron.[3]—*Rok.* Nient conissant

C., descent.

[2] MSS. of Y.B., R.

[3] The declaration was, according to the record, " quod quidam " Radulphus Gernoun fuit seisitus " de manerio de la Geronere, cum " pertinentiis, ad quod advocatio " prædicti Prioratus pertinet, tem- " pore pacis, tempore Henrici Regis, " proavi domini Regis nunc, et " ad illum præsentavit quendam " Simonem de Salynge per Con- " ventum ejusdem loci, licentia " ipsius Radulphi ad hoc obtenta, " electum, qui ad præsentationem " suam fuit admissus et installatus, " . . . . . qui quidem " Radulphus manerium illud ad " quod, &c., dedit quibusdam " Willelmo Gernoun et Isabellæ " uxori ejus tenendum ipsis Wil- " lelmo et Isabellæ, et heredibus de " corporibus suis exeuntibus, per " quod donum iidem Willelmus et " Isabella fuerunt inde seisiti, " . . . . et postea " prædicta Isabella obiit, post " cujus mortem Prioratus prædic- " tus vacavit per mortem prædicti " Simonis, &c., per quod prædictus " Willelmus Gernoun præsentavit " ad eundem Prioratum quendam " Thomam de Bello Campo per " Conventum prædictum licentia " ipsius Willelmi Gernoun electum, " qui ad præsentationem suam " fuit admissus et installatus. . . " . . . Et, vacante Prioratu " prædicto per mortem prædicti " Thomæ, idem Willelmus Ger- " noun præsentavit ad eundem " quendam Thomam de Chelmesho " per Conventum prædictum li- " centia ipsius Willelmi Gernoun " electum, qui ad præsentationem " suam fuit admissus et installatus, " . . . . . Et postea idem " Prioratus vacavit per mortem " prædicti Thomæ de Chelmesho, " per quod idem Willelmus Ger- " noun præsentavit ad eundem " quendam Henricum de Hegsete " per prædictum Conventum li- " centia ipsius Willelmi Gernoun " electum, qui ad præsentationem " suam fuit admissus et installatus, " post cujus mortem prædictus " Prioratus modo vacat, &c. Et " de ipsis Willelmo et Isabella " descendit manerium prædictum, " cum pertinentiis, ad quod, &c., " et advocatio prædicta cuidam " Johanni ut filio et heredi, &c, " qui quidem Johannes manerium " illud dedit quibusdam Henrico " Prentiz et Johanni personæ " ecclesiæ Sancti Gregorii Lon- " doniarum, reservando sibi feoda " militum et advocationes eccle- " siarum et Prioratus prædicti, " tenendum ipsis Henrico et " Johanni personæ, et heredibus " suis in perpetuum. Et de ipso " Johanne filio Willelmi descendit " advocatio prædicta per formam, " &c., isti Johanni Gernoun qui " nunc, &c., ut filio et heredi, &c. " Et ea ratione ad ipsum Johannem " pertinet ad prædictum Prioratum " præsentare."

No. 29.

A.D. 1345 *Rokel.* Not admitting that the advowson was appendant to the manor of "la Geronere," we tell you that
one Ralph Gernon, father of the Ralph of whom they
speak, was seised of the manor of Little Leighs, to
which the advowson of the Priory was appendant, and
presented, &c. From that Ralph it descended to the
Ralph whom they suppose to be donor, as to son, and
he had, and held it, and died seised of it. From
Ralph it descended to William as to son, to which
William he supposes the gift to have been made. That
William gave the manor of Little Leighs, to which the
advowson was appendant, to A., saving to himself fees
and advowsons, and afterwards gave the advowson to
one whose estate Robert Marny, the defendant, has.
And *Rokel* prayed a writ to the Bishop.[1]—*Notton.*
They do not take the non-appendancy of the patronage
to the manor of "la Geronere" for an answer to
which we shall be able to have a traverse, but by

---

[1] This plea differs materially
from that upon the roll. William
Marny was not the defendant but
a feoffee of the manor, exclusive
of the advowson.

No. 29.

qe lavoweson fuit appendant al maner de la Geronere, vous dioms qun R. Gernoun, pere Rauf de qi ils parlent, fuit seisi du maner de Petit Lesnes, a quei lavoeson de la Priorie fuit appendant, et presenta, &c. De R. descendi[1] a R., qils supposent estre donour, com a fitz, le quel out, et tient, et murust[2] seisi; de R. descendi[1] a W. come a fitz, a quel W. il suppose le doun estre fet, le quel W. dona le maner de Lesnes a quei lavoweson, &c., a A., sauvaunt a luy fees et avowesouns, et puis dona lavoesoun a un qi estat Robert Marny le defendant ad; et pria brief al Evesqe.[3]—*Nottone.* La desappendaunce de lavowere al maner de la Geronere ne pernount ils pas pur respons a quel nous purroms aver

---

[1] C., descent.

[2] C., muruyst.

[3] The plea was, according to the record, " non cognoscendo quod " advocatio Prioratus prædicti sit " pertinens manerio de la Geronere, " nec quod la Geronere sit mane- " rium, &c., dicit quod quidam " Radulphus Gernoun pater præ- " dicti Radulphi Gernoun, de cujus " seisina, &c., fuit seisitus de " manerio de Parva Lyes, ad quod " advocatio prædicti Prioratus fuit " pertinens tempore Henrici proavi " domini Regis nunc, et manerium " illud dedit cuidam Willelmo " Marny tenendum sibi et heredi- " bus suis de ipso Radulpho et " heredibus suis per servitium " militare in perpetuum, reser- " vando eidem Radulpho et here- " dibus suis feoda militum et " advocationes, &c., qui quidem " Radulphus obiit seisitus de " advocatione prædicta, post cujus " mortem præfatus Radulphus Ger- " noun intravit ut filius et heres, " et præsentavit ad Prioratum præ- " dictum præfatum Simonem de

" Salynge, &c. Et seisinam suam " de eadem advocatione continua- " vit tota vita sua. Et de ipso " Radulpho descenderunt feoda, " &c., et advocatio prædicta " cuidam Willelmo ut filio et " heredi, &c., qui quidem Willel- " mus præsentavit ad prædictum " Prioratum præfatum Thomam de " Bello Campo, et Thomam de " Chelmesho, et Henricum de " Hegsete. Et postmodum idem " Willelmus per finem in Curia " Regis levatum concessit feoda " militum et advocationem præ- " dictam cuidam Willelmo de " Teye et heredibus suis in " perpetuum, qui quidem Willel- " mus feoffavit inde præfatum " Johannem de Sancto Philberto " quondam virum, &c., et ipsam " Adam, tenendis sibi et heredibus " ipsius Johannis in perpetuum. " Et sic dicit quod ad ipsam, et " non ad prædictum Johannem " Gernoun pertinet ad prædictum " Prioratum præsentare, unde petit " judicium, et breve Episcopo, &c."

No. 29.

way of protestation, and, in case they will do so, we shall be ready to maintain the appendancy in accordance with our declaration. And whereas they say that the Ralph whom we suppose to have [been the donor], died seised, and continued seised without making any conveyance, we will aver that he gave the manor of "la Geronere," to which the advowson was appendant, as we have supposed; ready, &c.—*Thorpe.* The manor is not in dispute, nor could it now fall to an issue between us, but we will aver that he had, and held, and continued seised, *absque hoc* that he gave the advowson; ready, &c.—*Notton.* That averment is not admissible, for, if that which we say be true, that the manor to which the advowson was appendant was given with the appurtenances, the advowson passed; and since you have not taken issue or traverse on the appendancy, you must speak as to the gift of the manor to which the advowson was appendant.—WILLOUGHBY. Then you refuse the averment that the advowson was not given by the form of the gift.

No. 29.

travers, mes par voie de protestacion, et en cas qils vodrount,[1] nous serroms prest de meintenir lappend- aunce solonc nostre monstraunce. Et la ou ils dient qe R. qe nous supposoms qe muruyst seisi et con- tinua sanz demise faire, nous voloms averer qil dona le maner de Geronere, a quei lavowesoun, &c., solonc ceo qe nous avoms suppose; prest, &c.[2]— *Thorpe*. Le maner nest pas en debat, ne ceo ne poet chere entre nous a ore en issue, mes nous voloms averer qil out, et tient, et continua, &c., saunz ceo qil dona lavowesoun; prest, &c.[3]—*Nottone*. Cest averement nest pas resceivable, qar, sil soit voire ceo qe nous dioms qe le maner a quei lavowe- soun fuit appendant fuit done ove les appurtinances, lavoesoun passa; et quant sur lappendaunce vous navietz pas pris issue ne travers, il covient qe vous parletz al doun del maner, a quei, &c.—WILBY. Donqes refusetz laverement qe lavowesoun ne fuit pas done par la fourme.[4]

---

[1] C., vodreint.

[2] The replication was, according to the record, " quod ubi prædicta " Ada supponit præfatum Ra- " dulphum intrasse post mortem " prædicti patris sui, et obiisse " seisitum de advocatione illa ut " de feodo simplici, idem Ra- " dulphus dedit advocationem " illam, simul cum prædicto " manerio de la Geronere, in vita " sua, præfatis Willelmo Gernoun " et Isabellæ, prout ipse superius " supponit, absque hoc quod idem " Radulphus obiit inde seisitus, " sicut prædicta Ada dicit. Et

" hoc paratus est verificare, unde " petit judicium, &c."

[3] The rejoinder was, according to the record, " quod prædictus " Radulphus obiit seisitus de " advocatione illa in feodo simplici, " absque hoc quod ipse in vita sua " advocationem illam dedit præ- " fatis Willelmo et Isabellæ."

[4] According to the roll issue was joined upon the defendant's rejoinder. Afterwards, on a day given, the plaintiff failed to appear, and judgment was given for the defendant.

No. 30.

A.D. 1345.
Trespass.

(30.) § Trespass for John Stone in respect of his corn depastured.—The defendant justified the depasturing in the place mentioned as being his common. —And the plaintiff said that his corn was, at the time of the depasturing, in grain, and that in that case, even if there was any common, after the defendant had allowed so long a time to pass that the corn was in grain, it would not be permissible for him to depasture there until the corn had been cut, and that, even should judgment be given for the plaintiff, the effect would not be to deprive the defendant of his common, because afterwards he would have it as he had previously had.

No. 30.

A.D. 1345.
Trans.

(30.) [1] § Trans pur Johan Stone de ses blees [2]
pues.—Le defendant justifia le pestre illoeqes come
sa comune.[3]—Et le pleintif dit qe ses blees [2] furent,
al temps del pestre, engranes, ou, tut y avoit il
comune, apres ceo qil avoit suffert par tant de temps
qe les blees furent [4] engranes, il ne serreit pas con-
geable de pestre illoeqes tanqe les blees fuissent [5]
scietz, et tut soit ceo ajuge pur le pleintif, ceo nest
pas a tollir la comune al defendant, qar apres il
avera com devaunt avoit.[6]

---

[1] From L., H., and C. The
record found among the *Placita de
Banco*, Easter, 19 Edw. III.,
Rᵒ 62, d, probably relates to this
case, as the reporter may have
confounded the plaintiff's name
with that of the place (Stone). It
there appears that an action of
Trespass was brought by William
Motone, knight, against Joan late
wife of Robert le Seyntcler and
several others. It was alleged in
the declaration that the defendants,
" die dominica proxima post festum
" Translationis Sancti Thomæ,
" anno regni domini Regis nunc
" Angliæ decimo octavo, ...
" blada ipsius Willelmi Motone,
" videlicet, frumentum, ordeum,
" avenas, fabas et pisas . . . . .
" cum quibusdam averiis, videlicet,
" bobus, affris, vaccis, et bidenti-
" bus, depasti fuerunt, conculca-
" verunt, et consumpserunt."
There is a similar case on Rᵒ 91,d,
in which Hugh de Osevylle was
plaintiff.

[2] H., bledz ; C., bles.

[3] The plea in justification was,
according to the record, " quod
" ipsa [Johanna] habet liberum
" tenementum in villa de Stone,
" ad quod ipsa habet, et habere
" debet communiam pasturæ, &c.,

" in quodam campo, ...
" videlicet quolibet altero anno quo
" campus ille seminatur, &c., post
" blada messa et unita, quousque
" iterum seminatur, et quolibet
" secundo anno per totum annum,
" cum omminodis averiis, tanquam
" eidem libero tenemento pertinen-
" tem, ...
" quem quidem campum prædictus
" Willelmus anno regni domini
" Regis nunc decimo septimo
" seminaverat. Et in anno tunc
" proxime sequente, quando cam-
" pus ille warectus jacuisse debuit,
" idem campus seminatus fuit,
" per quod ipsa Johanna ante præ-
" fatum [*sic*] diem dominicam [*sic*],
" et eodem die, cum averiis suis
" campum prædictum intravit, et,
" communiam suam ibidem con-
" tinuando, averia sua depastus
" fuit, unde petit judicium si
" prædictus Willelmus occasione
" prædicta actionem de Trans-
" gressione versus eam habere
" debeat, &c." The others were
only aiding Joan.

[4] C., fuissent.

[5] L., furent.

[6] According to the record, the
replication was " . . . . .
" quod nec præfata Johanna nec
" tenentes liberi tenementi prædicti

No. 31.

(31.) § William de Clyntone and his wife brought a writ of Entry *sur disseisin* against Anthony Cyteroun and William la Zouche Mortimer and his wife. Heretofore Anthony took upon himself the tenancy, and vouched the other two named, &c., and they warranted; and, the death of the wife of William la Zouche having been returned, he revouched Hugh le Despenser, as son and heir of the wife, &c., and Hugh entered into warranty, and had aid of his co-parceners, who did not appear, and afterwards of the King. And now a writ *de procedendo* has come, and the demandant now counted against Hugh. And note that the writ *de procedendo* did not make any mention that the Original Writ was brought against any one else but Anthony alone; and, notwithstanding, it was adjudged by the COURT a sufficiently good warrant.—*Derworthy.* Judgment of the writ: for William, who is demandant, is Earl of Huntingdon, and is not described as Earl.— *Pole.* He does not demand in right of his Earldom, and moreover this writ was purchased before he was Earl.—*Derworthy.* His own act has abated his writ, just as if a clerk brings a writ, and, while his writ is pending, he is created a Bishop, his writ will abate.— But this was denied. — *Quære.* — Afterwards *Thorpe* prayed aid of Hugh's co-parceners anew, on the ground that he will in law have a new answer to a new count, and also that the previous judgment that he must answer alone, that is to say the judgment

No. 31.

(31.) [1] § William de Clyntone et sa femme porte- A.D. 1345.
rent brief dentre sur la disseisine vers Antone *Entre*
Cyteroun [3] et William la Souche Mortimer et sa *sur dis-*
seisine.[2]
femme. Autrefoith Antone enprist la tenance, et [Fitz.,
Proce-
voucha les autres ij nomes, &c., qe garrantirent; et, *dendo,* 2.]
la [4] mort la femme retourne,[5] revoucha Hughe le
Despenser com fitz et heir la femme, &c., qe entra,
et avoit eide de ses parceneres, qe ne vindreint pas,
et puis du Roi. Et ore brief *de procedendo* est venuz,
et le demandant counta ore vers luy. Et *nota* qe
le brief *de procedendo* ne fist pas mencion qe le
brief original fuit porte vers autre qe vers Antone
soulement; et, *non obstante*, par COURT ceo fuit agarde
bone garrant assetz.—*Derr.*[6] Jugement du brief: qar
W. qest demandant est Counte de Huntindone, nient
nome Counte.—*Pole.* Il ne demande pas en le dreit
de sa Counte, et auxint ceo brief fuit purchace
avant qil estoit Counte.—*Derr.*[6] Son fet demene ad
abatu soun brief, com si clerk porte brief, et pendaunt soun brief il est cree en Evesqe, son brief
abatera.—*Quod fuit negatum.*—*Quære.*—Puis *Thorpe*
pria eide de ses parceners [7] de rechief, qar a novel
counte par. lei il avera novel respons, et auxint le
primer jugement qil respoundreit soul, saver par

" habuerunt nec usi fuerunt habere
" communiam in prædicto campo
" . . . . . tanquam perti-
" nentem, &c."
 Issue was joined upon this.
 The verdict was " quod nec præ-
" dicta Johanna nec tenentes liberi
" tenementi quod eadem Johanna
" modo habet in Stone habuerunt
" communiam pasturæ in prædicto
" campo tanquam pertinentem ad
" liberum tenementum, &c." The
jury assessed the damages at 6s.
and judgment was given accordingly, with an award of a *Capias*
against the defendants.

[1] From L., H., and C. The
report is in continuation of Y.B.,
Mich., 14 Edw. III., No. 42, the
record being *Placita de Banco* of
that term, R° 341.

[2] The words sur disseisine are
from L. alone.

[3] L., and C., Cyfroun; H.,
Cyfrenoun.

[4] H., and C., lour.

[5] The words la femme retourne
are omitted from H. and C.

[6] H., *Derworthi.*

[7] C., parceneris.

Nos. 32, 33.

A.D. 1345. according to which we should recover *pro rata,* has lost its force so far as we are concerned.—This was not allowed.—Therefore he traversed the disseisin.

Statute Merchant.

(32.) § Execution was awarded on a statute merchant, and the lands were delivered by extent, and the extent was now returned.—*Grene.* You have here the debtors, who tell you that the lands are extended too low, and pray a re-extent.—HILLARY. On the contrary, you might well have a re-extent if the lands had been extended too high, for then the person who sued execution would have a remedy by such re-extent, but still that only on the first day, for if the extent and the livery had been made, and he accepted them without counterplea, on the first day on which the extent and the livery were returned, he would never afterwards have a remedy; but for the debtors the remedy is not given.—*Grene.* That would be a great mischief. —STONORE. It is not so, because it is your fault that you did not pay the money.—*Grene.* What remedy shall we have?—HILLARY. None, except by paying the money. And this he said by way of judgment, with the assent of his fellow-justices.

Debt.

(33.) § Debt, for the executors of Anthony late Bishop of Norwich, against a parson, counting that the Bishop and his predecessors, from time whereof there is no memory, had been seised of, and had had

Nos. 32, 33.

quel nous duissoms recoverir *pro rata*, ad perdu sa A.D. 1345.
force quant a nous.—*Non allocatur.*—Par quei il
traversa la disseisine.

(32.)[1] § Execucion fuit agarde sur statut marchaunt, Statut
et les terres par extent liveretz, et lextent ore re- marchaunt.[2]
tourne.—*Grene.* Vous avetz[3] cy les dettours qe vous
dient[4] qe les terres sount[5] estenduz trop bas et
prient reestent.—HILLAR.[6] *E converso,*[7] vous laveretz
bien, saver, si les terres fuissent estenduz trop haut,
celuy qe suyt execucion avera remedie par tiel reestent, et ceo unqore forqe al primer jour, qar si
lextent et la livere fuissent fetes et il lacceptast
sanz countreplee al primer jour qe lextent et le livere
fuissent retournes, jammes apres navereit remedie;
mes pur les dettours nest pas la remedie done.—
Grene. Ceo serreit graunt meschief.—STON. Noun
est pas, qar cest vostre defaut qe vous nussetz paie
les deners.—*Grene.* Quel remedie averoms nous?—
HILL. Nulle, forqe paier les deners. *Et hoc dixit*
par agard del assent ses compaignons.

(33.)[8] § Dette, pur les executours Antone nadgers Dette.
Evesqe de Northwiche, vers une persone, countaunt [Fitz.,
qe Levesqe et ses predecessours de temps[9] dount Jurisdic-
memore nest, furent seisiz, et avoint eu les primers tion, 22.]

---

[1] From L., H., and C.

[2] The marginal note in H. is Execucion.

[3] C., avietz.

[4] H., diount.

[5] H., fuissent.

[6] HILLAR. is omitted from C.

[7] The words *E converso* are omitted from H.

[8] From L., H., and C., but corrected by the record, *Placita de Banco,* Easter, 19 Edw. III., R° 334. It there appears that the action was brought by Michael de Hayntone, parson of the church of Matlock, Master Anthony de Goldesburghe, parson of the church of Hevingham, and John de Braydestone, parson of the church of Thorpe-by-Norwich, executors of the will of Anthony late Bishop of Norwich, who sue alone (certain co-executors not suing) against William de Wath, parson of the church of Great Cressingham.

[9] The words de temps are omitted from C.

No. 33.

the first fruits, within the diocese of Norwich, of churches on every voidance ; and he laid the seisin by the hand of the parson's predecessor, in respect of which first fruits, after the predecessor's death, the parson who is defendant paid to their testator part of the assessment of the church, and had a day for the payment of the residue, on which day he did not pay; and he had therefore been afterwards many times asked to pay, and had refused.—*Grene.* You see plainly how

No. 33.

fruites, deinz sa diocise de N., des eglises a ches- A.D. 1345.
qune voidance; et lia seisine par la mein le predecessour la persone, dount, apres la mort le predecessour,
la persone qest defendaunt paia a lour testatour
partie del taxe del eglise, et le remenant avoit jour
a paier, a quel jour il ne paia pas; par quei sovent
puis, &c.[1]—*Grene.* Vous veietz bien coment il ne

---

[1] The declaration was, according to the record, " quod Episcopus " Norwicensis, quicumque fuerit, et " omnes prædecessores sui Episcopi " Norwicenses, a tempore quo non " extat memoria, tale jus et " consuetudinem in Diœcesi sua " hactenus uti et habere con- " sueverunt quod de omnibus " ecclesiis infra Diœcesim Norwi- " censem, tam de patronagio alieno, " quam de patronagiis suis propriis, " personæ ecclesiarum prædicta- " rum taxas ecclesiarum, loco " primorum fructuum, Episcopis " qui pro tempore fuerint, quando- " cunque de novo per eos admissi " et instituti fuerint, solvere " tenentur, et eas hucusque solvere " consueverunt, de quibus quidem " taxis prædictus Antonius nuper " Episcopus, &c., cujus executores, " &c., fuit seisitus, et similiter " omnes prædecessores sui Episcopi " Norwicenses seisiti fuerunt a " tempore quo non extat memoria, " et quidam Willelmus de Ayre- " mynne quondam Episcopus Nor- " wycensis prædecessor prædicti " Antonii nuper Episcopi, &c , " cujus executores, &c., seisitus " fuit de taxa ecclesiæ de Cressyng- " ham Magna prædictæ per manus " cujusdam Rogeri de Ayremynne " quondam personæ ecclesiæ præ- " dictæ, &c., prædecessoris prædicti " Willelmi de Wath nunc personæ, " qui quidem Rogerus taxam illam " videlicet triginta marcas, loco " primorum fructuum, eidem Wil- " lelmo de Ayremynne quondam " Episcopo, &c., prædecessori præ- " dicti Antonii nuper Episcopi " soluit tempore quo de novo per " ipsum Willelmum de Ayremynne " quondam Episcopum, &c., ad- " missus et institutus fuerat in " ecclesia prædicta, &c. Et præ- " dictus Willelmus de Ayremynne " quondam Episcopus, &c., seisitus " fuit de taxa ecclesiæ prædictæ per " manus prædicti Rogeri præde- " cessoris, &c., et omnes præde- " cessores sui Episcopi Norwycenses " seisiti fuerunt per manus omnium " personarum ecclesiæ prædictæ " prædecessorum, &c., a tempore " quo non extat memoria. Et " postmodum prædicta ecclesia " vacavit per resignationem præ- " dicti Rogeri quondam personæ, " &c., per quod prædictus Antonius " quondam Episcopus, &c., cujus " executores, &c., contulit eidem " Willelmo de Wath nunc personæ, " &c., ecclesiam prædictam, quæ " est de collatione sua propria, die " Lunæ proxima post festum " Sancti Marci Ewangelistæ anno " regni domini Regis nunc Angliæ " tertiodecimo, et ipsum Rectorem " instituit in eadem, &c., quo die " idem Willelmus de Wath soluit " eidem Antonio nuper Episcopo, " &c., cujus executores, &c., apud " Norwycum, decem et octo marcas

No. 33.

he does not show any lay contract, but takes his action in respect of a matter which is entirely spiritual, of which this Court cannot have cognisance; judgment whether you ought to have cognisance. — *R. Thorpe*. Jurisdiction has been affirmed by the party because he has denied damage. Besides, even though it be the fact that you ought not to have cognisance to decide whether the Bishop shall have the first.fruits or not, we do not demand the first fruits, but we demand the amount assessed, of which he has paid a part, and has taken a day for the payment of the rest, and that is a lay contract. And an action for an annuity by prescription between persons of Holy Church can be maintained in this Court; consequently also it can be maintained in this case.—STONORE. An

No. 33.

moustre nulle[1] ley contracte, mes prent saccion de chose tut[2] espirituel, de quei ceste Court ne poet conustre; jugement si vous deivetz conustre.[3]—*R. Thorpe.* Jurisdiccion est afferme par partie, qar il ad defendu les damages. Ovesqe ceo, tut soit ceo qe vous ne deivetz conustre le quel Levesqe avera les primers fruictes[4] ou noun, nous demandoms pas les fruictes,[5] mes nous demandoms le taxe, dount partie il paia, et del remenant prist jour de paier, quel est une ley contracte. Et dune annuite entre persones de Seint Eglise par prescripcion laccion est meintenue ceinz; *per consequens* en ceo cas.[6]—STON.

"in partem solutionis triginta "marcarum eidem Antonio nuper "Episcopo, &c., pro taxa ecclesiæ "prædictæ sic debitarum, et tunc "cepit diem ab eodem Antonio "quondam Episcopo, &c., cujus "executores, &c., ad solvendum "residuum taxæ prædictæ ibidem, ". . . . . et prædictus Wil- "lelmus de Wath prædictas duo- "decim marcas prædicto Antonio "nuper Episcopo in vita ipsius "Episcopi, &c., seu prædictis "executoribus post mortem ipsius "Antonii nuper Episcopi, &c., licet "sæpius requisitus non reddidit, sed "eis hucusque reddere contradixit, "et adhuc contradicit, unde dicunt "quod deteriorati sunt, et damnum "habent ad valentiam quadraginta "librarum."

[1] nulle is from L. alone.

[2] L., tut de chose, instead of de chose tut.

[3] The plea to the jurisdiction was, according to the record, "Willelmus ". . . . defendit vim et "injuriam quando, &c., et dicit "quod prædicti executores non "debent inde ad hoc responderi, "&c., quia dicit quod, cum idem

"Willelmus sit persona ecclesias- "tica, et similiter idem Antonius "quondam Episcopus, &c., cujus "executores, &c., fuit Ordinarius "loci prædicti, et ipsi in narratione "sua prædicta non supponunt "prædictum debitum oriri de "aliquo laico contractu, per quod "Curia domini Regis hic cogni- "tionem placiti habere debeat, "immo mere de spiritualibus quæ "ad forum ecclesiasticum perti- "nent, petit judicium si prædicti "executores super tali demonstra- "tione responderi debeant, &c."

[4] C., fruitz.

[5] C., fruites.

[6] The replication was, according to the record, "quod prædictus "Willelmus ad calumniandum "jurisdictionem Curiæ modo ad- "mitti non debet, quia dicunt quod "idem Willelmus in Curia Regis "hic super demonstratione sua "prædicta vim, et injuriam, et "damna [et damna interlined] "defendit, sicque jurisdictionem "prædictam acceptando. Dicunt "similiter quod satis liquere potest "Curiæ quod prædictum debitum "originem sumpsit de laico con-

No. 33.

A.D. 1345. annuity is an annual payment, and by payment vests in freehold; and also, if it arises between parson and patron, there is a *quid pro quo*; and so there is a bargain of which the Court will have cognisance, and will be able to enquire. But in this case, according to your intendment, you are to be admitted to make Holy Church in bondage, whereas she is free.—*Thorpe.* We sued in Court Christian, and were ousted by Prohibition, and could not have Consultation; therefore, if you oust us, we shall be without remedy.—HILLARY. You will not rightly have any action.—*Grene, ad idem.* Tithes of a mill are by custom commonly converted into money when paid, and, although the nature of the tithes is changed, the money will nevertheless be demanded in Court Christian; so in the matter before us, though the first fruits be not demanded, but the amount due on the extent of the church in lieu of them, &c. And it is certain that the executors' testator would not have had any remedy in this Court in this case, nor consequently will they.—*Thorpe* denied this.—

Judgment. WILLOUGHBY gave judgment that the plaintiffs should be in mercy.—*Quære* as to the amercement, since the Court has not jurisdiction.

No. 33.

Annuite est annuel, et par paiement vest en franc- A.D. 1345. tenement; et auxint, sil sourde entre persone et patroun, il y ad *quid pro quo*; et issint bargayn de quei Court avera conissance et purra enquere. Més en ceo cas vous serretz resceu, a vostre entent, de fere Seint Eglise serve,[1] par la ou ele est fraunke. —*Thorpe.* Nous suymes en Court Christiene, et fumes ouste par Prohibicion, et ne poames aver Consultacion; par quei si vous nous oustetz[2] nous serroms saunz remedie.[3]—HILL. Par resoun vous naveretz nulle accion.—*Grene, ad idem.* Des dismes de molyn pur usage comunement[4] sount tournes en deners en paiement, et[5] tut soit la nature des dismes chaunge, les deners nepurquant serrount demandetz en Court Christiene; *sic in proposito*, tut ne soient pas les primers fruictes[6] demandetz, mes lextent del eglise en lieu de cel, &c. Et *certum est*[7] qe lour testatour ust eu nulle remedie ceinz en le cas, *nec per consequens* ceux.[8]—*Thorpe dedixit.*—WILBY agarda qe le *Judicium.*[9] pleintif fuit en la mercy.[10]—*Quære* del amerciement, *ex quo Curia non habet cognoscere.*

" tractu, maxime cum ipsi in
" narratione sua prædicta sup-
" ponunt prædictum Episcopum,
" &c., cujus executores, &c., et
" prædecessores suos Episcopos,
" &c., tale jus et consuetudinem a
" tempore quo non extat memoria
" habere, et similiter in hoc quod
" idem Willelmus soluit prædictas
" decem et octo marcas in partem
" solutionis prædictarum triginta
" marcarum, et cepit diem ad
" solvendum residuum, videlicet,
" prædictas duodecim marcas prout
" ipsi superius narrarunt, &c., unde
" petunt judicium et quod præ-
" dictus Willelmus respondeat, &c."

[1] C., seerf.

[2] H., oustres.

[3] H., recoverir.

[4] L., coment; the word is omitted from H.

[5] et is from H. alone.

[6] C., fruites.

[7] *est* is omitted from C.

[8] C., eux.

[9] The marginal note is from C. alone.

[10] The judgment was, according to the roll, "Quia videtur CURIÆ " quod prædictum debitum modo " petitum mere sumpsit originem " de spiritualibus, et non de laico " contractu unde Curia Regis hic " cognoscere possit, consideratum " est quod prædictus Willelmus " eat inde sine die, et prædicti " executores nihil capiant per " breve suum, sed sint in miseri- " cordia pro falso clameo, &c."

Nos. 34, 35.

(34.) § *Gaynesford.* John and Margaret his wife grant and render to A. and B. his wife for the lives of John and Margaret, so that after their death the same lands return to the heirs of Margaret. And the COURT refused to admit the fine, because, although there was a right saved on such a render, it could not return to those who divested themselves for their lives, nor to their heirs, nor to any one of them, inasmuch as the right was not in the heirs, and consequently it could not revert to them. And afterwards *Gaynesford* would have limited the right after their own death by way of remainder. And the COURT refused the fine, because the COURT could not admit it, because, *per* WILLOUGHBY and HILLARY, they could not limit to another by way of remainder that which could not rest in them by way of reversion.—Therefore the concord was refused.—See above, &c., a reversion granted by fine by one who had previously divested himself for his own life, &c.

Entry in
the *post.*

(35.) § Entry *sur disseisin* in the *post.—Pole.* Whereas he supposes that we entered after the disseisin effected on A., his ancestor, by one J., we tell you that J. leased the same land to D. for his life, with remainder to us, and after the death of D. we entered upon the remainder, and so our entry was by J., and so his writ ought to be in the *per*; judgment of the writ.—And because this statement was not denied by *Gaynesford*, HILLARY abated the writ.—*Quære*, because the writ was good, as it seems, through the mesne possession of D., so that the demandant could have elected to bring his writ either in the *per* or in the *post.*

Nos. 34, 35.

(34.) [1] § *Gayn.* Johan et Margarete sa femme grantent et rendent a A. et B. sa femme pur les vies Johan et Margarete, issint qapres lour descees mesme les terres retournent a les heirs Margarete. Et la COURT refusa la fyne, qar, tut y avoit dreit sauve sur tiel rendre, ceo ne poet retourner a eux qe se demistrent a lour vies, ne a les heirs de eux [ne dasqun de eux, par tant qe dreit ne fuit pas en les heirs, et *per consequens* ceo ne poet pas revertire a eux].[3] Et puis voleit aver taille par voie de remeindre le dreit apres lour decees demene. Et COURT refusa, pur ceo qe COURT ne ceo poet resceiver[4] qe ne poet demurer en eux par voie de reversion, ceo ne poaint ils tailler en autre par voie de remeindre par WILBY et HILL.—Par quei la pees fuit refuse.—*Vide supra, &c.*, reversion graunte par fyne par celuy qe soi avoit avant demise pur sa vie demene, &c.

A.D. 1345.
Finis.[2]
[Fitz.,
Fynes, 47.]

(35.) [1] § Entre sur disseisine en le *post.*—*Pole.* La ou il suppose qe nous entrames puis la disseisine fet a A., soun auncestre, par un J., nous vous dioms qe J. lessa mesme la terre a D.[6] a sa vie, le remeindre a nous, et apres la mort D.[6] nous sumes entre en le remeindre, et issint nostre entre par J., et issint serra soun brief en le *per*; jugement du brief.—Et pur ceo qe ceste chose ne fuit pas dedit par *Gayn.*, HILL. abatist le brief.—*Quære,* qar le brief fuit bone, a ceo qe semble, pur la mene possession de D.,[6] issint qe le demandant purreit aver eslieu soun brief en le *per* ou en le *post.*

Entre en
le *post.*[5]
[Fitz.,
Briefe,
469.]

---

[1] From L , H., and C.

[2] The marginal note is omitted from C.

[3] The words between brackets are omitted from H.

[4] L., vist, instead of ne ceo poet resceiver.

[5] The words en le *post* are from L. alone.

[6] C., A.

No. 36.

(36.) § Novel Disseisin in the King's Bench arraigned in Suffolk, in which there was pleaded in bar a recovery, in the mean time, by an Assise of Mort d'Ancestor. To this the plaintiff said that he should not be barred by that judgment, because the person against whom the recovery was had was not tenant of the freehold. The tenant said that the plaintiff ought not to be admitted to this plea, because the plaintiff previously brought an Assise of Novel Disseisin, as he now does, against the person supposed to be tenant in the Mort d'Ancestor, and then the tenant pleaded in bar the same mesne recovery that he (the tenant in the present Assise of Novel Disseisin) now does, and then the plaintiff alleged that he should not be debarred from his Assise by such a recovery, because the writ of Assise of Mort d'Ancestor was faulty, inasmuch as there was false Latin in it, that is to say *tenet* in the singular number where there ought to have been *tenent* in the plural number, and so the writ was bad, and consequently the record was null; and by that plea, which was peremptory, and upon which he himself heretofore abode judgment, he accepted the person against whom the writ was sued as tenant; judgment (said Counsel for the tenant) whether you shall now be admitted to say the reverse, or whether there ought to be an Assise. And they said also, for the tenant, that in the other Assise, according to the statement of the same plaintiffs on the first writ, the supposed tenant in the Mort d'Ancestor was affirmed to be tenant, because the same allegation [of false Latin] was then made in avoidance of the judgment. And while that first Assise was pending, being brought against the person who was supposed to be tenant in the Mort d'Ancestor, the plaintiff brought [the present] Assise against the same person that is now tenant, and took the same plea in annulment of the judgment [in the Assise of Mort d'Ancestor], and so, in no way denying the force of the judgment by reason of matter which falls under

No. 36.

(36.)[1] § Novele Disseisine en Bank le Roi arraine[2] A.D. 1345.
en Suffolk, ou fuit plede en barre par mene temps Novele
sur un recoverir par un Assise de Mordancestre. A Disseisine.
quei le pleintif dist qe par cel jugement il ne serra [19 Li.
pas barre, pur ceo qe celuy vers qi le recoverir se Ass., 4;
fist ne fuit pas tenant de franctenement. A quei Fitz.,
le tenant dist qil ne serra resceu, qar autrefoith le Assise,
pleintif porta un Assise de Novele Disseisine, come 84.]
ore fet, vers luy mesme, a quel temps il pleda en
barre par mesme le recoverir et par mesne temps,
come ore fet, a quel temps il alleggea qe par tiel
recoverir il ne serra[3] forclos Dassise, pur ceo qe le
brief Dassise de Mordancestre fuit vicious, en tant
qil y avoit faux latyn, saver *tenet* en le singuler
noumbre ou il duist aver este *tenent* en le plurel
noumbre,[4] issint le brief malveys, et *per consequens*
le recorde nulle; et par cele plee, quel fuit peremp-
torie, et sur quel il mesme autrefoith demura, il
accepta celuy estre tenant vers qi le brief fuit suy;
jugement si ore a dire le revers serretz resceu, ou
Assise deive estre. Et auxint disoint qen lautre
Assise mesmes les pleintifs disoint qen le primer
brief il fuit afferme tenant, pur ceo qadonqes fuit
allegge, en voidance del jugement. Et pendant cele
Assise vers celuy qest suppose qe duist aver este
tenant, le pleintif porta Assise vers mesmes ces qore
sount tenants,[5] et mesme[6] cel plee pristrent en
anientisement del jugement, et issint, nient dedisaunt
la force del jugement par chose qe chiet en fait,

---

[1] From L., H., and C. This case is noticed in 2 *Inst.* 25.

[2] So it appears to be in L., at any rate, rather than arrame, the interval between the first and second stroke being greater than that between the second and third, and the letter m being, in other places near, distinctly written. The reading in C. is arreyne.

[3] H., serreit.

[4] noumbre is from H. alone.

[5] MSS., pleintifs. In the *Liber Assisarum* the word is represented by the letter " t."

[6] mesme is from L. alone.

No. 37.

A.D. 1345. the head of fact, but taking his plea in law, he thereby waived his first writ because he purchased another, while that was pending, against another person, supposing the person against whom the second writ was brought to be tenant, and upon that he then abode judgment; judgment whether he can now be admitted to plead in annulment of the judgment in another way. The plaintiff said that by that plea the person against whom judgment was given in the Mort d'Ancestor was not accepted as being tenant, because he (the plaintiff) was non-suited, and, in the same first action, he could, after that plea in law in abatement of the writ, have said that the person was not tenant. And, inasmuch as he did not wait for judgment on the first exception, and judgment was not rendered against him, but the matter was ended by non-suit, it seemed to him that he was at liberty to plead in avoidance of the judgment, that is to say that the recoveree was not tenant, as above. And inasmuch as that fact was not denied he prayed the Assise.—And thereupon the King's Bench came to Westminster.—The plaintiff, as before, prayed the Assise.—*Grene.* The original writ is extinguished, because, by Statute,[1] assises shall be taken in their own county, and the Court is now in another county, and you can never send the original writ out of this Court; therefore you will not put us to answer. —And, after consideration by all the Justices, the Assise was awarded at large, because the defendant *nihil dicit, &c.*—And a *Nisi prius* was granted before Scot and his fellow-justices, or some of them, in Suffolk.—See below.[2]

Annuity.　　(37.) § A man brought a writ of Annuity against another, and counted that the defendant's father had granted to him an annuity of ten marks *per annum,*

---

[1] 9 Hen. III. (*Magna Charta*), c. 12.

[2] The reference is to Y.B., Trin. 19 Edw. III., No. 6.

No. 37.

et pernant soun plee en ley, par tant qil weyva A.D. 1345.
soun primer brief pur ceo qil purchacea autre,
pendant cel, vers autre persone, supposaunt ces vers
queux le secounde brief fut porte tenantz, et sur
ceo demura en jugement adonqes; jugement si ore
serra resceu danienter le jugement par autre voie.
Le pleintif dist qe par cel plee ne fuit pas accepte
celuy estre tenant vers qi le jugement fuit fait en
le Mortdancestre, qar il fuit nounsuy, et en mesme
le primer plee il pout apres cel plee en ley sur
labatement du brief, aver dit qe celuy ne fuit pas
tenant. Et desicome il ne atendist[1] pas jugement
sur la primere excepcion,[2] ne jugement ne fuit pas
rendu countre luy, mes termina par noun suite, luy
sembloit qil fuit a large de pledre en voidance de
jugement, saver qe celuy ne fuit pas tenant, *ut supra*.
Et desicome ceo ne fuit pas dedit, il pria Assise.
Et sur ceo le Baunk le Roi vint a Westmestre.—
Le pleintif, *ut prius*, pria Assise.—*Grene.* Loriginal
est amorti, qar par statut les assises serrount pris
en lour countes demene, et ore la place est en
autre counte, et vous ne maundretz jammes loriginal
hors de ceste place; par quei vous ne nous volletz
mettre a respondre.—Et par avys de toux les Justices
Lassise est agarde a large, *quia nihil dicit, &c.*—Et
Nisi prius grante devant Scot et ses compaignouns,
ou asqun de eux en Suffolk.—*Vide infra.*[3]

(37.)[4] § Un homme porta un brief Dannuite vers Annuite.
un autre, et counta qe le pere le defendant si avoit [Fitz., *Annuite*,
grante a luy une annuite de x marcz par an, et 26.]

---

[1] This reading is conjectural. In L. the word is atenast, in H. tendist, and in C. tendit.

[2] L., lexcepcion, instead of la primere excepcion.

[3] The words *Vide infra* are omitted from H.

[4] From L., H., and C.

Nos. 38, 39.

A.D. 1345. and had bound himself and his heirs to pay the aforesaid annuity from year to year. And the plaintiff
made *profert* of the deed of the defendant's father
which witnessed the fact. Thereupon the defendant
said that he had nothing by descent, upon which it
was found that he had two marks of rent by descent.
And, because the issue which he had taken was found
against the defendant, judgment was given that the
plaintiff should ⋅ recover the whole of the annuity
against him, because he ought to have pleaded in law
that he had only so much by descent, and have
charged that for the portion of the annuity.—And
quære whether it be law to charge him with the
entirety, because, in a Formedon, if the tenant plead
that he has nothing by descent, and it be found that
he has a part, but not to the full value of the demand,
the demandant will be barred only as to a portion.—
And therefore *quære*.—And so also in many other
cases.

Note.

(38.) § Note that a deed was denied, and there were
witnesses in the same deed, and process was made
against the witnesses, and the Sheriff returned that
they were dead. And the tenant said that one of them
was living, and this he wished to aver. And, because he
might in this way have delayed the demandant for
ever he was ousted from that answer, and process was
made against the jurors, &c.

Waste.

(39.) § Note that on a writ of Waste a wife was
admitted to defend on default of her husband, and
she pleaded that the vill was wrongly named as the
writ was brought. And because she had been admitted
to defend her right she was ousted from this plea.

Nos. 38, 39.

avoit oblige luy et ses heirs a paier lannuite avan- A D. 1345.
dite dan en an.[1] Et mist avant le fet son pere qe
le tesmoigna, ou le defendant dit qil navoit rien
par descente, ou trove fuit qil avoit deux marcz de
rente par descente. Et, pur ceo qe son issue fuit
trove countre luy, il fuit agarde qil recoverast tote
lannuite devers luy, pur ceo qil le dust aver plede
en ley qil navoit forqe tant par descente, et ceo
aver [2] charge pur la porcion.—Et *quære* si ceo soit
ley de luy charger del entier, qar en Fourme doun
sil plede qil nad rien par descente, et trove soit
qil ad parcelle, mes ne mye a la value demande,
il ne serra barre forqe pur la porcion.—*Et ideo
quære.*—Et auxint en plusours autres cas.

(38.) [3] § *Nota* qun fet fuit dedit, et il y avoint ^{Nota.[4]}
tesmoins en mesme le fet, et proces fuit fet vers ^{[Fitz.,
Proses,}
les tesmoins, et le Vicounte retourna qils furent ^{175.]}
mortz. Et le tenant dist qun fuit en vie, et ceo
voleit il averer. Et, pur ceo qil pout issint aver
delaye le demandant a toux jours, il fuit ouste de
cel respons, et proces fet vers lenqueste, &c.

(39.) [3] § *Nota* qen un brief de Wast la femme fuit ^{Wast.[5]}
resceu par la defaute son baron, et pleda qe la
ville fuit malement nome la ou le brief fuit porte.
Et pur ceo qele fuit resceu a defendre son dreit
ele fuit ouste.

---

[1] an is omitted from C.
[2] H., avera.
[3] From L., H., and C.

[4] The marginal note is omitted
from C.
[5] The marginal note in H. is
Nota.

No. 40.

(40.) [1] § Sir Adam de Everingham brought a writ of Naifty against two persons. And he appeared by attorney, and the warrant of attorney was in respect of a plea of Naifty. And he counted against them that tortiously they deny that they are his villeins who have fled from his villein-land since the Coronation of King Henry III., and tortiously for that one T.,[2] their grandfather, was the villein of his grandfather [3] who was seised of him as of his villein, in time of peace, &c., tallaging him high and low at his will, and as in ransom of flesh and blood, and in making him reeve, and harvest-bailiff, and taking from him aid for marrying his daughter, and other manner of villein issues, amounting to half a mark or more, as of fee and right. And he made the descent from his grandfather [4] to his father, and from his father to himself.[4] And in like manner he made the descent from T.[2] to A.[2] and so from A. to those two against whom the writ is brought. And if they will deny this, they wrongly deny it, for we tell you that our grandfather [3] brought a writ of Naifty against their grandfather in the time of King Edward I., in the tenth year of his reign, and counted against him that he was his villein, and the latter said that he could not deny it, and they and their father were born afterwards, and if they will deny it, we are ready to aver it by record.— *W. Thorpe* denied

---

[1] *See* above No. 12, p. 32.

[2] For the real names *see* p. 111, note 4.

[3] Father according to the record.

[4] From his father to himself according to the record.

No. 40.

(40.)[1] § Sire Adam Deveringham porta brief de Neifte vers deux. Et fuit par attourne, et le garrant fut *de placito Nativitatis.* Et counta devers eux qe atort dedient estre ses neifs qe sount fuis de sa neif terre puis le coronement le Roi H., et pur ceo atort qun T. lour aiel,[3] fuit le neif son aiel, et il seisi de luy come de son neif en temps de pees, &c., a tailler haut et bas a sa volunte, et come en rechat de char et de sank, et luy faire provost, et messer, et eide a sa fille marier, et autre manere dissue de villeyn, mountant a demi marc ou plus, come de fee et dreit. Et fist la descente de son aiel tanqe son pere et de son pere tanqe a luy, et de T. issint a A. et de A. issint a ceux deux vers queux, &c. Et sils le voillent dedire, atort le dedient, qar nous vous dioms qe nostre aiel porta un brief de Neifte vers lour aiel en temps le Roi E. laiel, lan de son regne x, et counta devers luy qil fuit son neif, et il dit qil ne poet ceo dedire, et ceux furent neez de puisne temps et lour pere, et sils le voillent dedire, prest daverer par recorde.[4]— *IT.*

---

[1] From L., H., and C., but corrected by the record, *Placita de Banco,* Easter, 19 Edw. III., R° 349. " Linc. Praeceptum fuit Vice- " comiti quod juste et sine dilatione " faceret habere Adæ de Everyng- " ham, de Laxtone, chivaler, Jo- " hannem filium Willelmi de " Westburghe de Newerke, et " Galfridum fratrem ejusdem Jo- " hannis, nativos et fugitivos suos, " cum omnibus catallis suis, et " tota sequela sua, ubicumque " inventi fuissent in balliva sua, " nisi essent in dominico Regis, " qui fugerunt de terra sua post " coronationem domini Henrici " Regis proavi domini Regis nunc, " &c., Ita quod loquela illa posita " fuit ad petitionem petentis per

" breve domini Regis ad hunc diem, " scilicet, a die Paschæ in xv dies, " &c."

[2] The words Brief de are from C. alone.

[3] H., lael, instead of lour aiel.

[4] The count was, according to the record, " quod prædicti Jo- " hannes et Galfridus injuste " dedicunt ipsos esse nativos suos, " quia dicit quod quidam Adam de " Everyngham, pater ipsius Adæ, " cujus heres ipse est, fuit seisitus " de quodam Willelmo de West- " burghe patre prædictorum Jo- " hannis et Galfridi, apud West- " burghe, ut de nativo suo, ut de " feodo et jure tempore . . . . " domini Regis nunc, talliando " ipsum alto et basso ad voluntatem

No. 40.

A.D. 1345. tort, and force, and the right, &c., and all manner of villenage, and will deny them, &c., and he said that whereas the demandant demands them as his villeins, they cannot be his villeins, because their father was a bastard.—And the other side said the contrary.—And so to the country.

No. 40.

Thorpe defendi tort et force et le dreit, &c., et totes A D. 1345. maneres de neiftes, et defendra, &c., et dit qe la ou il les demande come ses neifs qils ne purrount mie estre ses neifs, qar lour pere fuit bastard; prest, &c.[1]—*Et alii e contra* qe mulure.—*Et sic ad patriam.*

" ejusdem Adæ, et faciendo ipsum " præpositum suum, et capiendo " de ipso merchetum pro filiis et " filiabus maritandis, et redemp- " tionem carnis et sanguinis, et " alia servitia et consuetudines " nativas, et alia expletia ad " valentiam, &c., qui quidem " Adam, pater, &c., alias in Curia " domini Regis Edwardi avi domini " Regis nunc . . . . tulit " quoddam breve de naivitate " versus quendam Johannem atte " Maydenes, avum prædictorum " Johannis et Galfridi, et petiit " ipsum ut nativum et fugitivum " suum, &c., ad quod breve idem " Johannes venit in eadem Curia " &c., et cognovit de esse nativum " et villanum ejusdem Adæ, per " quod idem Adam tunc recuperavit " ipsum Johannem ut nativum " suum, cum omnibus catallis suis, " et tota sequela sua. Et de ipso " Ada descendit jus, &c., isti Adæ " qui nunc petit, &c. Et de præ- " dicto Johanne atte Maydenes " exivit prædictus Willelmus " pater prædictorum Johannis " filii Willelmi et Galfridi, qui " nunc petuntur, &c. Et, si præ- " dicti Johannes et Galfridus hoc " dedicere velint, ipse paratus est " verificare per recordum rotulo- " rum Justiciariorum de tempore " prædicto, &c."

[1] According to the record, the plea was " Johannes et Galfridus " defendunt jus suum et omnem " nayvitatem quando, &c. Et " dicunt quod ipsi liberi sunt et " liberæ conditionis, et similiter " prædictus Willelmus pater ipso- " rum, quem prædictus Adam " supponit fuisse nativum suum, " liber homo fuit, et liberæ condi- " tionis, quia dicunt quod idem " Willelmus fuit bastardus. Et " hoc parati sunt verificare, unde " petunt judicium, &c."

In the record there is a replica- tion (upon which issue was joined) " quod prædictus Willelmus pater, " &c., fuit filius prædicti Johannis " atte Maydenes nativi prædicti " Adæ patris sui ex legitimo " matrimonio procreatus, et geni- " tus, et non bastardus, sicut " prædicti Johannes et Galfridus " dicunt."

A verdict was found at *Nisi prius* " quod prædictus Willelmus " de Westburghe pater prædicto- " rum Johannis et Galfridi fuit " bastardus, et non ex legitimo " matrimonio procreatus, sicut " prædictus Adam superius sup- " ponit."

Judgment was thereupon given " quod prædictus Adam nihil " capiat per breve suum, sed sit in " misericordia pro falso clameo, " &c. Et prædicti Johannes et " Galfridus remaneant liberi et " liberæ conditionis, quieti de " prædicto Ada et heredibus suis " in perpetuum."

There is a similar case on

Nos. 41, 42.

A.D. 1345.

Novel
Disseisin.

(41.) § Note that John de Penerithe, barber, and his wife brought an Assise of Novel Disseisin, and made their plaint in respect of a certain number of feet in length and breadth. The tenant pleaded in bar a release from the sister of the plaintiff wife, whose heir the wife is, with warranty.—*Birton.* We shall not be put, as heir, to answer as to this deed, because the sister who is supposed to have executed the deed, had a son, J. by name, who is still living; ready, &c.—And the other side said the contrary.—It was found by the Assise that she had a son.—And the COURT enquired over as to the seisin and disseisin, which were found.—Therefore the plaintiff recovered seisin.—*Quære* whether, according to the rigour of the law, enquiry ought have been made over as to the seisin, or as to anything else but the damages.

*Quare
impedit.*

(42.) § The King brought a *Quare impedit* against the Prior of Bath, counting that it belonged to him to present inasmuch as the advowson was holden of him and appropriated, without his license, by the

Nos. 41, 42.

(41.) [1] § *Nota* qe Johan de [3] Penerithe,[4] barbour, A.D. 1345
et sa femme porterent Assise de Novele Disseisine, Assise de [2] Novele
et se pleindrent de certeinz pees en longure et lee. Disseisine.
Le tenant pleda en barre par relees de la soer la
femme pleintif, qi heir ele est, ove garrantie.—
Byrtone. A ceo fet, com heir, ne serroms mys a
respondre, qar cele qest suppose qe fist le fet ad
un fitz, J. par noun, en pleine vie; prest, &c.—*Et*
alii e contra.—Trove fut par Assise qele ad un fitz.
—Et COURT enquist outre de la seisine et disseisine,
quele fuit trove.—Par quei le pleintif, &c.—*Quære* [5]
si, *de rigore legis*, homme duist aver [6] enquis de la
seisine, ou dautre chose qe de damages.

(42.) [7] § Le Roi porta *Quare impedit* vers le Priour Quare
de Baaz, countant coment a luy appent [8] a presenter impedit.
[Fitz.,
par tant qe lavoeson fut tenu de luy et approprie, Briefe,
sanz son conge, par le Priour.[9]—*Huse* alleggea 470.]

R° 349, d, differing only in one
respect, viz., that the " nativi et
" fugitivi" claimed were " Thomas
" filius Willelmi de Westburghe de
" Newerke, et Margareta soror
" ejus."

[1] From L., H., C., and D.

[2] The words Assise de are from
L. alone.

[3] de is from C. alone.

[4] H., Penreth.

[5] *Quære* is omitted from C. and
D.

[6] D., avoir.

[7] From L., H., C., and D., but
corrected by the record, *Placita de
Banco*, Easter, 19 Edw. III.,
R° 282, d. It there appears that
the action was brought by the King
against the Prior of Bath, in respect
of a presentation to the church
of " Bathuiestone " (Batheaston ?
Somerset).

[8] C., appendoit.

[9] The declaration was, according
to the record, "quod quædam
" Matilldis Chaumflour fuit seisita
" de advocatione ecclesiæ prædictæ,
" ut de feodo et jure, tempore
" . . . Edwardi avi domini
" Regis nunc, et illam tenuit de
" eodem domino Rege in capite et
" ad eandem præsentavit quendam
" Martinum Chaumflour, clericum
" suum, qui ad præsentationem
" suam fuit admissus et institutus,
" . . . . . . quæ quidem
" Matilldis . . . . . dedit
" advocationem prædictam cuidam
" Waltero de Aune, tunc Priori
" Bathoniensi, tenendam sibi et
" successoribus suis in perpetuum,
" qui quidem Prioratus de funda-
" tione progenitorum domini Regis
" existit. Et postmodum, vacante
" ecclesia illa post mortem prædicti
" Martini, idem Walterus Prior,
" &c., eandem ecclesiam sibi et

No. 42.

A.D. 1345. Prior.—*Huse* alleged that the King had another *Quare impedit* pending in respect of the same presentation, and had taken the same title, &c.; judgment whether the King will be answered as to this writ purchased while the other is pending.—*Thorpe*. The King can bring as many writs as he may please, and one while another is pending, and so may an infant under age do.—And the writ was adjudged good. But the defendant was by judgment discharged of the first writ. —*Huse*. The King takes diverse causes in his declaration, that is to say, one that the advowson is holden of him, and another the appropriation which would be a cause even though the advowson were not holden of him.—And *Huse* was put to answer over.—And then *Huse* showed that before the Conquest there was an Abbot of Bath who then purchased the advowson from the King, and appropriated it, and he showed the King's charter, and a papal bull for the appropriation. Judgment, said he, whether the King will be answered, &c.

No. 42.

qe[1] le Roi ad un *Quare impedit* pendant de[2] mesme
le presentement, et ad pris mesme le title, &c.;
jugement si a cel brief purchace pendant lautre
voille le Roi estre respondu.—*Thorpe.* Le Roi poet
porter tauntes des briefs come luy plerra, et un
pendant un autre, et si fra un enfaunt deinz age.
—Et le brief agarde bone. Mes le defendant par
agarde fuit descharge del primer brief.—*Huse.* Le
Roi prent divers causes en sa moustrance, saver, un
qe lavoeson est tenue de luy, autre lappropriacion
tut ne fuit ele pas tenu de luy.—Et fuit mys outre.
—Et donqes il moustra qe devant la conqueste y
avoit Abbe de Baaz qe adonqes du Roi purchacea
lavoeson, et lappropria, et moustra chartre le Roi et
bulle del appropriacion. Jugement si le Roi voille
estre respondu, &c.[3]

" domui suæ de Bathonia ad
" manum mortuam appropriavit,
" in proprios usus tenendam,
" absque licentia ipsius Regis avi,
" &c., contra legem et consuetu-
" dinem regni, &c., per quod jus
" præsentandi ad eandem accrevit
" eidem Edwardo Regi avo, &c., et
" [the descent being traced to
" Edward III.] ea ratione pertinet
" ad ipsum dominum Regem nunc
" ad prædictam ecclesiam præ-
" sentare."

[1] D., coment.

[2] So in H. The other MSS.
vers.

[3] The Prior's plea was, according
to the record, " quod prædicta
" Matilldis Chaumflour non fuit
" seisita de advocatione ecclesiæ de
" Bathuiestone prædictæ, nec illam
" tenuit de domino Rege in capite,
" nec prædictus Martinus admissus
" fuit, &c., ad præsentationem
" ejusdem Matilldis, nec eadem
" Matilldis alienavit prædicto

" Waltero, &c., advocationem
" ecclesiæ prædictæ. Et, quo ad
" hoc quod dominus Rex sumit
" titulum suum de appropriatione
" ejusdem ecclesiæ per eundem
" Willelmum Priorem, &c., facta,
" dicit quod tempore Regis Wil-
" lelmi Conquæstoris et genitoris
" domini Regis nunc, quidem
" Abbas de Bathonia qui tunc fuit
" et ejusdem loci Conventus
" tenuerunt ecclesiam illam in
" proprios usus, &c. Et dicit quod
" ante tempus memoriæ quidam
" Robertus quondam Episcopus
" Bathoniensis qui tunc fuit per
" scriptum suum concessit et
" confirmavit, inter alia, ecclesiam
" illam cuidam tunc Priori de
" Bathonia prædecessori &c, et
" monachis ibidem. Et profert
" hic prædictum scriptum præfati
" Episcopi quod hoc testatur, &c.
" Et etiam ante tempus memoriæ
" quidam Alexander Papa tertius,
" qui tunc fuit per bullam suam,

No. 43.

(43.) § Trespass between the Abbot of Waltham, plaintiff and John de Gadesdene, prebendary, &c., of St. Paul, defendant, in respect of certain beasts taken. —*Thorpe.* We tell you that John is lord of the manor of B., within which manor he has, and he and his predecessors from all time have had, waifs and estrays, and that by grant of William the Conqueror, and in like manner by subsequent user, and allowance in the Court of Justices in Eyre, as a member of the lands annexed to the church of St. Paul. And those same beasts in respect of which he makes his plaint were waifs left by thieves within the same manor, wherefore he, as lord, having such a franchise, took them without tort.—*Notton.* We do not admit the grant of such a franchise to have been made to you, or to the church of St. Paul, nor the allowance in the Court of Justices in Eyre, of which you speak; but we say that the Abbot is lord of the half-hundred of Waltham, within which half-hundred the said manor is, and within which half-hundred the Abbot and his predecessors have, from all time, had view of frank-pledge, waifs and estrays, and also their view to be holden

No. 43.

(43.)[1] § Trans entre Labbe de Waltham, pleintif, A.D. 1345.
et Johan de Gadesdene,[2] provendrer, &c., de Seint Trans.
Pole, defendant, de certeins bestes pris. — *Thorpe.*
Nous vous dioms qe Johan est seignur del maner
de B., deinz quel maner il ad, et ly et ses predecessours de tut temps ount eu weyf et estray, et
ceo par grant William le Conquerour, et puis en
cea use et allowe en Eyre, come membre des terres
annex[3] al[4] eglise[5] de Seint Pole. Et[6] mesmes les
bestes dount se pleint[7] furent deinz mesme le maner
weyves[8] de larouns, par quei il com seignur qad
tiele fraunchise les prist sanz tort.—*Nottone.*[9] Nous
ne conissoms pas le grant fait a vous, ne al eglise
de Seint Pole, de tiele fraunchise, ne lalowaunce
en[10] Eyre, dount vous parletz; mes vous dioms qe
Labbe est seignur del demi hundred de Waltham,
[deinz quel demi hundred le dit maner est],[11] et[12]
deinz quel demi hundred Labbe et ses predecessours
de tut temps ount eu viewe de fraunk plegge, weyf[13]
et estrai, et auxint lour viewe a tenir deinz mesme[14]

" quam hic profert, inter alia,
" confirmavit eandem ecclesiam
" cuidam tunc Priori loci prædicti
" et ejus Conventui, &c. Et sic
" dicit quod ipse Prior et omnes
" prædecessores sui a tempore quo
" non extat memoria tenuerunt
" eandem ecclesiam in proprios
" usus, &c., absque hoc quod
" ecclesia illa appropriata fuit in
" forma qua dominus Rex supponit,
" &c."

Several adjournments follow on
the roll. Pleadings were resumed
in Easter Term in the 20th
year. After this there are more
adjournments from term to term,
and year to year, as far as Michaelmas Term in the 37th year, with
an adjournment to which Term
the case ends on the roll.

[1] From L., H., C., and D.

[2] L., Schaddesdene; H., and D., Chaddesdene.

[3] H., annexes.

[4] D., a la.

[5] D., esglise.

[6] H., ou.

[7] H., pleinount.

[8] D., weyfs.

[9] *Nottone* is omitted from C.

[10] L., fait en.

[11] The words between brackets are omitted from D.

[12] et is from H. alone.

[13] H., wayve; C., weyve; D., weyvfe.

[14] mesme is omitted from H. and D.

No. 43.

within the same half-hundred, and by virtue of such colour we took the same beasts until he took them with force, &c., *absque hoc* that the plaintiff or his predecessors have been seised of waifs and estrays in the half-hundred; ready, &c.—*Thorpe.* You see plainly how he claims by reason of a franchise, in which case he ought to have a special writ on his case; judgment of this writ which is no warrant to try such a franchise. —WILLOUGHBY. He might have a writ on his case, but this writ also is good; therefore answer.—*Thorpe.* They have not denied that our franchise was granted to the church of St. Paul, of which this manor is member, and parcel, as above, nor the allowance of it the Court of Justices in Eyre, and we have no need to say anything as to that which they allege concerning a franchise in their half-hundred. And, inasmuch as they say nothing as to our franchise within the manor, which would make an issue if they would deny it, and which we should be ready to maintain if they would deny it, but take a traverse on our possession, which could not make an issue in this case, inasmuch as the substance of the franchise and the right to it, which they have not denied to be in us, draw to themselves the possession, because possibly the case of an estray never occurred before the present time, therefore the non-seisin does not deprive us of our franchise, or disprove it; judgment.— *Notton.* Then you refuse the averment, and we demand judgment inasmuch as we have alleged our possession of the franchise throughout the whole of the half-hundred within which the said manor is in which the taking was effected; and we and our predecessors have been seised from all time, *absque hoc* that you have been seised, or your predecessor; and of that we

No. 43.

le demi hundred, et par tiel colour nous primes [1] A.D. 1345.
mesmes les bestes tanqil les prist a force, &c., sanz
ceo qe le pleintif ou ses predecessours ount este
seisiz en le demi hundred de weyf et estraye ; prest,
&c.—*Thorpe.* Vous veietz bien coment il cleyme par
resoun de fraunchise, en quel cas il avereit brief
especial sur son cas ; jugement de ceo brief quel
nest pas garrant a trier tiele fraunchise.—WILBY.
Il purreit aver [2] brief sur son cas, et auxint cest
brief est bon ; par quei responetz.—*Thorpe.* Ils
nount pas dedit nostre fraunchise grante al eglise
de Seint Pole, dount cel maner est membre et parcelle, *ut supra*, ne lallowaunce en Eyre, et ceo qils
parlent a la fraunchise deinz lour demi hundred
navoms mester a parler. Et desicome a nostre
fraunchise [3] deinz le maner, [4] quel freit issue sil le
le vodreint [5] dedire, et quel nous serroms prest de [6]
meintenir sils le vodreint [7] dedire, ne parlent [8] ils
pas, mes pernount [9] travers sur nostre possession,
quel en ceo cas ne poet faire issue, desicome le
gros et le droit de la [10] fraunchise, quel ils nount
pas dedit en nous, attreit a luy la possession, qar
par cas unqes ne vint le cas destray devant ore,
par quei la nounseisine ne toud ne desprove nostre
fraunchise ; jugement. — *Nottone.* Donqes refusetz
laverement, et demandoms [11] jugement desicome
nous avoms allegge nostre possession de fraunchise
par my et tut le demi hundred deinz quel le
dit maner ou la prise, &c., est ; et nous et
noz predecessours seisiz de tut temps, sanz ceo qe
vous fustes seisi, ou vostre predecessour ; et ceo

---

[1] L., preimes ; C., pernoms

[2] H., avoir.

[3] D., maner.

[4] D., la franchise, instead of le maner.

[5] H., voudront

[6] C., a.

[7] H., and C., voudrount; D., vodront.

[8] L., parlount.

[9] D., pernent.

[10] D., sa.

[11] The words et demandoms are omitted from C.

Nos. 44, 45.

A.D. 1345. have tendered averment, which averment you have refused; judgment.—*Thorpe.* And inasmuch as the franchise is not denied to be in us, as above, and if you will allege your possession of it within the manor we shall be ready to traverse it, while you do not maintain it, but speak of seisin within a half-hundred, as to which we have no need to say anything, because it would not make an issue in this plea, we demand judgment, &c.—And so to judgment.

Wardship.   (44.) § Note that a man brought a writ of Wardship against Gerard de Braybroke and against a woman. And the woman made default, and Gerard also. And as to the woman the Sheriff returned that she had nothing; and as to Gerard he returned the summons. And, process having been continued until the Grand Distress was returnable with regard to both, the Sheriff returned that the woman had nothing, and that Gerard had been distrained. And they were called, and did not appear, and therefore *Thorpe* prayed a Proclamation.—And the COURT said that he should not have a Proclamation with regard to the woman, because the Distress had not been served in her case, and she had not been distrained. Nor, said the COURT, can you have it in the case of Gerard, because we will never grant a Proclamation with regard to one unless there can be a Proclamation against both; and therefore continue to sue your process at common law,[1] for you will never have forjudger against the woman if the woman has not been distrained, nor against Gerard unless you should have it against the woman.

Note.   (45.) § Note that a wife who was admitted to defend her right on the default of her husband would have pleaded that a vill was wrongly named, and was not permitted to do, &c.

---

[1] *i.e.* not under the Statute 52 Hen. III. (Marlb.), c. 7, by which the Proclamation was given.

Nos. 44, 45.

avoms tendu daverer, quel averement vous avetz A.D. 1345.
refuse; jugement.—*Thorpe.* Et desicome la fraunchise
nest pas dedit a nous, *ut supra*, et si vous vodretz[1]
allegger vostre possession deinz le maner nous serroms prest a traverser, mes ceo ne meintenetz pas,
mes parletz a la seisine deinz un demi hundred a
quel nous navoms pas[2] mester[3] a parler, pur ceo
qe ceo ne serreit pas issue en ceo ple, jugement,
&c.—*Et sic ad judicium.*

(44.)[4] § *Nota* qun homme porta un brief de Garde Garde.
[Fitz.,
vers Gerard de Braybroke et vers une femme. Et *Proclama*
la femme fist defaut, et Gerard auxi. Et quant a *cion*, 5.]
la femme le Vicounte retourna qele navoit rienz; et
quant a Gerard il retourna la somons. Et proces
continue tanqe a la grand destresse vers lun et
lautre retournable, le Vicounte retourna qe la femme
navoit rienz, et qe Gerard fuit destreint. Et furent
demandez, et ne vindrent pas, par quei *R. Thorpe*
pria la Proclamacion.—Et la Court dit qil navereit
mie la Proclamacion vers la femme, qar la destresse
nest pas servy vers luy,[5] et ele nest pas destreint.
Ne vers Gerard vous ne le poietz mie aver, qar
nous ne grantroms[6] jammes Proclamacion vers lun
si la Proclamacion ne poet estre vers les deux; et
pur ceo suetz avant vostre proces a la comune ley,
qar devers la femme vous naveretz mie forjuger si
la femme ne fuit destreint, ne vers Gerard pas si
vous nel ussetz vers la femme.

(45.)[4] § *Nota* qune femme qe fuit resceu a defendre *Nota.*
son dreit[7] par la defaut son baron voleit aver plede
a mal nomer de ville, et ne fuit pas resceu, &c.[8]

---

[1] H., and C., vodriez.
[2] pas is from C. alone.
[3] C., mestier; D., meister.
[4] From L., H., C., and D.
[5] The words vers luy are omitted from D.

[6] So in D.; the other MSS., grantoms.
[7] The words son dreit are omitted from C.
[8] This report seems to be an abridgment of No. 39 above.

No. 46.

(46.) § A man brought a writ of Trespass against another in the King's Bench, and counted against him that he came with force and arms, on a certain day, and took from the plaintiff a hutch in which were contained ten quarters of wheat and ten charters, worth so much, tortiously and to the plaintiff's damage amounting to £20. And the defendant pleaded Not Guilty; ready, &c. And it was found that he was guilty, and to the plaintiff's damage of a certain amount.—*R. Thorpe.* You cannot give judgment on this verdict, because by his count he counts that the defendant carried off from him ten charters, and he does not say in his count what was contained in the charters, so that the Court could give judgment in accordance with the quantity of the tenements which were included in the charters, nor does he say that the charters belonged to him or were delivered to him to keep; and in case he had counted that the charters belonged to him it would have been right to award him greater damages, and also in accordance with the quantity of the land, whether greater or less. And on a writ of Detinue of a writing he ought to declare what was contained in the charters which he supposes to be detained from him : for according to the quantity which was included the damages ought to be increased or diminished.—*Moubray.* On a writ of Detinue of a writing my object is to demand the writing, and therefore I must declare what is contained in it, and that it belongs to me; and also if the writing be burnt I shall recover damages with due regard to the quantity of land which was included; but on a writ of Trespass the plaintiff's object is not to demand the charters, but to recover damages for the carrying of them away, so that in such case there is no need to specify by

No. 46.

(46.) [1] § Un homme porta brief de Trans devers A.D. 1345.
un autre en Bank le Roi, et counta devers luy qil Trans.
vint a force et armes, certein jour, et prist de luy
une huche en quel furent contenuz x quarters de
furment et x chartres, pris de tant, atort et a ses
damages de xx*li*. Et le defendant dit qil fuit de
rien coupable; prest, &c. Et trove fuit qil fuit
coupable a certeinz damages, &c.—*R. Thorpe*. Vous
ne poetz pas doner jugement sur cel verdit, qar par
soun counte il counta qil luy emporta x chartres,
et il ne dit mie ceo qe fut contenu [2] deinz les
chartres en soun counte, issint qe solonc la quantite
des tenementz qe furent compris deinz les chartres
Court purreit ajuger, ne qe les chartres attiendreint
a luy, ou luy furent bailles a garder, en quel cas
sil ust este counte qe les chartres attiendreint [3] a luy
il ust este resoun de luy aver agarde greyndre
damages, et auxint pur la quantite de la terre si
ceo fuit greyndre ou meindre. Et en brief de Detenue descript il duist counter ceo qe fuit contenue
deinz les chartres queux il supposa qe luy furent
detenutz; qar sur tiele quantite qe fuit compris
les damages deivent estre encrus [4] ou amenuses.—
Moubray. En brief de Detenue descript jeo su [5] a
demander lescript, et pur ceo il covient qe jeo
counte ceo qest contenu [6] deinz, et qil attient a moi;
et auxint si lescript soit ars jeo recoverai les [7]
damages, eaunt regarde a la quantite de la terre
qest compris; mes en brief de Trans il nest pas a
demander les chartres, mes recoverir damages pur
lemporter, [8] issint qen tiel cas il ne bosoigne [9] mie
de mettre en certein par counte ceo qest compris

---

[1] From L., H., C., and D.

[2] D., contenuz.

[3] H., ussent este.

[4] H., enquis; C., encrues; D.,
compris.

[5] H., suy; D., sui.

[6] L., contenue; D., contenuz.

[7] les is from C. alone.

[8] C., lenporter.

[9] C., bussoigne.

No. 46.

count what is included in the charters.—*Skipwith*. If the charters belonged to any one else, and not to you, it is not right that you should recover damages to so great an amount as if the charters were yours and related to your inheritance; and, therefore, when any one has to count, he must specify the particulars in his count, and, if they be not specified in the count, the Court has no warrant to give judgment upon it, even though the party accept the count in that form when he might have abated it; and now in this case the damages cannot by judgment be given by parcels, because they were not assessed by parcels by the verdict; therefore there is greater reason to go back, and make the parties plead anew, than to give judgment on a matter which is erroneous.—*Mutlow*. We saw in the Court of Common Pleas that a Replevin [1] was brought, and that the plaintiff counted that the defendant tortiously took his beasts, and did not say how many beasts, and, when the jury came to the bar and were charged, they said that the defendant took the plaintiff's beasts; and they were asked to say how many beasts; and they said two; and if they had not stated the number in particular, the plaintiff would not have recovered, nor would judgment have been given on that record, although the defendant accepted a bad count; no more ought you to give judgment when his count does not specify the quantity of land included in the charters.—Scot gave judgment that the plaintiff should recover his damages assessed by the jury.—In respect of this judgment a writ of Error was sued, as appears in Trinity Term in the twenty-first year, but nevertheless it was affirmed.— See there, and *quære*.

---

[1] The reference is probably to Y.B., Trin., 18 Edw. III., No. 42 (Rolls edition, pp. 390-394). The case was, however, one of Rescous, and not of Replevin.

No. 46.

deinz les chartres.—*Skip.*[1] Si les chartres fuissent
a autre, et ne mie a vous, il nest mie resoun qe
vous recoverez tauntes des damages com si les
chartres fuissent les vos et touchassent vostre heritage ; et, pur ceo, quant homme deit counter, il covient
qil mette en certein son counte, et sil ne soit pas
mys en certein la Court nad mie garrant a doner
jugement sur cele, tut accepte la partie tiele chose
la ou il pout aver abatu le counte ; et les damages
ore en ceo cas ne pount estre parcelles par jugement, qar ils ne furent pas parcelles par verdit ;
par quei il est greindre reson de retourner, et le
faire pleder de novel, qe de doner jugement sur une
chose erroigne.—*Mutl.* Nous veimes en la comune
Place qun *Replegiari* fuit porte, et il counta qil prist
ses avers atort, et ne dit mie combien des avers,
et quant lenqueste vint a la barre et furent charges,
ils disoint qil prist ses avers ; et demande fuit de
eux com bien des avers ; et ils disoint deux ; et
sils nussent dit le nombre en certein, il nust mie
recovere, ne jugement done sur cel recorde, tut
accepta le defendant un malveys counte ; nient plus
vous ne devetz quant son counte nest pas en certein de la quantite de la terre compris deinz les
chartres.—SCOT agarda qe le pleintif recoverast ses
damages taxes par lenqueste.—[De quel jugement
un brief Derrour fuit suy, *ut patet Trinitatis xxi.*,
et uncore fut afferme.—*Vide ibi, et quære.*][2]

---

[1] D., *Thorpe.*

[2] The words between brackets
are from L. alone.

TRINITY TERM

IN THE

NINETEENTH YEAR OF THE REIGN OF KING EDWARD THE THIRD AFTER THE CONQUEST.

TRINITY TERM IN THE NINETEENTH YEAR OF THE REIGN OF KING EDWARD THE THIRD AFTER THE CONQUEST.

Nos. 1, 2.

A.D. 1345.
Quare impedit.

(1.) § The Earl of Gloucester brought a *Quare impedit* against the Abbot of Chester, and they were at issue; and when the jury came the Earl was non-suited.—Stonore awarded a writ to the Bishop for the Abbot, without enquiry as to collusion.—*Quære.*—And note that, although the jury was ready in Court, he would not enquire as to damages (and yet prayer was made as to both points); but he ordered a writ to the Sheriff to enquire as to the value of the church for the damages.

Appeal.

(2.) § Appeal in the King's Bench. Heretofore the plaintiff was ousted from the suit because he was outlawed [for trespass],[1] and so was not in a condition to be answered, and therefore the defendant went without day. And afterwards that outlawry was reversed. And now the plaintiff sued a Re-attachment on the original writ.—*Grene.* The original writ is extinguished and abated; judgment whether you will put us to answer to this writ which has issued upon the other.—*Skipwith.* That plea is to the action: for, after a year has passed, suit shall not be had by way of Appeal. And it is certain that a party does not lose a real action or an action of Appeal by reason of outlawry on a writ of Trespass. Therefore this suit by way of Re-attachment shall be maintained, or none at all. But if the case had arisen on a plea of

---

[1] *See* Y.B., Mich., 18 Edw. III., No. 15, Rolls edition, p. 50, and p. 51, note 1.

DE TERMINO TRINITATIS ANNO REGNI REGIS EDWARDI TERTII A CONQUESTU DECIMO NONO.[1]

Nos. 1, 2.

(1.)[2] § Le Count de Gloucestre porta *Quare impedit* _{A.D. 1345.} vers Labbe de Cestre, et furent a issue; et quant *Quare impedit.* pais vint le Count fuit nounsuy.—STON. agarda brief al Evesqe pur Labbe saunz enquere de la collusioun. *Quære.*—*Et nota* qil ne voleit pas, coment qe lenqueste fuit prest en Court, enquere des damages; et si fuit lun point et lautre prie; mes il comanda brief al Vicounte[3] denquere de la value de leglise[4] pur damages.

(2.)[2] § Appelle en Bank le Roi. Autrefoith le _{Appelle.} pleintif fuit ouste de la suite pur ceo qil fuit utlage, et issint nient responable, par quei le defendant passa saunz jour. Et puis cele utlagerie fuit reverse. Et ore ad suy Reattachement hors del original. —*Grene.* Loriginal est amorty et abatu; jugement si a cest brief issue del autre nous voilletz[5] mettre a respondre.—*Skip.* Ceo plee est al accion: qar, après lan passe, homme na>vera pas suite[6] par voie Dappelle. *Et certum est* qe par utlagerie en brief de Trans partie ne perd pas accion real ne accion Dappelle. Donqes ceste suite par Reattachement serra meyntenue ou nulle. Mes si le cas fuit en

---

¹ The reports of this Term are from the Lincoln's Inn MS. (called L.), the Harleian MS. No. 741 (called H.), the Cambridge MS. Hh. 2. 3 (called C), and the Cambridge MS. Hh. 2. 4 called D).

² From the four MSS. as above.

³ So in D. The other three MSS. have Evesqe.

⁴ D., la esglise.

⁵ D., voleitz nous, instead of nous voilletz.

⁶ H., accion.

No. 3.

land, in which a new original writ could be had, he would possibly be put to a new original, and a Resummons would not lie for the purpose of reviving the first original; but in this case we shall not have a new original, because the year is passed; and there has been no negligence or fault in us, since our suit was, at the beginning, taken in time, and also because the outlawry, which was the obstacle, has been reversed.—BASSET. We have seen a writ of Appeal maintained after the year was passed, when the first writ had been abated by exception, and so possibly you will have it maintained.

Trespas.

(3.) § Trespass in respect of goods carried off, and the plaintiff's weir in Reculver forcibly broken down, and its timber carried off.—*Notton.* As to the goods, &c., and as to coming with force, &c., Not Guilty. And as to the weir we tell you that this weir is in the vill of Chislet, and he holds this weir of us at will, rendering to us yearly so many fish, &c.; and because the rent was in arrear we came, and took from the weir a certain instrument in the name of distress (judgment whether tort, &c.), *absque hoc* that we broke down his weir in Reculver, as he complains.—*Skipwith.* We complain in one vill, and he justifies the act in

No. 3.

plee de terre, ou homme purreit aver novel original, A.D. 1345.
par cas homme ly mettreit a novel original, et Resomons ne girreit pas pur resusciter loriginal ; mes
en le cas, pur ceo qe lan est passe nous averoms
pas loriginal[1]; et necligence[2] ne defaut ny ad pas
en nous, quant nostre suite fuit pris a comencement
en temps, et auxint qe[3] lutlagerie qe fuit obstacle
est reverse.—BASSET. Homme ad vieue brief Dappelle
meintenu apres lan, quant le primer brief fuit abatu
par chalange, et issint par cas averetz vous.

(3.)[4] § Trans des biens enportes, et son gorce en Trans.
R.[5] a force debruse, et le merym enporte.[6]—Nottone.
Quant as biens, &c., et venir[7] a force, &c., de rien
coupable. Et quant a gorce vous dioms qe cele[8]
gorce est en la ville de C.,[9] et cele gorce tient il
de nous a volunte, rendant par an tant des pessouns,
&c. ; et pur ceo qe la rente fuit arrere nous veni-
mes, et preimes del gorce un certein instrument en
noun de destresse, jugement si tort, &c., sanz ceo
qe nous debrusames soun gorce en R.[5] com il se
pleint.[10]—Skip. Nous pleignoms en une ville, et il

[1] H., original.

[2] D., negligence.

[3] qe is omitted from D.

[4] From the four MSS. as above, but corrected by the record, *Placita de Banco*, Trin., 19 Edw. III., R° 40, d. It there appears that the action was brought by Adam le Spicer of Reculvre (Reculver, Kent), against William de Thrul-leye, Abbot of St. Augustine, Canterbury, and others.

[5] MSS. of Y.B., A.

[6] The declaration was, according to the record, "quod prædicti Abbas " et alii . . . . . quendam " gurgitem ipsius Adæ apud " Reculvre fregerunt et maere- " mium inde scilicet, pilas et

" clayas, ad valentiam quidraginta " solidorum, ceperunt et asporta- " verunt . . . . . contra " pacem, &c."

[7] H., venus.

[8] H., and C., la ; D , le.

[9] MSS. of Y.B., B.

[10] The plea was, according to the record, " quo ad maeremium præ- " dictum seu aliud contra pacem, " &c., dicunt quod ipsi nihil " fecerunt contra pacem, et quo ad " præfatum gurgitem prædictus " Abbas dicit quod gurgis ille est " in villa de Chistolet, unde idem " Abbas est dominus, &c., et quod " prædictus Adam tenet gurgitem " illum ad voluntatem ipsius " Abbatis, reddendo inde eidem

No. 3.

another vill, to which plea we cannot have an answer, because issue cannot be joined on the question whether the weir is in the one vill or in the other; and therefore we will aver our writ.—*Sadelyngstanes.* We must be aided by plea on our act, because, if we were to say Not Guilty, it would be held to be not denied by us that the weir is in Reculver in accordance with his plaint, and that would not be right.—STONORE. And what if he has a weir in the one vill, and another in the other vill, and he makes his plaint respecting that in Reculver? Will you not answer to his plaint? Or is that an answer which you took in respect of the weir in Chislet when he makes his plaint in Reculver? But, if you are speaking the truth, the general issue "Not Guilty" will serve your purpose, because, on this writ, enquiry will be had only in respect of trespass committed in Reculver.—*Sadelyngstanes.* Enquiry will not be had by way of verdict as to which was the vill in which the tort was committed, unless special issue be joined upon that point, &c.

No. 3.

justifie le fet en autre ville, a quei nous ne poms ^{A.D. 1345.} aver respons, qar lissue ne se poet pas fere le quel le gorce soit en lune ville ou en lautre ; par quei nous voloms averer nostre brief. — *Sadl.* Il covient qe nous soioms eide sur nostre fet par plee, qar si nous deissoms de rien coupable serra tenu a nient dedit de nous le gorce estre en R.[1] come il se pleint, et ceo ne serra pas resoun. — STON. Et quei sil eit un gorce en lune ville et autre en lautre ville,[2] et il se pleint de[3] cele en R.[1]? Ne respondrez vous a sa[4] pleinte? [Ou est ceo respons qe vous priestes del gorce en C.[5] la ou il se pleint en R.[1]?][6] Mes, si vous dietz verite, general issue de rien coupable vous servira, qar homme enquerra forqe de trans fait en R.[1] a cest brief. — *Sadl.* Homme ne querra pas en quele ville le tort se fist, si especial issue[7] ne fuit sur ceo pris, par verdit, &c.[8]

" Abbati omminodos pisces in " eodem gurgite captos pretii " duodecim denariorum, et ultra, " et quia prædictus Adam piscatus " fuit in gurgite prædicto per quin- " decim dies ante prædictum diem " Sabati, &c., et cepit ibidem " viginti salmones, et viginti " congeros, pretii cujuslibet duo- " decim denariorum et ultra, et " eos prædicto Abbati non reddidit, ' idem Abbas cepit quoddam " ingenium quod vocatur Burroke " de prædicto gurgite, nomine " districtionis pro prædictis pisci- " bus a retro existentibus, sicut ei " bene licuit, absque hoc quod idem " Abbas seu alii gurgitem ipsius " Adæ apud Reculvre fregerunt, et " maeremium inde ceperunt et " asportaverunt, sicut idem Abbas " queritur. Et hoc parati sunt " verificare. Et petunt judicium, " &c."

[1] MSS. of Y.B., A.

[2] ville is omitted from L. and C.

[3] D., en.

[4] H., cele.

[5] MSS. of Y.B., B.

[6] The words between brackets are omitted from H.

[7] H., trans.

[8] The words *Et alii e contra* are added in H. According to the record, the replication upon which issue was joined was "quod præ- " dicti Abbas et alii gurgitem ipsius " Adæ apud Reculvre fregerunt et " maeremium inde ceperunt et " asportaverunt contra pacem, &c., " prout ipse per breve suum sup- " supponit." The *Venire* was awarded, but nothing further appears on the roll in relation to this case. There follows, however, a similar action agreeing in all respects with the above, except that the plaintiff was James de Newenham of Reculver.

No. 4.

A.D. 1345.
Formedon.
(4.) § Formedon.—*Grene.* We tell you that one A.[1] brought an Assise of Novel Disseisin against us, and is in possession by force of the recovery thereon ; judgment of this writ.—*Thorpe.* And, inasmuch as he does not deny that he was tenant on the day on which the writ was purchased, and does not allege any cause for the recovery before our writ was purchased, nor yet allege any execution in fact, which would give notice to us who are a stranger, we also demand judgment.—*Grene.* Then it is so. And suppose he put himself in possession without having execution, is he not in by force of the recovery?—KELSHULLE. If he has not had execution, then his entry is by disseisin.—*Grene.* You say what is contrary to law.—KELSHULLE. I have seen it so adjudged.—STOUFORD. Between those who are privies the entry is good enough, without execution ; but a stranger will have the averment that he entered by disseisin, and not by

---

[1] For the real names *see* p. 137, note 2.

No. 4.

(4.)[1] § Forme doun.—*Grene.* Nous vous dioms qun
A. porta un Assise de Novele disseisine devers nous,
et einz est par force del recoverir ; jugement de
ceo brief.[2]—*Thorpe.* Et, desicome il ne dedit pas
qil ne fuit tenant jour del brief purchace, ne il
nallegge cause del recoverir devant nostre brief purchace, ne unqore nallegge execucion en fet qe durra
notice a nous qe sumes estrange, jugement.—*Grene.*
Donqes est il issint. Et jeo pose qil se mist einz
sanz execucion, nest il pas einz par force del recoverir[3]?—KELL. Sil neit pas execucion, donqes est[4]
soun entre par disseisine. — *Grene.* Vous parletz
countre lei.—KELL. Jeo lai viewe issint estre ajuge.
—STOUF. Entre ces qe sount prives lentre est assetz
bon sanz execucion ; mes estrange avera averement
qil entra par disseisine, et noun pas par lexecucion;

---

[1] From the four MSS. as above, but corrected by the record, *Placita de Banco*, Trin., 19 Edw III., R⁰ 317, d. It there appears that the action was brought by Geoffrey le Wauncy of Aldworth against Gilbert de Sotesbroke in respect of tenements in Aldworth (Berks) alleged to have been given by Geoffrey le Wauncy to Geoffrey son of Geoffrey le Wauncy in tail. The descent alleged was from Geoffrey son of Geoffrey to John as son and heir, and from John to his brother, the demandant.

[2] The plea was, according to the record, "quod alias . . . "quidam Magister Walterus, per-" "sona ecclesiæ de Shalyngforde," "et Johannes Oliver, persona" "ecclesiæ de Fynchamstede, tuler-" "unt quandam Assisam novæ" "disseisinæ versus ipsum Gil-" "bertum, et questi fuerunt se" "disseisiri de prædictis tenementis" "nunc petitis, &c., quæ quidem

"Assisa inter eos tunc transivit,"
"et iidem Walterus et Johannes"
"Oliver seisinam suam de iisdem"
"tenementis super Assisam illam"
"per judicium . . . . versus"
"eum recuperaverunt, virtute"
"cujus judicii et executionis inde"
"factæ, ipsi Walterus et Johannes"
"positi fuerunt in seisinam"
"eorundem tenementorum, qui"
"ea adhuc tenent in forma præ-"
"dicta. Et sic dicit quod, pendente"
"inter ipsos Galfridum et Gil-"
"bertum brevi supradicto, ipse"
"Gilbertus amotus est de tene-"
"mentis illis per præfatum judi-"
"cium et executionem supra-"
"dictam, unde petit judicium de"
"isto brevi, &c."

[3] H., respons. The MS. appears to be corrupt from the commence-ment of *Thorpe's* speech to this point, many words being trans-posed, and so rendered unintel-ligible.

[4] D., est il.

Nos. 5, 6.

A.D. 1345. execution; therefore see whether you will allege execution or abide judgment in law.—*Grene* then alleged that execution had been effected, and that the person who recovered was tenant by force of the execution; ready, &c.—*Huse*. You were tenant on the day on which the writ was purchased, and have continued that estate; ready, &c.—And the other side said the contrary.

Dower.

(5.) § Dower, where elopement, without subsequent reconciliation, was pleaded in bar.—*Mutlow*. We tell you that her husband died at such a place, and we tell you that, without coercion of Holy Church, she had then dwelt a long time in his company; judgment, and we pray our dower.—*Grene*. And inasmuch as he has not denied the eloigning, &c., and she does not allege reconciliation, &c., which would be good cause for her endowment, we demand judgment.—STONORE, *ad idem*. She might, after the eloigning, have dwelt with her husband against his will, because possibly she had power over him.—*Mutlow*. She dwelt with her husband, and in his company, years and days, until his death, and with his good will, and with his consent, without coercion of Holy Church; ready, &c.—And the other side said the contrary.

Petition.

(6.)[1] § Robert Hovel[2] sued by Petition to the King, making his suggestion that an Assise was awarded

---

[1] This report is in continuation of Y.B., Easter, 19 Edw. III., No. 36.

[2] As the Assise was brought in Suffolk, the name is more probably Hovel or Hovell than the Welsh Hoel, or Houel, or Howel.

Nos. 5, 6.

par quei veietz si vous voilletz allegger lexecucion
ou demurer en ley.—*Grene* alleggea donqes execucion
estre fait, et qe lautre qe recoveri[1] est tenant par
force del execucion[2]; prest, &c.—*Huse.* Vous futes[3]
tenaunt jour du brief purchace, et cel estat avetz
continue; prest, &c.—*Et alii e contra.*[4]

(5.)[5] § Dowere, ou aloper[6] fuit plede en barre Dowere.
saunz estre recounseille.—*Mutl.* Nous vous dioms qe [Fitz., Dowere, 94.]
soun baroun muruyst a tiel lieu, et vous dioms qe,
saunz cohercion de Seint Eglise,[7] ele demura adonqes
grant[8] temps en sa compaignie; jugement et prioms
nostre dowere.—*Grene.* Et desicome il nad pas dedit
leloigner, &c., et ele nallegge pas recounseiller,[9] &c.,
qe serreit cause de son dowement, jugement.—Ston.,
ad idem. Ele purreit puis leloigner demurer ove[10]
soun baroun countre la[11] gree son baron, qar par
cas ele fuit meistre.—*Mutl.* Ele demura ove[10] son
baron, et[12] en sa compaignie, aunz et jours, tanqe
sa mort, et[13] par le[14] bon[15] gree son baron, et de
son assent, saunz cohercion de Seint Eglise; prest,
&c.—*Et alii e contra.*

(6.)[5] § Robert Hovel[16] suyt par Peticion au Roi, Peticion.
fesaunt sa suggestioun qune Assise en Bank le Roi [19 Li. Ass., 5.]

---

[1] H., respount.
[2] H., jugement.
[3] C., fuistes; D., fuites.
[4] The replication, upon which issue was joined, was, according to the record, " quod a die impetra-
" tionis brevis sui . . . .
" prædictus Gilbertus fuit tenens
" de prædictis tenementis, et
" semper continue seisinam suam
" inde continuavit usque ad hunc
" dicem, et adhuc inde seisitus
" est."
The award of the *Venire* appears on the roll, but nothing further.

[5] From the four MSS. as above.
[6] D., allouper.
[7] D., Esglise.
[8] C., grand.
[9] C., recounseillier.
[10] L., od.
[11] D., le.
[12] et is omitted from H.
[13] et is from C. alone.
[14] le is omitted from H.
[15] bon is omitted from C.
[16] D., Hovelle.

No. 6.

A.D. 1345. against him contrary to law in the King's Bench (see the Assise above), and also that some of the Justices awarded the Assise contrary to the unanimous opinion of their fellows. And the bill of Petition, enclosed in a letter under the Privy Seal, was sent to SIR WILLIAM SCOT, who said that this suit was a slander against the Court in so surmising dishonesty in its Justices. Therefore Robert was ordered into custody, and was put on mainprise to answer to the King.—SCOT said further:—This award of the Assise was made in accordance with the opinion of all the Justices of all the Courts, who told us that such award had often been made in like manner between other parties, and I have often seen it made myself. And others, our fellow-justices, said that we should prejudice this Court if we did not act in that manner; and therefore we hold the award of the Assise to be good. And we previously granted a *Nisi prius*, but, because we were not then certain as to the day, we gave a day over. But now you shall have a definite day in that same county in which the Assise was arraigned.—And he gave a day before himself and his fellows or some of them, the Saturday the morrow of St. John, at B.—And so note the *Nisi prius* in respect of an Assise which has not a day in the Bench, though the parties have.—And note that the whole suit by bill of Petition made to the King was solely upon the award of the Assise made upon the original writ which was extinguished by the removal of the [King's] Bench out of the county.—And SCOT said also that the plea pleaded in bar was naught.—And afterwards, before BASSET in the country, Hovel made default, and his wife prayed to be admitted to defend her right, and the plaintiff prayed the Assise.—And BASSET stayed proceedings, and would

No. 6.

fuit countre ley agarde vers ly (*ride supra* Lassise), <small>A.D.</small> 1345.
et auxint qe countre comune assent de ses com-
paignouns[1] asquns[2] des Justices agarderent Lassise.
Et la bille, enclos deinz la lettre south la targe,
fuit maunde a Mounsire WILLIAM SCOT, qe dit qe
ceste suite fuit fet en esclaundre de la Court, sur-
mettant issint fauxine[3] a les Justices. Par quei
Robert fuit comande en garde, et fuit par meinprise
de respondre au Roi.—SCOT dit outre qe cel agard
fuit fait [par avys de touz les Justices de totes les
Places, qe nous disoint qe sovent ad este fait][4] par
là manere entre autres parties, et issint lay jeo
viewe mesme estre fait. Et autres compaignons nous
disoint qe nous ferroms prejudice a ceste Place si
nous ne feissoms[5] par la manere ; par quei ceo qest
agarde nous le tenoms pur bon. Et nous grantas-
soms autrefoith *Nisi prius*, mes, pur ceo qe nous
fumes pas en certein de jour adonqes, nous donames
jour outre. Mes ore vous averetz jour en certein
en mesme le counte ou Lassise estoit arreyne.[6]—Et
dona jour devant luy et ses compaignouns ou
asquns[7] deux le Samady en lendemein Seint Johan
a B.—*Et sic nota Nisi prius* al Assise qe nad pas
jour en Bank, mes parties ount.—*Et nota* qe tote
la suite par bille[8] fait au Roi fuit soulement sur
lagarde del Assise fait sur loriginal amorti par remuement del Baunk hors del counte.—Et SCOT dit
auxint qe le plee plede en barre fuit un nient.—Et
puis, devant BASSET en pays, Hovelle[9] fit defaut,
et sa femme pria destre resceu, et le pleintif pria
Lassise.—Et BASSET sursist, et ne voleit prendre

---

[1] D., conpaignouns.
[2] C., asqun.
[3] D., faucine.
[4] The words between brackets are omitted from D.
[5] L., fesoimes ; H., fesoms ; D., feisoms.

[6] D., arraine (quite clearly written).
[7] D., asqun.
[8] The words par bille are omitted from D.
[9] H., Hovel.

No. 6.

A.D. 1345 not take the Assise.—Thereupon the wife appeared in
the King's Bench, and was admitted by judgment.—
Skipwith. Now you see plainly that the wife is admitted to defend her right, so that everything done or
pleaded before is null, and the wife is at liberty to plead
just as if everything had to be begun anew on the
original writ; and inasmuch as the original, which
was arraigned in Suffolk, is extinguished by the removal of the Court into another county, the original
has lost its force, unless it is otherwise by reason that
the parties were adjourned on some difficulty, and
that is the reason why you previously held the plea
in this Court, out of the same county. And now that
reason no longer exists; and therefore we understand
that you will not now proceed any further upon this
extinguished original.—*Pole.* We take your records to
witness that she has been admitted, and says nothing
further as a reason why there ought not to be an
Assise. And we pray the Assise. And that which she
says is to the jurisdiction of the Court, which she has
herself affirmed by her prayer to be admitted. Besides,
the matter is in a different condition from that in
which it would be if the writ had been arraigned
against her alone : for heretofore the Court has been
seised of the plea in this place, out of the county, for
sufficient cause, and has held the plea, which cannot
be taken away from it by her husband's default or by
her admission to defend. And, moreover, the writ is
brought against the husband, and the wife, and several
others, and process is continued against the others in
this Court, so that with regard to them it is necessary to
continue that which has been commenced.—SHARSHULLE
(Chief Baron of the Exchequer) came (into the Court of
King's Bench) and said :—The plea is not to the jurisdiction, because it is an established fact that in certain
cases all kinds of pleas are pleadable in this Court—a
writ of Right as well as other writs—but their exception
is that the original is extinguished. And the practice of

No. 6.

Lassise.—Sur quei en Bank le Roi la femme vint, et A.D. 1343.
fuit resceu par agarde.—*Skip*. Ore vous veietz bien[1]
qe la femme est resceu a defendre son dreit, issint
quant qest fait ou plede a devant est nulle, et la
femme a large auxi come tut fuit a comencer de
novel sur loriginal ; et desicome loriginal qe fuit
arreyne[2] en Suffolk, est amorti par remuement de
la Place en autre counte, loriginal ad perdu sa
force, sil ne fuit par cause qe sur asqun difficulte
qe les parties fuissent adjournes, et ceo fuit autrefoith la cause pur quei vous tenistes le plee en
ceste Place, hors de mesme le counte. Et ceste
cause cesse a ore ; par quei nous entendoms qe a
ore vous[3] ne voilletz nulle[4] plus avant[5] aler sur
cest original amorti.—*Pole*. Nous pernoms vos recordes qele est resceu, et autre chose ne dit pur
quei Assise ne deit estre. Et prioms Assise. Et
ceo qele parle est a la jurisdiccion de Court, quel
mesme ele ad afferme par sa prier destre resceu.
Ovesqe ceo, ceo est ore en autre cours qe si le
brief ust este arreyne[6] vers luy soul : qar devant
ces houres la Court sur cause[7] est seisi ceinz hors
del counte de plee, et lad tenu, quel par la defaut
soun baroun ne sa resceit ne poet estre tollet. Et
auxi le brief est porte vers le baroun, et la femme,
et plusours autres, et vers les autres le proces est
continue ceinz, issint qe quant a eux il covient
continuer ceo qest comence.—SCHAR. vint, et dit qe
le plee nest pas a jurisdiccion, qar certeine chose
est qe ceinz en cas toux maneres des plees sont
pledables, brief de Dreit, et autres briefs, mes lour
chalenge est qe loriginal est amorti. Et le cours

---

[1] bien is from D. alone.
[2] D., arraine.
[3] vous is from H. alone.
[4] H., nent. The word is omitted
from C,

[5] D., haut.
[6] L., arraine ; H., araine ; D.,
afferme.
[7] H., la cause.

No. 7.

this Court is that, when parties plead to the Assise, and it is not taken before the removal of the Court out of the same county, the original is extinguished by the removal of the Court. Therefore, since the Court adjourned the parties on a difficulty, and afterwards, when the Court was out of the County, they arrived at the opinion that the Assise should be awarded at large on plea of the parties, they ought to annul the original, and no more hold the plea than if they had awarded the Assise at the beginning.—*Pole.* The Justices of this Court do not hold Assises only in the manner limited by Statute,[1] but as they previously did in this Court before the making of the Statute.[1]—Scot. It would be a strange thing that we should lose jurisdiction, and should extinguish the original through the husband's default, and that we should have warrant to render judgment for the defendant, and not against him. Therefore, will you say anything else?—And then as to parcel she pleaded in bar, and as to parcel to the Assise.

Novel
Disseisin.

(7.) § Novel Disseisin, where land was given to a man and to his wife, and to the heirs male of his body, and they had issue two sons. The elder son had issue two daughters. The father died, and afterwards the elder son died, and after him the mother died, and after her death the younger son entered. The two daughters entered and ousted him, and he re-ousted the daughters, and enfeoffed Stephen de Catefelde, and Henry Stephen's son, against whom and the younger son the two daughters brought the Assise. And judgment was given that they should take nothing, &c.—*Quære*, if the elder son had survived, and attained to an estate by the limitation, whether the daughters would have had the inheritance by the limitation, which in words, extends only to males.

---

[1] 9 Hen. III. (*Magna Charta*), c. 12.

No. 7.

de ceste Place est qe quant parties pledent al Assise, et ele nest pas pris avant lour remuement de mesme le counte, qe par lour remuement loriginal est amorti. Donqes, quant sur difficulte ils ajournent les parties, et apres quant la Place fuit hors del counte, ils furent avises qe Lassise fuit agarde a large sur[1] plee des parties, ils duissent anienter loriginal, et nient plus tenir ple qe sils ussent agarde Lassise a comencement.—*Pole.* Les Justices de ceste Place ne tenent pas les Assises come est limite par statut soulement, mes solonc ceo qils firent a devant en ceste Place avant la fesaunce del estatut.—Scot. Il serreit merveille qe nous perdoms jurisdiccion, et amortiroms loriginal par la defaut le baroun, et qe nous averoms garrant a rendre jugement pur le defendant, et noun pas contre luy. Par quei[2] voil-letz autre chose dire?—Et donqes a parcelle ele pleda en barre, et de parcelle al Assise.

(7.)[3] § Novele disseisine, ou terre fuit done a un *Novele Disseisine.*[4] homme et a sa femme et a les heirs madles de son[5] corps, qavoint issue ij fitz. Leigne fitz avoit issue ij filles. Le pere murust,[6] et donqes leigne fitz murust,[6] et puis la mere devia, apres qi mort le fitz puisne entra. Les ij filles entrerent, et luy ousterent, et il reousta les filles, et feffa Estevene de[7] Catefelde, et Henre son fitz, vers queux et le fitz puisne les ij filles porterent Lassise. Et fuit agarde qeles preissent[8] rienz, &c.—*Quære,* si leigne fitz ust survesqui, et attendu estat par taille, si les filles ussent eu leritage par la taille[9] qe sestent par parole forqe en les madles.

---

[1] C., pur.
[2] The words par quei are omitted from C.
[3] From the four MSS., as above.
[4] H., *Assisa Novæ Disseisinæ.*
[5] L., lour.
[6] C., muruyst.
[7] de is from H. alone.
[8] H., pristrent.
[9] The words par la taille are omitted from D.

Nos. 8–11.

A.D. 1345.
Waste.

(8.) § Note that *Huse* alleged that a writ of Waste was brought against one on whose default at the Grand Distress the Sheriff was commanded to enquire as to the waste, and the waste was found, and therefore he lost, whereas he had never been summoned, attached, or distrained. And *Huse* produced a writ of *Audita Querela* on his case, and prayed a writ of Deceit.— HILLARY. Where have you seen a writ of Deceit granted on an *Audita Querela*?—*Huse.* You can do so without any writ, and the writ is only to prompt you to do that which the law wills. And the Abbot of Vaudey was in the same case, and there a writ of Deceit was granted.—STONORE. But that would be a strange thing after the action has been tried, and the party has had his judgment on verdict.— And afterwards, upon careful consideration, a writ of Deceit was granted.

Scire facias.

(9.) § *Scire facias* upon a recovery on a writ of Dower.—*Grene* prayed a writ to the Sheriff to enquire whether the husband died seised, and further as to the damages.—And he could not have it.—*Quære.*

Debt.

(10.) § Note that on a writ of Debt the defendant denied his deed, and it was found to be his deed, and therefore a *Capias* issued, at the suit of the King, *Alias*, and *Pluries*. And now an Exigent was prayed, and was not granted, but only a *Capias*.

Wardship

(11.) § Wardship, where the parties pleaded to issue to a jury, and a *Nisi prius* was granted thereupon before WILLOUGHBY, and the panel was returned before him by the *Habeas corpora*, and *Octo tales*, as if the whole array had been made by the bailiff of a liberty, and it was alleged for the defendant that the *Venire facias duodecim* had been returned, and the panel had been made and

Nos. 8–11.

(8.) [1] § *Nota* qe *Huse* alleggea qe brief de Wast A.D. 1345.
fuit porte vers un par qi defaut a la grant[2] des- Wast.
tresse maunde fuit au Vicounte denquere del wast, [Fitz., *Disceit*, 3.]
et le wast trove, par quei il perdist, la ou il estoit
unqes somons, attache, ne destreint.[3] Et moustra
brief de *Audita Querela* sur son cas, et pria brief
de Desceite.—[HILL. Ou avetz viewe granter brief
de Desceite][4] sur un *Audita Querela* ?—*Huse*. Vous
le[5] poietz faire sanz brief; et le brief nest forqe
exitacion a vous a faire ceo qe la ley voet. Et
Labbe de Vaude[6] fuit en mesme le cas, et illoeqes[7]
brief de Desceite grante.—STON. Et ceo serreit
merveille quant laccion est trie, et la partie avoit
son jugement sur verdit.—Et puis par bon avys
brief de Desceite fuit grante.

(9.) [1] § *Scire facias* hors dun recoverir sur brief *Scire facias*.
de Dowere.—*Grene* pria brief au Vicounte denquere
si le baron murust seisi, et outre des damages.—
Et non potuit habere.—*Quære.*[8]

(10.) [1] § *Nota* qen brief de Dette le defendant dedit Dette [9]
son fait,[10] et trove fuit son fait : par quei a la suite
le Roi *Capias* issit *sicut alias, sicut pluries*. Et ore
exigende fuit prie, et nest pas grante, mes *Capias*.

(11.) [1] § Garde, ou plede fuit al enqueste, sur quei Garde.
Nisi prius fuit graunte devant[11] WILBY, ou le panel
par le *Habeas corpora*, et *Octo tales*, fuit retourne
devant luy, com si tut[12] larray ust este fait par
baillif de fraunchise, et ou pur le defendant fuit
allegge qe le *Venire facias xij* et le panelle fuit fet

---

[1] From the four MSS., as above.
[2] C., grand.
[3] H., destreinz.
[4] The words between brackets are omitted from H.
[5] H., ne.
[6] H., W.
[7] D., illoesqes.
[8] *Quære* is omitted from L. and C.
[9] H., *Nota*.
[10] C., fet ; D., feat.
[11] H., and C., avant.
[12] D., tote.

No. 11.

A.D. 1345 returned into the Common Bench by the Sheriff, which
Sheriff was of affinity to the plaintiff, and therefore
that an inquest was not to be taken on such an array.
—And because WILLOUGHBY could not be apprised by
whom the first panel was made in virtue of the *Venire
facias*, because he had not the *Venire* of record before
him, he put the parties to proceed, and said that the
point should be saved to them in the Bench. Therefore he took the inquest, which found for the plaintiff,
who prayed his judgment thereupon in the Bench.
—*Thorpe* recited the challenge of the array which had
been made by the Sheriff, as above.—And it was inspected, and found to be an array made by the Sheriff.
—And *Thorpe* said:—We demand judgment, since
this challenge was not and could not be tried in the
country, whether without trial of it the Court ought
to render judgment on such a verdict: for that which
remained untried by reason of want of jurisdiction of
the Justice who took the inquest shall not turn to the
damage of the party, particularly since it was alleged
before judgment: for you can go back and take the
inquest anew just as if nothing had been done.—*Pole*.
We pray judgment on the verdict, for it was never
law to challenge the array of a panel after verdict.
And the words of the record are *Juratores de assensu
partium electi*, and therefore it is not right that he
should be heard with regard to any challenge. Besides, even if the inquest had had to be taken in this
Court, there would have been no challenge unless it
had been alleged that the Sheriff was a procurer and
maintainer, or had put in the polls on the nomination
of the party, and that so there was a challenge of the
polls, who should be tried, &c.—*Thorpe*. Let us be
agreed that the Sheriff was of affinity to the party.
And it seems that this was, as it were, not denied by
the party.—*Pole*. It would be contrary to law to hold

No. 11.

et retourne en Baunk par le Vicounte, le quel Vicounte est del affinite le pleintif, par quei sur tiel array enqueste ne fuit pas a prendre.—Et pur ceo qe WILBY ne pout estre appris par qi le primer panel fuit fet par force del *Venire facias*, pur ceo qil navoit pas cella de recorde devant luy, il les mist outre, et les dit qe ceo lour serreit sauve en Bank. Par quei il prist lenqueste qe chaunta pur le pleintif, sur quei en Bank il pria son jugement. —*Thorpe* rehercea, *ut supra*, le chalenge del array fet par Vicounte.—Et fuit quis, et trove larray fet par Vicounte :—Et demandoms jugement del houre qe cel chalenge ne fuit ne[1] ne poait en pays estre trie, si sanz triement de cel duissent sur tiel enqueste pris jugement rendre : qar ceo qe par noun-poaire del Justice qe prist lenqueste par *Nisi prius* remist nient trie ne tournera pas en damage de partie, nomement desicome cest allegge devant le jugement : qar vous poietz retourner et prendre lenqueste de novel com si rienz ust este fet.—*Pole.* Sur verdit nous prioms jugement, qar ceo ne fuit unqes ley apres verdit de chalenger array del panel. Et le recorde voet *Juratores de assensu partium electi*, par quei nest pas resoun qil soit escote[2] a nulle chalenge. Ovesqe ceo, tut ust lenqueste este a prendre ceinz, ceo nust pas este chalenge si homme nust allegge qe le Vicounte ust este procurour et meintenour, ou mys a denominacion de la partie les testes,[3] et auxint il[4] avoit le[5] chalenge a les testes qe furent tries, &c.—*Thorpe.* Soioms[6] a un qe le Vicounte fuit del affinite la partie. Et il semble qe ceo fuit com nient dedit [de la partie.—*Pole.* Ceo serreit countre

---

[1] L., pas.
[2] C., escute.
[3] The words les testes are omitted from D.

[4] H., qil.
[5] H., son ; the word is omitted from L. and D.
[6] H., Nous sumes.

No. 12.

as not denied this challenge of a party, which the Court could not try at that time, and which the Court ought to try *ex officio*, without putting the party to answer to the challenge.—WILLOUGHBY recorded that the party said, in the country, that the array was wholly made by the bailiff of a liberty, who was in receipt of fee and robes from the party (the reverse of which was found upon trial) and the party thereby accepted it as a fact that the office was not executed by the Sheriff.—*Thorpe.* Want of jurisdiction in the person who took the inquest ought not to turn to our damage; and if he could have tried the matter, and it had been tried, the whole array would certainly have been quashed; therefore now, when it can be tried, the proper course is to go back and try it.—And then the plaintiff's attorney was asked whether the Sheriff was of affinity to the plaintiff or not; and he said that he did not know.—And thereupon judgment was given that the array was not good.—Therefore a new *Venire facias* directed to the Coroners was awarded, and that was entered by reason of the non-denial of the party, and also it was entered that the writ issued to the Coroners on prayer of the plaintiff.—*Skipwith* prayed that the record might be amended, for (said he) we understand that you have said by way of judgment that we are to sue a writ to the Coroners.—WILLOUGHBY and the Clerks said that it will never be entered as either to the Coroners or to the Sheriff in particular, but in accordance with the manner in which the party may choose to pray it; for, if he so choose, he can have, at his peril, a *Venire facias* directed to the Sheriff.—Therefore he prayed a writ directed to the Coroners.—And, if the Justices will grant a day, he has a *Nisi prius.*

Right.   (12.) § The King brought a writ of Right, in respect of a fourth part of the advowson of the tithes of the church of St. Dunstan, against the Prior of the Hospital of St. John of Jerusalem, counting, by *R. Thorpe*, as

No. 12.

ley de tenir nient dedit]¹ cele² chalenge de partie, ^{A.D 1345.}
quel Court adonqes ne poet trier, et quel Court
doffice deit trier, sanz mettre partie a respondre al
chalenge.—WILBY recorda qe la partie en pays dit
qe larray de tut fuit fait par baillif de fraunchise,
quel fuit a fee et robes de la partie, et le revers
trie, acceptant par tant qe loffice ne fuit pas fet
par Vicounte.—*Thorpe.* Nounpoaire de cely qe prist
lenqueste ne nous deit tourner en damage; et sil
le poait aver trie, et il ust este trie, *certum est* qe
tut ust este quasse; *ergo* a ore, ou il poet estre
trie, il covient retourner et le trier.—Et puis fuit
demande del attourne le pleintif si le Vicounte fuit
del affinite le pleintif ou noun; qe dit qil ne savoit.
—Et sur ceo fuit agarde qe larray ne fuit pas bon.
—Par quei novel *Venire facias* fuit³ agarde a les
Coroners, et ceo fuit entre par cause del nient
dedire de la partie, et auxi qe par prier le pleintif
le brief issit as Coroners.—*Skip.* pria qe le record
fuit amende, qar par agarde nous entendoms qe
vous avetz dit qe nous suoms as Coroners.—WILBY,
et les clercs⁴ disoint qe jammes ne serra entre ne
as Coroners ne au Vicounte en certein, mes solonc
ceo qe la partie le voudra prier; qar, sil voudra, il
avera a son peril *Venire facias* au Vicounte.—Par
quei il pria brief as Coroners.—Et si Justices voleint
graunter jour⁵ il ad *Nisi prius.*

(12.)⁶ § Le Roi porta brief de Dreit, de la quarte ^{Dreit.⁷}
partie del avoweson⁸ des dismes del eglise de Seint ^{[Fitz.,
View,}
Dunstan, vers le Prior del Hospital Seint Johan, &c., ^{105.]}
countant⁹ de la seisine son auncestre, par *R. Thorpe,*

---

¹ The words between brackets
are omitted from H.
² C., tiel; D., tele.
³ C., and D., est.
⁴ L., and H., clers.
  jour is omitted from H.

⁶ From the four MSS., as above.
⁷ H., and D., Droit.
⁸ The words del avoweson are
omitted from C.
⁹ H., et counta.

No. 13.

to his ancestor's seisin of the entirety of the advowson, and he made the descent only as to the fourth part.—And exception was taken to this by *Birton*.— But the exception was not allowed, and therefore he demanded view.—*Thorpe*. There is only one church, &c., and if the advowson of the entirety were demanded, view would not be grantable; nor consequently is it now.—*Pole*. That is not a like case, because we cannot know of which fourth part of the tithes [the demand is made].—HILLARY. What you say is true; therefore you may have view.[1]

Cessavit.   (13.) § *Cessavit.*—*Birton.* We tell you that we have an estate only to ourself and the heirs of our body, &c., and that by gift from the demandant; judgment of the declaration, because, if the writ lies in this case, he must count in accordance with his case.— WILLOUGHBY. If he can have an action, the count is good enough.—And *Birton* was put to plead over.— Therefore he demanded judgment whether the writ lay against him who was thus tenant in tail.—*Blaykeston.* And, inasmuch as˙you have not denied that you hold of us, and have not denied the cesser for two years, which gives us the forfeiture against you, and no one can have any advantage of the limitation in tail except the issue in tail, [we also demand judgment].—*Birton.* Then it is so.—*Skipwith.* A writ of *Cessavit* rightly lies as well against tenant in fee tail as against tenant in fee simple: for, if my very tenant enfeoff any one in fee tail, with remainder over to another in fee simple, it is certain that he who is thus enfeoffed to hold in tail will be tenant to the chief lord; therefore, if a writ would lie against such a feoffee in tail, when a remainder is limited over, it will lie for the donor against the donee. —WILLOUGHBY. That does not follow, for if the donor be ousted from such a writ, it is by his own act; but

---

[1] *See* further Y.B., Easter, 20 Edw. III., where the record (*Placita de Banco*, R° 373, d) is cited, and Mich., 20 Edw. III.

No. 13.

A.D. 1345.

del entier del avoweson, et fist la descente de la quarte partie soulement. — Et[1] fuit chalenge par *Byrtone.*—*Sed non allocatur,* par quei il demanda la viewe. — *Thorpe.* Il ny ad qune eglise, &c., et si lavoweson del entier fuit demande, la viewe ne serreit pas grantable; *nec per consequens* a ore.— *Pole.*—*Non est simile,* qar nous ne poms saver de quele quarte partie des dismes.—HILL. Vous ditetz verite; par quei eietz[2] la viewe.

(13.)[3] § *Cessavit.*—*Birtone.* Nous vous dioms qe nous navoms forqe a nous et les heirs de nostre corps, &c., et ceo del doun le demandant; jugement de la moustrance, qar si le brief gise en le cas il countera solonc soun cas.—WILBY. Sil avera accion, le counte est assetz bon.—Et fuit mys outre.—Par quei il demanda jugement si le brief vers nous gise qe sumes issi tenant en la taille.—*Blayk.* Et desi- come vous navetz[4] pas dedit qe vous tenetz de nous, et le cesser par ij aunz, quel doune[5] la forfaiture devers vous, et de la taille nul homme navera lavantage forqe lissue en la taille.—*Birtone.* Donqes[6] est il issi.—*Skip.* Brief de *Cessavit* par resoun gist si bien vers tenant en[7] fee taille com en fee simple: qar si moun verroy tenant feffe un homme en fee taille, le remeindre outre a un autre en fee simple, *certum est* qil serra tenant a chief seignur qest issint feffe a tenir en la taille; par quei si brief girreit vers un tiel feffe en la[8] taille, quant le remeindre est taille outre, *ergo* pur le donour vers le done.— WILBY. *Non sequitur,* qar si le donour soit ouste de tiel brief, cest son fait demene; mes issint nest pas

Cessavit.
[Fitz.,
Cessavit,
30.]

---

[1] C., and D., qe.
[2] C., eit.
[3] From the four MSS., as above.
[4] L., and C., navietz.

[5] D., doun nous doune in later hand.
[6] C., and D., Et donqes.
[7] L., and C., de.
[8] la is from D. alone.

No. 14.

A.D. 1345. it is not so with regard to the chief lord, who is compelled by the act of another person to accept as his tenant the person enfeoffed in that manner.—And afterwards the writ abated by judgment.—*Quære*, if a remainder in fee simple had been limited over, whether the writ would lie.

Quid juris clamat. (14.) § *Quid juris clamat.* A lady against whom, &c., said that the conusor was her son, who had no estate except by limitation to her husband and herself and the heirs of their bodies, and demanded judgment, inasmuch as the conusor, after her death, would be put to claim by descent through her, whether by reason of his grant she should be put to attorn.—*Pole.* On the day on which the note of the fine was made she

No. 14.

de chief seignur, qest par autri fait chasce de accepter luy qest feffe par la manere destre son tenant.—Et puis par agarde le brief abatit.—*Quære* si le remeindre fuit taille de fee simple outre si le brief girreit. A.D. 1345.

Quid juris clamat.

(14.) [1] § *Quid juris clamat.* Une Dame vers qi,[2] &c., dit qe le reconissour[3] fuit son fitz, qe navoit forqe par une taille a son baroun et luy et les heirs de lour corps, et demanda[4] jugement, desicome le conissour,[5] apres sa mort, serra mys a clamer par descente par my luy, si par son grant ele serra mys dattourner.[6]—*Pole.* Jour de la note fet ele tient

[1] From the four MSS., as above, but corrected by the record, *Placita de Banco*, Trin., 19 Edw. III., R° 81, d. It there appears that the *Quid juris clamat* was brought by Thomas son of Maurice de Berkele, knight, against Amice de Beauchaumpe, in respect of the manor of Ivedene (Bucks), which Reginald de Monte Forti had granted to him by fine.

" Et prædicta Amicia quæsita " quid juris clamat in prædicto " manerio, et si se attornare " voluerit, &c."

[2] L., and C., qe.

[3] H., conissour.

[4] C., and D., demandoms.

[5] D., reconisour.

[6] According to the roll (which is illegible on one side) Amice pleaded " quod ipsa se attornare non debet, " quia dicit quod quidam Hugo . . . " . . . . forde, miles, " seisitus fuit de manerio prædicto, " cum pertinentiis, in dominico " suo ut de feodo, ... " . . . . . tam suam dedit " ipsi Amiciæ et heredibus suis de " corpore suo legitime procreatis, " . . . . " capitalibus dominis feodi, &c., " et reddendo inde præfato Hugoni " et Margeriæ un . . . . . . " . . . . . . utriusque ipsorum Hugonis et Margeriæ quinquaginta libras, et post decessum " . . . . " reddendo inde heredibus ipsius " Hugonis unam rosam ad festum " Nat . . . . " secularibus demandis Et si " contigerit prædictam Amiciam " sine herede . . . . " procreato . . . . decedere, " quod prædictum manerium, cum " omnibus pertinentiis suis ad . . " . . . . ux " . . . ejus si eadem Margeria " eum supervixerit ad totam vitam " ipsius . . . . ad heredes " ipsius Hugonis post decessum " ipsius Margeriæ, ... " . . prædictus Hugo obligavit se et " heredes suos ad warantizandum " prædictum manerium . . . . . . " . . . . prædictæ, &c., et " profert hic prædictam chartam " ipsius Hugonis, ... " . . . . prædicta testatur. " Et dicit quod postea . . . . " levavit quidam finis . . . .

No. 14.

A.D. 1345. held of our conusor for term of her life, in accordance with that which the note supposes; ready, &c.—*R. Thorpe.* You must say for term of life only, and not in fee tail as we say.—*Pole.* Then you refuse the averment, for we will not say anything else.—WILLOUGHBY to *Thorpe.* He pleads sufficiently to you, and you are rightly at a traverse.—*Thorpe.* That does not appear to us to be so : for we acknowledge a tenancy for term of life, and that in a certain manner, in respect of which tenancy we ought not to attorn by reason of the grant of the person who is conusor, and that point we put to judgment.—*Pole.* We shall not be put to plead, outside the note of the fine, to that which you say as to the entail, to which we are a stranger; and, inasmuch as we tender the averment that, on the day on which the note was made, you held for term of life, in accordance with that which the note supposes, which fact you do not deny, we demand judgment.—STONORE, *ad idem.* It is possible that, even though the tenancy was, at one time, such as you suppose by the entail, the tenancy has subsequently been changed : for the son may afterwards have come into possession, and have enfeoffed his mother for term of her life, and therefore the averment is admissible,

---

" . . . . Margeriam uxorem
" ejus querentes, et Amiciam
" Peverel deforciantem, ... :.
" . . . . unde
" placitum Conventionis summoni-
" tum fuit inter eos . . . .
" . . . . Margeria
" recognovit prædictum mane-
" rium, cum omnibus suis perti-
" nentiis, esse jus ipsius . . . . . .
" . . . . fine et
" concordia eadem Amicia con-
" cessit prædictis Hugoni et
" Margeriæ . . . . ·. . . .
" . . . habendum. et tenendum
" eisdem Hugoni et Margeriæ de

" prædicta Amicia et heredibus . .
" . . . .
" . . tota vita utriusque ipsorum
" Hugonis et Margeriæ, reddendo
" inde p . . . .
" . . Nativitatis Sancti Johannis
" Baptistæ pro omni servitio,
" consuetudine, et exactione, ad
" . . . . prædictos
" pertinente, et faciendo inde
" capitalibus dominis feodi illius
" pro . . . .
" prædictis omnia alia servitia quæ
" ad prædictum manerium perti-
" nent. Et p . . . .
" . . .·. . war . . . . eisdem

No. 14.

de nostre conissour a terme de sa vie solonc ceo A.D. 1345.
qe la note suppose; prest, &c.—*R. Thorpe.* Vous
dirretz a terme de vie soulement, et noun pas en
fee taille com nous dioms.—*Pole.* Donqes refusetz
laverement, qar nous ne voloms autre chose dire.—
WILBY a *Thorpe.* Il vous dit assetz, et par resoun
vous estes a travers.—*Thorpe.* Ceo nous semble pas:
qar nous conissoms tenance a terme de vie, et ceo
en manere, de qele tenance par son grant qest
connissour nous ne devoms attourner, et ceo mettoms
en jugement.—*Pole.* Nous serroms pas a vostre dit
de la taille, a quei nous sumes estrange, mys de
pleder hors de la note; et desicome nous tendoms
daverer qe, jour de la note, vous tenistes a terme
de vie solonc ceo qe la note suppose, quele chose
vous ne dedites pas. jugement.—STON., *ad idem.* Il
est possible qe tut fut la tenance tiele come vous
supposez par la taille a un temps qe puis la tenance est chaunge: qar le fitz puis[1] poet aver avenu[2]
et aver feffe sa mere a terme de sa vie, par quei
laverement est resceivable, a ceo qe semble, pur ceo

" Hugoni et Margeriæ prædictum
" manerium, cum pertinentiis, per
" p . . . .
" vita utriusque ipsorum Hugonis
" et Margeriæ. Et post decessum
" utriusque ipsorum . . . .
" . . . . manerium, cum
" pertinentiis, integre remaneret
" ad prædictam Amiciam et
" heredes suos . . . .
" . . . . Hugonis et Margeriæ
" tenendum de capitalibus dominis
" feodi illius per servitiæ quæ . .
" . . . . in
" perpetuum Et si contigerit quod
" prædicta Amicia obiret sine
" herede de corpore . . . .
" . . . . integre reman-
" eret propinquioribus heredibus

" ipsius Hugonis tenendum de . .
" . . . . servitia
" quæ ad illud manerium pertinent
" in perpetuum. Et profert hic
" partem finis . . . .
" Et sic dicit quod ipsa tenet
" manerium prædictum in feodo
" talliato juxta . . . .
" . . . . . etquod idem Reginaldus,
" &c., est filius ejusdem Amiciæ
" cui idem m . . . .
" . . . . dere debet per formam doni
" et finis prædictorum. Et petit
" judicium si per concess . . . . . .
" . . . . prædicto
" Thomæ attornare, &c."

[1] H., puisne.
[2] H., venu; the word is omitted
from D.

Nos. 15, 16.

A.D. 1345. as it seems, because the continuance of the estate tail is not proved, although at one time it existed, &c.—Therefore the averment was joined that she was tenant for term of life in accordance with that which the note supposes; ready, &c.—And the other said tenant in fee tail, as above, and not for term of life; ready, &c.—And the other side said the contrary.

Wardship of the body.

(15.) § Writ of wardship of the body. It was pleaded to issue to a jury whether the ancestor held of the plaintiff or not. It was found by the jury that the infant's ancestor held of the plaintiff by knight service, and that the infant was married, and that he was of the age of thirteen years only, and so *infra annos nubiles*, and that the value of the marriage, having regard to all the lands that he will have by descent, was 100 marks, and further that there were damages to the amount of thirty marks.—KELSHULLE, with the assent of his fellows, gave judgment that the plaintiff should recover the value of the marriage, and the damages as assessed, so that the whole should amount to six score and ten marks, &c.

Mesne.

(16.) § Note that Simon de Cattefelde brought a writ of Mesne against a Prior. It was prosecuted as far as the return of the Proclamation, when the Prior did not appear, and the question remained, until now, under consideration of the Court, whether judgment should be given or not, and so an *alias* Distress was now awarded, and not a forjudger, because the Prior ought not by his default to cause disherison to his church.

Nos. 15, 16.

qe la continuance[1] de la taille nest pas prove[2] A.D. 1345.
coment qe la taille a asqun temps y fuit, &c.—Par
quei laverement fuit joint qe tenant a terme de vie
solonc ceo qe la note suppose; prest, &c.[3]—Et lautre
qe tenant de fee taille *ut supra*, et noun pas a
terme de vie; prest, &c.—*Et alii e contra.*

(15.)[4] § Brief de Garde de corps. Plede fuit al Garde de corps.[5]
enqueste le quel launcestre tient del pleintif ou [Fitz.,
noun. Trove fuit par enqueste qe launcestre lenfant *Jugement,*
tient del pleintif par service de chivaler, et qe len- 172.]
fant est marie, et qil est del age de xiij aunz
soulement, et issint *infra annos nubiles,* et qe la
value del mariage, eaunt regarde a totes[6] les terres
qil avera par descente vaut c marcz, et outre les
damages de xxx marcz.—KELL., par[7] assent de ses
compaignouns, agarda qe le pleintif recoverast la
value del mariage, et les damages taxes, issint qe
tut courge en damage de $\frac{xx}{vi}$ et x marcz, &c.

(16.)[8] § *Nota* qe Simond de[9] Cattefelde porta Mene.
brief de Mene vers un Priour. Tant suy qe a la [Fitz.,
Proclamacion retourne il ne vint pas, et pendist en *Jugement*
avys de Court tanqore si le jugement se freit ou 171.]
noun, par quei fuit ore agarde destresse *sicut alias,*
et noun pas forjuger, pur ceo qe le Priour par sa
defaut ne[10] deit pas[11] desheriter sa eglise.

---

[1] H., tenance.

[2] H., peri.

[3] According to the record, the pleading was, "quod die levationis
"Notæ inter ipsum . . . .
"prædicto manerio . . . .
"eadem Amicia fuit tenens . . . .
". . . . ad terminum vitæ suæ
"tantum, sicut per Notam et præ-
"dictum breve suum supponitur,
"et non in feodo [talliato sicut]
"ipsa Amicia dicit."
  Issue was joined upon this.
  There were several adjournments, but nothing further appears
upon the roll.

[4] From the four MSS., as above.

[5] The words de corps are from
C. alone.

[6] L., toux.

[7] H., del.

[8] From L., C., and D.

[9] de is from C. alone.

[10] ne is from D. alone, and in a
later hand.

[11] pas is from D. alone, and in a
later hand.

No. 17.

A.D. 1345.
Debt.

(17.) § Debt brought by John de Kirketon against John de Godesfeld. And *profert* was made of a specialty. —*Sadelyngstanes.* By this deed indented you granted that, if we should not be of ill behaviour nor commit any trespass against you or yours, and should not be found guilty by twelve good men of such trespass, the deed, into the hands of whomsoever it had passed, should be held as null; and we tell you that we have not been of ill behaviour, and have not committed any trespass against you or yours; judgment whether an action, &c. And he alleged further that the obligation was delivered to one A.,[1] as to an impartial hand, on that condition.—*Skipwith.* We tell you that, since the

---

[1] For the real name *see* p. 161, note 5.

No. 17.

(17.)[1] § Dette porte par Johan de Kyrketone vers A.D. 1345.
Johan Godesfeld. Et especialte mys avant.—*Sadl.* Dette.
Par ceo fait endente vous grantastes qe si[2] nous
ne[3] nous[4] mesportames ne trans ne feimes a vous
ne a les voz, de quel trans nous serroms atteintz
par xij bones gentz, qe le fait en qi meins qil
devynt serra tenu pur nulle; et vous dioms qe nous
ne nous mesportames pas ne trans ne feimes a vous
ne a les voz; jugement si accion, &c. Et alleggea
outre qe lobligacion fut baille en owelle main sur la
condicion a un A.[5]—*Skip.* Nous vous dioms qe, puis

---

[1] From L., H., C., and D., but corrected by the record, *Placita de Banco*, Trin., 19 Edw. III., R⁰ 106. It there appears that the action was brought in the County of Lincoln by John de Kirketon against John de Godesfeld in respect of a debt of £20. The declaration ends " Et profert hic " in Curia quoddam scriptum sub " nomine prædicti Johannis de " Godesfeld quod prædictum debi- " tum testatur."

[2] L., H., and C., quant qe. This has originally been the reading in D. also, but has there been altered in a later hand to si, which agrees with the record.

[3] ne is from D. alone, in a later hand.

[4] nous is omitted from H. and D.

[5] The plea was, according to the record, " quod . . . . apud Horn- " castre ita convenit inter prædic- " tos Johannem de Kirketone et " Johannem de Godesfeld, vide- " licet, cum idem Johannes de " Godesfeld per scriptum suum " obligetur eidem Johanni de " Kirketone in prædictis viginti " libris solvendis eidem Johanni " de Kirketone, ad festum Sancti

" Michaelis prædictum, prout in " prædicto scripto continetur, præ- " dictum scriptum ex assensu " prædictorum Johannis et Jo- " hannis liberatum fuit cuidam " Roberto Brettone, chivaler, cus- " todiendum, sub tali conditione " quod si prædictus Johannes de " Godesfeld extunc versus præ- " dictum Johannem de Kirketone " vel aliquem suorum transgressus " fuisset vel male se haberet, et " inde per bonos et legales homines " inventus fuisset culpabilis quod " tunc prædictum scriptum obliga- " torium in suo robore existens per " prædictum Robertum Bretone " præfato Johanni liberaretur, et " si prædictus Johannes de Godes- " feld extunc prædicto [*sic*] Jo- " hanni de Kirketone seu aliquem " [*sic*] suorum transgressus non " fuisset quod prædictus Robertus " Bretone prædictum scriptum " penes se retineret, et scriptum " illud pro nullo haberetur, et " dicit quod ipse post diem præ- " dictum prædicto Johanni de " Kirketone nec alicui suorum " transgressus non fuit nec male " se habuit. Et hoc paratus est " verificare, unde petit judicium,

No. 17.

A.D. 1345. execution of this indenture, you, at such a place, beat A.[1] and B.[1] our servants, by reason whereof we lost their services for so much time, whereupon we brought a *Justicies* in the county court, in respect of the same obligation, against A.,[2] in whose custody it was, and he appeared, and alleged that he held it on condition, as above, &c., and prayed a garnishment against you, and had it. And you, being warned, did not appear, and therefore the deed of obligation was delivered to us; judgment, and we pray the debt and our damages.— *Sadelyngstanes.* You see plainly how his own deed purports that the obligation was to be held as null, except in case we committed a trespass, and were found guilty of that trespass, and he does not allege

---

[1] For the real names *see* p. 163, note 1.

[2] For the real name *see* p. 163, note 1.

No. 17.

la confeccion de cele endenture, a tiel lieu vous A.D. 1345. batistes A. et B. nos servantz, par quei nous per-dimes lour services par tant de temps, sur quei nous portames *Justicies* en counte de mesme lobliga-cion vers A., en qi garde, &c., qe vynt et alleggea qil lavoit par condicion, *ut supra*, &c., et pria gar-nisement vers vous et lavoit. Et vous garny ne venistes pas, par quei lescript del obligacion fut livere a nous; jugement, et prioms la dette et noz damages.[1]—*Sadl.* Vous veiez bien coment son fait demene voet qe lobligacion soit tenu pur nulle, sil ne fuit issint qe nous[2] trespassames, de quel trans nous fussoms[3] atteint, et il allegge nulle atteindre

---

" &c. Et profert hic in Curia " quoddam scriptum indentatum " sub nomine prædicti Johannis " de Kirketone, quod hoc testatur, " &c."

[1] The replication was, according to the record, " quod prædictus " Johannes de Godesfeld postea " . . . . . insultum fecit in quosdam " Laurentium le Hunte et Rogerum " le Warde, servientes ipsius Jo-" hannis de Kirketone, et ipsos " verberavit, vulneravit, et male " tractavit, per quod idem Jo-" hannes de Kirketone servitium " eorundem hominum et servien-" tium suorum per unum quarte-" rium anni amisit, per quod idem " Johannes de Kirketone postea " tulit quoddam breve domini " Regis quod dictur *Justicies* versus " prædictum Robertum Bretone " coram Vicecomite Lincolniæ in " Comitatu suo quod prædictum " scriptum ei redderet, qui quidem " Robertus ibidem placitando dixit " quod scriptum prædictum ei " liberatum fuit sub conditione " prædicta, et quod ipse paratus " fuit prædictum scriptum reddere " cui prædictorum Johannis de " Kirketone et Johannis de Godes-" feld Curia consideraverit, &c., " per quod prædictus Johannes de " Godesfeld postea præmunitus " fuit essendi ibidem ad certum " diem ad ostendendum si quid " pro se haberet vel dicere sciret " quare prædictum scriptum obli-" gatorium prædicto Johanni de " Kirketone liberari non deberet, " qui quidem Johannes de Godes-" feld tunc non venit, per quod per " considerationem Curiæ illius " prædictum scriptum ipsi Johanni " de Kirketone liberatum fuit, Et " sic, virtute scripti prædicti, et " pro eo quod idem Johannes de ' Godesfeld fecit prædictis ser-" vientibus ipsius Johannis de " Kirketone prædictam transgres-" sionem, petit ipse prædictum " debitum, una cum damnis, &c., " sibi adjudicari, &c."

[2] All the MSS., except D., nous ne.

[3] H., and C., fumes.

No. 18.

any conviction in our person; judgment whether the law puts us to answer to that which he has said, since he has not in the plea observed the condition which there is in his own deed.—*Skipwith.* And, inasmuch as you have not denied the trespass, as above, nor that heretofore you were warned to show cause why the obligation should not be delivered to us, at which time you ought to have appeared, and did not, and so it was through your default that the trespass was not tried then, we demand judgment, and pray the debt, &c.—STOUFORD to *Skipwith.* It seems to him that you ought first to sue a writ of Trespass, and convict him of trespass, and bring this writ afterwards, and not before. And, on the other hand, it seems to us that, since you are now ready to convict him of the trespass, that ought to suffice for you, and maintain your action. Are you willing on both sides that your plea should be entered in that manner?— *Sadelyngstanes* did not dare to abide judgment, but said that he did not beat the plaintiff's servants; ready, &c.—And the other side said the contrary.

Quare non admisit. (18.) § The King brought a *Quare non admisit* against the Bishop of Lincoln, in the King's Bench, counting that he had recovered his presentation against the Prior of Wymondham, who was an alien, by reason of the lands of the Priory having been seized into his hand, &c., and that he had thereupon sent his writ to the Bishop to admit his presentee.—*Skipwith.* We tell you that, long before the lands were seized into the

No. 18.

en nostre persone; jugement si a ceo qil ad dit, A.D. 1345. del houre qe par plee il nad servy la condicion en son fait demene, la ley nous mette a respondre.— *Skip.* Et, desicome vous navetz[1] pas dedit le trans, *ut supra,* et autrefoith qe vous̀ fuistes garny pur quei lobligacion a nous ne duist estre livere, a quel temps vous duissetz aver venu, et ne feistes pas, et issint vostre defaut qe le trans adonqes nust este trie, jugement, et prioms la dette, &c.—STOUF. a *Skip.* Il luy semble qe vous duissetz primes suyre brief[2] de Trans, et luy atteindre de trans, et apres porter ceo brief, et devant nient. [Et, dautre part, semble a nous, del houre qe vous estes a ore prest datteindre le trans, qe ceo vous deit suffire, et][3] meintenir vostre accion. Voillez vous dune part et dautre qe vostre plee soit entre par la manere?— *Sadl.* nosa demurer, mes dit qil ne batist pas ses servantz; prest, &c.—*Et alii e contra.*[4]

(18.)[5] § Le Roi porta *Quare non admisit* vers *Quare non* Levesqe de Nicol, en Baunk le Roi, countant coment *admisit.* il avoit recoveri son presentement vers le Prior de *Quare non* Wymondham alien, par cause des terres la Priorie *admisit,* seisiz en sa mein, &c., et sur ceo maunda brief[6] *7.]* al Evesqe de resceiver, &c.—*Skip.* Nous vous dioms qe longe temps devant qe les terres furent seisiz en

---

[1] L., and C., navietz.

[2] H., and D., par brief.

[3] The words between brackets are omitted from H.

[4] The rejoinder, upon which issue was joined, immediately follows the replication on the roll, viz:—" quod ipse non fecit præ-" dictis Laurentio et Rogero ser-" vientibus prædicti Johannis de " Kirketone prædictam transgres-" sionem, sicut prædictus Johannes " de Kirketone dicit."

After adjournments the defend-ant made default, and the verdict was taken against him by default at *Nisi prius.* The jury found that he was guilty of the trespass, and assessed the damages for non-payment of the debt at the appointed time at £4. Judgment was thereupon given for the plaintiff to recover the debt and damages, and the plaintiff had execution by *Elegit.*

[5] From L., C., and D.

[6] brief is from D. alone.

No. 18.

King's hand, and while they were in the Prior's hand, the same church was full of one A., who was presented by the Prior, who has continued that estate, and who is still parson imparsonee; and we do not understand that the King will be answered with regard to this writ brought against us.—*Thorpe.* You see plainly how he claims nothing in the patronage, and this writ is brought against him as minister and officer, in which case he cannot excuse himself by reason of the possession of another person, particularly inasmuch as he cannot judge of the King's title; and we pray that he be convicted of contempt.—*Skipwith.* Even though the Bishop be a minister, regard must be had to that which he can lawfully do; and beyond that, in respect of what he cannot lawfully do, no law will compel him. Now it is certain that if a parson be in possession by due process in accordance with the law of Holy Church, the Bishop will not be able to oust him without committing a tort against him; therefore even though one recover against another by consent, and without title, the Bishop is possibly not thereby compelled to admit his presentee, and oust one who has very possession: for one who should be so ousted would, notwithstanding the judgment of the King's Court, have a remedy against the Bishop in Court Christian, and would convict him of the tort.—Scot. The Bishop is bound by the law of Holy Church, and is also bound to execute the King's commands. Therefore, suppose the one law to be contrariant to the other, shall we therefore leave our judgments unexecuted, or would it therefore be right that the Bishop should be excused from executing the King's commands? as meaning to say that it would not be so.— And you know well that time does not run against the King; and therefore, whensoever he may recover, it is necessary, according to the opinion of some people, to admit his presentee. And I saw the Arch-

No. 18.

la mein le Roi, tanqe eles furent en la mein le A.D. 1345.
Prior, mesme leglise fuit pleine dun A. presente par
le Prior, qe cel estat ad continue, et unqore est
persone enpersone ; et nentendoms pas qe vers nous
le Roi veot a cest brief estre respondu.—*Thorpe.*
Vous veietz bien coment il ne cleyme rienz en
lavowere, et cest brief est porte vers luy come
ministre et officer, ou il ne se poet excuser par
autri possession, nomement desicome il ne poet al
title le Roi juger ; et prioms qil soit atteint del
contempte.—*Skip.* Tut soit Levesqe ministre, il fait
a regarder ceo qil poet de ley faire ; et outre ceo
qil ne purra pas faire nulle ley ne luy constreindra.
Ore est il certein qe si une persone soit einz en
possession par deuwe proces come atteint[1] par ley
de Seinte Eglise, Levesqe sanz tort fere a ly ne
ly purra ouster ; donqes tut recovere un[2] vers un
autre par consent et sanz title, par cas Levesqe
par tant nest pas arce de resceivere son presente,
et ouster celuy qad la verroy possession : qar cely
qe issint fut ouste, *non obstante* le[3] jugement de la
Court le Roi, avera remedie vers Levesqe en Court
Christiene, et ly atteindra del tort.—Scot. Levesqe
est oblige a la ley de Seinte Eglise, et auxint est
oblige de fere execucion des maundementes le Roi.
Donqes posetz qe lune ley soit contrariaunt a lautre,
lerroms nous par tant nos jugements nient executes,
ou serreit il par tant resoun qe Levesqe soi excusereit de faire execucion des maundementes le
Roi? *quasi diceret non.*—Et vous savetz[4] bien qe
temps ne court pas au Roi ; par quei quele houre
qil recovere il covient al entent dasquns resceivre
son presente. Et jeo vie Lercevesqe de Caunterbirs

---

[1] D., il atteint.
[2] un is from D. alone.
[3] le is from D. alone.
[4] C., saveretz.

No. 18.

bishop of Canterbury in a *Quare non admisit* for the King in this Court in a worse case than this Bishop is, and he would have been convicted of contempt in accordance with the opinion of all the sages of the law if the King had not pardoned him.—BASSET. The King the grandfather of the present King brought a *Quare non admisit*, before Roger Brabason, against Thomas de Corbrigge, Archbishop of York, in respect of a prebend in the Church of St. Peter of York, which he had recovered, and the Archbishop alleged that the Pope had a long time previously provided to the same prebend one whom he did not dare and had not the power to oust. And Brabason said to him: "That which you allege to be want of power we hold to be want of will." Therefore he was held guilty of contempt, and his temporalities were seized, and remained in the King's hand during all the life of that Archbishop.—*Mutlow.* The Bishop ought to do all that lies in his power, and to put the King's presentee in possession, and afterwards the dispute would remain between the clerks as to which of them had right.—SCOT. There are cases in which the Bishop will make a church void of a parson against the parson's will, and then he must afterwards make satisfaction to the parson.—THORPE (JUSTICE). That is true, and that may be in a case in which a Bishop encumbers a church within the period of six months. And it seems that, even though a Bishop be a minister, he must be adjudged to be of a different condition from that of a Sheriff, for if a writ be sent to a Sheriff to deliver seisin of any land by force of a recovery in a case in which the judgment has been against one who had nothing, it will not lie in the Sheriff's mouth to allege that he could not effect execution for such a reason: for, even though he deliver seisin, the person who is tenant is not thereby ousted; but some people think that a Bishop, in a case in which he ought to execute

No. 18.

en un *Quare non admisit* ceinz en pire cas pur le
Roi qe cest nest, et[1] ust este atteint del contempte
par avys de toux les sages si le Roi ne luy ust
fait grace.—BASSET. Le Roi laiel porta *Quare non
admisit,* devant Roger Brabasoun, vers Thomas Corbrige,[2] Ercevesqe Deverwyke, dune provandre en
leglise Seint Pere Deverwyke, qil avoit recoveri, et
Lercevesqe alleggea qe le Pape longe temps avant
avoit purvewe a mesme la provandre, &c., et il
nosast ne fuit de powere[3] de ly ouster. Et Brabasoun luy dit ceo qe vous alleggetz pur noun powere[3]
nous le tenoms pur[4] nient voler; par quei il fuit
atteint del contempte, et ses temporaltes seisiz, et
demurerent en la mein le Roi tote la vie cele
Ercevesqe.—*Mutl.* Levesqe duist faire ceo qen ly
est, et mettre le presente le Roi en possession, et
apres le debat serreit entre les clercs qi deux avoit
dreit.—SCOT. Il y ad cas ou Levesqe voidra leglise
dune persone maugre le soen, et si covient il apres
qil face gree a la persone.—THORPE (JUSTICE). Il
est verite, et ceo poet estre ou Evesqe encombre
leglise deinz le temps, &c. Et il semble qe, tut
soit Evesqe ministre, il serra ajuge dautre condicion
qun Vicounte, a qi si brief soit maunde de liverer
seisine dune terre par force dun recoverir, la ou
le jugement se tailla vers celuy qe rienz navoit, la
ne girreit il pas en bouche le Vicounte dallegger
qil ne poet pas faire execucion par tiele enchesoun:
qar, tut livere il la seisine, celuy qest tenant nest
pas par tant ouste; mes asquns gentz quident qe
Levesqe, la ou il deit faire execucion de brief le

---

[1] et is from D. alone.
[2] Corbrige is omitted from C.
[3] D., poair.
[4] pur is from C. alone.

No. 18.

the King's writ to admit the King's presentee, must first make the church void if it be full of any other person.—*Mutlow*. The King could take his title in a general way from the time of King Richard before the statute now lately made in the fourteenth year.[1]— THORPE (JUSTICE). Some people hold that statute to be of no effect to forclose the King, for it was never put in operation.—And so said SCOT, adding "And now for your answer over."—*Mutlow*. Then if the King takes his title from so remote a time, and recovers by very title on action tried, it is certain that the Bishop, who claims nothing in the patronage, cannot counterplead his title; and, even though the King recovers by default, the law holds good in that way. Now in this matter, although it is shown that the King recovered in right of the Priory and against the Prior who is admitted to be patron by right, so that the King's recovery puts him in possession of the patronage for the time during which the temporalities remain in his hand, and that by good title, and for that reason this presentation has accrued to him, nevertheless the Bishop has never to acknowledge the title on which the King recovered, and the writ which he receives does not mention it, so that the recovery, for anything that could fall under his notice, might as well have been in the time of the King's progenitors as in his own time; and therefore the Bishop could never be excused on the ground of such plenarty. And we tell you further that you are certified by the Official of the Court of Arches that he whom they allege to be parson never was parson, and that certificate has come into this Court by virtue of the King's writ.—*Skipwith*. There is no stress to be laid on that: for the party never put himself on any such issue, so that it is only *ex officio*.—*Seton*. You have also alleged by plea for the King that the Bishop took an Inquest of Office for the King's presentee, which was in his favour, and by

---

[1] 14 Edw. III., St. 4 (Clergy), c. 2.

No. 18.

Roi de resceivre le presente le Roi, qil covient primes A.D. 1345. voider leglise si ele soit pleine de nulle autre.— *Mutl.* Le Roi poet prendre son title generalment de temps le Roi Richard avant lestatut fait ore tard *anno xiiij.*—THORPE (JUSTICE). Ascuns gentz tenent cel estatut de nulle value de forclore le Roi, qar ceo ne fuit unqes mys en oevre.[1]—*Et sic dixit* SCOT. Ore outre vostre respons.[2]—*Mutl.* Donqes si le Roi prent son title de si haut temps, et recovere par verroy title sur[3] accion trie, *certum est* qe Levesqe ne[4] poet son title countrepleder qe rienz ne cleyme en lavowere; et, tut recovere le Roi par defaute, la ley se tient par la manere. Ore en cest matere, coment qil est moustre qe le Roi recoveri en la dreit de la Priorie et vers le Prior qest conu[5] patron de dreit, issint qe le recoverir le Roi luy mette en possession del avowere pur le temps qe les temporaltes demurent en sa mein, et ceo par bone title, par quei cel presentement luy est acru, nepurquant Levesqe nad jammes a conustre sur quel title le Roi recoveri, ne le brief qe luy vint ne fist pas mencion de cella, issint qe le recoverir,[6] pur rienz qe cherreit en notice de luy, purreit auxi bien estre en temps de ses progenitours comme de son temps demene; par quei par tiele plenerte il[7] se purrait jammes excuser. Et outre vous dioms qe par Lofficer des Arches estes vous ascerte qe celuy qils dient estre persone ne fuit unqes persone, et cest venutz ceinz par brief le Roi.—*Skyp.* Ceo nest pas a charger: qar partie se mist unqes en tiel issue, issi qe ceo nest forqe office.—*Setone.* Vous avetz[8] auxi[9] par plee allegge pur le Roi qe Levesqe prist enqueste doffice pur le presente le Roi, qe luy

---

[1] D., coure.
[2] L., and C., persone.
[3] C., soun.
[4] ne is omitted from D.
[5] D., com.

[6] L., and C., Roi.
[7] il is from D. alone.
[8] L., and C., avietz.
[9] auxi is omitted from C.

No. 18.

A.D. 1345. which the voidance and all the circumstances were found; and therefore the Bishop ought then, according to law, to have put the King's presentee in possession, and so that which he has admitted cannot excuse him in opposition to that which has been pleaded on behalf of the King.—WILLOUGHBY. The Bishop ought always, in such case, to execute the King's command, and the dispute will afterwards be between the clerks; and you may rest assured that with regard to the King the case is different from that which it is with regard to another person among the people, for the latter cannot affirm any tort in the Ordinary for encumbering the church, unless he previously brings a Prohibition or makes a presentation so that the Bishop may be apprised, whereas it is not necessary for the King to bring a Prohibition, because the Ordinary is bound to acknowledge the King's right. — *Skipwith.* Then, according to your statement, it would be law that even though a parson were in possession by ever so good a title, with the consent of his patron, who cannot deny it, he would be ousted on a *Quare impedit* brought for the King: for, in the Common Bench, you hold it to be law that, unless the Bishop ousts the one who is in, he cannot admit the presentee of the King or of any one else.—WILLOUGHBY. Yes. And that he can and ought to do. And in the *Quare non admisit* in the Common Bench,[1] the other day, if the Bishop of Exeter had not said that he admitted the presentee as soon as the writ came to him, he would have been found guilty of contempt; and so was Archbishop Thomas de Corbrigge, notwithstanding the fact that the benefice became void by reason of his creation in the Court of Rome, so that he ought to have given it in accordance with the Pope's prerogative; and notwithstanding the offence which he would otherwise have given to the Pope, which points were sufficiently argued, he was found

---

[1] Below No. 43 of the same term.

No. 18.

servy, et par quel voidaunce et totes les circumstaunces furent troves; par quei adonqes Levesqe de
ley duist aver mys le presente le Roi en possession,
et issint ceo qil ad conu[1] countre ceo qest[2] plede
pur le Roi ne luy poet excuser.—WILBY. Levesqe
deit toux jours el cas faire le comandement le Roi,
et le debat serra apres entre les clercs; et soietz
certein qil est autre du Roi qe dautre homme de
poeple, qe ne poet affermer tort en Ordinare par
encombrer, sil ne porte avant Prohibicion ou face
presentement issint qe Levesqe purra estre appris,
mes pur le Roi ne covient pas porter Prohibicion,
par quei Lordinare est tenuz de conustre le dreit
le Roi.—*Skyp.* Donqes, a vostre dit, ceo serreit ley
qe mesqe une persone fuit einz par ja si bone title,
par assent de son patron, qe ne purra dedire, a
un *Quare impedit* porte par le Roi serra ouste : qar
vous le tenetz ley en comune Bank qe si Levesqe
nouste cely qest einz autrement ne resceit il pas le
presente le Roi ne de nulle autre.—WILBY. Oyl.
Et ceo poet il et deit faire. Et en le *Quare non
admisit* en comune Bank lautre jour, si Levesqe
Dexcestre nust dit qil resceut a plus toust qe brief
ly vint, il ust este atteint de contempte; et si fuit
Lercevesqe Thomas de Corbrige, *non obstante* qe par
sa creacion en la Court de Rome le benefice se
voida, issint qe par la prerogatif le Pape le duist
doner; et *non obstante* loffence qil ust encoru vers
le Pape, come assetz fuit touche, si fuit il atteint

---

[1] C., conut. | [2] D., qil ad.

Nos. 19, 20.

A.D 1345. guilty of contempt.—Scot. Speak in some other way with regard to the King, for if you have not his pardon you are in a very hard case.—See, as to like matter, below, the case between the Lord the King and the Bishop of Exeter.[1]

Arraign-
ment on
Felony.

(19.) § John de Neuton was arraigned in the King's Bench by Thorpe for that he had been outlawed for a certain felony.—And he said that at the time at which the Exigent issued, and at the time of the indictment, he was in Britanny in the war.—And Thorpe asked him whether he was a clerk, and whether he had a charter of pardon of outlawry, and he said "No."—And he was remanded till the following day, and then questioned, as above, whether he could say anything wherefore they should not proceed to execution against him.— And he said that at the time of the issue of the Exigent, and before, and afterwards, he was imprisoned in York.—Thorpe. Yesterday you stated the contrary, that is to say, that you were in Britanny, and therefore you cannot be admitted to say this.—Therefore Thorpe commanded that he should be taken away [for execution]. — *Quære*, if he had held to his first answer that he was beyond sea, whether that would have availed him.—And note that by examination he was found to be very strongly suspected of various misdeeds.

Arraign-
ment on
abjura-
tion.

(20.) § Gilbert Gower was arraigned for that heretofore he was at such a church in Suffolk, and confessed that he had been consenting to and abetting the death of one A., and thereupon abjured the realm and is now found, without the King's license, in the King's realm. And he was asked whether he could say anything wherefore they should not proceed to execution.—And he made *profert* of a general charter

---

[1] Below No. 43 of the same term.

Nos. 19, 20.

del contempte.—Scot. Parletz dautre voie vers le A.D. 1345.
Roi qe si vous neietz grace de ly vous estes en
trop dure cas.—*Vide, de simili materia, infra inter
dominum Regem et Episcopum Exoniensem.*

(19.)[1] § Johan de Neutone fuit arrene[3] en Baunk Arrene sur
le Roi par Thorpe[4] de ceo qe pur certein felonie il felonie.[2]
fuit utlage.—Et dit qal temps del exigende issue, et [Fitz.,
Corone et
del enditement, il fuit en Breteigne[5] en la guere.[6]— Plees de
Corone,
Et Thorpe ly demanda sil fuit clerc ou[7] sil avoit 123.]
chartre, qe dit qe noun.—Et fuit remys tanqe len-
demeyn, et donqes aresone,[8] *ut supra,* sil savoit rienz
dire pur quei homme nirreit a execucion vers ly,[9]
qe dit qil fuit, al temps del exigende, et devant, et
puis, enprisone a Everwyke.—Thorpe. Here vous
conissastes le revers, saver,[10] qe vous fuistes en
Breteigne,[5] par quei vous ne serretz resceu a ceo
dire.—Par quei il comaunda de luy retrere.—*Quære*
sil soi ust tenutz a son primer respons qil fuit
outre miere, si ceo luy ust valu.—Et *nota* qe par
examinement il fuit trove trop suspeccionous de divers
malveites.

(20.)[11] § Gilbert Gowere fuit[13] arreyne[14] de ceo Arrene sur
qautrefoith il fuit a tiel eglise en Suffolk, et se abjura-
cion.[12]
conissat estre del assent et labbet de la mort un [Fitz.,
Corone et
A., et sur ceo forjura le Roialme, et ore est trove Plees del
sanz conge le Roi en sa terre, sil savoit rienz dire Corone,
pur quei homme nirreit a execucion; qe mist avant 124.]

---

[1] From L., H., C., and D.

[2] The words *sur felonie* are from L. alone.

[3] C., *arreyne.*

[4] Harl., *R. Thorpe.*

[5] H., *Bretayne*; D., *Bretaigne.*

[6] The words *en la guere* are omitted from H.

[7] D., *ou noun ou.*

[8] L., *arresone*; H., *aresonne.*

[9] The words *vers ly* are omitted from H. and D.

[10] D., *si*; the word is omitted from L. and H.

[11] From L., C., and D.

[12] The words *sur abjuracion* are from L. alone.

[13] *fuit* is from L. alone.

[14] L., *arrene.*

No. 21.

A.D. 1345 of pardon of all kinds of robberies, felonies, and
homicides, but it did not make any mention of abjuration.—And afterwards, on the following day, THORPE
arraigned him, as above, and asked him whether he
could say anything [wherefore they should not proceed
to execution].—And he said that he was Not Guilty,
and said further that he was not the person who had
made abjuration, but that it was another, and that his
name had been entered through malice, and thereof he
tendered averment.—THORPE. The Coroner has recorded
that you are the same person, and therefore you shall
not be admitted to that averment.—Yet nevertheless, *ex
abundanti cautela*, directions were given to make a search
as to whether the principal had been convicted.—And,
said THORPE, it was not necessary in this case, because
even though there had never been any act done such as
was alleged, still his confession condemned him; but
we do find that the principal was attainted by means
of outlawry, and the charter does not make any mention
of abjuration; it is therefore necessary to give judgment as the law requires, and as others have in the
same circumstances, that is to say that the charter
cannot avail him. And therefore take him away to
execution.—And note that it was said that the abjuration was made subsequently to the charter, but that
the felony must have been committed before the
charter; but this matter was not expressed in the
judgment.

Thief
attainted.

(21.) § Note that a thief was heretofore attainted,
and as he was going to the gallows he was rescued by
force. And he was sent back to prison and was now
questioned whether he could say anything [wherefore
they should not proceed to execution against him].
And he betook himself to his clergy, and was delivered
to the Ordinary. And note that he was first attainted
before the bailiff of a liberty, who could not effect
execution by reason of the prevention (caused by the

No. 21.

chartre general de totes maneres de roberies, felonies, _{A.D. 1345.} homicides, mes dabjuracion ele ne fit pas mencion. —Et puis, lendemein, THORPE ly arrena, *ut supra,* et demanda de luy sil savoit rienz dire, qe dit qil fuit de rien coupable, et outre dit qil nest pas mesme la persone, et ceo tendist daverer, mes autre qe luy fist labjuracion, et soun noun entre par malice.—THORPE. Le Coroner ad recorde qe vous estes mesme la persone, par quei a ceo ne serretz resceu.—Et unqore dabundance homme ad fet sercher si le principal fuit atteint.—Et ceo ne covendreit pas en ceo cas, qar tut ny avoit il unqes tiel fet fet,[1] unqore sa conissaunce luy dampne ; mes nous[2] trovoms le principal atteint par[3] utlagerie,[4] et la chartre ne fait pas mencion dabjuracion ; par quei il covient ajuger[5] come la lei demande, et come en mesme le cas les autres ount fait, saver qe le chartre ne luy poet lieu tenir. Et pur ceo retretz[6] le.—Et *nota* qe fuit dit qe labjuracion se fit puis la chartre, mes la felonie se[7] duist aver este fait devant la chartre ; mes ceste chose ne fuit pas mote en le jugement.

(21.)[8] § *Nota* qun laron autrefoith atteint, et come _{Laroun[9]} il ala vers[10] juise fuit rescous par force. Et remys _{atteint.} a la prisone, et ore arrene[11] sil savoit rienz dire, &c. Et il se prist a sa clergie, et est livere al Ordeigner. Et *nota* qil fuit primes atteint devant baillif de fraunchise, qe ne poait faire execucion pur

---

[1] The second fet is from C. alone.
[2] nous is omitted from D.
[3] D., et.
[4] D., utlaghe.
[5] L., eit, instead of il covient ajuger.

[6] C., retreetz ; D., retrez.
[7] C., qe.
[8] From L., H., C., and D.
[9] Laroun is from D. alone.
[10] vers is from L. alone.
[11] C., arreyne.

No. 22.

rescue). And he was afterwards brought by the same bailiff, who made the record.

Commission.

(22.) § A Commission issued to certain persons to enquire as to a nuisance committed in the river Lea, the course of which is from Ware to Waltham, and thence to the River Thames, and nuisances were recited as of trenches made to divert the course of the river, and also as of stakes, piles, &c., fixed in the course of the said river Lea, by reason whereof boats and ships which were wont to pass by the said river were prevented from passing by the said river, to the nuisance of the City of London and of the people coming thither. And enquiry was had as to the nuisance, and it was found in divers places.—And the whole matter was sent into the King's Bench by virtue of a writ. And there an order was made by precept to cause the ter-tenants to come on the Saturday next after the Quinzaine of the Trinity.—*Shipwith*. You see plainly how the nuisance is supposed to be in two counties, and you cannot lawfully make process out of the county in which you are sitting by precept without writ. And also according to law you ought to give a day in term in this case, and that you have not done ; and therefore we do not understand that you will put us to answer.—THORPE. As to a day in term, we do not lay any stress on that, because, after all the days of term are passed we can admit such an indictment, and make process while the Court is sitting. And, as to the precept which you mention, the nuisance is supposed to be in the same county; for though it could be added that the nuisance was committed to the nuisance of another county, ·still, if all the tort and the nuisance be committed in this county, we shall

No. 22.

lareste. Et puis fuit mene par mesme le baillif qe ^{A.D. 1345.}
fist le recorde.

(22.)[1] § Commission issit as certeinz gentz denquere ^{Com-}
del anusance fet en lewe[3] de la Leye, qe tient son ^{mission.[2]} ^{19 Li.}
cours de Warre a Waltham, et issint tanqal ewe de ^{Ass., 6;}
Tamise, et nusances reherces des trenches fetes pur ^{[Fitz.,} ^{Barre,}
bestourner le cours, et auxi peux, pilles, &c., fiches ^{279.]}
en le cours de la dite ewe de la Ley,[4] par quei
bateux et neefs qe sailent[5] par la dite ewe sount
destourbes a passer par la dite ewe, a nusance de
la Cite de Loundres et le poeple illoqes[6] venant.
Et la nusance enquis, et trove en divers lieux.—Et
tut maunde par brief en Baunk le Roi. Et illoeqes[7]
par precepte fuit commaunde a fere vener les terre
tenantz a[8] Samady proschein apres la xv de la
Trinite.—*Skip.* Vous veietz bien coment lanusance
est suppose en deux countes, et par precepte sanz
brief vous de ley ne poietz fere procees hors del
counte ou vous estes assis. Et auxint par ley vous
durretz jour de terme en le cas, et ceo navetz pas;
par quei nous nentendoms pas qe vous nous voilletz
mettre a respondre.—Thorpe. Quant au jour de
terme, nous le chargeoms pas, qar apres toux les
jours de terme passetz nous resceyveroms tiel enditement, et ferroms procees seaunt la place. Et
quant al precepte qe vous ditetz, qe lanusance est
suppose en mesme le counte; qar tut purreit estre
attreit qe lanusance fuit fait a damage dautre counte,
unqore si tut le tort et lanusance soit fet en ceo

---

[1] From L., C., and D. The
record of this case has been found
among the *Placita coram Rege*,
Trin., 19 Edw. III., R^o 51, and is
printed in full in the Appendix.

[2] D., Comissioun Danusance. In
C. the marginal note is, in a much
later hand, Commission de Sewers.

[3] C., lieu.

[4] L., &c., instead of de la Ley.
The words are omitted from D.

[5] C., sayleint; D., saillent.

[6] D., ilesqe.

[7] The words Et illoeqes are
omitted from D.

[8] D., le.

No. 22.

hold it to be a plea of the same county; therefore answer as to the nuisance committed in this county of Middlesex.—*Pole.* As to Maud who was the wife of Geoffrey Aleyn, it is presented that a ditch adjoining and between the said Maud's meadows has been made wider and deeper by a certain number of feet, but there is not thereby presented any certain act which could be called a nuisance or cause of stopping or diverting the river Lea; for possibly, even though the ditch be near, there may be twenty feet or more between the river and the ditch, and dry land between the two, and so nothing to cause a nuisance except by way of argument.—This exception was not allowed.— Afterwards exception was taken that it was not presented that Maud was tenant of the soil in which the nuisance was committed, and that ought to have been done, because process will be made against the tenant. —This exception was not allowed, because it is understood that it is her freehold by reason of the meadows which are hers on both sides of the ditch; and also by reason of the handywork which she has done it shall be understood that she is tenant of the soil.— Afterwards exception was taken on the ground that the nuisance was supposed to have been committed to the nuisance of London, which is a community like a single individual, and which could have an action in the name of the community as a single individual would have, in which case the King ought not to be made a party.—This exception was not allowed, because the words of the presentment are " to London and to the people."—Afterwards *Pole* said that, inasmuch as the tort was levied partly in the time of another person, he did not understand that she would be put to answer as to the time of that other person.—This exception was not allowed, because even though the penalty for that which was levied in the time of another person may be different from the penalty for that

No. 22.

counte, nous le tendroms com plee de mesme le
counte; par quei responez a ceo qest fait en ceo
counte de Middelsexe.—*Pole.* Quant a Maude qe fuit la
femme G.[1] Aleyn, il est presente qune fosse joinaunt
entre les prees la dite Maude est enlargy et fet
plus profounde de certeins pees, par tant nest pas
presente certein fait qe purreit estre dit nusance ne
cause destoper ne bestourner del ewe de la Ley;
qar par cas, tut soit le fosse juxt, il poet estre xx
pees ou plus entre lewe et le fosse, et seke terre
entre les deux, et issint nient anusant forqe par
argument.—*Non allocatur.*—Puis fuit chalenge de ceo
qe nest pas presente qil est tenant du soille ou
lanusance est fet; et ceo coviendreit estre fait, qar
vers luy procees se fra.—*Non allocatur,* qar il est
entendu qe ceo soit soun franc tenement pur les
prees qe sount a luy dune part et dautre; et auxint
pur le meineoure[2] quel ele ad fait serra entendu
qele est tenant del soille.—Puis est chalenge de ceo
qest suppose lanusance estre fait a Loundres, qest
une comune come une singulere persone qe poet
aver accion par noun de comune come une soul
persone avereit, en quel cas le Roi ne se deit pas
faire partie.—*Non allocatur,* qar le presentement voet
a Loundres et al poeple.—Puis, de ceo qe le tort
en partie fuit leve en autri temps, nentendi pas qe
dautri temps serra ele mys a respondre.—*Non
allocatur,* qar tut soit la penaunce divers de lever

---

[1] MSS. of Y.B., W. The record shows that the name was Geoffrey.

[2] C., meynure; D., menure.

No. 22.

which was levied in her own time, she must answer as to the whole.—Therefore she said that nothing had been done to the nuisance, &c.—And as to a nuisance committed in another place, because it was presented that three persons held the land, and one of them did not appear, a Distress was awarded against him, and the two who did appear had the same day.—And as to a Prioress it was presented that she and her predecessor had committed a nuisance by fixing piles in the river.—Exception was taken on the ground that her act and the act of her predecessor were supposed to have been done all at one time, which is impossible; and if they were done at different times, then it ought to have been determined in particular how much was done by one, and how much by the other; and thereupon they abode judgment.—Afterwards the jury came by process to try the issues pleaded to the country.—Thorpe, J. We ought to have the presenters in Court.—*Pole.* That is forbidden by Statute.—Thorpe. Yes, until the Parliament next after the Ordinance; and after that there was a Parliament, and nothing was done in relation to the matter, &c.—*Pole.* You see clearly how this is a nuisance upon which the jurors of the Inquest must form a judgment, and they cannot know about it without view; and the writ by which they are caused to come does not purport that they are to have view; therefore we do not understand that this warrant is sufficient.—Scot. Where are jurors to have view except in Assise, in which case the writ expresses it?—*Pole.* On a writ of Waste by reason of the necessity of view, and so in the case before us.—Thorpe. Our suit for the King is in lieu of a *Quod permittat prosternere*, in which case view will not be given to the jurors, but, if it were in the nature of an Assise, that would be different.—*Pole.* Certainly this suit is in the nature of an Assise.—Thorpe. Not so, for he would then be put without answer by the

No. 22.

fet en autri temps et[1] son temps demene, ele re- A.D. 1345.
spondra a tut.—Par quei ele dist qe rien fait
anusant, &c.—Et en autre lieu quant a nusaunce
fait, pur ceo qe presente fuit qe iij tiendrent la
terre, et un ne vint pas, distresse[2] agarde vers luy,
et les deux qapparount ount mesme le jour.—Et
quant a une Prioresse presente fuit qele et sa predecessoresse avoint par ficher[3] des pilles en lewe
fait nusance.[4]—Fuit chalenge pur ceo qe son fet et
le fet de sa predecessoresse est suppose estre fait
tut a un temps, qe ne poet estre; et si a divers
temps donqes duist il estre determine en certein
come bien fait par lune et come bien fait par lautre;
et sur ceo en jugement.—Puis vint lenqueste par
procees la ou fut plede au pays.—THORPE (JUSTICE).
Homme duist aver des presentours.—*Pole.* Cest defendu par statut.—THORPE. Oyl, tanqe au Parlement
proschein apres Lordinaunce; et puis Parlement fuit,
et rien de ceo fait, &c.—*Pole.* Vous veietz bien
coment cest une nusance qe covient estre juge par
ces del enqueste, et ceo ne pount ils saver sanz la
viewe; et le brief par quel ils sount fait venir nel
voet pas qils averount la viewe; par quei nentendoms
pas qe cel garrant soit suffisant.—SCOT. Ou averount
les jurours la viewe mes en Assise ou le brief le
voet?—*Pole.* En brief de Wast, pur la necessite, *et
sic in proposito.*—THORPE. Nostre suite pur le Roi
est en lieu de *Quod permittat,* en quel cas la viewe
ne se fra pas as jurours, mes sil fuit en nature
Dassise autre serreit.—*Pole.* Certes ceste suite est
en nature Dassise.—THORPE. Nanil,[5] qar donqes
serreit il ouste sanz respons par le presentement

---

[1]-D., qen.
[2] L., and C., demande.
[3] D., fischir.

[4] D., anusance.
[5] C., nanylle.

No. 22.

A.D. 1345. presentment alone : because in respect of usurpation made by the person who is himself tenant and in the time of the same King he will be put without answer. —*Pole* then took a challenge to the array, on the ground that it was made by the Sheriff of Middlesex, who is the deputy of the community of London, and removable by it, and it is the principal party.—This exception was not allowed, because it is the King's suit.—Afterwards the Inquest, being charged, could not agree. Therefore, after dinner, THORPE took the verdict at St. Clement's Church, by which verdict the nuisance was found partly as having been committed by those who had pleaded, and partly by others previously.—*Pole* said that the verdict had been taken out of Court, and not at a proper time.—SCOT. We can take a verdict by candle-light if the jury will not agree ; and if the Court were to move, we could take the jurors about in carts with us, and so Justices of Assise have to do.—THORPE. The nuisance is found, and therefore the COURT gives judgment that so much as has been levied by those who are parties to the nuisance be taken away at the cost of those who levied it, and that they be in mercy, and that so much of it as was levied by others be taken away by the Sheriff ; and sue you that the Sheriff make proclamation throughout all the places in which the nuisance was levied that those to whose injury the nuisance has been levied be aiding the Sheriff in taking it away.— And note that it was found by the inquest that the river Lea is the King's high-way.—And *R. Thorpe* prayed on the King's behalf that those who effected the handy-work, which could be only with force and arms, might be taken.—This was not allowed.—And nevertheless *Grene* touched the point that the law must rightly be the same in Nuisance as in Novel Disseisin, particularly when the nuisance is committed in the King's soil.

No. 22.

soulement : qar de purprise fet par mesme cely qest tenant et en temps de mesme le Roi ceo serra ouste sanz [1] respons.—Puis *Pole* prist chalenge al array, de ceo qil est fet par le Vicounte de Middel-sexe, qest depute et remuable par la comune de Loundres, qe sount principalment partie.—*Non allo-catur*, qar cest la suite le Roi.—Puis lenquest charge ne pount acorder ; par quei, apres maunger, THORPE prist le verdit al eglise Seint Clement, par quel nusance est trove, partie fet par ces qount plede, et partie par autres a devant.—*Pole* dist qe le verdit fuit pris hors de la place, et hors de temps.—SCOT. Nous prendroms enqueste ove chaundel si lenqueste ne voille acorder ; et si nous fuissoms a remuer nous les meneroms en charettes ove nous, et si duissent Justices des Assises.—THORPE. Trove est lanusance, par quei la COURT agarde qe ceo qest leve par eux qe sount parties al anusance soit ouste as coustages ceux qe le leverount, et eux en la merci, et ceo qe fuit leve par autres soit ouste par le Vicounte ; et suetz qe le Vicounte face crier par toux les places [2] ou lanusance fuit leve qe ces a qi nusance cest leve soient en eide au Vicounte del ouster.—Et *nota* qe par lenqueste est trove qe lewe de la Leye est haut estrete le Roi.—Et [*R.*] *Thorpe* pria qe ces qe firent le meynure qe ne poet estre forqe a force et armes qils soient pris pur le Roi. —*Non allocatur.*—*Et tamen Grene* toucha qe mesme la ley duist estre par resoun en Anusaunce qen Novele Disseisine, nomement quant lanusance est fet en le soille le Roi.

---

[1] D., de. | [2] places is from C. alone.

Nos. 23, 24.

A.D. 1345.
Fine.

(23.) § *Birton.* W., and A., his wife, grant and render all that they have of the right of J. to Thomas de Lincoln, to have and to hold to him and to his heirs, for the life of J., rendering for the first six years one rose, and afterwards two marks *per annum*; and Thomas grants that whensoever the rent may be in arrear it shall be lawful for them to distrain during the life of J.—*Quære* as to the distress.

Fine.

(24.) § A fine was levied by which one rendered to another, for the life of him to whom the render was made, to hold by the services of the eighth part of one knight's fee, and by so much rent, and suit to the court of the renderor, so that, after the decease of the renderee, so much should remain, by metes and bounds, to hold by the twentieth part of one knight's fee, and by certain rent, to such an one and the heirs of his body, to hold of the donor, and so severally to others, each performing for the donor the services due to the chief lords.—WILLOUGHBY. Will the tenant for term of life perform one service, and those who are in remainder other services?—*Grene.* Yes, the remainder in several parts is spread among several persons, and therefore the services must be apportioned.—HILLARY. Have you not cast and equally apportioned the services of those who are in remainder according to their portion of the tenancy, having regard to the tenancy of him from whom the render was made?—*Grene.* Certainly that is so; and moreover it is immaterial, because those who are in remainder will be able to hold by services other than those by which the person held to whom the render was first made.—WILLOUGHBY. Suppose that the land be holden over by knight service, then the person to whom the render was made and those in remainder will pay different scutages, and that is impossible.—*Grene.* You are not apprised of that.—For that reason the fine was afterwards admitted, with warranty and acquittal of services,

Nos. 23, 24.

(23.) [1] § *Birtone.* W. et A., sa femme, grantent et A.D. 1345.
rendent quant qils ount del dreit J. a Thomas de *Finis.*
Nichole, a aver et tener a luy et a ses heirs a la
vie J., rendant les primers vj aunz une rose, et
apres deux marcs par an; et Thomas grante quel
houre qe la rente soit arere qe lise a eux a destreindre pur la vie J.—*Quære* de la destresse.

(24.) [2] § Fyne se leva par quel un rendist a un *Finis.*
autre, a la vie celuy a qi le rendre se fist, par les [Fitz., *Fynes,*
services del oeptisme[3] partie dune fee de chivaler, et 71.]
par tant de rente, et suite a sa court, &c., issint
qapres son decees taunt par metes[4] et boundes re-
meigne, par vintisme[3] partie dune fee de chivaler,
et par certein rente, a un tiel et les heirs de son
corps, a tener del donour, et issint severalment as
autres, et fesant pur luy as chiefs seignours les
services dues.—WILBY. Fra le tenant a terme de
vie une service, et ces en le remeindre autres services?—*Grene.* Oyl, le remeindre severalment est
despendu en plusours, et pur ceo covient qe les
services soient apporciones.—HILL. Navetz jettu[5] les
services et apporcione owelement solonc lour porcion
de tenance de ces en le remeindre, eaunt regard a
la tenance de celuy de[6] qi le rendre se fist?—*Grene.*
Certes si est; et ceo ne toud ne doune unqore, qar
ces en le remeindre purrount tener par autres services qe le primer a qi le rendre se fist.—WILBY.
Mettetz qe la terre soit tenue outre par service de
chivaler, donqes ferra celui a qi le rendre se fist
et ces en le remeindre divers escuages, qe ne poet
estre.—*Grene.* De ceo nestes vous pas appris.—Par
quei, apres, la fyne est resceu, ove garrantie et

---

[1] From L., C., and D.
[2] From L., H., C., and D.
[3] D., utisme.
[4] C., meers.

[5] H., and D., gettu.
[6] The words celuy de are omitted from C.

No. 25.

A.D. 1345. but the words "performing to the chief lords," &c., were omitted, because it is impossible that they can pay different scutages —And then the fine was admitted. —*Quære*, therefore, how the tenant for life will pay scutage, for he will as a consequence do homage, and that is impossible.--But nothing was said as to this.

Petition.   (25.) § The heirs of John Difelde (or de Ifelde) sued by petition to the King to have certain lands. And after the delivery of the petition the King granted the lands to Thomas Dagworth, and to Eleanor his wife, for Eleanor's life; and therefore they were garnished, and they wished to have abated the bill on the ground that suit would be given against them at common law.—This exception was not allowed, because the King, as he himself recorded, was tenant on the day of the petition, &c., and their estate commenced while the petition was pending.—Therefore they afterwards produced a Protection for Thomas, and inasmuch as he was not a party, and the petition was only for the purpose of moving the King, the Protection was disallowed.— *Quære*, since he could have an answer as tenant by release, or in some other manner.—Afterwards *Derworthy* said : We tell you that, while the suit was pending, one of the heirs, that is to say one J., has died, and so the Petition is extinguished.—THORPE. This suit is made to our Lord the King, who will answer of his grace, and is not bound nor compelled to do so by law. It is his pleasure that the heir of the one who is dead be admitted to make the same petition, notwithstanding the death of his ancestor, for the King has so commanded us by his writ which is here.—*R. Thorpe.* The King could do so of his grace if he were himself tenant, but he cannot do so to the prejudice of another : for according to common right the petition is extinguished,-and consequently the tenants have the advantage that the demandants are put to sue against them according to common law by writ, of which

No. 25.

acquitance, et ceo fuit ouste fesaunt au chief seignur, A.D. 1345.
&c,, qar ceo ne purra pas estre qil fra divers
escuages.—Et donqes fuit ceo resceu.—*Ideo quære
qualiter* tenant a terme de vie fra escuage, qar *per
consequens* il freit homage, qe ne poet estre.—Mes
de ceo rienz ne fuit parle.

(25.) [1] § Les heirs Johan Difelde[2] suyrent par Peticion.
peticion au Roy daver certeinz terres. Et puis la
livere de la peticion le Roi granta les terres a
Thomas Dagworth, et a Elianore sa femme, a la vie
Elianore ; par quei ils furent garniz, et voleint aver
abatu la bille pur ceo qe suite serreit done vers
eux a la comune lei.—*Non allocatur*, qar le Roi,
come il mesme recorda, fuit tenant jour de la peticion,
&c., et lour estat comence pendant la peticion.—Par
quei apres ils moustrent avant proteccion[3] pur
Thomas, et par tant qil nest pas partie, mes soulement pur mover le Roi, la proteccion[3] fuit desallowe.
—*Quære*, desicomme il poet aver respons com tenant
par relees ou en autre manere.—Puis *Der.* Nous
vous dioms qe, pendant la suite, un des heirs, saver
un J. est mort, issint la peticion amorti.—Thorpe.
Ceste suite est fait vers nostre seignur le Roi, qe
voet de grace respondre, et nest lie ne arce par
ley. Il luy plest qe leir celuy qest mort soit resceu
a mesme la peticion, *non obstante* la mort sauncestre
qar il nous ad comaunde cella par son brief qe ci
est.—R.[4] *Thorpe.* Le Roi le poet faire de sa grace
sil fuit mesme tenant, mes en prejudice dautre nel
poet il pas faire : qar de comune dreit la peticiòn
est amorti, et *per consequens* les tenantz ount un
avantage qe les demandantz sount mys vers eux a
suire par[5] comune lei par brief,[6] quel avantage le

---

[1] From L., H., C., and D.
[2] C., Driffielde.
[3] L., and C., peticion.
[4] *R.* is omitted from H. and C.

[5] D., a la.
[6] The words par brief are omitted from D.

No. 26.

advantage the King ought not to deprive them. Besides, the King does not express in his writ that you are to proceed notwithstanding the non-age of the heir of the one who is dead, and, if the King had been apprised of the non-age of the person who now answers by guardian, it is possible that he would not have commanded you to proceed: for neither with regard to the King nor with regard to any other person is an infant under age in a condition to be answered as to the seisin of his ancestor.—*Derworthy.* Petitions are not to be regulated like any ordinary original writ; and it is certain that the treatment of a Petition is a matter of grace, and shall be regulated at the King's pleasure: for he can command that the heir shall continue the suit commenced by the heir's ancestor, and, if he so command, you must act accordingly, but it would be otherwise if this were an original writ.

Formedon. (26.) § Formedon. One to whom the reversion belonged was admitted to defend his right, and said by *Pole* that the demandant, and the demandant's mother, and one J., by a deed, which he produced, enfeoffed him who was thus admitted, with warranty. And he was put to state definitely in what way he was using the deed, whether as the demandant's deed, or as the ancestor's deed. And he stated that he used it as the demandant's deed.——*Huse.* We tell you that at the time of the execution of the deed we had nothing in the freehold; and we tell you that he had nothing by our feoffment; ready, &c.; judgment whether we shall be barred by this deed.—*R. Thorpe.* And inasmuch as he has confessed this deed, by virtue of which the land passed, and by which he, as well as the others, is bound to warrant, inasmuch as the deed is one, we pray judgment.—And at first *R. Thorpe* understood that the demandant had not alleged that he had nothing in the freehold, and therefore said that inasmuch as the demandant had confessed his

No. 26.

Roi ne les deit pas tollir. Ovesqe ceo, le Roi ne _{A.D. 1345.}
reherce pas en soun brief[1] *non obstante* le nounage
[leir[2] cely qest mort qe vous ailletz avant, et par
cas sil ust este appris de soun nounage][3] qore respond par gardein il nel ust pas comaunde : qar
nient plus devers le Roi qe devers autre persone
est enfant deinz age responable de la seisine son
auncestre.—*Der.* Les peticiouns ne serrount pas
reulles[4] com autre original; et il est certein qe cest
de grace et serra[5] reulle a la volunte le Roi : qar
il poet comaunder qe leir continue la suite comence
par son auncestre, et sil le comaunde vous le ferretz,
mes si cest fuit original autre serreit.

(26.)[6] § Forme doun. Un a qi reversion, &c., fuit ^{Forme-}
resceu, et dit par *Pole* qe le demandant, et sa mere, ^{doun.}
et un J. par ceo fet fefferunt ove garrantie cely qest
resceu. Et il fuit mys de user le fet en certein,
ou come le fet le demandant, ou come le fet sauncestre. Et il usa come le fet le demandant.—*Huse.*
Nous vous dioms qal temps de la confeccion nous
navioms rienz en le fraunctenement; et vous dioms
qil navoit rienz de nostre feffement; prest, &c.;
jugement si par ceo fet serroms barre.—[*R.*] *Thorpe.*
Et desicome il ad conu ceo fet par quel la terre
passa, et par quel il est tenuz a garrantir si bien
come les autres, desicome le fait est un, jugement.
—Et primes[7] [*R.*] *Thorpe* entendist qil nust pas
allegge qil navoit rienz en le fraunctenement, par
quei il dit qe desicome il avoit conu son fet, et qe

---

[1] The writ sent to the Justices of the King's Bench is on the *Rot. Lit. Claus.*, 19 Edw. III., p. 1, m. 4, d.

[2] leir is omitted from D.

[3] The words between brackets are omitted from H.

[4] C., roulles ; D., reullez.

[5] D., sil serra.

[6] From the four MSS , as above.

[7] L., puis qe ; D., prioms.

No. 26.

deed, and had confessed that the land passed by the deed, he should not be admitted to say that the person admitted to defend had nothing by feoffment from him without showing some particular fact as the reason. But, as it was recorded that the demandant alleged that he had nothing in the freehold at the time of the execution of the deed, *R. Thorpe* then said that the demandant's plea was double—one plea to the effect that he had nothing, and consequently could not deliver anything, another to the effect that, even though he had anything, he did not deliver it.—This exception was not allowed.—Therefore *Mutlow* said :—You and the others delivered the same land to us; ready, &c.—*Huse*. That is tantamount to saying that you had the land by feoffment from us; ready, &c., that you did not.— WILLOUGHBY. Even though you had nothing at that time, yet if you (the demandant) and the others came to the spot and gave livery in common, you performed by the livery all that had previously been wanting in you; therefore, is it the fact that you did give livery in common?—*Huse*. He had nothing by feoffment, or by livery, from us; ready, &c.—*R. Thorpe*. Suppose tenant for term of life and the person to whom the reversion belongs give and grant by deed, and livery is made by the tenant for term of life alone, is not that a good livery? And in that case everything passes— as well the right as the freehold. — WILLOUGHBY. Certainly it does so.—*R. Thorpe*. ·And also if tenant for term of years or at will make a feoffment, even though it be a disseisin to another person, the feoffment is good and complete between those who are parties; therefore in the matter before us, since the demandant has confessed that this is his deed, and that the land passed by the same deed, and the deed is completed by the putting to it of his seal, even though he never had had anything, he has affirmed the fact, so far as he is concerned, so strongly that

No. 26.

la terre par le fet passa, a dire qe nous navioms[1] A.D. 1345
rienz de soun feffement il ne serra resceu sanz fet
especial. Mes, quant recorde fuit qil alleggea qil
navoit rienz a la fesaunce en le franctenement, donqes
dit [R.] *Thorpe* qe son ple est double, un qil navoit
rienz, et *per consequens* rienz il poait[2] liverer, et
autre qe, tut avoit il, il[3] ne livera pas.—*Non allocatur.*
—Par quei[4] *Mutl.* Vous et les autres nous liverastes
mesme la terre ; prest, &c.—*Huse.* Tantamount qe
vous avietz de nostre feffement ; prest, &c., qe noun.
WILBY. Tut navietz rienz adonqes, et vous et les
autres venistes a la place et liverastes en comune,
ceo qe faillist devant en vous, vous le parfournistes
par la livere ; par quei est il issint qe vous liverastes
en comune ?—*Huse.* Il navoit rienz de nostre feffement nè livere ; prest, &c.—[R.] *Thorpe.* Jeo pose
qe tenant a terme de vie et cely a qi le reversion
appent dounent et grantent par fait, et la livere
soit fait par le tenant a terme de vie soulement,
nest ceo bone[5] livere ? Et tut passe, si bien le dreit
come le frauonctenement.—WILBY. Certes si fait.—
[R.] *Thorpe.*[6] Et auxint si tenant a terme daunz[7]
ou a volunte face feffement, tut soit il disseisine a
autre, entre eux qe sount parties le feffement est
bon et plein ; donqes en nostre matere, quant il ad
conu qe cest soun fet, et qe la terre passa par
mesme le fait, et issint le fait plein par mettre de
soun seal, tut navoit il unqes[8] rienz, il ad afferme
la chose, quant a luy, si fort qil est tenuz de

---

[1] All the MSS., except C., navoms.
[2] H., and D., poet.
[3] il is omitted from C.
[4] The words Par quei are omitted from D.
[5] D., sa.
[6] *Thorpe* is omitted from H.
[7] L., de vie.
[8] D., donqes.

No. 27.

he is bound to warrant, and consequently he can be barred.—*Huse*. We take your records to witness that the deed is used by way of establishing feoffment, and therefore he shall not be allowed to be aided in any other manner.—*Blaykeston*. Yes, we shall be aided by your confession.—WILLOUGHBY and HILLARY. He will always be able to affirm the fact, before issue is taken, in every possible way, and that by plea in law.—It is said that judgment was afterwards given that the demandant should take nothing, &c.—*Quære*.

Waste.

(27.) § Waste. It was found by verdict of jury, in a case in which the party had pleaded No Waste, that, as to a kitchen, which had been burnt by a strange woman, who did not know the defendant, because he lived in a different place, he had cut some oaks, in woods and in hedges round about the close, to rebuild that kitchen, and that the house was now in better condition than it had been before the burning. It was found also that he had felled a certain number of oaks, in woods and hedges round about the close, and sold them, and had felled some for the repair of houses, and had felled one which was still lying on the ground, and was not yet sold. —*Pole* prayed judgment on the verdict, because the burning of the house and everything which had been cut should now be adjudged to be waste according to the manner of the plea, because although it is found that part was cut for the repair of houses, which fact ought according to law to have been avowed by way of plea, and was not, he has lost that advantage inasmuch as he pleaded that no waste was committed, &c.—*R. Thorpe*. If the inquest had been taken by default, the Court would, on such a verdict, have adjudged that there was no waste; therefore also now, because the fact which is found is in accordance with our issue that there was no waste; and as to the

No. 27.

garrantir, et *per consequens* barrable.—*Huse.* Nous A.D. 1345.
pernoms vos recordes qe le fait est use par voie de
feffement, par quei destre eide par autre[1] manere
ne serra il resceu.—*Blayk.* Si serroms de vostre
conissaunce.—WILBY. et HILL. Toux jours affermera
il le fait avant lissue pris par totes les voies qil
purra, et ceo par plee en ley.—*Dicitur*[2] *quod post*
fut agarde qe le demandant ne prist riens, &c.—
Quære.[2]

(27.)[3] § Wast. Trove est par verdit denqueste, ou Wast.
plede fuit par partie qe nulle wast, qe quant a une [Fitz., Wast,
quisine,[5] quel fuit ars par une femme estraunge 30.][4]
nient sachaunt le defendant, pur ceo qil demura
aillours, pur refaire cele quisine il coupa des keynes
en boys et en hayes en viroun la clos, et qe la
mesoun est ore meillour qele nestoit avant larsone;
et qil avoit auxi abatu certein noumbre des keynes,
et vendu, en boys et hayes enviroun le clos, et
asquns abatu en amendement des mesouns, et un
abatu qe gist la unqore nient vendu.—*Pole* pria
jugement sur verdit, qar lardre de la mesoun et
quant qest coupe ore par la manere du ple serra
ajuge wast, qar coment qe trove soit qe partie fuit
coupe en amendement des mesouns, quel fait par
ley duist aver este avowe par plee, et ne fuit pas,
la ad il perdu lavantage par tant qil pleda nulle
wast fait, &c.—[*R.*] *Thorpe.* Si lenqueste ust este
pris par defaute, sur tiel[6] verdit Court ajugeast[7] qe
nulle wast; *ergo* a ore, pur ceo qe le fet trove est
acordant a nostre mise qe nulle wast; et quant a

---

[1] L. dautre, instead of par autre.

[2] The words from *Dicitur* to the
end are from D. alone. They are
in a different but apparently contemporary hand.

[3] From the four MSS., as above.

[4] In Fitzherbert's *Abridgment*
the case is represented as being of
the following Michaelmas Term.

[5] D., cuisine.

[6] D., cel.

[7] H., and D., ajugereit.

No. 28.

A.D. 1345. house which has been burnt it is found that the burning was done by a stranger, against whom we cannot have an action, and that it was not our fault, and the cutting of timber to rebuild that house is not waste.—WILLOUGHBY. The burning is waste for default of good keeping.—*R. Thorpe.* Quite recently it was found in this Court, on a writ of Waste, by inquest taken by default, that the Welsh had landed on the sea-coast and burnt a manor, and it was adjudged that this was no waste; for the same reason it is no waste in this case.—WILLOUGHBY. No, the party could not have made any opposition to the Welsh. But do you think that, if your household harbour a stranger who puts houses to fire and flame, it will not be adjudged waste? as meaning to say that it would. Therefore the burning is adjudged to be waste, and so the kitchen has been wasted. But the cutting of timber to rebuild the house is not waste. And as to the timber which is cut, and not sold, that is waste. And that which has been cut for repairs, notwithstanding that this was not pleaded, is adjudged to be no waste. Therefore the COURT gives judgment that the plaintiff do recover the place wasted, and treble damages, &c.—*Quære* whether he will recover the whole, since the hedges which are round about the close are wasted, for the cutting and selling are found in divers places throughout the hedges, &c.

Waste.   (28.) § Waste.—*Sadelyngstanes.* We hold nothing by lease from you; ready, &c.—*Skipwith.* And, inasmuch as you do not deny that we leased to you, judgment whether you shall be admitted to aver that you do not hold by lease from us.—*Sadelyngstanes.* Then you refuse the averment.—*Skipwith.* Yes, and we take your records to witness that the lease is not

No. 28.

la mesoun ars il est trove lardre[1] fait par une
estrange, vers qe nous ne poms aver accion, ne qe
ceo ne fuit pas nostre defaute, et le couper pur faire
cele mesoun nest pas wast.—WILBY. Larsoun est
wast pur defaute de bone garde.—[R.] *Thorpe.* Ore
tarde ceinz fuit trove, en brief de Wast, par enqueste
pris par defaute, qe les Galeys arriverent en cost la
mere et arderent un maner, et fuit ajuge qe nulle
wast; par mesme la resoun icy.—WILBY. Nanil,
contre les Galeys la partie ne poait aver mys des-
tourbaunce. Mes quidetz vous, si vostre meyne
herbergent un estraunge qe mette les mesouns en
feu et flambe, qe ceo ne serra pas ajuge wast? *quasi
diceret sic.* Par quei lardre est ajuge pur wast, et
issint la quisine waste. Mes le couper pur la mesoun
refere[2] nest pas wast. Et quant a ceo qest coupe,
et nient vendu, cest wast. Et ceo qest coupe en
amendement, *non obstante* qe ceo nestoit pas plede,
est agarde nulle wast. Par quei agarde la COURT qe
le pleintif recovere le lieu waste, et damages a treble,
&c.—*Quære* sil recovera tut, desicome les hayes qe
sount le clos enviroun, &c., sount wastes, qar le
couper et vendre est trove en divers lieux des hayes
par tut, &c.

(28.)[3] § Wast.—*Sadl.* Nous tenoms rienz de vostre
lees; prest, &c.—*Skyp.* Et, desicome vous ne deditez
pas qe nous ne lessames a vous, jugement si daverer
qe vous ne tenetz pas de nostre lees serretz resceu.
—*Sadl.* Donqes refusetz laverement.—*Skyp.* Oyl, et
pernoms voz recordes qe le lees nest pas dedit.—

---

[1] lardre is omitted from C.

[2] L., aparaler.

[3] From the four MSS., as above.
This seems to be the case which is
found among the *Placita de Banco*,
Trin., 19 Edw. III., R° 145. It
there appears that an action of
Waste was brought by Robert de
Foston, vicar of the church of
Louth (Luda), and four others,
against Matilda Sleght, of Louth.
It was alleged in the declaration
that the plaintiffs had demised a
messuage in Louth (Lincolnshire),
to the defendant for life.

Nos. 29–31.

A.D. 1345. denied.—*Sadelyngstancs* did not dare to abide judgment, but said that he had nothing by lease from the plaintiff; ready, &c.—*Skipwith.* We leased to you; ready, &c.—And the other side said the contrary.

Waste.   (29.) § Waste.—After the inquest had been taken by default, the defendant prayed, by *Huse,* that he might be allowed to plead before judgment, because he was under age.—HILLARY. You have not a day, and in this case one under age will have no more advantage in pleading than one of full age.

Replevin.   (30.) § Replevin between the Abbot of Our Lady of York, avowant, and the Prior of Drax, plaintiff, in which case the avowry was heretofore made [1] for five shillings of rent service. The Prior made *profert* of a deed of feoffment from the Earl of Lincoln, whose estate the Abbot has, by which deed his predecessor was enfeoffed at a rent of two shillings for all services, &c. And notwithstanding that the Abbot alleged the King's seisin, and that of Geoffrey Scrope as tenant of the manor to which the services are regardant, judgment was given that the plaintiff should recover his damages.—WILLOUGHBY said that he had seen judgment given on the same point between privy and privy, and between privy and stranger, and between stranger and stranger.

Replevin   (31.) § Replevin. After avowry had been made, the avowant on a subsequent day made default. And he was distrained to hear his judgment. And now he did not appear. Therefore judgment was given that the plaintiff should have his beasts quit, and his damages assessed by the COURT at one mark.

---

[1] *See* Y.B., Hil., 19 Edw. III., No. 39. The services are there said to have been cornage and the repairing of a mill-pool.

Nos. 29–31.

Sadl. nosa demurer, mes dit qil navoit rienz de son A.D. 1345.
lees; prest, &c.[1]—*Skyp.* Nous lessames a vous; prest,
&c.—*Et alii e contra.*

(29.) [2] § Wast.—Apres enqueste pris par defaute, Wast.
le defendant, par *Huse*, pria qil poet avant jugement [Fitz.,
Enfant,
pleder pur ceo qil est deinz age. — HILL. Vous 10.]
navietz [3] pas jour, et plus davantage de pleder navera
un deinz age en le cas qun de plein age.

(30.) [4] § *Replegiari* entre Labbe nostre Dame Replegiari.
[Fitz.,
Deverwyke, avowaunt, et le Prior de Drax, pleintif, Avowre,
ou lavowere fuit fait autrefoith pur vs. de rente 122.]
service. Le Prior mist avant fet de feffement le
Counte de Nicole, qi estat Labbe ad, par quel un
soun predecessour fuit feffe pur deux *s.* pur toux services, &c. Et *non obstante* qe Labbe alleggea[5] seisine
le Roi et Geffrey Scrope tenant del maner[6] a qi
les services sount regardauntz, fuit agarde qe le
pleintif recoverast ses damages.—WILBY dit qil ad
viewe entre prive [et] prive,[7] et prive et estraunge,
et estraunge et estraunge[8] mesme le point estre ajuge.

(31.) [4] § *Replegiari.* Apres avowere fait lavowaunt Replegiari.
[Fitz.,
a autre jour fist defaut. Et il fuit destreint doier Proscs,
son jugement. Et ore ne vint pas. Par quei fuit 36.]
agarde qe le pleintif ust ses avers quites, et ses
damages taxes par la COURT a un marc.

---

[1] According to the record the
defendant pleaded " quod ubi ipsi
" superius in narratione sua sup-
" ponunt ipsos dimisisse eidem
" Matilldi prædictum mesuagium,
" cum pertinentiis, tenendum ad
" vitam ejusdem Matilldis, eadem
" Matilldis nihil habuit in mesu-
" agio illo ex dimissione ipsorum
" Robert [&c.]" Issue was joined
upon this and the *Venire* awarded
but nothing further appears on the
roll.

[2] From L., C., and D.

[3] D., navetz.

[4] From L., H., C., and D.

[5] L., ad allege; D., ad. The
word is omitted from C.

[6] H., and D., manoir.

[7] prive is omitted from H. and D.

[8] The words et estraunge are
omitted from H. and D.

Nos. 32. 33.

A.D. 1345.
Error.

(32.) § Error on a writ of Account brought against Thomas son of Thomas de Radclyf.[1] And it was assigned as error that the plaintiff brought a writ in the name of Thomas son of Thomas, and his attorney had no warrant except in the name of Thomas de Radclyf, who must be understood to be another person. And error was also assigned in that no *Capias* was returned except one only, whereas by law three ought to have been returned before the Exigent, and were not, &c.—THORPE (J.). For these errors and others we admit him to peace, and annul the judgment.

Voucher.

(33.) § A tenant vouched, and the voucher was

---

[1] *See* Y.B., Hil., 19 Edw. III., No. 35 (pp. 510-512).

Nos. 32, 33.

(32.) [1] § Errour sur brief Dacompte porte vers A.D. 1345. Thomas le fitz Thomas de Radclyf. Et pur errour Errour. assigne fuit qe le pleintif porta brief par noun de Thomas le fitz Thomas, et son attourne navoit garrant forqe par noun de Thomas de Radclyf, qest entendu autre persone. Et auxint ou nulle *Capias* fuit retourne fors un soulement, et iij par ley duissent aver este retourne avant exigende, et ceo ne firent pas, &c.—THORPE. Pur ces errours et autres nous luy resceivoms a la pees, et anientissoms le jugement.[2]

(33.) [3] § Le tenant voucha, qe fuit countreplede qe Voucher. [Fitz., *Voucher*, 121.]

---

[1] From the four MSS., as above. The record of the proceedings in Error is among the *Placita coram Rege*, Trin., 19 Edw. III., R⁰ 109. The action of Account had been brought by Thomas son of Thomas de Radeclyfe against Thomas de Goushulle, who had been outlawed after non-appearance.

In the Court of King's Bench "Thomas filius Thomæ, quarto "die placiti, solemniter vocatus "[est], et non venit."

[2] According to the roll, judgment in the King's Bench was given as follows:—"Quia, visis et diligenter "examinatis recordo et processu "prædictis, videtur CURIÆ hic quod "Justiciarii erraverunt in hoc quod "ipsi consideraverunt quod præ- "dictus Thomas de Goushulle "utlagaretur ad sectam prædicti "Thomæ filii Thomæ de Rade- "clyfe, cum idem Thomas filius "Thomæ, pendente placito præ- "dicto, ad nullum diem placiti "fuit in Curia in propria persona, "nec per attornatum. quia in "recordo supradicto compertum

"est quod quidam Thomas de "Radeclyfe fecit attornatum suum "in placito prædicto Willelmum "de Boys versus prædictum "Thomam de Goushulle, sed non "prædictus Thomas filius Thomæ "de Radeclyfe. Item videtur CURIÆ "quod Justiciarii erraverunt in "hod quod ipsi consideraverunt "quod prædictus Thomas utla- "garetur ad sectam ipsius Thomæ "filii Thomæ, cum non fuit nisi "unum breve retornatum de "capiendo ipsum Thomam de "Goushulle in placito prædicto, "cum de jure semper tria brevia ad "capiendum defendentem debent "retornari in Curia antequam "breve de exigendo erit adjudican- "dum. Ideo utlagaria prædicta, ob "errores istos, et multos alios, in "recordo et processu prædictis "repertos, omnino revocetur et "adnulletur, et prædictus Thomas "de Goushulle ad legem com- "munem restituatur, et habeat "breve de pace sua proclamanda, "&c."

[3] From the four MSS., as above.

Nos. 34, 35.

counterpleaded on the ground that neither the vouchee nor any of his ancestors had anything in the tenements, &c. On another day the demandant confessed that the vouchee had been seised, and the vouchee was ready in Court and would have warranted, but he was not admitted to do so, because he had not a day in Court, but on the first day on which he was vouched he could have done so.—*Quære* as to the difference.

Formedon. (34.) § Formedon in the descender.—*Pole.* Your grandfather enfeoffed us, with warranty, by this deed; judgment whether you can demand anything contrary to the deed.—*Sadelyngstanes.* This same person, our grandfather, was donor, and gave to our mother in tail, as we suppose by our writ, and at that time she was under age, and so at the time of the execution of this deed he had nothing except by reason of nurture, the freehold resting in our mother, and so the taking of an estate by this deed was a disseisin; judgment whether you can bar us by the deed.—*Pole.* And inasmuch as you do not deny the deed, and your action is not taken on the disseisin, but is a writ affecting the right, judgment.—*Sadelyngstanes.* Then it is so.—*Pole* did not dare to abide judgment, but said that the demandant's grandfather was seised as of freehold at the time of the execution of the deed; ready, &c.—*Sadelyngstanes.* You shall not be admitted to that, for inasmuch as you do not deny the gift made by him to our mother, when she was under age, as above, without showing how he came to have the freehold, it cannot be understood that he did so. —WILLOUGHBY. Then you refuse the averment.— *Sadelyngstanes.* He had nothing except by reason of nurture, as above; ready, &c.—And the other side said the contrary.

Dower. (35.) § Note that on a writ of Dower the heir of

Nos. 34, 35.

luy ne nulle de ses auncestres rienz y avoint,[1] &c. A.D. 1345.
A un autre jour le demandant conust qil fuit seisi,
et le vouche fuit prest, et voleit aver garranti, et
nest pas resceu, pur ceo qil ny ad pas jour, mes
al primer jour qil est vouche il poet.—*Quære diversi-
tatem.*

(34.)[2] § Forme doun en descendre.—*Pole.* Vostre Forme
doun.
aiel par ceo fait nous feffa, ove garrantie; jugement
si countre le fait poietz rienz demander. —*Sadl.*
Mesme celuy nostre aiel fuit donour, et dona a
nostre mere en la taille, come nous supposoms par
nostre brief, a quel temps ele fuit deinz age, et
issint a la confeccion de cel fet il navoit rienz forqe
par resoun de nurture, le frauncteneme nt reposaunt[3]
en nostre mere, et issint la prise destat par ceo
fet disseisine; jugement si par le fet nous puissetz
barrer.—*Pole.* Et desicome vous ne deditez pas le
fet, et vostre accion nest pas pris de la disseisine,
mes est un brief de dreit, jugement.—*Sadl.* Donqes
est il issint. —*Pole* nosa demurer, mes dist qe son
aiel fuis seisi come de franctenement al temps de
la confeccion; prest, &c.—*Sadl.* A ceo ne serrez
resceu, qar desicome vous ne deditez pas le doun
fait par luy a nostre mere, quant ele fuit deinz age,
ut supra, saunz moustrer coment il avint al franctenement, il ne poet estre entendu, &c.—*Wilby.*
Donqes refusetz laverement.—*Sadl.* Il[4] navoit forqe
par resoun de nurture, *ut supra*; prest, &c.—*Et alii
e contra.*

(35.)[2] § *Nota* qen brief de[5] Dowere leire[6] le Count Dowere.
[Fitz.,
Proses
37.]

---

[1] H., navoint, instead of y avoint.
[2] From the four MSS., as above.
[3] C., and D., resposant.
[4] H., nosa demurer mes dit qil.

[5] The words brief de are omitted from D.
[6] leire is omitted from D.

No. 36.

A.D. 1345. the Earl of Atholl was vouched, his body and part of the lands being in the hand of A., and part of the lands in the King's hand, and part in the hands of others. And the voucher stood, and no process was to be made against the other guardians until the King should have signified his pleasure.

Entry   (36.) § Entry *sine assensu Capituli.—Rokel.* Your predecessor leased with the consent of the Convent, for see here their deed which witnesses the fact.—*Pole.* That is the deed of the Prior, and not of the Convent; ready, &c.—WILLOUGHBY. Then it is not the deed of the Prior and the Convent.—*Pole.* I confess that it is the deed of the Prior.—WILLOUGHBY. Even though it be his deed, if it be not the deed of the Convent, it is not their common deed.—Therefore *Pole* took issue in the form:—Not the deed of the Prior and Convent.

No. 36.

Dassels fuit vouche, qi corps et partie des terres A.D. 1345.
furent en la mayn A., et partie en la mayn le Roi,
et partie en meins des autres. Et le voucher estut,
et nulle procees fuit fait vers les autres gardeyns
tanqe le Roi avera maunde sa volunte.

(36.)[1] § Entre *sine assensu Capituli.*—*Rok.* Vostre Entre.
predecessour lessa par assent de Covent, qar veietz
cy lour fait qe le tesmoigne.[2]—*Pole.* Cest le fait le
Priour, et noun pas del Covent; prest, &c.—WILBY.
Donqes nest ceo pas le fait le Priour et le Covent?
—*Pole.* Jeo conusse qe cest le fait le Priour.—
WILBY. Tut soit il son fait, et ceo ne soit pas le
fait le Covent, ceo nest pas lour fait comune.[3]—Par
quei *Pole* prist lissue par la manere qe nient le
fait le Priour et Covent.[4]

---

[1] From the four MSS., as above, but corrected by the record, *Placita de Banco*, Trin., 19 Edw. III., R⁰ 114, d. It there appears that the action was brought by William, Prior of Kirkby Monachorum, against Agnes daughter of Adam Busshe of Kirkby, in respect of one messuage in Kirkby Monachorum (Monks' Kirby, Warwickshire), "in "quod eadem Agnes non habet "ingressum nisi per Petrum "Fraunceys, quondam Priorem de "Kirkeby Monachorum, prædeces-"sorem, &c."

[2] The plea was, according to the record, "quod prædictus Petrus "quondam Prior, &c., per nomen "fratris Petri Prioris de Kirkeby, "et ejusdem loci commonachi, per "scriptum suum, tradiderunt et "dimiserunt eidem Agneti et "cuidam Cristianæ sorori ejusdem "Agnetis prædictum mesuagium "..... habendum et tenendum "eisdem Agneti et Cristianæ, ad "terminum vitæ ipsarum Agnetis "et Cristianæ, de prædictis Petro

"Priore et successoribus suis, per "servitium septem solidorum per "annum, et obligarunt se et "successores suos ad warantizan-"dum, &c. Et profert hic præ-"dictum scriptum sub nomine "ipsorum Petri Prioris et Com-"monachorum, &c., quod hoc "testatur, &c., et in quo contine-"tur quod prædicti Petrus Prior "et Commonachi, &c., prædicto "scripto, ad modum cyrographi "confecto, sigillum domus suæ "adtunc apposuerunt, &c., unde "petit judicium si prædictus "Willelmus, Prior, &c., contra "scriptum prædictum, actionem "versus eam habere debeat, &c "

[3] L., en comune.

[4] The replication, upon which issue was joined, was, according to the record, "quod prædictum "scriptum non est factum prædic-"torum Petri nuper Prioris, &c., "prædecessoris, &c., et Commona-"chorum, sicut prædicta Agnes "superius allegavit."
The *Venire* was awarded as to

Nos. 37–40.

A.D. 1345.
Replevin.

(37.) § Note that St. Filbert's heir was prayed in aid in a Replevin by the plaintiff in Replevin, and was summoned. A Protection was now produced for the prayee.—*Pole.* Protection does not lie for the plaintiff, nor consequently for the prayee. — This exception was not allowed.—Therefore the Protection was allowed.

Note.

(38.) § Note that after the parties in a *Quare impedit* had pleaded to the inquest, when, on the second day afterwards, the plaintiff was essoined as being on the King's service, an objection was raised in the words of the Statute[1] "*postquam aliquis posuerit se in inquisitionem aliquam.*" — And notwithstanding this the essoin was adjudged, and a day was given.

Statute merchant

(39.) § *Birton* said that one had had execution on a statute merchant, and had levied the whole amount, as well as costs and charges, and twelve marks over, and prayed a *Scire facias* against him.—HILLARY. Our clerks say that in all past time in like cases the practice has been to grant a *Venire facias* to account, and never a *Scire facias.*—*Birton.* He will never come in virtue of that process, and I pray a *Scire facias* at my peril.—And afterwards the *Scire facias* to have back the land was granted to him, but it was said that, if his purpose had been to have an account, he would have had only a *Venire facias.*

Quare impedit.

(40.) § *Quare impedit* in which the plaintiff counted that a common ancestor had been seised of the manor to which the advowson was appendant, and presented, and that the descent was from him to two daughters,

---

[1] 13 Edw. I. (Westm. 2), c. 27.

Nos. 37–40.

(37.) [1] § *Nota* qe leire Seint Filbert [2] en un *Re-* A.D. 1345.
plegiari fuit [3] prie en eide par pleintif en *Replegiari,* *Replegiari.*
et il somons. Ore Proteccion fuit mys avant pur le *Protec-*
prie.—*Pole.* Proteccion ne gist pas pur le pleintif, *cion,* 74.]
nec per consequens pur celuy qest prie.—*Non allocatur.*
—Par quei ele fuit allowe.

(38.) [4] § *Nota* qe apres ceo qe les parties a un *Nota.*
Quare impedit avoint plede al enquest, et, al seconde [Fitz.,
Essone,
jour apres, le pleintif fuit essone de service le Roi, 21.]
statut fuit allegge *postquam aliquis posuerit se in in-*
quisitionem aliquam.—Et, *non obstante,* lessone fuit
ajuge et adjourne.

(39.) [5] § *Birtone* dist coment un avoit execucion Statut
par estatut marchaunt, et ad tut leve, mises et marchant.[6]
cóustages, et iiij marcz outre, et pria *Scire facias* [Fitz.,
Sugges-
vers luy.—HILL. Nos clercs dient qe tut temps en *tion,* 18.]
cea [7] ad este use en arrere *Venire facias* dacompter,
et unqes *Scire facias.*—*Birtone.* Il vendra jammes
par cel proces, et jeo le prie a moun peril.—Et
puis le *Scire facias* luy fuit grante a reaver la terre,
mes sil voleit aver lacompte fuit dit qil navera forqe
Venire facias.

(40.) [8] § *Quare impedit,* countant coment un comune *Quare*
impedit.
auncestre fuit seisi del maner a quei lavoeson est [Fitz.,
appendaunt, et presenta, et de luy descendi a ij filles, *Quare*
impedit,
59.]

---

the witnesses to the deed and
twelve jurors, but nothing further
appears on the roll, except adjournments.

[1] From the four MSS., as above.

[2] D., se joint, instead of Seint
Filbert.

[3] D., qe fut.

[4] From L., C., and D.

[5] From L., H., C., and D.

[6] The marginal note in H. is
Execucion.

[7] C., ceo, instead of en cea.

[8] From the four MSS., as above,
but corrected by the record, *Placita
de Banco,* Trin., 19 Edw. III.,
R⁰ 169. It there appears that the
action was brought by John son of
Peter de Bradestone against William
de Lambroke and Isabel his wife,
in respect of a presentation to the
church of Cloteworthe (Clatworthy,
Somerset).

No. 40.

A.D. 1345. who made partition of the manor; and he showed how he had the estate of the elder daughter, and that the church was now void through the death of the person presented by the common ancestor, so that it now belonged to him, as having the estate of the elder daughter, to present; and he did not make mention of any composition.—*Skipwith.* Judgment of the count, which supposes the advowson to be appendant to the manor, whereas by the partition of the manor

No. 40.

qe departirent le maner, et moustra coment il ad lestat leignesse, et qe leglise est ore voide par la mort le presente par le comune auncestre, issint a luy eaunt lestat leignesse attient a ore a presenter; et fist mencion de nulle composicion.[1]—*Skip*. Jugement de counte, qe suppose lavoeson estre appendant al maner,[2] ou par la purpartie del maner allegge *ut*

---

[1] The declaration was, according to the record, "quod quidam "Thomas de Arundel, frater et "heres Johannis de Arundel, fuit "seisitus de manerio de Clote- "worthe, cum pertinentiis, ad quod "advocatio ecclesiæ prædictæ per- "tinet, et de advocatione ecclesiæ "ejusdem manerii, tempore. . . . "domini Regis nunc, et ad eandem "ecclesiam præsentavit quendam "Ricardum de Hulleferon, cleri- "cum suum, ... post cujus "mortem prædicta ecclesia modo "vacat. Et de ipso Thoma "descendit manerium prædictum "ad quod, &c., et advocatio præ- "dicta cuidam Margaretæ et præ- "fatæ Isabellæ, ut filiabus et "heredibus, &c., quæ quidem "Margareta filia einecia, &c., "nupsit de cuidam Philippo de "Cloteworthe, et prædicta Isabella "nupsit se cuidam Simoni Chep- "man de Tauntone, inter quos "quidem Philippum, Margaretam, "et Simonem et Isabellam pur- "partia de manerio prædicto, cum "pertinentiis, ad quod, &c., facta "fuit. Et prædictus Simon obiit, "et prædicta Isabella nupsit se "præfato Willelmo de Lambroke. "Et postmodum prædicti Philippus "et Margareta propartem ejusdem "Margaretæ manerii prædicti, cum "pertinentiis, ad quod, &c., con- "cesserunt ipsi Johanni filio Petri "de Bradestone, tenendam sibi et "heredibus suis in perpetuum. "Et postmodum . . . . . levavit "quidam finis inter ipsum Jo- "hannem filium Petri, querentem, "et præfatos Philippum et Mar- "garetam, deforciantes, de medie- "tate manerii prædicti, cum "pertinentiis, per quem finem "idem Johannes recognovit præ- "dictam medietatem manerii ad "quod, &c., cum pertinentiis, esse "jus ipsius Margaretæ, ut illam "quam iidem Philippus et Mar- "gareta habuerunt de dono præ- "dicti Johannis, et pro illa, &c., "iidem Philippus et Margareta "concesserunt prædicto Johanni "prædictam medietatem, cum per- "tinentiis, et illam ei reddiderunt, "&c., habendam et tenendam "eidem Johanni de capitalibus "dominis, &c., tota vita ipsius "Johannis, et post decessum ipsius "Johannis prædicta medietas "manerii ad quod, &c., cum perti- "nentiis, integre remaneret Jo- "hanni filio prædicti Philippi et "Julianæ uxori ejus, et heredibus "de corporibus ipsorum Johannis "et Julianæ exeuntibus, et sic "dicit quod ipse tenet medietatem "manerii prædicti ad quod, &c., "in forma prædicta, per quod ad "ipsum pertinet ad præsens ad "prædictam ecclesiam præsen- "tare."

[2] D., manoir.

No. 40.

A.D. 1345. alleged as above it is supposed that the advowson remains in gross.—This exception was not allowed, because the advowson remains appendant as before.— *Skipwith.* You see plainly how he has supposed the advowson to remain between them in common, and he has not alleged any subsequent composition for them to present in turn; judgment whether this writ lies between them who so hold in common.—*Grene.* Then it is so; and we demand judgment inasmuch as you have not denied that partition was made of the manor to which the advowson is appendant, as above, nor that we have the purparty of the elder daughter. And we cannot have any other writ or recovery, because a Darrein Presentment does not lie, but a *Quare impedit* naturally does lie for us who are purchaser. And, if we had counted that there was a composition you would have had a traverse to that. And, inasmuch as you have not denied our title, we pray a writ to the Bishop.—WILLOUGHBY to *Skipwith.* Will you say anything else?—*Skipwith.* We demand judgment whether the writ lies between us who thus hold in common.—WILLOUGHBY. The COURT doth award that the plaintiff do have a writ to the Bishop.

No. 40.

supra il est suppose qe lavoweson demoert[1] un gros. A.D. 1345.
—*Non allocatur*, qar lavoweson demoert[1] appendant
come avant.—*Skip*. Vous veietz bien coment il ad
suppose lavoweson demurer entre eux en comune, et
il nad allegge nulle composicion apres par tourne;
jugement si entre eux qe issint tenent en comune
cest brief gise.[2]—*Grene*. Donqes est il issint; et demandoms jugement desicome vous navetz[3] pas dedit
la purpartie fait del maner,[4] a quei, &c., *ut supra*,
ne qe nous avoms[5] leignesse purpartie. Et autre
brief ne recoverir poms aver,[6] qar Drein[7] Presentement ne git pas, mes fait naturelment *Quare impedit*
pur nous qe sumes purchasours. Et, si nous ussoms
counte de composicion, vous ussetz eu a ceo travers.
Et, desicome vous navez[3] pas dedit nostre title, nous
prioms brief al Evesqe.[8]—WILBY a *Skip*. Voilletz
autre chose dire?—*Skip*. Nous demandoms jugement
si entre nous qe issint tenoms en comune le brief
gise.—WILBY. Si agarde la COURT qe le pleintif eit
brief al Evesqe, &c.[9]

---

[1] C., and D., demurt

[2] The plea was, according to the
record, "quod, cum prædictus Jo-
" hannes in narratione sua prædicta
" supponit manerium prædictum
" ad quod, &c., simul cum advoca-
" tione, &c., descendisse ipsi Isa-
" bellæ et præfatæ Margaretæ de
" præfato Thoma, communi ante-
" cessore, &c., ut filiabus et heredi-
" bus, &c., quod quidem manerium
" postea partitum fuit inter eas, et
" advocatio illa remansit præsen-
" tandi in communi, &c., unde
" petit judicium si breve istud de
" *Quare impedit* in hoc casu inter
" eos competit, &c."

[3] L., and C., navietz.

[4] D., manoir.

[5] D., navoms.

[6] D., avoir.

[7] C., Darrein.

[8] The replication was, according
to the record, "quod, ex quo præ-
" dicti Willelmus et Isabella ex-
" presse cognoverunt quod prædicta
" advocatio descendit præfatis Mar-
" garetæ et Isabellæ, ut filiabus et
" heredibus, &c., nec dedicunt quin
" ipse Johannes habet statum præ-
" dictæ Margaretæ filiæ eyneciæ,
" &c., nec quin ista est prima
" vacatio ecclesiæ prædictæ post
" mortem prædicti Ricardi per
" communem antecessorem, &c.,
" præsentati, per quod ad ipsum
" pertinet hac vice ad prædictam
" ecclesiam præsentare, unde petit
" judicium et breve Episcopo, &c."

[9] According to the roll the judgment was "Quia ex utraque parte
" partium prædictarum cognitum

No. 41.

A.D. 1345.
Dower.

(41.) § Dower which Hugh le Despenser and his wife brought against Thomas de Verdoun. And Thomas vouched the three sisters and the issue of the fourth sister as heirs of the husband, and also John Tibetot tenant by the curtesy of England in right of her issue, and they were to be summoned, &c. And because the issue was under age he made *profert* of the ancestor's deed, with warranty, &c.

No. 41.

(41.) [1] § Dowere qe Hughe le Despenser et sa
femme porterent vers Thomas de Verdoun, qe voucha
les iij soers et lissue la quarte soer [2] come heirs le
baron, et auxint Johan Tiptot tenant par ley Dengleterre en le dreit son issue, qe serront somons, &c.
Et pur ceo qe lissue est deinz age mist avant le
fait launcestre ove garrantie, &c. [3]

" est quod prædictus Thomas, com-
" munis antecessor, obiit seisitus
" de advocatione prædicta, quæ
" quidem advocatio descendit præ-
" fatæ Margaretæ filiæ eyneciæ et
" prædictæ Isabellæ in forma præ-
" dicta, et quod idem Johannes
" habet statum prædictæ Margaretæ
" sororis eyneciæ ad terminum vitæ
" suæ, &c., videtur Curiæ hic quod
" ad ipsum Johannem hac vice
" pertinet ad prædictam ecclesiam
" præsentare. Et ideo considera-
" tum est quod prædictus Johannes
" recuperet præsentationem suam
" ad ecclesiam prædictam versus
" eos, et habeat breve Episco, &c."
It was found upon writ of enquiry " quod prædicta ecclesia valet
" per annum, secundum verum
" valorem ejusdem, viginti marcas,
" et quod eadem ecclesia cœpit
" vacare in Festo Animarum ultimo
" præterito, et, quia tempus semes-
" tre elabitur ante recuperationem
" prædictam, consideratum est
" quod prædictus Johannes filius
" Petri recuperet versus eos damna
" sua, videlicet, valorem ecclesiæ
" duorum annorum." There was
an award of execution by *Elegit*.

[1] From L., C., and D., but corrected by the record, *Placita de
Banco*, Trin., 19 Edw. III., R° 260.
It there appears that the action was
brought by Hugh le Despenser and
Elizabeth his wife against Thomas
de Verdoun, knight, in respect of a

third part of the manor of Brendebradefelde (Bradfield Combust,
Suffolk), as her dower of the endowment of Giles de Badelesmere,
Elizabeth's former husband.

[2] soer is omitted from C.

[3] According to the record
" Thomas .... dicit quod prædic-
" tus Egidius de Badelesmere,
" quondam vir, &c. ..... per
" factum suum concessit, tradidit,
" et dimisit eidem Thomæ de Ver-
" doun ..... prædictum mane-
" rium de Brendebradefelde, unde,
" &c.,.... habendum et tenendum
" eidem Thomæ ad totam vitam
" suam de præfato Egidio et here-
" dibus suis, et obligavit se et
" heredes suos ad warantizandum,
" &c. Et profert hic prædictum
" factum quod hoc testatur, &c.
" Et sic dicit quod ipse tenet
" manerium prædictum, unde, &c.,
" ad terminum vitæ suæ, ex dimis-
" sione prædicti Egidii, et reversio
" inde, post mortem ipsius Thomæ
" ad quosdam Elizabetham, uxorem
" Willelmi de Bohun Comitis Nor-
" hamptoniæ, sororem et unam
" heredum prædicti Egidii, Matill-
" dem uxorem Johannis de Veer
" Comitis Oxoniæ, sororem et
" alteram heredum prædicti Egidii,
" Margeriam quæ fuit uxor Wil-
" lelmi de Roos de Hamelak,
" sororem et alteram heredum præ-
" dicti Egidii, et Johannem filium
" et heredem Margaretæ nuper

Nos. 42, 43.

(42.) § *Formedon.*—*Huse.* Whereas she makes her demand in respect of six messuages, there are only two messuages. And with respect to them he pleaded to issue on a traverse.—*Grene.* There are as many as we suppose, and we pray that it be so entered, so that his statement may not be held as not denied by us in accepting it as a fact that there are less.— Hillary. Your count is a definite statement contrary to that which he says, so that, whether the quantity be more or less, you will recover it.—*Grene.* It would follow from that by a release of two messuages he would bar me as to six, and so with regard to other answers.—*Huse.* No, in that case it would possibly be necessary for you to aver that your demand was greater, and your issue would be "not included" as to the four.—And afterwards it was ordered that the entry should be made.—But nevertheless the Clerks said that the *Venire facias* would be in accordance with the demand.

(43.) § *Quare non admisit* for the King against the Bishop of Exeter, counting that he recovered against

Nos. 42, 43.

(42.)[1] § Fourme doun.—*Huse.* Ou ele fait sa de- A.D. 1345.
mande de vj mies, &c., il ny ad qe ij mies. Et Fourme
de[2] doun.
de ceo pleda a issue sur travers.—*Grene.* Il y ad
taunt com nous supposoms, et ceo prioms qe soit
entre, qe ceo ne soit pas tenu a nient dedit de
nous, acceptaunt qil y ad meins.—Hill. Vostre
count est precees[3] countre son dit, issint qe eit il
plus ou meins vous le recoverez.—*Grene.* De ceo
ensuereit qe par relees de deux mies[4] il moi barreit
de vj, et issint par autres respons.—*Huse.* Nanylle,
vous averetz pur necessite daverer qe vostre demande
fuit plus par cas, et si serra vostre issue qe nient
compris quant a les iiij.[5]—Et puis fuit ceo comaunde
dentrer.—*Et tamen Clerici dixerunt* qe le *Venire facias*
serreit acordaunt a la demande.

(43.)[6] § *Quare non admisit* pur le Roi vers Levesqe *Quare non*
admisit.
Dexcestre, countant coment il recoverist vers le Prior [Fitz.,
Quare non
admisit,
8.]

" uxoris Johannis Tibetot, consan-
" guineum et alterum heredum
" prædicti Egidii, qui quidem Jo-
" hannes filius Margaretæ est infra
" ætatem. Et in forma illa vocat
" inde ad warantum ipsos Willel-
" mum Comitem, Elizabetham,
" Johannem Comitem, Matilldem,
" Margeriam, Johannem filium et
" heredem Margaretæ, et prædic-
" tum Johannem Tibetot, qui pro-
" partem prædicti Johannis filii et
" heredis Margaretæ tenet ad ter-
" minum vitæ suæ, per legem
" Angliæ, de hereditate ipsius Jo-
" hannis filii et heredis Margaretæ."
The vouchees were to be summoned in several counties. After
the sheriffs of all those counties
had twice failed to return the writs
directed to them "sicut pluries
" præceptum est cuilibet prædic-
" torum Vicecomitum quod sum-
" moneat, &c."

"Et dictum est attornato præ-
" dicti Thomæ quod sequatur suo
" periculo, &c."
[1] From L., H., C., and D.
[2] de is from L. alone.
[3] H., C., and D., procees.
[4] mies is omitted from D.
[5] L., and H., iij.
[6] From the four MSS., as above,
but corrected by the record, *Placita
de Banco*, Trin., 19 Edw. III., R° 91.
It there appears that the action
was brought by the King against
the Bishop of Exeter, on a recovery,
in *Quare impedit* against the Prior
of Totnes, of a presentation to the
church of Brixham (Devon), on the
ground that the Bishop refused to
admit the King's presentee Hugh
de Askham when a writ was delivered to him "in festo Sancti
" Silvestri" next following the
Quinzaine of St. Michael in the
18th year.

No. 43.

A.D. 1345. the Prior of Totnes, who was an alien, for the reason
that the temporalities of the Priory were seized into
his hand, whereupon he sent his writ to the Bishop
to admit his presentee, &c.—*Pole* denied the contempt
and damages, and said that a provisor, while the
temporalities of the Priory were in the hand of the
Prior, had been in possession of the same vicarage,
and had continued that estate until the time at which
judgment was rendered; and when the writ came to
him he gave institution to the King's presentee, and
put him in corporal possession, and he is now seised
on the King's presentation; judgment whether any
tort can be assigned in the Bishop's person, &c.—*Notton.*
He has first alleged plenarty by means of a provision,
which is, as it were, a mode of excuse for not having
admitted the King's presentee; and afterwards he
says that he has executed the King's command; and
so there are two answers, and each is contradictory
to the other; and we demand judgment for the King,
and pray that the Bishop be found guilty of the contempt.—*Pole.* Our answer is that we have executed the

No. 43.

A.D. 1345.

de Toteneys alien, par resoun des temporaltes la Priorie en sa mein seisiz, sur quei il luy maunda son brief de resceiver[1] son presente, &c.—*Pole* defendi le contempte et damages, et dit qun provisour, esteaunt les temporaltes de la Priorie en la mein le Priour, fuit possessione de mesme la vikarie, et cel estat continua tanqal temps del jugement rendu; et quant le brief luy vint il fist institucion al presente le Roi, et luy mist en corporel possession, et a ore seisi al presentement le Roi; jugement si tort en luy, &c.[2]—*Nottone.* Il ad allegge primes par provisioun plenerte qest comme excusacioun pur ceo qil ne poet resceiver[1] le presente le Roi; et puis dit qil ad fait le comaundement le Roi; et issint ij respons, et chesqun contrariaunt a autre; et demandoms jugement pur le Roi, et prioms qil soit atteint del contempte.[3]—*Pole.* Nostre respons est qe

---

[1] L., and H., resceivre.

[2] According to the record "Epis-"copus . . . . defendit vim et in-"juriam quando, &c. Et dicit "quod tempore quo advocatio "vicariæ prædictæ fuit in manu "prædicti Prioris, diu antequam "idem dominus Rex præsenta-"tionem suam ad vicariam præ-"dictam recuperavit, quidam Jo-"hannes Wrey, virtute cujusdam "provisionis ei a Curia Romana ad "vicariam prædictam factæ, posuit "se in eandem vicariam, et posses-"sionem suam in eadem continu-"avit quousque idem dominus Rex "breve suum prædictum de admit-"tendo prædictum Hugonem, cleri-"cum suum, &c., eidem Episcopo "mandavit. virtute cujus institu-"tionis idem Hugo modo est in "corporali possessione ejusdem. "Et hoc paratus est verificare, &c., "unde petit judicium si idem "dominus Rex aliquem contemp-

"tum in persona ipsius Episcopi "assignare posset, &c."

[3] According to the record (not always strictly grammatical) "Jo-"hannes [de Clone] qui sequitur, "&c., dicit quod in hoc quod idem "Episcopus dicit quod tempore quo "dicta advocatio fuit in manu præ-"dicti Prioris, et diu antequam "idem dominus Rex præsenta-"tionem suam, &c., recuperasset, "dictum Johannem Wrey prætextu "provisionis, &c., sibi factæ se "posuisse in eandem, et posses-"sionem, &c., in eadem continu-"asse quousque idem dominus Rex "breve suum de admittendo præ-"dictum Hugonem eidem Epis-"copo mandavit, sic supponendo "vicariam illam de prædicto Jo-"hanne Wrey virtute prædictæ pro-"visionis, &c., plenam extitisse "tempore quo advocatio, &c., fuit "in manu prædicti Prioris, et ita "recuperare ipsius domini Regis

No. 43.

King's command.—*Grene.* By your last answer it is to be understood that you admitted the King's presentee to a benefice which was void, and by the first answer that the vicarage was full; therefore, even though you did put the King's presentee in possession by parol, that putting in possession cannot take effect, because it was upon the possession of another person. And suppose you had pleaded nothing except that you admitted the King's presentee, and we had, on the King's behalf, maintained the contempt against you, and the fact had been so found by verdict, you would have been found guilty of the contempt because you had not excused yourself by plea; for the same reason you will be now in virtue of your confession.— *Blaykestone, ad idem.* When the King recovers, and commands the Bishop to admit his presentee, the Bishop is bound by law first to make the church void of every other person by whatsoever title he may be in possession, and then to put the King's presentee in possession, because otherwise he does not execute the King's command; and now it is to be understood by his plea that he put the King's presentee in possession upon the possession of another person, and that is by law no execution of the King's command. —*Skipwith.* And suppose a provisor were in possession, and the Bishop desired to oust him, and did everything in his own power, and the provisor defended himself by appeals to Rome, by reason of which the

---

" vacuum, et ita ipsum Episcopum,
" virtute brevis prædicti, prædictum
" Hugonem, propter possessionem
" prædicti Johannis prædictam,
" admittere non potuisse, et
" etiam quo ad hoc quod idem
" Episcopus superius allegavit se
" prædictum Hugonem per domi-
" num Regem præsentatum virtute
" brevis prædicti ad prædictam
" vicariam, quasi ad vicariam
" vacantem, admisisse, cum per
" placitum ipsius Episcopi vica-
" riam illam de prædicto Johanne
" plenam virtute provisionis, &c.,
" extitisse, et sic ipsum Johannem
" a possessione sua legitime non-
" dum amotum fuisse, et sic
" responsio ipsius Episcopi con-
" traria in se, multiplex, et incerta,

No. 43.

nous avoms fait le comaundement le Roi.—*Grene.*
Par vostre darrein respons est entendu qe vous resceustes le presente le Roi a benefice voide, et par
le primere respons qe la vikarie fuit plein ; par
quei, tut luy meistes en possession par parole, cel
mettre einz ne poet prendre effecte, qar ceo fuit sur
autri possession. Et jeo pose qe voùs ussetz rienz
plede mes qe vous resceustes le presente le Roi, et
nous ussoms, pur le Roi, meintenu le contempte sur
vous, et tiel fait sur verdit fuit trove vous serrez
atteint del contempte pur ceo qe par ple vous ne
vous excusastes pas ; par mesme la resoun a ore de
vostre conissaunce.—*Blayk., ad idem.* Quant le Roi
recovere, et comande al Evesqe de resceiver son presente, Levesqe par ley est tenutz primes de voider
leglise de chesqun autre par qicunqe title il soit
einz, et mettre einz le presente le Roi, qar autrement ne fait il pas le comandement le Roi ; et ore par
son plee est entendu qil mist einz le presente le
Roi sur autri possession, qest par ley nulle execucion
del comaundement le Roi.[1]—*Skyp.* Et jeo pose qun
provisour[2] fuit einz, et Levesqe luy voleit ouster, et
fist ceo qen luy fuit, et il par appeux soi defendist,

" et unde petit judicium pro Rege.
" Dicit etiam quod, advocatione
" prædicta in manu domini Regis
" sic existente, dicta vicaria vacavit,
" et vacans fuit diu antequam
" dominus Rex per breve suum
" versus prædictum Priorem præ-
" sentationem, &c., ad eandem,
" &c., recuperavit, usque prædic-
" tum diem Sancti Silvestri, quo die
" idem Hugo, ad prædictam vica-
" riam per dominum Regem præ-
" sentatus, prædictum breve de
" admittendo eidem Episcopo
" liberavit, et, ex parte domini
" Regis, ipsum Episcopum ut
" ipsum ad vicariam illam, virtute

" brevis prædicti, admitteret in-
" stanter requisivit, idem Episco-
" pus ipsum Hugonem admittere
" recusavit, et vicariam illam, ut
" Ordinarius, &c., occupavit, et
" fructus inde percepit a dicto die
" Sancti Silvestri usque diem
" Sancti Wolstani tunc proxime
" sequentem, quo die idem Episco-
" pus prædictum Johánnem Wrey
" in corporalem possessionem ejus-
" dem vicariæ per commissionem,
" &c., induxit, unde petit judicium
" pro domino Rege."
[1] The words le Roi are omitted
from C. and D.
[2] D., provisiour.

No. 43.

Bishop could not do anything, how could he excuse himself except in this way? But I say that it would be an excuse for him to do all that in him lies, and to let the King's presentee remove the other who is a provisor or any other person holding possession.— *Huse.* Even though it be, as we said at the beginning, that a provisor was in occupation at one time, he may have been deprived, or may have been dead, for anything that we said, at the time at which the King's writ came to us: for you have it not from us that the benefice was full when we effected execution of the King's command; but our answer is simply that we have executed the King's command, and that ought in law to be sufficient for us. And in a *Quare non admisit* it would not be a sufficient answer for a Bishop to say that the church was full, and that he could not therefore effect execution of the King's command, because according to law he must effect execution, and the parsons will afterwards plead between themselves.—Willoughby and Hillary denied this: because if the church were full of one who had a title antecedent to that which was the ground of the King's recovery, and the Bishop found that to be the case, he could not because of the King's command oust that one, and therefore that fact will be an excuse for him in a *Quare non admisit.—Huse.* That would indeed be a marvel—that a Bishop should try the King's title to find out whether it was higher or lower.—But afterwards *R. Thorpe* waived the demurrer for the King, and said that, at the time of the King's recovery, and when the Bishop received the writ to admit the King's presentee, the church was void, and the Bishop refused to admit his presentee, and the Bishop himself was a long time in occupation of the fruits of the benefice, and afterwards admitted a

No. 43.

par quei Levesqe ne poait rienz faire, coment soi A.D. 1345. excusereit il sil ne fuit par ceste voye? Mes jeo die qil serreit excuse de fere ceo qen luy fuit, et lesser le presente le Roi et lautre provisour[1] ou autre qe ocupa la possession tollir.[2]—*Huse.* Tut soit il issint com nous parlames a comencement qun provisour[1] ocupa a un temps, il poet estre prive ou mort, pur rienz qe nous dioms al temps qe le brief le Roi nous vint: qar vous navetz[3] pas de nous qe le benefice fuit pleine quant nous feimes execucion del mandement le Roi; [mes nostre respons est tut qe nous avoms fait le comaundement le Roi],[4] et ceo par ley nous deit suffire. Et a un *Quare non admisit* il ne serra pas respons pur Levesqe a dire qe leglise fuit pleine, par quei il ne poet faire execucion del mandement le Roi, qar de ley il fra[5] execucion, et les persones apres entreplederount.[6]— WILBY et HILL. *hoc negant*: qar si leglise fuit plein dun qavoit title de plus haut[7] qe ne fuit la cause del recoverir le Roi, et Levesqe trovast cella, par mandement le Roi il ne purra pas ouster celuy, par quei ceo serra excuse[8] pur luy al *Quare non admisit.* —*Huse.* Certes ceo serreit merveille qe Levesqe triereit le title le Roi le quel ceo fuit de plus haut ou plus bas.—Mes puis [R.] *Thorpe* weyva la demure pur le Roi, et dit qal temps del recoverir le Roi, et quant Levesqe resceut le brief de resceivre[9] le pre- sente le Roi, leglise fuit voide, et Levesqe refusa de resceivre[9] soun presente,[10] et il mesme[11] grant temps ocupa les fruitz, et apres resceut un provisour,[1] et

---

[1] D., provisiour.
[2] H., toller; C., toiler; D., toiller.
[3] L., and C., navietz.
[4] The words between brackets are omitted from D.
[5] C., preist.
[6] L., and C., entreplederent.
[7] D., haunt, or hauut.

[8] The word has originally been execucion in all the MSS., but the letters cuse have been substituted for ecucion in C., in a later hand.
[9] D., resceivere.
[10] D., le presente le Roi, instead of soun presente.
[11] D., mesmes.

No. 43.

provisor, and put the provisor in possession, by which act contempt is sufficiently proved, and (said *R. Thorpe*) we demand judgment whether the law puts us to answer as to any subsequent admission of the King's presentee, which cannot excuse the first contempt. —*Huse.* We tell you that we admitted the King's presentee, and gave him induction according· to the King's command, and that he is still in possession, &c., *absque hoc* that we or anyone on our behalf gave induction to any other person ; ready, &c.; judgment whether we can be convicted of contempt.—*R. Thorpe.* And we demand judgment, inasmuch as you have not denied that the vicarage was void at the time at which the writ came to you, and you do not discharge yourself of the contempt at that time, but say that you admitted the King's presentee, and you have not said that you admitted him on the same day, and so by your own confession you are convicted of contempt; judgment.—*Huse.* We take your records to witness that we said that on that same day on which the writ came to us we admitted him, &c., which day is and can only be understood to be the day of which you have counted, for there is no dispute between us as to the day on which the writ came to us.—And it was recorded on behalf of *Huse* that he had so said, but

No. 43.

luy mist en possession, par quel fait est assetz prove contempte, et demandoms jugement si a nulle resceit apres del presente le Roi, qe ne purra excuser le primer contempte, la ley les mette a respondre.— *Huse.* Nous vous dioms qe nous resceumes le presente le Roi et luy feimes induccion par comandement le Roi, et il possessione unqore, &c., sanz ceo qe nous feimes induccion, ou asqun de par nous, a nul autre; prest, &c.; jugement si de contempte, &c.— [*R.*] *Thorpe.* Et nous jugement, desicome vous navez[1] pas dedit la vikarie voide al temps quant le brief vous vint, et a cel temps vous deschargetz pas del contempte, mes parletz qe vous resceustes,[2] et navez[1] dit[3] qe a mesme le jour vous le resceustes,[2] et issint de vostre coinissance atteint del contempte; jugement.—*Huse.* Nous pernoms vos[4] recordes[5] qe nous deimes qe mesme le jour qe le brief nous vint nous luy resceumes, &c., quele chose nest ne poet estre entendu[6] mes a mesme le jour qe vous avietz counte, qar de jour nous sumes pas a[7] debat qe le brief nous vint.[8]—Et issint fuit recorde pur *Huse* qil avoit dit, et autrement de sa coinissance les

---

[1] L., and C., navietz.

[2] C., and D., resceutes.

[3] D., dedit.

[4] C., vos is omitted from C. and D.

[5] C., and D., recorde.

[6] C., entendue.

[7] D., en.

[8] According to the roll "Episco- "pus dicit quod idem dominus "Rex aliquem contemptum in "persona ipsius Episcopi per "aliquod præallegatum assignare "non potest, quia dicit quod die "quo dominus Rex breve suum "prædictum de admittendo præ- "dictum Hugonem ad vicariam "prædictam eidem Episcopo man-

"davit, videlicet prædicto die "Sancti Silvestri, idem Episcopus "eodem die ipsum Hugonem, "virtute brevis prædicti, ad eandem "vicariam admisit, et ipsum in "eadem instituit, et adhuc in "corporali possessione ejusdem "existit virtute institutionis præ- "dictæ, absque hoc quod idem "Episcopus prædictum Johannem "Wrey post eundem diem in "vicariam illam instituit, seu "ipsum instituendi in eadem aliis "vices suas commisit, prout idem "Johannes qui sequitur, &c., ei "imponit. Et hoc paratus est "verificare, &c., unde petit judi- "cium."

Nos. 44, 45.

A.D. 1345. otherwise the King's Serjeants would have abode judgment on his confession; but afterwards they imparled on the King's behalf, and said that he had encumbered after the prohibition, &c., as they had surmised against him on the King's behalf.

Conclusion of the *Scire facias*, in which one who had been admitted to defend his right was not allowed his age.[1]

(44.) § *Grene.* In a like case, on a previous occasion, one who had been admitted to defend his right was not allowed his age, and, although they allege a precedent, the reverse of this has never been adjudged; and we take your records to witness that they say nothing else, and we pray execution.— STONORE. We do not see that there is any disherison even if she have execution.—*R. Thorpe.* It is possible that the fine is void; and moreover we have our warranty, to claim which by *Warantia chartæ* we should be admitted before attaining our full age; and the law is the same although she claims only a term for life as if she were to claim a fee simple, and the mischief for the infant is equally great; and we take your records to witness that, if you give judgment that we shall not have our age, we shall be ready to answer.—STONORE. No, you say nothing else, and that we shall record, and we shall never give judgment for you to defend your right if it be not lawful for you to do so, and from us you will have but one judgment.—And afterwards, although the infant made his protestation that he was ready to answer if his age should not be allowed, yet because he said nothing else STONORE awarded execution, &c.

Judgment.

Dower.

(45.) § Dower. View was demanded.—*Birton.* Our demand is in respect of rent, and he is tenant of the rent, and not of the land; besides, he entered upon the rent by our husband.—*Huse.* We demand view of the land; and on a writ *De quibus* in respect of

---

[1] *See* Y.B., Mich., 18 Edw. III., No. 9.

Nos. 44, 45.

seriauntes le Roi voilleint aver demure; mes puis A.D. 1345. enparlerunt pur le Roi, et disoint qe puis la prohibicion, &c., il avoit encombre, come ils luy avoint pur le Roi surmys.[1]

(44)[2] § *Grene*. En autiel cas autrefoith celuy qad este resceu fuit ouste de son age, et, coment qils alleggent ensample, le revers fuit unqes ajuge; et pernoms vos recordes qautre chose ne dient, et prioms execucion.—STON. Nous veioms nulle desheritaunce tut eit ele execucion.—[R.] *Thorpe*. Par cas la fine est voide; et auxint nous avoms nostre garrantie, a quel par garrantie de chartre nous serroms resceu avant nostre age; et mesme la ley est coment qele cleyme forqe terme de vie, come si ele clamast fee simple, et owel meschief pur lenfant; et pernoms voz recordes qe, si vous agardez qe nous naveroms pas nostre age, prest serroms a respondre.—STON. Nanil, vous ditetz nulle autre chose, et ceo recordroms,[4] et nous agarderoms jammes qe vous defenderetz vostre dreit[5] si leal[6] ne vous soit, et de nous naveretz qun agarde.—Et puis, coment qe lenfant fist sa protestacion qil fuit prest, &c., si, &c.,[7] STON., pur ceo qil ne dit[8] autre chose, agarda *Judicium*. execucion, &c.

Marginal note: Residuum del *Scire* *facias* ou celuy qest resceu a defendre soun dreit est ouste.[3]

(45.)[2] § Dowere. Viewe demande.—*Birtone*. Nostre demande est de rente, et il est tenant de la rente, et noun pas de la terre; ovesqe ceo, il entra en la rente par nostre baron.—*Huse*. Nous demandoms la viewe de la terre; et en brief *De quibus* de rente

Marginal note: Dowere. [Fitz., *View*, 106.]

---

[1] A great number of adjournments follow, but nothing further appears on the roll.

[2] From the four MSS. as above.

[3] The marginal note is from C. and D. In L. it is Prier destre resceu, in H., Fines. In D. there are added the words "Cunstan Neville" in another but approximately contemporary hand.

[4] L., and H., recordoms.

[5] C., dit.

[6] H., ley.

[7] The words si, &c., are omitted from C.

[8] D., dedit.

Nos. 46, 47.

A.D. 1345. rent view will be had of the land.—WILLOUGHBY. Yes, on the understanding that he is tenant of the land; and it is not right that if you are tenant only of the rent you should have view of another person's freehold.—*Huse.* I cannot take an averment that I am not tenant of the land, or that I am not tenant of the rent, without myself ousting myself from view.—*Birton.* You can do so with the object of having view.—And afterwards view was granted.—See as to this a case in Hilary Term in the 19th year, above, in which view was granted.[1]

Dower.   (46.) § Dower. View was demanded where the husband had died seised.—*R. Thorpe.* It is no plea [to say that he died seised] unless you say of such an estate that he could endow you.—This exception was not allowed.

Appeal.   (47.) § Note that in an Appeal of Maihem for William White a Protection was produced for the defendant; and, notwithstanding that the party could recover only damages, the Protection was disallowed.

---

[1] The reference is to Y.B., Hil., 19 Edw. III., No. 29 (p. 492).

Nos. 46, 47.

homme avera viewe de la terre.—WILBY. Oyl, al A.D. 1345.
entent qil est tenant [de la terre; et]¹ il nest pas
resoun si vous soietz tenant de la rente qe vous
eietz la viewe dautri franctenement.—*Huse.* Jeo ne
puisse prendre averement qe jeo ne² su pas tenant
de la terre, ou qe jeo ne su pas tenant de la rente,
si jeo ne moi ouste mesme de la viewe.—*Birtone.*
Si poietz, al entent daver la viewe.—Et puis la
viewe fuit grante.—*De hoc Hillarii xix°, supra,* ou
la viewe fuit grante.³

(46.) ⁴ § Dowere. Viewe demande ou le baron Dowere.
muruyst seisi.—*R. Thorpe.* Ceo nest pas plee si vous [Fitz., *View*,
ne dietz de tiel estat qe dower vous⁵ poet.—*Non* 107.]
allocatur.

(47.) ⁶ § *Nota* qen Appelle de Maheym pur William Appelle.
White Proteccion fuit mys avant pur le defendant; [Fitz., *Protec-*
et, *non obstante* qe partie nest pas a recoverir forqe *cion,* 78.]
damages, la Proteccion fuit desallowe.

---

¹ The words between brackets are from H. alone.

² ne is from D. alone.

³ The last sentence is from L. alone.

⁴ From L., C., and D.

⁵ L., and C., nous.

⁶ From L., C., and D. The case appears to be that found among the *Placita coram Rege* (Rex) R° 23. The appeal was brought by William White of Holbeach against Simon son of Roger de Flete, and Laurence de Flete, knight, for abetting John Chouneson who had since fled.

Nothing is said in the roll as to a Protection, but the defendants pleaded "quod ipsi de abetto et "assensu prædictis vel hujusmodi "accessorio non debent respondere "quousque prædictus Johannes "Chounessone vel aliquis alius "appellatus de principali facto

"mahemii prædicti utlagaretur vel "alio modo convincantur. Et "petunt interim dimitti. Et eis "conceditur."

After outlawry of the principal, "idem Willelmus White instanter "separatim appellat prædictos "Simonem filium Rogeri et "Laurentium de Flete de abetto "et assensu mahemii prædicti."

The defendants pleaded Not Guilty, and issue was joined thereon to the country.

The defendants were allowed to be on mainprise, and each of the six mainpernors was responsible for their appearance, and "quod "præfato Willelmo White per "præfatos Simonem et Lauren-"tium nec per eorum procura-"tionem malum non eveniet, "videlicet, quilibet manucaptorum "prædictorum sub pœna xl*li*,"

Nos. 48–51.

A.D. 1345.
Account

(48.) § Note that on a writ of Account, after a verdict had passed at *Nisi prius* to the effect that the defendant had been the plaintiff's receiver, a Protection was produced in the Common Bench in order to delay judgment, and it was disallowed.

Aid-
prayer.

(49.) § Note that a tenant for term of life prayed aid, and the prayee was summoned and did not appear. A Protection was now produced for the tenant.—*Grene.* We pray that you record the non-appearance of the prayee.—HILLARY. That we cannot do, because we cannot enter on the roll *quod respondeat sine, &c.,* any more than we should record any default if a writ had been brought against two joint tenants and one of them had made default, and a Protection had been produced for the other.—And afterwards the parol demurred.

Trespass

(50.) § Note that on a writ of Trespass against several persons a Protection was produced for one, and the parol only demurred with regard to him alone.

*Quare in-
cumbravit.*

(51.) § *Quare incumbravit* for Theobald de Greneville against the Bishop of Exeter, in respect of the church of Kilkhampton, counting that the church became void on a certain day, and that, while the plea was pending, the Bishop encumbered.—*Gaynesford.*

Nos. 48–51.

(48.)¹ § *Nota* qen brief dacompte, apres enqueste A.D. 1345.
passe qil fuit resceivour pris par *Nisi prius*, Pro- Acompte.
[Fitz.,
teccion en Baunk fuit mys avant pur delaier le *Protec-*
jugement, et fuit desallowe. *cion*, 79.]

(49.)² § *Nota* qe tenant a terme de vie pria eide, Eide
qe fuit somons et ne vint pas. Ore Proteccion fuit prier.
[Fitz.,
mys avant pur le tenant.—*Grene.* Nous prioms qe *Protec-*
vous recordetz la noun venue le prie.—HILL. Ceo *cion*, 80.]
ne poms pas, qar nous ne poms pas entrer en roulle
*quod respondeat*³ *sine*, &c., nient plus qe si brief fuit
porte vers deux jointenantz et lun feist defaut, et
Proteccion fuit mys avant pur lautre, nous recordroms
nulle defaute.—Et puis la parole⁴ demura.

(50.)¹ § *Nota* qen brief de Trans vers plusours Trans.
[Fitz.,
Proteccion pur un fuit mys avant, et la parole de- *Protec-*
mura forqe vers luy soulement. *cion*, 81.]

(51.)⁵ § *Quare incumbravit* pur Thebaud Greneville *Quare in-
cumbravit.*
[Fitz.,
vers Levesqe Dexcestre⁶ del eglise de Kylhamtone,⁷ *Quare in-
cumbravit*
2.]
countant qe leglise se voida certein jour, et qe
pendant le plee, &c., il encombra.⁸—*Gayn.* Autrefoith

---

¹ From L., C., and D.

² From L., H., C., and D.

³ D., *respondeat parti.*

⁴ All the MSS. except D., proteccion. Parole is there written
on an erasure.

⁵ From L., H., C., and D., but
corrected by the record, *Placita de
Banco*, Trin., 19 Edw. III., R° 133.
It there appears that the action
was brought by Theobald de Greneville against John, Bishop of
Exeter, after Theobald s recovery
of his presentation to the church
of Kilkhampton (Cornwall) by
Assise of Darrein Presentment
against John de Ralegh, of Charles,
and Amy his wife, pending which

Assise, as alleged, the Bishop
encumbered the church.

⁶ H., de Excestre ; D., de E.

⁷ L., and H., Kykhamptone.

⁸ The conclusion of the declaration (in which it was alleged *inter
alia* that, pending the Assise, the
plaintiff on a certain day, in the
presence of certain persons "liber-
" avit eidem Episcopo breve
" domini Regis de prohibitione,
" &c., ne aliquem ad ecclesiam
" illam admitteret, pendente inter
" eos Assisa praedicta ") was
according to the roll that whereas
the plaintiff, in the presence of
certain persons " praefato Episcopo
praesentasset quendam Walterum

No. 51.

A.D. 1345 Heretofore the plaintiff brought another *Quare incumbravit*,[1] and counted that the church became void on a day other than that on which he now makes it to have become void, that is to say, then on a Friday, and now on a Tuesday; judgment of this count which is contrariant to the first.—This exception was not allowed, because the first *Quare incumbravit* was ended by non-suit, notwithstanding that it was said that this action is different from the other because the earlier or later occurrence of the vacancy may toll an action, or may possibly give one.—*Gaynesford.* We tell you that the church became void on a certain day—and he said when—and afterwards, on such a day, John de Ralegh and Amy his wife presented their clerk to us, before which time no presentation was made by you to us, and no prohibition came to us, and on their presentation, in accordance with the course of the law of Holy Church, we set on foot an inquest of office to enquire as to the vacancy, the litigiousness of the benefice, and the ability of the person, and other circumstances, and the office was in favour of the presentee; and therefore we admitted him by compulsion of the law of Holy Church; and we demand judgment whether the plaintiff can assign tort in our person.—*Blaykeston.* The prohibition was

---

[1] *See* Y.B., Mich., 17 Edw. III., No. 21 (Rolls edition, pp. 94-116), and *see* Y.B., Easter, 17 Edw. III., No. 3 (Rolls edition, p. 232).

No. 51.

il porta un autre[1] *Quare incumbravit*, et counta qe A.D. 1345. leglise se voida a autre jour qe ne fait a ore, saver par jour de vendredy, et ore le mardi; jugement de counte contrariaunt al primer.—*Non allocatur, quia terminabatur per non sectam, non obstante* qe fuit dit qe ceste accion varie del autre, qar la voidance plus toust[2] ou plus tard toudra accion ou durreit par cas.—*Gayn*. Nous vous dioms qe leglise se voida a certein jour—et dit quant—et apres a tiel jour Johan de Raly, et Amye sa femme presenterent a nous lour clerc, avant quel temps nul presentement par vous a nous ne fuit fait, ne nul prohibicion nous vint, et a lour presentement, par cours de ley de Seinte Eglise, liverames enqueste doffice denquere de la voidaunce, litigiousete,[3] et ablete[4] la persone, et autres circumstaunces, et office lui servy; par quei par cohercion de ley de Seint Eglise nous luy resceumes; et demandoms jugement si tort en nostre persono puisse assigner.[5]—*Blayk*. La prohibicion vous

---

" de Mertone, clericum suum,
" ipsum rogando ut præfatum
" Walterum ad ecclesiam prædic-
" tam admitteret, idem Episcopus,
" ipsum Walterum ad ecclesiam
" illam omnino admittere recusans,
" eandem ecclesiam infra tempus
" semestre de quodam Thoma
" Crosse incumbravit contra legem
" et consuetudinem regni Angliæ."

[1] autre is omitted from L. and H.

[2] toust is omitted from C.

[3] L., and D., litigiosite.

[4] C., hablete.

[5] The Bishop's plea was, according to the record (after a protestation as to the date of voidance) " quod die Lunæ proxima post " festum Omnium Sanctorum, anno " regni domini Regis nunc sexto- " decimo, prædicti Johannes et " Amia, asserentes dictam eccle-

" siam tunc esse vacantem, et quod " ad ipsos tunc pertinuit præsen- " tare ad eandem, eidem Episcopo, " ut loci illius Diocesano, dictum " Thomam Crosse ad ecclesiam " illam præsentarunt, supplicando, " caritatis intuitu, ut ipsum " Thomam ad eandem admitteret, " et canonice institueret in eadem, " qui quidem Episcopus inquisi- " tionem " [instead of " inquisiti- " onem " the words " ad instantem " requisitionem" have been written by mistake in the roll] " super " vacatione ecclesiæ prædictæ, jure " præsentantis, et aliis articulis " consuetis, prout moris est in hac " parte, prout de jure canonico " tenebatur, in pleno loci capitulo " fieri fecit, per quam inquisitionem " compertum fuit quod prædicti " Johannes et Amia veri patroni

No. 51.

A.D. 1345. delivered to you as above, and afterwards, while the plea was pending, and within the period of six months, you encumbered the church; ready, &c.— *Gaynesford.* We admitted, after office found, the presentee of John de Ralegh, *absque hoc* that any prohibition came to us on the day on which you have counted thereof; ready, &c.—*Blaykeston.* The day will not make an issue, for the question whether the prohibition was delivered one day or another is of no importance, if it was delivered before the time at which you admitted the presentee of the other person.— *R. Thorpe.* Will you not then maintain your count?— Stonore. You cannot, in any way, have an issue on the day.—*Blaykeston.* Inasmuch as we tender the averment that we delivered to him the prohibition before the day on which he has supposed that he admitted the presentee of John de Ralegh, and he refuses that averment, judgment. — Afterwards the issue accepted was whether the Bishop admitted the presentee of John de Ralegh before the prohibition or not.—And because the church was in Cornwall, and

No. 51.

fuit livere *ut supra*, et apres, pendant le plee, deinz ^{A.D. 1345.} les vj moys, encombrastes leglise ; prest, &c.—*Gayn.* Nous resceumes, apres office trove, &c., le presente Johan Raly, saunz ceo qe nulle prohibicion nous vint le jour qe vous avietz counte; prest, &c.—*Blayk.* Le jour ne fra pas issue, qar le quel ceo fuit livere un jour ou autre ny ad force, sil[1] fuit livere avant le temps qe vous resceustes le presente lautre.—[*R.*] *Thorpe.* Donqes ne voilletz vous pas meintenir vostre counte ?—STON. Vous ne poetz pas aver issue sur le jour en nulle manere.—*Blaik.* Desicome nous tendoms daverer qavant le jour qil ad suppose qil resceut le presente Johan Raly nous luy liverames la prohibicion, quel averement il refuse, jugement.— Puis lissue fuit resceu le quel il resceut le presente Johan Raly avant la prohibicion ou noun.[2]—Et pur ceo qe leglise fuit en Cornube et la livere de la

---

" ejusdem ecclesiæ extiterunt et in " possessione præsentandi, &c., et " quod ad ipsos ad eandem præsen- " tare spectabat, et quod dicta " ecclesia ad tunc non fuit litigiosa, " &c., per quod idem Thomas, " virtute articulorum per inquisi- " tionem prædictam compertorum, " versus ipsum Episcopum in " tantum prosequebatur quod idem " Episcopus die Sabbati in Festo " Sancti Petri in Cathedra anno " regni domini Regis nunc decimo " septimo, per compulsionem eccle- " siasticam, præfatum Thomam in " ecclesia prædicta instituit, et ei " literas inductionis inde fecit, " absque hoc quod idem Theo- " baldus, ante institutionem illam " eidem Thomæ sic factam, præ- " fatum Walterum de Mertone " ipsi Episcopo præsentaverat ad " eandem, seu aliqua prohibitio " domini Regis eidem Episcopo ne " aliquem ad ecclesiam admitteret,

" pendente inter partes prædictas " Assisa prædicta, ex parte prædicti " Theobaldi liberata fuit, prout " idem Theobaldus superius in " narratione sua supponit. Et hoc " paratus est verificare, unde petit " judicium, &c.''

[1] L., and H., sil ne.

[2] The replication was, according to the record, " quod prohibitio " Regis prædicta liberata fuit præ- " fato Episcopo . . . . . " ante prædictum diem Sabbati " quod idem Episcopus prædictum " Thomam instituit in eadem " ecclesia, ne idem Episcopus " aliquem admitteret in eandem, " pendente Assisa prædicta, prout " ipse superius narravit, et idem " Episcopus nihilominus infra " tempus semestre prædictam ec- " clesiam de prædicto Thoma " incumbravit, non obstante pro- " hibitione Regis prædicta." It was upon this that issue was joined.

No. 51.

A.D. 1345. the delivery of the prohibition was assigned in Devonshire, some would have had a jury from one county, and some from the other, and some from both counties.— Afterwards *Seton* said : — They have alleged that institution was made by the Bishop on St. Peter's day, and we fully admit it; therefore we shall not have any dispute on that point, but only as to the time of the delivery of the prohibition; and we will aver that it was before St. Peter's day; ready, &c.— *Derworthy.* The day cannot make an issue.—STONORE. They are at one with you as to the day on which you say that you made the induction; therefore the delivery of the prohibition before St. Peter's day or after makes the issue; therefore let a jury come from the neighbourhood in which the prohibition was delivered, that is to say, from the County of Devon. —And so it was done.[1]

---

[1] The conclusion of the report is in Y.B., Hil., 21 Edw. III., No. 7, fo. 3.

No. 51.

prohibicion assigne en Devene, asquns gentz voilleint A.D. 1345
aver eu pays del un counte, et asquns del autre, et
asquns de lun et lautre.—Puis *Setone*. Ils ount
allegge institucion fet par Levesqe le jour Seint
Piere, et nous le grantoms bien; par quei sur ceo
ne serroms pas en debat, mes sur le temps de la
livere de la prohibicion; et ceo voloms averer qavant
le jour Seint Piere; prest, &c.—*Der*. Le jour ne
fait pas issue.—STON. Ils sount un ovesqe vous de
mesme le jour [qe vous ditetz qe vous feistes la
induccion; par quei la livere de la prohibicion avant
le jour Seint Piere ou]¹ puis fait lissue; par quei
veigne pays del visne ou la prohibicion fuit livere,
saver de Devene.—*Et sic fuit*.²

---

¹ The words between brackets
are omitted from D.

² So in the roll " præceptum est
" Vicecomiti Devoniæ quod venire
" faciat, &c." A verdict was found
by Devonshire Jurors in the
Common Bench on the Quinzaine
of St. Hilary in the 21st year,
" quod prædictum breve Regis de
" prohibitione liberatum fuit præ-
" fato Episcopo . . . . die
" Jovis proxima post festum Sancti
" Hillarii, anno regni Regis nunc
" sextodecimo, ante præfatum diem
" Sabbati in festo Sancti Petri in
" Cathedra, quo die idem Epis-
" copus, prout superius in re-
" spondendo cognovit, instituit
" præfatum Thomam in ecclesiam
" prædictam, postquam prædictum
" breve de prohibitione ei libera-
" tum fuit. Et sic ecclesiam illam
" de eodem Thoma, infra tempus
" semestre, non obstante regia
" prohibitione prædicta, contra
" legem et consuetudinem regni
" Regis Angliæ, incumbravit. Quæ-
" siti ad quæ damna, &c, dicunt

" quod ad damnum prædicti Theo-
" baldi ducentarum marcarum."

Judgment was then given " quod
" prædictus Theobaldus recuperet
" versus præfatum Episcopum
" damna sua prædicta, et quod
" idem Episcopus deincumbret
" ecclesiam prædictam, et sit in
" misericordia, &c. Et præceptum
"·est Vicecomiti Devoniæ [Devoniæ
" interlined] quod distringat præ-
" dictum Episcopum per omnia
" quæ habet in balliva sua ad dein-
" cumbrandum ecclesiam illam."

" Postea die Veneris proxima
" post festum Nativitatis Sancti
" Johannis Baptistæ, anno regni
" domini Regis nunc Angliæ vice-
" simo secundo, dominus Rex
" mandavit Johanni de Stonore
" breve suum clausum de recordo
" et processu prædictis, cum omni-
" bus ea tangentibus, coram ipso
" domino Rege in Cancellaria sua
" mittendis, et coram eo mittuntur,
" et liberantur Bartholomæo atte
" Mede ad deferendum, &c." This
was possibly in relation to a second

Nos. 52, 53.

A.D. 1345.
Error.

(52.) § Error was sued by Thomas Gray and John Chasthowe on a Fresh Force in Newcastle-on-Tyne, and while the suit was pending, Thomas died; therefore Thomas son and heir of Thomas Gray and John Chasthowe sued a new *Scire facias* [*ad audiendum errores*] and they had a writ out of the Chancery.— *Mutlow.* You see plainly how this suit is made by them in common, that is to say, by a person who was party and by the heir of another person who was party, and they cannot join in one suit; judgment whether you will have any answer made to this suit taken by them in common.—THORPE (J.). Cannot the tenant who loses in an Assise, and one who was aiding in the disseisin have one writ of Error in common?— *Blaykeston.* I do not know; and even if it were so, still that would be because they were both aggrieved, at one and the same time, by the judgment; but the heir of the person who loses and the disseisor take their ground of action at different times, that is to say, one by descent, the other at the time of the judgment.—THORPE (J.). It is assigned for error that the party was neither attached nor summoned, and so it appears by the record; and we have since sent for a fuller record, and, when that was sent to us, we found no attachment or summons against the defendant; therefore we hold the process to be entirely without warrant; and therefore we reverse this process and entirely annul it, and we give judgment that restitution be made to the plaintiffs in Error.

Waste.

(53.) § Waste which Hugh le Despenser brought against Anthony Citroun. And, as to cutting certain

Nos. 52, 53.

(52.)[1] § Errour fut[2] suy par Thomas Gray et Johan Chasthowe[3] dun fresche force en Noefchastel sur Tyne, pendant quel suite Thomas morust; par quei Thomas fitz et heir Thomas et J. suirent novel *Scire facias* et avoint brief de la Chauncellerie.— *Mutl.* Vous veietz bien coment cest suite est fait par eux en comune, saver,[4] par celuy qe fuit partie et par leir de partie, qe ne se poient joindre en une suite; jugement si a ceste suite pris par eux en comune voilletz estre respondu.—THORPE. Ne poet le tenant qe perde par Assise et coadjutour a la disseisine aver un brief derrour en comune?—*Blaik.*[5] Jeo ne say; et tut fuit il issint, unqore ceo serreit pur ceo qils sount greves a un mesme temps par le jugement; mes leir cely qe perde et le disseisour pernount lour accion a divers temps, saver, lun par descente, lautre al temps del jugement.—THORPE. Pur errour est assigne qe la partie nest attache ne somons, et ceo pert par le recorde; et puis nous maundames pur plus plein recorde, et, quant ceo est[6] maunde[7] a nous, nous trovames[8] nul attachement ne somons vers le defendant; par quei nous tenoms le proces tut sanz garrant; par quei nous reversoms cel proces et lanientissoms de tut, et agardoms qils soient restitutz, &c.

(53.) [9] § Wast qe Hugh Despenser porta vers Antone Cytroun. Et, quant a couper de certeinz

---

[19 Li. Ass., 7; Fitz., Joindre en accion, 30.]

A.D. 1345.
Errour.
Fitz.
Wast.

writ of error (for the first *see* Y.B., Easter, 17 Edw. III., No. 4, Rolls edition, pp. 234-272) in relation to the judgment in Assise of Darrein Presentment on which the *Quare incumbravit* was founded. *See* Y.B., Easter, 22 Edw. III., No. 26, fo. 6b.

[1] From L., H., C., and D.
[2] fut is from D. alone.
[3] L., de Shathewe.

[4] saver is omitted from D.
[5] All the MSS. except D., BAUK.
[6] D., fut.
[7] C., recorde.
[8] L., and C., troveroms.
[9] From L., H., C., and D. The report is in continuation of No. 69 of Mich., 18 Edw. III. The record (*Placita de Banco*, Mich., 18 Edw. III., R° 294, d), is there cited.

No. 53.

trees, he avowed for the making of ploughs, harrows, folds, &c.; and upon that they abode judgment. And with respect to another parcel he pleaded that he cut by warrant from the plaintiff. And as to the residue he pleaded No Waste. And the plaintiff replied that, in addition to that which the defendant had avowed, he had committed waste to the amount which the plaintiff had surmised by count; ready, &c.—And the other side said the contrary.—And so a day was given over as well in respect of that upon which judgment was awaited as of the rest.—And afterwards HILLARY took the inquest at *Nisi prius,* and the jury found the cutting and selling beyond the number which the defendant had avowed, and found the price of each tree. And enquiry was also made and there was a finding of the number of the trees of which the defendant avowed the taking.—Thereupon *Notton* prayed judgment for the plaintiff.—*Seton.* There has been found the cutting of certain oak-trees in the lands of those who hold *in bondagio domini,* and also *in boscis domini,* and that cannot be understood to be the woods which Anthony holds, because he cannot be his own lord.— This exception was not allowed, because that which the jury said was only to mark the difference between the woods of the villeins and those of the lord.—Afterwards exception was taken on the ground that expulsion from the soil was found in the case of one who held in bondage, who might be a free man as well as a villein, on which point no definite enquiry had been had, and if he was a free man it is certain that there was no expulsion of a villein from the soil.— This exception was not allowed, because by the traverse which the defendant took to the count he accepted it as a fact that the person was villein, &c.—Afterwards *Grene* said:—We understand that you intend to give judgment in respect of that which has been found by verdict before you have given any judgment upon the matter which rests upon your

No. 53.

arbres, il avowa pur carues, herces, faudes, &c.; sur A.D. 1345.
quei ils demurerunt en jugement. Et dautre parcelle
qil coupa par garrant. Et del remenant nul wast.
Et le pleintif replia qe estre ceo qil avowa, &c., il
avoit waste a cel noumbre qil luy avoit surmys par
counte; prest, &c.—*Et alii e contra.*—Issint qe jour
est done outre si bien de cel qe demura en jugement come del remenant.—Et puis HILL. par *Nisi
prius* prist lenqueste, par quel trove fuit le couper
et vendre outre le noumbre qil avoit avowe, et pris
de chesqun. Et auxint fuit enquis et trove le
noumbre de ces qil avowa la prise.—Sur quei *Nottone*,
pur le pleintif, pria jugement. — *Setone*. Il y ad
trove couper de certeinz keynes en terres ces qe
tenent *in bondagio domini*, et auxint *in boscis domini*,
qe ne poet estre entendu des boys qe Antone tient,
qar il ne poet estre seignur a luy mesme.—*Non
allocatur*, qar ceo qe lenquest dit ne fut forqe a
difference des boys les vileins et du seignur.—Puis
est chalenge de ceo qe exil est trove dun qe tient
en bondage, qe poet estre un fraunk homme si bien
com villein, et ceo nest pas enquis en certein, et,
sil fuit fraunk, *constat* qe ceo nest pas exil.—*Non
allocatur*, qar par le travers qe le defendant prist al
count il accepta celuy vileyn, &c.—Puis *Grene*. Nous
entendoms qe vous voilletz rendre le jugement de
ceo qest trove par verdit devant qe vous eietz ajugge

No. 54.

A.D. 1345. judgment.—HILLARY. That is true.—*Notton.* They put themselves upon the inquest in respect of the same portion, and waste has been found, and so they have, in pleading, waived the advantage of their abiding judgment, and we pray judgment as to the whole upon the verdict.—*Grene.* Then you waive the advantage in respect of that in respect of which you previously abode judgment; judgment of your count.— WILLOUGHBY. You waived the advantage yourself by your plea, when you took for issue a traverse as to the whole, without excepting that which had been put to judgment; but I am quite sure that, if in pleading you had held to the point that the parcel on which the plaintiff, on your justification, abode judgment must be parcel of that in respect of which he complained, you might well have ousted him from the averment in respect of that parcel; but since you did not do so, but accepted his averment as to the whole, the abiding of judgment in law was waived both by him and by you; and that was the reason why the Court enquired as to the whole, because otherwise the inquest would not have been awarded before judgment had been given on the point which had been put to judgment.—*Quære,* for see below that an inquest was awarded on another cause.[1]—Afterwards WILLOUGHBY gave judgment that the plaintiff should recover the place wasted, and treble damages, and that entirely on the verdict of the jury.

Waste.   (54.) § The Earl of Hereford brought a writ of

---

[1] Referring possibly to the case No. 54, next below.

No. 54.

ceo qest en vos jugements.—HILL. Il est verite.—
Nottone. De mesme la porcion ils soi mistrent en
enqueste, et le wast trove, et issint ount ils en
pledaunt weyve lavantage de lour demure en jugement, et prioms jugement de tut sur verdit.—*Grene.*
Donqes vous weyvetz lavauntage de ceo dount autrefoith demurastes en jugement; jugement de vostre
count.—WILBY. Vous weyvastes[1] lavantage mesmes
par vostre ple, quant vous preistes lissue a travers
sur tut, sanz recouper cella qe fuit mys en jugement;
mes jeo say bien si en pledant vous ussetz pris a
cella qe la parcelle sur quei le pleintif sur vostre
justificacion se mist en jugement covendreit estre
parcelle de ceo dount il soi pleint, vous le puissetz
bien aver ouste del averement de cele parcelle; mes,
quant vous ne feistes pas, mes luy acceptastes al
averement de tut, la demure en ley fuit weyve de
luy et de vous; et ceo fuit la cause pur quei Court
enquist de tut, qar autrement ust pas lenqueste este
agarde avant qe ceo qe fuit mys en jugement ust
este ajugge.—*Quære*, qar *vide infra* qe lenqueste fuit
agarde sur autre cause.—Puis WILBY agarda qe le
pleintif recoverast le lieu waste et damages a treble,
et ceo tut sur verdit denqueste.

(54.)[2] § Le Count de Hereford porta brief de Wast wast.

---

[1] D., weyvez.

[2] From L., H., C., and D., but corrected by the record, *Placita de Banco*, Trin., 19 Edw. III., R° 131, d. It there appears that the action was brought by Humphrey de Bohun, Earl of Hereford and Essex, against Margaret late wife of John de Bohun, late Earl of Hereford and Essex, in respect of waste in the manor of Kynebauton (Kimbolton, Hunts), which she held in dower of his inheritance by endowment of his brother John, the particulars of which waste are set out in the declaration, and include "fodendo et puteos faciendo " in ducentis acris terræ in villa de " Kinebauton, quæ est parcella " manerii prædicti, et marleam et " arzillum inde vendendo pretii " viginti librarum, ... " et in boscis in eadem villa quæ " sunt parcella manerii prædicti " succidendo et vendendo octo " millia quercuum, pretii cujus- " libet duorum solidorum, viginti " millia querculorum, pretii cujus-

No. 54.

A.D. 1345. Waste against Margaret late wife of John, Earl of Hereford.—Exception was taken to the writ on the ground that the defendant was not described as Countess. —This exception was not allowed. — *Grene.* He has brought his writ supposing that we have committed waste of lands which we hold in dower in Kimbolton, and counting that we have committed waste in the manor of Kimbolton in the vill of Kimbolton, thus supposing the whole manor to be in Kimbolton; to that we say that the manor of Kimbolton extends into Kimbolton and three other vills, to wit, A., B., and C.; judgment of the writ.—*R. Thorpe.* We suppose the waste to be only in that part of the manor which is in Kimbolton, and therefore the writ is good. — *Grene.* Then you ought to have counted in a different manner, that is to say, that we had committed waste in part of the manor which extends into Kimbolton.—Afterwards this exception was waived, because the Court recorded that he counted that waste had been committed as in part of the manor.—Therefore *Seton* said :—As to waste committed before the thirteenth year of the King, the Earl released to Margaret, by this deed, all actions of Waste; and, as to the subsequent time we tell you, with regard to the lands, that there are pits in which the custom has been to dig mud and clay, and we dug mud in these pits in order to repair the walls of the manor which had fallen into decay. And as to the wood *Seton* justified the cutting for the purpose of repairing houses (and he stated definitely how many houses), and also for harrows and other necessaries;

No. 54.

vers Margarete[1] qe fuit la femme Johan Count de Hereford.—Le brief chalenge de ceo qele ne fuit pas nome Countesse.—*Non allocatur.*—*Grene.* Il ad porte son brief supposant qe nous avoms fait wast des terres qe nous tenoms en dowere en Kymbaltone, countant qe nous avoms fait wast en le maner[2] de Kymbaltone en la ville de Kymbaltone [supposant tut le maner en Kimbaltoun][3] la dioms nous qe le maner de K. sestent en K. et iij autres villes, saver, A., B., et C.; jugement du brief.—[*R.*] *Thorpe.* Nous supposoms pas le wast forqe en cele parcelle qest en K.; par quei le brief est bon.—*Grene.* Donqes duissetz[4] aver counte par autre manere, saver, qe nous ussoms fait wast en parcelle del maner qe sestent en K.—Puis le chalenge weyve, pur ceo qe Court recorda qil counta le wast estre fait come en parcelle del maner.—Par quei *Setone* dist:—Quant a wast fait avant le[5] xiij aun[6] le Roi, le Count ad relesse par ceo fait; et, quant al temps puis, vous dioms quant as terres il y sount putes ou homme soleit fower taye et arsille, et en celes putes fowames taye pur reparailler les mures del maner ruynous. Et quant a boys justifia le couper pur amendement des mesouns, et mist en certein come bien des mesouns, et auxint pur herces et autres necessaries;

" libet quatuor denariorum, quatuor
" millia et centum fraxinos pretii
" cujuslibet duorum solidorum,
" quatuor millia arabium pretii
" cujuslibet sex denariorum."
   [1] MSS. of Y.B., Margerie.

[2] D., manoir.
[3] The words between brackets are omitted from D.
[4] D., deussetz.
[5] le is from H. alone.
[6] aun is from H. alone.

No. 54.

and he prayed judgment whether tort could be assigned in that respect. And as to the rest he pleaded No Waste; ready, &c.

No. 54.

jugement si de ceo tort, &c. Et quant al remenant
nulle wast; prest, &c.[1]

---

[1] The plea was, according to the record, " quod idem Comes vice-" simo secundo die Aprilis anno " regni Regis nunc tertiodecimo, " .... per literas suas patentes et " indentatas, remisit, et relaxavit " ipsi Margaretæ omnimodas ac-" tiones vasti per ipsam in prædicto " manerio vel alibi a principio " mundi usque ad præfatum vice-" simum secundum diem Aprilis " facti. Et profert hic prædictas " literas præfati Comitis quæ hoc " testantur, &c. Et petit judicium " si idem Comes actionem de Vasto " de aliquo tempore ante præfa-" tum vicesimum secundum diem " Aprilis versus eam habere debeat, " &c. Et quo ad foditionem in " terra, &c., dicit quod est quædam " roda terræ infra manerium præ-" dictum in qua sunt putei in " quibus domini manerii prædicti '' semper hactenus licite fodebant " lutum pro reparatione murorum " et domorum in eodem manerio. " Et dicit quod ipsa fodebat licite " in eisdem puteis pro reparatione " murorum et domorum ibidem, " absque aliquo vasto inde facien-" do. Et quo ad vastum factum in " boscis dicit quod post datam " prædictarum literarum prædictus " Comes concessit cuidam Johanni " de Pertinhale quatuor quercus " pro maeremio in prædicto bosco, " et inde fecit literas suas patentes " ipsæ Margaretæ quod ipsa occa-" sione prædicta per præfatum " Comitem vel heredes suos inmo-" lesteretur (sic) seu gravaretur. " Et profert hic literas ejusdem " Comitis præmissa testante .... " Et dicit quod idem Comes con-" cessit cuidam Johanni de Fel-

" mersham. clerico, sex quercus in " eodem bosco et inde fecit similiter " literas suus patentes eidem Mar-" garetæ quod ipsa quieta foret de " vasto de eisdem, nec quod ipsa " per ipsüm Comitem vel heredes " suos occasione illa in aliquo " gravaretur, quas quidem literas " Comitis profert hic, ... unde " petit judicium si de quercubus " illis actionem de Vasto versus " eam habere debeat, &c. Et " quoad vastum, &c., in domibus " et gardinis dicit quod ipsa nullum " fecit vastum ... et de hoc ponit se " super patriam. Et Comes simili-" ter. Et quo ad vastum in boscis, '' &c., dicit quod fuerunt in eodem " manerio plures domus ruinosæ, " et plura alia quæ magna indige-" bant emendatione et reparatione [the particulars are here given] " pro quibus domibus et aliis, &c., " emendandis et reparandis ipsa " succidit quadringentas et triginta " quercus pretii cujuslibet sex " denariorum, et mille querculos " pretii cujuslibet unius denarii. " Et pro diversis clausuris circa "parcum et gardina ejusdem " manerii, et pro carectis, herciis, " et aliis necessariis, succidit ipsa " ducentos et quatuordecim quer-'· culos pretii cujuslibet unius " denarii, ducentas fraxinos et " centum arabes pretii cujuslibet " duorum denariorum, absque " vasto faciendo in eisdem boscis. " Et hoc parata est verificare, unde " petit judicium si idem Comes " actionem de Vasto in hoc casu " versus eam habere debeat, &c. According to the roll, the Earl replied " non cognoscendo quod " prædicta Margareta succidit

No. 55.

A.D. 1345.
Dower. (55.) § A writ of Dower in respect of rent was brought against several persons who made default.

No. 55.

(55.)[1] § Brief de Dowere de rente vers plusours, qe fount defaut. Deux de divers parcelles, com ceux

A.D. 1345

Dowere.
[Fitz.,
Resceit,
14.]

" tantas arbores ad reparationem " et emendationem domorum. " . . . . . et aliorum supra " contentorum quantas ipsa supe- " rius asserit in responsione sua " prædicta, dicit quod, post con- " fectionem prædictæ literæ de " acquietancia et quieta clama- " tione, prædicta Margareta fecit " vastum . . . . tam in terris quam " in boscis ibidem, &c."

Issue was joined upon this replications.

The jury found a special verdict at *Nisi prius* in Easter Term in the 20th year, partly in favour of the Earl and partly in favour of the Countess.

Afterwards "quia nondum visum " est Curiæ, &c., datus est eis dies " de audiendo inde judicio suo hic " in Octabis Sanctæ Trinitatis per " Justiciarios, &c. Ad quem diem " prædicta Margareta fecit se inde " essoniari de malo veniendi, &c. " Et habuit inde diem per essonia- " torem suum usque ad hunc diem " hic scilicet a die Sancti Michaelis " in xv dies proxime sequentes.

" Et modo venit tam prædictus " Comes quam prædicta Margareta " per attornatos suos. Et viso " veredicto inquisitionis prædictæ, " et intellecto, prædicta Margareta " dicit quod Inquisitio prædicta " sine waranto capta est pro eo " quod in brevi de Venire facias " xij, &c., quædam clausula in " hujusmodi brevibus usualis et " necessaria totaliter est omissa, " videlicet quod interim juratores " Inquisitionis prædictæ prædicta " tenementa vastata videant, per " quorum visum si vastum com-

" periatur ad exheredationem, &c., " factum, seisina de tenementis " vastatis liberari deberet, &c., et " etiam in Inquisitione prædicta " continetur quod quædam domus " certi pretii infra manerium præ- " dictum pro defectu custodiæ per " præfatam Margaretam adhibitæ, " combustæ fuerunt, et quod loco " domorum earundem adeo bonæ " domus per eandem Margaretam " modo constructæ sunt, et etiam " quod diversæ arbores certi pretii " in boscis prædicti manerii per " præfatam Margaretam succisæ " fuerunt, et quæ combustio et " succisio per juratores Inquisi- " tionis prædictæ tanquam vastum " per præfatam Margaretam factum " præsentatur, nullam mentionem " faciendo si domus illæ de arbori- " bus succisis sive aliis per præ- " fatam Margaretam alibi emptis " constructæ sint, et quæ, si &c., " ad diversum respectum referunt. " Propter quæ et alia in In- " quisitione prædicta amb[igua ? " edge of roll gone] visum est " Curiæ quod necesse est super " negotio prædicto iterato in- " quirere. Ideo præceptum est " Vicecomiti quod de novo venire " faciat hic a die Sancti Hillarii " in xv dies xij, &c., per quos, &c., " et qui nec, &c., ad recognoscen- " dum, &c., quia tam, &c. Et " interim prædicti juratores præ- " dicta tenementa vastata videant, " &c "

1 From L., H., C., and D. This may possibly be a continuation or another report of Y.B., Hil., 19 Edw. III., No. 29.

No. 55.

Two other persons severally prayed to be admitted to defend their right in respect of different parcels, on the ground that they were the persons to whom the reversion of the land out of which the rent issued belonged; and in so praying they alleged the death of certain of the tenants, that is to say, that one had died before the purchase of the writ, and another while the writ was pending, and they demanded judgment of the writ.—*Pole.* They pray to be admitted in respect of something which is not in demand, and, according to their statement, judgment would not be to their damage, for, if we recover without good title, they can discharge themselves when they have entered on their reversion.—STOUFORD, *ad idem.* If the tenants be dead, then those who pray to be admitted have not any reversion in expectancy; therefore to allege the death of the tenants is contrariant to their prayer, and so judgment will be of no effect, if that which they say is true, and to the damage of no one.— *Grene.* In praying to be admitted it is necessary to allege that matter, or else we shall never attain our purpose on account of the contradictoriness.— WILLOUGHBY. You will have it after the admission or never; and it seems that you suffer no damage even though judgment be rendered.—*R. Thorpe.* Suppose that the demandant has an action, and that we have warranty, we shall be deprived of our recovery to the value, which the law gives us, unless we are admitted. —WILLOUGHBY. You will have your warranty after the death of your tenant.—*R. Thorpe.* Never by a warranty which we have from a time earlier than that at which judgment was rendered, nor, if we had a release, should we ever have the advantage of pleading it after judgment.—*Huse.* What you say is contrary to law; for even though land were recovered against your tenant for term of life, where you were not a party, you would afterwards prevent execution

No. 55.

as queux la reversion appent de la terre dount, &c.,
severalment prierunt destre resceu, &c.; et en priant
alleggerent la mort dasqun des tenantz, et demanderent jugement du brief, saver, asqun mort avant le
brief et asqun mort pendant le brief.—*Pole.* Ils
prient[1] dautre chose qe nest en demande, et le
jugement a lour dit nest pas en damage de eux,
qar si nous recoveroms sanz title, ils soi[2] pount
descharger quant ils serrount entres en lour reversion.
—STOUF., *ad idem.* Si les tenantz soient mortz,
donqes nount ils pas reversion; par quei dallegger
lour mort est contrariaunt a lour prier, et si serra
le jugement de nulle value sils dient verite, ne a
nuly damage.—*Grene.* En priaunt il covient allegger
la chose, ou autrement nous navendroms pas pur la
contrariouste.—WILBY. Vous[3] laveretz apres la resceit ou jammes; et si semble qe vous nestes pas en-
damage tut soit le jugement rendu.—[*R.*] *Thorpe.* Jeo
pose qele eit accion, et qe nous eioms garrantie, nous
serroms forclos de nostre value, qe ley nous doune,
sil ne soit qe nous serroms resceu.—WILBY. Vous
averetz vostre garrantie apres la mort vostre tenant.
—[*R.*] *Thorpe.* Jammes par garrantie qe nous avoms
deigne temps qe le jugement se fist, ne, si nous
ussoms relees, nous averoms jammes lavantage del
pleder apres le jugement.—*Huse.* Vous ditetz countre
lei: qar mesqe terre fuit recoveri vers vostre tenant
a terme de vie, ou vous nestoietz pas partie, vous

---

[1] H., parlent.
soi is from L. alone.

[3] Vous is omitted from C.

No. 55.

of the same judgment by means of the release made to you before judgment.—*Grene*. I do not think so; but suppose that I am not admitted, and afterwards my tenant alienes in fee, or commits waste, and I recover, will not the charge continue for the natural life of my tenant, by force of the judgment?—KELSHULLE. No; when you have recovered you will plead in discharge.—HILLARY. He would not do so.—*Notton*. There is the same reason and the same mischief where there is loss of land as where there is loss of rent, and *e converso*, for the person to whom the reversion belongs; and for that reason voucher is given to the tenant of the land where rent is demanded.—*Skipwith*. It is not known whether it is the kind of rent in respect of which voucher would lie; and if one who has only a term for life in land pleads in chief, and cannot deny the demandant's action, or makes default by covin, he forfeits his tenancy; but if rent is demanded against him, even though he renders it, or cannot deny the action, he does not forfeit; therefore there is a difference between the two, and this is not a case within the words of the Statute[1]; for the tenant who makes default, and against whom judgment is given, will not have a *Quod ei deforciat*,[2] nor will the reversioner have a writ of Entry given by the Statute[3] where admission is given; nor is he within the mischief for which the Statute provides, because he will not by the judgment be ousted from his reversion, nor charged after the death of his tenant. Besides, even if it were law, in a case in which tenant for term of life has charged the land by his deed, that, notwithstanding a subsequent recovery by writ of Waste or recovery by Entry *in consimili casu*, the charge would continue during his natural life, in this case, nevertheless, it would not be so when recovery

---

[1] 13 Edw. I. (Westm. 2), cc. 3 and 4.

[2] 13 Edw. I. (Westm. 2), c. 4.

[3] 13 Edw. I. (Westm. 2), c. 3.

No. 55.

destourberetz execucion[1] apres de mesme le jugement A.D. 1345.
par le relees fait a vous avant le jugement.—*Grene.*
Ceo ne crey jeo pas; mes mettetz qe jeo ne soi
pas resceu, et apres mon tenant aliene en fee ou
fait wast, et jeo recovere, ne demura la charge pur
la vie naturelle mon tenant, par force del jugement?
—KELL. Noun; quant vous averetz recoveri vous
plederetz en descharge.—HILL. Noun freit.—*Nottone.*
Mesme la cause et meschief y ad de perde de la
terre qe de la rente, et *e converso*, pur cely a qi
la reversion appent; et pur ceo doun homme voucher
al tenant de la terre ou rente est demande.—*Skyp.*
Homme ne seet[2] sil soit tiel rente de quei[3] voucher
girreit; et si homme qe nad qe terme de vie en
terre plede en chief, et ne poet dedire laccion del
demandant, ou fet defaut par covyn, il forfait sa
tenance; mes si rente soit demande vers ly, tut
rende il ou ne puisse dedire, il ne forfet pas; donqes
y ad diversite entre les deux, et ceo nest pas en
cas de parole del estatut; qar le tenant qe fait defaut, et vers qi le jugement se fet, navera pas *Quare
deforciat*, ne celuy en la reversion brief Dentre come
statut doune ou la resceit est done; nen meschief
del estatut nest il pas, qar par le jugement il ne
serra pas ouste de sa reversion, ne charge apres le
decees son tenant. Ovesqe ceo, tut fuit il ley en
cas qe tenant a terme de vie quant il ad charge
par son fait la terre qe *non obstante* recoverir apres
par brief de Wast ou recoverir par Entre *in consimili
casu*, qe la charge demureit pur sa vie naturel, en
ceo cas, nepurquant, il ne serra pas issint quant

---

[1] C., lexecucion.
[2] D., sciet.

[3] C., dount, instead of de quei

No. 55.

is had against the tenant: for in the first case the charge would have to be claimed entirely in virtue of the deed of the tenant who could lawfully charge for his life; but in the other case it would have to be claimed on the ground of the demandant's own title upon which she recovered, and if she had no right to recover, the reversioner, as soon as he was in possession, would discharge the land.—WILLOUGHBY said that in case the tenant for term of life charged the land, the person to whom the reversion belonged, when he had recovered, as above, would discharge himself.—HILLARY emphatically denied this. — *R. Thorpe.* If neither *Quod ei deforciat* nor writ of Entry lies in respect of rent on such a recovery, admission should for that reason be granted all the more readily, on account of the mischief, and admission has very often been granted in the like case.—HILLARY. That is true.— WILLOUGHBY. That was never right, but *Volenti non fit injuria.*—HILLARY. At any rate we shall hold it as not denied that those who make default have only a term for life in the land.—And afterwards they were by judgment admitted; and they demanded judgment of the writ.—*Skipwith.* We tell you that those whose death you allege in abatement of the writ are the same persons against whom we previously had judgment by reason of their default; judgment whether you shall be admitted to such an exception after judgment has been delivered against them.—*R. Thorpe.* Your intention is by your recovery to charge the whole freehold in common, and though you have had judgment you will not have execution; nor would you, according to law, have had any judgment if the Court had been made acquainted with the facts, because judgment cannot in this case be given as if land had been demanded against several persons, inasmuch as each one can lose his own portion of land, and one who appears can defend only in accordance with the quantity which he

No. 55.

recoverir est taille vers le tenant : qar en le primer
cas la charge serra tut a clamer par le fait[1] le
tenant qe pout[2] charger de ley pur sa vie ; mes en
lautre cas serreit il a clamer par my son title demene sur quel il recoveri, et sil navoit pas dreit a
recoverir, quel houre qe cely en la reversion fuit
einz il la[3] deschargera.—WILBY dit qen cas qe le
tenant a terme de vie chargeast, qe cely a qi la
reversion appent, quant il avera recoveri, *ut supra*,
soi deschargera.—HILL. *instanter dedixit.*—[R.] *Thorpe.*
Si *Quare deforciat* ne brief Dentre ne gisent pas de
rente sur tiel recoverir, de taunt grauntera homme
le plustoust, pur la meschief, la resceite, et la resceite en tiel cas ad este grante molt[4] sovent.—HILL.
Il est verite.—WILBY. Ceo ne fuit unqes resoun,
mes *Volenti non fit injuria.*—HILL. Au meins nous
tendroms nient dedit qe ces qe fount defaut[5] nount
qe terme de vie en la terre.—Et puis par agarde
il fuit resceu ; et demanda jugement du brief.—*Skip.*
Nous vous dioms qe ces qi mort vous alleggetz al
abatement du brief sount mesmes les persones vers
queux nous avioms autrefoith jugement par lour defaut ; jugement si apres jugement taille vers eux a
tiel excepcion serretz resceu.—[R.] *Thorpe.* Vous estes
par vostre recoverir a charger tut le fraunk tenement en comune, et coment qe vous avietz jugement,
execucion navetz[6] pas ; ne par ley, si Court ust este
avise, vous eussetz eu nulle jugement, qar jugement
en le cas ne se poet pas faire come si terre fuit
demande vers plusours, qar de terre chesqun poet
perdre sa porcion, et un qe vint ne poet defendre

---

[1] D., laccion, instead of le fait.
[2] L., ne put.
[3] L., soi.
[4] molt is omitted from C.

[5] H., sont defendauntz, instead of fount defaut.
[6] L., navietz.

No. 55.

holds—that is to say, if three be named, one who makes default will lose a third part, and one who appears can defend only in respect of a third part; but with respect to rent each one can defend with regard to the entirety, and plead with the object of showing why no parcel should be charged. Therefore, since we can defend with regard to the entirety by plea, it is right that we should have a plea to the abatement of the writ with regard to the entirety.—WILLOUGHBY. Plead in discharge, if you will, for you will not abate the writ, and particularly after judgment. — *Grene*, with respect to one of the persons who had been admitted, said that one W. was seised of the land discharged, and enfeoffed him to hold discharged; and afterwards one A. acquired the land from which the rent issued, and enfeoffed the person who is admitted and his wife, to hold to them and their heirs, and he afterwards leased to the persons on whose default he is admitted, and he vouched himself as the assign of A., who should be summoned, &c. And with respect to the other person who had been admitted he alleged that in the time of King Henry III. a fine was levied between H. son of Baldwin de Wake, and Baldwin de Veer, of certain lands in Bourne and Deeping, by which fine Baldwin released to H. all his right, &c., for which release H. granted and rendered to this same Baldwin all his lands in the Isle of Guernsey, to hold of him, &c., by the services due for half a knight's fee, and yielding six pounds a year at Bourne, which is the same rent whereof the demandant demands her dower. And Baldwin granted that whensoever the same rent should be in arrear, if it was because the Isle of Guernsey had been devastated by war, it should be lawful for H. and his heirs to distrain in all his lands in Thrapston, in which vill the writ of Dower is now brought. And we tell you, said *Grene*, that the demandant's husband

No. 55.

mes solonc la quantite qil tient, saver, si iij soient
nomes, un qe fait defaut perdra la terce partie, et
un qe vint ne purra defendre forqe la terce partie ;
mes de rente chesqun purra defendre lentier et
pleder pur quei nulle parcelle serra charge. Par quei,
quant nous poms defendre lentier par ple, il est
resoun qe nous eioms plee al abatement du brief
del entier.—WILBY. Pledetz en descharge si vous
voilletz, qar vous nabateretz pas le brief, et nomement apres jugement.—*Grene*, quant al un qe fuit
resceu, dit qun W. fuit seisi de la terre descharge,
et luy feffa a tener descharge ; et puis un A. avynt[1]
a la terre dount, &c., et feffa celuy qest resceu et
sa femme a eux et ses heirs, et il apres lessa a
ces par qi defaut il est resceu, et voucha luy mesme
com assigne A. qe serra somons, &c. Et quant a
lautre qest resceu il alleggea coment en temps le
Roi H. fyne se leva entre H. le fitz Baudewyn de
Wake, et Baudewyn de Veer, des certeinz terres en
Brun et Depyng, par quel fyne Baudewyn relessa
a H. tut soun dreit,[2] &c., pur quel relees H. graunta
et rendist a mesme celuy Baudewyn toux ses terres
en Lille de Gernesey a tener de luy, &c., par les
services par[3] un demi fee de chivaler, et rendaunt
vj *li.* par an a Brun, quel est mesme la rente dount
ele demande son dowere.[4] Et Baudewyn graunta qe
quele houre qe mesme la rente fuit arere, sil ne
fuit qe Lille de G. fuit destruit par geer, qe lirreit
a H. et ses heirs destreindre en totes ses terres de
Trapestone,[5] en quele ville le brief de Dowere est
porte ore. Et vous dioms qe son baron avoit lestat

---

[1] H., and C., auxint ; D., avient.
[2] dreit is omitted from C.
[3] The words les services par are from D. alone.

[4] H., dowere en L.
[5] H., Tapilton.

No. 55.

had H.'s estate, and that her husband was seised of the same rent through the tenants of Guernsey; and we demand judgment, inasmuch as the lands in Thrapston are not charged as to the freehold of this rent, but only to distress as above, whether you can maintain this action against the ter-tenants of Thrapston.—*Skipwith.* You see plainly how we are a stranger to the fines, and we have nothing to do with that which he says about rent in Guernsey, because that is not what we are demanding; and we demand judgment inasmuch as we shall be ready to maintain our husband's possession in Thrapston so that our husband could endow us, if he will deny it, as to which he makes no answer, and we pray seisin of our dower.—STOUFORD, *ad idem.* What issue or traverse will he have to that which you have said?—*R. Thorpe.* He can confess that the rent of which we speak is the same, and maintain that the land in Thrapston is charged because the Isle of Guernsey is devastated, or else he can say that his demand is in respect of another rent; and he must do one or other, inasmuch as we have admitted the possession of the husband.— *Grene, ad idem.* We will aver that her husband was not seised of any other rent, so that he could endow her, in Thrapston; ready, &c.—*Skipwith.* We say that you do not answer to our demand.—*Grene.* You have delivered an averment to us on the seisin of your husband, to which, if you will hold to it, we shall have a traverse, &c.—*Skipwith.* As to the voucher you see plainly how he has been admitted to defend with respect to the land, and vouches with respect to the rent, which voucher is not grantable for him; also our demand is one as for rent charge, so that to admit one to vouch and another to plead to the action in respect of another parcel would be to suppose that our action is severable, which it cannot

No. 55.

H., et qe son baron fuit seisi de mesme la rente
[par les tenantz de Gernesey; et demandoms jugement, desicome les terres de Trapestone ne sount
pas charges del frank tenement de ceste rente],[1]
mes soulement a la destresse *ut supra*, si vers les
terre tenantz de Trapestone puissetz ceste accion
meintenir.—*Skip.* Vous veietz bien coment a les fines
nous sumes estraunge, et ceo qil parle de rente en
Gernesey nous navoms qe faire, qar ceo ne demandoms pas; et demandoms jugement desicome
nous serroms prest de meintenir la possession nostre
baron en Trapestone, sil le voleit dedire, si qe dower
nous pout, a quei il ne respond pas, et prioms
seisine de nostre dowere.—STOUF., *ad idem.*[2] Quel
issue ou travers avera[3] il a ceo qe vous avietz dit?—
[R.] *Thorpe.* Il poet conustre qe cest mesme la rente
dount nous parloms, et meintener qe la terre de
Trapestone est charge par tant qe Lille de Gernesey
est destruit, ou autrement dire qe sa demande est
dautre rente; et lun covient il qil face, desicome
nous avoms conu la possession son baron.—*Grene,
ad idem.* Nous voloms averer qe son baron ne fuit
pas seisi dautre rente si qe dower la pout en Trapestone; prest, &c.—*Skip.* Nous dioms qe vous responez pas a nostre demande.—*Grene.* Vous avetz[4]
livere un averement a nous sur la seisine vostre
baroun, a quel si vous voilletz tener nous averoms
travers, &c.—*Skip.* Quant al voucher vous veietz
bien coment il est resceu de la terre, et vouche de
rente, qe nest pas grantable[5] pur luy; auxint nostre
demande est une come de rente charge, issint qe
seoffrir un a voucher et autre de pleder al accion
dautre parcelle qe serreit a supposer nostre accion

---

[1] The words between brackets are omitted from H.

[2] The words *ad idem* are omitted from D.

[3] L., ad; C., doun (interlined in later hand).

[4] C. and D., avietz.

[5] L. and D., garrauntable

No. 55.

be in respect of this rent.—But this last argument was not held good. — *Skipwith*. Also he vouches himself, supposing himself to have a right to a fee simple, and he does not vouch in order to save the estate of another person; and also he vouches in respect of an estate which he supposes that he took jointly with his wife, and he does not show how a sole estate could afterwards have accrued to him; and also he vouches himself as the assign of one A., and does not show that he at any time made any estate to A.; therefore, for all these reasons, the voucher is not grantable.—*Grene*. Cannot anyone vouch as assign even though the person whose assign he says he is has not any warranty higher up? as meaning to say that he can. But if anyone vouches as assign it is a good answer to say that he never had anything by assignment from the person as whose assign he vouches.—*Skipwith*. It has not been seen that anyone has vouched himself in respect of a fee simple for any other cause than for the purpose of saving the estate of another person, or an estate tail.—Stonore. Is it not to your advantage when he passes over this Roger by whom he entered, and vouches over?—*Skipwith*. But, Sir, since Roger could not, on the matter shown, have voucher of him, he, as Roger's assign, cannot have voucher of himself. —*R. Thorpe*. Possibly he would not have warranty, but that is no affair of yours, but, in order to maintain the voucher, the previous sole seisin suffices.— Willoughby.—It does not.—*Grene* then alleged that at an earlier time he enfeoffed Roger so that, as Roger's assign, he vouched himself.—*Skipwith*. As to that which he pleads in bar, you have heard how he alleges fines, and also speaks of rent issuing out of lands in Guernsey, to which matter we are altogether a stranger; and as to that which is alleged to the effect that our husband was not seised of the rent in

No. 55.

estre severable, qe ne poet estre de ceste rente.— A.D. 1345
Sed ista ultima ratio non allocatur.—*Skyp.* Auxint il
vouche luy mesme la ou il luy[1] suppose estre en
dreit de fee simple, et ne vouche pas pur sauver
autri estat; et auxint vouche dun estat quel il sup- [Fitz.,
pose qil prist joint ove sa femme, et ne moustre *Voucher,*
122.]
pas coment soul[2] estat puis luy serreit acru; et
auxint vouche, come assigne un A., luy mesme, et
ne moustre pas qil a nul temps fist estat a A.; par
quei par totes cestes resouns le voucher nest pas
grantable.[3]—*Grene.* Ne poet homme voucher come
assigne coment qe celuy qi assigne il soi dist estre
neit garrantie[4] par amount? *quasi diceret sic.* Mes
si homme vouche come assigne il est bon respons
a dire qil navoit unqes rienz del assignement celuy
come qi assigne il vouche.[5]—*Skyp.* Homme nad pas
view homme voucher luy mesme de fee simple par
nulle cause sil ne fuit pur sauver autri estat ou
estat taille.—STON. Ne fait il pas pur vous quant
il treshaut celuy Roger par qi il entra, et vouche
outre?—*Skyp.* Mes, Sire, quant Roger ne pout sur
la matere moustre aver voucher de luy, il, come
assigne Roger, ne pout aver le voucher de luy mesme.[6]
—[R.] *Thorpe.* Par cas il navereit pas garrantie, mes
ceo nest pas a vous, mes a meintener le voucher la
soul seisine devant suffit.—WILBY. Noun fait.—*Grene*
alleggea donqes qe de temps plus haut il feffa Roger,
issint come assigne Roger vouche luy mesme.—*Skip.*
Quant a ceo qil plede en barre vous avietz entendu
coment il allegge fynes, et auxint parle de rente
issaunt des terres en Gernesey, a quele chose nous
sumes tut estraunge; et a ceo qe[7] allegge est qe
nostre baron ne fuit seisi come de franktenement de

---

[1] luy is omitted from L. and H.
[2] D., son.
[3] L., and D., garrauntable.
[4] C., graunte.

[5] L., soi fait.
[6] mesme is omitted from D.
[7] All the MSS. except D., qil.

No. 55.

Thrapston as of freehold, it is a traverse of our action; we will aver that our husband was seised of the rent, in respect of which we have made our demand, so that he could endow us; ready, &c.—*R. Thorpe.* If you will have judgment on our confession you can do so quite well, for we fully confess to you that your husband levied the rent by distress in Thrapston for default of payment, and then there will be no need to have an averment; but to aver in general terms the seisin of your husband where it is in a manner confessed, is not right, because it is certain that even though our land in Thrapston be charged to distress as we understand, still the freehold of the rent is in this case adjudged to be issuing from the land from which it was first issuing; and if you were to have such a general averment you would be endowed twice over of one and the same thing.—*Skipwith.* If he were to allege that the rent was issuing from lands in another vill in which I could have suit and writ, then his exception would go no farther than to my writ, but he assigns matter on which I shall never have an action elsewhere, and therefore his answer deprives me of an action with regard to the rest.—HILLARY. The King's writ runs in Guernsey.—STONORE. You are demandant; consider whether you will admit that you demand dower of the same rent of which he confesses that you are entitled to dower, or of another.—*Skipwith.* The colour which there is for having me put to answer to him is on the ground that the rent might be levied by distress in Thrapston; but now the distress, according to their own statement, did not extend to our husband, because he is supposed to be assign according to their statement, and distress extends only to the party and his heirs; therefore it seems that the distress will not put me out of my writ, that is to say, prevent me from averring, in general terms, my husband's seisin. — WILLOUGHBY,

No. 55.

rente en Trapestone, cest a travers de nostre accion; A.D.1345
nous voloms averer qe nostre baron fuit seisi de la
rente dount nous avoms fait nostre demande si qe dower
nous poet; prest, &c.—[R.] *Thorpe.* Si vous voilletz
de nostre conissance aver jugement[1] vous poietz bien,
qar nous vous conissoms bien qe vostre baron par
destresse leva la rente en T. pur defaut de paiement, et donqes ne bosoignera[2] pas daver averement;
mes[3] generalment[4] daverer la seisine vostre baron,
ou en manere cest conu, nest pas resoun, qar il
est certein, tut soit nostre terre charge en T. a la
destresse a ceo qe nous entendoms, unqore le franktenement de la rente est en ceo cas ajugge estre
issaunt de la primere terre dount ele est issaunt;
et si vous averetz tiel averement general[5] vous serretz
dune mesme chose deux foith dowe.—*Skyp.* Sil
alleggeast qe la rente fuit issaunt des terres en
autre ville ou jeo purroi aver suite et brief, donqes
irreit sa excepcion forqe a mon brief, mes il doune
matere qe jammes naverai jeo accion aillours, par
quei son respons moi toude accion a remenant.—
Hill. Brief le Roi court en Gernesey.—Ston. Vous
estes demandant; veietz si vous voilletz conustre qe
vous demandetz dowere de mesme la rente qil vous
conust ou dautre.—*Skyp.* Le colour qil y ad pur
quei jeo serrai mys a respondre a luy cest pur tant
qe la rente purreit par destresse estre leve en T.;
mes ore la destresse, par lour dit demene, sestendist
pas a nostre baron, qar il duist estre assigne a ceo
qils dient, et la destresse sestent forqe a la partie
et ses heirs; donqes semble qe la destresse ne moi
mettra pas hors de moun brief, saver, generalment
daverer la seisine mon baron.—[Wilby. Quidetz vous

---

[1] D., L., and 25,184, travers.
[2] C., bussoignera.
[3] mes is omitted from D.

[4] D., general.
[5] C., generalment.

No. 55.

Do you suppose that an assign will not be able to distrain in such a case.—*Skipwith.* No, Sir, no more than he will be able to deraign warranty.—WILLOUGHBY. What you say is contrary to law; therefore will you say anything else?—*Skipwith.* Seised in his demesne as of fee, &c., so that he could endow her, &c., of rent issuing out of the lands in Thrapston, other than that rent of which you speak; ready, &c.—And the other side said the contrary.—And they were compelled to take this issue by the COURT.—*Skipwith.* As to the voucher, you see plainly how he vouches himself, and that in respect of an estate of fee simple, in which case voucher is not given except in order to save the estate of another person, as one of joint tenancy, or an estate tail, and he is not in such case; judgment whether he ought to have this voucher of himself.—*R. Thorpe.* We who are admitted to defend have alleged a reason for the voucher in order to save the estate of another person, that is to say, of our wife: for if we vouch and are warranted, we shall hold to the value jointly with our wife, because it is certain that, if the tenant for term of life were dead, and we were in possession on our reversion, we should hold jointly with our wife.—STONORE. Yes, you would then hold according to the first course; but now, so long as your demise lasts, which puts your wife to her action, you cannot say that she holds the reversion or anything else jointly; therefore this voucher cannot be to her advantage against all the world; therefore answer. —And he was ousted from the voucher by judgment.— And he pleaded in bar as above, and the same traverse was taken.—Veer was admitted to defend on the default of some of the tenants, and Bruys was admitted on the default of others.

No. 55.

qe lassigne en tiel[1] cas ne purra destreindre?—*Skyp.* A.D. 1345
Noun, Sire, nient plus[2] qe derrener garrantie.][3]—
WILBY. Vous parletz countre ley; par quei voilletz
autre chose dire?—*Skyp.* Seisi en soun demene come
de fee, &c., si qe dower la pout, &c., de rente
issaunt des terres en Trapestone, autre qe cele rente
qe vous parletz; prest, &c.—*Et alii e contra.*—Et a
ceo furent chacetz[4] par COURT.—*Skyp.* Quant al
voucher, vous veietz bien coment il vouche luy mesme,
et ceo destat de fee simple, en quel cas voucher
nest pas done sil ne fuit pur sauver[5] autri estat
come de jointenance ou asqun autre estat taille, et
il nest en tel cas; jugement si de luy mesme ceo
voucher deive aver.—[R.] *Thorpe.* Nous qe sumes resceu avoms allegge cause[6] del voucher pur sauver autri
estat, saver, de nostre femme: qar si nous vouchoms
et soioms garranti nous tendroms la value joint ove
nostre femme, qar *certum est* si le tenant a terme
de vie fuit mort, et nous fuissoms einz en la reversion, nous tendroms joint ove nostre femme.—
STON. Oyl, adonqes vous le tendretz en le primer
cours; mes a ore, tanqe[7] vostre demise dure, la
quele mette vostre femme a saccion, vous ne poietz
dire qele tient joint reversion ne autre chose; par
quei ceo voucher ne[8] purra estre pur tut le mound
en avantage de luy; par quei responez.—Et fuit
ouste del voucher par agarde.—Et pleda en barre
ut supra, et mesme le travers pris.—Veer[9] resceu
par defaut des asquns des tenantz, et Bruys resceu
par defaut des autres.

---

[1] D., ceo.
[2] plus is omitted from C.
[3] The words between brackets are omitted from H.
[4] C., chasce.
[5] H., and C., salver. The word is omitted from D.

[6] cause is omitted from D.
[7] D., tauntqe.
[8] ne is omitted from H.
[9] L., Vere.

Nos. 56–58.

A.D. 1345.

Prayer to be admitted.

(56.) § Note that Gerard de Lisle, who was heretofore admitted to defend his right, now had a Protection produced for him.—*R. Thorpe.* He appears by attorney, and he is a party on his own prayer, without any process having been made against him, and therefore protection is not allowable for him.—This exception was not allowed.—Therefore the Protection was allowed.

Prayer to be admitted.

(57.) § Note that in a case in which the Earl Marshal and his wife had on a previous occasion prayed to be admitted to defend their right by reason of the default of their tenant for term of life, and, because the demandant was then essoined, a day was given until now, and now the demandant is essoined, as against the tenant, as being on the King's service, and also, by another essoin, as against those who prayed to be admitted, the COURT asked the essoiner to which essoin he would hold; and he said to the essoin as against the tenant.—*Pole.* And, inasmuch as the tenant whose default was heretofore recorded is now out of Court, and has not a day, the demandant cannot be essoined as against him; therefore, inasmuch as the demandant does not appear, judgment on his nonsuit, and we pray that it be recorded for the King's advantage.—WILLOUGHBY. As against whom should he be essoined? Those who pray to be admitted are not admitted yet, and so are not parties; therefore the tenant, even though he shall not be called, is party to the demandant, and no one else is.—Therefore the essoin was adjudged, and a day was given.—And those who prayed to be admitted proffered themselves by attorney; and that is recorded in order to save to them the advantage hereafter.

Prayer to be admitted.

(58.) § Note that an infant prayed to be admitted

Nos. 56–58.

(56.)[1] § *Nota* qe Gerard del Ille[3] qe fuit resceu a defendre son dreit autrefoith ore[4] proteccion fuit mys avant pur luy.—[*R.*] *Thorpe.* Il est par[5] attourne et est partie, sanz proces vers luy fait, a sa prier demene, par quei pur luy proteccion nest pas allowable.—*Non allocatur.*—Par quei la proteccion est allowe.

A.D. 1345.
Prier destre resceu.[2]

(57.)[6] § *Nota* qe ou le[8] Count Mareschal et sa femme[9] autrefoith par defaut de lour tenant a terme de vie prierunt destre resceu, et pur ceo qe le demandant fuit adonqes essone, jour fuit done tanqa ore, et ore le demandant est essone de service le Roi vers le tenant, et auxint par autre essone vers ces qe prierunt, demande fuit par COURT de essoignour,[10] a quel essone il soi voleit tenir, qe dit al essone vers le tenant.—*Pole.* Et desicome le tenant qi defaut autrefoith fuit recorde est ore hors de Court, et nad pas jour, le demandant vers luy ne poet estre essone; par quei, desicome il ne vint pas, jugement de sa nounsuite, et ceo prioms qe recorde soit pur le Roi.—WILBY. Vers qi serreit il essone? Ces qe prierunt ne sount[11] pas resceu unqore, et issint nient parties; par quei le tenant, tut ne serra il pas demande, est partie al demandant, et nul autre.—Par quei lessone fuit ajugge et ajourne.—Et ces qe prierunt se profrirent par attourne; et ceo est recorde pur sauver a eux autrefoith lavantage.

Prier destre resceu.[7]
[Fitz., *Essone,* 22.]

(58.)[6] § *Nota* qun enfant, par defaut de tenant a

Prier destre resceu.[12]

---

[1] From L., H., C., and D.

[2] The marginal note in D. is *Nota.* H. has none.

[3] H., Isle; C., Ile.

[4] ore is omitted from D.

[5] par is omitted from L. and H. In C. it is interlined in a later hand.

[6] From L., C., and D.

[7] The marginal note in C., and D. is *Nota.*

[8] C., and D., les heirs le.

[9] The words et sa femme are from L. alone.

[10] D., essoneour.

[11] C., serrount.

[12] The marginal note in D. is *Nota.*

No. 59.

to defend his right by reason of the default of a tenant for term of life, and alleged, when so praying, that the demand was less in number of acres than the writ supposed. And he prayed to be admitted on the ground of a grant of the reversion made to his ancestor by a deed, of which *profert* was made, and attornment, &c.—*Seton.* The supposed grantor did not grant the reversion by this deed; ready, &c.—*R. Thorpe.* Though that is not an issue, ready, &c., that he did. —And the other side said the contrary.—And security for the issues was found by four mainpernors.—And seisin was awarded of the residue in respect of which the infant did not pray to be admitted, because it is not in his power to say that the demand is less than is supposed in the writ.

Error.　　(59.) § John Gysors, and his co-parceners, that is to say, his brother's sons, sued a writ of Error on a forejudger on a writ of Mesne given against him and his brother, whose heirs sue, on the ground that the seignory is partible between males by custom; and

No. 59.

terme de vie, pria destre resceu, et alleggea en priaunt qe la demande est meins en noumbre des acres qe le brief suppose. Et pria par cause dun grant de reversion fet a son auncestre par fait, qe fuit mys avant, et attournement, &c.—*Setone.* Il ne granta pas par ceo fet la reversion ; prest, &c.— [*R.*] *Thorpe.* Tut ne soit ceo pas issue, prest, &c., qe ci.—*Et alii e contra.*—Et seorte trove des issues par iiij meinpernours.—Et del remenant, dount il ne pria pas, seisine agarde, qar il ne poet dire qe la demande soit meins.

(59.)[1] § Johan Gisors et ses parceners, saver, les fitz son frere, suyrent brief Derrour sur forjuger en brief de Mene taille vers luy[2] et son frere, qi heirs suent, pur ceo qe la seignurie est departable entre

---

[1] From L., H., C., and D. It appears in the *Placita coram Rege*, Trin , 19 Edw. III., R° 55, that there were proceedings in Error on a judgment given in the Common Bench in Hilary Term, 19 Edw. III., (*Placita de Banco*, R° 245 of that term). An action of Mesne was brought by John de Wenlyngburghe against John Gysors and Henry his brother for acquittal of services demanded by Queen Philippa in respect of tenements "in villa " de Sancto Botolpho " (Boston, Lincolnshire). After certain process, proclamation, and defaults, judgment was given in the Common Bench " quod prædicti Johannes " Gysors et Henricus amittant " servitium prædicti Johannis de " Wenlyngburghe de tenementis " prædictis, et idem Johannes de " Wenlyngburghe, omissis præ- " dictis Johanne Gysors et Henrico " mediis, &c., amodo sit inten- " dens prædictæ Reginæ capitali " dominæ, &c., de eisdem servitiis " quæ prædicti Johannis Gysors et " Henricus, medii, &c., ei facere " consueverunt." See also Y.B., Easter, 19 Edw. III., No. 14.

Error was sued by the above-named John Gysors, and by John and Henry, sons and heirs of the above-named Henry. They assigned for error in the judgment " quod idem Henricus tempore " redditionis judicii prædicti, et " diu ante, fuit mortuus, &c., " dicunt enim quod idem Henricus " obiit apud Londonias, in parochia " Sancti Jacobi de Carlichithe, in " warda de Vintria, in vigilia " Sanctæ Katerinæ, anno regni " Regis nunc decimo septimo, unde " dicunt quod ipsi erraverunt in " tantum quod ipsi reddiderunt " judicium versus ipsum Henricum, " ut versus hominem vivum, cum " idem Henricus tempore reddi- " tionis judicii prædicti et diu ante " fuit mortuus, &c."

[2] L., eux.

No. 59.

he assigned for error the fact that his brother was dead at the time at which the judgment was rendered. —*Skipwith*. John cannot now allege the death since he could have alleged it before judgment; and, inasmuch as he has out-stayed his time, judgment.—BASSET. If a writ is brought against two joint tenants, and one dies, and judgment is afterwards rendered against them, will not the other afterwards have a writ of Error?—*Skipwith*. Certainly not, because he could have abated the writ.—*Grene*. In a case in which summons is testified by the Sheriff, it does not lie in the mouth of any one to allege the death of the party, for judgment was given on that point recently in the Common Bench on a *Præcipe* brought against several persons in respect of a rent charge.—THORPE (JUSTICE) to *Skipwith*. Will you accept the averment? for if you will aver that the brother is living, we are discharged from giving judgment, and if you will not, we shall give judgment.—*Skipwith*. We abide your judgments as whether he shall be admitted to his averment, and particularly whether on this writ of Mesne he can have the averment any sooner than on a *Præcipe quod reddat*.—BASSET. One of them could not have acquitted the services without the other; therefore, if he could not have pleaded anything, even if he had appeared, it is not right that he should be ousted from a writ of Error through his nonappearance.—*Skipwith*. He could have alleged the death of the other, or else have pleaded as to the liability to acquit; and I am quite sure that they are aided in this suit by their several right; for otherwise the heirs of both would never join in this suit, but by survivorship the whole would accrue to the one that survived; and if the case were such that they had had a joint estate, the one who survived, and who could have come and have abated the writ, or pleaded as to the right, would never now have such suit,

No. 59.

madles par usage; et assigna pur errour la mort A.D. 1345. son frere al temps del jugement rendu.—*Skyp*. Johan ne poet la mort allegger del houre qil pout aver allegge cella avant le jugement; et, desicome il ad sursis son temps,[1] jugement.—BASSET. Si brief soit porte vers ij jointenantz, et lun moert, et jugement apres est rendu vers eux, navera lautre apres brief Derrour?—*Skyp*. Noun certes, qar il pout aver abatu le brief.—*Grene*. La ou somons est tesmoigne par Vicounte, dallegger la mort gist en nuly bouche, qar ceo fuit agarde en Comune Baunk ore tarde en *Præcipe* porte vers plusours dune rente charge.— THORPE, JUSTICE, a *Skyp*. Voilletz laverement? qar si vous voletz averer la vie celuy, nous sumes descharge del jugement, et, si noun, nous lajuggeroms. —*Skyp*. Nous demuroms en voz jugements sil avendra, et nomement en cest brief de Mene si[2] pout aver laverement plus toust qen *Præcipe quod reddat*.—BASSET. Lun ne poet pas aver acquite sanz lautre; donqes, tut ust il venuz, sil ne pout rienz aver plede, par sa noun venue n'est pas resoun qil soit ouste Derrour.—*Skip*. Il pout aver allegge la mort lautre, ou autrement aver plede al acquitance; et jeo sai bien ils soi eident en ceste suite par lour several dreit; qar[3] autrement les heirs lun et lautre se joindreint jammes en ceste suite, mes par survivre tut acrestereit en celuy qe survivereit; et, sil fuit en cas qils ussent eu joint estat, celuy qe survesquit,[4] et qe poet aver venu, et[5] aver abatu le brief, ou plede en dreit, il navera jammes tiéle suite,

---

[1] L., jour.
[2] All the MSS. except C., il.
[3] C., quant.

[4] L., and D., survivereit.
[5] C., and D., ou.

No. 59.

nor consequently will he now have it as to a moiety; since it is several, the one who was party cannot have the suit, nor the others who have undertaken the suit together with him who has no action; but possibly they might have, by another writ, suit as to the moiety which belongs to them.—*Grene.* It would be an extraordinary thing to divide the matter into parcels, for the seignory is one, and must be one; and I say that, although it has been said that if there are two joint tenants, and they lose by default, whereas one was dead at the time at which judgment was rendered, the one who survives will not have a writ of Error, but is ousted from it by his own default, &c., the fact is not so, because, even though he should come before judgment, and allege the death of his companion, he would not be admitted, nor would he have Assise by reason of the execution of the judgment, if he was ejected from any parcel, but, because by survivorship the whole would accrue to him, he would have a writ of Error with respect to the whole.—*R. Thorpe.* That is not law, and I am quite sure that one who loses by default can well assign error in law, but never error in fact, because judgment has been rendered on his default, and his own default is the cause of his loss. —*Grene.* The reverse is law, for we saw judgment rendered against a man and his wife on an Assise which was taken by default (and that was Wickham's case) and the husband afterwards reversed it by way of Error, and in that case this matter was well argued. —*R. Thorpe.* In Assise one does not lose by default; therefore the cases are not alike.—Scot. Whatever may be said, we thoroughly understand that, in all the cases which you mention, one may appear before judgment, and allege that the other is dead, but it does not therefore follow that they will not have a writ of Error to reverse the whole judgment rendered on the writ which was always bad by reason of the death

No. 59.

nec per consequens a ore de la moite ; del houre qe A.D. 1345.
cest several, celuy qe fuit partie ne poet aver la
suite, ne les autres qount enpris la suite ov luy qe
nulle accion nad, ne pout a cest brief aver accion ;
mes par cas de la moite afferrant a eux ils averount
par autre brief sa suite.—*Grene.* Ceo serreit merveille de parceller la chose, qar la seignurie est une,
et covient estre une[1] ; et jeo die qe coment qe
homme[2] parle qe si deux jointenantz y soient, et
ils perdent par defaut, la ou lun a un temps del
jugement rendu est mort, qe celuy qe survyst navera
pas brief[3] Derrour, mes est ouste par sa defaut
demene, &c., il nest pas issint, qar, mesqil venist
avant jugement, et alleggeast la mort son compaig-
noun, il ne serra pas resceu, ne il navera pas Assise
par lexecucion del jugement, sil fuit ouste de nulle
parcelle, mes, pur ceo qe par survivre tut acrestreit[4]
a luy, de tut avera il Errour.—[*R.*] *Thorpe.* Ceo nest
pas ley, et jeo say bien qe celuy qe perde par defaut il assignera errour de ley bien, mes errour de
fait jammes, qar le jugement est rendu sur sa defaut, et sa defaut demene est la[5] cause de sa perde.
—*Grene.* Le revers est ley, qar nous veimes jugement rendu vers un homme et sa femme sur une
Assise qe fuit pris par defaut, et fuit ceo le cas de
Wykham, et apres le baron le reversa par voie
Derrour, et la fuit ceste matere bien parle.—[*R.*] *Thorpe.*
En Assise homme ne perde pas par defaut ; *ideo
non est simile.*—Scot. Quei qe homme parle, nous
entendoms molt bien qen toutz les cas qe vous
parletz qe lun purra venir avant jugement et allegger
la mort lautre, mes de ceo nensuit pas qils naver-
ount[6] brief Derrour de reverser tut le jugement
rendu sur le brief qe[7] tut temps fuit malveis par

---

[1] une is omitted from C.
[2] C., qomme, instead of qe homme.
[3] brief is omitted from C.

[4] All the MSS. except L., afferreit.
[5] la is omitted from C.
[6] L., and H., averount.
[7] L., and C., et.

No. 59.

of one of the persons named.—*Birton*. This suit cannot be severed, even though the plaintiffs have several right; and there are some matters of fact which abate a writ even without plea, and some which do so only by plea; for instance, the death of a party abates a writ even without plea, so that if the demandant will not await the day which has been given him in Court, he can waive his writ, and purchase another, and maintain it, notwithstanding that the latter writ was purchased while the other was pending; and there are other matters of fact which must be pleaded, as, for instance, if a woman takes a husband while the writ is pending, that fact must be alleged by the party, and, unless he does so, he cannot assign that fact as error; therefore in this matter the writ was abated by death without any plea, and the fault that there was in that this writ was prosecuted was the plaintiff's fault.—THORPE (JUSTICE). In the opinion of some, in a *Præcipe* brought in respect of land, in which the matter is clearer, and in which severance can well be made, one of the joint tenants who survives will have a writ of Error upon a judgment rendered on default, as above, and, even though he cannot do so, there is hardly any mischief, because he can have a writ of Deceit, and a writ of Right; but in this case a writ of Deceit does not lie for the purpose of regaining that which was lost, but only for having damages against an officer, nor does a writ of Right lie, because of the judgment; it would therefore be a strong measure if he were ousted from this suit.—*R. Thorpe*. The point on which we abide judgment is whether one who was party to the judgment, and through whose default the judgment was given, ought to be answered as to this suit.—THORPE (JUSTICE). The COURT holds it as not denied that one of the parties was dead, for that is assigned as error in fact, and is not denied, and although it is said that the other person who was

No. 59.

mort dun des nomes.—*Birtone.* Ceste suite ne poet A.D. 1345.
estre severe, tut eient les pleintifs several dreit; et
il y ad asqune chose en fait qe abate brief tut saunz
plee, et asqune chose qe noun pas forqe par plee,
come mort de partie abate brief tut sanz plee, issint
qe, si le demandant ne voille attendre le jour qe
luy est done en Court, il poet weyver son brief, et
purchacer autre, et le meintener, *non obstante* qe
ceo fuit purchace pendant un autre; et autre chose
en fait qe covient estre plede, come si femme
pendant son brief prent baron, ceo covient estre
allegge par partie, et sil ne face nient de[1] ceo ne
poet il assigner errour; par quei en ceste matere
par mort le brief fuit abatu tut saunz ple, et la
defaute qe cel brief fuit pursuy fuit la defaut le
pleintif.—THORPE, JUSTICE. Al entent dasquns, en
Præcipe porte de terre qest plus clere et poet bien
estre severe, lun des jointenantz qe survyst avera
Errour sur jugement taille par defaut, *ut supra*, et
tut ne poet il pas il ny ad gers de meschief, qar
il avera brief de Desceit et brief de Dreit; mes en
ceo cas brief de Desceit ne gist pas pur reaver ceo
qe fuit perdu, mes soulement damages vers ministre,
ne brief de Dreit, pur le jugement; par quei il
serreit fort sil fuit ouste de ceste suite.—*R. Thorpe.*
Nostre demure est sil qe fuit partie al jugement, et
par qi defaut le jugement se fist sil deive a ceste
suite estre respondu.—THORPE, JUSTICE. COURT tient
a nient dedit qun des parties fuit mort, qar cest
assigne pur errour en fet, et nest pas dedit, et
coment qest parle qe cely qe fut partie pout aver

---

[1] H., and C., et de.

No. 59.

party could have alleged this matter before judgment, that is not clear, and particularly in this case of a matter touching seignory; and even though he could have done so, and did not, the fact is not of sufficient strength to oust him from this suit, nor yet to oust the heirs; therefore this COURT doth award that the judgment be reversed, and we do entirely annul it, and do restore the plaintiffs to their seignory, and do adjudge that the tenant of the demesne be attendant unto them as he was to have been before the judgment.

No. 59.

allegge la chose avant jugement, ceo nest pas clere, ^{A.D. 1345.} et nomement en ceste matere de chose seignurel; et tut le pout il faire, et ne fist pas, ceo nest pas si fort qe luy ouste de ceste suite, ne les heirs nient plus; par quei agarde ceste COURT qe le jugement soit reverse, et nous lanientissoms de tut, et restituoms les pleintifs a lour seignurie, et les tenantz del demene entendantz a eux com il dust aver este avant le jugement.[1]

---

[1] According to the King's Bench roll John de Wenlyngburghe pleaded "quod ipse non intendit "quod prædictus Johanues Gisors "ad istud breve captum in com-"muni cum heredibus ipsius "Henrici responderi debeat, &c., "quia dicit quod de jure communi "post mortem ipsius Henrici secta "tantomodo esse deberet præfato "Johanni et non in communi cum "heredibus ipsius Henrici, &c."

The pleadings are then continued as follows :—"Et Johannes Gisors, "et Johannes et Henricus dicunt "quod quidam Johannes Gisors "pater ipsius Johannis Gisors, et "avus prædictorum Johannis et "Henrici, fuit seisitus de servitiis "prædictis simul cum aliis terris "et tenementis in villa de Sancto "Botolpho, quæ quidem servitia, "terræ, et tenementa in eadem "villa, quæ sunt de feodo de "Richemonde, sunt partibilia inter "masculos, &c. Et dicunt quod "post mortem præfati Johannis "Gisors eadem servitia, simul cum "aliis terris et tenementis in eadem "villa, descenderunt præfatis Jo-"hanni Gisors et Henrico ut filiis "et heredibus, &c. Et sic dicunt "quod post mortem ipsius Henrici "secta sua data est in communi "præfato Johanni Gisors cum "heredibus ipsius Henrici, &c.

"Et Johannes de Wenlynburghe, "protestando quod ipse non cog-"noscit ipsum Henricum esse "mortuum tempore redditionis "judicii prædicti, prout prædicti "Johannes Gisors, Johannes, et "Henricus superius supponunt, "dicit, ut prius, quod prædictus "Johannes Gisors ad istud breve "responderi non debet, &c., quia "dicit quod exquo proclamatio in "prædicto brevi de *Medio* ad præ-"fatam quindenam Sancti Hillarii "anno supradicto versus ipsum "Johannem testificata fuit, quo "tempore idem Johannes venire "potuisset et allegasse mortem "ipsius Henrici pro brevi cassando, "quo tempore idem Johannes non "venit, sed patiebatur judicium "prædictum esse versus ipsum "redditum, petit judicium si idem "Johannes ad istud breve respon-"deri debeat, &c. Et quo ad præ-"dictos Johannem et Henricum "petit judicium exquo ipsi tulerunt "breve istud in communi cum "præfato Johanne Gisors, ubi "secta ipsorum Johannis et Hen-"rici esse debet per se, et non in "communi, pro portionibus suis, "petit judicium si ad istud breve "responderi debeant, &c.

"Et Johannes Gisors, et Jo-"hannes et Henricus dicunt quod "exquo prædictus Johannes de

No. 60.

A.D. 1345.

Detinue of a writing.

(60.) § Detinue of a writing was brought by the Prior of St. Oswald against William de Brokelesby, in which the declaration was that the writing was delivered to him upon a certain condition, that is to say, that if the Prior should pay to Peter Maule, the fifth, £10, &c., it should be re-delivered to him; and he said that he paid, &c.—William de Brokelesby said that he did not know whether the covenants had been kept or not, and prayed a *Scire facias* to be directed to Peter. And Peter was warned by a writ, reciting the whole matter, to show whether he could say anything wherefore the writing should not be delivered to the Prior. And Peter appeared.—*Seton*. We tell you

No. 60.

(60.)[1] § Detenue descript porte par le Prior de
Seint Oswald vers William de Brokelesby, countant
qe ceo luy fuit livere sur certein condicion qe sil
paiast a Piers Maule le quinte x*li.*, &c., qe ceo luy
serreit livere ; et dit qil paia, &c.—W. Brokelesby
dist qil ne savoit si les covenauntz[2] furent tenuz
ou noun, et pria garnissement vers Piers, qe fuit
garny par brief, reherceaunt tut, &c., sil savoit rienz
dire pur quei lescript ne serreit livere al Prior, qe

A.D. 1345.
Detenue
descript.
[Fitz.,
Garnishe,
et Garnish-
ment, 36.]

" Welyngburghe non dedicit mor-
" tem ipsius Henrici pendente
" proclamatione præedicta versus
" ipsos Johannem et Henricum, per
" cujus mortem breve illud per
" legem omnino fuit cassatum,
" petunt quod prædictum judicium
" versus ipsum Henricum redditum
" revocetur, et pro nullo habeatur,
" &c."

After an adjournment, the plaintiffs in Error " dicunt, ut prius,
" quod prædictus Henricus Gisors
" obiit pendente proclamatione
" quam idem Johannes de Wen-
" lyngburghe prosequebatur versus
" ipsos Johannem Gysors et Henri-
" cum, et hoc prætendunt verificare,
" &c., quam quidem verificationem
" prædictus Johannes omnino re-
" cusat, et petunt judicium, &c."

" Et quæsitum est a præfato
" Johanne de Wenlyngburghe si
" ipse verificationem prædictam
" velit necne, &c."

" Et Johannes de Wenlyng-
" burghe dicit, ut prius, quod
" exquo prædictus Johannes Gisors
" ante judicium super prædicto
" brevi de *Medio* non venit nec
" mortem ipsius Henrici allegavit,
" quo tempore idem Johannes
" venisse potuit et allegasse mor-
" tem supradictam in forma præ-
" dicta, petit præcise judicium si

" ad aliquam verificationem patriæ,
" quam prædicti Johannes et alii
" superius prætendunt, admitti
" debeant."

Judgment was therefore given
as follows :—

" Et quia, visis recordo et pro-
" cessu prædictis, videtur Curiæ
" quod exquo prædictus Johannes
" de Wenlyngburghe non dedicit
" mortem prædicti Henrici tempore
" quo prædictum judicium reddi-
" tum fuit versus ipsos Henricum
" et Johannem Gisors, et verifica-
" tionem prædictam omnino ad-
" mittere recusat, nec aliud dicit
" quare judicium illud revocari non
" debet, consideratum est quod
" prædictum judicium revocetur et
" adnulletur, et prædictus Jo-
" hannes de Wenlyngburghe amodo
" sit intendens et respondens præ-
" dictis Johanni Gisors, Johanni
" et Henrico, filiis prædicti Henrici
" Gisors, de eisdem consuetudini-
" bus et servitiis quæ idem Jo-
" hannes de Wenlyngburghe præ-
" fatis Johanni Gisors et Henrico
" facere solebat, &c., ante judicium
" versus ipsum Johannem Gisors
" et Henricum super prædicto
" brevi de *Medio* redditum, &c."

[1] From L., H., C., and D.
[2] L., condicions.

No. 60.

A.D. 1345. that the Prior ought to have paid £50, and he has not paid, and therefore the writing ought not to have been delivered to him.   And *Seton* showed further that if the payment was not made, it was for Peter to have the writing, and prayed that it might be delivered to him.—*Grene.* You speak of a different condition, and, as between the defendant and us, we are agreed with respect to the condition supposed by our declaration, so that, if the defendant has accepted the condition as being different from that which it was, he has charged himself with regard to you; but inasmuch as you plead a different condition, with regard to which you cannot recover on this writ, we pray that the writing be delivered to us: for if it be as you say, even though we recover against the defendant, he will by his own folly be put to answer to you when you employ an action of Detinue against him, and you are warned only to answer whether you have anything to say wherefore, according to the covenants, with regard to which we are agreed as between the defendant and us, the deed should not be delivered to us; therefore to plead a different condition would be unwarranted by this original writ.—WILLOUGHBY. The garnishment is for him to show whether he can say anything wherefore the writing should not be delivered to you, and as to that he gives a sufficient answer wherefore; and although the defendant may, to his own damage, have accepted a statement which is false, he shall not, on that account, be ousted from his answer.—*Thorpe.* Nor shall be admitted to oust us from the advantage which is admitted in our favour by the defendant, who can by law charge himself both to the garnishee and to us; and if we were to take issue with him on a different condition we should abate our count.— STOUFORD (JUSTICE). What you say is true, and therefore you can maintain your declaration against the garnishee; and it must be so in this matter, because

No. 60.

vint.—*Setone.* Nous vous dioms qe le Prior duist ^{A.D. 1345.} aver paie 1*li.*, et il nad pas paie, par quei a luy ne duist lescript aver este livere. Et moustra outre qe si le paiement ne fuit pas fait qe a ly attenoit[1] daver le, et pria qe lescript fuit livere a Piers.— *Grene.* Vous parletz dautre condicion, et entre[2] le defendant et nous sumes a un de la condicion sup- pose par nostre moustrance, issint qe sil ad accepte la condicion autre qele ne fuit, il soi ad charge devers vous; mes desicome vous pledetz autre[3] con- dicion a quei a cest brief vous ne poietz recoverir, nous prioms qe lescript soit a nous livere: qar sil soit come vous parletz, tut recoveroms nous vers luy, il serra mys par sa folie demene de respondre a vous quant vous useretz accion de Detenue vers luy, et vous nestes pas garny mes de respondre si vous eietz rienz a dire pur quei,[4] solonc les coven- auntes, dount entre le defendant et nous sumes a un, le fait a nous ne serra livere; par quei de pleder autre condicion serra desgarranti de cest original.—WILBY. Le garnissement est sil sache rienz dire pur quei lescript ne serra a vous livere, et a ceo dist il assetz[5] pur quei; et coment qe le de- fendant en damage de ly eit accepte un faux, par tant ne serra il pas ouste de soun respons.—[*R.*] *Thorpe.* Ne il ne serra pas resceu de nous ouster del avant- age qe nous est conu par le defendant, qe de lei se poet charger et vers[6] luy et vers nous; et si nous preissoms issue ove luy sur autre condicion nous abateroms nostre count.—STOUF., JUSTICE. Vous ditetz verite, et pur ceo vous poietz meintener vers luy vostre moustrance; et ceo covient il en ceste

---

[1] L., attient; H., attynt.
[2] H., and D., outre.
[3] D., dautre.

[4] D., quoi.
[5] D., asseth.
[6] L., devers, instead of et vers.

No. 61.

he is made a party to you, and the opposition to your purpose is entirely in him. And how will you be able to have judgment now without answering to his statement? as meaning to say, in no way: for you must have judgment either upon confession or upon verdict on a plea in traverse found in your favour, and there is now no one else against whom you can demand judgment but against him.—WILLOUGHBY to *Grene*. Answer. —*Grene*. The condition was for the payment of £10 which have been paid; ready, &c.—*Seton*. The condition for the re-delivery of the writing was the payment of £50, which have not been paid; ready, &c.—And the other side said the contrary.—And the jury will come from the place in which the delivery of the deed was made.

Resummons on a writ of Wardship.

(61.) § A Resummons on a writ of Wardship was sued by a man and his wife against Edmund who was the son of William atte Park, on the ground that, while the plea was pending, Edmund's father died, and process was continued until they recovered the wardship against Edmund by default, after proclamation, together with damages, and thereupon heretofore the husband and wife prayed execution by *Elegit* of the goods and chattels and a moiety of the lands of William the father, as appears by the roll. Afterwards the husband died, and the wife now sued a *Scire facias* against Edmund for him to show cause why she should not have execution against him in respect of the damages.—*Grene*. Heretofore she and her husband

No. 61.

matere, qar il est fait partie a vous, et la des- A.D. 1345.
tourbaunce de vostre purpos est tut en luy. Et
coment purretz aver jugement a ore sanz respondre
a son dit? *quasi diceret nullo modo* : qar ou covient
aver jugement sur conissaunce[1] ou sur verdit par
plee en[2] travers trove pur vous, et il ad ore nul
autre vers qi vous poietz demander jugement forqe
devers luy.—WILBY a *Grene*. Responez.—*Grene*. La
condicion fuit sur paiement de x*li.* queux sount
paietz ; prest, &c.—*Setone*. La condicion de la livere
fuit de[3] paiement de l[4]*li.* qe ne sount pas paietz ;
prest, &c.—*Et alii e contra.*—Et pays vendra del
lieu[5] ou la livere se fist del fait.[6]

(61.)[7] § Resomons en brief de Garde fuit suy par Resomons
en brief de
Garde.
un homme et sa femme vers Edmond qe fuit le fitz
William atte[8] Park, pur ceo qe pendant le plee son [Fitz.,
Scire
facias,
119.]
pere muruyst, et procees tant continue qils recoverirent
vers luy par defaut apres la proclamacion et damages,
sur quei autrefoith le baron et sa femme eslurrent[9]
les biens et chateux et la moite des terres William
le pere, come piert par roulle. Puis le baron murust,
et la femme suyt ore *Scire facias* vers Edmond pur
quei ele navera execucion vers ly des damages.—
Grene. Autrefoith ele et son baron eslurrent[9] en

---

[1] L., sa conissaunce ; H., vostre
conisaunce.

[2] L., ou.

[3] L., sur.

[4] L., C., and D., xl.

[5] The words del lieu are omitted
from H. and D.

[6] The words del fait are omitted
from H.

[7] From L., H., C., and D., but
corrected by the record, *Placita de
Banco*, Trin., 19 Edw. III., R° 323.
It there appears that, whereas
Andrew de Medestede and Margaret
his wife had recovered against

Edmund son and heir of William
atte Park, of Aillecote, 50 marks
for damages in an action of Wardship in respect of Robert the son
and heir of Henry de Ayllecote, and
execution had not been had, a
Scire facias was directed to the
Sheriff of Devonshire to warn the
said Edmund at the suit of the
said Margaret (Andrew being now
dead) in respect of 49 marks out of
the fifty.

[8] H., C., and D., del.

[9] D., eslirent.

No. 61.

A D. 1345. definitely elected to have execution of the lands and chattels of the father; judgment of this writ.—WIL LOUGHBY. That was the election of the husband, who foolishly so elected, and it does not oust the woman from suing better execution. — *Grene.* By law she would have suit, if anyone would, in respect of the father's lands and chattels, because he was a party to the original writ.—WILLOUGHBY. He was not a party to the judgment, and rest assured that a person other than the one against whom judgment was rendered will not be charged.—*Grene.* Judgment of the writ which does not make mention of the original writ sued against the father. — This exception was not allowed.—Therefore he said that it is a chattel that has been recovered by the husband, because the whole falls under the head of damages, as appears by the record, and in that case the husband's executors will have the suit, and not the wife.—STOUFORD. That would be to suppose that she would have execution for the benefit of another person, whereas she has to deraign for her own profit, because the case is different from what it would have been if the husband had been seised. — WILLOUGHBY. Yes, for she will have execution just as well as she would have an action by writ of Wardship. And suppose that, while the writ for the husband and his wife was pending, the husband had died, who would have a Resummons—the wife or the executors?—*Grene* and *R. Thorpe* said that a Resummons would not lie in that case, because the wife would not be either heir or executor, for whom alone the Statute[1] operates.—WILLOUGHBY. Say something else.—*Grene.* You see plainly how the original writ was brought against our ancestor, and we tell you that the person who brought the writ had nothing in the seignory, but that our father then had the seignory, to hold to him and his wife, and that in fee tail, and

---

[1] 13 Edw. I. (Westm. 2), c. 35.

No. 61.

certein daver execucion des terres et chateux le pere;
jugement de ceo brief.—WILBY. Ceo fuit la eleccion
le baron qe folement eslust, qe ne ouste pas la
femme a suire meuth.—*Grene.* De ley ele avereit
suite, si nulle avereit, des terres et chateux le pere,
qar il fuit partie al original.—WILBY. Il ne fuit
pas partie al jugement, et autre qe celuy vers qi
le jugement se fit ne serra charge, soietz certein.—
Grene. Jugement du brief qe ne fet pas mencion
del original suy vers le pere.—*Non allocatur.*—Par
quei il dit qe cest chatel recoveri par le baron, qar
tut chiet en damage, com piert par le recorde, en
quel cas les executours le baron averount la suite
et noun pas la femme.—STOUF. Ceo serreit a supposer qele avereit execucion a autri oeps, la ou ele
est a derrener a son profit demene, qar il est autre
qe si le baron ust este seisi.—WILBY. Oyl, qar si
bien come ele avereit accion par brief de Garde
avera ele execucion. Et mettetz qe, pendant le brief
pur le baron et sa femme, le baron ust devie, qi
avera Resomons, le quel la femme ou les executours?
—*Grene* et [*R.*] *Thorpe* disoint qe Resomons girreit pas
en le cas, qar la femme ne serreit heir ne executour,
pur eux soulement statut oevre. — WILBY. Ditetz
autre chose.—*Grene.* Vous veietz bien coment
loriginal fuit porte vers nostre auncestre, et vous
dioms qil navoit rienz en la seignurie qe porta le
brief, mes nostre pere adonqes avoit la seignurie a
luy et a sa femme, et ceo en fee taille, entre queux

No. 62.

A.D. 1345. that we are their issue, and that our mother is still living, and we tell you that we were never summoned or attached, and knew nothing of the proclamation, and never had anything in the wardship; and we also tell you that nothing ever descended to us in fee simple from our ancestor; judgment whether an action for damages lie against us.—*Huse.* He had assets by descent; ready, &c.—Stouford. There is no necessity to aver that, where he was himself a party to the loss.—Willoughby. That may be so, but since the parties wish it, we also are willing.—And he gave them a day on the traverse.

Wardship. (62.) § A writ of Wardship was brought in respect of the heir of Stephen de Buterleye.—*Grene.* We tell

No. 62.

nous sumes issue, et nostre mere unqore en vie, et
vous dioms qe nous unqes fumes somons ne attache,
ne rienz savioms de la proclamacion, ne unqes rienz
avioms en la garde; et auxint vous dioms qe unqes
rienz nous descendist en fee simple de nostre auncestre; jugement si vers nous accion des damages,
&c.[1]—*Huse.* Il avoit assetz par descente; prest, &c.
—STOUF. Ceo ne bosoigne[2] pas daverer la ou il
fuit mesme partie a la perde.—WILBY. Poet bien
estre, mes puis qe les parties le volent nous le
voloms.—Et sur le travers les dona jour.[3]

(62.)[4] § Brief de Garde del heir Estevene de Garde.
Boterle.—*Grene.* Nous vous dioms qe launcestre tient

---

[1] According to the roll, on the return of the *Scire facias,* and appearance of the parties, Edmund pleaded " quod, cum prædicta " Margareta petit versus eum " executionem de prædictis dena- " riis, et nititur ipsum Edmundum " onerare de eisdem ut filium et " heredem prædicti Willelmi, ipse " Edmundus, ut heres ejusdem " Willelmi, de denariis illis onerari " non debet, quia dicit quod nihil " ei descendit per descensum " hereditarium in feodo simplici " de eodem Willelmo. Et hoc " paratus est verificare, &c., unde " petit judicium, &c."

[2] C., bussoigne.

[3] The replication was, according to the roll, " quod terræ et tene- " menta descenderunt eidem Ed- " mundo post mortem prædicti " patris sui per descensum heredi- " tarium in feodo simplici de eodem " Willelmo patre, &c., et de quibus " idem Edmundus seisitus fuit die " impetrationis brevis sui de *Scire* " *facias."* Issue was joined upon this, and a verdict was found at *Nisi prius* "quod terræ et tenementa " descenderunt prædicto Edmundo " post mortem prædicti Willelmi " patris sui per descensum heredi- " tarium in feodo simplici de eodem " Willelmo apud Ayllecote, et de " quibus idem Edmundus seisitus " fuit prædicto die impetrationis " prædicti brevis de *Scire facias,* " prout prædicta Margareta sup- " ponit."
Execution by *Elegit* was accordingly awarded.

[4] From L., H., C., and D., but corrected by the record, *Placita de Banco,* Trin., 19 Edw. III., R° 326. Tt there appears that the action was brought by Walter de Heptone, knight, against William de Shobe- done and Burga his wife in respect of the wardship of Robert son and heir of Stephen de Buterleye, on the ground that Stephen held of Walter tenements in the vill of Shelderton (Salop) by knight service.

No. 62.

A.D. 1345. you that the ancestor held of the Countess of March, certain land, to wit, &c.,[1] by a prior feoffment, and she leased her estate to us; judgment whether an action lies against us.—*Huse.* Such an answer was not given at common law, and it is not given by statute,[2] except to the lord; judgment whether the law puts us to answer.—WILLOUGHBY. And will you not say anything else?—*Huse.* We tell you as to this land which they allege to be holden by prior feoffment (though we do not admit the prior feoffment) that Stephen, on the day on which he died, held the same land jointly with his wife, who is now the defendant's wife, in fee tail; judgment whether you can allege priority of feoffment by reason of land which he held jointly.

---

[1] *See* p. 287, note 2. | [2] 13 Edw. I. (Westm. 2), c. 16.

No. 62.

A.D. 1345.

de la Countesse de la Marche[1] certein terre, saver, &c., par eigne feffement, la quel nous lessa soun estat; jugement si vers nous accion, &c.[2]—*Huse*. Tiel respons ne fuit pas a la comune ley, et ceo nest pas done par statut forqe al seignur; jugement si la ley nous mette a respondre.—WILBY. Et autre chose ne voletz dire?—*Huse*. Nous vous dioms qe cele terre qils dient[3] estre tenu par priorite, &c., nient conissant la priorite, &c., qe Estevene, jour qil murust tient mesme la terre joint ove sa femme, qest ore la femme le defendant, en fee taille; jugement si par cause de terre qil tient joint puissetz priorite allegger.[4]

---

[1] All the MSS. except C., Mareschal, instead of de la Marche.

[2] The plea was, according to the record, "quod prædictus Stephanus "pater prædicti Roberti, cujus "heres ipse est, tenuit unam caru-"catam terræ, cum pertinentiis, "in villa de Ouldone de quadam "Johanna de Mortuo Mari Comi-"tissa Marchiæ, per servitium "militare, per antiquius feoffamen-"tum quam tenuit prædicta tene-"menta in villa de Sheldertone "de prædicto Waltero, &c., quæ "quidem Comitissa per scriptum "suum dedit et concessit custodiam "et maritagium prædicti Roberti "prædictis Willelmo et Burgæ "usque ad legitiman ætatem ipsius "Roberti. Et proferunt hic in Curia "prædictum scriptum quod hoc "testatur, ... unde petunt "judicium si prædictus Walterus "aliquid in prædicta custodia "exigere possit, &c."

[3] L., and H., diount.

[4] The replication, commencing with a protestation as to the priority of feoffment, was "quod "quicquid est in villa de Ouldone "est infra manerium de Ouldone "in dominico et in servitio, in "reversione et eleemosyna, de quo "quidem manerio integro, cum "pertinentiis, quidam Johannes "de Bromfelde fuit seisitus "in dominico ut in dominico, "in servitio ut in servitio, in "reversione ut in reversione, in "eleemosyna ut in eleemosyna, "qui quidem Johannes prædictum "manerium integrum, cum perti-"nentiis, sicut prædictum est, dedit "et concessit cuidam Ricardo "Dobyn, personæ ecclesiæ de "Buterleye, Tenendum sibi et here-"dibus suis in perpetuum, per quæ "donum et concessionem idem "Ricardus seisitus fuit de manerio "prædicto integro, cum pertinen-"tiis, sicut prædictum est, et idem "Ricardus prædictum manerium "integrum, cum pertinentiis, dedit "et concessit prædicto Stephano et "prædictæ Burgæ, tunc uxori suæ, "tenendum sibi et heredibus de 'corporibus suis exeuntibus, quæ "quidem Burga nunc est uxor "prædicti Willelmi, et nominatur "in brevi, et sic prædictus

No. 63.

A.D. 1345.
Annuity. (63.) § The Bishop of Winchester brought a writ of Annuity, in respect of the arrears of an annuity of twenty marks, against the Archdeacon of Surrey, and alleged in his declaration that he and his predecessors as Bishops had been seised by the hand of the defendant and of the defendant's predecessors from time whereof there was no memory.—*Skipwith* denied tort and force, and said that the plaintiff had counted against the defendant as Archdeacon, which is a name of office

No. 63.

(63.)[1] § Levesqe de Wyncestre porta brief Dan- A.D. 1345.
nuite des arerages dune annuite de xx marcs vers Annuite.
Lercedeken de Surrey, countant qe luy et ses pre- [Fitz., Jurisdic-
decessours Evesqes furent seisiz par la mein le tion, 28.][2]
defendant et ses predecessours de temps dount il[3]
ny ad memore.[4]—Skyp. defendi tort et force, et dit
qil ad counte vers Ercedekene qest noun doffice et

" Stephanus, die quo obiit, non
" fuit solus tenens prædictæ Comi-
" tissæ, nec aliquid habuit in
" prædictis tenementis in dominico
" neque in servitio, in reversione
" seu in eleemosyna nisi conjunctim
" cum prædicta Burga tunc uxore
" sua, nunc uxore prædicti Wil-
" lelmi, et quæ quidem Burga
" simul cum prædicto Willelmo
" viro suo nunc sunt tenentes de
" prædicto manerio integro, cum
" pertinentiis, ut prædictum est,
" ut de jure prædictæ Burgæ, &c.
" Et ex quo prædicti Willelmus et
" Burga cognoverunt prædicta
" tenementa in villa de Sheldertone
" teneri de prædicto Waltero per
" servitium militare, petit judicium,
" et prædictam custodiam, et damna
" sua sibi adjudicari, &c."
According to the record there was
a rejoinder " quod prædictus
" Stephanus fuit solus tenens
" prædictæ Comitissæ de prædicta
" carucata terræ, cum pertinentiis,
" in Ouldone, die quo obiit, sicut
" iidem Willelmus et Burga supe-
" rius allegarunt, absque hoc quod
" prædicta Burga tunc aliquid
" habuit in eadem nisi ut uxor
" prædicti Stephani, sicut prædic-
" tus Walterus dicit."
Issue was joined upon this, and
the Venire awarded, but nothing
further appears on the roll except
an adjournment.

[1] From L., C., and D., but
corrected by the record, Placita de
Banco, Trin., 19 Edw. III., R° 373.
It there appears that the action
was brought by the Bishop of
Winchester against William Inge,
Archdeacon of Surrey, in respect
of arrears of an annual rent of
50 marks.
[2] In Fitzherbert's Abridgment,
the case is represented as being
of the following Michaelmas Term.
[3] D., y.
[4] The declaration was, according
to the record, " quod quidam Jo-
" hannes de Stretforde, nuper
" Episcopus Wyntoniensis, præde-
" cessor suus, seisitus fuit de annuo
" redditu prædicto per manus præ-
" dicti Willelmi nunc Archidiaconi,
" ut de jure ecclesiæ suæ Sancti
" Swythini Wyntoniæ . . . . . .
" et similiter omnes Episcopi
" Wyntonienses, prædecessores sui,
" a tempore quo non extat memoria,
" fuerunt seisiti de eodem annuo
" redditu per manus Archidia-
" conorum Surreiæ prædeces-
" sorum prædicti Archidiaconi
" nunc . . . . . usque
" undecim annos ante diem
" impetrationis brevis sui . . . .
" quod prædictus Willelmus nunc
" Archidiaconus annuum redditum
" illum ei subtraxit, et ei reddere
" contradixit."

No. 63.

A.D. 1345. and of dignity, and, said *Skipwith*, we do not understand that the Court will take cognisance.—*Huse.* And, inasmuch as he does not answer, judgment against him as one who is undefended.—*Grene.* "Archdeacon" is a name of office as of an official who has no reason for the existence of his office except spiritual corrections, and so it cannot be understood that such a charge as an annuity is by law due by reason of such an office, for the plaintiff has not brought a writ against him as against parson or prebendary who might be charged by construction of law; therefore we understand that the Court will not take cognisance.—STONORE. The King is bound to do right to all, and you have paid, and so effected a charge, and in time of vacancy, if that which the plaintiff says is true, the King will have this profit.—WILLOUGHBY. You will not deny that if he were to show the commencement of the annuity by lay contract, the Court would take cognisance, notwithstanding the fact that he is neither parson nor prebendary; therefore your exception ought to be put in that manner, and he could then abide judgment on the question whether title of prescription ought not to suffice.—*R. Thorpe.* The fact that he has a right is no proof that he will recover in this Court, but we understand, on the contrary, that you will not take cognisance of such matters between spiritual persons.—STONORE. Rest assured that on a title of prescription we will take cognisance in this Court on this writ.—WILLOUGHBY, *ad idem.* Will you say anything else? Answer.—*Skipwith* denied the damages, and then said that the Archdeacon, by reason of his office, had to levy annually, partly in Rome pennies, partly in St. Swithin's farthings, and partly in synodal money, to the amount of twenty marks, and inasmuch as this is a spiritual matter, we do not understand that the Court will take cognisance.—*Huse.* He has denied the damages, thus accepting the jurisdiction of the Court; judgment.—

No. 63.

de dignite, et nentendoms pas qe la Court voille conustre.—*Huse.* Et desicome il ne respond pas, jugement de luy come de noun defendu. — *Grene.* Ercedekene est noun doffice come official qe nad pas resoun doffice forqe correccions espirituels, et issint ne poet estre entendu tiel charge par ley due par resoun de tiel office, qar il nad pas porte brief vers luy come persone ou[1] provandrer, qe purreit par entent de ley estre charge; par quei nous entendoms qe Court ne voet conustre.—STON. Le Roi est tenutz de faire dreit a toux, et vous avietz paie et issint charge, et en temps de vacacion, sil die voire,[2] le Roi avera[3] ceo profit. — WILBY. Vous dedirretz pas qe sil moustrast comencement de ley contracte qe la conustra, *non obstante* qil nest ne persone ne provandrer ; donqes duist vostre chalenge estre pris par la manere, et il poet demurer si title de prescripcion ne deit suffire.—[*R.*] *Thorpe.* Ceo nest pas prove pur ceo qil ad dreit qil recovera ceinz, mes nous entendoms qe de teles choses entre persones espiritueles vous ne voiletz conustre.— STON. Soietz certein qe sur title de prescripcion nous voloms ceinz conustre sur ceo brief.—WILBY, *ad idem.* Voiletz autre chose dire? Responez.—*Skyp.* defendi les damages, et puis dist qe Lercedekene, par cause de soun office, est a lever annuelment partie en Rome penies, partie en ferlinges Seint Swythan, partie en deners sinodals, a la mountaunce de xx marcs, et nentendoms pas, desicome ceste chose est espiritual, qe Court voille conustre.—*Huse.* Il ad defendu les damages, acceptant jurisdiccion ; jugement.

---

[1] C., en.
[2] C., veire.

[3] C., avereit.

No. 63.

A.D. 1345. *Grene.* There are cases of annuity pleaded in Court Christian, such as between parson and vicar, and between parson and patron, proceedings in which the Court there will not stay by reason of the King's prohibition, and that is the purport of the Statute *Circumspecte agatis.*[1]—HILLARY. That is not a statute sealed.—WILLOUGHBY. No, the Prelates made it themselves,[2] and in both the cases which you have mentioned this Court will take cognisance on a title by prescription; therefore answer.—And this was by judgment of the COURT.—*Grene.* We tell you that in respect of the money, as above, which amounts to twenty marks a year, there was a dispute between the Bishop's predecessor and us, and the Archdeacon granted to the Bishop twenty marks annually for the Bishop's life, which the Archdeacon paid during the Bishop's time, *absque hoc* that the Bishop and his predecessors have been seised of any other annuity from all time; ready, &c.—*Huse.* We are altogether a stranger to that which you say as to Rome pennies, &c., and to our predecessor's contract, and we have no need to say anything with regard to it; but, whereas you say that we and our predecessors have not been from all time seised, &c., ready, &c., that they have.— *Grene.* Ready, &c., that they have not been seised of any other annuity than

---

[1] 13 Edw. I. (*Circumspecte agatis*). | [2] *See*, however, 2 Inst., 487.

No. 63.

—*Grene.* Il y sount cas come[1] entre persone et A.D. 1345.
viker, entre persone et patroun, de annuite plede en
Court Cristiene qe par prohibicion le Roi la Court
illoeqes ne surserra pas, et ceo voet lestatut *Cir-*
cumspecte agatis.—Hill. Ceo nest pas estatut enseale.[2]
—Wilby. Noun, les prelates le firent mesmes, et
en toux deux les cas qe vous avietz mis[3] ceste
Court sur title de prescripcion voet conustre ; par
quei responez.—Et ceo fuit par agarde.—*Grene.* Nous
vous dioms qe pur les deners,[4] *ut supra*, qe amountent
a xx marcs par an, debat y avoit entre soun predecessour et nous,[5] et il granta a ly pur sa vie
xx marcs annuelment, &c., les queux il paia en soun
temps, sanz ceo qe ly et ses predecessours dautre
annuite de tut temps ount este seisi ; prest, &c.[6]—
Huse. A ceo qe vous parletz de Rome penies, &c.,
et al contract nostre predecessour nous sumes tut
estrange, et navoms mester[7] a ceo parler ; mes la
ou vous ditetz qe nous et nos predecessours de tut
temps navoms pas este seisi, &c., prest, &c., qe ci.
—*Grene.* Prest, &c., qe noun dautre annuite qe nous

---

[1] come is omitted from C.

[2] By a curious mistake the reading in Fitzherbert's *Abridg-ment* is neusable.

[3] mis is omitted from C.

[4] D., deners.

[5] C., and D., nostre predecesour.

[6] The plea was, according to the record, " quod tempore quo præ-
" dictus Johannes fuit Episcopus
" loci prædicti discordiæ et con-
" tentiones motæ fuerunt inter
" prædictum Johannem Episcopum
" et ipsum nunc Archidiaconum,
" quæ quidem discordiæ sedatæ
" fuerunt inter eos in hunc modum,
" scilicet, quod, toto tempore quo
" idem Johannes extunc foret.
" Episcopus ibidem, ipse nunc
" Archidiaconus solveret ei quan

" dam annuam pensionem viginti
" marcarum per annum, de qua
" annua pensione idem Johannes
" Episcopus fuit seisitus per manus
" ipsius Archidiaconi nunc toto
" tempore quo idem Johannes fuit
" Episcopus ibidem tantum, absque
" hoc quod idem Johannes Episco-
" pus seu prædecessores sui seisiti
" fuerunt de aliquo alio annuo red-
" ditu viginti marcarum per manus
" ipsius Archidiaconi seu præde-
" cessorum suorum, ut de jure
" ecclesiæ suæ Sancti Swithini
" prædictæ, a tempore quo non
" extat memoria, sicut prædictus
" Episcopus nunc supponit. Et
" hoc paratus est verificare, &c.,
" unde petit judicium, &c."

[7] C., meistier.

No. 64.

A.D. 1345. that of which we have spoken.—*Huse.* We have nothing to do with that which you allege, because it does not refer to the annuity which we demand.—WILLOUGHBY, *ad idem.* You must come to a traverse of the plaintiff's statement, if you wish to have issue, because he has no need to answer to that which you have said.—*Grene.* We will confess that the Bishop and his predecessors were from all time seised of Rome pennies, &c., *absque hoc* that they were seised of any other annuity.—STONORE. Rome pennies, &c., which you allege had to be paid to the Bishop, and that for the benefit of other persons, that is to say, of the Court of Rome, do not extend to his demand. —Therefore by compulsion of the COURT he took issue that the Bishop's predecessors had not been seised from time whereof memory is not; ready, &c.—And the other side said the contrary.

Ad terminum qui præteriit. (64.) § *Ad terminum qui præteriit* on a lease made by the grandfather, and the demandant had nothing to prove the lease.—*Sadelyngstanes.* This same person, your grandfather, enfeoffed us in fee simple by this

No. 64.

navoms parle.—*Huse.*　Nous navoms qe faire de ceo A.D. 1345.
qe vous alleggetz, qar ceo refert pas al annuite qe
nous demandoms.—WILBY, *ad idem.*　Il vous covient
estre a travers del pleintif, si vous voletz aver lissue,
qar a ceo qe vous avetz dit il nad mester[1] a respondre.—*Grene.*　Nous voloms conustre qe luy et
ses predecessours de tut temps furent seisiz de Rome
penies, &c., sanz ceo qe dautre annuite furent seisiz.
—STON.　Rome penies, &c., qe vous alleggetz qe
duissent estre paietz al Evesqe, et ceo a autri
oeps, saver, al Court de Rome, ceo sestent pas a
sa demande.—Par quei par chace de COURT il prist
issue qe nient seisi de temps dount memore nest;
prest, &c.—*Et alii e contra.*[2]

(64.)[3] § *Ad terminum qui præteriit* du lees laiel, *Ad termi-*
et le demandant navoit rienz du lees.—*Sadl.*　Mesme *num qui*
præteriit.
cely vostre aiel par ceo fait nous feffa en fee simple;

---

[1] C., meistier.

[2] According to the record issue
was joined upon the replication
" quod prædictus Johannes de
" Stretforde, prædecessor suus,
" fuit seisitus de prædicto annuo
" redditu, quem ipse modo petit, per
" manus prædicti Willelmi nunc
" Archidiaconi Surreiæ, apud Farn-
" ham in eodem Comitatu, jure
" ecclesiæ suæ Sancti Swithini
" prædictæ, et similiter omnes
" Episcopi Wyntonienses, præde-
" cessores sui, a tempore quo non
" extat memoria, seisiti fuerunt
" de eodem annuo redditu per
" manus Archidiaconorum Surreiæ
" ibidem qui pro tempore fuerunt,
" ut de jure ecclesiæ suæ prædictæ,
" sicut ipse superius in narratione
" sua prædicta supponit."
The award of the *Venire*, but
nothing further, appears on the
roll.

[3] From L., C., and D., but
corrected by the record, *Placita
de Banco*, Trin., 19 Edw. III.,
R° 419, d.　It there appears that
the action was brought by George
Monbochier, knight, and Isabel his
wife, against Thomas son of Thomas
" de Hedone juxta Madersay " in
respect of one messuage and one
bovate of land in " Evertone
" juxta Madersay, in quæ idem
" Thomas non habet ingressum
" nisi per Thomam de Hedone
" juxta Madersay, cui Ermetruda
" de Madersay, proavia prædictæ
" Isabellæ, cujus heres ipsa est,
" illa dimisit."　The descent is
traced in the count from Ermetrude
" cuidam Isabellæ, ut filiæ et
" heredi, &c., et de ipsa Isabella
" . . . cuidam Gerardo ut filio
" et heredi, &c., et de ipso Gerardo
" . . . isti Isabellæ ut filiæ et heredi
" qui nunc petit simul, &c."

No. 65.

deed; judgment whether you can be admitted to say that he leased for a term, or ought to have an action contrary to the deed.—*Skipwith*. Nothing passed by this deed; judgment whether you can bar me by such a deed.—*Sadelyngstanes*. You shall not be admitted to that in opposition to the fact that you have by the writ supposed à demise made by your ancestor, and you have nothing but empty air to prove the term, and we prove by the deed that the conveyance was of a fee.—*Skipwith*. Then you refuse the averment; and we demand judgment.—*Sadelyngstanes*. The tenements passed; ready, &c.—And the other side said the contrary.

Avowry.

(65.) § The Prior of the Hospital of St. John of Jerusalem avowed on the ground that he was lord of the manor of Melchbourne, within which manor, according to custom, whosoever brews ale, and offers it for sale, shall pay to the lord, for every brewing, three gallons of ale, and if the payment of the ale be in arrear the lord shall distrain; and he laid

No. 65.

jugement si vous serretz resceu a dire qil lessa a A.D. 1345
terme, ou si countre le fait accion, &c.[1]—*Skyp.* Rienz
ne passa par ceo fait, &c.; jugement si par tiel fait
moi puissetz barrer.—*Sadl.* A ceo ne serretz resceu
countre ceo qe vous avietz suppose la demise vostre
auncestre par le brief, et vous navietz qe vent a
prover le terme, et nous par son fet le provoms de
fee. — *Skyp.* Donqes refusetz laverement; et demandoms jugement.—*Sad.* Qe les tenementz passe-
rent; prest, &c.—*Et alii e contra.*[2]

(65.) [3] § Le Prior del Hospital avowa par la re- Avowere.
soun qil est seignur del maner de Melchebourne,
deinz quel maner par usage qi qe brace et mette
a vent cervoise,[4] de chesqun bracer fra au seignur
iij galouns de cervoise,[5] et si la cervoise [5] soit arrere
il destreindra; et lia seisine de mesme le mies

---

[1] The plea was " quod eadem
" Ermetruda in pura viduitate
" sua, dum sola fuit, dedit, con-
" cessit, et charta sua confirmavit
" prædicto Thomæ de Hedone præ-
" dicta tenementa, cum pertinen-
" tiis, habenda et tenenda eidem
" Thomæ et heredibus suis in
" perpetuum, et obligavit se et
" heredes suos ad warantizandum
" eidem Thomæ, heredibus, et suis
" assignatis prædicta tenementa,
" cum pertinentiis, in perpetuum,
" et profert hic in Curia quandam
" chartam sub nomine prædictæ
" Ermetrudæ proaviæ, quæ hoc
" testatur, &c., unde petit judicium
" si contra factum prædictæ pro-
" aviæ, &c., quod feoffamentum
" prædictum factum in feodo, et
" warantiam prædictam testatur,
" actionem versus eum inde habere
" debeant, &c."

[2] The replication, upon which
issue was joined, was " non pos-

" sunt dedicere quin prædicta
" charta sit factum prædictæ
" Ermetrudæ proaviæ, &c., sed
" dicunt quod ipsi per chartam
" illam ab actione sua excludi
" non debent, &c., quia dicunt
" quod prædictus Thomas de
" Hedone nunquam aliquid habuit
" in tenementis prædictis virtute
" chartæ illius."

Nothing further appears on the
roll except the award of the *Venire*
and an adjournment.

[3] From L., H., C., and D., but
corrected by the record, *Placita
de Banco*, Trin., 19 Edw. III.,
R° 332, d. It there appears that
the action was brought by John le
Barkere of Melchbourne against
the Prior of the Hospital of St. John
of Jerusalem in England, in respect
of the taking of a horse.

[4] C., cerveise ; D., servoise.

[5] C., cerveise.

No. 65.

seisin by the tenants of the house held by the plaintiff, and also generally throughout the whole manor from all time ; and, because the plaintiff brewed and sold, the Prior avowed for the ale in arrear.—*Sadelyngstanes.* Your predecessor, by this deed, enfeoffed our ancestor, &c., of the messuage in which, &c., to hold by different services in lieu of all manner of services and customs; judgment whether contrary to the deed you can avow. —WILLOUGHBY. This avowry is not made by reason of

No. 65.

tenantz, &c., et auxint generalment pur tut le maner ^{A.D. 1345.} de tut temps; et pur ceo qe le pleintif bracea et vendist, pur la cervoise[1] arrere avowa.[2]—*Sadl.* Vostre predecessour par ceo fait feffa nostre auncestre, &c., par autres services del mies en quel, &c., pur toux maneres des services et custumes; jugement si countre le fait puissetz avower.[3]—WILBY. Ceste avowere nest

---

[1] C., cerveise.

[2] The Prior's avowry was, according to the record, " quod ipse est " dominus manerii de Melche- " bourne, infra quod manerium est " talis consuetudo quod domini " dicti manerii habebunt de omni- " bus braciatoribus infra manerium " prædictum de qualibet bracina " cervisiæ braciata venditioni tres " lagenas melioris cervisiæ quotiens " braciaverint, &c., et si eædem " tres lagenæ melioris cervisiæ ad " aliquam bracinam a retro fuerint, " seu iidem braciatores eas solvere " noluerint, extunc dominus mane- " rii prædicti per consuetudinem " prædictam pro eisdem tribus " lagenis cervisiæ de qualibet " bracina a retro existentibus " potest distringere, et districtiones " retinere quousque de eisdem, &c , " ei fuerit satisfactum. De quo " quidem proficuo secundum con- " suetudinem prædictam capiendo " omnes prædecessores prædicti " Prioris domini manerii prædicti " a tempore quo non extat memoria " fuerunt seisiti, et etiam ad " distringendum infra manerium " prædictum pro prædictis tribus " lagenis cervisiæ de qualibet " bracina braciata venditioni quo- " tiens illas a retro fore contigerit, " &c., et similiter prædictus Prior " nunc dominus manerii prædicti " fuit seisitus de prædicto proficuo,

" capiendo per manus quorundam " Rogeri filii Willelmi atte Lee, " Ricardi le Bakere, et Elenæ la " Bakere, et etiam per manus " omnium aliorum qui infra præ- " dictum manerium cervisiam " venditioni braciaverunt, &c. Et " quia prædictus Johannes bracia- " vit cervisiam venditioni infra " manerium prædictum . . . . " et tres lagenas melioris cervisiæ " de eadem bracina præfato Priori " domino manerii prædicti, contra " consuetudinem prædictam, sol- " vere recusavit, idem Prior per " . . . . ballivum ipsius Prioris " cepit prædictum equum."

[3] The plea was, according to the record, " quod quidam frater " Willelmus de Totehale, quondam " Prior, &c., prædecessor Prioris " nunc, fuit seisitus de uno co- " tagio, cum pertinentiis, in villa " de Melchebourne post tempus " memoriæ, &c., quod quidem " cotagium idem Prior dedit, " concessit, et charta sua confirma- " vit cuidam Johanni Siccori de " Melchebourne patri prædicti " Johannis le Barkere cujus heres " ipse est, habendum et tenendum " eidem Johanni Siccori et heredi- " bus suis de se legitime procreatis, " libere, quiete, bene, et in pace, " in perpetuum, Reddendo inde " annuatim eidem Willelmo Priori " et successoribus suis quadraginta

No. 65.

tenancy as for something due to the lord from his tenant, but is a claim made generally throughout the manor, as well in respect of the fee of any other person as in respect of the Prior's own fee; therefore this deed does not oust him from this avowry; therefore sue the return on his behalf, and let the plaintiff be in mercy.—*Quære.*

No. 65.

pas fet par cause de tenance com de chose due[1] au seignur par son tenant, mes generalment est. clame deinz le maner si bien dautri fee com de son fee demene; par quei ceo fet ne luy ouste pas de ceste avowere; par quei suetz retourn, et le pleintif en la merci.[2]—*Quære.*

" denarios ad duos anni terminos, ". . . . et in obitu suo et " heredum suorum tertiam par- " tem omnium bonorum suorum " mobilium pro omni servitio " sæculari, consuetudine, et de- " manda, quod quidem cotagium " est illud idem mesuagium in " quo idem Prior modo advocat " captionem prædictam, &c. Et " petit judicium, ex quo prædictus " Willelmus, quondam Prior, &c., " prædecessor prædicti Prioris " nunc, fuit seisitus de prædicto " mesuagio post tempus memoriæ " omnino exonerato, et illud " mesuagium prædicto Johanni " Siccori patri, &c., per chartam " suam dedit in forma prædicta, " faciendo servitia supradicta pro " omnibus servitiis, consuetudini- " bus, et demandis, et etiam " per eandem chartam concessit " quod idem Johannes et heredes " sui forent quieti de omnibus " servitiis et demandis in charta " illa non contentis, &c., si idem " Prior pro aliis consuetudinibus " super ipsum de jure advocare " posset, &c. Et profert hic in " Curia chartam prædicti Willelmi " quondam Prioris, &c., præde- " cessoris, &c., sigillo suo signatam " præmissa testantem."

[1] C., dowe; D., dewe.

[2] According to the record the

Prior replied " quod ex quo præ- " dictus Johannes non dedicit " prædictam consuetudinem infra " manerium prædictum a tempore " quo non extat memoria, tam de " illis qui non sunt tenentes dicti " manerii quam de illis qui tene- " menta . tenent infra manerium " prædictum, et non habendo " respectum ad tenenciam in " eodem manerio sed solomodo ad " consuetudinem infra manerium " prædictum usitatam, nec quin " idem Prior et omnes prædeces- " sores sui de prædicto proficuo " capiendo secundum consuetudi- " nem prædictam, a tempore quo " non extat memoria, fuerunt seisiti, " prout idem Prior superius advo- " cando supponit, et quicquid idem " Johannes superius placitando " allegavit est omnino ad ex- " onerandum tenementum suum " prædictum, et nihil ad consuetu- " dinem prædictam in manerio " prædicto hactenus usitatam ad- " nihilandum, petit judicium et " returnum sibi adjudicari, &c."

Then follows the judgment in these words : — " Per quod con- " sideratum est quod prædictus " Johannes le Barkere nihil capiat " per breve suum, sed sit in " misericordia, &c. Et prædictus " Prior habeat returnum prædicti " egui, &c."

MICHAELMAS TERM

IN THE

NINETEENTH YEAR OF THE REIGN OF
KING EDWARD THE THIRD
AFTER THE CONQUEST.

MICHAELMAS TERM IN THE NINETEENTH YEAR OF THE REIGN OF KING EDWARD THE THIRD AFTER THE CONQUEST.

No. 1.

A.D. 1345.
Scire facias.

(1.) § *Scire facias*: Wengrave's case. The writ was not served, and the Sheriff was admitted, after exception by a party, to amend the return, that is to say, whereas he ought to have garnished Alice late wife of W., &c., he returned that he had garnished Alice the wife. Afterwards the tenant prayed aid of a man and his wife, as being tenant for term of life by lease from them; and the aid-prayer was counterpleaded on the ground that it had not been shown that the lease had been made by fine, because such a deed made by husband and wife *in pais* is held to be entirely the deed of the husband.—This exception was not allowed. —Therefore aid was granted by judgment.

DE TERMINO MICHAELIS ANNO REGNI REGIS EDWARDI TERTII A CONQUESTU DECIMO NONO.[1]

No. 1.

(1.)[2] § *Scire facias* : Wendegrave. Le brief ne fuit
pas servy, et le Vicounte fuit resceu, apres chalange
de partie, damendre le retourn, saver, ou il dust
aver garny Alice qe fuit la femme W., &c., il retourna qil avoit garny Alice la femme. Puis le
tenant pria eide dun homme et sa femme com tenant a terme de vie de lour lees; et fuit countreplede pur ceo qe ceo ne fuit pas moustre le lees
estre fet par fine, car par fait en pays tiel lees
fait par baron et sa femme est tut ajugge le fait
le baron.—*Non allocatur.*—Par quei eide par agarde
est graunte.[3]

A.D. 1345.
*Scire
facias.*
[Fitz.,
Aide, 27.]

---

[1] The reports of this Term are
from the Lincoln's Inn MS. (called
L.), the Harleian MS. No. 741
(called H.), the Cambridge MS.
Hh. 2. 3 (called C.), and the
Cambridge MS. Hh. 2. 4 (called D.).

[2] From L., H., C., and D. The
record may be that found among
the *Placita de Banco*, 19 Edw. III.,
R° 58, d. It there appears that a
fine was levied *sur don grant et
render* between John de Wengrave and Christiana his wife,
plaintiffs, and John Thurberne,
chaplain, deforciant, in respect of
tenements in Wengrave and Rolle-
sham (Wingrave and Rowsham,
Bucks), which were rendered to John
and Christiana for their lives, with
successive remainders to Thomas
son of John de Wengrave and Ma-

tilda his wife in special tail, and to
John brother of Thomas in fee. The
Scire facias was brought by Matilda,
who alleged that John de Wengrave
and Christiana, and Thomas son
of John were dead, and that
William Bibet of Weston Turville,
tailor, had entered on a portion of
the tenements.

[3] According to the record William
Bibet (or Bybet) as tenant for life
prayed and had aid of William atte
Putte of Berkhamsted and Joan
his wife, by whose demise he held,
and to whom the reversion belonged,
but the prayees did not appear.
Then William Bibet " dicit quod
" ubi prædicta Matilldis per breve
" istud de *Scire facias* petit execu-
" tionem de quadraginta et tribus
" acris terræ, et duabus acris prati

No. 2.

A.D. 1345.

Jurata utrum.

(2.) § *Jurata utrum* in Bath and Walcote. The Bailiff of the Liberty of Bath said that, although the writ was brought in Bath and in another vill, all the tenements demanded are in Bath alone, and prayed cognisance of the plea. And on the ground that the demand was in two vills, and the liberty extends only into one vill, the COURT was minded to hold the plea in this Court of Common Bench.—*Huse.* You have here the tenant, who joins himself with the bailiff in maintenance of the franchise, and they tell you, as the bailiff did at first, that the whole of the tenements are in Bath, and therefore the bailiff prays cognisance as above.—HILLARY. Where have you heard of a tenant joining himself with a bailiff in maintenance of a franchise ? You will never see such a thing. And what would happen if the issue were taken ?—*Huse.* The issue can well be taken between the demandant and them ; and, if the finding be for the demandant, he will recover the land, and, if the other way, the cognisance will be granted.—*Birton, ad idem.* It is not right that the cognisance should be lost through the feigning of another vill in the writ : for in that way no one will ever have cognisance except at the pleasure of the demandant ; and in this matter the plea is not to the abatement of the writ ; and it seems

No. 2.

(2.)[1] § Jure de *Utrum*[2] en Baaz et Walcote. Le
baillif del fraunchise de Baaz dit qe coment qe le
brief fuit porte en Baaz et en une autre ville
qe toux les tenementz demandetz sount en Baaz
soulement, et pria la conissance. Et pur ceo qe la
demande fuit en deux villes, et la fraunchise sestendi
forqe en lune ville, la Court fuit del avys daver
tenu le plee ceinz.—*Huse.* Vous avietz ci le tenant,
qe se joint au baillif en meintenance de la fraunchise,[3]
et vous dient, come le baillif primes dit, qe tut est
en Baaz, et pur ceo le[4] baillif pria la fraunchise,
ut supra.—Hill. Ou avietz vous oy le tenant se
joindre au baillif en meintenance de la fraunchise?
Vous le verretz jammes. Et quei avendreit si lissue
fuit pris?—*Huse.* Entre le demandant et eux lissue
purra bien estre pris; et si trove fuit pur le demandant il recovrera terre, et si dautre part la
fraunchise serra grante.—*Birtone, ad idem.* Par
feindre dune autre ville el brief nest pas resoun qe
la fraunchise serra perdu: qar issint navera homme
jammes fraunchise forqe a la volunte le demandant;
et en ceste matere ci le plee nest pas al abatement

"et dimidia virtute finis prædicti,
"&c., tenementa illa non conti-
"nentur in prædicto fine. Et hoc
"paratus est verificare, unde petit
"judicium, &c.

"Et Matilldis dicit quod tene-
"menta prædicta unde ipsa per
"breve suum petit executionem,
"&c., sunt contenta in prædicto
"fine."

Issue was joined upon this, but
on the day given "eadem Matilldis
"non potest dedicere quin prædicta
"tenementa unde præfata Matill-
"dis modo petit executionem, &c.,
"non continentur in prædicto fine.
"Ideo prædictus Willelmus eat
"inde sine die."

[1] From L., H., C., and D., but

corrected by the record, *Placita de
Banco*, Mich., 19 Edw. III., R° 278.
It there appears that the action
was brought by William de Kelle-
seye, parson of the chapel "Sanctæ
"Wereburgæ juxta Bathoniam"
against Thomas de Stote, citizen
of Bath and Matilda his wife,
Bathinus le Dyere and Christina his
wife, Adam de Farleye and Margery
his wife, and the Prior of Bath, in
respect of 15½ acres of land and
3 acres of meadow in Walcote and
Bath.

[2] L., dutrum instead of de
Utrum.

[3] The words en meintenance de
la fraunchise are from L. alone.

[4] C., qe le.

A.D. 1345

Jure de Utrum.[2]

[Fitz.,

Conu-saans, 84.

No. 2.

A.D. 1345. that on the demandant's non-denial—that is to say
his confession that the whole of the tenements are in
Bath—the cognisance is grantable.—WILLOUGHBY. What
does the tenant say?—*Huse.* He says that the whole
of the tenements are in Bath, because Walcote is only
a part of Bath.—WILLOUGHBY. That plea is to the
abatement of the writ.—*Birton.* Even if the writ
were bad, that would not take away the franchise.—
WILLOUGHBY. Who will be parties to try this matter?
—And afterwards, without giving any reason, HILLARY
ousted the bailiff from the cognisance.—Therefore one
tenant vouched another tenant, and said that there
never was any such person as the demandant supposed
to have aliened.[1]—And upon that they were at issue
by compulsion of the Court.—Another tenant alleged
that Walcote is in Bath.—*Grene.* Walcote is not in
Bath; ready, &c.—*Huse.* You must maintain that they
are two different vills, for a *Jurata utrum* is not
maintainable in a hamlet.—WILLOUGHBY. He has met
your objection, and you are at issue, for your plea
exacts the condition "and if it be found, &c."—*Huse.*
Walcote is in Bath, and if it be found, &c.—WIL-
LOUGHBY. Now you are at issue, &c.

---

[1] For the demandant's count or declaration *see* p. 309, note 5.

No. 2.

A.D. 1345.

du brief; et il semble qe sur nient dedire le demandant, saver, qe tut est en Baaz, [la fraunchise
est grantable.—WILBY. Quei dit le tenant?—*Huse.*
Il dit qe tut est en Baaz][1] qar W. nest qe parcelle
de Baaz.—WILBY. Cele plee est al abatement du
brief.—*Birtone.* Et tut fuit le brief malveis, ceo ne
toudra pas la fraunchise.—WILBY. Qi serra partie a
trier ceste chose?—Et puis, *absque causa*, HILL. luy
ousta de la fraunchise.—Par quei un tenant voucha
un autre[2] et dit qil ny avoit unqes nulle tiel persone come le demandant suppose qe aliena.—Et sur
ceo sount a issue par chace de Court.—Un autre
alleggea[3] qe Walcote est en B.—*Grene.* W. nest pas
en B.; prest, &c.—*Huse.* Il covient qe vous meintenetz qils sount[4] deux divers villes, qar Jure de
Utrum nest pas meintenable en hamelle.—WILBY. Il
vous seert a vostre chalenge, et voüs estes a issue,
qar vostre plee demande et si trove soit, &c.—*Huse.*
W. est en B., et si trove soit, &c.—WILBY. Ore
estes a issue, &c.[5]

---

[1] The words between brackets are omitted from D.

[2] The Prior according to the record made default, and there was an award of "Jurata quo ad eum "capiatur per ejus defaltam." Thomas and Matilda vouched the Prior to warrant. Nothing appears on the roll as to the claim of cognisance by the Bailiff of the Liberty of Bath.

[3] alleggea is omitted from C.

[4] The words qils sount are omitted from C.

[5] The declaration was, according to the record, "quod quidam "Ricardus quondam persona ca- "pellæ prædictæ fuit seisitus de "prædictis tenementis, cum perti- "nentiis, in dominico suo ut de "feodo et jure capellæ suæ præ- "dictæ, tempore pacis, tempore

"Her.rici Regis, proavi domini "Regis nunc, ... qui "quidem Ricardus eodem tempore "tenementa prædicta alienavit, "&c."

The plea of Bathinus et Christina was "quod, ubi prædictus Willel- "mus per breve suum supponit "prædictam terram versus eos "petitam fore in Walcote et "Bathonia, eadem tenementa sunt "quædam mansiones, et sunt in "Bathonia. Et hoc parati sunt "verificare per juratam, &c. Et "si, &c., tunc dicunt quod terra "illa est laicum feodum ipsorum "Bathini et Christinæ, et non "libera eleemosyna pertinens ad "capellam Sanctæ Wereburgæ "prædictam." Issue was joined upon this.

The plea of Adam and Margery

Nos. 3–5.

A.D. 1345.
Writ of
Right.

(3.) § Note that the tenant demanded view on a writ of Right.—*Birton* alleged that the same tenant had recovered against himself the same tenements by default after default, and so was in the case of the Statute[1] which deprived him of view.—But because this writ of Right is not a writ given by the Statute[2] on a loss by default, but is a writ at common law, he had view by judgment.

Statute
mer-
chant:
*Audita
Querela.*

(4.) § Note that executors sued execution upon a statute merchant made to their testator, and the debtor sued an *Audita Querela*, and produced their testator's acquittance, which they denied; and it was found that the acquittance was the testator's deed; and the jury were asked to what the damages amounted, which having been found, the debtor prayed his damages against the executors.—*Birton.* The executors are in a different case from that of the testator himself, for they were bound to sue on the statute, because they could not know of any such acquittance, and therefore it is not right that damages should be recovered against them.—And to this the COURT agreed.—Judgment was then given that he should not recover any damages.

Writ *de*

(5.) § Note that a successor brought a writ *de quibus*

---

[1] 13 Edw. I. (Westm. 2), c. 48. | [2] 13 Edw. I. (Westm. 2), c. 3.

Nos. 3–5.

A.D. 1345.
Dreit.
[Fitz.,
View,
108.]

(3.)¹ § *Nota* qen brief de Dreit le tenant demanda la viewe.—*Birtone* alleggea qe mesme le tenant recoverist vers luy mesme mesmes les tenementz par defaut apres defaut, issint en cas destatut qe ly toude la viewe.—Mes pur ceo qe ceo nest pas brief done par statut sur le perde, mes est un brief a la comune ley, il avoit la viewe par agarde.

Statut
mar-
chant:
*Audita
Querela*.²
[Fitz.,
Damage,
98.]

(4.)¹ § *Nota* qe executours suyrent execucion hors dun estatut marchant fait a lour testatour, et le dettour suyt *Audita Querela*, moustraunt acquitance de lour testatour, quel ils dedisoint; et trove fuit qe son fait; et enquis a queux damages, sur quei il pria ses damages vers les executours.—*Birtone*. Les executours sount en autre cas qe le testatour mesme, qar ils furent tenutz de suyre lestatut, pur ceo qils ne poaint saver de tiel acquitance, et pur ceo nest il pas resoun qe damages soient recoveris vers eux.—Et a ceo acorda la COURT.—Puis agarda fut qil recoverast nul damage.

(5.)³ § *Nota* qe le successour porta un brief *de* Brief *de*

---

was " quod, ubi prædictus Willel- " mus per narrationem suam præ- " dictam supponit quendam Ri- " cardum, quondam personam " capellæ prædictæ, fuisse seisitum " de terra versus eos petita, ut de " jure capellæ prædictæ, et eam " alienasse, &c., nunquam fuit " aliquis ib persona capellæ præ- " dictæ, prædecessor, &c., qui " vocabatur Ricardus. Et si, &c., " tunc dicunt quod terra illa est " laicum feodum ipsorum Adæ et " Margeriæ et non libera elee- " mosyna pertinens ad capellam " Sanctæ Wereburgæ prædictæ." Issue was joined also on this plea. Nothing further appears on the roll, except adjournments.

¹ From the four MSS., as above.

² The words *Audita Querela* are from H. alone, which omits the words Statut marchant.

³ From the four MSS., as above. There is a case among the *Placita de Banco*, Mich., 17 Edw. III., R° 379, in which the result is different from that stated in the report with regard to the damages, but which, nevertheless, may be worth citing. The action was brought by John son of Laurence le Coroner against Adam de Trewelone, clerk, in respect of tenements in Bekenesfeld (Beaconsfield, Bucks) " de " quibus idem Adam injuste et " sine judicio disseisivit Lauren- " tium le Coroner, patrem prædicti " Johannis, cujus heres ipse est." The tenant traversed the dis-

No. 6.

in respect of a disseisin effected on his predecessor The disseisin was found by inquest, and enquiry was made further as to the damages.—*Gaynesford* prayed judgment and his damages, and he was forjudged of the damages by judgment.—*Quære.*—*Est reus errore lapidem qui gestat in ore.*

Intrusion.   (6.) § Note that in an Intrusion on Wardship brought by two persons severance was made by judgment, by reason of the non-suit of one of them. And also the point was touched that the like would be done on a writ of Ravishment of Ward. And afterwards the issue taken was whether the defendant held of the plaintiff by knight service. And the plaintiff had counted, as to his damages, with respect to the whole, but he had made no definite demand for himself alone after the severance.

No. 6.

quibus dune disseisine fait a son predecessour. La
disseisine trove par enqueste, et enquis outre des
damages.—[*Gayn.* pria jugement et ses damages],[2]
et fuit forjuge des damages par agarde.—*Quære.*—
Est reus errore lapidem qui gestat in ore.[3]

(6.)[4] § *Nota* qen Intrusion de garde[5] porte par deux
la severaunce par agarde se fist par la nounsuite del
un. Et auxint fuit touche qe se freit en garde ravise,
&c. Et puis lissue fuit pris le quel il tient par
service de chivaler.[6] Et counta a ses damages del
entier, mes demande en certein navoit il pas.[7]

---

seisin, and the jury found " quod " prædictus Adam injuste et sine " judicio disseisivit præfatum "Laurentium patrem prædicti " Johannis de prædictis tene- " mentis sicut idem Johannes per " breve suum supponit, ad dam- " num ejusdem Johannis sexaginta " solidorum."

The judgment was " Ideo con- " sideratum est quod prædictus " Johannes recuperet inde seisi- " nam suam et damna sua præ- " dicta."

[1] The marginal note is omitted from C.

[2] The words between brackets are omitted from C.

[3] The last sentence is omitted from H.

[4] From the four MSS., as above. The case appears to be that found among the *Placita de Banco*, Mich., 19 Edw. III., R° 56, d. The action was originally brought by John son of Thomas de Esenhulle and Mauger le Vavasour, and continued by the first named plaintiff, against William son and heir of Robert Rynel " quare, cum custodia unius " mesuagii, duarum carucatarum " terræ, et decem libratarum

" redditus, cum pertinentiis, in " Buckeby, usque ad legiti- " mam ætatem heredis præ- " dicti, ad ipsum Johannem et " Maugerum le Vavasour pertineat, " eo quod prædictus Robertus " prædicta mesuagium, terram, et " redditum de eis tenuit per servi- " tium militare, ac iidem Johannes " et Maugerus in plena et pacifica " seisina ejusdem custodiæ diu " extiterint, idem Willelmus, infra " ætatem existens, se in prædicta " mesuagium, terram, et redditum " intrusit, et custodiam illam " præfato Johanni detinet."

[5] The words de garde are omitted from D.

[6] The plea upon which issue was joined was, according to the record, " Willelmus venit . . . " et dicit quod prædictus Johannes " actionem versus eum habere non " debet, quia dicit quod ipse non " tenet de eo tenementa prædicta " per servitium militare sicut idem " Johannes per breve suum sup- " ponit."

[7] The declaration was according to the record on behalf of the plaintiff John alone, and its con- clusion was that " prædictus Wil-

Nos. 7, 8.

A.D. 1345.

*Quare
impedit.*

(7.) § The King brought a *Quare impedit* against the Prior of Wenlock by reason of the temporalities of the Priory being in his hand, and counted that a certain predecessor of the Prior presented, &c.—*Pole.* The presentee was not admitted nor instituted on his presentation, &c.; ready, &c.—*Thorpe.* Do you mean that to be your answer?—*Pole.* Yes, since you do not show any right in you, nor that the King is seised, &c.—And afterwards *Thorpe* accepted the issue.[1]

*Scire
facias.*

(8.) § The King brought a *Scire facias* against the Abbess of Wilton, in respect of the prebend of Chalke, upon a recovery had by him on a *Quare impedit* by reason of the temporalities of the Abbey having been in the hand of King Edward his grandfather, and another *Scire facias* against J.[2] "*dictam præbendam incumbenti injuste, &c.*"—*Huse.* As to the Abbess, she tells you that, immediately after the judgment, the King gave and granted the same prebend to A., his clerk,[3] and by judicial writ commanded the Ordinary to admit his clerk, in virtue of which gift and grant the Bishop admitted him, and installed him, and he was seised in that manner for years and days, and so the judgment was executed; judgment whether the King ought to have execution a second time.—*R. Thorpe.* You see plainly how the King takes his suit

---

[1] For the conclusion of this case *see* below No. 78.

[2] For the real name *see* p. 321, note 2.

[3] For the real name *see* p. 315, note 6.

Nos. 7, 8.

(7.)¹ § Le Roi porta *Quare impedit* vers le Prior A.D. 1345.
de Wellok² par resoun des temporaltes de la Priorie *Quare*
en sa mein, countant qun son predecessour Priour, *impedit.*
&c., presenta, &c.—*Pole.* Il ne fuit pas resceu ne
institut a son presentement, &c.; prest, &c.—*Thorpe.*
Ceo voilletz pur respons—[*Pole*]. Et de puis qe vous
ne moustretz pas dreit en vous ne qe le Roi est
seisi, &c.—Et puis *Thorpe* prist lissue.

(8.)³ § Le Roi porta *Scire facias* vers Labbesse de *Scire*
Wiltone, de la provandre de Chalke, hors dun re- *facias.*
coverir qe se tailla pur luy sur *Quare impedit* par *Quare*
resoun des temporaltes Labbey en la mein le Roi *impedit,*
E.⁴ son aiel, et autre *Scire facias* vers J. *dictam* *60.]*
præbendam incumbenti injuste, &c.⁵—Huse. Quant al
Abbesse, ele vous dist qe, freschement apres le jugement, le Roi dona et granta mesme la provandre a
A. son clerc, et par brief de jugement comaunda al
Ordeigner de resceivre son clerc, par force de quel
doun et grant Levesqe luy resceut, et luy enstalla,
et il aunz et jours seisi par la manere, issint le
jugement execut; jugement si autrefoith execucion
deive aver.⁶—[*R.*] *Thorpe.* Vous veietz bien coment

" lelmus, infra ætatem existens, se
" in prædicta mesuagia, terram, et
" redditum intrusit, et custodiam
" illam præfato Johanni et Mau-
" gero, qui, &c., detinet, unde
" dicit quod deterioratus est, et
" damnum habet ad valentiam
" centum librarum."

¹ From the four MSS., as above.

² C, Weltok.

³ From the four MSS., as above,
but corrected by the record, *Placita
coram Rege*, Mich., 19 Edw. III.,
Rᵒ 104. It there appears that the
Scire facias was directed to the
Sheriff of Wiltshire in respect of
execution of a recovery had by
the King, against Constance late

Abbess of Wilton, of his presentation to the prebend of Chalke in
the church of St. Edith of Wilton,
" quæ vacat, et ad suam spectat
" donationem, ratione Abbatiæ de
" Wiltone nuper vacantis, et in
" manu domini Edwardi quondam
" Regis Angliæ avi Regis nunc
" existentis."

⁴ The words le Roi E. are from
L. alone.

⁵ As to the *Scire facias* against
the incumbent *see* below p. 321.

⁶ According to the roll the Abbess
pleaded " quod dominus Rex, re-
" center post judicium pro ipso
" Rege redditum, per literas suas
" patentes dedit et concessit præ-

No. 8.

for having execution in respect of a presentation, and the Abbess does not allege any execution of any presentation made by the King, but speaks of a gift and a grant, which is not a presentation : for the Bishop was not, by force of such a gift, compelled by law to admit the person to whom the King gave, but with regard to a *Quare non admisit* could have excused himself on the ground that no one was presented to him ; therefore we pray execution.—*Huse.* There is no other form in the

No. 8.

le Roi prent sa suite daver execucion dun presente- A.D. 1345.
ment, et il nallege execucion de nul presentement
fait par le Roi, mes parle de doun et grant, qe
nest pas presentement : qar Levesqe par force de
tiel doun ne fuit par ley arte[1] de resceivre celuy
a qi le Roy dona, mes a un *Quare non admisit* se
ust excuse pur ceo qe nul fuit presente a luy ; par
quei nous prioms execucion.[2]—*Huse.* Il ny ad autre

" bendam prædictam cuidam Wil-
" lelmo de Raundes, clerico suo,
" et mandavit breve suum de
" judicio ex causa judicii prædicti
" Episcopo Sarum, loci Ordinario,
" quod idem Episcopus idoneam
" personam ad præbendam prædic-
" tam admitteret, qer quod præfa-
" tus Episcopus, virtute literarum
" illarum et brevis prædicti, præ-
" dictum Willelmum ad præben-
" dam prædictam admisit, et ipsum
" instituit et installavit in eadem,
" et idem Willelmus per dies et
" annos tenuit præbendam prædic-
" tam in forma prædicta virtute
" judicii et recuperationis prædic-
" torum, et petit judicium si
" dominus Rex executionem vir-
" tute judicii prædicti ad præsens
" habere debeat, &c."

[1] H., and C., arce.

[2] The replication on behalf of
the King was, according to the
roll, " quod dominus Rex ab
" executione sua ratione prædicta
" præcludi non debet, quia dicit
" quod in hoc quod prædicta
" Abbatissa in responsione sua
" allegat quod dominus Rex post
" recuperare suum prædictum
" dedit et concessit per literas suas
" patentes præbendam prædictam
" præfato Willelmo de Raundes,
" virtute quarum literarum et
" brevis de judicio præfato Epis-

" copo directorum, idem Episcopus
" ad donationem ipsius Regis ad
" dictam præbendam ipsum Willel-
" mum admisit, et ipsum in eadem
" instituit et installavit, et ex quo
" prædicta Abbatissa non dedicit
" recuperare prædictum versus
" dictam Constanciam nuper Abba-
" tissam, &c., ut in jure ipsius
" Constanciæ nuper Abbatissæ,
" ratione temporalium Abbatiæ
" prædictæ in manu domini Ed-
" wardi quondam Regis Angliæ,
" avi, &c., existentium, sibi accres-
" cente, et non in jure Coronæ suæ,
" in quo casu dominus Rex. præ-
" sentare debet clericum suum
" ad Episcopum loci per verba
" præsentationis, quæ quidem præ-
" sentatio debet esse warantum pro
" Episcopo loci Ordinario ad hujus-
" modi præsentatum admittendum,
" de quo nihil ostendit, nec quod
" prædictus Willelmus præsentatus
" fuit ad præbendam prædictam
" per verba præsentationis, nec
" quod in prædicto brevi de judicio
" per quod idem Episcopus ipsum
" Willelmum admisit nomen ipsius
" Willelmi inserebatur, nec dictæ
" literæ de donatione prædictæ
" præbendæ quas ipsa Abbatissa
" allegat eidem Willelmo esse
" factas ullam mentionem faciunt
" de judicio alias pro ipso domino
" Rege reddito, prætextu cujus

No. 8.

Chancery for presenting to a prebend but *dedimus et concessimus,* and if there were any, still, even though the King should present by words which are not formal, the Bishop must admit the presentee; and with regard to a *Quare non admisit* he could not have excused himself, and the King could present by parol without any presentation in writing whatever. (And this was admitted.) Therefore when the Bishop had a judicial writ to admit the King's clerk, and by the King's deed he was apprised to whom the King had made donation, and so apprised who it was that he ought to admit, and did admit that person, it cannot be understood that that person was admitted otherwise than by force of the judgment.—THORPE (JUSTICE). When the King makes such a collation of a prebend to his clerk, it is void, and therefore it is the custom in Chancery to make another patent to the Bishop to admit the clerk; now in your matter the judicial writ was not a warrant to the Ordinary to admit any particular person, nor was the collation made to the clerk,

No. 8.

fourme de presenter a provandre en la Chauncellerie forqe par *dedimus et concessimus*, et tut y avoit il, unqore, tut presentereit le Roi par paroles nient fourmels, Levesqe luy coviendreit resceivre; et al *Quare non admisit* il ne soy ust pas excuse, et par parole tut sanz presentement en lescript le Roi poet presenter. *Quod fuit concessum.* Donqes quant Levesqe avoit brief de jugement de resceivre le clerc le Roi, et par le fait le Roi il fuit appris a qi le Roi avoit done, et issint appris qi il duist resceivre, et luy resceut, il ne poet estre entendu qil fuit resceu forqe par force de jugement.—Thorpe, Justice. Quant le Roi fait un tiel collacion a son clerc dune provandre, cella est voide, et pur ceo homme use en Chauncellerie de faire autre patent al Evesqe de resceivre le clerc; ore en vostre matere le brief de jugement ne fuit pas garrant al Ordener[1] de resceivre nulle certeine persone, ne la collacion fait

---

" judicii dictus dominus Rex præsentationem suam ad dictam " præbendam recuperavit, neque " aliquid Curiæ ostendit quod " cederet in præjudicium seu " damnum ipsius Abbatissæ si " executio judicii prædicti versus " eam fieret, eo quod nihil in præ- " sentatione prædicta ad præsens " clamat, et sic judicium prædic- " tum non est executum, petit " judicium pro domino Rege, et " breve Episcopo, &c."

Other matters were also alleged " pro jure Regis declarando" concluding with the traverse " absque hoc quod prædictus Wil- " lelmus de Raundes institutus " fuit et installatus in præbenda " prædicta ad præsentationem " domini Regis, et hoc paratus est " verificare pro domino Rege."

After further pleadings the Abbess said " quod judicium alias " pro domino Rege reddditum " . . . . fuit executum de " quodam Willelmo de Raundes, " et hoc parata est verificare."

Then follows the pleading on behalf of the King, on which issue was joined, " quod prædictum " judicium non fuit executum de " prædicto Willelmo de Raundes."

The jury afterwards found at *Nisi prius* " quod judicium pro " domino Rege de præsentatione ad " præbendam infra nominatam " versus Constanciam nuper Abba- " tissam de Wiltone nunquam fuit " executum in persona Willelmi de " Raundes."

Judgment was therefore given for the King.

[1] L., Ordeigner; H., and D., Ordiner.

No. 8.

which was not directed to the Ordinary, any warrant; by what warrant then was he admitted? as meaning to say by none.—*Notton*. Presentation and collation are of different natures, for to presentation appertain examination of the person presented, and inquest of office, but to collation only corporal induction; therefore, if the King, not being apprised that it belonged to him to present, made such a collation, even though the clerk was thereby admitted, it does not follow that the King will [not] have his presentation a second time: for although the King, where he has a right to present, may make a ratification for one, or two or three persons, where each ratification has the effect of a presentation, yet he is not thereby ousted from his presentation after the death of those persons. Besides, if the King gives and grants to me any land, which I hold in his right for my life, unless the King is apprised what right he has, whether in reversion or in any other manner, the right does not pass; no more in the matter before us.—*Moubray*. It cannot be denied that the clerk was admitted in virtue of the King's command; therefore the admission cannot be understood to have been otherwise than by force of the judgment: for, if otherwise, then the King was an usurper, and he is now tenant of the advowson in his own right, and consequently no judgment delivered for him in right of another person is executory.—*Huse*, as to the other *Scire facias*, took exception to the writ, on the ground that the writ lies only against one who is patron and who can have an answer, whereas by this writ it is supposed that the defendant has nothing, &c. And afterwards *Huse* gave the answer as above, that the judgment was executed.—*R. Thorpe*. You see plainly that he does not affirm his possession by title against the King, nor does he claim anything in the patronage; therefore we pray a writ to the Bishop making mention of his disclaimer. — Scot. Even

No. 8.

au clerc, qe ne fuit pas directe a luy, ne fuit pas A.D. 1345. garrant; par quel garraut fuit il adonqes resceu? *quasi diceret* par nulle.—*Nottone.* Presentement et collacion sount de divers natures, qar a presentement appent examinement de la persone, et enqueste doffice, et a collacion forqe corporel induccion; par quei si le Roi, nient appris qe a luy appendist a presenter, fist une tiel[1] collacion, tut fuit le clerc par cele resceu, nensuit pas qil avera autrefoith son presentement: qar mesqe le Roi, la ou il ad dreit a presenter, face ratificacion a une persone, ou deux ou iij persones, ou chesqun est leffecte dun presentement, unqore par tant nest il pas ouste de son presentement apres la mort des persones. Ovesqe ceo, si le Roi moi doune et grante une terre, qe jeo tienk en son dreit pur ma vie, si le Roi ne soit appris quel dreit il ad, le quel en reversioun ou en autre manere, le dreit ne passe pas; *neque in proposito.*— *Moubray.* Ne poet estre dedit qe le clerc ne fuit resceu par my le maundement le Roi; donqes ne serra entendu forqe par force del jugement: qar si autrement donqes fut le Roi purpernour, et est tenant a ore del avoweson en son propre dreit, et *per consequens* nul jugement taille pur luy en autri dreit executore.—*Huse* a lautre *Scire facias* chalengea le brief de ceo qe le brief ne gist forqe vers celuy qest patroun et qe poet aver respons, et par ceo brief est suppose qil nad rienz, &c. Et puis dona mesme le respons *ut supra*, qe le jugement fuit execut.[2] —[R.] *Thorpe.* Vous veietz bien coment il nafferme pas sa possession par title vers le Roi, ne rienz ne cleime en la patronage; par quei nous prioms brief al Evesqe fesaunt mencion de son desclamance.[3]—

---

[1] tiel is omitted from D.

[2] According to the roll (R⁰ 104, d) the second *Scire facias* was against Lambert de Noulesholt, clerk, "possessioni dictæ præbendæ in-

" juste incumbenti." His plea was in the same terms as that of the Abbess.

[3] The replication, on behalf of the King, was, according to the roll,

X

No. 8.

A.D. 1345. though you had judgment, you would not have a writ to the Bishop until the plea against the Abbess has been determined.—*R. Thorpe.* There are two separate writs; therefore, &c.; and even if there were only one writ, it is not contrary to what is right to grant a writ to the Bishop with regard to the one before the other has pleaded, and so we had one in the Common Bench for Hugh le Despenser: for against the one recovery may be had in a *Quare impedit* within the period [of six months], and against the other possibly after the period has expired; how could the damages be dealt with in that case?—*Huse.* We have had the writ of *Scire facias* served upon us, and so by law we shall have an answer; and it is not in this case as in a case of *Quare impedit*, because inasmuch as you make us a party to show cause why execution should not be had, you give us the advantage, and we said that we are prebendary.—THORPE, J. We have spoken to all the sages of the law, and we are unanimously agreed that inasmuch as you do not affirm your possession, nor show that execution will be any damage to you, the defendant, therefore do you who are for the King sue execution against the defendant.

No. 8.

Scot. Mesqe vous ussetz jugement vous averetz pas A D 1345 brief avant qe le plee soit termine vers Labbesse.— [*R.*] *Thorpe.* Il y sount deux briefs, par quei, &c.; et tut ny avoit forqe un brief, il nest pas countre resoun de granter brief al Evesqe vers lun avant qe lautre eit plede, et issint avioms en Comune Baunk pur Hughe le Despenser : qar devers lun en *Quare impedit* homme recovera deinz le temps, et vers lautre par cas apres le temps ; coment freit homme des damages donqes ?—*Huse.* Nous sumes garny, et issint de ley averoms respons ; et il est autre cy qen *Quare impedit*, qar par tant qe vous nous fetes partie pur quei execucion ne se deit faire si nous donetz[1] vous lavantage, et nous deimes[2] qe nous fumes provandrer.—Thorpe. Nous avoms parle a touz les sages, et sumes dun acord desicome vous naffermetz pas vostre possession, ne moustretz qe lexecucion serra damage a vous, par quei devers luy suetz execucion.[3]

" quod ex quo prædictus Lambertus " in responsione sua nihil clamat " in patronatu præbendæ prædictæ, " nec per placitum suum facit " ipsum præbendarium ejusdem " præbendæ, nec aliquem alium " titulum ad eandem præbendam " injustam occupationem suam " ejusdem præbendæ sibi per breve " Regis impositam excusantem se " habere allegavit, nec aliquid " aliud dicit ad excludendum " dominum Regem ab executione " sua, petit judicium pro domino " Rege, et breve Episcopo, &c."

[1] H., donoms.

[2] H., dioms.

[3] According to the roll judgment was given as follows : — " Quia " videtur Curiæ quod idem Lam- " bertus nihil dicit in exclusione " executionis judicii prædicti, con-

" sideratum est quod idem dominus " Rex habeat inde executionem, et " breve Episcopo Sarum quod, non " obstante reclamatione ipsius " Lamberti, ad præsentationem " domini Regis ad præbendam " prædictam idoneam personam " admittat, &c."

The matter did not, however, end here, for after the judgment on the *Scire facias* against the Abbess there is the following entry on the roll :—

" Postea, scilicet, termino Pas- " chæ anno regni Regis nunc " Angliæ quadragesimo secundo, " quia datum fuit domino Regi " intelligi quod, licet judicium " inde tunc redditum fuit, executio " tamen inde adhuc restat faci- " enda, præceptum fuit Vicecomiti " quod non omitteret, &c., quin

No. 9.

A.D. 1345.
Recordari. (9.) § *Recordari jacias loquelam* from a Court of Ancient Demesne, *quia clamat tenere ad communem legem.* The tenant who sued the *Recordari* was

No. 9.

(9.) [1] § *Recordari* hors daucien demene, *quia clamat* A.D. 1345.
tenere ad communem legem Le tenant qe suyt le *Recordari.*

" per probos, &c., scire faceret
" Abbatissæ de Wiltone quæ nunc
" est, et Thomæ Orgrave clerico,
" qui præbendam prædictam modo
" tenet, quod essent coram domino
" Rege a die Paschæ in quinque
" septimanas tunc proxime sequen-
" tes ubicumque, &c., ad ostenden-
" dum si quid pro se haberent vel
" dicere scirent quare dominus
" Rex executionem judicii prædicti
" juxta considerationem Curiæ
" suæ prædictæ habere non debeat,
" ad quas quidem quinque septi-
" manas Paschæ coram domino
" Rege apud Westmonasterium
" veniunt servientes domini Regis
" ad placita, et Michael Skyllynge
" qui pro domino Rege in hac
" parte sequitur similiter venit. Et
" Vicecomes retornavit prout inse-
" quitur :—Scire feci Abbatissæ de
" Wiltone infrascriptæ et Thomæ
" Orgrave, clerico, quod sint
" coram domino Rege ubicumque
" fuerit in Anglia ad diem in brevi
" contentam ad faciendum quod
" breve istud requirit, per Thomam
" Cuttynge et Johannem Bubbere
" Quæ quidem Abbatissa per Wal-
" terum Perlee attornatum suum,
" et Thomas Orgrave, in propria
" persona sua, sic præmuniti
" veniunt.
    " Et prædictus Thomas Orgrave
" dicit quod dominus Rex nunc
" (per literas suas patentes, quas
" profert hic in Curia, in hæc
" verba :—Edwardus Dei gratia
" Rex Angliæ, dominus Hiberniæ
" et Aquitaniæ, omnibus ad quos
" præsentes literæ pervenerint
" salutem. Sciatis quod dedimus
" et concessimus dilecto clerico
" nostro Thomæ de Orgrave præ-

" bendam de Chalke in ecclesia
" collegiata de Wiltone vacantem,
" et ad nostram donationem
" spectantem ratione Abbatiæ de
" Wiltone nuper vacantis et in
" manu domini Edwardi quon-
" dam Regis avi nostri existentis,
" habendam cum suis juribus et
" pertinentiis quibuscunque. In
" cujus rei testimonium has
" literas nostras fieri fecimus
" patentes. Teste me ipso apud
" Westmonasterium x die Novem-
" bris anno regni nostri quadra-
" gesimo primo) præsentavit eum
" ad præbendam prædictam, vir-
" tute cujus præsentationis idem
" Thomas ad præbendam illam per
" loci Ordinarium admissus fuit, et
" canonice inductus, et installatus
" in eadem, et sic judicium prædic-
" tum in persona ipsius Thomæ
" executum fuit.
    " Et prædicta Abbatissa, per
" attornatum suum prædictum
" similiter dicitquod judicium præ-
" dictum in persona ipsius Thomæ,
" virtute literarum prædictarum,
" executum fuit in forma prædicta,
" &c. Unde non intendunt quod
" dominus Rex alias executionem
" judicii prædicti versus eos habere
" debeat, &c.
    " Et tam prædicti servientes
" domini Regis, &c., quam prædic-
" tus Michael qui sequitur, &c.,
" hoc non dedicunt.
    " Ideo iidem Abbatissa et
" Thomas Orgrave eant inde sine
" die, salvo semper jure domini
" Regis, si quod, &c."
[1] From the four MSS., as above,
but corrected by the record, *Placita
de Banco*, Mich., 19 Edw. III.,
R° 538. It there appears that the

No. 10.

A.D. 1345. essoined.[1]—*R. Thorpe.* The essoin does not lie, because on a previous occasion the tenant sued another *Recordari,* and did not appear to maintain the cause of it, and therefore the parol was remanded to the Court of Ancient Demesne, so that even if she were now in Court she would not be answered as to this writ, nor could she for any reason maintain the cause, because, in that case, it would follow that a demandant would never bring to an end a cause in a Court of Ancient Demesne, and therefore he can never have more than one *Recordari.*—*Moubray.* This writ is possibly in respect of other land, and of a different demand from that in the first writ, and the essoiner cannot be a party to try that fact.—*R. Thorpe.* If the essoin lies, she will afterwards be non-suited, and will bring another *Recordari,* and will be essoined, and so the process will be infinite, and that will be too great a mischief. And in the alternative course there is no mischief, because she will afterwards have an Assise of Novel Disseisin if she be ousted.—STONORE. You wish it to be understood that she could not maintain the tenements to be at common law if she were in Court, but possibly she could do so, and therefore we shall allow the essoin against you, and shall adjourn it, and we shall give you a day of grace.—And so it was done.—See below.[2]

Voucher.   (10.) § The Archbishop of Canterbury vouched to

---

[1] For the names of the parties *see* p. 325, note 1.

[2] No. 52 of the same term.

No. 10.

Recordari fuit essone.[1]—[*R.*] *Thorpe.* Lessone ne A.D. 1345.
git pas, qar avant ces houres il suyt un autre *Re-*
cordari, et ne vint pas pur meintener la cause, par
quei la paroule estoit remaunde en aunciene demene,
issint qe tut fuit il ore en Court il ne serra pas
respondu a cest brief, ne par nulle resoun ne pout[2]
meintener la cause, qar issint ensuereit qe demandant
jammes vendra a fine en auncien demene, et pur
ceo il navera jammes forqe un *Recordari.*—*Moubray.*
Par cas cest brief est dautre terre, et dautre demande qe ne fuit le primer, et a ceo trier ne purra
lessoignour estre partie.—[*R.*] *Thorpe.* Si lessone gise
il serra apres nounsuy, et portera autre *Recordari*, et
serra essone, et issint le procees infinit, qe serra
trop grant meschief. Et dautre part nad il pas
meschief, qar il avera autrefoith[3] Assise de Novele
Disseisine sil soit ouste.—STON. Vous entendretz qil
meintendra pas les tenementz estre a la comune lei
sil fuit en Court, mes par cas il freit, et pur ceo
nous ferroms pur vous et adjourneroms lessone, et
vous durroms[4] jour de grace.—*Et ita factum est.*[5]—
Vide infra, &c.

(10.)[6] § Lercevesqe de Canterbirs voucha a garrant Voucher.[7]

[Fitz., *Proses,* 38.]

Recordari facias loquelam was
directed to the Sheriff of Berkshire,
in respect of the *loquela* which
was "in Curia Abbatis de Bello
"Loco Regis de Chepyngfaren-
"done inter Margaretam de
"Eggardeseye petentem et Mar-
"ciliam atte Berewe de Shultone
"tenentem, de uno mesuagio
"et duabus virgatis terræ, cum
"pertinentiis, in Shultone, ...
"quia prædicta Marcilia clamat
"tenere mesuagium et terram
"prædicta ad communem legem."

[1] According to the record, on the
day appointed, "a die Sancti Jo-
"hannis Baptistæ in xv dies tam

"prædicta Margareta quam præ-
"dicta Marcilia fecerunt se esso-
"niari."

[2] The words ne pout are from
D. alone, and are there interlined
in a different hand.

[3] autrefoith is from H. alone.

[4] D., dorroms.

[5] According to the record, "Et
"habuerunt inde diem per esson-
"catores suos hic ad hunc diem,
"scilicet, a die Sancti Martini in
"xv dies."

[6] From the four MSS., as above.

[7] The marginal note in H. is
Non omittas.

Nos. 11, 12.

A.D. 1345. warrant Robert de Wodhous.—*Moubray*. Let the voucher stand. And we tell you that heretofore a *Non omittas propter libertatem* has been awarded on this original writ; and therefore we pray that the clause *Non omittas* may be inserted in the *Summoneas ad warantizandum*.—HILLARY. He has vouched in this county, and in others, and if he elects suit to summon the vouchee in the same county in which the original writ is brought, a *Non omittas* may well be granted; but if he wishes to sue in another county, you cannot have it, and the tenant must elect in which counties he will sue.—*Richemunde*. Sir, it seems that, even though he wished to sue only in the same county, inasmuch as this is a new process against a person other than the one who was previously a party, a *Non omittas* will not be grantable.—HILLARY. Yes, it will.

Detinue of chattels.

(11.) § Cecilia de Manestone brought a writ of Detinue of chattels against a parson, and counted as to a delivery by herself.—*Huse*. She did not deliver any chattels to us, nor do we detain any from her; ready, &c., by our law.—*Notton*. Do you mean that to be your answer?—*Huse*. Yes, certainly, since you have counted as to a delivery made by yourself.—*Notton*. And inasmuch as this matter is not such a private contract but that it would naturally fall within the knowledge of the country, judgment whether wager of law lies.—WILLOUGHBY. And, because you have refused the wager of law, take nothing by your writ, but be in mercy.

Trespass.

(12.) § Ralph de Wyndesore, prebendary of South

Nos. 11, 12.

Robert de Wodhous.—*Moubray.* Estoise le voucher. A.D. 1345.
Et vous dioms qe avant ces hures [1] *Non omittas
propter libertatem* ad este agarde a ceste original, par
quei en le *Summoneas ad warantizandum* prioms qe le
Non omittas soit.—HILL. Il ad vouche en cel counte [2]
et autres, et sil elise la suite de luy somondre en
mesme le counte ou loriginal est porte *Non omittas*
serra bien grante; mes sil voudra suir en autre counte
vous laveretz pas, et le tenant eslirra ou il voudra
suir.—*Rich.* Sire, il semble qe, tut vodreit il suir en
mesme le counte, pur ceo qe cest un novel procees
vers autre qe devant ne fuit pas partie, *Non omittas*
ne serra pas grantable. [3]—HILL. Si serreit.

(11.) [4] § Cecile de Manestone porta brief de [5] De- Detenue
tenue des chateux vers une persone, countant de de
son baille demene. —*Huse.* Nulles chateux nous [6] [Fitz.,
bailla, ne nulles ne luy detenoms [7]; prest, &c., par Ley, 51.]
nostre ley.—*Nottone.* Ceo voilletz pur respons?—
Huse. Oyl, certes, quant vous avietz counte de baille
fait par vous mesmes.—*Nottone.* Et desicome ceste
chose nest pas si prive contracte qe naturelement il
chiet [8] en conissance de pays, jugement si la ley gise.
—WILBY. Et pur ceo qe vous avietz refuse la ley,
pernetz rienz par vostre brief, mes soietz en la mercy.

(12.) [9] § Rauf [10] de Wyndesore, provandrer de Mal- Trans.
[Fitz.,
Attourne,
77.]

---

[1] C., heures.
[2] C., countee.
[3] D., garrantable.
[4] From the four MSS., as above.
[5] The words brief de are from D.
alone.
[6] L., ne ly; H., luy; C., ly,
instead of nous.
[7] L., H., and C., detient.
[8] H., gist.
[9] From the four MSS., as above,
but corrected by the record, *Placita
de Banco*, Mich., 19 Edw. III.,

R° 92, d. It there appears that
the action was brought by Thomas
Martyn of Lindfield against
Ralph de Wyndesore " Canonicus
" in ecclesia de Suthmallyng "
who, as alleged in the writ, " apud
" Suthmallyng cepit et imprison-
" avit et ipsum in prisona,
" quousque finem per viginti libras
" pro deliberatione sua habenda
" fecisset, detinuit."

[10] MSS., of Y.B., William, or W.

Nos. 13, 14.

A.D. 1345 Malling, alleged against one B.,[1] in defence to a writ of Trespass, that he ought not to be answered, because he was a villein of Ralph's prebend.—*Gaynesford.* Free, &c.—*R. Thorpe.* If it appears to the Court that Ralph can without prejudice make an attorney in this case, he would gladly do so.—KELSHULLE. Others have done so in the like case.—STOUFORD. He may do so now well enough without prejudice as to pursuing the averment which he has tendered, that is to say, that the plaintiff is his villein.—Therefore by allowance of the COURT Ralph made his attorney.

Quid juris clamat. (13.) § A *Quid juris clamat* was brought against a woman, supposing that she held for term of her life, and that after her death the tenements were revertible. And it was supposed by the note of the fine that another person was to hold after the death of the woman, if he should survive her, for his life, and then the reversion was saved which was granted to the plaintiff.—*Grene.* This writ is not warranted by the note.—*R. Thorpe.* Suit cannot be taken against one who has nothing, nor could his attornment vest the reversion.—And, notwithstanding, the writ abated for the variance.

Formedon. (14.) § Formedon. The manor of Windsor, except so much, was demanded, and it was supposed by the count that the whole manor was given; and the writ also was in the words "*quod*" such an one "*dedit*," without making any exception, in accordance with the demand.—*R. Thorpe.* He counts that the manor,

---

[1] For the real name *see* p. 329, note 9.

Nos. 13, 14.

lyng, allegea countre un B. a un brief de Trans A.D. 1345.
qil ne duist estre respondu, qar il est villein de sa
provandre.¹—*Gayn.* Fraunk, &c.²—[*R.*] *Thorpe.* Sil
semble a la Court qe Rauf³ purra sanz prejudice
en ceo cas fere attourne il le freit volunters.—KELL.
Autres lount fet en mesme le cas.—STOUF.⁴ Si purra
ore assetz bien sanz prejudice a pursuyr ceo qil ad
tendu, saver, qil est villein.—Par quei par avys de
COURT Rauf³ fist son attourne.⁵

(13.) ⁶ § *Quid juris clamat* porte vers une femme, *Quid juris clamat.*
supposant qele tient a termé de sa vie, et qapres [Fitz.,
son decees les tenementz furent⁷ revertibles. Et par *Variauns,*
la note est suppose qautre⁸ tendra après la mort la 82.]
femme, sil survive, pur sa vie, et donqes la reversion
sauve quel fuit granfe al pleintif.—*Grene.* Cest brief
nest pas garraunti de la note.—[*R.*] *Thorpe.* La suite
ne purra estre pris vers celuy qe rienz ad, ne son
attournement ne purra vestir reversion.⁹—Et, *non
obstante,* le brief abatist pur la variaunce.

(14.) ⁶ § Fourme doun. Le maner¹⁰ de Wyndesore, Fourme
forpris tant, fuit demande, et par count fuit suppose doun.
lenter estre done, et auxint le brief voleit *quod* un [Fitz.,
tiel *dedit* sanz fere forpris acordant al demande.— *Amende-*
[*R.*] *Thorpe.* Il counte qe le maner, forpris tant, *ment,* 65; *Briefe,* 243.]

---

¹ The plea was, according to the
record, "quod ipse non debet ei
"inde ad istud breve seu ad aliquod
"aliud respondere, quia dicit quod
"idem Thomas est villanus ipsius
"Radulphi ecclesiæ de Suth-
"mallynge, unde petit judicium,
"&c."

² The replication (upon which
issue was joined) was, according
to the record, "quod ipse est liber
"et liberæ conditionis."

³ MSS., of Y.B., William, or W.

⁴ D., *Nottone.*

⁵ In D., the word *Quære* is added
at the end. After the award of
the *Venire,* the words of the roll
are "Et super hoc prædictus
"Radulphus ponit loco suo Gal-
"fridum de Suttone vel Nicholaum
"de Risyng de prædicto placito,
"&c."

⁶ From the four MSS., as above.

⁷ D., sount.

⁸ L., qe lautre.

⁹ reversion is omitted from C.

¹⁰ D., manoir.

No. 15.

except so much, was given, and that is not in accordance with the writ, and the cases are different where the exception is in the gift of a manor and where the exception is only in the tenancy.—*Richemunde.* I counted at first that such an one gave the manor, except so much, and afterwards I found upon examination that the whole manor had been given ; therefore, before any exception was taken, I amended the count, supposing that the whole was given.—And that was recorded on behalf of *Richemunde.*—And nevertheless it seems that the count was good in having counted that so much only was given as was supposed by the writ to be demanded.—Afterwards it was alleged that there was no such vill without addition.—This exception was not allowed, because nothing was demanded in a vill, but it was a manor which was demanded.— Therefore *R. Thorpe* alleged that there are divers manors, and no one of them without addition, in the county, &c. ; judgment of the writ.—Upon this a traverse was taken.

(15.) § Two parceners brought a writ of Aiel on the seisin of one who was grandfather to one of them, and cousin to the other, it being supposed by the count that the one who was cousin was great-great-grandfather, and exception was taken to this on the ground that he could not be understood to be cousin.—The exception was not allowed, because there is no other form of writ, inasmuch as a great-great-grandfather is in Chancery made cousin according to their custom.— *Birton.* On a previous occasion the demandant brought a writ, by the name of I. son "*Eudonis,* against our father, and now he brings a writ against us supposing his father to have had the name of Ivo and himself to be the son "*Ivonis.*"—*Sadelyngstanes.* What issue was taken on that plea?—And, after the rolls had been searched, it was found that the plea between the parties had been continued on another exception until

No. 15.

A.D. 1345.

fuit done, qest desacordant au brief, et il ad diversite la ou forprise est en le doun dun maner et la
ou il ny ad qe forprise en la tenance.—*Rich.* Jeo
countay primes qun tiel dona le maner, forpris tant,
et puis par examinement jeo trovay qe tut le maner
fuit done; par quei, avant chalange, jeo amenday le
counte, supposant tut estre done.—Et ceo fuit recorde
pur *Rich.*—*Et tamen* il semble qe le count fuit
bon daver counte tant fuit done come par brief fuit
suppose estre demande soulement.—Puis fuit allegge
qil ny ad nulle tiele ville sanz adjeccion.—*Non
allocatur*, qar rienz est demande en ville mes maner.
—Par quei il alleggea qil y ad divers maners, et
nul sanz adieccion en le counte, &c.; jugement du
brief.—Sur quei, &c., travers est pris.

(15.)[1] § Deux parceners porterunt brief Daiel de la
seisine laiel al un et cosyn al autre, supposant par
count celuy qe fuit cosyn estre tresaiel, qe fuit
chalenge, qil ne pout estre entendu cosyn.—*Non
allocatur*, qar il ny ad autre fourme de brief, pur
ceo qe tresaiel en Chauncellerie par lour oeps[3] est
fet cosyn.—*Birtone.* Autrefoith le demandant porta
brief par noun de I. fitz *Eudonis*[4] vers nostre pere,
et ore porte il brief vers nous supposant son pere aver
noun I. et luy estre fitz *Ironis*.[5]—*Sadl.* Quel issue
prist cel plee?—Et, roulles quis, trove fuit qe le
plee entre parties fuit continue sur autre chalenge

Aiel.[2]
[Fitz.,
*Joindre en
Accion*,
31.]

---

[1] From the four MSS., as above.
[2] L., Brief daiel; H., Deux
parceners; D., Ayel.
[3] In D. the word us has been
substituted for oeps in a different
hand.
[4] H., E.
[5] H., I.

Nos. 16–18.

A.D. 1345. the writ abated by the death of a party.—Stonore.
If your father accepted a bad writ as being good, is
that any reason why you should abate a good writ?—
Birton. Since the demandant affirmed, on a previous
occasion, that the father had a different name, and
continued his suit by that name, it seems that he shall
not be admitted to say that the father had another
name.—Hillary. Answer to this writ.—*Birton.* They
demand on the seisin of the great-great-grandfather,
who is out of possession, and in respect of whose seisin
no writ lies but a writ of Right; judgment whether the
writ lies.—This exception was not allowed, but Willoughby and Hillary put him to answer.

View de-
manded.

(16.) § View was demanded, and it was counterpleaded on the ground that, on a previous occasion,
on another writ in respect of the same tenements, the
tenant, as then tenant, performed his law as to non-
summons, and thereby abated the first writ, and so is
apprised of the demand. — Willoughby. The writ
abated on the ground of non-summons; therefore,
since no summons was made, the tenant cannot know
what land was in demand: therefore let him have
view.

View de-
manded.

(17.) § View was demanded, and it was counterpleaded on the ground that the demandant, on a
previous occasion, recovered by default against the
same person against whom the writ is brought, who
thereupon brought a writ of Deceit. The deceit was
found and therefore judgment was given that the
tenant should have back his land, and so the matter
was within the case of the statute.[1] And, notwithstanding, view was granted.

Cessavit.

(18.) § Note that in a *Cessavit*, after the verdict had
passed for the demandant, the tenant tendered the

---

[1] 13 Edw. I. (Westm. 2), c. 48.

No. 16–18.

tanqe par mort de partie le brief abatist.—STON. A.D. 1345.
Si vostre pere accepta un malveis brief bon, est il
resoun par taunt qe vous abatetz un bon brief ?—
Birtone. Quant il afferma son pere autrefoith aver
autre noun, et continua sa suite par cel noun, si
semble il qil ne serra resceu a dire qil avoit autre
noun.—HILL. Responez a ceste brief.—*Birtone.* Ils
demandent de la seisine le tresaiel qest hors de
possession et de qi seisine nul brief ne gist forqe
brief de Dreit ; jugement si le brief gise. — *Non
allocatur,* mes WILBY et HILL. luy mistrent a respondre.

(16.)[1] § Viewe[3] demande, et countreplede pur ceo
qautrefoith a autre brief de mesmes les tenementz
come tenant il fist sa ley de noun somons, et par
tant abatist le primer brief, et issint appris de la
demande.—WILBY. Le brief abatist par noun somons;
donqes quant nul somons fut fait il ne poet saver
quele terre fuit en demande ; par quei eit la viewe.

Viewe
demande.[2]
[Fitz.,
View,
109.]

(17.)[1] § Viewe[3] demande, et countreplede pur ceo
qe le demandant autrefoith recoverist par defaut vers
mesme cestuy vers qi le brief est porte, sur quei il
suyt par brief de Desceit. La desceit trove, par
quei fuit agarde qil reust[5] la terre, et issint en cas
destatut. Et, *non obstante,* la viewe fuit grante.

Vewe
demande.[4]
[Fitz.,
View,
110.]

(18.)[1] § *Nota* qen *Cessavit,* apres enqueste passe
pur le demandant, le tenant tendist arrerages et

Cessavit.
[Fitz.,
Suerte, 3.]

---

[1] From the four MSS., as above.
[2] demande is from L. alone.
The marginal note in D. is Dowere.
[3] The word Dowere is inserted
before Viewe in D.

[4] demande is omitted from C.
The marginal note in D. is Dowere.
[5] D., reut.

No. 19.

arrears, and damages, and surety was found, that is to say, two other persons bound their lands to distress, and they stated where they had lands. And the demandant accepted the surety.

Debt.

(19.) § A writ of Debt was brought on an obligation bearing date at Chester, and the plaintiff counted that the defendant bound himself at Chester.—*Skipwith* challenged the jurisdiction on the ground that the deed in virtue of which the action was used could not be tried in this Court (of Common Bench), and consequently this Court ought not to take cognisance of the plea; but (said *Skipwith*) on such a deed bearing date at a place in which the King's writ does not run, the plaintiff should bring his writ in the place in which the deed can be tried; and in case the debtor has nothing there, it is the plaintiff's own folly that he accepted such a deed.—WILLOUGHBY. A writ of Debt should be brought in the place in which the party can best be brought to answer; and, although the King's writ does not run at Chester, nevertheless Chester is within the King's power, and he could send thither to try the deed if it were denied; therefore answer.—*Skipwith*. Not his deed; ready, &c.—And the other side said the contrary.—WILLOUGHBY. Now we will consider how this will be tried.—And afterwards he directed a writ to be sent to the Justice of Chester, or his *locum tenens*, to try the deed.

No. 19.

damages, et soerte fuit trove, saver, qe deux autres A.D. 1345. obligerunt lour terres a la destresse, et disoint ou ils avoint terres.[1] Et le demandant accepta la soerte.

(19.)[2] § Dette porte par obligacion portant date a *Dette.* Cestre, et counta qe le defendant soi obligea a Cestre.[3] [Fitz., *Jurisdic-* —*Skip.* chalengea jurisdiccion pur ceo qe le fet par *tion,* 29; quel laccion est use[4] ne poet ceinz estre trie, et *Triall,* 66.] *per consequens* ceste Court ne deit conustre; mes sur tiel fait[5] portant date ou le brief le Roi ne court pas il portera brief illoeqes[6] ou le fait purra estre trie; et en cas qil neit rienz illoeqes cest sa folie qe prist tiel fait.—WILBY. Brief de Dette serra porte ou partie meuthe purra estre mene en respons; et coment qe brief le Roi ne court pas a Cestre, nepurqant cest deinz le powere[7] le Roi, qe purra maunder illoeqes[6] de trier le fait sil fuit dedit; par quei responez.—*Skyp.* Nient son fait; prest, &c. —*Et alii e contra.*—WILBY. Ore nous aviseroms coment ceo serra trie.—Et puis comanda brief al[8] Justice de Cestre, ou son lieu tenant, de trier le fait.[9]

---

[1] terres is omitted from C.

[2] From the four MSS., as above, but corrected by the record, *Placita de Banco,* Mich., 19 Edw. III., R° 254. It there appears that the action was brought in the Common Bench as in the County of Nottingham by John Bars, citizen and merchant of Chester, against William de Melburne, late parson of a church.

[3] The declaration was, according to the record, "quod prædictus " Willelmus . . . . . apud " Cestriam per scriptum suum " concessit se teneri et obligari " prædicto Johanni in . . sex " libris . . e . . . . præ- " dictus Willelmus, licet sæpius

" requisitus, prædictas sex libras " prædicto Johanni nondum red- " didit, sed ei hucusque reddere " recusavit . . . . Et profert " hic prædictum scriptum sub " nomine ipsius Willelmi, quod " hoc testatur, cujus data est apud " Cestriam, &c."

[4] D., usee.

[5] D., feat.

[6] L., and H., illeoqes.

[7] H., and D., poaire.

[8] L., H., and D., as.

[9] According to the record, the defendant pleaded "quod scriptum " illud non est factum suum," and the roll continues "Et, quia data " scripti prædicti est apud Cestriam " in Comitatu Cestriæ, mandatum

No. 20.

A.D. 1345, (20.) § Note that in the King's Bench an outlawry
Note con- for felony was reversed on the ground that the party
cerning
Outlawry was in prison[1] at the time at which the outlawry was
pronounced, and therefore he prayed a writ to have
his chattels delivered to him.—*R. Thorpe.* In virtue

---

[1] There is a reference in the margin of the Harleian MS. to the Statute of Westminster the fifth c. 12, meaning apparently, 5 Edward III., c. 13.

No. 20.

(20.)[1] § *Nota* qen Bank le Roi une utlagerie de
felonie fuit reverse par tant qe la partie fuit en
prisoun al temps del utlagerie pronuncie, par quei
il pria brief de liverer a luy[3] ses chateux.[4]—[*R.*]

A.D. 1345.
Nota de
Utlagerie.[2]
[Fitz.,
*Forfay-
ture,* 19.]

"est Edwardo Principi Walliæ,
"Duci Cornubiæ, et Comiti Cestriæ,
"aut ejus Justiciario Cestriæ, aut
"ipsius Justiciarii locum tenenti
"ibidem, quod per sacramentum
"xij, &c., de visneto prædicto per
"quos rei veritas melius sciri
"poterit, et qui nec, &c., præ-
"dictum Johannem nec prædictum
"Willelmum aliqua, &c., in præ-
"sentia prædictarum partium ad
"hoc præmunitarum, si interesse
"voluerint, inquirat si prædictum
"scriptum sit factum ipsius Wil-
"lelmi nec ne. Mandatum est
"etiam eisdem Principi [&c. as
"above] recordum placiti prædicti,
"una cum prædicto scripto dedicto,
"ad inquirendum super præmissis,
". . . . . et inquisitionem
"quam, &c., scire faciant hic in
"Octabis Sancti Hillarii per
"literas suas sigillatas, remittentes
"hic ad præfatum terminum præ-
"dictum scriptum dedictum, et
"breve Regis quod eis inde venit."
Nothing further appears on the
roll, except an adjournment.

[1] From the four MSS., as above,
but corrected by the record, *Placita
coram Rege*, "*Rex*," R° 32, d. It
there appears that Richard de
Wegenholt was indicted for felony
before Justices of Oyer and
Terminer in Suffolk, that a *Capias*
issued, and that, after it was
returned "Non est inventus," he
was outlawed in the County Court
of Suffolk.

[2] The words *Nota* de are omitted
from C., and the words de Utlagerie
are omitted from H. and D.

[3] The words a luy are omitted
from D.

[4] According to the roll "Modo
". . . apud Westmonasterium
"venit prædictus Ricardus de
"Wegenholt et reddidit se prisonæ
"Marescalciæ Regis hic in Curia,
"&c., occasione prædicta, qui com-
"mittitur Marescallo, &c. Et
"statim per Marescallum ductus
"venit. Et quæsitum est ab eo si
"quid pro se habeat vel dicere
"sciat quare ad judicium super
"utlagaria prædicta versus eum
"procedi non debeat in hac parte,
"qui dicit quod utlagaria prædicta
"ei nocere non debet, dicit enim
"quod ipse, prædicta die Lunæ
"proxima post festum Sancti
"Jacobi Apostoli, quando utlagaria
"prædicta in dicto Comitatu
"Suffolciæ in ipsum extitit pro-
"mulgata, et diu ante, et post,
"captus fuit et in prisona domini
"Regis Staffordiæ certis de causis
"detentus, ita quod ad Comitatum
"tentum prædicta die Lunæ,
"quando utlagaria prædicta in
"ipsum extitit promulgata, nullo
"modo comparere potuit seu se
"ibidem reddidisse, &c.

"Et super hoc dominus Rex
"misit Justiciariis suis hic quan-
"dam certificationem per Willel-
"mum de Clyntone, Comitem
"Huntygndoniæ, et Custodem
"forestæ suæ citra Trentam,
"factam, imprisonamentum præ-
"dictum testificantem una cum
"brevi eidem Willelmo de certifi-
"catione prædicta in Cancellaria
"Regis mittenda directo." The

No. 21.

of the Exigent issued againt him, even though he were acquitted of the felony, the chattels will be forfeited; therefore, even though the outlawry be reversed, it is not thereby proved that the chattels are not forfeited unless the fact were that the imprisonment had been proved to be at the time at which the Exigent issued; and that is not proved, but only imprisonment at the time at which the outlawry was pronounced.

Assise of Nuisance. (21.) § Assise of Nuisance in respect of a way stopped. And there was pleaded in bar unity of pos-

No. 21.

A.D. 1345.

Thorpe. Par lexigende issue sur luy, tut fuit il acquite de la felonie, les chateux serrount forfaites; donqes, tut soit lutlagerie reverse, par tant nest pas prove qe les chateux ne sount pas forfaites sil ne fuit issint qe lenprisonement fuit[1] prove al temps qe lexigende issit; et ceo nest pas prove, mes soulement quant lutlagerie fuit pronuncie.[2]

(21.)[3] § Assise Danusaunce dun chimyn estope. Et fuit plede en barre par unite de possession de

Assise Danu-sance.[4]
[Fitz. *Nusauns* 3.]

writ to the Earl of Huntingdon, and his certificate in return are set out at length, as well as a writ to the Justices of the King's Bench, reciting the above facts, and directing them "quod, inspecta certifica-" tione prædicta, ulterius super " adnullationem utlagariæ præ-" dictæ fieri facerent quod de jure " et secundum legem et consuetu-" dinem regni nostri Angliæ fuerit " faciendum.

" Et idem Ricardus de Wegen-" holt petit quod utlagaria prædicta " non cedat ei in præjudicium, sed " potius revocetur et adnulletur " juxta tenorem brevis domini " Regis prædicti, &c.

" Et quia, inspectis recordo et " processu utlagariæ prædictæ, nec " non certificatione prædicti Wil-" lelmi de Clyntone, compertum " est quod prædictus Ricardus de " Wegenholt, tempore utlagariæ " prædictæ, et diu ante, et post, in " prisona domini Regis Staffordiæ " supradicta extitit detentus, et " non est juri consonum quod " aliquis de regno Regis utiagetur " dum in prisona sic existat, " consideratum est quod utlagaria " prædicta in ipsum Ricardum, ut " præmittitur, promulgata revo-cetur, et penitus adnulletur, et " idem Ricardus de Wegenholt ad

" communem legem regni Angliæ " restituatur, et terras et tenementa " sua [an erasure after sua, which " word is also written on an " erasure], si quæ in manum Regis, " occasione utlagariæ prædictæ, " capta fuerint, rehabeat, &c."

[1] H., and D., ne fust.

[2] According to the roll, after the reversal of outlawry Richard de Wegenholt had the King's pardon as to " sectam pacis nostræ quo ad " nos pertinet pro feloniis, ... " ac etiam utlagarias si quæ in " ipsum his occasionibus fuerint " promulgatæ . . .

" Et super hoc idem Ricardus " de Wegenholt dicit quod terræ " et tenementa sua in Comitatu " Bukinghamiæ seisita sunt, &c., " occasione utlagariæ prædictæ, et " petit breve Vicecomiti Buking-" hamiæ de terris et tenementis " suis prædictis sibi liberandis, &c. " Et ei conceditur. Et præcep-" tum est Vicecomiti Bukinghamiæ " quod omnia terras et tenementa " ipsius Ricardi seisita, &c., " occasione prædicta, &c., rehabere " faciat eidem Ricardo, &c."

Nothing is said about chattels.

[3] From the four MSS. as above.

[4] The marginal note in L. is Assise only; in H., Assise de Nusaunce; in C., Anusaunce only.

No. 22.

A.D. 1345. session of both lands (that is to say, of the land in which, and of the land to which, the way was claimed) in the time of King Edward I. To this the plaintiff said that there had always before been a way out of this land to a mill-pool to which he claims to use it, and that the person in whom the defendant alleges unity of possession had daughters who made partition of his inheritance, and that, upon the allotment of the purparties, the mill, with the way, was allotted to one whose estate the plaintiff has, and so he was seised, &c.—SHARSHULLE. Assise of Nuisance lies only for that which is appendant, for it does not lie to have an easement as in gross except by specialty, and judgment to that effect has often been given by the sages of the law. Therefore, which will you do—aid yourself and have the assise charged as in respect of something appendant, or on the other hand rely on the partition, to the effect that it serves you for title? For, on making partition between parceners, rent or other profit in the purparty of another parcener cannot be reserved without a specialty.—*Skipwith.* The parcener is tenant of the estate of her ancestor, and for the same reason for which the ancestor had the way to the mill the one who holds will, in respect of her estate, have the same way.—*Grene.* Yes, and therefore, according to the opinion of many, this plea is never a bar.—SHARSHULLE. Can not one have a way even without any land, and can he not have an Assise in respect of that way? Suppose then that you had a way by grant from me where you had no freehold, and afterwards purchased land, would you not have an Assise by reason thereof? as meaning to say that he would.[1]

Assise of Novel Disseisin.

(22.) § Assise of Novel Disseisin in which a deed of

---

[1] There is a reference in the Harleian MS. to Y.B., Hil., 21 Edw. III., No. 5, fo. 2, as the conclusion of this case. The Assise was awarded.

No. 22.

lune terre et de lautre, saver,[1] en quel et a quel,
&c., en temps laiel le Roi. A quei le pleintif dit
qe tut temps devant il y avoit chimyn outre[2] cele
terre al estanke[3] del molyn a[4] quel il cleyme pur
le faire, et qe cely en qi il allegge la unite de
possession avoit filles qe departirent son heritage, et
qe sur lallotement de la[5] purpartie le[6] molyn ov
le chimyn fuit allote a un qi estat le pleintif ad,
et issint fuit il seisi, &c.—Schar. Assise Danusance[7]
ne git forqe dappendance, qar desement aver come
un[8] gros par especialte[9] ne git il pas, et ceo ad
este ajuge sovent par les sages. Par quei le quel
voilletz, eider et charger[10] lassise com de chose
appendant, ou autrement par force de la purpartie
qe ceo vous seert pur title? Qar entre parceners sur
purpartie faire homme ne[11] poet reserver rente et
autre profit en autri purpartie sanz especialte.—
Skyp. La parcenere est tenant del estat son auncestre, et par mesme la resoun qe launcestre avoit
le chimyn au molyn avéra ele qe tient, de son estat,
mesme le chimyn.—*Grene.* Oyl, et pur ceo, al entent de plusours, ceo nest[12] unqes barre.—Schar.
Ne poet homme aver chimyn tut sanz terre, et de
cel chimyn ne poet il aver Assise? Mettetz donqes
qe vous avietz un chimyn de mon grant la ou vous
navietz nul franktenement, et puis vous purchacetz
terre, naverez vous Assise par cause de cele? *quasi
diceret sic.*[13]

(22.)[14] § *Assisa Novæ Disseisinæ* ou fait launcestre

---

[1] saver is omitted from H. and C.

[2] L., and D., entre.

[3] D., et lestanke, instead of al estanke.

[4] a is omitted from L.

[5] la is from D. alone.

[6] C. de.

[7] H. de Nusaunce.

[8] L., and D., dun.

[9] L., reson despecialte.

[10] H., chacer; C., chascer.

[11] ne is from D. alone.

[12] H., and C., ne fuit.

[13] MSS. of Y.B., *non.* But this does not seem to agree with the context.

[14] From the four MSS., as above.

No. 23.

the plaintiff's ancestor, with warranty, was pleaded in bar. And it was alleged that he had nothing, except jointly with the plaintiff for their lives. And this was an Assise before HILLARY. And afterwards the plaintiff was barred as to one moiety, and recovered the other moiety by judgment.—See among the *Recorda*.[1]

Assise of Novel Disseisin.

(23.) § Assise of Novel Disseisin. Cauntele's case. It was pleaded in bar that the tenements were given to W. and to K. his wife for their lives, and after their death to W. the son of W. and the heirs of his body, and, if he should die without heir of his body, to R. his brother and the heirs of his body, and, if R. should die without heir of his body, to the right heirs of W. the father, and that W. the son and R. died without issue, and, after the death of W., one A., daughter and heir of W. the father, granted the reversion to the tenant, and that K. attorned, and afterwards leased her estate to the plaintiff, and K. is now dead, and therefore the tenant entered upon his reversion; judgment whether an Assise, &c. The plaintiff said that R. the son of W. survived W. his father, and at that time the fee simple was in him as of his purchase, and showed that she in virtue of whose grant the tenant claims the reversion was of the half-blood to R., and therefore R.'s right resorted to the plaintiff as to uncle and heir of the whole blood, and prayed the assise for damages.—*Skipwith*. If an action had to be used in respect of this right, no other person would have an action but the right heir of W. the father, and that would be our grantor: for even though it were the fact that the fee simple had been in R. (which does not appear to be the case, for the time of the fee simple appears to have been then in suspense) still, inasmuch as he had not possession in his own person, that right cannot give an action, nor

---

[1] A reference apparently to some collection of extracts.

No. 23.

ove garrantie fuit plede en barre. Et fuit allegge qil navoit rienz si noun joint ove le pleintif a lour vies. Et ceo fuit une Assise devant HILL. Et puis par agarde il fuit barre de la moite et recoverist lautre moite.—*Vide inter recorda.*[1]

(23.)[2] § *Assisa Novæ Disseisinæ.* Cauntele. Plede *Assisa*
fuit en barre coment les tenementz furent dones a *Novæ*
Disseisinæ.
W. et a K. sa femme a lour vies, et apres lour decees a W. le fitz W. et les heirs de son corps, et si, &c., a R. son frere et les heirs de son corps, et si, &c., as dreits heirs W. le pere, et coment[3] W. le fitz et R. devierunt sanz issue, et apres la mort W. une A. fille et heir W. le pere graunta la reversion al tenant, et K. sattourna, et puis lessa son estat al pleintif, et K. est ore mort, par quei il[4] entra en sa reversion ; jugement si assise, &c. Le pleintif dist qe R. le fitz W. survesquit W. son pere, a quel temps le fee pure fuit en luy come de son purchace, et moustra qe cele[5] par qi graunt le tenant cleime la reversion fuit del demi sank a R., par quei le dreit de R. resorti al pleintif com a uncle et heir del entier sank, et pria assise pur damages.—*Skyp.* Si accion fuit a user[6] de cel dreit, nul autre avereit accion forqe le dreit heir W. le pere, et ceo serreit nostre granteresse : qar tut fuit il qe fee pure ust este en R., come il semble pas, qar le temps de fee pure fuit suspensif adonqes, unqore, par tant qil ne fuit pas possessione en luy, cel dreit ceo ne poet doner accion, *nec per consequens*

---

[1] The last sentence is omitted from H.

[2] From the four MSS. as above.

[3] D., counta coment

[4] H., ele.

[5] L., celuy.

[6] L., ueser.

No. 24.

A.D. 1345. consequently a right to his heir.—*R. Thorpe.* There is no doubt but that he had a right, and that by purchase, which could not by any possibility descend to her of the half blood : for the case is quite different from that which it would have been if R. had had such a right by descent from W. his father.—And afterwards the parties came to terms.—According to the opinion of the COURT the plaintiff would have been barred.—See fully among the *Recorda.*

Con- (24.) § A writ of Conspiracy was brought against a
spiracy. man and his wife, and others, on the ground that the defendants procured and abetted a woman to sue an Appeal of the death of her husband against the plaintiff, with regard to which appeal he passed quit. And the record was to the effect that the woman was non-suited. And a writ issued to the Sheriff and to the Coroners to certify ·whether they had an indictment, and none was found, and for that reason he passed quit, but the words of the writ were "*acquietatus fuit.*" —*R. Thorpe.* The writ supposes an acquittal, whereas it is still possible that he may be convicted of the same act by way of indictment; judgment of the writ,

No. 24.

dreit a son heir.—[*R.*] *Thorpe.* Il nest pas doute
qil navoit dreit, et ceo par purchace, quele par nulle
possibilite[1] poet descendre a cele[2] del demi sank :
qar il est tut autre qe si R. ust eu tiel dreit par
descente de W. son pere.—*Et postea concordarunt.*—
Per opinionem Curiæ le pleintif ust este barre.—
Vide inter recorda plene, &c.

(24.)[3] § Brief de Conspiracie porte vers un homme Con-
et sa femme, et autres, de ceo qe les defendantz spiracie.
procurent et abetterent une femme de suir une
Appel de la mort son baron vers le pleintif, a quel
Appel il passa quites.[4] Et le recorde fuit qe la
femme[5] fuit noun suy. Et brief issit a Vicounte et
as[6] Coroners de certifier sils avoit enditement, et
nul trove, par quei il passa quites, mes le brief
voleit *acquietatus fuit.*—[*R.*] *Thorpe.* Le brief suppose acquitaunce, ou possible est unqore qe par
enditement de mesme le fait il serra soille ; juge-

---

[1] C., purchace.

[2] L., celuy.

[3] From the four MSS., as above.
The record is probably that found
among the *Placita coram Regè,*
Mich., 19 Edw. III., R° 78. It
there appears that an action of Conspiracy was brought by Eustace de
Foleville against Richard Chaumberleyn, William Whelchare, and
several other persons, among whom
were Thomas Tochet of Asshewelle
and Joan his wife.

[4] According to the roll the
declaration was that the defendants
" die Lunæ post festum Sancti
" Michaelis anno regni Regis nunc
" decimo septimo, conspiratione
" inter ipsos apud Wymundewolde
" præhabita, ipsum Eustachium
" per Ceciliam quæ fuit uxor Alani
" Damysele de morte prædicti

" Alani quondam viri sui in Curia
" Regis per breve retornabile coram
" ipso Rege in Octabis Purifica-
" tionis beatæ Mariæ anno regni
" Regis nunc decimo octavo in
" Comitatu Rotelandiæ appellari,
" et ipsum in prisona Marescalciæ
" Regis coram Rege a quindena
" Sancti Johannis Baptistæ tunc
" proxime sequente usque in
" Octabas Sancti Hillarii proxime
" sequentes, scilicet anno regni
" Regis nunc decimo nono, quo
" die idem Eustachius per con-
" siderationem Curiæ Regis inde
" quietus recessit, detineri falso et
" maliciose procurarunt contra
" formam ordinationis in hujus-
" modi casu provisæ."

[5] femme is omitted from C.

[6] as is from D. alone.

No. 25.

because the writ lies only where the plaintiff has been acquitted, and, if it could lie in the present case, it would be in another form, that is to say, "*ivit sine die.*"—WILLOUGHBY. At any rate he passed quit as to this Appeal, because the woman, with regard to what was to follow, lost her action by the non-suit.—Afterwards exception was taken to the writ as brought against a woman, because it cannot be understood in law that a woman could be supposed to conspire, and particularly a *feme covert*, for, if this writ were good, for the same reason one would be good if it were brought against a husband and wife alone, and it could not be understood that a wife, who is at the will of her husband, could conspire with him, because the whole would be accounted the act of the husband. —And the writ was adjudged to be good.

Quid juris clamat. (25.) § A *Quid juris clamat* was brought against a lady by Peter de Gildesburgh.—*Grene.* Whereas the reversion is granted to Peter for his life, the remainder being to others in fee tail, &c., the lady is ready to surrender in a particular manner, if the Court can permit it, that is to say, saving to herself £20 *per*

No. 25.

ment du brief, qar le brief ne git pas mes ou le
pleintif est acquite, et sil girreit en le cas ou il
est ceo serreit sur autre fourme, saver, *ivit sine die.*
—WILBY. Au meins il passa quites a cel Appel,
qar la femme a remenant perdist accion par la
nounsuite.— Puis le brief est chalenge porte vers
femme, qar de ley ne poet estre entendue qe femme
duist conspirer, nomement femme covert, qar si cest
brief fuit bone, par mesme la reson sil fuit porte
soul vers le baron et sa femme, et ceo ne serreit
pas entendu qe femme, qest a la volunte son baron,
purra ove luy conspirer, pur ceo qe tut serreit
acompte le fait le baron.[1]—Et le brief est agarde bon.[2]

(25.)[3] § *Quid juris clamat* vers une dame par Piers *Quid juris clamat.*
de Gildesburghe.—*Grene.* La[4] ou la reversion est [Fitz.,
grante a P. pur sa vie, le remeindre as autres en *Surrendre* 8.]
fee taille, &c., la dame est prest a rendre en manere
si la Court la poet soeffrer,[5] saver, salvaunt[6] a luy

---

[1] According to the roll, the defendants, Richard Chaumberleyn and William Whelchare (who alone appeared) " singillatim petunt judi- " cium de brevi, &c., quia singilla- " tim dicunt quod in prædicto " brevi supponitur conspirationem " prædictam fieri per ipsos Ri- " cardum Chaumberleyn, et Wil- " lelmum Whelchare, et prædictos " Thomam Tochet et Johannam " uxorem ejus, et alios in brevi " prædicto nominatos, ex quo iidem " Thomas et Johanna uxor ejus, " dummodo ipsa cooperta sit de " ipso Thoma viro suo sunt una et " eadem persona, et conspiratio " non potest fieri nisi inter diversas " personas, quod nullo modo potest " intelligi inter ipsum Thomam et " præfatam Johannam, quæ sunt " una et eadem persona."

[2] According to the roll a day was given to the parties in the King's Bench on the Quinzaine of St. Hilary. On that day there was a further adjournment " datus est " eis dies," but the words on the roll which have followed the word " dies " have been erased, and nothing further appears in this place. There is, however, a sub-sequent entry on the same skin to the effect that the plaintiff " obtulit " se quarto die versus prædictos " Thomam Tochet et Johannam " uxorem ejus et alios in prædicto " brevi nominatos," who did not appear. There was an award of *Distringas, alias,* and *pluries* to have their bodies, but nothing more.

[3] From L., C., and D.

[4] La is omitted from C.

[5] D., seoffrer.

[6] L., sauvant; D., savant.

No. 26.

annum for her life.—WILLOUGHBY. Who will be able to charge the land to the lady?—*Grene.* When the surrender is made on that condition, it is reasonable that the land should be charged.—WILLOUGHBY. Will the tenant in tail be charged with the rent after Peter's death?—*Grene.* It is right that he should be, because he would not have the land by virtue of the fine until after the lady's death, and if he has it before her death by means of the surrender, it is right that he should be charged with the rent reserved on the surrender.—WILLOUGHBY. This surrender does not extend to any one but the person to whom the surrender is made.—HILLARY. Certainly it does so.—WILLOUGHBY. It does not.—*Grene.* Suppose Peter had a fee simple in the reversion, would not the charge reserved on the surrender be good?—as meaning to say that it would—consequently it is so in this case.—WILLOUGHBY. It would not be good.—And the surrender in that manner was refused.—Therefore the lady attorned.

Quod permittat. (26.) § The Prior of Haverholme brought a *Quod permittat* in respect of common of pasture as in gross. —*Moubray,* as to a certain number of acres, alleged joint tenancy, and as to the rest said "never seised as appendant," for he understood that the Prior had claimed the common as appendant.—*Skipwith.* You

No. 26.

xx*li.* par an pur sa vie.—WILBY. Qi purra charger
la terre a la dame?—*Grene.* Quant le rendre est
fait sur la condicion il est resonable.—WILBY. Serra
le tenant en la taille apres la mort P. charge de
la rente?—*Grene.* Cest resoun, qar il navereit la
terre par la fyn tanqe apres la mort la femme, et
si par le rendre il avera devant, resoun est qil soit
charge de la rente reserve par le rendre.—WILBY.
Cele[1] rendre sestent a nulle forqe a celuy a qi le
rendre est.—HILL. Certes si fait.—WILBY. Noun
fait.—*Grene.* Jeo pose qe P. ust fee simple en la
reversion, ne serreit pas la charge bone reserve sur
le rendre?—*quasi diceret sic—per' consequens* a ore.—
WILBY. Noun serreit.—Et la rendre par la manere
refuse.—Par quei la dame attourna.

(26.)[2] § Le Priour de Haverholme porta *Quod* *Quod*
permittat.
permittat de comune de pasture come gros.[3]—*Moubray,*
quant a certein noumbre des acres alleggea jointenance, et quant al remenant dist qunqes seisi come
appendant, qar il entendist qil ust clame come
appendant.—*Skyp.* Vous veietz bien coment la noun

---

[1] D., cest.

[2] From L., H., C., and D., but
corrected by the record, *Placita de
Banco*, Mich., 19 Edw. III., R⁰ 199.
It there appears that the *Quod
permittat* was brought by William
Prior of Haverholme against David
son of David de Fletwyke, knight.

[3] The count was, according to
the record, that " Henricus nuper
" Prior, &c., prædecessor, &c., fuit
" seisitus de communia prædicta
" in Leuesyngham, videlicet com-
" muniandi in tribus partibus
" duarum millium acrarum terræ,
" cum omnimodis averiis suis,
" quolibet anno post blada messa,
" vincta, et asportata, quousque

" dictæ terræ iterum reseminentur,
" et in quarta parte ejusdem terræ
" per totum annum, et in ducentis
" acris prati quolibet anno post
" fena falcata, levata, et asportata,
" usque ad festum Purificationis
" beatæ Mariæ, et in quingentis
" acris moræ per totum annum,
" ut de jure ecclesiæ suæ beatæ
" Mariæ de Haverholme, tempore
" pacis, tempore Edwardi Regis
" avi domini Regis nunc, &c., et
" de qua, David de Fletwyke pater
" prædicti David filii David de
" Fletwyke, cujus heres ipse est,
" injuste et sine judicio disseisivit
" Henricum nuper Priorem de
" Haverholme."

No. 27.

A.D. 1345. see plainly how non-seisin would deprive us of the action altogether, and therefore we pray to be discharged of any plea in abatement of the writ: for seisin in one part is seisin throughout, and gives an Assise throughout, and consequently non-seisin in one part is non-seisin throughout.—HILLARY. He will not have to plead as to a parcel which he holds jointly; and therefore answer.—*Skipwith*. Sole tenant; ready, &c. And as to that parcel and the rest he has not answered, for we claim as in gross.—*Moubray*. I did not understand that. What have you to prove the common?—*Skipwith*. You shall not be admitted to that. And afterwards he passed on, and made himself a title.—And *Moubray* traversed the seisin.—And the other side said the contrary.

Assise. (27.) § The Prior of the Hospital of St. John of Jerusalem brought an Assise, and it was found by verdict that a Commander of the Hospital had by deed enfeoffed the defendant for his life, yielding a

No. 27.

seisine est a toller[1] laccion en tut, par quei de plee A.D. 1345.
al brief nous prioms estre[2] descharge : qar seisine
en une parcelle est seisine par tut, et doun Lassise
par tut, et *per consequens* noun seisine en une parcelle est noun seisine par tut.—HILL. Il pledra pas
a la parcelle quel il tient joint ; et pur ceo responez.—*Skyp.* Soul tenant ; prest, &c. Et quant a
la parcelle et del remenant il nad pas respondu,
qar nous clamoms come gros.—*Moubray.* Ceo nentendi jeo pas. Quei avetz de la comune ?--*Skyp.*
Vous navendretz pas. Et puis passa et[3] se[4] fist
title.—Et *Moubray* traversa la seisine.[5]—*Et alii e
contra.*[6]

(27.)[7] § Le Prior del Hospital de Seint Johan Assise.
[19 Li.
Ass., 9 ;
Fitz.,
Feffements
et Faits,
68.]
porta Assise, et trove fuit par verdit qun Comandour
del Hospital avoit feffe par fait le defendant[8] pur

---

[1] L., a tollire ; D., attollir, instead of a toller.

[2] D., destre.

[3] The words passa et are omitted from D.

[4] H., and C., ceo.

[5] According to the record, the plea was " quod prædictus Prior " de communia prædicta actionem " versus eum habere non debet, " quia dicit quod cum prædictus " Prior per narrationem suam " supponit prædictum Henricum " nuper Priorem, prædecessorem, " &c., seisitum fuisse de communia " prædicta, idem Henricus nuper " Prior, &c., prædecessor, &c., " nunquam fuit seisitus de eadem " communia, sicut prædictus Prior " dicit, et hoc paratus est verificare, " &c., unde petit judicium, &c."

[6] According to the record there was a replication, upon which issue was joined, " quod prædictus David " eum ab actione sua prædicta per " hoc excludere non debet, quia

" dicit quod prædictus Henricus " nuper Prior, &c., prædecessor, " &c., fuit seisitus de communia " prædicta sicut ipse per breve " suum supponit."

The *Venire* was awarded, but nothing further appears on the roll, except an adjournment.

[7] From the four MSS., as above, but corrected by the record, *Placita de Banco*, Mich., 19 Edw. III., Rº 140. It there appears that the action was brought before Justices of Assise in the County of Somerset by the Prior of the Hospital of St. John of Jerusalem in England against William Caleware, in respect of one messuage, six acres of land, and two acres of meadow, in Mertok (Martock).

[8] C., defendant, but on an erasure and in a later hand ; D., tenant on an erasure and in a different hand. In the other two MSS., the reading is pleintif.

No. 27.

certain rent, in the time of the Prior's predecessor, and that the present Prior was seised of that rent and received it. And the Assise said that by custom such Commanders could lease a term by roll of Court, but not a freehold, and that the Prior did not know of this lease [for life], and also that the Commander took *gersuma* for entry. And there was touched by the

No. 27.

sa vie, rendant certein rente, en temps le predecessour
le Prior, de quel le Prior qore est fuit seisi et la
resceut. Et disoint qe par usage tiels Comaundours
pount lesser terme par roulle de Court, mes noun
pas frank tenement, et qe le Prior ne savoit de cel
lees, et auxint qe le Comaundour prist gersome[1]
pur lentre.[2] Et fuit touche par COURT qe par nul

---

[1] H., and D., gersone.

[2] The Assise was taken by default, and, according to the record, the verdict was " quod " quidam Robertus de Nafforde " quondam fuit Magister et Præ- " ceptor de Temple Coumbe per " prædictum Priorem deputatus, " ibidem commoraturus ad volun- " tatem ipsius Prioris, et ad " voluntatem suam ammotivus. Et " dicunt quod in manerio de Temple " Coumbe habetur talis consuetudo " quod Magister et Præceptor " ejusdem manerii qui pro tempore " fuerit potest dimittere et ab " antiquo dimittere consuevit tene- " menta quæ tenentur de prædicto " manerio in Bondagio, quando- " cumque hujusmodi tenementa in " manum ipsius Prioris per mortem " ea tenentium in bondagio con- " tigerit devenire, quibuscumque " personis qui ea de Præceptore qui " pro tempore fuerit capere volu- " erint tenenda in bondagio per " rotulum Curiæ per certa servitia " solvenda, et non per scriptum, " nec per aliud factum nisi per " Rotulum Curiæ, sed alia tene- " menta quæ sunt de dominicis " terris manerii prædicti dimitti " non possunt per Præceptorem " nec dimitti consueverunt. Et " dixerunt quod tenementa præ- " dicta fuerunt de dominicis terris " manerii prædicti. Et dixerunt " quod prædictus Robertus de

" Nafforde dimisit tenementa præ- " dicta prædicto Willelmo ad " terminum vitæ suæ per Rotulum " Curiæ manerii prædicti tenenda " per servitia sex solidoram et octo " denariorum per annum, nec non " per quatuor libras pro ingressu " habendo in tenementis illis, præ- " dicto Priore de dimissione illa " nihil sciente, quas quidem " quatuor libras prædictus Willel- " mus soluit prædicto Roberto pro " ingressu prædicto. Et dixerunt " quod idem Robertus soluit præ- " dicto Priori finem et redditum " prædictos inter alios redditus " manerii prædicti. Dixerunt etiam " quod idem Willelmus nunquam " habuit aliquem alium statum " in tenementis illis, et petierunt " discretionem Justiciariorum. Re- " cognitores quæsiti de damnis " prædicti Prioris si disseisina " adjudicetur, et quantum prædicta " tenementa valent per annum, qui " assederunt damna, si, &c., ad " viginti et sex solidos, et octo " denarios, et dixerunt quod tene- " menta prædicta valent per " annum, ultra redditum prædic- " tum, sex solidos et octo denarios. " Et dixerunt quod prædictus Prior " seisitus fuit de redditu prædicto " inter alios redditus manerii præ- " dicti tempore Magistri qui nunc " est, post ammotionem prædicti " Roberti de Nafford quondam " Magistri, &c. . . . . ."

No. 28.

A.D. 1345. COURT the point that by no custom could bailiff or steward lease a freehold.—*Gaynesford.* It is a common custom throughout the whole realm to make such leases through stewards and others deputed by the lords; and since the defendant paid a fine for his entry, and the Prior himself· has since accepted his rent, it is not right that he should be ousted, and it would be an evil precedent.—Nevertheless the Prior recovered.

Quod permittat. (28.) § The Prior of Haverholme brought a *Quod permittat villanos facere sectam ad molendinum.—Grene.* What have you in proof of this suit and profit which you claim in our freehold?—*R. Thorpe.* In the time of the King's grandfather a fine was levied between your grandfather and our predecessor, by which your ancestor acknowledged the suit to the mill to be the right of our predecessor, and of his church, &c., as that which our predecessor had before by grant from his more remote ancestor, &c., and so our predecessor was seised.—*Grene.* And inasmuch as he does not produce fine, or transcript of fine, or any other specialty, judgment whether he ought to be answered.

No. 28.

A.D. 1345.

usage poet baillif ne seneschalle lesser fraunctenement.—*Gayn.* Ceo cy est comune usage par tote la
terre de faire tiel lees par seneschalles et par autres
deputes par les seignours; et quant il paia fine pur
son entre, et puis le Prior mesme ad accepte sa
rente, ceo nest pas resoun qil soit ouste, et ceo
serreit malveys ensample.[1]—*Non obstante* le Prior
recoverist.[2]

(28.)[3] § Le Prior de Haverholme porta *Quod per-*
mittat villanos facere sectam ad molendinum.—*Grene.*
Quei avetz de cele suite et profit qe vous clametz
en nostre franktenement?—[*R.*] *Thorpe.* En temps
laiel le Roi fine se leva entre vostre aiel et nostre
predecessour, par quel vostre auncestre conissat la
suite estre le dreit nostre predecessour, et de sa
eglise, &c., com ceo qe nostre predecessour avoit
avant del grant son auncestre paramount, &c., et
issint seisi.—*Grene.* Et desicome il ne moustre fine,
ne transcript,[4] ne autre especialte, jugement sil deive

Quod
permittat.

---

[1] D , ensaunple.

[2] After the verdict, according to the record, " super hoc dies datus " fuit prædicto Priori de audiendo " judicio suo apud Welles die Jovis " proxima post festum Sancti " Laurentii, &c. Ad quem diem " . . . . venit præ- " dictus Prior per . . . attorna- " tum suum, et datus fuit eis dies " de audiendo judicio suo super " veredicto prædicto hic a die " Sancti Michaelis in xv dies, &c. " Et modo venit prædictus Prior, " per attornatum suum, et petit " judicium super veredicto præ- " dicto.
" Ideo consideratum est quod " prædictus Prior recuperet inde " seisinam suam per visum recog- " nitorum Assisæ prædictæ, et

" damna sua prædicta. Et præ- " dictus Willelmus in misericordia, " &c."
There is a similar case, but with different defendants, on R° 140, d The result was the same. There is again another against other defendants with the same result on R° 158.

[3] From the four MSS., as above, but corrected by the record, *Placita de Banco*, Mich., 19 Edw. III., R° 199, d. It there appears that the action was brought by the Prior of Haverholme against David son of David de Fletwyke, knight, " quod permittat villanos suos de " Leusyngham facere sectam ad " molendinum ipsius Prioris de " Leusyngham."

[4] D., transescript.

No. 29.

A.D. 1345. *R. Thorpe.* And we also pray judgment since we allege a fine, which he does not deny, and which, if he would deny it, we would verify by record; and we pray seisin, and our damages.—And afterwards *Grene* passed on, and traversed the seisin.—And the other side said the contrary.

Annuity.

(29.) § A writ of Annuity was brought for the Prioress of Haliwell (or Holywell), on an ordinance of the Ordinary, against a parson, on which the count was that, on submission to the Ordinary by the parson's predecessor of a dispute respecting tithes between him and the Prioress's predecessor, who claimed tithes, the Ordinary ordained that the parson should have the tithes on condition of paying the annuity, &c., to the Prioress and her successors, in virtue of which ordinance her predecessors and she

No. 29.

estre respondu.—[*R.*] *Thorpe.* Et nous jugement, A.D. 1345.
del houre qe nous alleggeoms fine, quel il ne dedit
pas, et quel, sil voudra dedire, nous voloms averer par
recorde; et prioms seisine, et noz damages.—Et puis
Grene passa, et traversa la seisine.—*Et alii e contra.*[1]

(29.)[2] § Annuite pur la Prioresse de Haliwelle, sur Annuite.
ordinance dordeigner, vers une persone, countaunt qe
par submission del predecessour la persone sur debat
des dismes entre luy et la predecessoresse la Prioresse,
qe clama dismes, qe ordeigna qe la persone avereit
les dismes, fesaunt a la Prioresse et ses successours,
&c., lannuite, &c., par force de quel ordinaunce ses

---

[1] According to the record the count was " quod quidam Simon " de Pykworthe, quondam Prior de " Haverholme, prædecessor, &c., " fuit seisitus de prædicta secta " ad prædictum molendinum per " manus villanorum prædicti " David, scilicet per manus Wil- " lelmi Riche villani ejusdem " David, de omnimodis bladis " molendis et provenientibus de " uno mesuagio et una bovata " terræ cum pertinentiis in " Leusyngham" and in like manner by the hands of fifteen other villeins named, each in respect of one messuage and one bovate of land in the same vill, " et similiter per manus omnium " terrarum et tenementorum præ- " dictorum tenentium, ad sextum " decimum vas, ut de feodo et jure " ecclesiæ ipsius Prioris beatæ " Mariæ de Haverholme, tempore " pacis, tempore Edwardi Regis " avi domini Regis nunc, ... " quousque prædictus David per " octo annos ante diem impetra- " tionis brevis . . . . prædictos " villanos suos prædictam sectam

" ad prædictum molendinum facere " non permisit, sed illam hucusque " subtraxit." The plea was " quod, " cum prædictus Prior superius in " narratione sua supponit prædic- " tum Simonem de Pykworthe " nuper Priorem, &c., prædeces- " sorem, &c., seisitum fuisse de " prædicta secta per manus præ- " dictorum Willelmi Riche, villani, " et aliorum villanorum ipsius " David, in forma prædicta, idem " Simon nuper Prior, prædecessor, " &c., non fuit seisitus de prædicta " secta per manus prædictorum " villanorum. Et hoc paratus est " verificare, &c., unde petit judi- " cium, &c."
Then follows a replication, upon which issue was joined, " quod " prædictus Simon nuper Prior, " prædecessor, &c., fuit seisitus de " prædicta secta, ut de jure ecclesiæ " suæ prædictæ, per manus villa- " norum prædictorum, prout ipse " superius versus eum narravit."
The award of the *Venire* and one subsequent adjournment only appear on the roll.

[2] From the four MSS., as above.

No. 30.

A.D. 1345. were seised, &c., until the parson withdrew the annuity; and she made *profert* of a deed in witness of the facts. —*Notton.* You see plainly how she has taken for title the ordinance of the Ordinary, and has not counted in what place the ordinance was made, and, if that ordinance were traversed, it could not, according to her count, be tried; judgment of the count.—And the Court agreed that the count was faulty in that particular.—And afterwards *Notton, gratis*, passed on, and prayed aid of the Prioress of Haliwell and of the Ordinary.—*Grene.* He ought not to have aid of the Prioress, because she is herself a party, and it cannot in accordance with any law be understood that she could join in aid against herself; and aid of the Ordinary, without aid of the patron, is not grantable; therefore in this case aid is not grantable either of the one or of the other.—Kelshulle. If the parson cannot have aid of the Ordinary without having aid of the patron, and he cannot be a party alone, he must therefore have aid of both.—Stouford, *ad idem.* Even though the Prioress be herself plaintiff, aid of her is grantable from several points of view.— Willoughby. Let him have aid.

Annuity.   (30.) § William de Edyngton, Warden of the Hospital of St. Cross near Winchester, brought a writ of Annuity against a parson on a title by prescription.

No. 30.

predecessoresses et luy seisiz, &c., tanqe, &c.; et A.D. 1345.
mist avant fait tesmoignant, &c.—*Nottone*. Vous
veietz bien coment il ad pris pur title lordinaunce
dordeigner, et il nad pas counte en quel lieu lordinaunce se fist, quele ordinaunce, si ele fuit traverse,
par son count ne poet estre trie; jugement de
counte.—Et la COURT assentist qe count en ceo
pechea.[1]—Et puis *Nottone*, *gratis*, passa, et pria eide
del Prioresse de Haliwelle et del Ordeigner.—*Grene*.
De la Prioresse ne deit il eide aver, qar ele est
mesme partie, et par nulle ley serra entendu qele
se joindreit[2] en eide countre luy mesme; ne del
Ordeigner saunz patroun eide nest pas grantable;
par quei en ceo cas leide nest pas grantable de lun
ne lautre.[3]—KELL. Si la persone ne poet aver eide
del Ordeigner sanz aver eide del patroun, et il ne
poet soul estre partie, donqes covient qil eit eide
de lun et lautre.[4]—STOUF., *ad idem*. Tut soit la
Prioresse pleintif mesme, a divers[5] regardes eide est
grantable de luy.—WILBY. Eit leide.

(30.)[6] § William de Edyngtone, gardein del Hospital Annuite.
[Fitz.,
de Seint Croys juxt[7] Wyncestre, porta brief Dannuite *Ayde de*
vers une persone sur title de prescripcion.[8] La per- *Roy*, 5;
Proses,
39.]

---

[1] L., pecchea.

[2] H., joindra.

[3] D., del autre.

[4] D., de lautre.

[5] C., diverses.

[6] From the four MSS., as above, but corrected by the record, *Placita de Banco*, Mich., 19 Edw. III., R° 359, d. It there appears that the action was brought by William de Edyntone "Custos domus "Sanctæ Crucis juxta Wynto- "niam," against John Mouner, parson of the church of Stockton (Wilts) in respect of arrears of an annuity of 100*s*.

[7] D., juste.

[8] The declaration was, according to the record, "quod quidam "Robertus de Maydenston, quon- "dam Custos domus prædictæ, "prædecessor ipsius Custodis nunc, "fuit seisitus de prædicto annuo "redditu centum solidorum, ut "de jure domus suæ Sanctæ "Crucis prædictæ, per manus "cujusdam Nicholai Romeyn, "quondam personæ ecclesiæ de "Stoktone prædictæ, prædecessoris, "&c., ... et similiter "omnes Custodes domus prædictæ, "prædecessores, &c., fuerunt

No. 31.

A.D. 1345. The parson prayed aid of the King by reason of the temporalities of the Bishopric of Winchester (of whose patronage he held the church) being in the King's hand, and aid of the Bishop of Salisbury, the Ordinary, &c.—*Grene.* The King has nothing in the patronage except wardship; and suppose any one were guardian by reason of the non-age of an heir, aid of him would not be grantable, nor will it now be granted of the King in this case.—WILLOUGHBY. In the case which you put aid would be granted of the heir, and the parol would demur by reason of his non-age; but in this case the defendant cannot have aid of any one else; therefore let him have aid of the King, &c.— And a Summons to the Ordinary was awarded before suit was made to the King: for according to what was said the case is different from that which it is in Dower where the heir or others are prayed in aid.

Avowry for a heriot.

(31.) § Avowry for a heriot claimed by title of pre-

No. 31.

A.D. 1345.

sone pria eide du Roi par resoun des temporaltes levesqe[1] de Wyncestre en sa mein, de qi patronage il tient leglise, et del Evesqe de Sarum, Ordeigner, &c.[2]—*Grene.* Le Roy nad rienz en le[3] patronage forqe garde; et mettetz qun fuit gardein par noun age dun heir, eide de luy ne serra pas grantable, neque a ore du Roi en ceo cas.—WILBY. En vostre cas eide serreit graunte del heir, et par son[4] noun age la parole demureit; mes en ceo cas il ne poet aver eide dautre; par quei eit leide du Roi, &c. Et somons agarde vers Ordeigner avant la suite fait[5] vers le Roi: qar a ceo qe fuit dit cest altre[6] qen Dowere ou leir ou[7] autres sount prietz en eide.[8]

(31.)[9] § Avowere pur heriete lie par title de pre-

" seisiti de eodem annuo redditu,
" ut de jure domus suæ prædictæ,
" per manus personarum ecclesiæ
" prædictæ, qui pro tempore
" fuerunt, a tempore quo non extat
" memoria usque viginti et novem
" annos ante diem impetrationis
" brevis sui."

[1] C., levesche.

[2] According to the record " Jo-
" hannes . . . . dicit quod,
" tempore quo ipse institutus fuit
" in ecclesia sua prædicta, invenit
" ecclesiam suam de prædicto
" annuo redditu exoneratam, quæ
" quidem ecclesia est de patronatu
" Episcopi Wyntoniensis, cujus
" quidem Episcopatus temporalia
" adnunc sunt in manu domini
" Regis post mortem Adæ nuper
" Episcopi loci prædicti, unde dicit
" quod non potest ecclesiam suam
" prædictam, sine domino Rege, et
" Episcopo Sarum, ejusdem ecclesiæ
" Ordinario, onerare, et petit
" auxilium de domino Rege et
" Episcopo Sarum prædicto."

[3] D., el instead of en le.

[4] H., and C., sa.

[5] fait is omitted from C.

[6] altre is from L. alone.

[7] D., et.

[8] According to the roll " Ideo
" ipse Episcopus Sarum sum-
" moneatur quod sit hic a die
" Sancti Martini in xv dies per
" Justiciarios, &c., ad responden-
" dum simul, &c., si, &c., ...
" et interim loquendum est cum
" domino Rege, &c."

A writ *de procedendo*, reciting the above matters, was afterwards sent to the Justices on the prayer of the plaintiff. The Bishop of Salisbury (the prayee in aid) did not appear. The defendant there-fore pleaded alone, and traversed the alleged seisin, upon which traverse issue was joined.

[9] From the four MSS., as above.

[10] The words pur heriet are from L. alone.

No. 31.

scription in accordance with a custom within a fee.—
Grene. We tell you that the avowant's grandfather
was seised of the same tenements in the time of the
King the grandfather of the present King, and that
what he calls a fee consists only of some small hold-
ings now held of him, and at that time the whole was
in the hand of his ancestor, who enfeoffed such an
one, and such an one his wife, in fee tail, by this
deed, to hold by certain services in lieu of all services;
judgment of this. avowry which is made as in respect
of a seignory and tenancy in fee simple.—*Mutlow.*
That plea is three-fold : one that by reason of our
ancestor's possession in the time of Edward I., the
tenements are not, with regard to us, from all time
subject to heriot, as we suppose by our avowry; the
second is the tenancy in tail; the third is the deed
which discharges ; therefore we pray that he be compelled
to hold to one.—*Pole* took his plea in this form :—
Inasmuch as the plaintiff makes his plaint in respect
of his beast, and we⁻ have avowed as in respect of
our own beast, and he does not maintain that it
is his beast in accordance with his plaint, and so he
departs from his plaint, judgment. — *Grene.* Shall
I not have a plea to your avowry.?—WILLOUGHBY.
Yes, you will have one ; but take one definite plea in
particular.—*Grene* held to the plea that the avowant
had seignory only in fee tail; judgment of the avowry
alleging it to be in fee simple.—*Mutlow.* And, inasmuch as he is a stranger in whose mouth such a plea
does not lie [we pray judgment].—*Grene.* We tell you
that he, and his ancestors, and those· whose estate he
has in the seignory were never seised of a heriot to
be taken from the ter-tenant of the land which we
hold ; ready, &c.—*Mutlow.* Then you do not deny that
the tenements are of the fee of Boseville, nor that the
custom is such throughout the fee.—*Grene.* I have
nothing to do with that, for, even though all the

No. 31.

scripcion sur usage deinz un fee.—*Grene.* Nous vous A.D. 1345.
dioms qe laiel lavowaunt fuit seisi de mesmes les
tenementz en temps le Roi laiel, et ceo qil appelle
fee ne sount qe petites tenures ore tenuz de luy,
et adonqes tut fuit en la mein son auncestre, le
quel feffa un tiel et une tiel sa femme en fee taille
par ceo fait, a tenir par certeins services pur toux
services; jugement de ceste avowere qest fait come
de seignurie et tenance de fee simple.—*Mutl.* Ceo
plee est treble: une qe pur la possession de nostre
auncestre en temps laiel qe les tenementz vers nous
de tut temps, come nous supposoms par lavowere,
ne sount pas herietables; autre la tenance en taille;
le terce le fait qe descharge; par quei nous prioms,
&c.—*Pole* prist le plee disicome le pleintif se pleint
de sa beste, et nous avoms avowe come de nostre
propre beste, et ele ne meintient pas qele est sa
beste come il se pleint, et issint depart il de sa
pleint, jugement.—*Grene.* Navera[1] jeo plee a vostre
avowere?—WILBY. Si averetz, mes pernetz une plee
en certein.—*Grene* se tient a ceo qil navoit qe
seignurie de fee taille; jugement del avowere de fee
simple.—*Mutl.* Et desicome il est estraunge en qi
bouche tiel plee ne gist pas.—*Grene.* Nous vous
dioms qe luy et ses auncestres et ces qi estat il
ad en la seignurie furent[2] unqes seisi de heriet de
terre tenant qe nous tenoms; prest, &c.—*Mutl.*
Donqes deditetz vous pas qe les tenementz sount del
fee de Boseville, ne qe lusage est tiel par my le
fee.[3]—*Grene.* Jeo nay qe faire de cel, qar, tut

---

[1] H., and D., naverai.
[2] furent is from D. alone.

[3] L., and C., feffe.

No. 32.

others paid heriot, my holding would not therefore be charged.—*Mutlow.* If tenements within a fee are partible, &c., if there be one holding which has by possibility never undergone partition, because perhaps there was never more than one male, as soon afterwards as there are two the land will be partitioned; so in the case before us, the non-seisin will not prejudice the case if the custom be general.—HILLARY. Is it possible to understand that one tenant has continued his tenancy in this land since time of memory, as in the case which you suppose in which there was never but one heir male? as meaning to say that it was not possible. And if it could be shown in your parallel case that there were two males, and that the elder had the whole of the land, in that way there would be an ouster of the custom; so also in this matter non-seisin tolls the right to heriot, as it seems. And suppose that you had yourself been seised, and had enfeoffed the tenant, would you have a heriot? Certainly not.—*Mutlow.* Is it not possible that, since time of memory, no tenant died seised until now, because each tenant aliened? Then if the custom be general throughout the whole of the fee, the non-seisin in this parcel will not make it of other condition than that of which all the rest is.—HILLARY. Then you refuse the averment.—They were adjourned, *prece partium,* on the avowry.

Scire facias. (32.) § The Abbot of Ramsey sued a *Scire facias* to have execution of damages recovered by his predecessor in a *Quare impedit*; and the writ purported that he recovered on verdict; and the record purported that,

No. 32.

A.D. 1345.

paiassent toux autres heriet, par tant ne serreit pas ma tenance charge.—*Mutl.* Si tenementz deinz une fee soient departables, &c., sil y eit une tenance qunqes ne fuit departie pur possibilite par cas qe unqes navoit qun mal, quant[1] apres qe deux y soient la terre serra departie; *sic in proposito,* la noun seisine ne grevera pas si lusage soit[2] general.—HILL. Est il possible dentendre qun tenant eit continue puis temps de memore[3] sa tenance en cele terre, come el cas qe vous supposetz qil ny avoit[4] qun heir madle? *quasi diceret non.* Et si homme purra moustrer en vostre semblaunce qe ij madles y furent, et leigne avoit tote[5] la terre, par tant serra ouste de la custume; auxint en ceste matere la noun seisine toude heriete, a ceo qe semble. Et poses qe vous mesmes fuistes seisi[6] et ussetz feffe le tenant, averetz heriet? Noun certes.—*Mutl.* Nest il possible qe, puis temps de memore,[3] nul tenant avant ore muruyst seisi, pur ceo qe chesqun tenant aliena? Donqes si lusage soit general par my tut le fee, la noun seisine en cele parcelle nel fra dautre condicion qe tut le remenant nest.—HILL. Donqes refusetz laverement.—*Adjournantur, prece partium,* sur lavowere.

(32.)[7] § Labbe de Rameseye suyt *Scire facias* daver execucion des damages recoveris par soun predecessour en un *Quare impedit*; et le brief voet[8] qil recoverist sur verdit[9]; et le recorde voet,[8] pur ceo

Scire facias. [Fitz., Scire facias, 120;

---

[1] L., quel; H., quel houre.
[2] L., H., and C., ne soit.
[3] D., memoire.
[4] L., and C., ad.
[5] C., tut.
[6] C., seisiz.
[7] From the four MSS., as above, but corrected by the record, *Placita de Banco,* Mich., 19 Edw. III., R° 483, d.

[8] D., veot.
[9] According to the roll the recital in the *Scire facias* was " cum " quidam Abbas de Rameseye, præ-" decessor Abbatis de Rameseye " qui nunc est, in Curia Domini " Regis Edwardi nuper Regis " Angliæ patris domini Regis nunc, " anno regni sui decimo octavo, " coram Justiciariis ipsius Regis

No. 32.

because the opposite party would not count against his predecessor, that party and his pledges were in mercy, and his predecessor had a writ to the Bishop. And the record purported further that, because he was a man of Religion, and there was an Assise of Darrein Presentment pending between the parties in respect of the same church, enquiry should be had by that Assise as to collusion, and as to the value of the church; and so it was done before MUTFORD at *Nisi prius.—Notton.* It is proved by the record that the damages were not recovered upon verdict, because he recovered his presentation and damages by judgment of this Court for a cause other than by verdict; judgment of this writ, which is not warranted by the record. And also the words of the writ are "*prout per quandam juratam inter eos captam est compertum,*" whereas the-inquest was only one of office.—And, notwithstanding this, the writ was adjudged good.—*Quære.* —*Skipwith.* We tell you that the Abbot's predecessor sued a *Fieri facias,* and that the damages were levied by the Sheriff of our goods and chattels, and delivered to him; judgment whether you ought to have execution.—*Blaykeston.* He alleges matter which ought to

No. 32.

A.D. 1345.
Variauns 83.]

qe son adversere[1] ne voleit pas counter vers son predecessour, qe luy et ses plegges furent en la mercy, et qe son predecessour ust brief al Evesqe. Et pur ceo qil fuit homme de Religioun, et il y avoit une Assise de drein[2] presentement pendaunt entre les parties de mesme leglise, qe par cele Assise homme enquerreit de la collusion, et de la value del eglise; et issint fuit fait devant MUTEFORDE par *Nisi prius.—Nottone.* Par le recorde est il prove qe les damages ne furent pas recoveris sur verdit, qar il recoverist son presentement et damages par agarde de ceste Court par autre cause qe sur verdit; jugement de ceo brief qe nest pas garranti del recorde. Et auxint le brief voet[3] *prout per quandam juratam inter eos captam est compertum,* la ou lenqueste ne fuit forqe doffice.—Et, *non obstante,* le brief est agarde bon.—*Quære.—Skyp.* Nous vous dioms qe son predecessour suit le *Fieri facias,* et les damages furent leves par le Vicounte[4] de nos biens et chateux, et a luy liveretz; jugement si vous execucion deivetz aver.[5]—*Blayk.* Il allegge chose qe coviendreit estre

---

" patris, &c., de Banco, apud
" Eboracum, per considerationem
" ejusdem Curiæ Regis patris, &c.,
" recuperasset versus Adam filium
" Thomæ de Brauncestre quater-
" viginti libras pro damnis suis
" quæ habuit occasione quod præ-
" dictus Adam injuste impedivit
" ipsum præsentare idoneam per-
" sonam ad ecclesiam de Braun-
" cestre, prout per quandam
" juratam coram dilecto et fideli
" dicti patris Regis nunc Johanne
" de Mutforde apud Norwycum
" inde inter eos captam convictum
" fuit, prædictus Adam sexaginta
" et quindecim libras de prædictis
" quaterviginti libris prædicto præ-
" decessori prædicti Abbatis qui
" nunc est, nec etiam prædicto

" Abbati qui nunc est, nondum
" soluit, prout ex insinuatione
" ipsius Abbatis qui nunc est
" accepit Rex," &c.

[1] D., adversare.

[2] C., derryne.

[3] D., veot.

[4] H., Levesqe, instead of le Vicounte.

[5] According to the roll the plea was " quod quidam Simon quon-
" dam Abbas de Rameseye, præde-
" cessor Abbatis nunc, tempore
" Edwardi Regis patris domini
" Regis nunc, secutus fuit breve
" suum *Fieri facias* versus prædic-
" tum Adam Vicecomiti Norffolciæ
" qui tunc fuit, scilicet, Egidio de
" Wathesham, qui quidem Vice-
" comes virtute brevis illius

No. 32.

A.D. 1345. be averred by record; and you will not find on the roll that any writ issued, or that the roll was marked, and he does not produce any tally or acquittance; therefore we pray execution.—*Notton.* I cannot, according to common intendment, have any tally or acquittance in respect of that which the Sheriff levied; and if, by default of the clerks, the roll be not marked, I shall not on that account be charged; and since I have tendered the averment that his predecessor was seised, which fact they do not deny, judgment.—HILLARY. Execution ought to be averred by record, because writs of execution are returnable; and the words of the writ are " *et habeas ibi denarios,*" and if the Sheriff did not produce the money in Court he would be amerced.—WILLOUGHBY. Because you (the defendant) have not an acquittance or any other specialty which discharges you, and your answer ought to have been averred by record, therefore do you who are for the Abbot sue execution for him.

No. 32.

avere par recorde; et en roulle vous troveretz pas A.D. 1345 qe brief issit ne roulle merche, ne il ne moustre taille ne acquitance; par quei nous prioms execucion.[1] —*Nottone*. De ceo qe le Vicounte leva, jeo ne puisse aver taille ne acquitance de comune entente; et si roulle ne soit pas merche par defaute des clercs jeo ne serra[2] pas par taunt charge; et del houre qe jay tendu daverer qe soun predecessour fuit seisi, quele chose ils ne dedient pas, jugement.—HILL. Lexecucion duist estre avere par recorde, qar tiels briefs sount retournables; et le brief voet *et habeas ibi denarios*, et si le Vicounte nel feist il serreit amercie.—WILBY. Pur ceo qe vous navetz pas acquitance ne autre[3] especialte qe vous descharge, et vostre respons serreit avere par recorde, par quei suetz execucion pur Labbe.[4]

" denarios prædictos de bonis et " catallis ipsius Adæ fieri fecit, et " denarios illos prædicto Simoni " quondam Abbati prædecessori, " &c., soluit apud Brauncestre et " Bertone Byndyche in eodem " Comitatu, et hoc paratus est " verificare, &c. Et petit judicium " si Abbas qui nunc est iterum " executionem denariorum prædic- " torum habere debeat, &c."

[1] According to the roll the repli- cation was " quod . . . ad talem " verificationem admitti non debet, " &c., quia dicit quod quodlibet " breve *Fieri facias* est retornabile " coram Justiciariis coram quibus " judicium redditum fuit, et in " Curia de recordo ubi breve illud " emanavit, et etiam in quolibet " brevi illius naturæ continetur " quod Vicecomes haberet denarios " in brevi contentos ad diem et " locum in brevi specificatos, ad " reddendum illi cui damna adjudi- " cata fuerunt, &c."

[2] C., serray.

[3] L., nulle autre.

[4] According to the roll the judg- ment was " Ex quo idem Adam " nihil ostendit Curiæ nec per " recordum rotulorum, nec per " retornum brevium, seu acquietan- " tiam Vicecomitis qui tunc fuit, " vel acquietantiam Abbatis, &c., " nec aliquid aliud dicit, quamvis " per Curiam sæpius requisitus, et " etiam compertum est in rotulis " de Banco hic quod prædictus " Abbas prædecessor Abbatis " nunc secutus fuit breve " suum *Fieri facias* a tempore " judicii redditi usque ad annum " domini Regis nunc quintum " decimum versus prædictum " Adam de denariis prædictis, &c., " per quod videtur CURIÆ quod " verificatio quam prædictis, Adam " prætendit non est admittenda, " &c.,

" Ideo consideratum est quod " prædictus Abbas qui nunc, &c.,

No. 33.

A.D. 1345.
Intrusion. (33.) § A writ of Intrusion was brought by J. Bluet against W. Colstan, supposing his entry to have been by abatement after the death of K. to whom A., the father of J. Bluet, had leased for K.'s life.—*Seton.* We tell you that A., your father, by this deed which is here, gave the same tenements to this same K., who was our father, and to C. his wife, and to the heirs of their bodies, and that we are their issue, and that A. bound himself and his heirs to warranty; judgment whether such a writ lies against us.—*Moubray.* We shall not be barred by this deed, because nothing passed; ready, &c.—*R. Thorpe.* And inasmuch as you do not show anything to prove the lease supposed by your writ, and we make *profert* of a specialty which proves the conveyance to have been made in a different manner, judgment whether you shall be admitted to such an avoidance of the deed.—*Moubray.* Is it not possible that the lease was made by another deed, or without deed, as our writ supposes, and that nothing passed by the deed pleaded in bar? And if this deed was executed while K. was in seisin, he gives me such an avoidance by the manner in which he has used the deed.—HILLARY. On this writ you will not have such an avoidance, nor on a writ of Entry *ad terminum qui præteriit,* for if you execute in my favour a charter conveying fee simple, and afterwards make livery of the land to me, without deed indented, only for term of life, the whole will pass in accordance with the purport of the charter.—WILLOUGHBY. Yes, certainly. And it would be strange, unless one intended to change the ancient

No. 33.

(33.)[1] § Intrusioun porte par J. Bluet vers W. Colstan, supposant soun entre par abatement apres la mort K. a qi A.[3] son pere[4] lessa a sa vie.—*Setone.* Nous vous dioms qe A. vostre pere, par ceo fait qe ci est, dona mesmés les tenementz a mesme cesti K., qe fuit nostre pere, et a C. sa femme, et les heirs de lour corps, entre queux nous sumes issue, et obligea luy et ses heirs a la garrantie; jugement si tiel brief vers nous gise.—*Moubray.* Par ceo fait nous ne serroms barre, qar rienz ne passa; prest, &c. — [R.] *Thorpe.* Et desicome vous ne moustretz rienz del lees suppose par vostre brief, et nous mettoms avant especialte qe prove le lees en autre manere, jugement si a tiel voidaunce del fait serretz resceu.—*Moubray.* Nest il possible qe le lees se fist par autre fait, ou saunz fet, come nostre brief suppose, et qe par ceo fait rienz ne passa? Et si ceo fet fuit fait en seisine, par la manere qil ad use le fait il moi doune tiel voidaunce.—HILL. En cest brief vous naveretz pas tiel voidaunce, nen[5] brief de[6] Entre[7] *ad terminum qui præteriit*, qar si vous fetes[8] a moy chartre de fee, et puis moi liveretz saunz fait endente la terre, forqe terme de vie, tut passera solonc purport de la chartre.—WILBY. Oyl, certes. Et il serreit merveille, si homme ne voleit chaunger les aunciens leys, de

A.D. 1345.

Intru-sioun.[2]

[Fitz., *Estoppell*, 184.]

" habeat executionem judicii prius " redditi, &c."

The Abbot had award of execution by *Elegit.*

Afterwards, however, probably with a view to proceedings in Error, " dominus Rex misit breve suum " hic clausum Johanni de Stonore " Justiciario de prædictis recordo " et processu mittendis coram " domino Rege in Cancellaria sua. " Et mittuntur per J. de Aultone " in Cancellariam, &c."

[1] From the four MSS., as above.

[2] The marginal note is omitted from C.

[3] L., un A.

[4] L., auncestre.

[5] C., ne.

[6] The words brief de are from L. alone.

[7] D., autre.

[8] D., feistes.

No. 34.

laws, to take, without *profert* of any specialty to show the lease, such an averment in avoidance of the deed which is pleaded in bar ; but on a writ of Entry founded on disseisin you would attain your purpose.—STOUFORD. And inasmuch as the lease supposed by his writ may be consistent with that which he alleges in avoidance of the deed, it would be strange, and contrary to reason, to oust him from such an answer.—HILLARY asked *Seton* whether he used the deed as a bar by reason of the warranty, or on the other hand to oust the demandant from the averment of the lease supposed by his writ.—*R. Thorpe.* We demand judgment whether the writ lies.

Cui in vita.

(34.) § Five persons brought a writ of [*Sur*] *cui in vita*, demanding two parts of certain lands.—*Gaynesford* alleged non-tenure, partly on the ground that the demandants themselves held, assigning to them a different addition of surname, and partly that a stranger held. —*Notton.* With regard to part he alleges non-tenure, saying that a stranger holds, and that is to the abatement of the whole writ ; and with regard to part he alleges it, saying that we hold in our own person ; to which will he hold ?--*Gaynesford.* I can allege non-tenure in twenty ways.—STOUFORD, *ad idem.* Although he might have pleaded your own seisin to the action, he would not do so, but he pleads in another manner to the writ ; therefore answer.—*Notton.* We tell you that heretofore we brought a [*Sur*] *cui in vita*, and demanded this land, and other lands, and with respect to part we recovered, and with respect to part the demise was traversed by the tenant, and it was found that the husband did not demise to the person supposed by the writ ; therefore our writ abated ; therefore we immediately framed this present writ against him in respect of the same parcel in respect of which he abated our writ as tenant ; judgment whether he shall

No. 34.

prendre, saunz especialte moustrer del lees, tiel avere- A.D. 1345
ment en voidaunce del fait qest plede en barre;
mes a un brief Dentre foundu sur la disseisine vous
averetz vostre purpos.—STOUF. Et quant le lees
suppose par son brief poet esteer ove ceo qil allegge
en voidaunce del fait, serreit merveille et countre
resoun de luy ouster de tiel respons.—HILL. demanda
de *Setone* le quel il usa le fait pur barre par la
garrantie ou autrement de luy ouster daverer le lees
suppose par son brief.—[*R.*] *Thorpe.* Nous demandoms
jugement si le brief gise.

(34.)[1] § V porterent brief de[2] *Cui in vita* demand- *Cui in*
antz les deux parties de certeinz terres.—*Gayn.* *vita.*
alleggea noun tenue, partie en les demandantz par [Fitz.,
Briefe,
autre adjeccion de surnoun, partie en estrange.— 244.]
Nottone. De parcelle il allegge nountenure en
estrange, qest al[3] abatement de tut[4] le brief, et de
parcelle en nostre persone demene; a quel se voet
il tener?—*Gayn.* Javerai xx nountenures.—STOUF.,
ad idem. Tut purreit il pleder vostre seisine demene
al accion, il ne voleit pas, mes plede par[5] autre
maner au brief; par quei responez.—*Nottone.* Nous
vous dioms qautrefoith nous portames *Cui in vita,*
et demandames cele terre et autres, et de parcelle
nous recoverimes, et de parcelle [le lees fuit traverse
par luy, et trove fuit qe le baroun ne lessa point
a celuy qe fuit suppose par le brief; par quei nostre
brief abatist; par quei freschement nous][6] avoms
conceu vers luy cest brief de mesme la parcelle de
quel il abatist nostre brief come tenant; jugement

---

[1] From the four MSS., as above.
[2] The words brief de are omitted
from H. and D.
[3] L., and D., en.

[4] C., tote.
[5] D., en.
[6] The words between brackets
are omitted from H.

No. 34.

be admitted to allege non-tenure.—*Gaynesford.* You shall not be admitted to say that it was in respect of the same parcel, because we tell you that heretofore the five demanded as they say, and that at that time two of the five were non-suited and severed by judgment, and the other three demanded three parts of the land, and that which the five demand now is the two parts which are the share of the two who were non-suited, and that fact appears by the present demand by the description of two parts ; and also they now demand something else, that is to say moor and pasture, in respect of which the first writ was not abated as above.—*Notton.* Whether the quantity be greater or less, we now demand the same tenements in respect of which our writ abated on the previous occasion ; therefore we demand judgment whether you shall be admitted [to plead non-tenure].—*Huse.* Since the two were non-suited on the first writ, those two could have had writs for themselves alone in respect of those two parts, or the five could have had a writ in accordance with their present demand, and the three who previously recovered could be barred, and the two could recover their portion ; therefore, although the five have brought their writ and demanded two parts, that demand can only be understood to be of the same two parts that are the share of the two who were non-suited on the first writ.—*R. Thorpe.* Since they now demand two parts of so much land, that can only be understood in the sense that a third part is excepted from the whole, for in an Assise the plaint would in such a case be in respect of two parts of land divided into five parts ; therefore it seems that they are demanding part of that of which they are themselves tenants through their recovery. On the other hand, since, on the first writ, the demise supposed to have been made by the husband was traversed, that was a plea to the action though they say that it

No. .34.

si dallegger nountenure serra il resceu.—*Gayn*. Qe A.D. 1345.
ceo fuit de mesme la parcelle ne serretz resceu, qar
nous vous dioms qautrefoith les v demanderunt come
ils dient,[1] a quel temps les deux de les[2] v furent
nounsuitz et severetz par agarde, et les iij demanderent les iij[3] parties, et ceo qils demandent a ore
ces sont les deux parties afferaunt a les deux qe
furent nounsuitz, et ceo piert par la demande a ore
par noun des deux parties; et auxint ils demandent
a ore autre chose, saver more et pasture, de quei
le primer brief ne fuit pas abatu *ut supra*.—*Nottone*.
Soit il plus ou meins, nous demandoms a ore
mesmes les tenementz dount nostre brief abatist
autrefoith; par quei jugement si vous serrez resceu.
—*Huse*. Quant deux furent nounsuitz al primer brief,
celes deux poaint de celes deux parties aver eu a
per eux [briefs, ou les v solonc ceo qore demandent,
et les iij qautrefoith recoverirent estre barre, et les
deux recoverir lour porcion][4]; donqes tut eient les
v porte brief et demande les ij parties, ceo ne poet
estre entendu mes mesmes les ij parties qe afferrount
a les ij qe furent nounsuitz al primer brief.—*R.
Thorpe*. Quant ils demandent a ore les deux parties
de tant de terre, ceo ne serra entendu[5] mes qune
terce partie est forpris del entier, qar en Assise en
tiel cas la pleinte serreit de ij parties devise[6] en v
parties; par quei il semble qils demandent parcelle
de ceo qils sount mesmes tenantz par lour recoverir.
Dautre part, quant en le primer brief le lees suppose par le baron fuit traverse, ceo fuit[7] al accion

---

[1] L., ore ils demandent, instead of ils dient.

[2] les is omitted from C. and D.

[3] The words demanderent les iij are omitted from C.

[4] The words between brackets are omitted from H.

[5] C., entencion.

[6] D., devisetz.

[7] L., ne fuit.

No. 34.

was only to the entry, so that even though this demand could be understood to be in respect of the same thing in respect of which the first writ abated, yet that is not in a condition to be aided by a writ purchased immediately afterwards, because that rule holds good only where the first writ abated by reason of a dilatory exception, and not where there was a plea to the action.--WILLOUGHBY. The plea was only to the writ, for although the husband did not demise to the person alleged, he possibly did demise to some one else.—*R. Thorpe.* For that there would be another action.—*Birton.* When the five brought the first writ, and through the non-suit of the two the other three recovered three parts, it must be understood that they recovered to hold. in severalty, because they could not be supposed to hold in common with their deforcer; therefore, when the Sheriff came to make livery, he possibly found by extent that one acre was of greater value than any of the four other acres, and then he could and he ought to have made livery according to the value, and not according to the number of acres, so that the recovery had by the three does not prove that they had three parts except only having regard to value, and not to the number of acres; and when some parceners have been non-suited, and some have recovered, it is afterwards, on bringing another writ, at their election to demand the whole or only a portion of that which was not previously recovered, and that in any manner they may please, that is to say by the description of a moiety or otherwise; therefore the demand made by the description of such a number of acres does not prove that they are demanding the same two parts which are the share of the two who were previously non-suited, and so the manner in which the demand is made is immaterial with regard to the non-tenure alleged. — WILLOUGHBY to *Notton.* Will you say anything else?—*Notton.* As to the moor

No. 34.

coment qils dient qe ceo fuit forqe al entre, issint A.D. 1345.
qe tut poait il estre entendu de mesme la chose
dount le primer brief abatist, unqore ceo nest pas
en cas destre eide par brief freschement purchace,
qar cele reule se tient soulement ou le primer brief
abatist par excepcion dilatorie, et noun pas par plee
al accion.—WILBY. Le plee ne fuit forqe al brief,
qar tut ne lessa il pas a mesme celuy, il lessa a
autre par cas.—[R.] *Thorpe.* Ceo serreit autre accion.
—*Birtone.* Quant les v porterent le primer brief et
par nounsuite de les ij les iij recoverirent les iij
parties, ceo coviendreit estre a tenir en severalte,
qar ils ne duissent pas tenir en comune ove lour
deforceour; donqes quant le Vicounte vint pur faire
la livere il trova par extent qune acre valust plus
qautres iiij acres par cas, il poait et devereit liverer
solonc la value, et noun pas par noumbre des acres,
issint qe le recoverir de iij ne prove pas qils avoint
les iij parties forqe soulement eaunt regarde a value,
et noun pas a noumbre des acres; et quant asquns
des parceners furent nounsuitz et asquns recoverirent,
apres a un autre brief, il est a lour choise a demander tut ou parcelle de ceo qe ne fuit pas autrefoith recoveri, et ceo par quel manere qils voleint,
saver, par moite ou autrement; par quei la demande
par tiele quantite des acres ne prove pas qils demandent mesmes les deux parties qafferrent a les
deux qe devant furent nounsuitz, et issint la manére
de la demande ne toude ne doune quant a la nountenure allegge.—WILBY a *Nottone.* Voilletz autre chose
dire?—*Nottone.* Quant a la more et pasture, pleine-

No. 34.

A.D. 1345. and pasture, fully tenant; ready, &c. And, as to the rest, these are the same tenements in respect of which he, as tenant, previously abated our writ; judgment whether to this writ purchased immediately afterwards he shall be admitted to allege non-tenure.—STONORE. You demand twenty acres of land, and also two parts of certain acres of moor, pasture, and wood; as to the land, deliver yourself with respect to that first, because it seems to the tenant that it should be demanded by the description of two parts of five parts of fifty acres of land; for by the record of the demand in the first writ it is proved that the five demanded fifty acres of land, and through the non-suit of the two who were severed the three recovered three parts, that is to say, in effect, thirty acres, so that afterwards there remained only twenty to be demanded; therefore it is necessary to see whether they are to be demanded substantively as a certain number of acres or as two parts of five parts. And I say that the demandant can elect; therefore with regard to that we adjudge the writ to be good.—*R. Thorpe.* And even though the writ be good from that point of view, still the writ brought by the five solely in respect of the portion which is the share of the two is bad.—STONORE. No, it is necessary that all the heirs should demand, and when the five have recovered they will hold this portion and the rest in common, and will then make partition.—*R. Thorpe.* The two alone will have the writ, and, in tracing the descent, will make mention of the recovery had by their co-parceners.—WILLOUGHBY. It is necessary that all the heirs should demand, and STONORE has answered you on that point.—STONORE to *Notton.* Now show for what reason, with regard to the moor, pasture, and wood, which you demand by the description of two parts, whereas by such a demand nothing is excepted from the whole

No. 34.

ment tenant; prest, &c. Et, quant al remenant, ces A.D. 1345. sount mesmes les tenementz dount autrefoith il come tenant abatist nostre brief; jugement si a ceo brief freschement purchace serra resceu dallegger nountenure.—STON. Vous demandetz xx acres de terre, et auxint les deux parties [1] de certeins acres de more, pasture, et boys; quant a la terre, deliveretz cella primes, qar il semble al tenant qe ceo serra demande par noun de deux parties de v parties de l acres de terre; qar par le recorde de la demande el primer brief est prove qe les v demanderunt l acres de terre, et [2] par la nounsuite de deux qe furent severetz les iij recoverirent les iij parties, saver, en effecte, xxx acres, issint qe apres ne remistrent a demander forqe xx; donqes fet a regarder le quel ceo serra demande come un gros par noumbre des acres, ou par noun de ij parties [3] de v parties. Et jeo die qe le demandant poet eslire; par quei en dreit de ceo nous agardoms le brief bon.—[R.] *Thorpe.* Et tut soit le brief bon a cel regarde, unqore le brief porte par les v de la porcion soulement afferraunt a les deux est malveis. — STONOR. [4] Nanil, il covient qe toux les heirs [5] demaundent, et quant les v ore averount recoveri ils tendrount cel, et le remenant en comune, et donqes le departirent.—[R.] *Thorpe.* Les deux soulement averount le brief, et en la descente ferrount mencion del recoverir fait par lour parceners.—WILBY. Il [6] covient qe toux les heirs demandent, et STON. vous ad respoundu a cella.— STON. a *Nottone.* Ore moustretz par quele resoun, quant a la more, pasture, et boys, qe vous demandetz par noun de ij parties, [3] ou del entier par tiel demande rienz est forpris forqe une terce partie

---

[1] MSS., la moite, instead of les deux parties.

[2] H., qar.

[3] MSS., moite, instead of ij parties.

[4] C., *Nottone.*

[5] H., coheirs.

[6] H.. Y.

No. 35.

but a third part, and how you can so demand it, because it seems that your demand should, on your facts, be for two parts of five parts, for so much and no more remained not recovered on the first writ; but now you are demanding that which you have already recovered.—*Notton.* As to that they have alleged non-tenure, which falls under the head of fact, and so have accepted the form of the demand.—*R. Thorpe.* We take the record to witness that you allege it yourself.—*Notton.* The allegation was made with respect only to the land; and it is possible, for anything that we have said, that the first writ was in respect of

Judgment. tenements other than this moor.—And nevertheless the COURT abated the writ in its entirety.

Præcipe. (35.) § *Præcipe.*—*R. Thorpe* alleged non-tenure on the day of the purchase of the writ.—*Seton.* And inasmuch as he does not allege non-tenure in him this day, and so his exception is not complete, we pray judgment.—*R. Thorpe.* Suppose I were to say that I am not tenant, and that I was not tenant on the day on which the writ was purchased, and you were to say that I am and was, enquiry would be made only as to the day of the date of the writ; and since, upon issue joined, enquiry will not be made as to any other time, the exception which is given as to that same time is sufficiently complete.—WILLOUGHBY. So it appears to some people, because if there be any tenancy while the writ is pending which maintains it, that will come from the demandant when his writ is made to be false at the time of its purchase.—HILLARY. In the case which *R. Thorpe* puts enquiry will be made whether he was tenant at any time since the writ was purchased.— *R. Thorpe* denied that, and said that he would be put to mischief if he came into possession by purchase while the writ was pending, in which case the writ would be good, unless the statement came from the

No. 35.

coment vous le poietz demander, qar il semble qe ^{A.D. 1345.} vostre demande sur vostre fait serreit de les ij parties[1] de v parties, qar tant et nient plus fuit remys nient recoveri el primer brief; mes ore demandetz vous ceo qe vous avietz devant recoveri.—*Nottone.* Quant a cella ils ount allegge nountenure qe chiet en fait, issint acceptant la forme de la demande.—[*R.*] *Thorpe.* Nous le pernoms del record qe vous mesmes alleg- getz.—*Nottone.* Ceo ne fuit pas allegge forqe a la tèrre; et poet estre, pur rienz qe nous avoms dit, qe le primer brief fuit des autres tenementz qe de cele more, &c.—Et, *non obstante,* COURT abatist tut[2] *Judicium.*[3] le brief.

(35.)[4] § *Præcipe.*—[*R.*] *Thorpe* alleggea nountenure *Præcipe.* jour du brief purchace.—*Setone.* Et, desicomme il nallegge pas nountenure huy ceo jour en luy, et issint sa excepcion nient pleine, jugement.—[*R.*] *Thorpe.* Jeo pose qe jeo deisse qe jeo ne su pas tenant ne fu jour du brief purchace, [et vous deissetz qe si],[5] homme nenquerreit forqe jour de la date du brief; et quant en issue homme nenquerra dautre temps lexcepcion est assetz pleine qest done de mesme le temps.—WILBY. Ceo semble a asquns gentz, qar sil y eit asqune tenance pendant le brief, qe le meintient, ceo vendra del demandant, quant son brief est faux al temps del purchace.—HILL. En le cas qe [*R.*] *Thorpe* mette homme enquerra de chesqun temps sil fuit tenant puis[6] le[7] brief purchace.—[*R.*] *Thorpe dedixit illud,* et dit qil serreit mys a meschief sil avenist par purchace pendant le brief, en quel cas le brief serreit bon, sil ne venist

---

[1] All the MSS., except D., la moite, instead of les ij parties.

[2] tut is omitted from L. and H.

[3] The marginal note is from D. alone.

[4] From the four MSS., as above.

[5] The words between brackets are omitted from D.

[6] L., and D., jour.

[7] All the MSS., except H., de,

No. 36.

A.D. 1345. demandant in order to maintain his writ, because (said *Thorpe*), if I have purchased while the writ was pending, the same law which maintains the writ gives me my voucher, notwithstanding the averment which is given by statute[1] that before the writ was purchased the vouchee had nothing; and if such matter did not come from the demandant I should lose my voucher. —STONORE. You do not show his writ to be false, nor do you assign any matter to show how it could be better than it is; and if you have come into possession by descent or otherwise while the writ has been pending, which tenancy does not maintain his writ, it is for you to say that you will have the advantage of abating it.—*R. Thorpe* alleged non-tenure on the day on which the writ was purchased and this day.—Against this the demandant maintained that he was tenant the whole time; ready, &c.—And the other side said the contrary.

Quare impedit.

(36.) § A *Quare impedit* was brought for the King against an Abbot, on the ground that one John held the advowson of the King the father of the present King, and presented, and aliened, without the King's license, to the Abbot's predecessor.—*Huse.* We tell you that John did not hold the advowson of the King, &c.; and we tell you that the Abbot and his predecessors have held the same church to their own use from time whereof memory does not run.—*R. Thorpe.* That John held of the King, and that you and your predecessors have not held the church to your own use from time whereof memory does not run, ready, &c.—*Huse.* Those are two issues.—*R. Thorpe.* By your answer you give us both; therefore will you accept the averment?—*Huse*, *gratis*, maintained both.

---

[1] 3 Edw. I. (Westm. 1), c. 40.

No. 36.

del demandant pur meintener son brief, qar si jay A.D. 1345.
purchace pendant le brief, mesme la ley qe meintent le brief moi doune mon voucher, *non obstante*
laverement qest done par statut qe avant le brief
porte le vouche navoit rienz; et si tiele[1] matere ne
venist del demandant jeo perdroi[2] mon voucher.—
Ston. Vous ne fauxetz[3] pas son brief, ne donetz
matere coment il poet estre meillour qil nest; et
si vous soietz[4] avenu par descente ou autrement
pendant le brief, quele tenance ne meintent pas son
brief, a vous est a dire qe voilletz aver lavantage
dabatre, &c.—[R.] *Thorpe* alleggea la nountenure
jour de brief purchace et ore.—Countre quei le demandant meintient qe pleinement tenant; prest, &c.
—*Et alii e contra.*

(36.)[5] § *Quare impedit* pur le Roi vers un Abbe, *Quare impedit.*[6]
pur ceo qun Johan tient lavoeson du Roi le pere,
et presenta, et aliena, sanz conge du[7] Roi,[8] al predecessour Labbe.—*Huse.* Nous vous· dioms qe J. ne
tient pas lavoeson du Roi, &c.; et vous dioms qe
Labbe et ses predecessours ount tenu[9] mesme leglise
en propre oeps de temps dount memore[10] ne court.
—[R.] *Thorpe.* Qe J. la tient du Roi, et qe vous et
voz predecessours navietz pas tenu[9] leglise en propre
oeps de temps dount memore ne court,[11] prest, &c.
—*Huse.* Ces sount deux issues.—[R.] *Thorpe.* Par
vostre respons vous nous donetz lun et lautre; par
quei voilletz laverement?—*Huse, gratis*, meintent lun
et lautre.

---

[1] L., la.
[2] C., perdray.
[3] D., faucetz.
[4] H., ne soiez.
[5] From the four MSS., as above.
[6] The marginal note is omitted from C.
[7] L., le.

[8] The words du Roi are omitted from D.
[9] D., tenuz.
[10] D., memoire.
[11] H., tut temps, instead of temps dount memore ne court; D., "&c.," instead of dount memore ne court.

Nos. 37–39.

A.D. 1345.
Dower.
(37.) § William Blake and Isabel his wife brought a writ of Dower against William Lavenham and Maud his wife. The demand was previously made and entered, and exception was now taken to it on the ground that it did not express on whose endowment the dower was demanded.—And, because the writ serves for that, the exception was not allowed.—*Seton.* On a previous occasion Isabel brought a writ of Dower against us, and this writ was purchased while the other was pending (and *Seton* showed how); judgment. *Haveryngton.* The husband was not a party to that first writ; besides, we tell you that the first writ of Dower was brought by Isabel while she was sole, and by the taking of a husband her writ abated in law just as much as by death; and immediately afterwards her husband and she brought this writ.—WILLOUGHBY. And because that which you allege was only the act of the woman, that is to say, the taking of a husband, &c., the COURT adjudges that you do take nothing by this writ, and that you be in mercy.

Note :
Nisi prius.
(38.) § Note that a *Nisi prius* was granted before Justices of Assise, notwithstanding that WILLOUGHBY, who belongs to the Court [of Common Pleas], wished to have granted it before himself. And the reason was that he had many times previously granted it before himself, and did not go to the appointed place.

*Præcipe
quod
reddat.*
(39.) § A *Præcipe quod reddat* was brought in respect of twenty acres of land.—*Notton.* There are only ten acres, and in respect thereof we vouch to warrant.— *Grene.* Let the voucher stand. But we will aver that there are twenty acres, and, since he does not answer as to ten acres, judgment; and we pray seisin.—*Notton.* Be it greater or less, we vouch in respect of the

Nos. 37–39.

(37.)[1] § William Blake[2] et Isabele sa femme porterent brief de Dowere vers William Lavenham[3] et Maude[4] sa femme. La demande autrefoith fait et entre, et ore[5] chalenge de ceo qil ne voet pas de qi dowement.—Et, pur ceo qe le brief seert a ceo, *non allocatur.—Setone.* Autrefoith Isabele porta brief de Dowere vers nous, et cest brief est purchace pendant lautre—et moustra coment—jugement.—*Har.* Le baron ne fuit pas partie a cel primer brief; ovesqe ceo, nous vous dioms qe le primer brief de Dowere fuit porte par Isabele quant ele fuit sole, et par la prise del baroun soun brief abatist en ley si bien come par mort; et freschement apres son baron et luy porterent cest brief.—WILBY. Et pur ceo qe ceo qe vous alleggetz ne fuit forqe[6] le fait la femme, saver, la prise del baron, &c., agarde la COURT qe vous ne preignez rienz par cest brief, et soietz en la mercy.

A.D. 1345. Dowere. [Fitz., *Briefe,* 245; *Dowere,* 95.]

(38.)[1] § *Nota* qe *Nisi prius* fuit grante devant Justices des Assises, *non obstante* qe WILBY, qest de la place, le voleit aver graunte devant luy mesme. Et la cause fuit pur ceo qe sovent devant il lavoit graunte, et ne vint pas illoeqes.

Nota[7]: *Nisi prius.*[8]

(39.)[1] § *Præcipe quod reddat*[9] porte de xx acres de terre.—*Nottone.* Il ny ad qe x acres, et de ceo vouchoms a garrant.—*Grene.* Estoise le voucher. Mes nous voloms averer[10] qil y ad xx acres, et de puis qe a les x acres il respond pas, jugement; et prioms seisine.—*Nottone.* Soit ceo plus ou meins

Præcipe quod reddat.[9] [Fitz., *Voucher,* 123.]

---

[1] From the four MSS., as above.

[2] L., Blayk; H., Blac; D., Blaik.

[3] D., Lamenham.

[4] L., Margerie; H., M.

[5] ore is omitted from D.

[6] L., rienz forqe.

[7] The word *Nota* is from L. and H. alone.

[8] The words *Nisi prius* are from C. and D. alone.

[9] The words *quod reddat* are from L. alone.

[10] H., meyntener.

Nos. 40, 41.

demand.—*Grene.* According to your interpretation, by a release which extends only to one acre you would bar me in respect of twenty, and that cannot be.— STONORE. No, in that case you will possibly have an averment; but in this case he vouches in respect of the demand, and the vouchee will be summoned to warrant the demand; and if he warrants the whole there is no mischief, and if he escapes from warranty in respect of parcel you will then have the advantage of having seisin of it; and it is right that you should have the advantage then, but not now.— *Birton.* Is it not possible that the voucher is given with respect to part, and is not given with respect to another part? How then can the demandant have the advantage of counterpleading the voucher in respect of part unless he can say that there is a greater quantity?—HILLARY. You will not have the averment now, but your statement may be entered as representing your protestation.

Note:
Voucher
to
warrant.

(40.) § Note that one who was vouched entered into warranty as one who had nothing by descent.—*R. Thorpe.* Assets descended to him, of which he was seised on the day of the voucher; ready, &c.—HILLARY. Your statements, both on the one side and on the other, shall be entered by way of protestation; but averment on that point cannot be made between you, because it is necessary to answer the demandant.— And so it was done.

*Præcipe
quod
reddat.*

(41.) § A *Præcipe quod reddat* was brought against the wife of W. Casse, and one A.; and A. made default after default. The woman said that she was tenant of the whole, *absque hoc* that A. had anything, and that she was ready to answer. The demandant tendered the averment that they held jointly; ready, &c.—And the other side said the contrary.—At *Nisi prius* the woman made default, and now the demandant prayed

Nos. 40, 41.

nous vouchoms de la demande.—*Grene.* A vostre
entent, par relees qe sestent soulement a une acre
vous moi barretz de xx, qe ne poet estre.—Ston.[1]
Nanyl, la averetz averement par cas; mes en ceo
cas il vouche de la demande, et le vouche serra
somons de garrantir la demande; et sil garrante
tut il ny ad pas meschief, et sil estuert[2] de parcelle[3] de ceo donqes averetz lavantage daver seisine;
et adonqes est il resoun qe vous eietz lavantage,
mes a ore nient.—*Birtone.* Nest il pas possible qe
de parcelle le voucher est done, et de parcelle nient?
Coment[4] donqes avera le demandant avantage de
countrepleder le voucher de la parcelle sil ne purreit
dire qil y avoit plus?—Hill. Vous naveretz pas
laverement a ore, mes pur vostre protestacion vostre
dit purra estre entre..

(40.)[5] § *Nota* qun qe fuit vouche entra come celuy
qe rienz nad par descente.—[*R.*] *Thorpe.* Assetz
luy descent, de quei il fuit seisi jour de voucher;
prest, &c.—Hill. Vostre dist dun part et dautre
serra entre par protestacion; mes averement sur ceo
ne se fra pas entre vous, qar il covient respondre
al demaundaunt.—*Et ita factum est.*

(41.)[5] § *Præcipe quod reddat*[8] porte[9] vers la femme
W. Casse, et un A., qe fit defaut apres defaut. La
femme dit qele[10] est tenant del entier, sanz ceo qe
A. rienz ad, prest a respondre. Le demandant tendist daverer qils tiendrent[11] joint; prest, &c.—*Et
alii e contra.*—Al *Nisi prius* ele fit defaut, et ore

Nota[6]:
Voucher a
garrant.[7]
[Fitz.,
Voucher,
124.]

*Præcipe
quod
reddat.*[8]
[Fitz.,
Jugement,
173.]

---

[1] C., *Nottone.*

[2] L., estureit; H., estuereit;
D., esturt.

[3] The words de parcelle are
omitted from D.

[4] Coment is from H. alone.

[5] From the four MSS., as above.

[6] *Nota* is omitted from L.

[7] The words Voucher a garrant
are from L. alone.

[8] The words *quod reddat* are
from L. alone.

[9] porte is omitted from L.

[10] C., qil.

[11] H., tyndrent; C., tiendreint;
D., tiegnent.

No. 42.

A.D. 1345. seisin of a moiety on the default of A., and a *Petit Cape* in respect of the other moiety on the default of the woman.—And the COURT awarded seisin of a moiety, and a *Petit Cape* in respect of the other moiety. But it was extraordinary that judgment was not respited in respect of the whole, because the woman might subsequently save the default, and it is possible that she was tenant of the whole.—*Quære* what remedy she will have if she be sole tenant of the entirety, and be ousted by this judgment.

Waste.   (42.) § A writ of Waste was brought against a husband and his wife, supposing that they had both committed waste after a demise made to the woman and her first husband.—*Skipwith.* We tell you that since the last marriage no waste has been committed; judgment of this writ which supposes that both have committed waste: for in respect of waste committed before the marriage by the woman while she was sole the writ should be in the form "*ostensuri quare*" the woman has committed waste just as much as in a case of a writ of Entry.—WILLOUGHBY. In a case in which a *feme sole* has committed a disseisin or a trespass, and has afterwards taken a husband, will not a writ of Assise or a writ of Trespass after she has taken a husband be brought against them supposing the disseisin or the trespass in their two persons? as meaning to say that it would. So also in this case. Therefore, if you will abide judgment your plea is to the action.—*Skipwith.* The plaintiff will have an action by a different writ and in a different form in accordance with his case.—WILLOUGHBY. Will you say any-

No. 42.

le demandant pria sur la defaut A. seisine de la A.D. 1345. moite, et de lautre moite petit *Cape* par la defaut la femme.—Et COURT agarda seisine de la moite, et petit *Cape* del autre moite. *Quod mirum fuit*, qe le jugement nust este respite de tut, qar la femme purra sauver[1] la defaute apres, et poet estre qele tient le tut.—*Quære* quele remedie ele avera si ele soit tenant soulement del entier, et soit ouste par ceo jugement.

(42.)[2] § Wast porte[3] vers le baron et sa femme, Wast. [Fitz., *Briefe*, 246.] supposant lun et lautre aver fait wast dun lees fet al primer baron et la femme.—*Skyp.* Nous vous dioms qe puis la drein[4] esposaille nulle wast fait; jugement de ceo brief supposant qe lun et lautre ount fait wast : qar de wast fait avant les esposailles par la femme sole le brief serreit *ostensuri quare* la femme ad fet wast si bien come en cas Dentre dun brief.—WILBY. En cas qe femme sole eit fait une disseisine ou trans, et puis prent baron, ne serra brief Dassise ou de Trans apres ceo[5] qele eit pris baron porte vers eux supposant la disseisine ou trans en eux deux ? *quasi diceret sic.* Auxint en ceo cas. Par quei, si vous voilletz demurer, vostre plee est al accion.—*Skyp.* Il avera accion par autre brief et dautre forme acordant a son cas.—WILBY. Voilletz

---

[1] D., aver sauve.

[2] From the four MSS., as above, but corrected by the record, *Placita de Banco*, Mich., 19 Edw. III., R⁰ 344. It there appears that the action was brought by Matilda late wife of John Ingleys of Lincoln, William le Porter and Isabel his wife, John de Hibaldestone and Alice his wife, Walter Get, and Geoffrey de Whytone against Walter de Dalderby, of Lincoln, and Margaret his wife, " de placito " quare de domibus in suburbio " Lincolniæ, quas tenent ad vitam " ipsius Margaretæ, ex dimissione " quam Johannes Savage inde " fecit eidem Margaretæ, et Ricardo " Longe, quondam viro suo et " heredibus ipsius Ricardi fratris " prædictarum Matilldis, Isabellæ, " et Aliciæ, et avunculi prædic- " torum Walteri Get, et Galfridi, " cujus heredes ipsi sunt, fecerunt " vastum, &c."

[3] porte is from H. alone.

[4] C., darrein.

[5] ceo is from H. alone.

No. 43.

A.D. 1345 thing else ?—*R. Thorpe.* If you adjudge this writ to be good, you will then by your judgment award that the husband shall be charged with damages for a tort committed by his wife.—WILLOUGHBY. Why not ?— *Skipwith.* Since the death of our first husband no waste has been committed ; ready, &c.—And the other side said the contrary.

Escheat   (43.) § John Mynyot brought a writ of Escheat against Thomas Ughtred in respect of the manor of Islebeck, supposing that one William de Iselbeke held of him, and committed felony, for which he was outlawed. And he assigned the felony as having been committed in the eighteenth year of the King the father of our Lord the King that now is, and the outlawry was pronounced in the eleventh year of the King that now is.—*Moubray.* We tell you that, in the

No. 43.

autre chose dire ?—[*R.*] *Thorpe.* Si vous agardez ^{A.D. 1345.}
ceo brief bon, donqes par le jugement vous agarderez
qe le baron serra charge des damages pur tort fait
par sa femme.—WILBY. Pur quei nient ?—*Skyp.*
Puis la mort nostre baron nulle wast fait[1]; prest,
&c.[2]—*Et alii e contra.*[3]

(43.)[4] § Johan Myniot porta brief Deschete vers Eschete.
Thomas Ughtred del maner de Iselbeke, supposant
qun W. tient de luy, et fit felonie, pur quele il fuit
utlage. Et assigna la felonie lan xviij le Roi pere
nostre seignur le Roi qore est, et lutlagerie pronuncie lan xj[e 5] le Roi qore est.[6]—*Moubray.* Nous

---

[1] fait is from H. alone.

[2] According to the record the plea was "quod ipsi, post mortem "prædicti Ricardi quondam viri "ipsius Margaretæ, non fecerunt "aliquod vastum . . . in præ- "dicto mesuagio, ad exheredati- "onem ipsorum Matilldis,Isabellæ, "Aliciæ, Walteri Get, et Galfridi. "Et hoc parati sunt verificare, &c. "Et petunt judicium si de aliquo "vasto tempore prædicti Ricardi "facto respondere debeant, &c."

[3] According to the record there was a replication, upon which issue was joined, "quod prædicti Wal- "terus de Dalderby et Margareta "fecerunt vastum prædictum post- "mortem prædicti Ricardi, ad "exheredationem ipsorum Matill- "dis, Isabellæ, Aliciæ, Walteri "Get, et Galfridi." The *Venire* was awarded, but nothing further appears on the roll. The reports of this year are not continued beyond No. 42 in H.

[4] From L., C., and D., but corrected by the record, *Placita de Banco*, Mich., 19 Edw. III., R° 621. It there appears that the action was brought by John Mynyot,

knight, against Thomas Ughtred, knight, in respect of the manor of Iselbeke (Islebeck, Yorks), with cer- tain exceptions, which William de Iselbeke held of the demandant.

[5] MSS. of Y.B., xij°.

[6] According to the record it was stated in the count that the claim was " eo quod prædictus Willelmus " feloniam fecit, pro qua utlagatus " fuit, et inde producit sectam, et " unde idem Willelmus indictatus " fuit coram domino Rege apud " Eboracum, Termino Michaelis " anno domini Regis nunc decimo, " de eo quod idem Willelmus " furtive cepit viginti solidos de " quodam Alano de Kyrkeby, apud " Kyrkeby Wyske, die Martis " proxima post festum Sancti " Michaelis anno regni Regis " Edwardi patris domini Regis " nunc Regis decimo octavo, " prætextu cujus indictamenti præ- " dictus Willelmus postea, pro eo " quod non comparuit, positus fuit " in exigendo ad utlagandum, &c., " et ea occasione fuit utlagatus " per breve domini Regis, quod " quidem breve retornatum fuit " coram domino Rege apud Ebora-

No. 44.

A.D. 1345. tenth year of King Edward the father of the King
that now is, this same William became an adherent of
Robert Bruce and the Scots, enemies of the King, for
which cause he forfeited to the King the father.
Therefore that King seised the same manor, and
continued that estate, and died seised, and after his
death our Lord the King that now is entered and
enfeoffed S. Simioun, who enfeoffed us, and so the
King the father was seised, at the time at which you
suppose the felony to have been committed, by reason
of a forfeiture of earlier date; judgment whether you
ought to be answered as to this writ.—*Skipwith.* That
is tantamount to saying that he did not hold of us
on the day on which the felony was committed;
ready, &c., that he did.

Avowry
for relief. (44.) § Avowry for relief was made upon a Prior
who was plaintiff, on the ground that one C. held of
the avowant's ancestor so much land by homage, fealty,
and scutage, that is to say, when the scutage ran at
the rate of forty shillings per knight's fee, forty shillings, and so on in proportion, and by certain services,
of which services the ancestor was seised, and this C.
enfeoffed the plaintiff's predecessor[1] to hold to him
and his successors, whereupon a dispute arose between
the avowant's ancestor and the said predecessor, &c.,
and thereupon the avowant's ancestor confirmed to the
predecessor by a deed indented, which was produced,
the same tenements to hold to him and his successors
of the ancestor and his heirs by the same services,
and by relief to be paid after the death or cession of
every Prior elected and installed, that is to say, so
much as was in proportion to such a quantity; and

---

[1] As to what the avowry really was *see* p. 397. note 3.

No. 44.

vous dioms qe, lan x le Roi E. pere le Roi qore A.D. 1345.
est, mesme celuy W. soi aherda a Robert Bruis et
les Escotz, enemys le Roi, par quel acheisoun[1] il
forfist au Roi le pere. Par quei il seisist mesme le
maner, et cel estat continua, et muruyst seisi, apres
qi mort nostre seignur le Roi qore est entra et
feffa S. Simioun,[2] qe nous feffa, et issint le Roi le
pere seisi, al temps qe vous supposez la felonie estre
fait, par forfeture deigne temps; jugement si a ceo
brief devetz estre respondu.—*Skyp.* Tantamount qil
ne tient pas de nous jour de la felonie fet; prest,
&c., qe si.[3]

(44.)[4] § Avowere pur releef sur un Prior pleintif, Avowere pur re-leef.[5]
et pur la resoun qun C.[6] tient del auncestre lavow-
aunt tant par homage, feaute, et escuage, saver,
quant lescu court a xl*s.*, xl*s.*, &c.,[7] et par certeinz
services, des queux services, &c., le quel feffa le
predecessour le pleintif a luy et a ses successours,
dount surdit debat entre soun auncestre et le dit
predecessour, &c., et sur ceo soun auncestre conferma
al predecessour mesmes les tenementz a tener a luy
et ses successours de luy et ses heirs par mesmes
les services, et par releef apres mort ou cessioun
de chesqun Prior eslieu et installe, saver, tant qe[8]
affiert a la quantite de tant par ceo fet endente;

"cum in Octabis Sancti Michaelis
"anno regni domini Regis nunc
"undecimo."

[1] D., achaisoun.

[2] C., Simonde; D., Simone.

[3] C., cy; D., ci. After the count
all that appears upon the roll is:—
"Et Thomas . . . . . venit.
"Et super hoc dies datus est ei
"hic a die Paschæ in xv dies in
"statu quo nunc, &c."

[4] From L., C., and D., but
corrected by the record, *Placita*
de Banco, Mich., 19 Edw. III.,
R° 414, d. It there appears that
the action was brought by Robert,
Prior of Christ Church Twyneham,
against Robert Fitz Payn and John
le Gust, in respect of a taking of
ten oxen.

[5] The words pur releef are from
L. alone.

[6] D., E.

[7] The words xl*s.*, &c., are
omitted from C.

[8] D., come.

No. 44.

A.D. 1345. the avowant was seised of these services, and his ancestor had been seised by the hand of the same predecessor of one hundred shillings for relief. And the avowry made the descent of the seignory to the avowant; and because the homage, fealty, and scutage, and the rent, &c., and also the relief after the death of Edmund, Prior elected and installed, that is to say, one hundred shillings for the relief in arrear, he avowed upon the Prior who is plaintiff as upon his very tenant in the place in which the Prior makes his plaint as to the taking, and in the avowant's own fee. —*Grene*. We have counted that he is seised of the

No. 44.

et des queux services il seisi, et launcestre fuit seisi A D. 1345.
par la mein mesme celuy predecessour de c*s.* pur
releef. Et fist la descente de la seignurie al avowaunt; et pur ceo qe lomage, feaute, et escuage, et
la rente, &c., et auxint le releef apres la mort E.,[1]
Priour eslieu et installe, saver,[2] c*s.* pur releef arrere,
il avowe sur le Priour qest pleintif come sur soun
verroy tenant en lieu ou il se pleint, &c., et deinz
soun fee.[3]—*Grene.* Nous avoms counte qil est seisi;

---

[1] MSS. of Y.B., W.

[2] L., et.

[3] The avowry was, according to the record, " quod quidam Jo-
" hannes quondam Prior Christi
" ecclesiæ de Twynham, præde-
" cessor prædicti Prioris nunc,
" tenuit manerium de Estyngtone
" . . . . de quodam Roberto
" le Fitz Payn, patre ipsius Roberti
" le Fitz Payn, cujus heres ipse est,
" per homagium, fidelitatem, et ad
" scutagium domini Regis quadra-
" ginta solidorum, cum acciderit,
" quadraginta solidos, et ad plus
" plus, et ad minus minus, et per
" servitium duodecim denariorum
" . . . . annuatim solvendorum,
" de quibus servitiis idem Robertus
" pater, &c., fuit seisitus per manus
" prædicti Johannis Prioris, ut per
" manus veri tenentis sui. Et, pro
" eo quod prædictus Johannes
" Prior feodum præfati Roberti
" patris, &c., intravit sine assensu
" et voluntate ejusdem Roberti,
" contentio mota fuit inter eosdem
" Robertum patrem, &c., et Jo-
" hannem Priorem et ejusdem
" loci Conventum, qua quidem
" discordia postmodum inter eos
" sedata et concorditer pacificata,
" præfatus Robertus pater, &c., per
" quoddam scriptum inter ipsos
" indentatum concessit et con-

" firmavit præfatis Priori et Con-
" ventui et eorum successoribus
" totam terram quæ est prædictum
" manerium, ... tenendum
" deo eodem Roberto et heredibus
" suis, et faciendo et solvendo eidem
" Roberto et heredibus suis ser-
" vitia supradicta, et etiam rele-
" vium post mortem vel cessionem
" cujuslibet Prioris, &c., ita quod
" idem relevium post installa-
" tionem proximi Prioris subse-
" quentis præfato Roberto patri,
" &c., et heredibus suis integre
" persolveretur. Et profert hic
" prædictum scriptum indentatum
" sigillo prædictorum Prioris et
" Conventus signatum, quod hoc
" testatur, &c., de quo quidem
" relevio, videlicet, de centum
" solidis post mortem prædicti
" Johannis Prioris, &c., præfatus
" Robertus pater, &c., fuit seisitus
" per manus cujusdam Ricardi
" proximi Prioris subsequentis
" postquam idem Ricardus electus
" fuit et installatus, &c. Et de
" ipso Roberto patre, &c., de-
" scenderunt prædicta servitia isti
" Roberto ut filio et heredi qui
" nunc advocat, &c., qui quidem
" Robertus nunc fuit seisitus de
" servitiis prædictis, et de relevio,
" &c., per manus cujusdam Ed-
" mundi quondam Prioris, &c.,

No. 45.

A.D. 1345. beasts; let him wage the deliverance.—*Huse.* As to three of the cows[1] we do wage it, and as to the rest we cannot wage it, because they have died of the common murrain.—*Grene.* We pray a *Withernam.*— *R. Thorpe.* No, you have passed beyond that, after deliverance has been waged by compulsion from your-self.—WILLOUGHBY. That is true; and therefore we have only to see by whose default the beasts have died.—*Grene.* He put them in the pound, so that we could not have view of them, or feed them; ready, &c. —*Huse.* Dead of the common murrain, and not by our default; ready, &c.—And the other side said the contrary.—WILLOUGHBY. Now answer to the avowry.— *Grene.* He has avowed for a relief as upon his very tenant, and he falls back upon a specialty which sounds in covenant; judgment of this avowry which is repugnant, &c.

Præcipe :
View.

(45.) § A *Præcipe* was brought by a husband and his wife. View was demanded, and was counterpleaded on the ground that on a previous occasion the wife brought a like writ against the same person, and that after view the writ abated because she had taken a husband. And because a different person, that is to

---

[1] oxen according to the record.

No. 45.

gage[1] la deliveraunce.—*Huse.* Quant a iij vaches A.D. 1345.
nous gageoms, et quant al remenant nous ne poms
gager, qar ils sount mortes de comune[2] moryn.—
Grene. Nous prioms le *Withernam.*—[*R.*] *Thorpe.*
Nanil, cella estes vous passe apres ceo qe la deliveraunce par vostre chace demene est gage.—WILBY.
Il est verite; et pur ceo il[3] ny ad a veer mes en
qi defaute ils sount mortez.—*Grene.* Il les enparka,
issint qe nous ne poames aver la viewe, ne les
pestre; prest, &c.—*Huse.* Mortez de comune moryn,
et noun pas en nostre defaut; prest, &c.—*Et alii e*
contra.—WILBY. Ore responez al avowere.—*Grene.*
Il ad avowe pur releef com sur son[4] verrai[5] tenant,
et descent sur une especialte qe soune en covenant;
jugement de ceste avowere repugnant, &c.

(45.)[6] § *Præcipe* porte par le baron et sa femme. *Præcipe*[7]
Viewe demande, et countreplede par tant qautrefoith [Fitz.,
la femme porta autiel[9] brief vers mesme la per- *View,*
sone, et apres viewe le brief sabatist pur ceo qele 111.]
avoit pris baron. Et pur ceo qautre, saver, le baron,

" proximi prædecessoris prædicti
" Roberti nunc Prioris, &c., ut per
" manus veri tenentis sui, &c. Et
" quia homagium et fidelitas ejus-
" dem Roberti nunc Prioris, et
" etiam redditus prædictus per duos
" annos ante diem captionis præ-
" dictæ, et etiam centum solidi de
" relevio post mortem præfati
" Edmundi nuper Prioris, proximi
" prædecessoris ejusdem nunc
" Prioris, postquam idem nunc
" Prior proxime subsequens electus
" fuit et installatus, &c., eodem die
" captionis, &c., ipsi Roberto le
" Fitz Payn aretro fuerunt, pro
" relevio illo ipsi aretro sic existente
" advocat ipse ˙captionem prædic-
" tam super prædictum nunc
" Priorem ut super verum tenentem

" suum, &c. Et quo ad septem
" boves de prædictis bobus, &c.,
" dicit quod illi septem boves
" obierunt communi morina tunc
" temporis accidenti, &c. Et quo
" ad tres boves, &c., vadiat ei
" deliberationem illorum boum."
Nothing further appears on the
roll, except adjournments.

[1] D., gagetz.
[2] The words mortes de comune
are omitted from L.
[3] L., and C., qil.
[4] son is from D. alone.
[5] C., verroy.
[6] From the three MSS., as above.
[7] *Præcipe* is omitted from L.
[8] Vewe is from L. alone.
[9] L., and C., autre.

Nos. 46–49.

A.D. 1345. say, the husband, is now demandant on this writ, and was not a party to the first writ, view is granted.

Writ on Statute merchant. (46.) § A writ on a statute merchant was returned " *Clericus est,*" and the plaintiff prayed a writ to the Bishop to levy *de bonis ecclesiasticis, &c.* And he could not have it, because it is not given by the Statute.[1] Therefore he was told that he should have a writ to the Sheriff to deliver the debtor's lands to him.

Account. (47.) § A writ of Account was brought touching receipts in divers counties. The receipt of the whole amount having been traversed, the plaintiff sued jury-process in two counties, and no jury-process was had in a third county. And now one jury came ready to give its verdict. It was alleged that the whole was discontinued because the plaintiff had not sued jury-process in one of the counties.—*Birton.* The parties have a day, and the process between them has been well continued ; therefore, even though no jury-process has been had in one county, still with regard to the others a verdict must be taken.—HILLARY gave judgment that the plaintiff should take nothing by his writ, but should be in mercy.

Note: Account. (48.) § Note that in Account, where the inquest was to be taken by the defendant's default, a Protection was produced for him.—*Gaynesford.* He has not a day.—This exception was not allowed, but the Protection was allowed.

Voucher. (49.) § A husband and his wife were vouched.— *Moubray.* Neither the husband, nor the wife, nor the wife's ancestors ever had anything, &c.—*Seton.* The averment does not extend to the husband's ancestors as well as those of the wife ; therefore this counter-plea is not warranted by Statute.[2]—And afterwards he accepted the averment *gratis.*

---

[1] 13 Edw. I. (*De Mercatoribus*). | [2] 3 Edw. I. (Westm. 1), c. 40.

Nos. 46–49.

est ore demandant a ceo brief, et ne fuit pas partie A.D. 1345.
au primer brief, la viewe est graunte.

(46.)[1] § Brief sur estatut marchaunt retourne Brief sur[2] estatut
Clericus est, et le pleintif pria brief al Evesqe de mar-
lever *de bonis ecclesiasticis, &c. Et non potest habere,* chaunt.
eo quod non datur per statutum. Par quei dist luy [Fitz., *Execucion,*
fuit qil avereit brief au Vicounte de liverer ses 79.]
terres, &c.

(47.)[1] § Acompte de resceit en divers countes.[3] Acompte.
La resceit de tut traverse, le pleintif suyt vers les
enquestes en deux countes,[3] et en le terce counte[4]
nulle procees ne fuit fait vers lenqueste. Et ore un
enqueste vint prest a passer. Fuit allegge qe tut
est discontinue pur ceo qen un des countes[3] le
pleintif nad pas suy.—*Birtone.* Les parties ount jour,
et le procees entre eux bien continue; par quei
mesqe en un counte[4] rienz soit fait vers lenqueste,
unqore vers les autres il[5] covient prendre lenqueste.
—HILL. agarda qe le pleintif prist rienz par soun
brief, mes fuit en la merci.

(48.)[1] § *Nota* qen Acompte, ou lenqueste fuit a *Nota* :[6]
prendre par defaute del defendant, proteccion pur Acompte.[7] [Fitz.,
luy fuit mys avant.—*Gayn.* Il nad pas jour.—*Non* *Proteccion,*
allocatur, sed Protectio allocatur.[8] 82.]

(49.)[1] § Le baron et sa femme furent vouches.— Voucher.
Moubray. Le baron, ne la femme, ne les auncestres
la femme navoint unqes rienz, &c.—*Setone.* Laverement ne sestent pas al auncestre le baron si bien
come de la femme; par quei ceo nest pas garranti
par statut.—Et puis *gratis* il resceut laverement.

---

[1] From the three MSS., as above.
[2] The words Brief sur are from C. alone.
[3] C., countees.
[4] C., countee.

[5] D., y.
[6] *Nota* is from L. alone.
[7] Acompte is omitted from L.
[8] The last three words are from D. alone.

Nos. 50, 51.

A.D. 1345.
Scire facias.

(50.) § *Scire facias* in the King's Bench. There was pleaded in bar a fine levied in the Court of the Abbot of Reading, that is to say, a writ of Covenant brought in the Common Bench, and by allowance of cognisance of the plea determined in the Abbot's Court; and the record was produced *sub pede sigilli.—R. Thorpe.* To a fine alleged in such a Court no law puts us to answer : for this fine was levied without warrant, because even though the Abbot had warrant and cognisance, by point of his franchise to hold pleas, it does not therefore follow that he can admit fines and make them of record ; and if the Abbot were himself a party to this plea he would lose his franchise for the admission of the fine.—They were adjourned.

Trespass.

(51.) § Trespass in respect of goods carried off.— *Grene.* We tell you that J.,[1] against whom the writ is brought, was parson of the church of A.,[2] and that J.[1] let his church to the plaintiff and another to farm, at a certain rent to be paid to him yearly, and upon condition to uphold and repair buildings, &c., and that, if they should fail in payment, it should be lawful for him to re-enter the parsonage, and abide there at their cost for a month, until satisfaction had been made to him, and that, if at the end of the month satisfaction had not been made to him, it should be lawful for him to take all the goods found therein, and to sell them, and make his profit thereof ; and, because the covenants were broken, on account of his farm being in arrear and of satisfaction not having been made to him after the expiration of the month, he re-entered (and *Grene* said through whose default this was), and the goods in respect of which the plaint is made were the plaintiff's, and were

---

[1] For the real name *see* p. 403, note 3, and p. 405, note 2.

[2] For the real name *see* p. 405, note 2.

Nos. 50, 51.

(50.) [1] § *Scire facias* en Baunk le Roi. Plede fuit A.D. 1345 *Scire facias.* en barre une fyne leve en la Court Labbe de Redynges, saver, brief de Covenant porte en Comune Bank, et par allowaunce termine en la Court Labbe; et le recorde est mys avant *sub pede sigilli.*—[*R.*] *Thorpe.* A fyne allegge en tiel Court nulle ley nous mette a respondre : qar ceo fuit leve sanz garrant, pur ceo qe tut avoit Labbe garrant et conissance, par point de franchise de tener plees, par tant nensuit il pas qil purra resceivre [2] fines et les faire de recorde; et si Labbe mesme fuit partie a ceo plee il perdreit sa fraunchise pur la resceit de la fyne.—*Adjornantur.*

(51.) [3] § Trans des biens enportes.—*Grene.* Nous Trans. [Fitz., *Barre,* 280.] vous dioms qe J., vers qi le brief est porte, est persone del eglise de A., le quel J. lessa sa eglise al pleintif et a un autre a ferme, rendant a luy certein par an, et de sustener mesouns et re-parailler, &c., issint qe sils faillassent [4] de la paie qe lirreit a luy de reentrer la personage, et demurer a lour coustage par un moys, tanqe soun [5] gree luy fuit fait, et si a la fin del moys gree ne luy fuit fait qe lirreit a ly de prendre toux les beins leinz [6] trovetz, et vendre, et de ceo faire soun profit; et pur ceo qe les covenantes furent enfreintes, pur sa [7] ferme arere et son gree nient fait apres le moys il reentra, et dit en qi la defaut fuit, et les biens dount il soi pleint furent au pleintif, et illoeqes [8]

---

[1] From the three MSS., as above.

[2] D., resceivere.

[3] From the three MSS., as above, but corrected by the record, *Placita de Banco*, Mich., 19 Edw. III., R° 460, d. It there appears that the action was brought by John Hervy, of Ashwell, chaplain, against Walter Broun, clerk. The declaration was " quod prædictus

" Walterus . . . . . clausum " ipsius Johannis apud Chilter-" diche fregit, et bona et catalla " sua . . . cepit et asportavit."

[4] C., defaillassent.

[5] soun is omitted from D.

[6] C., luy einz.

[7] D., la.

[8] D., illeosqes.

No. 51.

A.D. 1345. found there; therefore the defendant seized them as being his own goods by virtue of the covenant; and (said *Grene*) we demand judgment whether tort can be assigned in respect of this taking. And *Grene* made *profert* of a deed indented in witness of these facts.—*Gaynesford*. We tell you that he took our goods,

No. 51.

trovetz; par quei il les seisi come ses biens propres A.D. 1345.
par force del covenant; et demandoms jugement si
tort de cele prise, &c. Et mist avant fet endente
ces[1] tesmoignant.[2]—*Gayn.* Nous vous dioms qil prist

---

[1] D., ceo.

[2] The plea was (after a traverse of the breaking of the close, upon which issue was joined) " quo ad bona et catalla, &c., dicit " quod idem Walterus nuper fuit " persona ecclesiæ de Chilterdiche, " quo tempore inter ipsum Wal- " terum, per nomen Walteri Broun " rectoris ecclesiæ de Chilterdiche, " et prædictum Johannem, et " quendam Thomam de Asshewelle, " personam ecclesiæ de Warlee " septem ollarum, ... per " scriptum ipsorum Walteri, Jo- " hannis, et Thomæ, inter eos " indentatum convenit in hunc " modum, videlicet, quod prædictus " Walterus concessit, et ad firmam " tradidit, et dimisit prædictis " Johanni et Thomæ totam eccle- " siam suam de Chilterdiche, cum " omnibus suis pertinentiis, juri- " bus, et obventionibus dictæ " ecclesiæ qualitercunque incum- " bentibus, Habendam et tenendam " prædictis Johanni et Thomæ et " suis assignatis a festo Sancti Mi- " chaelis Archangeli tunc proxime " futuro usque ad finem trium " annorum proxime sequentium " plenarie completorum, Reddendo " inde annuatim præfato Waltero, " vel suo procuratori, durante " termino prædicto, decem libras " solvendas ad festa Natalis " Domini, Paschæ, Nativitatis " Sancti Johannis Baptistæ, et " Sancti Michaelis, - per æquales " portiones, Qui quidem Johannes " et Thomas per scriptum suum " prædictum concesserunt pro se " et executoribus suis quod si ipsi " in solutione prædictæ firmæ " aliquo termino in parte vel in " toto defecissent quod tunc bene " liceret prædicto Waltero eandem " ecclesiam reingredi, et eam simul " cum omnibus bonis et catallis " ibidem inventas in manus suas " capere et tenere, vivendo interim " ad custus prædictorum firmari- " orum quousque eidem Waltero " vel assignatis suis de prædicta " firma, una cum damnis habitis " occasione detentionis ejusdem " firmæ, plenarie fuisset satisfac- " tum, Concedentes ulterius per ' scriptum prædictum quod si " prædictam firmam vel aliquam " partem ejusdem ultra unum " mensem aretro existere contin- " geret quod tunc bene liceret præ- " dicto Waltero vel assignatis suis " omnia bona et catalla in prædicta " rectoria existentia in manus suas " capere et penes se retinere in " perpetuum, vel ea pro voluntate " sua vendere. Et profert hic in " Curia quandam partem prædicti " scripti indentati quæ præmissa " testatur. Et, quia sexaginta et " decem solidi, de terminis Paschæ, " et Nativitatis Sancti Johannis " Baptistæ, in primo anno termini " prædicti, eidem Waltero a retro " fuerunt, . . . intravit ipse " . . . in rectoria prædicta, " et bona et catalla ibidem existen- " tia in manus suas cepit, et de eis " pro voluntate sua disposuit, prout ' ei virtute scripti prædicti licuit.

No. 52.

A.D. 1345. and that without cause; ready, &c. — WILLOUGHBY. Answer as to your deed.—*Gaynesford.* Whereas he says that his farm was in arrear, there was nothing in arrear, and so he took our goods *de son tort demesne;* ready, &c.—*Grene.* The farm was in arrear; ready, &c.—And the other side said the contrary.

Recordari. (52.) § The *Recordari facias loquelam* out of a Court of Ancient Demesne, which appears above in this Term.[1] The tenant had a day now by essoin, and came ready to maintain the cause of the removal into the Common Bench.—*R. Thorpe* recited, as before, that by reason of non-suit on another *Recordari* the tenant had lost the advantage with respect to the whole of this plea.— WILLOUGHBY. So it appeared on the previous occasion, but because judgment could not be given to that effect in the absence of the party, there was an adjournment; and, therefore, is there now anything else that you have to say?—And afterwards STONORE said:—We have inspected the roll, and we find that, after she was essoined, and had a day, a non-suit was adjudged, which was not her fault; therefore she shall be admitted to maintain the cause.—And the cause assigned was that she and the ter-tenants, from time whereof there is no memory, had held the same land at com-

---

[1] *See* p. 324.

No. 52.

nos biens, et sanz cause; prest, &c.—WILBY. Re- A.D. 1345.
sponez a vostre fait.—*Gayn.* La ou il dit qe sa
ferme fuit arere, il ny avoit rienz arere, et issint
de son tort demene il prist noz biens; prest, &c.—
Grene. La[1] ferme fuit arere; prest, &c.—*Et alii e
contra.*[2]

(52.)[3] § Le *Recordari* hors[4] dauncien demene, *ut* Recordari.
patet supra isto termino. Ore il ad jour par essone.
Le tenant vint prest a meintener la cause.—[*R.*]
Thorpe rehercea, *ut prius*, qe par la nounsuite a
lautre *Recordari* il perdist[5] lavantage a tut ceo ple.
—WILBY. Ceo sembloit autrefoith, mes pur ceo qe
ceo ne poait estre ajuge en vostre absence, &c.; et
pur ceo savetz autre chose dire?—Et puis STON.
Nous avoms viewe roulle, et trovoms qapres ceo qil fuit
essone, et avoit jour, un nounsuite fuit agarde, qe nest
pas sa defaut; par quei il serra resceu de meintener
sa cause.—Et la cause fuit pur ceo qe luy et les
terre tenantz, de temps dount memore[6] nest, ount
tenuz mesme la terre a la comune ley.[7]—[*R.*] *Thorpe.*

" Et hoc paratus est verificare,
" unde petit judicium si prædictus
" Johannes actionem de Trans-
" gressione occasione prædicta
" versus eum habere debeat."
  [1] D., Sa.
  [2] According to the record issue
was joined on the plaintiff's
replication : — " Johannes, non
" dedicendo scriptum prædictum
" esse factum suum, dicit quod
" prædictus Walterus de injuria sua
" propria fecit eidem Johanni præ-
" dictam transgressionem, prout
" ipse superius versus eum queritur,
" absque hoc quod prædicta firma
" eidem Waltero aretro fuit, prout
" ipse superius asserit."
  The *Venire* was awarded, and
the defendant admitted to main-

prise, but nothing further appears
on the roll.
  [3] From the three MSS., as above,
but corrected by the record, *Placita
de Banco*, Mich., 19 Edw. III.,
R° 538. The report is in continuation of No. 9 above.
  [4] hors is from D. alone.
  [5] D., perdit.
  [6] D., memoire.
  [7] According to the roll " prædicta
" Marcilia dicit quod ipsa tenet
" prædicta mesuagium et terram
" ad communem legem, ut ea quæ
" ipsa et omnes antecessores sui,
" ac alii mesuagium et terram illa
" tenentes, a tempore quo non extat
" memoria, semper hactenus ad
" communem legem tenuerunt, et
" non secundum consuetudinem

Nos. 53, 54.

mon law.—*R. Thorpe.* That is not a cause, unless she were to assign some special fact, such as a fine, or that plea touching the land had been held in this Court.—WILLOUGHBY. Yes, it is; and she surmises against you that the land is frank fee, and has from all time been pleadable at common law, and that she will aver. Will you accept the averment?—*R. Thorpe.* Ancient Demesne, pleadable by little writ of Right; ready, &c.—STONORE. You must say "and not holden according to common law."—And *Thorpe* did so.—And the other side said the contrary.

Cui in vita.

(53.) § *Cui in vita* against a woman.—*Blaykeston.* One Alice Pye gave the same tenements to our husband and us and the heirs of our husband, and so we have only a term for life, the fee resting in J. son and heir of our husband, and we pray aid of him.—*Huse.* For such a cause you ought not to have aid, because this Alice, on whose gift, &c., is the same person on whose seisin we demand, and so the cause of your aid-prayer would be a bar of our action.—*Blaykeston.* I cannot plead to your action without the person in whom the right is.—WILLOUGHBY. Let her have the aid.

Præcipe quod reddat.

(54.) § *Præcipe quod reddat* three messuages, and so much land, except a third part of one messuage. And, because the demand should be in the form *duas partes*

Nos. 53, 54.

Ceo nest pas cause, sil ne donast asqun fait especial, A.D. 1345
come fyne, ou qe la terre ust este plede ceinz.—
WILBY. Si est il; et[1] il vous surmette qe frank
fee de tut temps pledable a la comune ley, et ceo
voet il averer. Voilletz laverement?—⌊R.⌋ *Thorpe.*
Auncien demene, pledable par petit brief de Dreit;
prest, &c.—STON. Vous dirretz et noun pas tenu a
la comune ley.—*Et ita fecit.—Et alii e contra.*[2]

(53.)[3] § *Cui in vita* vers une femme.—*Blayk.* Une *Cui in*
Alice Pye dona mesmes les tenementz a nostre *vita.*
baroun et nous et les heirs nostre baroun, et issint [Fitz.,
navoms qe terme de vie, le fee reposant en J. fitz *Counter-
plee de*
et heir nostre baroun, et prioms eide de luy.—*Huse.* *Ayde,* 5.]
Sur tiel cause ne devetz[4] eide aver,[5] qar cele Alice,
de qi[6] doun, &c., est mesme la persone de qi[7] seisine
nous demandoms, et issint la cause de vostre eide
prier serreit barre de nostre accion.—*Blayk.* Jeo ne
puisse pleder a vostre accion sanz celuy en qi le
dreit est.—WILBY. Eit leide.

(54.)[3] § *Præcipe quod reddat*[8] iij mies et tant de *Præcipe
quod
reddat.*[8]
terre, forpris[9] la terce partie dun mies. Et pur ceo
la demande serreit *duas partes unius mesuagii,* et [Fitz.,
Briefe,
247.]

"manerii prædicti, et petit quod
"loquela illa in curiam prædictam
"ulterius non deducatur, &c."

[1] The words Si est il; et are
omitted from D.

[2] According to the record, the
pleading upon which issue was
joined, was "quod tenementa præ-
"dicta sunt de antiquo dominico
"Coronæ domini Regis de manerio
"prædicto de Chepyngfarendone,
"et ibi placitari debent secundum
"consuetudinem manerii prædicti,
"et non placitabilia ad communem
"legem, prout prædicta Marcilia
"superius asserit."

Marcilia, the tenant, afterwards

made default, and judgment was
given: — "loquela prædicta re-
"mittater ad curiam prædictam,
"ut ibi deducatur secundum con-
"suetudinem manerii, &c."

There is a precisely similar case,
but with a different demandant,
and a different tenant, on R⁰ 539.

[3] From the three MSS., as above.

[4] L., and C., deivetz.

[5] D., avoir.

[6] D., qe.

[7] D., qy.

[8] The words *quod reddat* are
from L. alone.

[9] D., forprise.

No. 55.

unius mesuagii, and not made by an exception of a third part of one messuage, the writ abated.

Avowry.   (55.) § Avowry on the plaintiff on the ground that she held of our lord the King by certain services, and that he was seised by her hand, &c., and that our lord the King granted her services to the avowant, by reason of which grant she attorned in respect of rent and suit of court; and the defendant avowed for fealty in arrear.—*Grene.* What have you to show the grant? —HILLARY. You have attorned to him, and therefore he has not to show any specialty to you.—*Grene.* The attornment is nothing to the purpose, because he would avow by reason of the King's grant, even without attornment.—HILLARY. If you had not attorned, it would have been necessary for him to show the King's grant, but not so now; therefore answer.

No. 55.

noun pas par forprise de la terce partie del mies, A.D. 1345.
le brief abatist.

(55.)[1] § Avowere sur le pleintif pur ceo qil tient Avowere.
de nostre seignur le Roi par certeinz services, et [Fitz.,
il seisi par sa mein, &c., et nostre seignur le Roi *de faits,*
granta ses services al avowant, par quel grant il *fins, et*
attourna de rente et suite; et pur la feaute arere 69.]
avowa.[2]—*Grene.* Quei avetz del grant?—Hill. Vous
estes attourne a luy, par quei a vous nel deit il
pas moustrei.—*Grene.* Lattournement nest pas a
purpos, qar il avowereit par grant du Roi tut sanz
attournement.—Hill. Si vous ne fuissetz pas attourne,
il coviendreit moustrer le grant le Roi, mes ore
nient; par quei responez.[3]

---

[1] From the three MSS., as above, but corrected by the record, *Placita de Banco*, Mich., 19 Edw. III., R° 465, d. It there appears that the action was brought by Joan de Fulham, Prioress of Clerkenwell, against Thomas atte Hethe and John atte Hale, in respect of a taking of one horse and one cow at Tottenham.

[2] The avowry was, according to the record, " quod prædicta " Priorissa tenuit de domino Rege " nunc unum mesuagium et ducen- " tas acras terræ, et sex acras prati, " cum pertinentiis, in Totenham, " per fidelitatem, et servitium " triginta et duorum solidorum et " decem denariorum per annum, ". . . . et faciendi sectam ad " curiam ipsius domini Regis de " Totenham, ... de quibus " servitiis idem dominus Rex nunc " fuit seisitus per manus prædictæ " Priorissæ, ut per manus veri " tenentis sui. Et postea idem " dominus Rex concessit prædicto " Thomæ ad terminum vitæ suæ,

" servitium prædictæ Priorissæ, " cum omnibus terris et tene- " mentis, redditibus et servitiis, " quæ habuit in Totenham, vir- " tute cujus concessionis eadem " Priorissa se attornavit prædicto " Thomæ de redditu prædicto. Et " quia fidelitas prædictæ Priorissæ " ei a retro fuit die captionis " prædictæ cepit ipse prædictum " equum. Et quia prædicta secta " ei a retro fut per tres annos ante " diem captionis prædictæ cepit " ipse prædictam vaccam."

[3] According to the record, the Prioress pleaded . . . . " quod " ipsa tenuit de domino Rege " tenementa prædicta ut diversas " tenuras per separabilia servitia, ". . . . . et hoc parata " est verificare, unde petit judicium " si prædictus Thomas ad advocare " suum prædictum, per quod sup- " ponit prædictam Priorissam " tenere tenementa prædicta ut " unam tenuram, et per unum " servitium, responderi debeat."

The replication, upon which

No. 56.

A.D. 1345.
Annuity. (56.) § Annuity.—*Mutlow*. We tell you that at such a place we prayed the plaintiff to be with us on a certain *dies amoris*, &c., at such a place, and we also at that place prayed him to be with us on another

No. 56.

(56.)[1] § Annuite.—*Mutl.* Nous vous dioms qe a
tiel lieu nous luy priames destre ove nous a un
jour des amys, &c., a tel lieu, et auxint illoeqes[2]
lui[3] priames destre ove nous a un autre jour et[4]

---

issue was joined, was "quod præ-
"dicta Priorissa tenuit de domino
"Rege tenementa prædicta ut
"unam tenenciam, et per unum
"servitium, sicut ipse superius
"advocando asserit, et non per
"diversas tenencias et diversa
"servitia, sicut prædicta Priorissa
"dicit."

The jury found "quod prædicta
"Priorissa tenuit tenementa præ-
"dicta per diversas tenuras, et per
"separabilia servitia, et non per
"unam tenenciam. Quæsiti ad
"quæ damna prædicta captio facta
"fuit, &c., dicunt quod ad damnum
"prædictæ Priorissæ viginti soli-
"dorum."

Judgment was accordingly given
for the Prioress to recover the
damages.

[1] From the three MSS., as above,
but corrected by the record, *Placita
de Banco*, Mich., 19 Edw. III.,
R° 367. It there appears that the
action was brought by John de
Chisenhale, clerk, against the
Abbbot of Burton-on-Trent, in
respect of arrears of an annuity of
40s.

The declaration was, according
to the record, "quod, cum quidam
"Willelmus quondam Abbas de
"Burtone, prædecessor, &c., et
"ejusdem loci Conventus . . . .
"per scriptum suum concessissent
"eidem Johanni, pro consilio suo,
"auxilio, et labore, in suis agendis,
"in futuro adhibendis, quadraginta
"solidos de domo sua de Burtone
"annuatim, ad vitam suam, in

"forma prædicta percipiendos, . . .
"prædictus Abbas nunc per decem
"et septem annos ante diem
"impetrationis brevis . . . .
"prædicto Johanni reddere contra-
"dixit, et adhuc contradicit."
Profert was made of the deed
which is set out at length. It is
therein stated "quia ad defen-
"sionem et tuitionem jurium
"ecclesiæ nostræ nos vigiles decet
"esse non remissos propter adver-
"santium insidias, quæ maxime
"invaluerunt his diebus, pro
"quibus evitandis necessario eo
"magis requiritur consilium peri-
"torum, nos, considerantes in-
"dustriam et prudentiam dilecti
"nobis in Christo Domini Johannis
"de Chisenhale, clerici, nobis in
"domo nostra necessariam in futu-
"rum fore simul et opportunam,
"dedimus et concessimus, . . .
"quadraginta solidos Sterlingorum
"de domo nostra Burtone annua-
"tim ad totam vitam suam in
"forma prædicta percipiendos, . . .
"quos quidem quadraginta solidos
"annuos ad rogatum domini nostri
"Regis Dominus Ricardus de
"Lustehulle de nobis percipere
"consuevit, et, ad cessionem ac
"requisitionem ipsius Ricardi.
"dictos quadraginta solidos annuos
"in personam prædicti Johannis,
"ut præmittitur, fecimus trans-
"ferri."

[2] D., illeosqes.

[3] lui is from D. alone.

[4] et is from D. alone.

No. 57.

A.D. 1345. day, and at another place, and he refused, and therefore this conditional annuity is extinguished; judgment
whether an action lies.—*R. Thorpe.* He alleges two
matters which fall under the head of fact; let him
hold to one.—And he was put to do this by judgment.
—*Mutlow.* We requested him to be at B. on such a
day, and he refused.—*R. Thorpe.* He did not request
us; ready, &c.—And the other side said the contrary.

Wardship.   (57.) § Wardship of twenty-four shillings of rent,
supposing that the infant's ancestor held the same
rent of the plaintiff by knight service.—*Mutlow.* We
tell you that the infant's ancestor was seised of the
land, and held it of you, and leased the same land,
out of which the rent arises, to one J.[1] for his life,
rendering to the ancestor and his heirs the same rent
of which you now demand wardship, and so J.[1] held
the land of you; judgment of your declaration.—This
exception was not allowed, because the plaintiff could

---

[1] For the real names *see* p. 417, note 2.

No. 57.

a autre lieu, et il refusa, par quei ceste annuite A.D. 1345.
condicionel est esteint; jugement si accion, &c.—
[R.] *Thorpe.* Il allegge deux choses qe chesent en
fait; se teigne al un.—Et a ceo fuit mys par
agarde.—*Mutl.* Nous luy requeimes destre a B. a
tel jour, et il le refusa.[1]—[R.] *Thorpe.* Il nous
requist pas; prest, &c.—*Et alii e contra.*[2]

(57.)[3] § Garde de xxiiij[4]*s.* de rente, supposant qe Garde. [Fitz.,
launcestre tient de luy mesme la rente par service *Garde,*
de chivaler.—*Mutl.* Nous vous dioms qe launcestre, 40.]
&c., fuit seisi de la terre, et la tient de vous, et
lessa mesme la terre dount, &c., a un J. a sa vie,
rendant a luy et ses heirs mesme la rente dount
vous demandetz garde, et issint tient il de vous la
terre; jugement de vostre moustrance.—*Non allocatur,*

---

[1] The plea was, according to the
record, "quod prædictus annuus
"redditus concessus fuit eidem
"Johanni pro consilio, auxilio, et
"labore suo in agendis ipsius
"Abbatis in futurum adhibendis,
"et dicit quod Willelmus quondam
"Abbas de Burtone prædecessor
"suus [on a stated day] requisivit
"ipsum Johannem essendi apud
"Tamworthe . . . ad quendam
"diem amoris inter ipsum Willel-
"mum Abbatem et Willelmum de
"Dacre, personam ecclesiæ de
"Prestecote, ad consulendum et
"auxiliandum ipsi Abbati in nego-
"tiis suis ibidem. . . . . . .
"Et prædictus Johannes venire
"ibidem ad prædictum diem, . .
"sicut requisitus fuit, omnino re-
"cusavit, &c. Et hoc paratus est
"verificare, unde petit judicium,
"&c."

[2] The replication upon which
issue was joined, was, according
to the record, "quod ipse non fuit

"requisitus per prædictum Willel-
"mum Abbatem essendi apud
"Tamworthe ad consulendum,
"auxiliandum, et laborandum, ad
"prædictum diem amoris, sicut
"prædictus Abbas dicit."
Nothing further, beyond the
award of the *Venire*, appears on
the roll.

[3] From the three MSS., as above,
but corrected by the record, *Placita
de Banco*, Mich., 19 Edw. III.,
R° 485, d It there appears that
the action was brought by John
son of John de Swaby against John
son of William atte Halleyate, of
Swaby, and Emma his wife, and
Matilda their daughter, in respect
of the wardship of 24*s.* of rent in
Swaby (Lincolnshire), "quæ ad
"ipsum Johannem filium Johannis
"pertinet, eo quod Robertus filius
"Hugonis de Cokeryngtone reddi-
"tum prædictum de eo tenuit per
"servitium militare, &c."

[4] MSS. of Y.B., xiiij.

No. 57.

A D. 1345 not have any other count upon such a writ.—*Mutlow* repeated that which was said above, and said further :— the infant's ancestor granted to the three persons who are defendants the same rent together with the reversion of the land for their lives by this deed; judgment whether the writ lies against them in respect of their freehold.—*Skipwith*. That plea is double : one is our tenant's lease, the other that the ancestor held the land of us, and not the rent.—WILLOUGHBY. He produces his deed; answer.—*Skipwith*. Then that demise of which he speaks is his answer, and as to that we tell you that it was made by collusion in order to deprive us of the wardship; ready, &c.; judgment.— *Mutlow*. Then you do not deny that it is the land which is holden of you, and not the rent.—*Skipwith*. It is proved by this that his answer was double.— HILLARY to *Skipwith*. Consider whether you have any other matter, and do not encumber yourself with that which is naught.—They were adjourned, *prece partium*.

No. 57.

qar autre count sur tiel brief navera il pas.—*Mutl.* A.D. 1345. rehercea *ut supra*,[1] et dit outre qe launcestre lenfant granta a les iij qe sount defendantz mesme la rente ensemblement ove la reversion de la terre a lour vies par ceo fait; jugement si devers eux de lour franc tenement le brief gise.[2]—*Skyp.* Ceo plee est double: une la demise nostre tenant, autre qil tient la terre de nous, et noun pas la rente.— WILBY. Il moustre soun fait; responez.—*Skyp.* Cele demise dount il parle est soun respons donqes, et a ceo vous dioms qe ceo fuit par collusion a tollir nous la garde; prest, &c.; jugement.—*Mutl.* Donqes deditetz[3] vous pas[4] qe la terre est tenu[5] de vous, et noun pas la rente.—*Skyp.* Par ceo est il prove bien qe soun respons fuit double.—HILL. a *Skyp.* Veietz si vous avetz[6] autre matere, et nencombretz vous pas dune nient.—*Adjornantur prece partium.*[7]

---

[1] D., "&c.," instead of *ut supra*.

[2] The plea was, according to the record, "quod prædictus Robertus, "per nomen Roberti de Cokeryng- "tone Manens in Raytheby, fuit "seisitus de uno tofto. duobus "croftis, et una bovata terræ, cum "pertinentiis, in Swaby, in do- "minico suo ut de feodo et jure, "et tenementa illa tenuit de præ- "dicto Johanne de Swaby, sed, non "cognoscendo quod tenementa "illa tenuit de eo per servitium "militare, dicunt quod ipse tene- "menta illa dimisit cuidam Simoni "filio Gilberti le Taillour de Swaby, "et Ricardo fratri ejus, tenenda ad "terminum vitæ ipsorum Simonis "et Ricardi, tenenda de ipso "Roberto per servitium viginti et "quatuor solidorum per annum, "qui sunt prædicti viginti et "quatuor solidi unde prædictus "Johannes de Swaby superius "clamat habere custodiam, &c. "Et postea idem Robertus reddi- "tum illum ac reversionem tene- "mentorum prædictorum concessit "et dimisit prædictis Johanni filio "Willelmi, Emmæ, et Matilldi, "tenenda ad totam vitam ipsorum "Johannis, Emmæ, et Matilldis, "virtute cujus concessionis præ- "dicti Simon et Ricardus se "attornaverunt prædictis Johanni "filio Willelmi, Emmæ, et Matilldi. "Et sic dicunt quod ipsi tenent "prædictum redditum. Et petunt "judicium de brevi, &c."

[3] D., dites.

[4] pas is omitted from D.

[5] D., tenuz.

[6] L., eietz.

[7] Nothing appears on the roll, after the plea, except adjournments.

Nos. 58, 59.

(58.) § A *Cui in vita* was brought, by two *Præcipes*, in the *post*. And, after view, *Sadelyngstanes* said, for one of the tenants, that the demandant had a different name, and this was counterpleaded on the ground that he could not be admitted to plead it after view.—*Sadelyngstanes*. She now appears in her own person, and she previously appeared by attorney, who could not plead a mistake in the name of his own principal.—WILLOUGHBY. You cannot have any advantage from that; therefore answer.—*Sadelyngstanes* said, for the other tenant, that the demandant could have a good writ in the *per* and *cui*, and mentioned the degrees; judgment (said he) of the writ in the *post*.—*Notton* mentioned all the mesne possessions and conveyances which maintained his writ in the *post*.—*Sadelyngstanes*. Inasmuch as the Statute[1] purports that a writ in the *post* shall not be maintained where it could be within the degrees, and we have given him a good writ within the degrees, which fact he does not deny, judgment.—STONORE. He has maintained his writ sufficiently well. Answer.

(59.) § Thomas Talbot brought a *Quid juris clamat* against the Countess of Pembroke, who came upon the Grand Distress, and had oyer of that writ, and afterwards of the *Venire facias*, and that by judgment, because the writ of *Venire facias* was in the nature of an original writ against her, and that writ of *Venire facias* was in lieu of a Resummons, as the parol had previously been put without day by a Protection, and therefore she prayed oyer of the first *Venire facias*, and had it. And because there was a variance between the first *Venire facias* and the second, and also because the last *Venire facias* did not determine for what purpose she was to come into Court, the Countess, by judgment, went without day.

---

[1] 52 Hen. III. (Marlb.), c. 29.

Nos. 58, 59.

(58.)[1] § *Cui in vita* par deux *Præcipe* en le *post.* A.D. 1345.
Et, apres viewe, *Sadl.*, pur lun, dist qele ad autre *Cui in vita.*
noun, et fuit countreplede qil navendra pas apres [Fitz.,
viewe.—*Sadl.* Ele[2] est ore en propre persone, et *Briefe,*
devant fuit par attourne, qe ne poait pleder a mes- 248.]
pressioun del noun soun mestre.[3]—WILBY. De ceo
naveretz nulle avantage ; par quei responez.—*Sadl.*,
pur lautre, dist qe le demandant avereit bon[4] brief
en *per* et *cui*, et dona les degres ; jugement du
brief en le *post.*—*Nottone* dona tant des possessions
et demises menes qe meintent le brief en le *post.*—
Sadl. Desicome lestatut voet qe brief en le *post* ne
serra meintenu la ou il poet estre deinz les degrees,
et nous lavoms done bon brief deinz les degres,
quele chose il dedit pas, jugement.—STON. Il ad
meintenu soun brief assetz. Responez.

(59.)[1] § Thomas Talbot porta *Quid juris clamat* vers *Quid juris clamat.*
la Countesse de Penbroke,[5] qe vint par la grant[6]
destresse, et de cel[7] brief avoit loy,[8] et puis del
Venire facias, et ceo par agarde, pur ceo qe ceo fuit
com loriginal devers luy, quel brief de *Venire facias*
fuit en lieu de Resomons, qar la parole a devant
fuit sanz jour par proteccion, par quei ele pria oy[9]
del primer *Venire facias, et habuit.* Et pur ceo qil
y avoit variaunce entre le primer *Venire facias* et le
seconde, et auxint qe le darrein *Venire facias* ne
determina pas a quei fere ele vindreit en Court, par
agarde la Countesse ala sanz jour.

---

[1] From the three MSS., as above.
[2] Ele is omitted from C.
[3] D., meistre.
[4] C., soun.
[5] C,, Penebroke.
[6] C., grand.
[7] C., cest.
[8] C., loye.
[9] D., oye.

No. 60.

(60.)[1] § *Grene*. This writ by which the King has commanded you to proceed is no warrant to you to proceed, because you see plainly how it is supposed in the charter in virtue of which aid was prayed [of the King] that a certain rent was reserved to the King upon the King's gift, and the King does not recite that in his writ, and so the King is not apprised of the damage to himself nor of the loss which there would be to him as the effect of a recovery, for, if the demandant recovers by reason of his right of earlier date, the seignory reserved by the King's gift is extinguished. And suppose a tenant for term of life, by lease from the King, or a tenant in fee tail, prays aid of the King, and the King commands you to proceed, and does not mention in his writ that the reversion belongs to him, even though he commands you by other words of the writ to proceed, you will nevertheless stay proceedings; so also in this case.—STONORE. When the reversion is in the King, that is one of the causes for which aid of the King is grantable; but in this case the rent reserved is not a cause for granting aid; therefore answer.—*Grene*. We tell you that the tenements are in the Welshry, and, before the conquest of Wales, were pleadable in the Court of the Prince of Wales, and after that conquest the King the grandfather of the present King ordained that tenures of Wales, that is to say, baronies and earldoms, should be pleadable in his own Court, and the nearest Sheriffs should effect execution; and we tell you that, while this writ was pending, the King has granted the Principality of Wales to his son, to hold with all the franchises as fully as Llewellyn held them, and the Prince now has his Justices, Chancery, &c., there;

---

[1] This report is in continuation of Y.B., Hil., 19 Edw. III., No. 12 (Talbot *v.* Wylyntone and wife), where the record is cited. The matter relating to jurisdiction and to the Principality of Wales is there printed from the roll (p. 425, note 3).

No. 60.

(60.)[1] § *Grene.* Ceo brief par quel le Roi vous ad A.D. 1345.
mande daler avant nest pas garrant a vous daler Brief *de*
avant, qar vous veietz bien coment en la chartre[3] *Proce-*
dendo.[2]
par quel leide fuit prie est suppose qe certein rente
par le doun le Roi luy est reserve, et le Roi en
soun brief ne reherce pas cella, et issint le Roi
nient appris de soun damage ne de la perde qil
avereit par force del recoverir, qar, si le demandant
recovere de soun dreit plus haut, la seignurie reserve par le doun le Roi est esteint. Et jeo pose
qe tenant a terme de vie, du lees le Roi, ou en fee
taille, prie eide du Roi, et le Roi vous mande.[4]
daler avant, et ne fait pas mencion en soun brief
qe la reversion est a ly, tut vous mande[5] il par
autres paroles del brief daler avant, unqore vous
suserretz ; auxint en ceo cas.—STON. Quant la reversion est en le[6] Roi, cest une des[7] causes pur
quei eide est grantable du Roi ; mes en ceo cas la
rente reserve nest. pas cause del eide ; par quei
responez.—*Grene.* Nous vous dioms qe les tenementz
sount en la Galescherie, et avant la conquest de
Gales pledable en la Court le Prince, et apres la[8]
conquest le Roi laiel ordeigna qe les tenures de
Gales, saver,[9] Baronies et Countes, serreint pledables
en sa Court demene, et les Vicountes plus procheins
freint execucion ; et vous dioms qe, pendant ceo
brief, le Roi ad grante la Principalte[10] de Gales a
soun fitz, a tenir ove totes les fraunchises si entiere-
ment come Leulyn les tient, et le Prince ore ad
ses Justices, Chauncellerie, &c., illoeqes ; et nenten-

---

[1] From the three MSS., as above.
[2] In C. the marginal note is *Residuum* entre Gilbert Talbot, &c. ; in D. it is *Residuum*, Talbot.
[3] C., charge.
[4] D., ad mande.

[5] C., comaunde.
[6] D., au, instead of en lc.
[7] D., de les.
[8] C., and D., le.
[9] D., et.
[10] C., Princialte.

Nos. 61, 62.

A.D. 1345. and we do not understand that you will take cognisance in this Court. And he made *profert* of a writ in witness of his statement.—*Skipwith.* The woman who has been admitted to defend her right, and has prayed aid of the King, has accepted the jurisdiction, and the Prince is not a party, and does not claim cognisance; and you are not apprised that the tenements are in Wales, except by the statement of one who has no power to make the allegation; therefore, &c.

Covenant: the case of the Abbot of Fountains.

(61.) § WILLOUGHBY. Because it appears to us that this covenant is of record, and is binding between the parties and their successors, the COURT doth award that the Prior do recover his damages of one hundred pounds; and, even though he may have suffered damage to a greater extent, yet, because he has not counted of any greater amount, he shall have that only.—*Grene.* We pray that the Abbot be distrained to keep the covenant.—WILLOUGHBY. You will not have that.—*Skipwith.* Then we pray an *Elegit* against the Abbot.—WILLOUGHBY. Sue that, and you shall have it.—And afterwards, in the same term, the COURT refused an *Elegit* for an Abbot who recovered damages, to wit, the Abbot of Ramsey.

Scire facias.

(62.) § Two persons were convicted of disseisin, and, after the expiration of a year, a *Scire facias* was sued against them to have execution of the damages. The Sheriff returned that one was dead, and that the other had been warned. And the latter said that he should

Nos. 61, 62.

doms pas qe ceinz voilletz conustre. Et mist avant A.D. 1345.
brief tesmoignant soun dit.—*Skyp.* La femme qest
resceu, et ad prie eide du Roi, ad accepte la jurisdiccion, et le Prince nest pas partie, ne le chalenge;
et vous nestes pas appris qe les tenementz sount
en Gales, forqe par dit de celuy qe nel poet allegger;
par quei, &c.[1]

(61.)[2] § WILBY. Pur ceo qe nous semble qe cel Cove-
covenant est de recorde, et lie entre les parties et Foun-
lour successours, agarde la COURT qe le Prior re- tayns.[4]
covere ses damages de c*li*.[5]; et, tut soit il de plus *Abbe*, 13.]
en damage, pur ceo qil nad counte de plus,[6] il
avera soulement cella.—*Grene.* Nous prioms qil soit
destreint a tener le covenant.—WILBY. Ceo naveretz
vous pas.—*Skyp.* Nous prioms *Elegit* donqes vers [Fitz.,
Labbe.—WILBY. Suetz le, et vous laveretz.[7]—Et puis, *Execucion*,
en mesme le terme, COURT via un *Elegit* pur un
Abbe qe recoverist damages, saver,[8] Labbe de Rame-
sey.

(62.)[9] § Deux furent atteintz de disseisine, et *Scire*
Scire facias, apres lan, fuit suy vers eux daver exe- [Fitz.,
cucion des damages. Le Vicounte retourna qe lun *Execucion*,
est mort, et lautre est garny. Et dit qil ne serra 81.]

---

[1] The reports of this Term end
here in D., fo. 252 b, but there are
catch words, which show that the
MS. originally contained the case
next following (No. 61). On fo. 253
of the MS. reports of Michaelmas
Term, 23 Edw. III. begin.

[2] From L., and C. This is the
conclusion of the report No. 15 of
Easter Term, 16 Edward III.
(pp. 182-190). The record, *Placita*
de Banco, Easter, 16 Edw. III.,
R° 132 is printed in the Appendix
to Y.B., 16 Edw. III., Part I.
(pp. 287-290). The action was

brought by Richard, Prior of
Wartre, against the Abbot of
Fountains.

[3] Covenant is from L. alone.

[4] Fountayns is from C. alone.

[5] For the words of the judgment
as they appear on the roll *see* Y.B.,
16 Edw. III., Part I., p. 290.

[6] This so appears in the record.
Y.B., 16 Edw. III., Part I., p. 288.

[7] The execution by *Elegit* also
appears on the roll. Y.B., 16 Edw.
III., Part I., p. 290.

[8] L., vers.

[9] From L., and C.

No. 62.

not be put to answer until the heir and the ter-tenants of the other had been warned.—*Seton.* He is by law chargeable with the whole, and so is each of them; and, even though execution had been awarded against both of them, the Sheriff could have levied the whole of one of them.—Scot. It seems to the one who has been warned that, although the Sheriff could have done that, it does not therefore follow that we should do so by judgment, inasmuch as our judgment with regard to execution must be in accordance with the first judgment, which judgment charges all their lands in common.—*R. Thorpe.* The reason which you give would be sufficiently binding if a *Scire facias* were sued against this one as ter-tenant, but it is not: for, inasmuch as he committed the tort himself, he is chargeable, even if he have no land.—*Notton.* If the Sheriff were to levy the whole of him, and the other were sufficient, the one of whom the whole had been levied would have suit and remedy in respect thereof against the Sheriff, and that has been seen to be the case.—*Grene, ad idem.* If two persons be bound in a statute merchant, and one of them be taken, on his prayer his fellow obligee will be taken—and that, too, whether the plaintiff wishes it or not; and the reason is that one shall not be charged alone. And in Debt also one shall never be charged alone by judgment. And it has been seen in a case such as that in which we now are, in which there was a conviction of disseisin with force and arms, and two were taken, and one of them died, that the other paid his fine before satisfaction was made to the plaintiff, because execution of the damages will fall upon the ter-tenants of the other, and they ought not to be taken.—Baukwell. That is not law; and in cases of Debt and Statute merchant, it is no wonder that it is as you say, because the obligation is in common.—And afterwards, because the Court was minded to adjourn the parties

No. 62.

pas mys a respondre tanqe les heirs et terre tenantz
del autre fuissent garniz.—*Setone.* Celuy de ley est
chargeable del entier, et chesqun de eux; et, tut ust
execucion este agarde vers lun et lautre, le Vicounte
pout aver leve tut de lun.—Scot. Semble a luy qe,
tut pout le Vicounte ceo aver fait, de ceo nensuit
pas qe nous par agarde le devoms faire, desicome
nostre agarde sur lexecucion serra acordant al primer
jugement, le quel jugement charge tut lour terres
en comune.—[*R.*] *Thorpe.* Vostre resoun liereit bien
si *Scire facias* fuit suy vers cest com terre tenant,
mes il nest point: qar, par tant qil fist mesme le
tort, il est chargeable, tut neit il pas terre.—*Nottone.*
Si le Vicounte levast tut de luy, et lautre fuit [1]
suffisant, celuy de qi tut fuit leve avereit suite et
remedie de cel vers le Vicounte, et ceo ad homme
view.—*Grene, ad idem.* Si deux soient lies en estatut
marchaunt, et lun soit pris, a sa prier soun com-
paignon serra pris, et auxint tut voleit le pleintif
ou noun; et cest pur ceo qe lun soul ne serra pas
charge. Et auxint en Dette lun soul ne serra jammes
charge par agarde. Et homme ad viewe qen tiel
cas com nous sumes, ou la disseisine fuit atteint a
force et armes, et deux fuissent pris, et lun muruist,
qe lautre fist sa fyne avant qe gree fuit fait al
pleintif, pur ceo qe execucion des damages cherra
sur les terre tenantz de lautre, qe ne duissent pas
estre pris.—Bauk. Ceo nest pas ley; et en cas de
Dette et Statut marchaunt nest pas merveille, qar
lobligacion est en comune.—Et, puis pur ceo qe Court
voleit aver adjourne les parties sur lexecucion, le

---

[1] C., est.

No. 63.

A.D. 1345. with regard to execution, the plaintiff prayed further a writ against the heir and ter-tenants of the other.

Assise of Darrein Present-ment.   (63.) § Assise of Darrein Presentment in respect of the church of A.[1]—*Derworthy.* A.[2], our father, presented one J.,[2] in the time of the King the father of the King that now is, and he was admitted, &c., by reason of whose death the church is now void. And before him our great-grandfather[2] presented, &c. And before him our great-great-grandfather[2] presented, &c., in the time of King Henry III. And *Derworthy* made the descent of the advowson to be from A.[2] to the plaintiff.—*Huse.* We tell you that one W.[3] was seised, in the time of King Henry III., of two parts[4] of the vill of P.,[3] to which the advowson of two parts of the church is appendant, and presented to the two parts of the same church, &c., and that in the time of the same King. From W.[1] *Huse* made the descent to R.,[3] who

---

[1] For the name of the church *see* p. 427, note 1.

[2] For the names *see* p. 427, note 3.

[3] For the real names *see* p. 429, note 2.

[4] A moiety according to the record.

No. 63.

pleintif prist outre brief vers les heirs et terre A.D. 1345.
tenantz de lautre.

(63.)[1] § Darrein Presentement del eglise de A.— Darrein Presentement.
Der. A., nostre pere, presenta un J. en temps le
Roi pere le Roi, &c., qe fuit resceu, &c., par qi
mort leglise, &c. Et devant luy nostre besaiel
presenta, &c. Et devant ly[2] nostre tresaiel presenta, &c., en temps le Roi Henre. Et fist la descente del avoweson de A. al pleintif.[3]—*Huse.* Nous
vous dioms qun W., en temps le Roi Henre, fuit
seisi de deux parties de la ville de P., a quei lavoeson de les deux parties del eglise est appendant,
et presenta a les deux parties de mesme leglise, &c.,
et en temps de mesme le Roi. De W. fist la de-

---

[1] From *L.*, and *C.*, but corrected by the record, *Placita de Banco,* Mich , 19 Edw. III., R° 486, d. It there appears that the Assise was brought by "Laurentius de "Sancto Martino" against John "de Sancto Laudo" in respect of the church of Maydene Nywetone (Maiden Newton, Dorset).

[2] ly is omitted from C.

[3] According to the record Lauren-tius "dicit quod quidam Regi-"naldus de Sancto Martino, avus "ipsius Laurentii, cujus heres "ipse est, fuit seisitus de advoca-"tione ecclesiæ prædictæ, et præ-"sentavit ad eandem ecclesiam "quendam Thomam de Forde, "clericum suum, qui ad præsenta-"tionem suam fuit admissus et "institutus . . . . tempore "Edwardi Regis, avi domini Regis "nunc, per cujus mortem prædicta "ecclesia modo vacat. Et in "proxima vacatione ejusdem qui-"dam Willelmus de Sancto Mar-"tino proavus ipsius Laurentii, "cujus heres, &c., præsentavit ad "eandem quendam Henricum de "Stauntone, clericum suum, qui "ad præsentationem suam fuit "admissus et institutus . . . . "tempore Henrici Regis, proavi "domini Regis nunc. Et in "proxima vacatione præcedente "idem Willelmus præsentavit ad "eandem quendam Jordanum de "Sancto Martino, clericum suum, "qui ad præsentationem suam "fuit admissus et institutus . . . . "tempore prædicti Henrici Regis, "&c. Et in proxima vacatione "præcedente, &c., quidam Jor-"danus de Sancto Martino, "triavus ipsius Laurentii, præsen-"tavit ad eandem quendam "Robertum de Strengestone, cleri-"cum suum, qui ad præsentati-"onem suam fuit admissus, &c., "tempore pacis, tempore prædicti "Henrici Regis, &c. Et de præ-"dicto Reginaldo descendit jus "præsentandi, &c., cuidam Lau-"rentio ut filio et heredi, &c. Et "de ipso Laurentio descendit jus "præsentandi, &c., isti Laurentio "ut filio et heredi, &c., qui nunc "clamat, &c."

No. 63.

presented, &c., to the same two parts of the church, which R.[1] gave the two parts of the vill, with the appurtenances to one T.[1] in fee tail, of whom the woman against whom the writ is brought[2] is issue in tail. This T.[1] leased the two parts of the vill, &c., to one K.[1] for a term of years, at which time A.[1] their ancestor of whom they speak presented J.,[1] &c.,¯ *absque hoc* that the others whom they mentioned were admitted on their presentation, &c.; and we demand judgment whether by reason of an usurpation effected in the time of our ancestor, who was tenant in tail, and during the time of the termor, you ought to have an Assise.—*Derworthy.* You see plainly how he con-

---

[1] For the real names *see* p. 429, note 2.

[2] The writ was not brought against her, but against her son, according to the record. *See* p. 429, note 2.

scente a R. qe presenta, &c., a mesmes les ij parties, A.D. 1345.
le quel dona les deux parties de la ville, ove les
appurtenances, a un T. en fee taille, de qi la femme
vers qi le brief est porte est issue en taille, quel
T. lessa les deux parties de la ville, &c., a un K.
a terme daunz, a quel temps A., lour auncestre, de
qi ils parlent, presenta J., &c., sanz ceo qe les
autres dount ils parlent furent resceu a lour presentement, &c. ; et demandoms jugement si par
purprise fet en temps nostre auncestre, qe fuit tenant
en taille, et en temps le termer si vous deivetz[1]
Assise aver.[2]—*Der.* Vous veietz bien coment il conust

---

[1] C., devetz.

[2] According to the record the plea was " quod quidam Alexander " de Chyverel, triavus ipsius " Johannis, cujus heres ipse est, " fuit seisitus de medietate villæ " de Maydene Nywetone, ad quam " advocatio duarum partium eccle- " siæ prædictæ pertinebat, qui ad " duas partes ecclesiæ prædictæ " præsentavit quendam Simonem " de Mantestone, clericum suum, " qui ad præsentationem suam fuit " admissus, &c., tempore Regis " Henrici, &c., proavi, &c. Et de " ipso Alexandro descendit medie- " tas illa villæ prædictæ, ad quam, " &c., cuidam Johanni ut filio et " heredi, &c., qui, vacantibus " duabus partibus ecclesiæ præ- " dictis per mortem præfati " Simonis, præsentavit ad easdem " quendam Adam de Kaukeberge, " clericum suum, qui ad præsenta- " tionem suam fuit admissus, &c., " tempore prædicti Henrici Regis, " &c. Et, vacantibus duabus " partibus ecclesiæ prædictis per " mortem ejusdem Adæ, præfatus " Johannes filius Alexandri præ- " sentavit ..d easdem quendam

" Galfridum de Melbourne, cleri- " cum suum, qui ad præsenta- " tionem suam fuit admissus, &c., " tempore Edwardi Regis, avi, &c. " Qui quidem Johannes postea " prædictam medietatem villæ, ad " quam, &c., dedit cuidam Henrico " de Braundestone, clerico, tenen- " dam sibi et heredibus suis in " perpetuum. Et vacantibus dua- " bus partibus ecclesiæ prædictis " per mortem prædicti Galfridi, " idem Henricus præsentavit ad " easdem quendam Thomam de " Stauntone, clericum suum, qui " ad præsentationem suam fuit " admissus, &c., tempore prædicti " Regis avi, &c. Et postea idem " Henricus dedit prædictam medie- " tatem villæ ad quam, &c., cuidam " Alexandro Chyverel, avo ipsius " Johannis de Sancto Laudo, et " Dionisiæ uxori ejus, et heredibus " de corporibus suis exeuntibus. " Qui quidem Alexander medieta- " tem illam, ad quam, &c., quibus- " dam Roberto Steel et Waltero de " Mynterne concessit tenendam ad " terminum decem annorum. Et " de ipso Alexandro descendit jus, " &c., cuidam Johannæ ut filiæ et

No. 63.

A.D. 1345. fesses the last presentation to have been made by our ancestor, and would avoid it on the ground of usurpation, but that answer does not lie in the mouth of any one except of the person who is possessor of the patronage, and he does not make himself to be that, because he claims only a part of the advowson; judgment whether such a plea lies in his mouth.—*R. Thorpe.* Do you mean to abide judgment on that?—*Derworthy.* He takes two different reasons to show usurpation, one that the presentation was made in the time of his ancestor who was tenant in tail, the other that it was in the time of a termor; let him hold to one.—*R. Thorpe.* He shall not be admitted to that, because by his first exception he has accepted our answer as being one.—*Derworthy* afterwards maintained that the presentation had been in one of his more remote ancestors, but this was traversed by the other side.—And thereupon the Assise was awarded.

No. 63.

la darrein presentement a nostre auncestre, et le voet voider par purprise, quel respons gist en nully bouche forqe de celuy qest possessour del avowere, et il se fait pas tiel, qar il cleyme forqe parcelle de lavoweson[1]; jugement si tiel ple en sa bouche gise.—[*R.*] *Thorpe.* La voilletz demurer?—*Der.* Il prent deux causes de purprise, une pur ceo qe le presentement se fist en temps soun auncestre tenant en taille, autre pur ceo qe ceo fuit en temps de termer; se teigne[2] al un.—[*R.*] *Thorpe.* A ceo navendra il pas, qar par soun primer chalenge il ad accepte qe nostre respons est un.—*Der.* puis meintent le presentement en un de ses auncestres paramount, qe fuit traverse par eux.—Et sur ceo lassise agarde.[3]

" heredi, &c., quæ quidem Johanna " statum suum quem habuit in " medietate prædicta, ad quam, " &c., cum accidisset, &c., reddidit " isti Johanni de Sancto Laudo, " versus quem, &c., ut filio præ- " dictæ Johannæ et heredi ap- " parenti prædictorum Alexandri " et Dionisiæ, in feodo talliato " supradicto. Et dicit quod præ- " dictus Thomas de Stauntone, " quem ipse supponit præsenta- " tum fuisse per prædictum Wil- " lelmum de Sancto Martino, " antecessorem, &c., fuit eadem " persona quam prædictus Henri- " cus de Braundestone præsen- " tavit, &c., ad prædictas duas " partes ecclesiæ, &c. Et dicit " quod prædicta præsentatio de " prædicto Thoma de Forde facta " non debet dici nisi quædam " præsentatio purprisa infra termi- " num prædictorum decem anno- " rum, et tempore prædicti " Alexandri tenentis in feodo " talliato, &c., absque hoc, &c.,

" quod prædicti Robertus de " Strengestone, Jordanus, Thomas " de Stauntone, et Thomas de " Forde admissi fuerunt et instituti " in ecclesia prædicta ad præsenta- " tionem prædictorum antecesso- " rum prædicti Laurentii, sicut " idem Laurentius superius suppo- " nit. Et hoc paratus est verificare, " unde petit judicium, &c."

[1] C., avoweson, instead of de lavoweson.

[2] C., tiegne.

[3] The replication, upon which issue was joined, was, according to the record, " Laurentius, non cog- " noscendo advocationem ecclesiæ " prædictæ fuisse pertinentem ad " medietatem villæ prædictæ, nec " prædictam præsentationem fac- " tam de præfato Thoma de Forde " factam fuisse per purprisam " infra terminum tenentium ad " terminum annorum, &c., nec " quod aliquis antecessor prædicti " Johannis, unquam præsentavit " aliquam personam ad duas partes

Nos. 64, 65.

A.D. 1345.
Cessavit.

(64.) § *Cessavit*, supposing that another person held
of the demandant, and that the tenements ought to
revert to the demandant by reason of the cesser of
the person against whom the writ was brought.—
Richemunde. Judgment of the writ, because it does
not suppose any privity between the person who is
supposed to be your tenant and us, as by entry.—
WILLOUGHBY. This writ serves for the lord when his
very tenant enfeoffs another, or is disseised by another
who ceases to render the services; therefore, will you
say anything else?

Cessavit.

(65.) § John Moubray, knight, brought a *Cessavit*
against A., who appeared, and tendered the arrears
for two years.—*Seton.* The arrears for the whole time
must be tendered, and damages also; and we tell you
that the rent is in arrear for four years.—WILLOUGHBY.
Your writ supposes the cesser to have been for two
years, and therefore it is sufficient to tender the
amount due for that time; and, if more be in arrear, you
must impute it to your own folly that you did not
purchase your writ in time.—*Seton.* This writ is given
for want of distress, and that which could be levied
by distress, if the land were open to distress, must,
according to law, be tendered, if the land is to be

Nos. 64, 65.

(64.) [1] § *Cessavit*, supposant qautre tient de luy, et qe par cesser de cest vers qi le brief est porte les tenements deivent revertir. — *Rich.* Jugement [2] du brief, qe suppose nulle privite entre celuy qest suppose vostre tenant et nous, come par entre.—WILBY. Cest brief seert pur le seignur quant soun verroy tenant feffe autre, ou est disseisi par autre qe cesse; par quei voilletz autre chose dire?

(65.) [1] § Johan Moubray, chivaller, [3] porta *Cessavit* vers A., qe vint, et tendist les arrerages de deux aunz.—*Setone.* Il covient tendre les arrerages de tut temps, et damages; et vous dioms qe la rente est arere par iiij aunz.—WILBY. Vostre brief suppose le cesser par deux aunz, par quei a cel tendre pur cel temps suffit; et, si plus soit arere, rettetz a vostre folie qe vous nussetz purchace vostre brief par temps.—*Setone.* Cest brief est done par defaute de destresse, et ceo qe poait par destresse estre leve, si la terre fuit overt, serra tendu par ley, si la terre

---

" ecclesiæ prædictas, dicit quod
" prædictus Thomas de Stauntone
" fuit admissus et institutus in
" ecclesia prædicta per prædictum
" Willelmum de Sancto Martino,
" proavum prædicti Laurentii, et
" non per prædictum Henricum de
" Braundestone, clericum, cujus
" statum ipse allegat se habere,
" &c."
After some adjournments the defendant failed to appear, and the assise was taken by default, the verdict being " quod prædictus " Reginaldus de Sancto Martino, " avus prædicti Laurentii, cujus " heres ipse est, fuit seisitus de " advocatione ecclesiæ prædictæ et " ultimo præsentavit ad eandem " præfatum Thomam de Forde, " clericum suum, qui ad præsen-

" tationem suam fuit admissus et
" institutus in ecclesia prædicta
" tempore pacis, tempore prædicti
" Edwardi Regis avi domini Regis
" nunc, per cujus mortem prædicta
" ecclesia vacavit. Et dicunt quod
" tempus semestre jam transactum
" est. Quæsiti quantum prædicta
" ecclesia valet per annum secun-
" dum verum valorem, &c., dicunt
" quod valet per annum quinqua-
" ginta libræ."
Judgment was therefore given for the plaintiff to recover his presentation, and have a writ to the Bishop, and £100 damages, being two years' value of the church.

[1] From L., and C.

[2] Jugement is omitted from C.

[3] chivaller is from C. alone.

No. 66.

A.D. 1345. saved.—And afterwards the tender was admitted *gratis,* and two other persons charged their lands as security, &c.

Dower.　　　(66.) § Dower against a guardian. And the demandant made her demand in respect of a third part of certain messuages, land, meadow, &c.—*Grene.* A fine was levied between the husband[1] and A.,[1] his first wife, of the one part, and one J.[1] of the other part, of the manors of P.[2] and W.,[2] which are the same tenements of which she demands her dower, and by that fine J.[1] granted and rendered the manors to them and to the heirs of their bodies, &c., and the infant who is in the wardship of the tenants is their issue ; judgment whether this demandant, who is the husband's second wife, ought to have dower of such an estate.—*Moubray.*

---

[1] For the real names *see* p. 435, note 4.

[2] For the names of the manors *see* p. 435, note 4.

No. 66.

serra sauve.—Et puis *gratis* le tendre fuit resceu, et A.D. 1345 autres deux [1] pur soerte chargerent lour terres, &c.

(66.) [2] § Dowere vers gardein. Et fist sa demande Dowere. par noun de terce partie de certein mies, terre, pree, &c.—*Grene.* Fine se leva entre le baron et A., sa primere femme, dune part, et un J. dautre part, de maners de P. et W., qe sount mesmes les tenementz dount ele demande soun dowere, par quel J. granta et rendi les maners a eux et a les heirs de lour [3] corps, &c., entre queux cesty qest en sa garde est issue ; jugement si ceste qest sa seconde femme de tiel estat deive dowere aver. [4]—*Moubray.*

---

[1] 'deux is from L. alone.

[2] From L., and C., but corrected by the record, *Placita de Banco*, Mich., 19 Edw. III., R° 509. It there appears that the action was brought by Margaret late wife of William de Holbroke, knight, against Richard de Brewes, knight, and John de Brewes, parson of the church of Stradbroke, guardians of the land of the heir of William de Holbroke, knight, in respect of a third part of 160 acres of land, 12 acres of meadow, 10 acres of pasture, and three acres of wood in East Bergholt, "Brendewenham" Raydon, Capel, Stratford, and Little Wenham (Suffolk).

[3] C., lours.

[4] The plea was, according to the record, "quod prædicta tenementa, "unde, &c., sunt parcella mane- "riorum de Brendewenham et "parva Wenham, et faciunt "maneria prædicta. Et quo ad "illa, &c., dicunt quod prædicta "Margareta non debet inde dotem "habere, quia dicunt quod alias " . . . . levavit "quidam finis inter prædictum

" Willelmum de Holbroke, quon- " dam virum, &c., ex cujus dota- " tione, &c., et Amiciam tunc " uxorem ejus querentes, et Jo- " hannem de Breouse personam " ecclesiæ de Stradebroke et Wil- " lelmum personam ecclesiæ de " parva Wenham deforciantes, de " prædictis maneriis de Brende- " wenham et parva Wenham, " cum pertinentiis, et advocatione " ecclesiæ ejusdem manerii de " parva Wenham, unde placitum " Conventionis, &c., per quem " finem prædictus Willelmus de " Holbroke recognovit prædicta " maneria, cum pertinentiis, et " advocationem prædictam esse " jus ipsius Johannis, ut illa quæ " idem Johannes et Willelmus, " persona, &c., habuerunt de dono " ipsius Willelmi de Holbroke, et " pro hac recognitione, &c., iidem " Johannes et Willelmus, persona, " &c., concesserunt prædictis Wil- " lelmo de Holbroke, et Amiciæ " prædicta maneria, cum pertinen- " tiis, et advocationem prædictam, " et ea illis reddiderunt, ... " habenda et tenenda eisdem

No. 66.

A.D. 1345 He is a stranger, in whose mouth such a plea does not lie.—HILLARY. He is guardian of the issue in tail. Answer.—*Moubray*. We tell you that there are the manors of P.[1] and W.,[1] which have always been manors, and that the tenements whereof we demand dower are not the manors, nor parcel of the manors; ready, &c.; judgment, and we pray seisin.—*Skipwith*. That is tantamount to saying that the tenements are not included in the fine.—*Moubray*. The fine speaks of the manors, and we grant that there are such manors, &c.; but our demand has nothing to do with the manors, and therefore our answer is a different kind of plea from that of "not included'; and since there are such manors, and the fine is levied of the manors, nothing passed by the fine except the manors. —HILLARY. If you levy a fine of certain tenements by the description of a manor, when in fact there never was such a manor, is not the fine good?— *Moubray*. Yes, it is; but when there is a manor, which existed in previous times, and a fine is levied of the manor, that is quite a different case from that

---

" Willelmo de Holebroke et " Amiciæ et heredibus masculis de " corporibus ipsorum Willelmi et " Amiciæ exeuntibus, de capi- " talibus dominis, &c., ita quod si " iidem Willelmus et Amicia " obierunt sine herede masculo " de corporibus suis exeunte, tunc " post decessum ipsorum Willelmi " de Holbroke et Amiciæ prædicta " maneria, cum pertinentiis, et " advocatio prædicta integre re- " manebunt rectis heredibus ipsius " Willelmi de Holbroke, tenenda " de capitalibus dominis, &c. Et " proferunt hic partem prædicti " finis qui hoc idem testatur, &c. " Et dicunt quod prædicti Willel- " mus de Holbroke et Amicia

" habuerunt quendam Ricardum ' filium et heredem ipsorum " Willelmi et Amiciæ inter ipsos " procreatum, qui modo est infra " ætatem, ratione cujus minoris " ætatis prædicta tenementa unde, " &c., quæ faciunt maneria præ- " dicta, ut prædictum est, sunt in " custodia ipsorum Ricardi et " Johannis. Et petunt judicium " si prædicta Margareta, quæ est " secunda uxor ipsius Willelmi de " Holbroke, de tali statu dotem de " prædictis tenementis sic datis in " forma prædicta habere debeat, " &c."

[1] For the real names *see* p. 439, note 1.

No. 66.

Il est estrange, en qi bouche tiel ple ne gist pas. A.D. 1345.
—HILL. Il est gardein lissue en la taille. Responez.
—*Moubray.* Nous vous dioms qil y ad les maners
P. et W., qe tut temps ount este maners, et qe les
tenementz dount nous demandoms le dowere ne sount
pas les maners, ne parcelle des maners; prest, &c.;
jugement, et prioms seisine.—*Skyp.* Taunt amount
qe nient compris. — *Moubray.* La fine parle des
maners, et nous grantoms qils y sount tiels maners,
&c.; mes nostre demande nest rienz des maners,
par quei nostre respons est autre manere de plee qe
nient compris; quant tiels maners y sount, et la fine
est leve des maners, rienz passe par les fines forqe
les maners.—HILL. Si vous levetz fine de certeinz
tenementz par noun du maner, la ou unqes ne fuit
ceo maner, nest la fine bone?—*Moubray.* Si est;
mes quant il y ad maner a devant, et fine soit leve
del maner, est tut autre qe si unqes maner y fuit,

No. 67.

A.D. 1345. where there never was any manor, and a render is made by fine by the description of a manor.—WIL-LOUGHBY. You are demurring about nothing. He tells you that the fine was levied of the same tenements; therefore answer to that.—*Moubray* repeated as above, and said "and so not included"; ready, &c.—And the other side said the contrary.

Formedon in the descender.
(67.) § John de Segrave and his wife, and Edward Montagu and his wife brought a Formedon in the descender, in virtue of the gift of the King the father of the present King. The tenant confessed the action. *Rokele*. We tell you that the tenant leased the same

No. 67.

et homme par fine rende par noun de maner.—A.D. 1345.
WILBY. Vous demuretz sur nient. Il vous dit qe la
fine se leva de mesmes les tenementz; par quei
responez vous a cella.—*Moubray* rehercea *ut supra*,
et dit qe issint nient compris; prest, &c.[1]—*Et alii
e contra.*[2]

(67.)[3] § J. Segrave et sa femme, E. Mountagu,[5] Fourme
et sa femme porterent Fourme doun en descendre descen-
par le doun le Roi le pere.[6] Le tenant ne pout dre.[4]
[Fitz.,
dedire.[7]—*Rokele.* Nous vous dioms qe le tenant lessa Resceit,
15.]

[1] The replication was, according to the record, "quod maneria de "Brendewenham et parva Wen-"ham ab antiquo, et a tempore quo "non extat memoria, extiterunt, "et quod prædicta tenementa "unde, &c., non sunt parcella "prædictorum maneriorum, nec "faciunt maneria prædicta. Et "sic dicit quod prædicta tene-"menta unde, &c., non continentur "in prædicto fine. Et hoc parata "est verificare, unde petit judi-"cium, &c."

[2] According to the record there was a rejoinder, upon which issue was joined, "quod prædicta tene-"menta unde, &c., continentur in "prædicto fine, &c."

There was afterwards a verdict, at *Nisi prius*, "quod prædicta "tenementa non sunt parcella "prædictorum maneriorum, nec "faciunt prædicta maneria, nec "continentur in prædicto fine. Et "dicunt quod prædictus Willelmus, "quondam vir prædictæ Mar-"garetæ, fuit seisitus de prædictis "tenementis in dominico suo ut "de feodo simplici, et inde obiit "seisitus de tali statu. Quæsito a "præfatis juratoribus ad quæ "damna, dicunt ad damnum "viginti marcarum."

Judgment was therefore given "quod prædicta Margareta re-"cuperet inde seisinam suam "versus eos, &c., et damna sua "prædicta."

[3] From L., and C., but corrected by the record, *Placita de Banco*, Mich., 19 Edw. III., R° 475, d. It there appears that the action was brought by John de Segrave and Margaret his wife, and Edward "de Monte Acuto" and Alice his wife, against Adam Broun and Margery his wife, in respect of the manor of Dykeleburghe (Dickle-borough, Norfolk) "quod Ed-"wardus nuper Rex Angliæ, pater "domini Regis nunc, dedit Thomæ "de Brothertone, nuper Comiti "Norffolciæ, et heredibus de cor-"pore suo exeuntibus, et quod, "post mortem prædicti Comitis, "præfatis Margaretæ et Aliciæ, "filiabus et heredibus ejusdem "Comitis, descendere debet."

[4] The words en descendre are from C. alone.

[5] C., Mountagew.

[6] MSS. of Y.B., laiel, instead of le pere.

[7] According to the roll the tenant confessed the action, and the demandants had judgment to recover their seisin.

No. 67.

tenements to Robert de Morle, for a term of years, by this deed, and that term is unexpired, and this suit is feigned, &c., and we pray the benefit of the Statute of Gloucester.[1]—HILLARY. Robert does not appear either by attorney or in his own person; therefore let the demandants recover their seisin.—And soon afterwards *Rokele* produced a writ of attorney for Robert, making mention of the case, and prayed that execution might

---

[1] 6 Edw. I. (Glouc.), c. 11.

No. 67.

mesmes les tenementz a Robert Morle, a terme daunz, A.D. 1345. par ceo fait, quel terme dure, et ceste suite est feint, &c., et prioms benefice del estatut de Gloucestre. —HILL. Robert nest pas par attourne nen propre persone, par quei recoverent sa seisine. — Et tost apres *Rokele* moustra brief dattourne pur R., fesaunt mencion del cas, et pria qexecucion ne se fist pas.[1]

[1] According to the roll, " Postea " venit quidam Johannes de la " Rokele et protulit partem cujus- " dam indenturæ testificantem " quod prædictus Adam dimisit " manerium prædictum, cum per- " tinentiis, cuidam Roberto de " Morle, chivaler, tenendum ad " terminum decem annorum, de " quo quidem termino elapsi sunt " duo anni, et per formam statuti " nuper apud Gloucestre editi " petiit quod executio judicii " suspendatur usque ad finem " termini prædicti." Rokele also made *profert* of the King's writ close directed to the Justices, dated the 20th of November in the 19th year of the reign :—" Cum in " statuto nostro apud Gloucestre " dudum edito inter cætera con- " tinetur quod si quis in Civitate " nostra Londoniarum dimiserit " tenementum suum ad terminum " annorum, et ille cujus est " liberum tenementum se faciat " implacitari per collusionem, et " fecerit defaltam post defaltam, " aut reddere voluerit, ad facien- " dum terminarium admittere [*sic*] " terminum suum, Maior et ballivi " inquirant per probos et legales " homines de visneto, in præsentia " terminarii et petentis, utrum " petens juste implacitet tenentem " an per collusionem et fraudem " ad faciendum terminarium ad- " mittere[*sic*] terminum suum, et,

" si inveniatur per inquisitionem " quod petens juste movit placitum " suum, statim perficiat judicium, " et, si inveniatur quod petens " implacitaverit tenentem per " fraudem ad auferendum termi- " nario terminum suum, remaneat " terminarius in termino suo, et " executio judicii pro petente sit " suspensa usque post terminum " completum. Eodem modo fiat " de æquitate in tali casu coram " Justiciariis, si terminarius hoc " vendicet ante judicium, prout in " statuto prædicto plenius con- " tinetur. Jamque ex parte dilecti " et fidelis nostri Roberti de Morle " nobis sit, graviter conquerendo, " monstratum quod, cum ipse " teneat manerium de Dikele- " burghe cum pertinentiis, ad " terminum decem annorum, ex " dimissione Adæ Broun, Johannes " de Segrave et Margareta uxor " ejus, Edwardus de Monte Acuto " et Alicia uxor ejus, per fraudem " et collusionem inter eosdem " Johannem, Margaretam, Ed- " wardum, et Aliciam, et præfatos " Adam et Margeriam uxorem ejus " habitas, machinantes excludere " prædictum Robertum de termino " suo prædicto implacitent coram " vobis per breve nostrum præfatos " Adam et Margeriam de manerio " supradicto, per quod ex parte " ejusdem Roberti nobis est cum " instantia supplicatum ut, cum

No. 68.

A.D. 1345. be stayed.—WILLOUGHBY. You come too late, as you come after judgment has been rendered.—*Rokel.* I mentioned the matter before judgment, and, even if I had prayed this before judgment, I should not have hindered the judgment, but only execution; therefore the effect of the statute is to delay execution; therefore it seems that, since I have come before execution, I have come in sufficiently good time.—STONORE. The statute purports otherwise; and your writ also which you bring supposes that you ought to have come before judgment, because a matter which has been adjudged is not feigned. And it can hardly be said that the statute takes effect in a *Scire facias* upon a fine or upon a judgment. Now with regard to this matter the King's gift is of record; therefore, even if you had come before judgment, you would possibly not have been heard; *a fortiori* you will not now. Therefore do you, the demandants, sue execution.

Waste.   (68.) § A writ of Waste was brought against a man

No. 68.

WILBY. Vous venetz trop tard, apres jugement rendu. A.D. 1345.
—*Rokele.* Jeo le parlay avant jugement, et, tut usse
jeo venu avant jugement, ne usse pas destourbe
jugement, mes soulement execucion; donqes leffecte
del[1] estatut est a destourber execucion; par quei il
semble qe quant jeo su venutz avant execucion. qe
assetz su jeo venu par temps.—STON. Lestatut est
autre; et vostre brief auxint qe vous portetz suppose
qe vous duissetz vener avant jugement, qar chose
juge nest pas feint. Et en *Scire facias* suy hors
dune fine ou dun jugement a peyn si lestatut teigne[2]
lieu. Ore en ceste matere le doun le Roi est de
recorde; par quei, tut ussetz venutz avant jugement,
par cas vous ne serretz pas oy; a plus fort a ore.
Par quei suetz execucion.[3]

(68.)[4] § Wast porte vers un homme et K. sa Wast.

[Fitz.,
Wast,
317.]

" ipse diversis arduis negotiis
" nostris per præceptum nostrum
" multipliciter intendat, per quod
" ipse ad jam instantem quin-
" denam Sancti Martini ad quem
" [sic], præfatus Adam et Margeria
" defaltam facere seu alias mane-
" rium prædictum reddere velle
" verisimiliter præsumitur, &c.,
" hujusmodi fraudem et collusi-
" onem coram vobis calumniando
" juxta formam statuti prædicti,
" Nos, pro eo quod evidenter nobis
" constat quod prædictus Robertus,
" occasione prædicta, ad diem
" prædictum coram vobis per-
" sonaliter venire non potest, ad
" fraudem et collusionem calumni-
" andum juxta formam ejusdem
" statuti, concessimus eidem Ro-
" berto quod ipse loco suo faciat
" . . . . . . attornatos suos
" ad hujusmodi fraudem et collu-
" sionem in placito prædicto
" calumniandum, qui quidem Ro-
" bertus . . . .

" loco suo Willelmum de Berghe
" et Galfridum de Westone ad
" fraudem et collusionem præ-
" dictas . . . .
" . . . . . perdendum in
" præmissis, et ad omnia alia et
" singula faciendum quæ idem
" Robertus faceret . . . . .
" . . . . præ-
" dictos Willelmum et Galfridum
" vel alterum ipsorum loco ipsius
" Roberti ad . . . ."
The writing has perished at the
sides and bottom of the roll.

[1] C., par.

[2] C., tiegne.

[3] The roll is, for the most part,
illegible at the end.

[4] From L., and C., but corrected
by the record, *Placita de Banco*,
Mich., 19 Edw. III., Rᵒ 486. It
there appears that the action was
brought by Thomas de Cantebrigge
against William de Langeleye and
Mabel his wife, in respect of waste
in houses, woods, and gardens in

No. 68.

A.D. 1345. and K.[1] his wife, supposing that the wife held, by lease from T.[1] the plaintiff, for her life. — *Sadelyng-stanes.* We tell you that one W.,[2] who was the feoffor of T. the plaintiff, long before T. had anything in the tenements, made a recognisance, &c., to one A.,[2] which A. sued against K., while she was sole, and had execution of a moiety of this land, and died seised of that estate, and his executors are seised of that estate this day; and we do not understand that we ought to be charged in respect of the time when that execution was had by virtue of a recovery of earlier date than is the estate of T. the plaintiff, and we also tell you that before execution was had we committed no waste. And as to the other moiety we tell you that K., while she was sole, leased her estate, a long time before this writ was purchased, to R.[2] and to his heirs, which R. is tenant in that manner; and we do not understand that we ought to be charged in respect of the time since that lease. And as to the time before the lease made to R., no waste was committed. — *Gaynesford.*

---

[1] For the names *see* p. 443, note 4.

[2] For the real names see p. 445, note 5.

No. 68.

femme, supposant qe la femme tient, du lees T. le A.D. 1345. pleintif, a sa vie.—*Sadl.* Nous vous dioms qun W., qe fuit feffour T. le pleintif, longe temps avant qe T. rienz y avoit, fist une reconisance, &c., a un A., le quel A. suyt vers K. quant ele fuit sole, et avoit execucion de la moite de ceste terre, et muruist seisi de cel estat, et ses executours de cel[1] estat huy ceo jour seisi; et nentendoms pas qe de temps qe cel execucion fuit fait par force dun recoverir de plus haut qe nest lestat T. qest pleintif deivoms estre charge, et auxint[2] avant[3] lexecucion fait nulle wast, &c. Et quant a lautre moite nous vous dioms qe K., tanqe come ele fuit sole, lessa soun estat, longe temps avant cest brief purchace, a R. et a ses heirs, quel R. est tenant par la manere; et nentendoms pas qe de temps puis le lees devoms[4] estre charge. Et quant de temps devant le lees fait a R., nulle wast, &c.[5]—*Gayn.* Nous voloms averer

---

Fulham (Middlesex), which the plaintiff demised to Mabel for her life.

[1] C., tiel.

[2] auxint is from L. alone.

[3] L., devant.

[4] L., ne devoms.

[5] The plea was, according to the record, "quod quidam Ricardus "de Clare nuper fuit seisitus de "prædictis tenementis, cum perti- "nentiis, in dominico suo ut de "feodo, et fecit quandam recogni- "tionem in Curia hic cuidam "Ricardo de Chissebeche de quad- "raginta et octo libris certo "termino solvendis, &c., qui qui- "dem Ricardus de Clare dedit "tenementa prædicta præfato "Thomæ tenenda sibi et heredibus "suis, &c., et idem Thomas eadem "tenementa dimisit præfatæ Ma- "billæ, dum sola fuit, tenenda ad "totam vitam ejusdem Mabillæ. "Et postea, pro eo quod prædictus "Ricardus de Clare denarios præ- "dictos termino statuto non soluit, "præfatus Ricardus de Chissebeche "secutus fuit executionem, virtute "recognitionis prædictæ, versus "præfatam Mabillam, et habuit "executionem, videlicet, medieta- "tem prædictorum tenementorum, "per liberationem Vicecomitis, "virtute brevis Regis quod dicitur "*Elegit*, tenendam, &c., quousque, "&c., qui quidem Ricardus de "Chissebeche obiit, et quidam "Thomas atte Vyne, executor "testamenti ejusdem Ricardi, "statum quem habuit in eisdem "tenementis concessit quibusdam "Antonio Gysors et Johannæ uxori "ejus, unde eadem Johanna post "mortem prædicti Antonii adhuc "est tenens, &c. Unde dicunt

No. 69.

A.D. 1345. We will aver that those against whom our writ is brought have committed waste.—WILLOUGHBY.   Answer to that which he has pleaded.—*Gaynesford.*   We tell you that, before R. or A. had anything in the tenements, the defendants committed the waste; ready, &c. —And the other side said the contrary.

Præcipe.   (69.) § *Præcipe quod reddat* by two *Præcipes* alleging the seisin of the demandant's brother.—*Pole.*   We tell you that his brother, with regard to whose seisin he demands, was a bastard.—*Gaynesford.*   You cannot say that, because on a previous occasion we brought a like writ against you, and, after view, you abated our writ on the ground of non-tenure, whereupon we immediately brought this writ; judgment, inasmuch as by the demand of view the descent was affirmed by

No. 69.

qe ces vers queux nostre brief est porte ount fait A.D. 1345.
wast.—WILBY. Responez a ceo qil ad plede.—*Gayn.*
Nous vous dioms qe, devant qe R. ou A. rienz y
avoint, ils firent le wast; prest, &c.—*Et alii e contra.*[1]

(69.)[2] § *Præcipe* de la seisine le frere par deux *Præcipe.*
Præcipe.—*Pole.* Nous vous dioms qe soun frere, de [Fitz., Estoppell,
qi seisine, &c., fuit bastard.—*Gayn.* Ceo ne poietz 185.]
dire, qar autrefoith nous[3] portames autiel brief vers
vous, et, apres la viewe, abatistes nostre brief par
nountenue, sur quei freschement nous avoms porte
cest brief; jugement, desicome par la viewe demande
la descente fuit afferme par vous, si ore de luy

"quod ipsi non debent onerari de
"aliquo vasto in medietate illa, &c.
"Et hoc parati sunt verificare, &c.
"Et quo ad aliam medietatem, &c.,
"dicunt quod prædicta Mabilla
"statum suum quem habuit in
"eadem dimisit præfato Antonio
"et heredibus suis, de qua quidem
"medietate quidam Jacobus filius
"et heres ejusdem Antonii adhuc
"est tenens, &c. Et dicunt quod
"a tempore dimissionis prædictæ
"ipsi Willelmus et Mabilla de
"aliquo vasto inde facto non
"debent inquietari. Et quo ad
"tempus ante, &c., dicunt quod
"ipsi non fecerunt aliquod vastum
"in medietate illa. Et hoc parati
"sunt verificare, unde petunt
"judicium, &c."

[1] The replication, upon which
issue was joined, was, according to
the record "quod antequam præ-
"dicta medietas tenementorum,
"&c., devenit ad manus prædicti
"Ricardi de Chissebeche virtute
"executionis prædictæ, vel præ-
"dicta alia medietas in possessio-
"nem prædicti Antonii per con-
"cessionem præfatæ Mabillæ, &c.,
"prædicti Willelmus et Mabilla

"fecerunt venditionem, &c., in
"prædictis tenementis, prout ipse
"superius per breve et narrationem
"suam prædictam supponit."
The award of the *Venire* follows,
the jurors having to view the tenements wasted before the day given,
but nothing further appears on the
roll.

[2] From L., and C., but corrected
by the record, *Placita de Banco*,
Mich., 19 Edw. III., R° 486. It
there appears that a writ of Entry
was brought by Richard de Brockhampton against Ralph atte More
and Sarah his wife, in respect of
certain tenements, and against
Alice de Brockhampton in respect
of certain other tenements, in
Estfysshebourne (East Fishbourne,
Sussex), "in quæ iidem Radulphus,
"Sarra, et Alicia non habent
"ingressum nisi per Willelmum
"de Brokhamptone, qui illa eis
"dimisit, qui inde injuste et sine
"judicio disseisivit Willelmum
"filium Willelmi de Brokhamp-
"tone, fratrem prædicti Ricardi,
"cujus heres ipse est."

[3] nous is from L. alone.

No. 70.

A.D. 1345. you, whether you shall now be admitted to bastardise him. — *Pole.* This is another writ. Besides, even though view had been granted on the same writ, still after view we should have this exception, which is to the action; and we take your records to witness that he does not deny the fact.--WILLOUGHBY. You cannot challenge him, and therefore he cannot be said to be at one with you; and it appears to us that you cannot be admitted to make the plea. — *Pole.* As to this *Præcipe* we will imparl; and as to the other *Præcipe* the tenant tells you that the person on whose seisin the demandant demands was a bastard.

Account.   (70.) § Account against guardian in socage.—*Grene.* Whereas you say that the lands descended to you through your father, and that we snatched the posses-

No. 70.

bastarder serretz resceu.—*Pole.* Cest un autre brief. A.D. 1345.
Ovesqe ceo, tut ust viewe este graunte a mesme le
brief, unqore apres la viewe nous averoms cest
chalenge, qest al accion; et pernoms vos recordes qil
nel dedit pas.—WILBY. Vous le poetz pas chalenger,
par quei il serra pas a un ovesqe vous; et il nous
semble qe vous navendretz pas.—*Pole.* Quant a cest
Præcipe nous enparleroms; et quant a lautre *Præ-*
cipe le tenant vous dist qe celuy de qi seisine il
demande fuit bastard.[1]

(70.)[2] § Accompte vers gardein en sokage.[3]—*Grene.* Acompte
La ou vous ditetz qe les terres vous descendirent
par vostre pere,[4] et qe nous happames la possession

---

[1] According to the record, Alice's
plea was " quod, ubi prædictus
" Ricardus petit mesuagium illud
" de seisina præfati Willelmi filii
" Willelmi, ut frater et heres ejus-
" dem Willelmi, &c., idem Willel-
" mus quem nominat Willelmum
" filium Willelmi fuit bastardus,
" per quod fratrem et heredem
" habere non potuit. Et hoc
" parata est verificare, unde petit
" judicium, &c."
According to the record there
was a replication, upon which
issue was joined, "quod prædictus
" Willelmus filius Willelmi, de
" cujus seisina, &c., legitimus fuit
" et non bastardus."
The *Venire* was awarded, but
nothing further appears on the
roll, except adjournments.

[2] From L., and C., but corrected
by the record, *Placita de Banco*,
Mich., 19 Edw. III., R° 592, d.
It there appears that the action
was brought by Robert de Beverle
and Joan his wife against Geoffrey
State of Ipswich.

[3] According to the record the

declaration was " quod cum præ-
" dictus Galfridus habuisset in
" custodia sua unum mesuagium,
" sexaginta acras terræ, septem
" acras prati, et decem solidatas
" redditus, cum pertinentiis, in
" Braunforde et Blakenham, de
" hereditate ipsius Johannæ,
" ratione minoris ætatis ejus-
" dem Johannæ, quæ tenentur
" in socagio de Episcopi Eliensi,
" per fidelitatem et servitium
" decem solidorum per annum pro
" omni servitio, ... per-
" cipiendo inde exitus et expletia
" inde provenientia, idem Gal-
" fridus, licet sæpius requisitus,
" prædictæ Johannæ, postquam
" eadem Johanna ad plenam
" ætatem pervenit, dum sola fuit,
" nec eidem Johannæ et prædicto
" Roberto viro suo, rationabilem
" compotum suum de exitibus de
" terris et tenementis illis . . . .
" provenientibus semper hucusque
" reddere contradixit, et adhuc
" reddere contradicit."

[4] C., auncestre.

No. 71.

A.D. 1345. sion as next friend, as to that we tell you that your father had not anything in the tenements except in right of R.[1] his wife; judgment whether such a writ lies against us.—*Skipwith.* Ready, &c., that she had nothing except as wife of our ancestor.—*Grene.* You must maintain the estate of your ancestor through whom you claim by descent, and not take issue on the wife's estate.—WILLOUGHBY. He destroys your answer which you have pleaded in bar, and that suffices for him.—*Skipwith.* Our ancestor was sole seised, *absque hoc* that R.[1] had anything in the tenements except as wife; ready, &c.—And the other side said the contrary.

Trespass.   (71.) § Trespass for an Abbot plaintiff. It was alleged that he was excommunicated, and thereupon a letter of the Bishop was produced to prove it.—*Grene.* The letter testifies excommunication through the information and notice of a person other than the Bishop himself; judgment whether you can rebut us by this testimony.

---

[1] For the real name *see* p. 451, note 1.

No. 71.

come prochein amy, a ceo vous dioms qe vostre ^{A.D. 1345}
pere navoit rienz en les tenementz forqe de dreit
R. sa femme; jugement si tiel brief vers nous gise.[1]
—*Skyp.* Qele navoit rienz mes come femme[2] nostre
auncestre, prest, &c.—*Grene.* Il covient meintenir
lestat vostre auncestre par my qi vous clametz par
descente, et noun pas prendre issue sur lestat la
femme.—WILBY. Il destruit vostre respons qe vous
avetz plede en barre, et ceo luy suffit.—*Skyp.* Nostre
auncestre fuit soul seisi, sanz ceo qe R. rienz y
avoit, mes com femme; prest, &c.—*Et alii e contra.*[3]

(71.)[4] § Trans pur un Abbe pleintif. Fuit allegge ^{Trans}
qil fuit escomenge, et sur ceo lettre Levesqe
moustre. —*Grene.* La lettre tesmoigne escomenge-
ment par informacion et apprise dautre persone qe
del Evesqe mesme; jugement si par ceste tesmoig-
naunce nous puissetz reboter.

---

[1] The plea was, according to the record, "quod Walterus de West-"hale, pater prædictæ Johannæ, "cujus heres ipsa est, nihil habuit "in prædictis tenementis unde "prædicti Robertus et Johanna "supponunt ipsum Galfridum "habuisse custodiam, &c., nisi ut "de jure Agnetis uxoris suæ, "matris prædictæ Johannæ, ra-"tione cooperturæ, &c., qui quidem "Walterus obiit, post cujus mor-"tem prædicta Agnes mater, &c., "nupsit se eidem Galfrido State, "et ita dicit quod eodem tempore "quo prædicti Robertus et Jo-"hanna supponunt ipsum seisitum "fuisse de eisdem tenementis "nomine custodiæ, ratione minoris "ætatis prædictæ Johannæ, ipse "seisitus fuit de eisdem tene-"mentis ut de libero tenemento, "ratione cooperturæ, &c., absque "hoc quod ipse unquam aliquid "habuit in eisdem tenementis. "nomine custodiæ, ratione minoris "ætatis prædictæ Johannæ nunc "uxoris Roberti, &c. Et hoc "paratus est verificare, unde petit "judicium, &c."

[2] femme is omitted from C.

[3] The replication, upon which issue was joined. was according to the record "quod prædictus "Galfridus fuit seisitus de præ-"dictis tenementis, nomine custo-"diæ, ratione minoris ætatis "prædictæ Johannæ, prout ipsi "superius versus cum narraverunt, "absque hoc quod prædicta Agnes "mater prædictæ Johannæ un-"quam aliquid habuit in eisdem "tenementis nisi ut uxor, &c."

The *Venire* was awarded, but nothing further appears on the roll.

[4] From L., and C.

Nos. 72–74.

A.D. 1345.

Præcipe.

(72.) § *Præcipe* brought without the degrees. The tenant made default after default.—*Grene* prayed seisin. —*Pole.* The writ is faulty and defective: for the words "*unde queritur*" and the whole of the preceding clause are wanting, so that you have no warrant to render judgment on this writ.—*Grene.* For whom do you speak?—STONORE. It is for us to look to this; and it appears that the writ is so defective that, even though the parties may be agreed, the COURT cannot render judgment on this writ.

Indict-
ment.
Judgment
on one
who com-
mitted a
trespass in
the pre-
sence of
the
Justices.

(73.) § N. of Carlisle, tailor, was indicted in the King's Bench for that he, in the presence of the Justices, threatened and struck the jurors of an in-quest. And he appeared and put himself upon the King's mercy. And, after consideration by the whole COUNCIL, THORPE gave judgment that his right hand should be cut off, and his lands and chattels forfeited, and that he should be imprisoned for life.—But after-wards the COURT said that execution should be stayed until the King had signified his pleasure.—And note that the King immediately gave the land, as forfeit, to another person.—*Quære* as to forfeiture of land in this case.

Dower.

(74.) § The Lady de Montagu brought a writ of Dower. The tenant vouched to warrant William son and heir of William de Montagu. Exception was taken

Nos. 72–74.

(72.)[1] § *Præcipe* porte hors des degres. Le tenant A.D. 1345.
fit defaute apres defaute.—*Grene* pria seisine.—*Pole*. *Præcipe*.
Le brief est vicious et defectif : qar *unde queritur*
et tote la clause devant y faut, issint qe vous
navietz pas garrant de rendre jugement sur ceo
brief.—*Grene*. Pur qi parletz vous ?—Ston. Cest a
nous a veer ; et il semble qe le brief est si defectif
qe, tut soient parties dun acord, Court ne poet
rendre jugement sur ceo brief.

(73.)[1] § N. de Cardoille, taillour, fuit endite en Endite-
Baunk le Roi de ceo qil, en presence des Justices, Judicium
manacea et ferist les jurours dune enqueste, qe vint pur celuy
et se mist en la grace le Roi. Et, par avys de tut[4] en
le Counseille, Thorpe agarda qe la mein destre fuit presence
coupe, terres et chateux forfaitz, et il a perpetuel Justices.[3]
prisoun.—Mes puis Court dist qe execucion cessera [Fitz.,
tanqe le Roi avera[5] comaunde ceo qe lui plerra.— 174.]
Et *nota* qe le Roi dona sa terre come forfait tan-
toust a un autre.[6]—*Quære* de forfeture de terre *in
hoc casu*.

(74.)[7] § La Dame de Mountagu[8] porta brief de Dowere.
Dowere. Le tenant voucha a garrant W. fitz et Voucher,
heir W. Mountagu.[9] Le voucher chalenge de ceo 125.]

---

[1] From L., and C.

[2] Enditement is from L. alone.

[3] The words after Enditement are from C. alone.

[4] L., tote.

[5] avera is omitted from C.

[6] The words a un autre are omitted from L.

[7] From L., and C., but corrected by the record, *Placita de Banco*, Mich., 19 Edw. III., R° 495. It there appears that the action was brought by Catharine late wife of William " de Monte Acuto," late Earl of Salisbury, against John Loterel, knight, in respect of a third part of tenements in " Estcoker " (East Coker, Somerset), and against John Inge, knight, in respect of a third part of the manor of Donheved (Donhead) of the endowment of the said late Earl. There is, on the same roll, a similar action between the same parties respecting dower claimed of the Isle of Lundy (Devon).

[8] C., Mountagew.

[9] C., Mountagew. According to the record " Johannes Loterel alias " dixit quod ipse tenet tenementa " unde, &c., ad terminum vitæ

No. 74.

to the voucher on the ground that the vouchee was under age, and in the King's wardship, in which case he ought to be vouched as being in the King's wardship. And this exception was taken by the vouchee, who produced a writ reciting that W. de Montagu held of the King *in capite*, and that his son was, by Inquest of Office on *Diem clausit extremum*, in the seventeenth year of the King's reign, found to be fifteen years of age, and that his lands are now in the King's wardship.—*Huse*, for the demandant, prayed her dower.—*Derworthy*. We tell you that on the day of the voucher the vouchee was without the wardship of any one, so that, so far as we are concerned, there was no defect in the voucher; and we tell you that the King granted by his patent to W., the vouchee's ancestor, that his heir should be out of wardship.—*R. Thorpe*. It is to be understood that one who is under age, and in the King's wardship, is in the King's wardship for the whole time after the death of his ancestor; therefore, since the King records that the vouchee's lands are now in his hand by reason of wardship, they must be understood to have been in his hand from the time that the right of wardship accrued to him, that is to say, since the death of the ancestor.— WILLOUGHBY. It is possible enough that on the day of the voucher he was out of wardship of any one, and that the King has since seized, and in that case

No. 74.

qil qest vouche est deinz age, et en la garde le
Roi, en quel cas il serreit vouche en la garde le
Roi. Et cel chalenge fuit done par le vouche, et
mist avant brief reherceaunt qe W. Mountagu[1] tient
en chief du Roi, et qe soun fitz par office sur *Diem
clausit extremum* fuit lan xvij trove del age de xv
aunz, et qe ses terres sount ore en la garde le Roi.
—*Huse*, pur la demandante, pria soun dowere.—*Der*.
Nous vous dioms qe jour de voucher le vouche fuit
hors de chesquny garde, issint qen nous ny avoit
pas defaute en le voucher; et[2] vous dioms qe le
Roi par soun[3] patent granta a W. soun auncestre
qe soun heir serreit hors de garde.—[*R*.] *Thorpe*.
Celuy qest deinz age et en la garde le Roy il est
entendu qe tut temps puis la mort soun auncestre
en la garde le Roi; par quei de puis qe le Roi
recorde qore ses terres sount par resoun de garde
en sa mein, ils serrount tut le[4] temps entendu en
sa mein qe dreit de garde luy acrust, saver, puis
la mort launcestre.—WILBY. Il est assetz possible
qe jour de voucher il fuit hors de chesquny garde,
et qe puis le Roi ad seisi, et donqes soun voucher

" suæ, ex dimissione Willelmi de
" Mountagu, Comitis Sarum, qui
" quidem Comes eadem tenementa
" concessit per scriptum suum
" tenenda ad terminum vitæ ejus-
" dem Johannis, et obligavit se et
" heredes suos ad warantizandum,
" &c. Et protulit hic quoddam
" scriptum sub nomine prædicti
" Comitis quod hoc testabatur.
" Et in forma illa vocavit inde ad
" warantum Willelmum filium et
" heredem prædicti Comitis, &c.,
" infra ætatem, &c., . . . Et
" Johannes Inge dixit quod ipse
" tenet prædictum manerium unde,
" &c., ad terminum vitæ suæ, et
" per unum annum ulterius, ex-

" dimissione Willelmi de Moun-
" tagu, Comitis Sarum, qui illud
" manerium ei dimisit per scriptum
" suum quod hic profert, et quod
" hoc testatur, &c., tenendum ad
" terminum vitæ ejusdem Jo-
" hannis, reversione inde ad præ-
" dictum Comitem et heredes suos
" spectante. Et in forma illa
" vocavit inde ad warantum præ-
" dictum heredem infra ætatem
" existentem, . . . qui modo
" venit per summonitionem per
" custodem suum."

[1] C., Mountagew.
[2] et is omitted from C.
[3] C., sa.
[4] le is from C. alone.

No. 74.

the tenant's voucher is good; and, if the King has seized since, it would rather be right that the tenant should revouch than that he should lose his land, inasmuch as there was no fault in him.—*R. Thorpe.* It would be an extraordinary thing to revouch, and delay the demandant; but, at any rate, judgment cannot be rendered in respect of lands which are in the King's hand without command from himself. —*Grene.* It is to the King's advantage that the voucher should stand, because on that voucher the heir can vouch over, and, if he were vouched as being in wardship, he could not vouch over. And put it at the worst that can happen, that judgment will now be given against the heir, no execution will be had of lands which are in the King's hand.—Afterwards there came a writ reciting that all the time after the death of the ancestor the lands had been in wardship.—Therefore exception was taken to the voucher as above.—And then the tenant alleged discontinuance of process on the voucher, because the vouchee was vouched by the name of William son and heir of William de Montagu, Earl of Salisbury, and in the subsequent process the words " Earl of Salisbury " were omitted.

No. 74.

est bon ; et, si le Roi eit puis seisi, il serreit plus
toust resoun qe le tenant revouchereit qil perdreit
sa terre, la ou nulle defaut fuit en luy.—[R.] *Thorpe.*
Il serreit merveille de revoucher, et delaier la demandante ; mes au meins des terres qe sount en la
mein le Roi ne poet jugement estre rendu sanz
mandement de luy mesme.—*Grene.* Il est pur le
Roi qe le voucher estoise,[1] qar sur ceo voucher leire
poet voucher outre, et sil fuit vouche en garde il
vouchereit pas outre. Et mettetz qapys [2] qe purra
estre qe le jugement se taillera ore vers leire, nulle
execucion se freit des terres qe sount en la mein
le Roi.—Puis brief vint reherceaunt qe tut temps
puis la mort launcestre les terres furent en garde.
—Par quei le voucher fuit chalenge *ut supra.*—Et
donqes le tenant alleggea discontinuance del proces
sur le voucher, qar il fuit vouche par noun de W.
fitz et heir W. Mountagu,[3] Count de Sarum, et en
le proces puis Count de Sarum est entrelesse.[4]

---

[1] estoise is omitted from C.

[2] L., qe appis.

[3] C., de Mountagew.

[4] According to the record, immediately after the voucher, " Super
" hoc prædicti Johannes Loterel et
" Johannes Inge calumniant pro-
" cessum de loquela ista, quia dicunt
" quod prædictus Willelmus filius
" et heres Willelmi alias vocatus
" fuit per nomen Willelmi filii et
" heredis Willelmi de Mountagu
" Comitis Sarum, et breve quod
" exiit de rotulis ad summonen-
" dum eundem heredem facit
" mentionem ad summonendum
" Willelmum filium et heredem
" Willelmi de Monte Acuto nuper
" Comitis Sarum, quod quidem
" breve non concordat rotulo, et
" sic processus iste discontinuatur,
" &c.

" Dies datus est tam prædictæ
" Katerinæ quam prædictis Jo-
" hanni Loterel et Johanni Inge,
" et etiam prædicto Willelmo filio
" Willelmi, hic in Crastino Purifica-
" tionis beatæ Mariæ in statu quo
" nunc, salvis, &c. Et interim
" scrutetur processus, &c."
After a further adjournment.
the demandant, and John Inge,
and the vouchee (by guardian)
appeared, " Et Willelmus dicit
" quod, ubi prædictus Johannes
" Inge vocavit ipsum ad warantum
" ut extra quamcumque custodiam,
" corpus ejus et terræ sunt in
" custodia domini Regis, et fuerunt
" antequam idem Johannes voca-
" vit inde ipsum ad warantum, &c.,
" videlicet, ante mensem Paschæ
" anno regni Regis nunc decimo
" nono, super quo dominus Rex

No. 75.

A.D. 1345. (75.) § Wardship against several persons. Some
Wardship. appeared, and Proclamation issued against the others,
by reason of their default, and they did not appear.
And those who were in Court by the *Idem dies* said

No. 75.

(75.)[1] § Garde vers plusours. Les unes vindrent et vers les autres par lour defaut proclamacion issit, qe vindrent pas.[2] Et les autres qe sount en Court

A.D. 1345
Garde.
[Fitz.,
Proclama-
cion, 10.]

" misit hic breve suum quod " testatur quod idem Willelmus, " die obitus prædicti Comitis patris " sui, videlicet in Crastino Nativi- " tatis Sancti Johannis Baptistæ " anno regni ejusdem Regis decimo " septimo, fuit ætatis quindecim " annorum, et, ratione minoris " ætatis ejusdem heredis, corpus " ejusdem heredis et omnia terræ " et tenementa quæ fuerunt præ- " dicti Comitis die obitus sui, et de " quibus obiit seisitus in dominico " suo ut de feodo, fuerunt in manu " ejusdem Regis, et tempore " confectionis ejusdem brevis, " videlicet, vicesimo quarto die " Novembris anno regni sui decimo " nono, extiterunt, per quod liquet " Curiæ hic quod corpus prædicti " heredis, et terræ et tenementa " quæ fuerunt prædicti Comitis die " quo obiit, prædicto die quo idem " heres vocatus fuit ad warantum, " &c., fuerunt in custodia domini " Regis, unde petit judicium si in " hoc casu warantizare debeat, &c."

" Et Johannes Inge non potest " hoc dedicere, &c."

Judgment was therefore given as follows : — " Quia compertum est " per præmissa in prædicto brevi " contenta quod prædictus heres, " terræ, et tenementa sua prædicta, " prædicto die quo vocatus fuit ad " warantum, &c., fuerunt in " custodia domini Regis, &c., et " idem heres vocatus fuit, &c., " extra quamcumque custodiam, " &c., consideratum est quod " prædicta Katerina recuperet " dotem suam prædictam versus " præfatum Johannem Inge, et

" prædictus Willelmus eat quietus " de vocare prædicto. Et prædic- " tus Johannes Inge in miseri- " cordia, &c."

[1] This and the report next following (No. 76) appear to be different reports of the same case. This is placed at the end of the term in the MSS., but has been transferred, because it relates chiefly to an earlier portion of the case, and No. 76 chiefly to a later portion. Comparison with the record is thus rendered easier. Both reports are from the two MSS., L. and C., and the record is among the *Placita de Banco*, Mich., 19 Edw. III., Rº 594. It there appears that the action was brought by the " Prior ecclesiæ " Sanctæ Trinitatis de Norwyco " against Richard de Worthstede, together with John de Leem the younger, and Roger de Brexton, in respect of the wardship of 6 mes- suages, one mill, and 60 acres of land in Worthstede (Worstead) and Dilham (Norfolk) " quæ ad ipsum " Priorem pertinet, eo quod Jo- " hannes de Worthstede mesuagia, " molendinum, et terram prædicta " tenuit de Willelmo de Claxtone, " quondam Priore ecclesiæ prædic- " tæ, prædecessore prædicti Prioris. " per servitium militare, &c."

[2] According to the roll " Et ipse " [Ricardus] non venit. Et præ- " ceptum fuit Vicecomiti quod " distringeret eum per omnes " terras, &c., ita quod haberet " corpus ejus hic ad hunc diem, " . . . . et similiter quod in " tribus plenis comitatibus suis

No. 76.

A.D. 1345. that the others who made default on the Proclamation had nothing in the wardship. And the plaintiff counted against them, and a traverse was taken on the tenancy. And there was touched the point that by the Proclamation sued against some of the defendants the plaintiff discontinued his process, because in such a case suit should always be at common law by Distress.—*Quære.*

Wardship.   (76.) § Wardship.—*Grene.* As to part, the ancestor did not hold of the plaintiff; and, as to the rest, the ancestor enfeoffed us to hold of the chief lord of the fee, by virtue of which feoffment we are the plaintiff's tenant, and we have tendered our services to him

No. 76.

par le *Idem dies* disoint qe les autres qe fount A.D. 1345
defaut a la proclamacion nount rien.[1] Et le pleintif
counta vers eux, et travers pris sur la tenance.[2]
Et fuit touche qe par la proclamacion suy vers les
unes le pleintif discontinua soun proces, qar la suite
en tel cas serreit toux jours a la comune lei par
destresse.—*Quære.*

(76.)[3] § Garde.—*Grene.* Quant a parcelle, laun- Garde
cestre ne tient pas del pleintif; et, quant al remenant, il nous feffa a tenir de chief seignour de
fee, par force de quel feffement nous sumes tenant
al pleintif, et avoms tendu nos services sovent, &c.[4]

" publice proclamationem faceret
" quod prædictus Ricardus veniret
" hic ad præfatum terminum, præ-
" dicto Priori inde responsurus si,
" &c. Idem dies datus fuit præ-
" dictis Johanni et Rogero. . .
" . . . . Et Vicecomes modo
" mandat quod prædictus Ricardus
" districtus est, &c., et quod in
" tribus plenis comitatibus pro-
" clamari fecit in forma prædictæ."

[1] According to the roll " præ-
" dictus Prior petit seisinam de
" tertia parte custodiæ prædictæ
" per defaltam prædicti Ricardi,
" &c. Et Johannes et Rogerus
" dicunt quod prædictus Prior
" seisinam de tertia parte prædictæ
" custodiæ habere non debet, quia
" dicunt quod ipsi tenent integre
" custodiam prædictam, et tenue-
" runt die impetrationis brevis,&c.,
" et parati sunt eidem Priori inde
" respondere."

[2] *See* the report next following
(No. 76).

[3] *See* p. 459, note 1.

[4] According to the roll, after the
Prior's declaration, which was in
accordance with the writ, John and

Roger pleaded "quod prædicta tene-
" menta, unde, &c., non sunt nisi
" duo mesuagia, et triginta acræ
" terræ tantum, unde unum mesua-
" gium et decem acræ terræ sunt
" integre in prædicta villa de
" Dilham, et, non cognoscendo
" prædicta tenementa teneri per
" servitia prædicta, &c., quo ad
" mesuagium et terram in prædicta
" villa de Dilham dicunt quod
" prædictus Johannes de Worth-
" stede non tenuit de prædicto
" Willelmo de Claxtone, quondam
" Priore, &c., prædecessore, &c.,
" die quo obiit, &c. Et, quo ad
" prædicta mesuagium et viginti
" acras terræ residua in prædicta
" villa de Worthstede, dicunt quod
" prædictus Johannes de Worth-
" stede diu in vita sua feoffavit
" ipsos Johannem de Leem et
" Rogerum de prædictis tenementis,
" habendis et tenendis eisdem
" Johanni de Leem et Rogero et
" heredibus suis in perpetuum in
" feodo simplici, per quod iidem
" Johannes de Leem et Rogerus,
" ut tenentes prædictorum tene-
" mentorum sæpius obtulerunt

No. 76.

many times, &c.—*R. Thorpe.* As to their statement that the infant's ancestor did not hold of us, ready, &c., that he did. And as to the rest, in respect of which they allege a feoffment, we tell you that it was a feigned feoffment made by collusion for the purpose of depriving us of our wardship; ready, &c.—*Grene.* As to that, the ancestor did not hold of you at the time of his death; ready, &c.—*R. Thorpe.* Even though you waive your plea, and will not say anything as to the feoffment, we tell you that there was a feigned feoffment, &c., and so the ancestor held of us; ready, &c.—WILLOUGHBY. He does not now aid himself by the feoffment, nor mention it, but traverses your writ in general terms, wherefore it is not necessary for you to mention the feoffment.—*R. Thorpe.* It is necessary for me to allege it, because otherwise a lord who claims wardship would never be aided by a feigned feoffment, because possibly the feoffee would not plead the feoffment, but would traverse the writ, and thence it would follow that the Statute[1] and the clause[2] of the Statute would be set at naught; therefore, although he does not mention the feoffment, it must be in evidence on our issue, and we pray that it be entered.—And so it was.—And the other side said, on the contrary, that the infant's ancestor did not hold of the plaintiff.

---

[1] 18 Edw. I. (*Quia emptores*).
[2] "Si partem aliquam earundem terrarum seu tenementorum alicui " vendiderit, feoffatus illam teneat " immediate de capitali domino " (c. 2).

No. 76.

—[*R.*] *Thorpe.* Quant a ceo qils dient qe launcestre
lenfant ne tient pas de nous, prest, &c., qe si. Et
quant al remenant qils alleggent feffement, nous
vous dioms qe ceo fuit feffement feint par collusion
pur nous tollir la garde; prest, &c.—*Grene.* Quant
a cel, il ne tient pas de vous al temps de sa mort;
prest, &c.—[*R.*] *Thorpe.* Tut weyvetz vous vostre
plee, et ne voilletz parler del feffement, nous dioms
qil y avoit feffement feint, &c., et issint tient
launcestre de nous; prest, &c.—WILBY. Il ne seide
pas a ore ne parle del feffement, mes traverse
generalment vostre brief, par quei il ne bosoigne
pas qe vous parletz del feffement.—[*R.*] *Thorpe.* Il
covient qe jeo lallegge, qar autrement seignour qe
cleime garde ne serreit jammes eide par feint feffement, qar le feffe ne pledra pas le feffement, mes
par cas traversera le brief, et de ceo ensuereit qe
lestatut et la clause de lestatut serreit anienti; par
quei, tut ne parle il del feffement, il covient qil
soit en evidence a nostre issue, et ceo prioms qe
soit entre.—Et issint fuit.[1]—*Et alii e contra* qe
launcestre lenfant ne tient pas del pleintif.

" eidem Willelmo de Claxtone,
" quondam Priori, &c., præde-
" cessori, &c., servitia de prædictis
" tenementis debita et consueta.
" Et sic dicunt quod prædictus
" Johannes de Worthstede non
" tenuit de prædicto Willelmo de
" Claxtone, quondam Priore, præ-
" decessore, &c., prædicta tene-
" menta, die quo obiit. Et hoc
" parati sunt verificare, unde
" petunt judicium."

[1] According to the roll the Prior
replied " non cognoscendo quod
" prædicti Johannes et Rogerus
" obtuleruut eidem Willelmo de
" Claxtone, quondam Priori, &c.,
" aliqua servitia, dicit quod prædicta
" tenementa, unde, &c., sunt in

" prædicta villa de Worthstede,
" exceptis sex acris terræ in præ-
" dicta villa de Dilham. Et dicit
" quod prædictus Johannes de
" Leem et Rogerus   .   .
"   .   .   .   .   ."
[The roll is here in part illegible
by reason of erasures and inter-
lineations] " fuerunt per prædic-
" tum Johannem de Worstede de
" prædictis tenementis unde, &c.
" in prædictis villis de Worthstede
" et Dilham per fraudem et collu-
" sionem, ad auferendum eidem
" Willelmo de Claxtone, quondam
" Priori, &c., prædecessori, &c.,
" custodiam prædictorum tene-
" mentorum. Et sic dicit quod
" prædictus Johannes de Worth-

No. 77.

A.D. 1345.
*Quare
impedit.*
(77.) § A *Quare impedit* was brought for the King against the Abbot of Abingdon, and the count on the King's behalf was that one J.[1] was seised and presented, and held the advowson of the King, and aliened the advowson to the Abbot's predecessor without the King's license, &c.—*Derworthy.* We do not admit the alienation, nor that the advowson was held *in capite* of the King; but we tell you that, whereas he takes his title on the ground that J.[1] was seised and presented, &c., the person whom they mention was not admitted, &c., on J.'s[1] presentation; ready, &c.—*R. Thorpe.* And inasmuch as you have not denied that J.[1] was seised of the advowson, and that alienation was made by him, we demand judgment, and pray a writ

---

[1] For the full name *see* p. 465, note 3.

No. 77.

(77.)[1] § *Quare impedit* pur le Roi vers Labbe de A.D. 1345.
Abyndone, et counta qun J. fuit seisi, et presenta, *Quare impedit.*
et tient du Roi lavoweson, et aliena al Abbe lavowe-
son[2] sanz conge le Roi, &c.[3]—*Der.* Nous conissoms
pas lalienacion, ne qe lavoeson soit tenuz en chief
du Roi; mes vous dioms qe ou il prent soun title
qe J. fuit seisi et presenta, &c., celuy de qi ils
parlent nestoit pas resceu, &c., al presentement J.;
prest,[4] &c.[5]—[*R.*] *Thorpe.* Et desicome vous navietz
pas dedit qe J. fuit seisi del avoeson, et alienacion
fait par luy, jugement, et prioms brief al Evesqe.[6]—

" stede tenuit de prædicto Willelmo " de Claxtone quondam Priore, " &c., prædecessore, &c., prædicta " tenementa."

Issue was joined upon this, and the *Venire* awarded, but nothing further appears on the roll.

[1] From L., and C., but corrected by the record, *Placita de Banco*, Mich., 19 Edw. III., R⁰ 539. It there appears that the action was brought by the King against the Abbot of Abingdon " quod ipse " simul cum Henrico de Stoke " Abbatis permittat ipsum Regem " præsentare idoneam personam " ad ecclesiam de Farnebergh " (Farnborough, Berks).

[2] The words al Abbe lavoweson are from C. alone.

[3] According to the record the declaration was " quod quidam " Johannes de Ellesfelde fuit " seisitus de advocatione ecclesiæ " prædictæ ut de feodo et jure, " . . . tempore domini Edwardi " Regis avi domini Regis nunc, qui " illam tenuit de ipso domino Rege " avo, &c., in capite, et ad eandem " præsentavit quendam Robertum " de Brightewelle, clericum suum, " qui ad præsentationem suam fuit " admissus et institutus

" tempore ejusdem Edwardi Regis " avi, &c., post cujus mortem " ecclesia prædicta modo vacat, " &c. Et postmodum idem Jo- " hannes de Ellesfelde advoca- " tionem ecclesiæ prædictæ dedit " cuidam tunc Abbati de Abyndone, " prædecessori prædicti Abbatis " nunc, absque licentia domini " Regis, &c., per quod jus ad eccle- " siam prædictam præsentandi " accrevit prædicto domino Ed- " wardo Regi avo, &c." The descent is then traced from Edward I. to Edward III.

[4] prest is from C. alone.

[5] The plea was, according to the record, " Abbas, . . . non cog- " noscendo quod advocatio præ- " dicta tenebatur de domino Rege " in capite, nec quod prædictus " Johannes de Ellesfelde fuit " seisitus de advocatione prædicta, " dicit quod prædictus Robertus " de Brightwelle non fuit admissus " et institutus in ecclesia prædicta " ad præsentationem prædicti Jo- " hannis de Ellesfelde, sicut " dominus Rex supponit. Et hoc " paratus est verificare, &c."

[6] The corresponding words of the record are " quod exquo prædictus " Abbas non dedicit quin prædicta

No. 77.

to the Bishop.—*Derworthy.* I shall not by law be put to answer that, since I have destroyed the possession of the person through whom you claim the presentation.—And thereupon to judgment.—They were adjourned.

No. 77.

Der. Jeo ne serray par ley a ceo mys a respondre, ^{A.D. 1345.}
del houre qe jay destruit la possession de luy par
qi vous clametz le presentement.[1]—*Et super hoc ad
judicium.—Adjornanter.*[2]

"advocatio tenetur de domino
" Rege in capite, nec quin prædictus
" Johannes de Ellesfelde fuit
" seisitus de advocatione illa, nec
" quin eadem advocatio alienata
" fuit sine licentia domini Regis,
" . . . . petit judicium
" pro domino Rege, et breve
" Episcopo, &c."

[1] The words of the record are
" quod in brevi de *Quare impedit,*
" &c., nullus responderi debet ad
" excludendum aliquem de præ-
" sentatione sua, nisi allegaverit
" admissionem et institutionem
" Episcopi de aliquo clerico ad
" alicujus præsentationem, &c.
" Et dominus Rex in demonstra-
" tione sua prædicta nullum alium
" titulum, &c., allegat ad istud
" breve de possessione, &c., nisi
" tantum admissionem et institu-
" tionem de præfato Roberto de
" Brightwelle, ad præsentationem
" prædicti Johannis de Ellesfelde
" factam, &c., ad quem titulum
" evacuandum in hac parte idem
" Abbas superius dixit et adhuc
" dicit quod prædictus Robertus
" non fuit admissus et institutus
" in ecclesia prædicta ad præsenta-
" tionem prædicti Johannis de
" Ellesfelde sicut dominus Rex
" superius supponit. Et hoc para-
" tus est verificare. Quam quidem
" verificationem dominus Rex non
" admittit, per quod intendit quod
" titulus domini Regis in hac parte
" omnino destructus est et adnulla-
" tus, unde petit judicium, &c."

[2] According to the roll, after two
adjournments, there were the

following further pleadings "Abbas
" dicit, ut prius, quod prædictus
" Robertus non fuit admissus et
" institutus in ecclesia prædicta
" ad præsentationem prædicti Jo-
" hannis de Ellesfelde, immo fuit
" admissus, &c., ad præsenta-
" tionem cujusdam Nicholai quon-
" dam Abbatis, &c., prædecessoris
" prædicti Abbatis nunc, qui qui-
" dem Nicholaus seisitus fuit de
" advocatione prædicta, et ipse et
" predecessores sui et successores
" sui seisiti fuerunt de advocatione
" prædicta de tempore a quo non
" extat memoria, absque hoc quod
" prædictus Johannes aut aliquis
" antecessorum suorum unquam
" aliquid habuit in advocatione
" illa. Et hoc paratus est verifi-
" care, &c.

" Et Johannes [de Clone] qui
" sequitur [pro domino Rege] dicit
" quod prædictus Abbas alias
" placitavit aliud placitum, et
" moratus fuit præcise in judicium,
" &c., per quod idem Abbas ad
" istam responsionem seu aliquam
" aliam quam ad priorem respon-
" sionem suam admitti non debet.
" Et sic per istas ultimas verifica-
" tiones quas modo prætendit vi-
" detur primam responsionem suam
" penitus reliquisse, unde petit
" judicium et breve Episcopo, &c."

After a great number of further
adjournments during which the
King's attorney, John de Clone, was
succeeded by John de Gaunt, and
he in turn by Michael Skyllyng,
" testatum est eis hic quod præ-
" dictus Abbas mortuus est. Et

No. 78.

A.D. 1345

*Quare
impedit.*

(78.) § A *Quare impedit* was brought for the King against the Prior of Wenlock, counting of a presentation by one W.,[1] the Prior's predecessor, to the chapel, &c., and that by reason of the war between the King and the French the King had seised the temporalities of the Priory, because the Prior was an alien, and they were previously, on the same original writ, at issue to the country in respect of the presentation, and thereupon they had a day now.—*Notton* counted a different count, for the King, on a different presentation.—*Mutlow* recited as above, and demanded judgment whether he should be admitted, after issue joined, to count a different count on the same original.—WILLOUGHBY, by judgment, put *Mutlow* to answer over.—*Mutlow.* We tell you that in the time of King John there was one W. who was seised of the manor to which the advowson is appendant, and (on the settlement of a dispute [between] Joliberd our predecessor, and W.), our predecessor, for himself and his successors, granted that W. and his heirs should retain the advowson, to present in such a manner that W. and his heirs should upon every vacancy present their clerk to the Prior and to his successors, and that the Prior for the time being should present over to the Ordinary the same clerk, by the description of the person presented by W. or his heirs, and that when the presentee

---

[1] For the real name *see* p. 469, note 3.

No. 78.

(78.) [1] § *Quare impedit* pur le Roi vers le Prior
de Wenlok, countant del presentement un W., predecessour le Prior, al chapelle, &c., et par resoun
de la guere[2] entre le Roi et ses de Fraunce le Roi
seisi, &c., par tant qe le Prior est alien, &c., et
sur le presentement furent autrefoith, en mesme
loriginal, a issue de pays, et sur ceo avoint jour a
ore.—*Nottone* counta pur le Roi autre count sur
autre presentement.[3]—*Mutl.* rehercea *ut supra*, et
demanda jugement si a mesme loriginal il serra
resceu, apres issue, de counter autre counte.—WILBY,
par agarde, luy mist outre.—*Mutl.* Nous vous dioms
qen temps le Roi Johan il y avoit un W. qe fuit
seisi del maner a quei lavoeson est appendant, et,
sur debat appeser Joliberd nostre predecessour et
luy, nostre predecessour pur luy et ses successours,
graunta qe W. et ses heirs retendreint lavoweson,
issint a presenter qe W. et ses heirs presentereint
a chesqun voidaunce lour clerc al Priour et a ses
successours, quel Prior mesme le clerc, par noun
de presente par W. et ses heirs presentereint outre

A.D. 1345.
*Quare
impedit.*
[Fitz.,
*Preroga-
tive*, 18.]

"idem Michael non potest hoc
" dedicere. Ideo quo ad hoc breve
" nihil fiat ulterius, salvo jure
" Regis alias, &c."

[1] From L., and C. This report
is the conclusion of No. 7 above.
The case appears to be that found
among the *Placita de Banco*, Mich.,
19 Edw. III., R° 58. The action
was brought by the King against
the Prior of Wenlock in respect of
a presentation to the chapel of
Baggesoure (Badger, Salop).

[2] C., gere.

[3] The declaration here was,
according to the roll, " quod
" quidam Henricus quondam Prior
" de Wenloke, prædecessor, &c.,
" fuit seisitus de advocatione
" capellæ prædictæ, ut de feodo et

" jure Prioratus sui prædicti, tem-
" pore . . . Edwardi Regis,
" patris domini Regis nunc, et
" præsentavit ad eandem quendam
" Philippum de Strethay, clericum
" suum, qui ad præsentationem,
" &c., admissus fuit, &c., ...
" post cujus mortem capella præ-
" dicta jam vacat, et postmodum
" temporalia ejusdem Prioratus
" devenerunt in manum domini
" Regis nunc, occasione guerræ
" inter ipsum Regem et illos de
" Francia motæ, eo quod Prior
" alienigena est et de potestate
" Franciæ, et, temporalibus præ-
" dictis sic in manu domini Regis
" nunc existentibus, prædicta
" Capella vacavit post mortem
" prædicti Philippi."

No. 78.

should be admitted he should do fealty and pay forty pence *per annum* to the Prior. And *Mutlow* showed how at all times afterwards the presentations were made in that manner, and that the presentation from which the King took his title was so made also, *absque hoc* that the person from whom the King took his title was admitted on the presentation of the Prior's predecessor as in right of his Priory; ready, &c. And, said *Mutlow*, we do not understand that in respect of such a presentation and title the King will be answered. —*Grene.* You see plainly that the Prior is a stranger to the right, which, according to his statement, is supposed to abide in the heirs of W.; and he produces nothing in proof of the agreement which he mentions, and claims nothing in the patronage; and, even though he were privy, &c., still, according to his own confession, the Prior would be the patron on whose presentation the parson would be admitted, and W.'s heirs would be only the nominators of the clerk, and that gives them nomination only, and not patronage; therefore we demand judgment for the King.—STOUFORD, *ad idem.* If the Prior claims as patron, then it belongs to the King to present for the time being, and, if he does not claim anything in the patronage, then this answer does not lie in his mouth.—*Mutlow.* We show that the patronage is in W.'s heirs, and we show that the presentation made by our predecessor was not made by him as patron, but in right of another person, and so we destroy the King's title, and he does not maintain it; judgment.—WILLOUGHBY. You are a stranger to that which you allege, and, even were you privy, it would be of no avail; and, in such circumstances, and if you had your lands delivered to you, &c., you would yourself present, and therefore do you who are for the King sue a writ to the Bishop for the King, &c.

No. 78.

al Ordeigner, et quant il serreit resceu il freit feaute
et xl deners par an al Priour. Et moustra coment
tut tens puis les presentements furent faitz par cele
manere, et qe le presentement dount le Roi prent
soun title auxi, &c., sanz ceo qe celuy dount le
Roi prent soun title fuit resceu al presentement
soun predecessour come de dreit de sa Priorie; prest,
&c. Et nentendoms pas qe sur tiel presentement
et title le Roi voille estre respondu.—*Grene.* Vous
veietz bien coment il est estrange a dreit quel duist
demurer, a ceo qil dist, en les heirs W.; et del
acord dount il parle rien ne moustre, et en lavowere
rien ne cleime; et, tut fuit il prive, &c., unqore, de
sa conissance demene, le Prior serreit avowe a qi
presentement la persone serreit resceu, et les heirs
W. forqe nomours du clerc, qest forqe denominacion
et noun pas patronage; par quei nous demandoms
jugement pur le Roi.—STOUF., *ad idem.* Si le Prior
cleyme come avowe, donqes appent au Roi a presenter pur le temps, et, sil ne cleime rienz, donqes
ne git pas cel respons en sa bouche.—*Mutl.* Nous
moustroms qe lavowere est en les heirs W., et
moustroms qe le presentement nostre predecessour
ne fuit pas come patron mes en autri dreit, et
issint destruoms le title le Roi, quel title il ne
meintent pas; jugement.—WILBY. Vous estes estrange
a ceo qe vous alleggetz, et, tut fuistes vous prive,
il ne vaudra pas; et, sur tiel fait, vous presenterez
mesmes, et si vous ussetz vos terres deliveretz, &c.,
par quei suetz brief al Evesqe pur le Roi, &c.[1]

---

[1] According to the roll, the Prior "nihil dicit quare dominus Rex "præsentationem suam ad Capel-"lam prædictam ratione prædicta "habere non debeat.
"Ideo consideratum est quod "dominus Rex recuperet versus "eum præsentationem suam ad "Capellam prædictam, et habeat "breve Episcopo Herefordensi, loci "Diocesano, &c."

No. 79.

A D. 1345
Writ on
the
Statute.
(79.) § W.[1] brought a writ on the Statute[2] which
enacts that it is not lawful for any one save the King
and his officers to take a distress outside his fee, &c.,
and alleged that the defendant,[1] not being the King's
officer, took his beasts against the peace.—*Skipwith.*
We tell you that in the County Court one A.[3] attached
a plaint of the taking of beasts against Philip de
Somerville, whose villein the plaintiff is, and of whom
Philip is seised as of his villein; and, because view of
the beasts could not be had, a *withernam* was ordered, and
a precept came to J.[3], against whom the writ has been
brought, to take a *withernam*, as bailiff, and he therefore took the same beasts which belonged to Philip,
and were found in the plaintiff's possession; judgment
whether he can assign tort in respect of that taking.
—*Pole.* Whereas he says that he took Philip's beasts,

---

[1] For the real names *see* p. 473, note 1.

[2] 52 Hen. III. (Marlb.), c. 15.

[3] *See* p. 473, note 4.

No. 79.

(79.)[1] § W. porta brief sur statut, qe ne list a nulle homme sauf au Roi et ses ministres de prendre destresse hors de soun fee, &c., et le defendant, qe nest pas ministre, prist ses avers *contra pacem*.[2]—*Skyp*. Vous dioms qen Countee[3] un A. attacha une pleinte de prise des avers vers Phelippe de Somer-ville, qi villeyn le pleintif est, et il seisi de luy come de soun villein; et pur ceo qe la viewe ne poet estre fait des bestes, le *withernam* fuit comande, et precepte vint a J., vers qi le brief fuit porte, com baillif, de prendre *withernam*, par quei il prist mesmes les bestes queux furent a P., et en la pos-session le pleintif trovetz; jugement si de cele prise puisse tort assigner.[4]—*Pole*. La ou il dit qil prist

A.D. 1345.
Brief sur statut.
[Fitz., Barre, 281;
Recapcion, 9.]

[1] From L., and C., but corrected by the record, *Placita coram Rege*, Mich., 19 Edw. III., R° 73, d. It there appears that the action was brought by Richard Fyldynge against John son of Nicholas de Alrewas, Henry his brother, William de Glascote, and several others.

[2] According to the record the declaration was " quod, cum de " communi consilio regni Regis " Angliæ provisum sit quod non " liceat alicui districtiones facere, ex " quacumque causa, extra feodum " suum, nec in Regia via, aut com-" muni strata, nisi domino Regi, et " ministris suis specialem auctori-" tatem ad hoc habentibus, prædicti " Johannes [&c.], qui ministri " domini Regis non sunt, ut " dicitur, extra feodum suum, apud " Alrewas, . . . averia præ " dicti Ricardi, videlicet duos " equos, duo jumenta, et duas " vaccas, contra formam provi-" sionis prædictæ, ceperunt et " imparcaverunt, et ea adhuc " imparcata detinent, contra legem

" et consuetudinem regni domini " Regis nunc Angliæ, et contra " pacem, &c."

[3] L., Conte.

[4] According to the record all the defendants pleaded Not Guilty as to the taking of the horses and cows, and issue was joined upon that plea, " Et quo ad captionem " prædictorum jumentorum præ-" dictus Willelmus de Glascote " dici quod tunc temporis ipse " fuit ballivus juratus Comitatus " prædicti, et dicit quod prædictus " Johannes filius Nicholai se " questus fuit versus quendam " Philippum de Somerville, in " Comitatu prædicto, de averiis " ipsius Johannis filii Nicholai " captis et injuste detentis, de " quibus quidem averiis prædictus " Johannes filius Nicholai delibera-" tionem nec visum habere potuit, " per quod præceptum fuit omnibus " et singulis ballivis Comitatus " prædicti quod deliberationem " facerent, &c., de averiis prædic-" tis, qui quidem ballivi in pleno " Comitatu responderunt quod

No. 79.

A.D. 1345. he took our beasts, as we have complained; ready, &c.
—*Skipwith.* And, inasmuch as you do not deny that
you are Philip's villein, in which case, even though
they were your beasts, with regard to effecting execution, they would be adjudged to be the beasts of the
lord, and so the averment is not admissible, and inasmuch as you have not denied that we are an officer,
which fact is contrary to your writ, we demand judgment of your writ, because against an officer you
would have a Replevin and not this writ; and instances
of this have been seen.—*R. Thorpe.* Yes, I saw a bill

No. 79.

les bestes P., il prist noz bestes, come nous sumes
pleint; prest, &c.[1]—*Skyp.* Et, desicome vous ne
deditetz pas qe vous nestes le villein P., en quel
cas, tut fuissent ils voz bestes, quant a execucion
faire, ils serreint ajuges les[2] bestes le seignour, et
issint laverement nient resceivable, et vous navietz
pas dedit qe nous sumes ministre, qest a contrarie
de vostre[3] brief, jugement de vostre brief, qar vers
ministre vous averetz *Replegiari*, et noun pas cel[4]
brief; et ceo ad homme view.[5]—[*R.*] *Thorpe.* Oyl,

" averia prædicta elongata fuerunt,
" ita quod visum de eis habere non
" potuerunt, ita quod deliberatio
" per eos fieri non potuit, per quod
" per judicium Comitatus prædicti
" consideratum fuit quod idem
" Johannes filius Nicholai haberet
" de averiis ipsius Philippi in
" wythernamium ad valentiam,
" &c., per quod prædictus Willel-
" mus, et prædictus Henricus frater
" Johannis filii Nicholai assignati
" fuerunt per commissionem Vice-
" comitis ad faciendum execu-
" tionem judicii prædicti, quam
" quidem commissionem ipse Hen-
" ricus protulit hic in Curia sigillo
" Vicecomitis signatam. Et dicunt
" quod prædicti duo equi, de quibus
" prædictus Ricardus queritur,
" tempore captionis prædictæ,
" fuerunt jumenta ipsius Philippi
" in possessione ejusdem Ricardi
" tunc nativi ipsius Philippi, et
" ipse Philippus adtunc de præ-
" dicto Ricardo ut de nativo suo
" [seisitus fuit],et adhuc est,et idem
" Ricardus tenet terras et tene-
" menta de ipso Philippo in villen-
" agio. Et sic dicunt quod ipsi
" ceperunt jumenta prædicta, quæ
" fuerunt prædicti Philippi, in
" forma prædicta, virtute judicii
" Comitatus prædicti et Commis-

" sionis prædictæ, &c., et hoc parati
" sunt verificare, et petunt judicium
" si prædictus Ricardus aliquam
" injuriam in personis ipsorum
" Willelmi et Henrici ratione præ-
" dicta assignare possit, &c.

" Et prædicti Johannes filius
" Nicholai et alii dicunt quod ipsi
" venerunt in auxilium prædic-
" torum Willelmi et Henrici ad
" executionem prædictam facien-
" dum, &c."

[1] According to the record the
replication was, " quod averia
" prædicta fuerunt averia ipsius
" Ricardi, sicut ipse superius
" queritur, et hoc paratus est
" verificare, &c."

[2] C., come.

[3] C., nostre.

[4] C., tiel.

[5] The pleading is, on the roll,
" quod, ex quo ipse Ricardus non
" dedicit quin est nativus ipsius
" Philippi, et idem Philippus die
" captionis prædictæ seisitus fuit
" de prædicto Ricardo ut de nativo
" suo, et per legem terræ averia
" ipsius Ricardi sunt averia ipsius
" Philippi domini sui ad volun-
" tatem et ad executiones per
" præceptum domini Regis facien-
" das, et non dedicit quin captio
" prædicta facta fuit per prædictos

No. 79.

abated before PARUYNGE[1] for the same reason.—W. THORPE (JUSTICE). That was extraordinary, because, when any one avows an act he will plead justification, when it is the act of an officer as well as when it is the act of another.—*R. Thorpe.* You will not plead matter affecting realty on writs of Trespass here in the King's Bench in the same manner as they do in the Common Bench.—SHARSHULLE.[2] If it were law to plead matter affecting realty down there, it would be strange if it were not so here.—*R. Thorpe.* And so it used to be; but if you make a change in this respect, I am quite content.—SCOT. We should be more disposed to act in that way on this writ than on another containing the words " *vi et armis, &c.*"—*Pole* returned to their plea, and said:—*Skipwith* is taking two pleas, one surmising against us that we have not denied that we are Philip's villein, which is one plea by itself, the other that inasmuch as he is an officer the writ does not lie.—But no importance was attached by the COURT to this plea to the writ.—And the point was touched that the defendant ought always to affirm that he is an officer, if he is one.—*Pole.* If he had confessed the ownership to be in us, and had avowed as in respect of our beasts on the ground that we are a villein, he would have put us to answer whether we were a villein or not, and on that we should have abode judgment with him ; but when he says that they were Philip's beasts in our possession, as Philip's servant or groom, he gives us the opportunity of maintaining the ownership to be in us in accordance with our plaint.—W. THORPE (J.). He does not deny that you have ownership such as a villein has in relation to his lord, but execution can be had of a villein's beasts, and that he puts to judgment; and if he had taken the plea in the manner in which you

---

[1] As to this name *see* Y.B., Easter and Trinity, 18 Edw. III. (Rolls edition), Introd., pp. xxxv-xxxvii.

[2] *See* p. 478, note 1.

No. 79

jeo[1] vie devant PARU. une bille estre abatu par A.D 1345.
mesme la resoun.—[W.] THORPE (JUSTICE). Ceo fuit
merveille, qar quant il avowe un fait homme pledera[2]
a justificacion dun ministre si bien come dautre.—
[R.] *Thorpe.* Vous ne pledretz pas en le realte en
briefs de Trans cy el Bank le Roi si avant comme[3]
ils fount en Comune Bank.—SCHAR. Sil serreit ley
la aval de pleder en realte, il serreit merveille sil
ne fuit ici.—[R.] *Thorpe.* Et issint soleit il estre;
mes si vous chaungetz cele matere il moi pleist
bien.—SCOT. Nous le froms plus avant en cest brief
qen un autre *vi et armis, &c.*—*Pole* resorti a lour
plee, et dist qe *Skyp.* prent deux plees, un sur-
mettant a nous qe nous navoms pas dedit qe nous
sumes villein P., qest un ple a per luy, un autre
qe par taunt qil est ministre qe le brief ne gist
pas.—Mes cel ple au brief nest pas charge par
COURT.—Et si fuit il touche qe le defendant coviendreit affermer touz jours qil est ministre.—*Pole.* Sil
ust conu la proprete a nous, et ust avowe come de
nos bestes par tant qe nous sumes villein, il nous
mettreit a respondre si nous fuissoms villein ou noun,
et la demureimes en jugement ovesqe luy; mes
quant il dist qils furent les avers P. en nostre
possession, come servant ou garsoun a P.. il nous
doune de meintener la proprete a nous come nous
pleignoms.—[W.] THORPE. Il ne dedit pas qe vous
navietz proprete tele come villein ad vers soun
seignur, mes des bestes le villein execucion est a
faire, et ceo mette il en jugement; et sil ust pris
le plee par la manere qe vous tailletz ore, unqore

" Willelmum ballivum juratum et
" per prædictum Henricum balli-
" vum virtute commissionis præ-
" dictæ, et ratione wythernamii
" prædicti in possessione prædicti
" Ricardi, &c., nativi prædicti

" Philippi capti, petunt judicium,
" &c."
[1] C., je.
[2] pledera is omitted from C.
[3] comme is omitted from C.

No. 80.

A.D. 1345. now limit it, still the same point would be put to judgment; therefore consider whether you will say anything else.—SHARSHULLE.[1] If you be a villein, it is best for you to be non-suited.—*Pole* imparled, and said that he was free, and of free condition; ready, &c —And the other side said the contrary.

False Judgment.   (80.) § False Judgment. The suitors appeared, and brought their record, and delivered it to the Clerk, and afterwards departed.—*Grene* prayed that the parties might be called, and assigned errors.—HILLARY. Where are the suitors who ought to acknowledge the record?—*Grene.* They have delivered up the record to the Court, and it is before you on the file.—HILLARY. They will be distrained to produce their record here. —*Grene.* That cannot be, since you are yourselves in possession of it: for you are apprised that they cannot bring the record which remains before you.— HILLARY. They will be distrained, and, when they

---

[1] It is uncertain whether the judge was Sharshulle or not. Michaelmas Term in this year extended from the 10th of October to the 28th of November. Sharshulle, after having been Chief Baron of the Exchequer for some months, was re-appointed to the Common Bench, as second Justice, on the 10th of November, 1345. In Michaelmas Term, therefore, he must have been holding one of those two offices, and could hardly have been a Justice of the King's Bench. He does not, however, appear to have sat in the Common Bench before Hilary Term in the following year. The only other judge whose name was at all similar, at this time, was Scardeburgh, who, having been a Justice of the King's Bench in England, was appointed Chief Justice of the King's Bench in Ireland in July, 1344, but had been succeeded in that office by John le Hunte on the 1st of August, 1345.

No. 80.

mesme le point serreit mys en jugement; par quei A.D. 1345.
veietz si vous voilletz autre chose dire.—SCHAR. Si
vous soietz villeyn il vaut plus destre nounsuy.—
Pole enparla et dist qe fraunk, et de fraunk estat;
prest, &c.—*Et alii e contra.*[1]

(80.)[2] § Faux Jugement. Les suiters vindrent, et Faux jugement. [Fitz., *Proses,* 40.]
porterent lour recorde, et le livererent al Clerc, et
apres departirent.—*Grene* pria qe les parties fuissent
demandetz, et assigna errours.—HILL. Ou sount les
suyters qe duissent avower le recorde?—*Grene.* Ils
ount livere le recorde suys a la Court, et cest la
devant vous en filace.[3]—HILL. Ils serrount destreints
daver cy lour recorde.—*Grene.* Ceo ne poet estre,
quant vous mesmes estes seisi: qar vous estes appris
qils ne pount porter le recorde quel demurt devant
vous.—HILL. Ils serrount destreints, et, quant ils

---

[1] The entry on the roll continues as follows:—

" Prædictus Ricardus Fyldynge,
" protestando quod ipse non cog-
" noscit prædictum Willelmum de
" Glascote esse ballivum juratum,
" nec prædictum Henricum filium
" Nicholai habere talem commis-
" sionem, nec prædictum wyther-
" namium esse adjudicatum versus
" prædictum Philippum, dicit quod
" ipse, die captionis prædictæ, fuit
" liber homo et liberæ conditionis,
" et hoc paratus est verificare.

" Et Willelmus et Henricus
." dicunt quod prædictus Ricardus,
" die captionis prædictæ, fuit
" nativus ipsius Philippi, et idem
" Philippus seisitus de ipso Ricardo
" ut de nativo suo, sicut iidem
" Willelmus et Henricus dicunt."

Issue was joined upon this and the *Venire* awarded, but nothing further appeared on the roll except an adjournment.

[2] From L., and C. The case may probably be identified as that which appears among the *Placita de Banco*, Mich., 19 Edw. III., R° 630. It there appears that the Sheriff of Devonshire was directed to distrain the suitors of the King's Court of Exeter (twenty-nine in number, all of whom are named) " et quod haberet corpora eorun- " dem hic ad hunc diem, &c., ad " faciendum recordum loquelæ quæ " fuit in eadem Curia per breve " Regis de Recto, inter Johannem " Coke, spicer, et Beatricem quæ " fuit uxor Ricardi Beaufou ten- " entem de uno mesuagio, cum " pertinentiis, in Exonia unde idem " Johannes queritur sibi falsum " factum fuisse judicium in eadem " Curia."

The Sheriff's return and certain adjournments appear on the roll. but nothing further.

[3] C., filaz.

Nos. 81, 82.

A.D. 1345. appear, if they will acknowledge this as their record, they will be excused; but possibly they will disavow it.—Therefore HILLARY ordered the Clerk to enter the Distress.

Dower.

(81.) § Dower was brought against a certain person, and the demand made was for a third part of three parts, &c. And the same demandant demanded against that same person and another, by another writ of Dower, a third part of a moiety of the same tenements. And exception was taken on the ground that she demanded parcel of the same thing twice over. Therefore she had to abridge her demand. And she was admitted to do this, notwithstanding that it was after exception taken by party.

Note as to Trespass.

(82.) § Note that when a writ of Trespass is without day by Protection, or in any other manner, a *Venire facias* will be had when the parol is reattached, and the party who is defendant will by that process lose the advantage of an essoin, because essoin does not lie on a *Venire facias*.

Nos. 81, 82.

vendrount, sils voillent avower cest pur recorde, ils A.D. 1345.
serrount excuses; mes par cas ils le voleint des-
avower.—Par quei il comanda au clerc dentrer la
destresse.

(81.)[1] .§ Dowere porte vers un, et la demande fait Dowere.
de la terce partie des iij parties, &c. Et vers
mesme celuy et un autre, par autre brief de Dowere,
mesme la demandante demanda la terce partie de
la moite de mesmes les tenementz. Et fuit chalenge
de ceo qele demanda parcelle deux foith dune mesme
chose. Par quei ele abreggera sa demande. Et a
ceo est resceu, *non obstante* qe ceo fuit apres chalenge
de partie.

(82.)[1] § *Nota* qe quant brief de Trans est sanz *Nota* de [2]
jour par proteccion, ou en autre manere, homme Trans. [Fitz.,
avera *Venire facias* quant la parole serra reattache, *Proses,*
et partie defendant par cel proces perdra avantage 41.]
del essone, pur ceo qen *Venire facias* ele ne git pas.

---

[1] From L., and C.

[2] The words *Nota* de are from L. alone.

APPENDIX.

APPENDIX.

Record of the Case, Trinity, 19 Edward III., No. 22.

(*Placita coram Rege*, Trin., 19 Edw. III., R° 51.)

Dominus Rex mandavit breve suum clausum Justiciariis hic in hæc verba :—Edwardus Dei gratia Rex Angliæ et Franciæ, et Dominus Hiberniæ, dilectis et fidelibus suis Willelmo Scot et sociis Justiciariis ad placita coram nobis tenenda assignatis salutem. Quasdam inquisitiones per dilectos et fideles nostros Johannem de Cherletone, Willelmum de Forde, et Ricardum de Burtone de mandato nostro factas, et in Cancelaria nostra retornatas, vobis mittimus sub pede sigilli nostri, mandantes quod, inspectis inquisitionibus prædictis, et vocatis coram vobis in hac parte evocandis, ulterius fieri faciatis quod de jure et secundum legem et consuetudinem regni nostri Angliæ fore videritis faciendum. Teste me ipso apud Westmonasterium, quarto die Junii, anno regni nostri Angliæ decimo nono, regni vero nostri Franciæ sexto.

Commissio præfatis Johanni et sociis suis inde directa sequitur in hæc verba :—Edwardus Dei gratia Rex Angliæ et Franciæ, et Dominus Hiberniæ, dilectis et fidelibus suis Johanni de Cherletone, Willelmo de Forde, et Ricardo de Burtone salutem. Quia datum est nobis intelligi quod quamplures homines de Comitatibus Essexiæ et Middelsexiæ, in diversis locis in aqua vocata la Leye, quæ currit a villa de Ware usque ad Waltham Sanctæ Crucis, et ab inde usque Civitatem nostram Londoniarum, in qua quidem aqua naves et batelli, cum victualibus a diversis partibus usque dictam Civitatem pro sustentatione Communitatis Civitatis illius, et aliorum ad eandem confluentium, totis temporibus retroactis transire consueverunt, pilas, claias, exclusas, et alia ingenia diversa pro captione piscium fixerunt et imposuerunt, necnon aquam illam per diversas trencheas in terris suis in quibusdam aliis locis factas currere faciunt, et rectum cursum aquæ illius diverterunt, per quod transitus hujusmodi navium et batellorum per aquam prædictam impeditur, ad dictorum Communitatis Civitatis illius et aliorum ad eandem Civitatem sic confluentium grave damnum et jacturam manifestam, Nos, volentes indemnitati populi nostri prospicere in hac parte, assignavimus vos, et duos vestrum, ad inquirendum per sacramentum proborum et legalium hominum de Comitatibus prædictis, per quos rei veritas melius sciri poterit, super præmissis omnibus et singulis, et aliis circumstantiis ea tangentibus, plenius veritatem. Et ideo vobis mandamus quod, ad certos dies et loca quos vos vel duo vestrum ad hoc provideritis, inquisitiones super præmissis faciatis, et eas distincte et aperte factas nobis sub sigillis vestris vel duorum vestrum, et sigillis eorum per quos factæ fuerint, sine dilatione mittatis, et hoc breve. Mandavimus enim Vicecomitibus nostris Comitatuum prædictorum quod, ad certos dies et loca quos vos vel duo vestrum eis scire faciatis, venire faciant coram vobis, vel duobus vestrum, tot et tales probos et legales homines de ballivis suis per quos rei veritas in præmissis melius sciri poterit et inquiri. In cujus rei testimonium has literas nostras fieri fecimus patentes. Teste me apud Claryngdone xx die Julii anno regni nostri Angliæ decimo septimo, regni vero nostri Franciæ quarto.

Midd. Inquisitio capta coram præfato Johanne et sociis suis in Comitatu Middelsexiæ sequitur in hæc verba:—

Inquisitio capta coram Johanne de Cherletone et sociis suis Justiciariis domini Regis apud Westsmethefelde extra Baram in Comitatu Middelsexiæ, die dominica proxima post festum Sancti Lucæ Evangelistæ anno regni Regis Edwardi tertii post Conquestum decimo octavo, virtute cujusdam commissionis eis directæ, de his qui diversas pilas, claias, exclusas, et alia ingenia diversa pro captione piscium in aqua vocata la Leye fixerunt et imposuerunt, necnon de omnibus illis qui aquam prædictam per diversas trencheas in terris suis seu in aliis locis factas currere faciunt, et rectum cursum aquæ illius diverterunt, per quod transitus navium et batellorum per dictam aquam de la Leye impeditur, ad damnum et jacturam Communitatis Civitatis Londoniarum et aliorum ad eandem confluentium, ac etiam ad damnum et jacturam diversorum hominum de Comitatu Middelsexiæ prædicto, per sacramentum Willelmi atte Wodehalle, Thomæ de Nortone, Johannis Dixy, Johannis May, moleward, Johannis de Bysterlee, Johannis de Hendone, Gregorii de Wyke, Simonis Hern, Johannis Dobelyn, Petri atte Gate, Johannis le Hert, et Johannis de Herlestone, qui dicunt per sacramentum suum quod est quoddam fossatum vocatum Louediche juxta le Eldeforde, in villa de Stebbenhethe in Comitatu Middelsexiæ, inter prata Matilldis quæ fuit uxor Galfridi Aleyn ex utraque parte, et solebat esse latitudinis ad caput dicti fossati juxta la Leye sex pedum tantum, et profunditatis duorum pedum tantum, et solebat obturari

cum quinque pilis quondam positis per Stephanum Asswy
tenentem duorum molendinorum vocatorum landmilnes, pro
aqua de la Leye in cursu suo recto conservanda, ne aqua de
la Leye diminueretur, quod quidem fossatum extendit se ad
[*for* de?] dicta aqua de la Leye usque ad aquam vocatam Rothulvespond, quod quidem fossatum oblargatum est cum manuopere tempore quo Johannes Hauteyn fuit tenens de dictis
pratis, videlicet tempore domini Regis Edwardi patris domini
Regis nunc, per duos pedes, et dictum fossatum elargatum
fuit cum manuopere tempore domini Regis Edwardi nunc,
tempore quo Gilbertus de la Bruere fuit tenens pratorum prædictorum per quatuor pedes. Et etiam dictum fossatum elargatum fuit, tempore domini Regis Edwardi nunc, per Galfridum
Aleyn et Matilldem uxorem ejus, in vita ejusdem Galfridi,
per duos pedes. Et similiter dictum fossatum elargatum est
per eandem Matilldem, nunc tenentem pratorum prædictorum,
in viduitate sua, post decessum dicti Galfridi, per quatuor pedes.
Et per eandem Matilldem dictum fossatum factum est profundius quam solibat [*sic*] esse per duos pedes, ad nocumentum
omnium illorum cum navibus et batellis in dicta aqua de la
Leye transeuntium. Item dicunt quod Le[ti]cia de Markam,
nuper Priorissa de Stratforde, et Isabella Blounde, nunc Priorissa,
posuerunt octodecim pilas in aqua de la Leye prædicta, juxta
pontem de Stratforde, in villa de Bramleghe, tempore Regis Edwardi nunc, ad nocumentum et impedimentum cum navibus et
batellis suis per eandem aquam transeuntium. Item dicunt
quod eadem Isabella nunc Priorissa in alio loco in eadem villa
posuit in aqua eadem xij pilas, tempore Regis Edwardi nunc, ad
nocumentum ut supra. Item dicunt quod eadem Isabella nunc
Priorissa posuit in prædicta aqua apud Bramleghe xx pilas, et
in eadem villa in alio loco xx pilas, tempore Regis Edwardi
nunc, ad periculum et nocumentum omnium transeuntium cum
navibus et batellis suis. Item dicunt quod Ricardus de Wight,
quondam Abbas de Stratforde, fecit quandam hayam in introitu
aquæ Tamisiæ in villa de Westhamme in aqua de la Leye, for-
titudine cujus hayæ rectus cursus aquæ de la Leye divertitur
super Comitatum Middelsexiæ, et rectus cursus aquæ omnino
obturatur per duodecim perticatas, pertica continente xvj pedes
et dimidium, et terra ibidem ita elevatur et exaltatur quod vix
aliqua navis in prædicta aqua de la Leye potest transire, nec
pisces Tamisiæ in prædicta aqua possunt intrare per fortitudi-
nem et injuriam ipsius Abbatis, ad damnum Regis et Communitatis Civitatis Londoniarum, et nocumentum populi, ut supra,
quod nocumentum per Willelmum de Coggeshale nunc Abbatem
continuatur. Item dicunt quod Johannes de Triple, tempore
Regis nunc, posuit in cursu aquæ de la Leye in Stebbenhethe-

mershe tresdecim pilas, ad nocumentum ut supra. Item dicunt quod Ricardus de Bynteworth, nuper Episcopus Londoniensis, contra Trendlehope in Stebbenhethe posuit in prædicto cursu novem pilas anno regni Regis Edwardi nunc quarto-decimo, et Radulphus nunc Episcopus Londoniensis dictum nocumentum adhuc continuat, ad nocumentum ut supra. Item dicunt quod Isabella nunc Priorissa de Stratforde juxta Redhope in Brembeleghe posuit septem pilas in aqua prædicta ad nocumentum ut supra. Item dicunt quod Radulphus quondam Prior de Crist cherche Londoniarum apud le Warewal in Brambeleghe posuit undecim pilas, tempore Regis Edwardi patris Edwardi nunc, ad nocumentum ut supra, et Nicholaus nunc Prior dictum nocumentum continuat. Item dicunt quod prædictus Radulphus quondam Prior de Crist cherche apud molendinum suum in Brambeleghe in cursu aquæ prædictæ posuit sex pilas, tempore Regis Edwardi patris Regis Edwardi nunc, ad nocumentum ut supra, et Nicholaus nunc Prior continuat dictum nocumentum. Item dicunt quod prædictus Radulphus quondam Prior de Crist cherche juxta manerium suum de Bremlehalle in Bremleghe posuit septemdecim pilas, et in alio loco in eadem villa juxta pilas prædictas posuit tresdecim in cursu aquæ prædictæ, tempore Regis Edwardi patris Regis Edwardi nunc, ad nocumentum ut supra, et dictum nocumentum per Nicholaum nunc Priorem continuatur. Dicunt etiam quod apud Stratforde in parochia de Brambeleghe habetur quædam exclusa aquæ de la Leye vocata Fouremulleloke, quæ quidem exclusa primo posita fuit per Henricum de Bedike, tempore Regis Edwardi avi Regis nunc, unde Thomas Bedike, Priorissa de Haliwelle, et Isabella nunc Priorissa de Stratforde sunt tenentes, quæ claudit et retinet aquam prædictam per quatuor pedes in altitudine plus quam reliquæ exclusæ superius in prædicta aqua de Lye positæ retinent. Et dicunt quod illa exclusa facit aquam prædictam recurrere et divertere, ita quod molendina quæ sunt superius per eandem aquam posita non possunt molere dummodo aqua ibidem sic retinetur, ad nocumentum Civitatis prædictæ Londoniarum. Et per eandem exclusam aqua divertitur ita quod recurrit in prata adjacentia, per quod fenum crescens multum destruitur, ad nocumentum tenentium et Civatatis Londoniarum. Dicunt etiam quod per eandem exclusam via regia apud Stratforde dimergitur, ad nocumentum omnium per illud transeuntium, et similiter ad nocumentum et impedimentum omnium cum navibus et batellis per prædictam aquam de la Leye transeuntium, et istud nocumentum et impedimentum ab illo tempore usque nunc continuatur. In cujus rei testimonium prædicti Jurati huic Inquisitioni, die, et anno, et loco supradictis, sigilla sua apposuerunt.

Et super hoc, tam pro domino Rege quam pro aisiamento et commodo populi sui partium prædictarum, &c., præceptum fuit Vicecomiti Middelsexiæ quod venire faceret coram domino Rege, die Lunæ proxima post tres septimanus Sanctæ Trinitatis, ubicumque, &c., prædictos Matilldem, Priorissam de Stratforde, Abbatem de Stratforde, Johannem de Tripelle, Episcopum Londoniensem, Priorem de Crist cherche, Thomam Bedyke, et Priorissam de Haliwelle, ad respondendum domino Regi quare prædicta nocumenta in aqua prædicta per ipsos posita et continuata amoveri non deberent, et ulterius, &c.

Ad quem diem Vicecomes modo retornavit quod prædicta Matilldis attachiata est per Hugonem Lambyn et Johannem Adam, et Priorissa per Nicholaum atte Wyke et Willelmum Marwan, et prædictus Abbas per Rogerum le Taillour et Willelmum de Motwelle, et prædictus Johannes de Tripelle per Ricardum Underwode et Willelmum atte Welle, et prædictus Episcopus per Willelmum atte Fenne et Ricardum de Haddele, et prædictus Prior per Thomam Roghe et Adam Kippeye, et prædictus Thomas per Willelmum Perkyn et Thomam Freman, et prædicta Priorissa de Haliwelle per Thomam Mantel et Johannem de Hedone, qui quidem Matilldis et alii solemniter vocati non veniunt. Ideo ipsi in misericordia, &c. Et præceptum est Vicecomiti quod distringat prædictos Matilldem et alios per omnes terras, &c., et quod de exitibus, &c., et quod habeat corpora eorum coram domino Rege, die Sabbati proxima ante festum Nativitatis Sancti Johannis Baptistæ, ubicumque, &c., ad respondendum domino Regi in forma prædicta, &c., et ulterius, &c.

Ad quem diem veniunt coram domino Rege tam Johannes de Lincolnia qui sequitur pro domino Rege, quam prædicti Matilldis quæ fuit uxor Galfridi Aleyn, Abbas de Stratforde, Priorissa de Stratforde, Johannes de Tripelle, Prior de Cristchirch, et Priorissa de Haliwelle, per Johannem de Lokyngtone, attornatum suum, et prædictus Episcopus et Thomas de Bedyke non veniunt, &c.

Et super hoc quæsitum est ab eis pro domino Rege si quid pro se dicere sciant quare prædicta nocumenta et impedimenta, &c., amoveri non debeant, &c.

Et prædicta Matilldis, quo ad hoc quod præsentatum est quod ubi quoddam fossatum vocatum Louedich juxta le Eldeforde in villa de Stebenhethe inter prata prædictæ Matilldis ex utraque parte solebat esse latitudinis ad caput dicti fossati juxta le Leye sex pedum tantum, et profunditatis duorum pedum tantum, et solebat obturari cum quinque pilis quondam positis per Stephanum Asswy, tenentem duorum molendinorum vocatorum Landmulnes, pro aqua prædicta in suo cursu con-

servanda, ne aqua illa diminueretur, quod quidem fossatum
elargatum est cum manuopere tempore quo Johannes Hauteyn
fuit tenens de dictis pratis, videlicet, tempore domini Edwardi
nuper Regis Angliæ patris, &c., per duos pedes, et dictum
fossatum elargatum fuit cum manuopere, tempore domini Regis
nunc, per quatuor pedes, tempore quo Gilbertus de la Bruere
fuit tenens prædictorum pratorum, et etiam dictum fossatum
elargatum fuit, tempore ejusdem domini Regis nunc, per Galfridum Aleyn et prædictam Matilldem, in vita ipsius Galfridi,
per duos pedes, et similiter dictum fossatum elargatum est
per ipsam Matilldem, nunc tenentem pratorum prædictorum, per
quatuor pedes, et per eandem Matilldem dictum fossatum factum est profundius quam solebat esse per duos pedes, ad nocumentum omnium illorum cum navibus et batellis in dicta aqua
transeuntium, &c., dicit quod ipsa nihil fecit nec continuavit
in elargando prædictum fossatum, ad nocumentum Civitatis
Regis Londoniarum, in prædicta aqua de la Leye, nec ad impedimentum hominum neque per terram neque per aquam prædictam cum navibus et batellis transeuntium, sicut superius
præsentatum est. Et de hoc ponit se super patriam, &c.

Et prædicta Priorissa de Stratforde, quo ad hoc quod præsentatum est quod, ubi prædicta Isabella nunc Priorissa de Stratforde posuit in prædicta aqua apud Redhope septem pilas, et
etiam quod eadem nunc Priorissa posuit in eadem aqua duodecim pilas in alio loco in eadem villa, et etiam quo ad hoc
quod, ubi præsentatum est quod prædicta Leticia quondam
Priorissa de Stratforde, posuit in prædicta aqua apud Brambeleghe viginti pilas, et in eadem villa in alio loco viginti pilas,
ad nocumentum et impedimentum, &c., dicit quod ipsa nihil
fecit nec continuavit in prædicta aqua ad nocumentum sive
impedimentum hominum per prædictam aquam cum navibus et
batellis transeuntium, sicut superius præsentatum est. Et de
hoc similiter ponit se super patriam, &c.

Et prædictus Johannes de Tripelle, quo ad hoc quod præsentatum est superius quod idem Johannes posuit in cursu aquæ
prædictæ in Stebbenhethmersshe tresdecim pilas ad nocumentum, &c., dicit quod ipse nihil posuit in cursu aquæ prædictæ
ad nocumentum sive impedimentum navium et batellorum per
prædictam aquam transeuntium, sicut superius præsentatum
est. Et de hoc ponit se super patriam, &c.

Et prædictus nunc Prior de Cristchirche, quo ad hoc quod
præsentatum est quod ipse continuavit quoddam nocumentum
undecim pilarum positarum in prædicta aqua per prædictum prædecessorem suum apud Warewal, et etiam quod ipse continuavit
quoddam aliud nocumentum sex pilarum positarum per prædictum prædecessorem suum in eadem aqua apud molendinum

suum de Brambeleghe, et etiam quod ipse continuavit quoddam aliud nocumentum decem et septem pilarum positarum
in prædicta aqua per prædictum prædecessorem suum apud
Brambehalle, et etiam quod ipse continuavit quoddam aliud
nocumentum tresdecim pilarum in prædicta aqua per prædictum
prædecessorem suum positarum in alio loco in eadem villa,
dicit quod omnes pilæ prædictæ positæ in prædicta aqua de
la Leye per prædictum prædecessorem suum, &c., positæ
fuerunt in eadem aqua per prædictum prædecessorem suum
ad salvationem terrarum ipsius Prioris juxta aquam illam
jacentem, et aliorum hominum partium illarum, et non ad
nocumentum sive impedimentum hominum cum navibus et
batellis per aquam illam transeuntium sicut superius præsentatur. Et de hoc similiter ponit se super patriam.

Et prædictus Johannes de Lincolnia, qui sequitur pro domino
Rege, similiter.

Ideo veniat inde Jurata coram domino Rege, die Mercurii
proxima post festum Nativitatis Sancti Johannis Baptistæ,
ubicunque, &c., ad recognoscendum, &c.

Et præceptum fuit Vicecomiti quod distringeret prædictos
Episcopum et Thomam de Bedyke, per omnes terras, &c.

Et Vicecomes returnavit quod mandavit Nicholao le Clerke
de Waletone, ballivo libertatis Abbatis Westmonasterii, qui
nullum inde sibi dedit responsum.

Ideo præceptum est Vicecomiti quod non omittat propter
eandem libertatem Abbatis Westmonasterii quin distringat eos
per omnes terras, &c., contra eundem diem, &c.

Ad quem diem Mercurii veniunt coram domino Rege tam
prædictus Johannes de Lincolnia, qui sequitur pro domino
Rege, quam prædicti Matilldis, Priorissa de Stratforde, Johannes
de Tripelle, et Prior de Cristchirche, per prædictum attornatum
suum, et similiter juratores, videlicet, Maurillus de Saunforde,
Johannes atte Castel, Thomas de Nortone, Hugo Bussy,
Radulphus Onlay, Johannes atte Mersshe, Radulphus Balde-
wyne, Rogerus atte Lofte, Willelmus Vykere, Hugo de Depe-
dene, Willelmus Bisshope, et Gregorius de Wyke veniunt, qui
dicunt super sacramentum suum quod habetur quoddam fossatum vocatum Louediche juxta le Eldeforde in villa de
Stebbenhethe, in Comitatu prædicto, quod jacet inter prata
prædictæ Matilldis ex utraque parte, et solebat esse latitudinis
ad caput dicti fossati juxta la Leye sex pedum tantum, et
profunditatis duorum pedum tantum, et solebat obturari cum
quinque pilis, quod quidem fossatum elargatum est cum manuopere tempore quo Johannes Hauteyn fuit tenens per duos
pedes, tempore Edwardi Regis patris, et similiter per quatuor
pedes tempore quo Gilbertus de la Bruere fuit tenens, tempore

Edwardi Regis nunc, et per Galfridum Aleyn et prædictam Matilldem, in vita ipsius Galfridi, per duos pedes, tempore Regis nunc, et idem fossatum elargatum est per eandem Matilldem, post mortem ipsius Galfridi, per iiij pedes, et per eandem Matilldem factum est profundius quam solebat esse per duos pedes et plus, tempore Edwardi Regis nunc, ad grave nocumentum Regis et omnium illorum cum navibus et batellis per aquam prædictam transeuntium, et dicunt quod cursus aquæ prædictæ per nocumentum prædictum in tantum exsiccatur quod nocumentum illud nullo modo potest permitti nisi cursus aquæ illius continue diminuatur.

Et dicunt quod septem pilæ positæ fuerunt apud Redhope in aqua prædicta, et xij pilæ positæ fuerunt per Isabellam nunc Priorissam de Stratforde, et quod quadraginta pilæ positæ fuerunt per Leticiam quondam Priorissam de Stratforde in aqua prædicta, et continuatæ per eandem nunc Priorissam, ad nocumentum omnium illorum per aquam illam transeuntium.

Et dicunt quod prædictus nunc Prior de Cristchirche continuavit nocumentum xj pilarum positarum per Radulphum quondam Priorem, &c., positarum apud Warewal in Brambele in aqua prædicta, et similiter positionem septem pilarum apud molendinum suum de Brambele positarum per prædictum prædecessorem suum, et similiter quod idem Prior continuavit positionem xvij pilarum positarum per prædictum prædecessorem suum in aqua prædicta juxta le Brambelehalle, et continuavit nocumentum xiij pilarum positarum in prædicta aqua per prædictum prædecessorem suum, ad nocumentum omnium illorum in aqua prædicta transeuntium, et quod prædictus Johannes non posuit aliquas pilas in aqua prædicta, ad nocumentum sive impedimentum, sicut superius præsentatum est.

Ideo consideratum est quod prædictum fossatum sic elargatum et profundatum in latitudine et profunditate per prædictam Matilldem tempore suo ad custagia ipsius Matilldis obstruatur et emendetur, et eadem Matilldis in misericordia pro obstructione et profundatione fossati illius, et alia prædicta nocumenta facta in fossato prædicto temporibus quibus prædicti Galfridus, Gilbertus, et Johannes Hauteyn fuerunt tenentes ejusdem fossati similiter obstruantur et emendentur ad custagia domini Regis, et prædictæ xix pilæ positæ per prædictam Isabellam nunc Priorissam amoveantur et deleantur ad custagia ipsius Priorissæ, et eadem Priorissa in misericordia, &c., et quod prædictæ xl pilæ positæ per prædictam Leticiam quondam Priorissam amoveantur et evellantur ad custagia domini Regis, et quod omnia nocumenta continuata per prædictum nunc Priorem de Cristchirche similiter amoveantur ad custagia domini Regis, &c.

Et præceptum est Vicecomiti quod publice proclamari faciat per totam ballivam suam quod omnes illi de Comitatu suo ad quorum nocumentum et impedimentum et obstructiones prædicta in aqua prædicta facta fuerunt sint ibi, ad aliquem certum diem per ipsum Vicecomitem eis præfixum, in auxilium ipsius ad prædicta nocumenta, impedimenta, et obstructiones, in eadem aqua per prædictos Matilldem, Priorissam, et Priorem facta et continuata amovenda, obstruenda, et penitus evellenda, &c., et qualiter, &c., idem Vicecomes scire faciat coram domino Rege, a die Sancti Michaelis in xv dies, ubicunque, &c.

Ad quem diem Vicecomes mandavit quod breve adeo tarde, &c. Ideo sicut prius præceptum est Vicecomiti quod publice, &c., in forma prædicta, et qualiter, &c., Vicecomes scire faciat coram domino Rege, a die Sancti Hillarii in xv dies, ubicunque, &c.

Ad quem diem Vicecomes non misit breve. Ideo, sicut pluries, fiat breve eidem Vicecomiti in forma prædicta, et qualiter, &c., Vicecomes scire faciat coram domino Rege, a die Paschæ in xv dies, ubicunque, &c.

Ad quem diem Vicecomes retornavit quod breve Regis sibi inde venit adeo tarde, &c.

Ideo sicut pluries fiat breve eidem Vicecomiti in forma prædicta, &c., et qualiter, &c., Vicecomes scire faciat domino Regi, a die Sanctæ Trinitatis in xv dies, ubicunque, &c.

Ad quem diem coram domino Rege prædictus Vicecomes retornavit quod breve Regis sibi inde venit adeo tarde, &c.

Ideo sicut pluries fiat breve eidem Vicecomiti in forma prædicta juxta considerationem prædictam, &c., et qualiter, &c., Vicecomes scire faciat domino Regi, a die Sancti Michaelis in xv dies, ubicunque, &c.

Ad quem diem coram domino Rege Vicecomes Middelsexiæ retornavit quod, prout insequitur, &c., virtute istius brevis illud fossatum vocatum Louediche juxta le Eldeforde in villa de Stebbenhethe, quod Matilldis quæ fuit uxor Galfridi Aleyn elargavit per quatuor pedes, quod quidem fossatum jacet inter prata ipsius Matilldis ex utraque parte, et quod solebat esse latitudinis dicti fossati juxta la Leye sex pedum tantum, et profunditate duorum pedum tantum, et quod solebat obturari in quinque pilis, et quod eadem fieri fecit profundius quam solebat esse per duos pedes et plus, tempore suo, irradicari et emendari fecit ad custagia ipsius Matilldis, prout in brevi isto præcipitur, et similiter dictum fossatum elargatum per Johannem Hauteyn per duos pedes, et per Gilbertum le Bruere elargatum per quatuor pedes, et per Galfridum Aleyn in vita sua elargatum per duos pedes, temporibus quibus ipsi fuerunt tenentes prædictorum pratorum eadem nocumenta ad custagia domini Regis irradicari et emendari fecit, ita quod prædictum fossatum nunc est prout in antiquo tempore, ut prædictum, esse solebat in latitudine et profunditate, prout in brevi isto præcipitur, unde summa expensarum et custagiorum ex parte domini Regis factorum circa dicta nocumenta in dicto fossato per prædictos Johannem, Gilbertum, et Galfridum facta irradicanda et emendanda est xl*d*. Sed alia nocumenta et impedimenta in isto brevi contenta facta et continuata in prædicta aqua de la Leye per Isabellam nuper Priorissam de Stratforde, et Leticiam quondam Priorissam de Stratforde, ac etiam per Nicholaum nunc Priorem de Cristchirche, amoveri et evelli juxta hujus brevis tenorem nullo modo facere potui propter maximum diluvium et elevationem aquæ, que continue fuerunt in partibus illis a die receptionis hujus brevis usque nunc ad returnum ejusdem brevis.

Ideo sicut pluries præceptum est Vicecomiti quod omnia nocumenta [et] impedimenta per prædictam nunc Priorissam de Stratforde in prædicta aqua posita ad custagia ipsius Priorissæ amoveri et evelli faciat, et etiam prædictas quadraginta pilas positas per prædictam Leticiam quondam Priorissam de Stratforde ad custagia domini Regis nunc amoveri et evelli faciat, et etiam quod omnia nocumenta et impedimenta in aqua prædicta per prædictum nunc Priorem de Cristchurche continuata amoveri faciat et avelli, et publice proclamari faciat in forma prædicta, ut prædictum est, quod omnes illi, &c., ad quorum, &c., quod tunc, &c., et qualiter, &c., scire faciat domino Regi a die Sancti Hillarii in xv dies, ubicunque, &c.

INDEX OF MATTERS.

INDEX OF MATTERS.

A

ABATEMENT OF WRITS:
See VILLEIN.

(*Cessavit.*) The writ does not lie for donor against donee in tail, and, if brought, will abate, 152-154.

If A. brings the writ against B. and supposes that C., and not B., holds of him, and that the tenements ought to revert to him by reason of B.'s cesser, it is good where C. has enfeoffed B., or has been disseised by B., 432.

(*Cui in vita.*) A writ brought in the *post* may be good, if sufficient mesne possessions and conveyances are shown, though it might possibly have been framed in the *per* and *cui*, 418.

(Dower.) When judgment by default has been given against some out of several tenants in respect of rent, the writ, as a whole, will not be abated on the plea of reversioners admitted to defend their right, in respect of the land out of which the rent issues, that those particular tenants are dead, 252-254.

(Entry.) If the writ is brought in the *post*, when it should have been brought in the *per*, it abates. *See* ABATEMENT OF WRITS (*Cui in vita*).

If the writ be brought in the *post* and the tenant make default after default, and seisin be prayed, and it be alleged in Court that the writ is

ABATEMENT OF WRITS—*cont.*
faulty and defective through the omission of the words *unde queritur*, and others which should precede them, it is not necessary for counsel, when asked, to state on whose behalf he makes the objection, but the Court will examine the writ, and if it be found faulty, as alleged, will refuse to render judgment on it, 452.

(Formedon in the descender.) If the action be brought in respect of rent, and a manor be put in view as the land out of which the rent is to be taken, and the tenant plead non-tenure of a part of the manor in abatement of the writ, it will abate if the fact be as alleged by him, 78-82 ; 83, note 1.

(*Præcipe quod reddat.*) Where non-tenure is alleged in the case of part of a manor demanded, the quantity must be clearly defined, but in other cases a plea of non-tenure, if not denied, suffices to abate the writ, 28-30.

Where non-tenure is pleaded in abatement of the writ, it must be pleaded with respect to time subsequent to the purchase of the writ as well as to that day, 382-384.

Where two messuages and two thirds of another messuage are demanded, and the demand is expressed as of three messuages, except a third part of one messuage, instead of *et duas partes unius mesuagii*, the writ abates, 408-410.

AID OF THE KING—*cont.*

When on a writ of Annuity, brought against a parson, he prayed aid of the King, because his church was of the patronage of a Bishop, and the temporalities of the Bishopric were in the King's hand, the aid was granted, 360-362.

Where there is a reversion in the King, aid of the King is grantable, but not when there is only a rent reserved, 420.

AIEL:

The writ may be brought by two parceners on the seisin of an ancestor who was the grandfather of one, and the "cousin" (or great-great grandfather) of the other, 330-332.

AMENDMENT:

Where, in Formedon, the count was inconsistent with the writ, and the demandant's counsel discovered this in time, and before exception had been taken, he was permitted to amend it, 330-332.

ANCIENT DEMESNE:

When, on a *Recordari facias loquelam* brought by a tenant to remove a cause out of a Court of Ancient Demesne into the Common Bench, on the ground that the tenements are frank fee and pleadable at common law, the demandant tenders the averment "Ancient Demesne pleadable by little writ of Right" it is insufficient, and he must add "and not pleadable at common law," 406-408; 407, note 2.

See ESSOIN; MONSTRAVERUNT.

ANNUITY:

If the action be brought on the grant of the defendant's ancestor, and the defendant plead that he has nothing by descent, and it be found that he has rent by descent, but to a less amount than that of the annuity, judgment is given for the plaintiff to recover the whole, 106-108.

ANNUITY—*cont.*

Where both the plaintiff and the defendant are spiritual persons the Common Bench nevertheless has jurisdiction, and will take cognisance, if the alleged title be prescription, in which case the defendant's only plea is a traverse of the alleged seisin from time immemorial, 288-294.

Where an annuity for life had been granted by an Abbot and Convent on condition that the grantee should give his advice and assistance when required, and the Abbot's successor pleaded that the grantee had been asked to give such advice and assistance on a certain day and at a certain place, and also on a certain other day and at a certain other place, it was held that he must hold to one or the other only. Issue was then joined on a traverse of one, 412-414; 415, notes 1 and 2.

See AID; AID OF THE KING.

APPEAL:

Where judgment has been given that an appellee is to go without day because the appellor has been outlawed for trespass, and is therefore not in a condition to be answered, and the outlawry has been subsequently reversed, *quære* can the appellor proceed by way of Reattachment on the same original writ? 130-132.

APPEAL OF MAIHEM:

Protection is not allowed to a defendant in, 226.

An accessory need not answer, until the principal has been convicted, 227, note 6.

Defendants in, allowed to be out on mainprise, 227, note 6.

ARRAIGNMENT:

See ABJURATION OF THE REALM; BENEFIT OF CLERGY; OUTLAWRY.

COMMON :

Claim of common of pasture in a field every second year on which it was sown, after the corn had been cut and made into sheaves, until it was again sown, 90 ; 91, note 3.

Claim of common of pasture in gross, for all kinds of beasts, in arable land every year after the crops had been cut and carried until the land was resown, and in meadow land every year after the hay had been cut and carried until the Feast of the Purification, and in moor land during the whole year, 350-352 ; 351, note 3.

COMMON BENCH :

Jurisdiction of the. *See* ANNUITY.

CONFIRMATION :

See CHARTER.

CONSPIRACY :

If a writ of Conspiracy be brought against a man and his wife and several others, and it be pleaded that a *feme covert* cannot be supposed to conspire because husband and wife are in law one and the same person, that is no sufficient answer, and the writ will be held good, 346-348 ; 349, note 1.

CONTEMPT OF COURT :

See INDICTMENT.

CORONER :

Record of. *See* ABJURATION OF THE REALM.

COURT ROLL :

See NOVEL DISSEISIN.

COUSIN :

A great-great-grandfather is a cousin according to the forms of the Chancery writs, 330.

COVENANT :

Where the action was brought by a lessee for years who had been ousted, and who made *profert* of the

COVENANT—*cont.*

deed containing the covenants, and the defendant pleaded that the plaintiff had broken all the covenants, it was held that this was a good plea, and that the defendant need not particularise. When, however, it was found by verdict that the plaintiff had duly observed all the covenants except one touching the payment of rent on a certain day, on which day he had only paid a part, the Court gave judgment in his favour, with damages, 16-18; 19, note 2.

After judgment upon non-suit by Justices of Assise a record can be made of a covenant between the parties, and a writ of Covenant lies thereon, 422.

CUI IN VITA :

See ABATEMENT OF WRITS; AID.

CUSTOM :

If there is an admitted custom existing from time immemorial in a manor that the lord should have a certain profit, and he by charter enfeoffs any one of a messuage to hold by certain other services in lieu of all secular services, customs, and demands, and it is expressed in the charter that the feoffee and his heirs shall be quit of all services and demands not therein mentioned, the custom is nevertheless not thereby affected, and the lord can distrain for the profit in accordance with the custom of the manor, 296-300 ; 301, note 2.

If there is a custom to take a heriot within a certain fee, and the lord has at some time enfeoffed one to hold by certain services in lieu of all services, and no seisin of the heriot is shown since the time of the feoffment, *quære* whether nonseisin tolls the right to the heriot, 362-366.

D

DAMAGES:
See AUDITA QUERELA ; DEBT ; ENTRY
de quibus; QUARE IMPEDIT ; SCIRE
FACIAS ; TRESPASS ; WARDSHIP.

DARREIN PRESENTMENT:
Pleadings in Assise of, where the
plaintiff claimed on a presentation
by his ancestor, who was seised of
the advowson, and the defendant
pleaded that this presentation was
by usurpation, and that he had the
estate of one who held a moiety of
a vill to which the advowson of two
parts of the church was appendant,
426-430; 429, note 2 ; 431, note 3.

DEBT:
Process on writ of, 146.
The deed of obligation was delivered
to a third person to keep, on
condition that if the defendant
should misbehave or commit any
trespass against the plaintiff or any
of his dependents, and be convicted
thereof by a jury, it should be
delivered to the plaintiff, but that
if the defendant should not commit
any such trespass the deed should
be retained by the third person,
and held as null, and the defendant
pleaded that he had not misbehaved
or committed any such trespass.
The plaintiff replied that the
defendant assaulted his servants
and that he had lost their services,
that he had brought a *Justicies* in
the County Court against the third
person for the delivery of the deed,
that the defendant had been warned
to show cause there why it should
not be so delivered, and that, on
the defendant's default, judgment
had been given that the deed
should be delivered to the plaintiff.
The plaintiff prayed, in the

DEBT—*cont.*
Common Bench, judgment that he
should have the debt and damages.
It was argued on behalf of the
defendant that he could not be put
to answer because he had not been
convicted of the trespass by a jury.
It was, however, held by the Court
that he must deny the trespass
alleged against him, and issue was
joined on his denial. The jury
found that he had committed it,
and judgment was given for the
plaintiff to recover the debt and
damages, 160-164; 165, note 4.
A writ of Debt should be brought in
the place in which the defendant
can best be brought to answer,
though the obligation on which it
is founded may have been executed
elsewhere, and even in a County
Palatine, 336.
See EXECUTORS ; FIRST FRUITS.

DECEIT:
Where, on a writ of Waste, waste had
been found, and the defendant had
never been summoned, attached, or
distrained to appear, and had sued
a writ of *Audita Querela*, and had
thereupon prayed a writ of Deceit,
it was granted, as the *Audita
Querela* was used only to prompt
the action of the Justices, 146.

DEED:
See HABENDUM ET TENENDUM:

DETINUE:
Venue in, where it was alleged on the
one hand that a charter was delivered to a particular person at a
particular place, and on the other
hand that it was delivered to a
different person in a different
county. See VENUE.
A. alleges the delivery of a writing to
B. on condition that it is to be re-
delivered to him when he has paid
a certain sum to C., and the due
payment of the money. B., against

DETINUE—*cont.*

whom the action is brought, pleads that he does not know whether the condition is fulfilled. A *Scire facias* issues for C. to show cause why the writing should not be delivered to A. C. appears, and alleges that the condition was for the payment of a larger sum than that mentioned by A., and prays that the writing may be delivered to himself. Issue is then joined between A. and C. with respect to the condition, and the jury is to come from the place in which the writing was delivered by A. to B., 276-280.

If the plaintiff alleges delivery of chattels by his own hand to a bailee, who offers to wage his law that the plaintiff did not deliver any chattels to him and that he does not detain any, the plaintiff must accept the wager of law, or, if not, judgment will be given against him, 328.

DISTRESS :

An action was brought on the statute 52 Hen. III. (Marlb.), c. 15, for taking a distress outside the defendants' fee. The defendants pleaded that they had taken the distress by virtue of a judgment of *rithernam* given in the County Court, and of a commission from the Sheriff to take it, and that the mares of which the distress consisted were those of the person against whom the judgment had been given, and were found in the possession of the plaintiff, who was that person's villein. After several pleadings on both sides issue was in the end joined on the question whether the plaintiff was, on the day of the taking, the villein of the person named, and that person was seised of him as of his villein, 472-478; 479, note 1.

DIVORCE :

See FRANKMARRIAGE.

DOMESDAY BOOK :

See MONSTRAVERUNT.

DOWER :

Demand of a moiety of a fifth part of the tronage of a town, in action of, 66.

Where elopement, without subsequent reconciliation, was pleaded in bar, the demandant was allowed the replication (without using the word reconciliation) that she had dwelt with her husband, and in his company, years and days, until his death, and that without coercion of Holy Church, 138.

Admission to defend in action of for rent. *See* RECEIPT.

If a widow, being sole, bring a writ of Dower, and afterwards marry, and the husband and wife bring another writ of Dower while the first is pending, they will take nothing by it, 386.

It was pleaded that the tenements described as so many acres of land, &c., constituted two manors, and that the demandant's husband and a previous wife had levied a fine by which the manors were granted and rendered to them and the heirs male of their bodies, with remainder to the right heirs of the husband, and they had a son and heir still under age, and judgment was demanded whether the demandant ought to have dower of tenements so given. The replication was that the manors had been in existence before time of memory, that the tenements were not parcel of the manors, and so were not included in the fine, and issue was joined on the rejoinder that the tenements were so included. After a verdict that they were not included in the fine, judgment was given for the demandant, 434-438; 439, notes 1 and 2.

Abridgment of demand in, 480.

See VIEW; VOUCHER.

E

ENTRY:
When the writ should be in the *per*, when in the *post*, and when in either form, 102.
See ABATEMENT OF WRITS.

ENTRY, *ad terminum qui præteriit*:
Writ of, in respect of a bedelary of a soke, 76.
Where the demandant had no evidence of the lease for a term, and the tenant pleaded a feoffment of the tenements in fee by the demandant's ancestor to the tenant's father, with warranty, and the demandant did not deny the charter of feoffment, but alleged that nothing passed by it, issue was joined on the question whether the tenant's father had anything by force of the charter, 294-296 ; 297, note 2.

ENTRY, *de quibus*:
Damages in, recovered when the disseisin was effected on the demandant's ancestor, but not when on the demandant's predecessor. *Quære*, 310-312 ; 311, note 3.

ENTRY *sine assensu Capituli*:
Where a lease of a Prior and Convent was pleaded in bar, and it was alleged in reply that the lease was that of the Prior and not of the Convent, the issue joined was that the deed was not the deed of the Prior and Convent, 204.

ERROR:
Judgment in the County of Chester reversed on writ of Error to the King's Bench, 66-74 ; 75, note 4.
Where the attorney of a plaintiff in Account had been misdescribed as his father's attorney, and judgment of outlawry had been given against

ERROR—*cont.*
the defendant after the return of one writ of *Capias* only, instead of three, before the issue of the Exigent, the outlawry was reversed upon writ of Error in the King's Bench, 200 ; 201, note 2.
Where a writ of Error to the King's Bench is sued by two defendants in Fresh Force in a borough, and one of them dies while the suit is pending, his heir and the other may join and sue a new *Scire facias ad audiendum errores*. If error be found, judgment is given by the Court of King's Bench that the plaintiffs in Error have restitution, 236.
Where a writ of Error was brought to reverse a judgment in Mesne, it was assigned for error that, at the time at which the judgment was given, one of the two defendants was dead. It was argued that the other defendant ought to have pleaded the death in the Court below, before judgment, in abatement of the writ, and that therefore a writ of Error did not lie. It was, however, held that, as the death was not denied, the writ of Error did lie, and the judgment was reversed, 264-274 ; 275, note 1.
See NOVEL DISSEISIN.

ESCHEAT:
Where the writ was grounded on the outlawry for felony of one who held of the demandant, and it was pleaded that before his outlawry and before the commission of the felony he had already forfeited to the King through having been adherent to the King's enemies, 392-394.

ESSOIN:
Allowed in *Quare impedit* to the plaintiff, as being on the King's service, two days after issue had been joined to the country, notwithstanding the Statute Westm. 2, c. 27, 206.

ESSOIN—*cont.*

When there is a prayer to be admitted to defend, on the default of the tenant for life, and the demandant is essoined, his essoin is as against the tenant, and not against the person who prays to be admitted, because the latter, until admitted, is not a party, 264.

An essoin lies for a tenant who has sued a *Re. fa. lo.* to remove a cause from a Court of Ancient Demesne, even though he may have sued another *Re. fa. lo.* on a previous occasion, and may have failed to appear to maintain it, and the parol may have been remanded to the Court of Ancient Demesne, 324-326; 406.

ESTOPPEL:

Judgment in Assise of Mort d'Ancestor is an estoppel when another Assise of Mort d'Ancestor is brought by the same demandant against the same tenant in respect of the same tenements, notwithstanding the fact that it may have been pleaded as a new plea after another plea had been decided in the demandant's favour, 66-74; 75, note 4.

If a *Præcipe quod reddat* abates after view, on the ground of non-tenure, and the demandant immediately brings another writ, the tenant is estopped from pleading that the person on whose seisin and disseisin the action was brought was a bastard, because he accepted the descent by the demand of view on the first writ, 446-448.

EXCOMMUNICATION:

Quære whether it can be proved by a Bishop's letter, which reports only upon the information of another person, and not of the Bishop himself, 450.

EXECUTION:

See ABBOT; ABJURATION OF THE REALM; OUTLAWRY; SCIRE FACIAS; STATUTE MERCHANT; WARDSHIP.

EXECUTORS:

When a writ of Debt is brought by executors, and a day has been given *prece partium,* the executors are entitled to an answer without producing the will, 30.

See AUDITA QUERELA.

EXTENT:

See STATUTE MERCHANT.

F

FALSE JUDGMENT:

The suitors of a court in which it was alleged that a false judgment had been given appeared in the Common Bench, and brought the record, and left it with the Clerk of the latter Court, and departed. They were then called, and, as they were not present, they were distrained to produce the record, and on their re-appearance they would have the option of acknowledging the record which was in court or disavowing it, 478-480.

FEOFFMENT:

A feoffment by several persons who have nothing in the land, if followed by livery, is good, as between the parties, 192.

A feoffment by tenant for life and reversioner is good, if livery is made by the tenant for life alone, 192.

A feoffment by tenant for term of years or at will, though it may be a disseisin to anyone else, is good as between the parties, 192.

NISI PRIUS:

When a Justice of the Common Bench had several times granted a *Nisi prius* before himself, and had failed to go to the appointed place at the appointed time, and again wished to grant one before himself, the Court granted it before Justices of Assise, 386.

NON OMITTAS:

See PROCESS.

NON-TENURE:

See ABATEMENT OF WRITS (*Præcipe quod reddat*).

NOVEL DISSEISIN:

Assise of, in respect of the rent of a moiety of a mill, 12-14.

A defendant pleaded in bar a release of all personal actions, and the plaintiff replied that he had been seised and disseised since the execution of the release, and the Assise was taken without any title having been made for the plaintiff, who had a verdict in his favour and recovered, and a writ of Error was brought on the ground that the Assise ought not to have been taken without a title having been shown. It was held that the recovery was good, 34.

A. brought an Assise of Novel Disseisin against C., to which C. pleaded in bar that A. had in the mean time recovered by Mort d'Ancestor, and A. replied that the record of the Mort d'Ancestor was null, because C. was not tenant of the freehold, and C. rejoined that A. had accepted C. as tenant because he had pleaded in abatement of the writ on the ground of false Latin, and A. was non-suited. A. brought another Assise of Novel Disseisin against B. who pleaded in bar the mesne recovery against C., and A. replied, as before, that the recoveree in the Mort d'Ancestor was not tenant of the freehold, and

NOVEL DISSEISIN—*cont.*

prayed the Assise. It was held that A. was entitled to this replication, notwithstanding the plea in abatement of the writ in the previous Assise, and the Assise was awarded at large, 104-106.

An Assise of Novel Disseisin having been arraigned in the King's Bench when that Court was in Suffolk, the Court, after hearing certain pleadings, adjourned to Westminster. It was there pleaded, on behalf of the tenant, that the original writ was extinguished because according to Magna Charta assises must be taken in their own county, and the writ, once in the King's Bench, could not be sent out of it. The Justices, not only of the King's Bench, however, but of all the Courts unanimously decided that the Assise should be taken at large, "*quia nihil dicit*," and a *Nisi prius* was granted before the Chief Justice of the King's Bench and his fellow-justices, or some of them, in Suffolk, 104-106; 140.

At *Nisi prius*, before a puisne Justice of the King's Bench (husband and wife being defendants) the wife prayed to be admitted to defend on default of her husband, and the Justice would not take the Assise. She then appeared in the King's Bench, and was admitted. It was again pleaded that the Court had no jurisdiction, and that the original writ was extinguished, but the wife, having been admitted, was allowed to plead as to parcel in bar, and as to parcel to the Assise, 142-144.

Where the defendant pleaded in bar a release from the plaintiff's sister, whose heir the plaintiff was, and the plaintiff alleged that the sister had a son who was still living, issue was joined thereon, and the Assise

P

PARTITION:

Where two brothers purchased a mill, to hold to themselves and their heirs, and they agreed to accept the decision of a third person in settlement of a dispute touching repairs, and he marked the mill-post, and it was agreed that one brother should repair on one side of the mark and the other brother on the other side, this was held to be a good partition or sever-ance, without any specialty, so that the heir of one of the brothers could recover his moiety of the rent when the mill was leased, 12-14.

PETITION TO THE KING:

Where the petitioner suggested, in his petition, that the taking of an Assise had been awarded in the King's Bench contrary to law by some of the Justices in opposition to the opinion of their fellows, and the fact was that the award was made in accordance with the opinion of the Justices of all the Courts, and the petition was sent enclosed in a letter, under the Privy Seal, to the Chief Justice of the King's Bench, he declared it to be a slander against the Court, and ordered the petitioner into custody. The petitioner was then put on mainprise to answer to the King, 138-140.

Where several petitioners pray resti-tution of land, and the King subsequently grants the land away to others, the bill of petition will not abate on the ground that there is a common law remedy against the grantees, because the King was tenant on the day of the petition.

PETITION TO THE KING—*cont.*

Nor is the petition extinguished by the death of one of the petitioners, if it be the King's pleasure that the heir of the deceased shall continue the suit commenced by his ancestor, 188-190.

PLEADING:

See ACCOUNT; AMENDMENT; ANCIENT DEMESNE; ANNUITY; COVENANT; DEBT; DISTRESS; DOWER; ENTRY *sine assensu Capituli*; ESTOPPEL; FORMEDON; FORMEDON IN THE DE-SCENDER; MONSTRAVERUNT; NAIFTY; NOVEL DISSEISIN; QUARE IMPEDIT; QUARE INCUMBRAVIT; QUARE NON ADMISIT; QUID JURIS CLAMAT; TRES-PASS; VOUCHER; WARDSHIP; WASTE.

PRÆCIPE QUOD REDDAT:

Where the writ was brought against A. and B., as joint tenants, and B. made default after default, and A. appeared and claimed to be tenant of the whole, and issue was joined on that point, and A. afterwards made default at *Nisi prius*, judg-ment was given for the demandant to have seisin of the moiety in re-spect of which B. had made default after default, and a *Petit Cape* was awarded in respect of the other moiety on A.'s default. "*Quod mirum fuit*" says the reporter, 390.

See ABATEMENT OF WRITS; ESTOPPEL; VIEW; VOUCHER.

PRECE PARTIUM:

See EXECUTORS.

PROCEDENDO:

Writ of, 420.

PROCESS:

Upon writ of Wardship, 122.

Upon writ of Debt on obligation, 146.

Where a *Non omittas propter liber-tatem* has been awarded on the original writ, and the tenant vouches to warrant, the *Non omittas* clause may be inserted in the *Summoneas*

PROCESS—*cont.*

    ad warantizandum, provided that the vouchee is to be summoned only in the county in which the original was brought, but not otherwise, 326-328.

    On writ of Trespass, 480.

PROFERT :

    Where, in Replevin, the avowry was that the King had granted the plaintiff's services to the avowant, to whom the plaintiff had attorned, it was held that the avowant need not produce the grant in Court, though it would have been otherwise if there had been no attornment, 410.

PROTECTION :

    Not allowed to a grantee of lands, when other persons are suing by petition to the King, and not by original writ, for restitution of the same lands, 188.

    Allowed for prayee in aid in Replevin, 206.

    Not allowed to appellee in Appeal of Maihem, 226.

    Not allowed to defendant in Account in the Common Bench, after a verdict has been given at *Nisi prius* that he was the plaintiff's receiver, 228.

    Allowed for tenant, when prayee in aid has been summoned, and has not appeared, 228.

    When a Protection is allowed for one of several defendants in Trespass, the parol demurs with regard to him alone, 228.

    Allowed for one who had been admitted to defend, 264.

    Allowed for a defendant in Account after a default, 400.

PUNISHMENT :

    See INDICTMENT.

Q

QUARE IMPEDIT :

    Where it was alleged on behalf of the King, who was plaintiff, that an advowson was held of him *in capite*, and that it had been appropriated, without his license, by a Prior and Convent, and the plea was that one A. had been seised of it and had granted it to the House to hold in frankalmoign, and that the King himself had subsequently given his license to the House to appropriate, and that so it was held in frankalmoign of A.'s heir, the replication upon which issue was joined was (without any reference to the alleged license) that the Prior held the advowson immediately of the King. The jury having found that it was held in frankalmoign of A.'s heir, and not immediately of the King, judgment was given for the Prior, 38-42 ; 43, note 6.

    Judgment in the case, Easter, 18 Edw. III., No. 15, 58.

    Where it was alleged by the plaintiff that the Bishop had conferred a church (to which the plaintiff had the right of presentation) by reason of the elapsing of the period of six months, and that the church had become vacant through the resignation of the person upon whom it was conferred, and it was alleged by the defendant, an alien Prior, that the King, after having seized the advowsons, &c., of the Priory had recovered a presentation against him by *Quare impedit*, he was compelled to traverse (by an *absque hoc*) the collation by the Bishop on the ground of lapse of time, 58-64 ; 59, note 3.

QUARE IMPEDIT—*cont.*

admitted nor instituted on the predecessor's presentation, 314.

Where the action was brought by the King against an Abbot, on the ground that A. had held the advowson of the King and had aliened it to the Abbot's predecessor without license, and the Abbot pleaded that A. did not hold it of the King and that the Abbot and his predecessors had held it before time of memory *in proprios usus*, the King was allowed to plead the two issues that A. did hold of him and that the Abbot and his predecessors had not held the church *in proprios usus* before time of memory, 384.

Quære, when a title is grounded (*inter alia*) on the admission and institution of the presentee of a particular person, and the defendant tenders the averment that the particular clerk was not admitted and instituted on that person's presentation, which averment the plaintiff will not meet, whether the defendant is entitled to judgment, 464-466 ; 465, notes 3, 5, and 6 ; 467, note 1.

Where issue has been joined with respect to a particular presentation, and the King is plaintiff, a new count may be afterwards counted, or declaration made, and in respect of a different presentation, 463.

See ESSOIN; SCIRE FACIAS (On judgment in *Quare impedit*).

QUARE INCUMBRAVIT :

The plaintiff alleged that the Bishop had encumbered the church, while an Assise of Darrein Presentment was pending, and that he had on a certain day delivered a writ of Prohibition to the Bishop forbidding him to admit any one to the church while the plea was pending. The Bishop acknowledged that he had instituted one who was not the plaintiff's presentee, but denied that

QUARE INCUMBRAVIT—*cont.*

he had received any Prohibition while the plea was pending. Issue was joined on the plaintiff's replication that the Prohibition was delivered to the Bishop before the day (named) on which he had instituted, 228-234.

QUARE NON ADMISIT :

When a Bishop, against whom the writ is brought by the King, pleads that the church was full before the King's title accrued, it is not a sufficient answer, because he is bound, as minister and officer, to execute the King's commands, and any subsequent dispute will be between the clerk previously in possession and the King's presentee admitted in obedience to the King's writ. If the Bishop refuses to admit the latter he is guilty of contempt, 164-174. But *see* also 214-224.

A Bishop cannot escape the consequences of a contempt unless he can show, in a *Quare non admisit*, that he admitted the King's presentee on the day on which he received the King's writ commanding him so to do, 214-224 ; 223, note 8.

QUID JURIS CLAMAT :

Where the tenant pleaded that the conusor in the fine was her son who had no estate except by limitation to her husband, and herself, and the heirs of their bodies, and that after her death he would be put to claim by descent through her, and demanded judgment whether she should be put to attorn, and it was alleged on the other side that on the day on which the fine was levied she held of the conusor for term of life only, as supposed in the note of the fine, issue was joined on the question whether she held for life only or in tail, 154-158.

Where the tenant held for her life,

SEVERANCE:
  See INTRUSION ON WARDSHIP.

SEWERS:
  Commission of, and subsequent proceedings thereon in the King's Bench, 178-184; 485-494.

SHERIFF:
  Amendment of return by, 304.

SLANDER:
  Of the Court of King's Bench. *See* PETITION TO THE KING.

STATUTES CITED:
  9 Hen. III. (*Magna Charta*), c. 12, 106; 144.
  52 Hen. III. (Marlb.), c. 15, 472.
  ——————— c. 29, 418.
  3 Edw. I. (Westm. 1), c. 40, 381; 400.
  ——————— c. 43, 12.
  6 Edw. I. (Glouc.), c. 11, 440 (*See* STATUTES, CONSTRUCTION OF.)
  13 Edw. I. (Westm. 2), c. 3, 250; 310.
  ——————— c. 4, 250.
  ——————— c. 16, 286.
  ——————— c. 23, 12.
  ——————— c. 27, 206.
  ——————— c. 35, 282.
  ——————— c. 48,310; 334.
  ——————— (*De mercatoribus*), 400.
  ——————— (*Circumspecte agatis*), 292.
  18 Edw. I. (*Quia emptores*), 462.
  4 Edw. III., c. 7, 12.
  5 Edw. III., c. 13, 338.
  14 Edw. III. St. 4 (Clergy), c. 2, 170.

STATUTES, CONSTRUCTION OF:
  Although the Statute of Gloucester (6 Edw. I.). c. 11, provides only that execution shall be suspended where a tenement has been demised for a term of years, and the freeholder causes himself to be impleaded by collusion and makes default after default, or confesses the action, for the purpose of causing the termor to lose his term, yet the termor must make his claim before judgment is given, and cannot otherwise have the benefit of the act, 438-442.

STATUTE MERCHANT:
  After the debtors' lands have been delivered, in execution, to the obligee, the debtors cannot have a re-extent on the ground that the lands were extended too low, and they have no remedy except by payment of the money. On the other hand the obligee may have a re-extent if he alleges in time that the lands have been extended too high, 94.

  Where execution has been had on a statute merchant, and the debtor alleges that a certain sum in excess of the debt has been levied, as well as costs and charges, a *Scire facias* to have back the land is granted to him, but only a *Venire facias* when he wishes to have an account, 206.

  If to the writ of execution the Sheriff returns " *Clericus est,*" the creditor cannot have a writ to the Bishop to levy *de bonis ecclesiasticis*, but he will have a writ to the Sheriff to deliver the debtor's lands to him, 400.

  See AUDITA QUERELA.

SUR CUI IN VITA:
  See ABATEMENT OF WRITS.

SURRENDER:
  See QUID JURIS CLAMAT.

T

TAIL MALE:
  See NOVEL DISSEISIN.

TRESPASS:
  Action of, where the plaintiff alleged a depasturing of his corn, and the defendant justified it in the particular place as being his common, 90; 91, notes 1, 3, and 6.

VENUE—*cont.*

pleaded that the charter had been delivered to a different person in a different place and county, and issue was joined on that plea, a *Venire* was directed to the Sheriffs of both counties to cause the jurors to come, 24-28; 29, note 1.

Where, in *Quare incumbrarit*, it was alleged that a writ of Prohibition had been delivered to the Bishop in one county, though the church was in another county, and issue was joined on the question whether he had encumbered the church after the Prohibition had been delivered to him, the *Venire* was directed to the Sheriff of the county in which the delivery was alleged, 232-234; 235, note 2.

See DETINUE.

VIEW :

Prayed and granted of a bedelary of a soke, 76.

Prayed and granted where the demand, in writ of Right of advowson, was of the fourth part of the tithes of a church, 150-152.

Granted where rent was demanded by writ of Dower, 224-226.

On Writ of Right, 310.

Where a previous writ has abated on the ground of non-summons, the tenant will have view when a second writ is brought in respect of the same tenements, 334.

Where the tenant has lost by default on a previous writ, and has brought a writ of Deceit and regained his land, and the same demandant brings another writ in respect of the same tenements against the same tenant, the latter will have view, the statute of Westminster the second, c. 48, notwithstanding, 334.

Where a *feme sole* brings a *Præcipe quod reddat*, and the tenant has view, and the writ afterwards

VIEW—*cont.*

abates because she has taken a husband, and the husband and she bring a new writ against the same tenant in respect of the same tenements, view will be again granted, because the husband was not a party to the first writ, 398-400.

A mistake in a demandant's name cannot be pleaded after view, even though the demandant may have appeared before view by attorney, and after it in person, 418.

VILLEIN :

Where one holding in common with others has, in a *Nuper obiit*, confessed himself to be a villein in Court, and has after adjournment made default, and his co-tenants then allege the same matter, the writ abates against all, 56-58.

See DISTRESS ; NAIFTY ; TRESPASS.

VOUCHER :

Where a tenant vouched, and the voucher was counterpleaded, and on a subsequent day the demandant withdrew his counterplea, and the vouchee was in Court ready to warrant, he was not admitted to do so, because he had not a day in Court, 202.

If, in Dower, the husband's heir be vouched, when his body and part of the lands are in the hands of one person, and part in the hands of the King and of other persons, the voucher stands, but no process issues until the King has signified his pleasure, 202-204.

In Dower, tenant for life by lease from the husband vouches as reversioners three sisters and the issue of a fourth sister, deceased, as the husband's heirs, and also the husband of the deceased sister, who is tenant by the curtesy of England, 212; 213, note 3.

A., having been admitted, on the default of B., to defend as rever-

VOUCHER—*cont.*

sioner of land charged with rent, alleges that C. was seised of the land discharged, and enfeoffed him to hold discharged, that afterwards D. acquired the land out of which the rent issued and enfeoffed A. and his wife in fee. A. afterwards leased to B., and now wished to vouch himself as assign of D. As, however, voucher in respect of an estate of fee simple must be for the purpose of saving the estate of another person, as in case of joint tenancy, or estate tail, and as A. has demised to B., and A.'s wife could recover only by an action of *Cui in vita* after A.'s death, she does not hold the reversion jointly with him, and his voucher could not save any estate to her, and is therefore not allowed, 254-262.

Where, in a *Præcipe quod reddat*, the demand is for 20 acres, and the tenant alleges that there are only 10 acres, and vouches to warrant, and the demandant does not counterplead, but tenders the averment that there are twenty acres, and demands seisin of the remaining ten, the averment will not be accepted, but the vouchee will be summoned to warrant the demand, 386-388.

Where a vouchee enters into warranty as one who has nothing by descent, and the tenant tenders the averment that he had assets by descent on the day of the voucher, the statements on both sides may be entered by way of protestation, but the averment cannot be admitted because it is necessary to answer the demandant, 388.

Where husband and wife were vouched, and the counterplea was that neither the husband, nor the wife, nor the wife's ancestors had anything, the averment was accepted

VOUCHER—*cont.*

gratis, though no mention was made of the husband's ancestors, 400.

If, in Dower, an infant be vouched as being out of wardship, when he is in fact in the wardship of the King, judgment will be given for the demandant to recover her dower against the tenant, and the vouchee will go quit of the voucher, 452-458 ; 457, note 4.

See PROCESS.

W

WAGER OF LAW:
    See DETINUE.

WALES :
    Questions of jurisdiction relating to, 420-422.

WARDSHIP :

Process on writ of, where two defendants have made default, and one has been served with the Grand Distress, and the other has not, 122.

Where it was found that the heir was married, but was of the age of thirteen years only, and so *infra annos nubiles*, and the value of the marriage was assessed by the jury at a definite sum, and the damages at another definite sum, judgment was given that the plaintiff should recover the value of the marriage and the damages as assessed, so that the whole sum recovered should amount to the total value of the marriage and the damages added to it, 158.

Husband and wife bring writ of Wardship. A defendant (A.) dies, and they have Resummons against his son and heir (B.), against whom they recover, and they pray execution of damages, by *Elegit*, of the goods and a moiety of the lands of

WARDSHIP—*cont.*

A. On the death of her husband the wife sues a *Scire facias* (on the ground that execution has not been had) to have execution of the damages against B. It is held that the *Elegit* was the election of the husband, and did not prevent a better execution for her. B. then had to plead that nothing had descended to him in fee simple from A. A jury having found, after issue joined, that lands and tenements did so descend to him, execution was awarded against him, 280-284.

Where wardship was claimed in respect of rent, it was pleaded that the infant's ancestor held of the plaintiff's ancestor the tenements out of which the rent issued, and demised them to certain tenants for their lives at the rent mentioned, and afterwards granted the rent and the reversion of the tenements to the defendants for their lives, that the lessees attorned to them, and that so they held the rent, and they prayed judgment of the writ. There was an adjournment, *prece partium*, 414-416; 417, note 2.

Proclamation on writ of, 458-460.

If the defendant has pleaded a feoffment in virtue of which he alleges that he is the plaintiff's tenant, and that he has tendered the services due for the tenements, and the plaintiff has replied that the feoffment was feigned and made by collusion for the purpose of depriving him of his wardship, the defendant cannot waive his plea and rejoin simply that the ancestor did not hold of the plaintiff at the time of his death, but issue will be joined on the plaintiff's statement that the feoffment was made by fraud and collusion, and that so the ancestor did hold of the plaintiff, 460-462; 463, note 1.

WASTE:

If a fire is caused by a stranger who is harboured by the tenant's household, it is waste, by reason of want of good keeping by the tenant, 194-196.

But if a fire is caused by a hostile incursion of foreigners or rebels, it is no waste, because the tenant could not oppose them, 196.

The cutting of timber to rebuild or repair a house is no waste, 196.

If a tree is felled, and left lying on the ground, and not sold, it is waste, 194-196.

Where a writ of Waste was brought against one to whom the plaintiff alleged that he had leased the tenements for life, the defendant pleaded that he had nothing by lease from the plaintiff, and issue was joined on the plea, 196-8.

The defendant pleaded in justification, as to part of the waste alleged, that he had cut down certain trees for the purpose of making ploughs, harrows, folds, &c., and the plaintiff prayed judgment whether such a justification could be good without any special warrant shown. With regard to other waste alleged the defendant pleaded that he had cut trees by warrant from the plaintiff, and with regard to the residue No Waste. The plaintiff replied that the defendant had cut down a greater number of trees and of greater value than he had confessed, and issue was joined upon this question of fact. The jury found that the defendant had committed waste in excess of that which he had confessed. It was held that the issue in law had been waived on both sides when the defendant joined issue on the averment of fact in the plaintiff's replication, and judgment was given for the plaintiff to recover the tenements wasted, and treble

INDEX OF PERSONS AND PLACES.

INDEX OF PERSONS AND PLACES.

M

Madersay, "Ermetruda" de, her daughter Isabel, her grandson Gerard, and her great-grand-daughter Isabel, 295, note 3.

Maiden Newton, or Maydene Nywetone (Dorset), the church, and parsons of, 426-430; 427, notes 1 and 3; 429, note 2; 431, note 3.

Manestone, Cecilia de, plaintiff in Detinue, 328.

Mante, Thomas, 489.

Mantestone, Simon de, clerk, 429, note 2.

March, Joan de Mortuo Mari (or Mortimer), Countess of, 286; 287, note 2.

Marny, William, 86, notes 1 and 2; 87, note 3.

Marshal, the Earl, and his wife, 264.

Martock, or Mertok (Somerset), lands in, 353, note 7.

Martyn, Thomas, of Lindfield, plaintiff in Trespass, 328-330; 329, note 9.

Marwan, John, 489.

May, John, moleward, 486.

Maydenes, John atte, 111, note 4.

Medestede, Margaret, late wife of William de, sues Scire facias on judgment in Wardship, 280-284; 281, note 7.

Melbourne, Geoffrey de, clerk, 420, note 2.

Melburne, William de, defendant in Debt, 336; 337, note 2.

Melchbourne (Beds), a custom in the manor of, 290-300.

Mersshe, John atte, 491.

Mertone, Walter de, 229, note 8; 231, note 5.

Monbochier, George, and Isabel his wife, demandants in Entry ad terminum qui præteriit, 294-296; 295, note 3.

Monks' Kirby, or Kirkby Monachorum (Warwickshire), messuage in, 205, note 1.

——— ———, William, Prior of, demandant in Entry sine assensu Capituli, 204; 205, note 1.

——— ———, Peter Fraunceys, Prior of, 205, note 1.

Montagu, or Mountagu, or Mountagew, or de Monte Acuto, Edward, and Alice his wife, 438-442; 439, note 3; 441, note 1.

Montagu, Catherine, late wife of William de, or "de Monte Acuto," Earl of Salisbury, otherwise described as Lady de Montagu, demandant in Dower, 452-458; 453, note 7.

———, William, son and heir of William de, Earl of Salisbury, 452; 453, note 9. 457, note 4.

Monte forti, Reginald de, 155, note 1.

More, Ralph atte, and Sarah his wife, tenants in writ of Entry, 447, note 2.

Morle, Robert de, knight, 440; 441, note 1.

Mortimer, William la Zouche, 92.

Motone, William, knight, plaintiff in Trespass, 90; 91, note 1.

Motwelle, William de, 489.

Moubray, John, knight, demandant in Cessavit, 432-434.

Mouner, John, parson of the church of Stockton, defendant in Annuity, 360-362; 361, note 6.

Mundy, Thomas, of Woodstock, plaintiff in Debt, 30-32; 31, note 7.

Mynterne, Walter de, 429, note 2.

Mynyot, John, knight, demandant in Escheat, 392-394; 393, note 4.

N

Nafforde, Robert de, Master, and Commander or Preceptor of Temple Combe, deputed by the Prior of the Hospital of St. John of Jerusalem in England, 355, note 2.

Neuton, John de, 174.

Newcastle-on-Tyne, Fresh Force in the borough of, 236.

Newenham, James de, of Reculver, 135, note 8.

Newmarket, the manor of, 23, note 6.

Norfolk, Thomas de Brotherton, Earl of, 439, note 3.

Y

Z

LONDON:

PRINTED FOR HIS MAJESTY'S STATIONERY OFFICE,
BY MACKIE AND CO. LD.

[8381.—750.—9/1906.]

Lightning Source UK Ltd.
Milton Keynes UK
UKHW04f0256061018
329919UK00001B/75/P